Business Ethics and Strategy
Volume II

The International Library of Essays in Public and Professional Ethics
Series Editor: Seumas Miller and Tom Campbell

Business Ethics and Strategy
Volume II

Edited by

Alan E. Singer

University of Canterbury, New Zealand

ASHGATE

© Alan E. Singer 2007. For copyright of individual articles please refer to the Acknowledgements.

All rights reserved. No part of this publication may be reproduced, stored in a retrieval system or transmitted in any form or by any means, electronic, mechanical, photocopying, recording or otherwise without the prior permission of the publisher.

Published by
Ashgate Publishing Limited
Gower House
Croft Road
Aldershot
Hampshire GU11 3HR
England

Ashgate Publishing Company
Suite 420
101 Cherry Street
Burlington, VT 05401-4405
USA

Ashgate website: http://www.ashgate.com

British Library Cataloguing in Publication Data

Business ethics and strategy
   Vols. 1 & 2. - (The international library of essays in
   public and professional ethics)
    1.Business ethics 2.Business planning 3.Strategic planning
    I.Singer, Alan E.
    174.4

Library of Congress Control Number: 2007921640

ISBN 13: 978–0–7546–2609–1

Printed in Great Britain by TJ International Ltd, Padstow, Cornwall

Contents

PART XV   PERFORMANCE (CORPORATE SOCIAL AND FINANCIAL PERFORMANCE)

PART XVI   IMPLEMENTATION (IMPLANTING ETHICAL STRATEGY)

Acknowledgements

The editor and publishers wish to thank the following for permission to use copyright material.

Blackwell Publishing Limited for the essays: William D. Oberman (2004), 'A Framework for the Ethical Analysis of Corporate Political Activity', *Business and Society Review*, **109**, pp. 245–62. Copyright © 2004 Center for Business, Ethics at Bentley College; Samuel B. Graves and Sandra A. Waddock (2000), 'Beyond Built to Last . . . Stakeholder Relations in "Built-To-Last" Companies', *Business and Society Review*, **105**, pp. 393–418. Copyright © 2000 Center for Business, Ethics at Bentley College.

Copyright Clearance Center for the essays: Edward Soule (2002), 'Managerial Moral Strategies – In Search of a Few Good Principles', *Academy of Management Review*, **27**, pp. 114–24; LaRue Tone Hosmer (1995), 'Trust: The Connecting Link Between Organizational Theory and Philosophical Ethics', *Academy of Management Review*, **20**, pp. 379–403.

Cornell for the essay: Joshua D. Margolis and James P. Walsh (2003), 'Misery Loves Companies: Rethinking Social Initiatives by Business', *Administrative Science Quarterly*, **48**, pp. 268–305. Copyright © 2003 Administrative Science Quarterly.

Harvard Business School of Publishing for the essay: C.K. Prahalad and Allen Hammond (2002), 'Serving the World's Poor, Profitably', *Harvard Business Review*, pp. 48–57.

IOS Press for the essays: Alan E. Singer (1997), 'Game Theory and the Evolution of Strategic Thinking', *Human Systems Management*, **16**, pp. 63–75. Copyright © 1997 IOS Press; Alan E. Singer and Jerry Calton (2001), 'Dissolving the Digital Dilemma: Meta-Theory and Intellectual Property', *Human Systems Management*, **20**, pp. 19–33. Copyright © 2001 IOS Press; Milan Zeleny (1995), 'Human and Social Capital – Prerequisites for Sustained Prosperity', *Human Systems Management*, **14**, pp. 279–82. Copyright © 1995 IOS Press.

John Wiley & Sons, Ltd for the essays: Jay B. Barney and Mark H. Hansen (1994), 'Trustworthiness as a Source of Competitive Advantage', *Strategic Management Journal*, **15**, pp. 175–90. Copyright © 1994 John Wiley & Sons, Ltd; Christopher J. Robertson and Andrew Watson (2004), 'Corruption and Change: The Impact of Foreign Direct Investment', *Strategic Management Journal*, **25**, pp. 385–96. Copyright © 2004 John Wiley & Sons, Ltd; Karen Schnatterly (2003), 'Increasing Firm Value through Detection and Prevention of White-Collar Crime', *Strategic Management Journal*, **24**, pp. 587–614. Copyright © 2003 John Wiley & Sons, Ltd; Abagail McWilliams and Donald Siegel (2000), 'Corporate Social Responsibility and Financial Performance: Correlation or Misspecification?', *Strategic Management Journal*, **21**, pp. 603–09. Copyright © 2000 John Wiley & Sons, Ltd.

Philosophy Documentation Center for the essays: Jerry M. Calton and Lawrence J. Lad (1995), 'Social Contracting as a Trust-Building Process of Network Governance', *Business Ethics Quarterly*, **5**, pp. 271–95. Copyright © 1995 Business Ethics Quarterly; John Dobson and

Judith White (1995), 'Toward the Feminine Firm: An Extension to Thomas White', *Business Ethics Quarterly*, **5**, pp. 463–78. Copyright © 2001 Kluwer Academic Publishers; Leonard J. Weber (1996), 'Citizenship and Democracy: The Ethics of Corporate Lobbying', *Business Ethics Quarterly*, **6**, pp. 253–59. Copyright © 1996 Business Ethics Quarterly; J. Brooke Hamilton, III and David Hoch (1997), 'Ethical Standards for Business Lobbying: Some Practical Suggestions', *Business Ethics Quarterly*, **7**, pp. 117–29. Copyright © 1997 Business Ethics Quarterly; George G. Brenkert (1998), 'Trust, Morality and International Business', *Business Ethics Quarterly*, **8**, pp. 293–317. Copyright © 1998 Business Ethics Quarterly; R. Edward Freeman (1998), 'Poverty and the Politics of Capitalism', *Ruffin Series: New Approaches to Business Ethics* (published as a special issue of *Business Ethics Quarterly*), **1**, pp. 31–35. Copyright © 1998 Business Ethics Quarterly; Patricia H. Werhane (1998), 'Moral Imagination and the Search for Ethical Decision-Making in Management', *Ruffin Series: New Approaches to Business Ethics* (published as a special issue of *Business Ethics Quarterly*), **1**, pp. 75–98. Copyright © 1998 Business Ethics Quarterly; Robert C. Solomon (1999), 'Game Theory as a Model for Business and Business Ethics', *Business Ethics Quarterly*, **9**, pp. 11–29. Copyright © 1999 Business Ethics Quarterly; Ken Binmore (1999), 'Game Theory and Business Ethics', *Business Ethics Quarterly*, **9**, pp. 31–35. Copyright © 1999 Business Ethics Quarterly; Patricia H. Werhane and Michael Gorman (2005), 'Intellectual Property Rights, Moral Imagination, and Access to Life-Enhancing Drugs', *Business Ethics Quarterly*, **15**, pp. 595–613. Copyright © 2005 Business Ethics Quarterly.

Sage Publications for the essay: Marc Orlitzky, Frank L. Schmidt and Sara L. Rynes (2003), 'Corporate Social and Financial Performance: A Meta-analysis', *Organization Studies*, **24**, pp. 403–41. Copyright © 2003 Sage Publications.

Springer Publishing for the essays: Ronald Paul Hill (2002), 'Stalking the Poverty Consumer: A Retrospective Examination of Modern Ethical Dilemmas', *Journal of Business Ethics*, **37**, pp. 209–19.Copyright © 2002 Kluwer Academic Publishers; D.B. Resnick (2003), 'A Pluralistic Account of Intellectual Property', *Journal of Business Ethics*, **46**, pp. 319–35. Copyright © 2003 Kluwer Academic Publishers; Peter Pruzan (2001), 'The Question of Organizational Consciousness: Can Organizations Have Values, Virtues and Visions?', *Journal of Business Ethics*, **29**, pp. 271–84. Copyright © 2001 Kluwer Academic Publishers; W. Gary Simpson and Theodor Kohers (2002), 'The Link Between Corporate Social and Financial Performance: Evidence from the Banking Industry', *Journal of Business Ethics*, **35**, pp. 97–109. Copyright © 2002 Kluwer Academic Publishers; Gedeon J. Rossouw and Leon J. van Vuuren (2003), 'Modes of Managing Morality: A Descriptive Model of Strategies for Managing Ethics', *Journal of Business Ethics*, **46**, pp. 389–402. Copyright © 2003 Kluwer Academic Publishers; Ronald R. Sims and Johannes Brinkman (2003), 'Enron Ethics (Or: Culture Matters More than Codes)', *Journal of Business Ethics*, **45**, pp. 243–56. Copyright © 2003 Kluwer Academic Publishers; Sandra Waddock (2004), 'Creating Corporate Accountability: Foundational Principles to Make Corporate Citizenship Real', *Journal of Business Ethics,* **50**, pp. 313–27. Copyright © 2004 Kluwer Academic Publishers.

Every effort has been made to trace all the copyright holders, but if any have been inadvertently overlooked the publishers will be pleased to make the necessary arrangement at the first opportunity.

Series Preface

'Ethics' is now a considerable part of all debates about the conduct of public life, in government, economics, law, business, the professions and indeed every area of social and political affairs. The ethical aspects of public life include questions of moral right and wrong in the performance of public and professional roles, the moral justification and critique of public institutions and the choices that confront citizens and professionals as they come to their own moral views about social, economic and political issues.

While there are no moral experts to whom we can delegate the determination of ethical questions, the traditional skills of moral philosophers have been increasingly applied to practical contexts that call for moral assessment. Moreover this is being done with a degree of specialist knowledge of the areas under scrutiny that previously has been lacking from much of the work undertaken by philosophers.

This series brings together essays that exhibit high quality work in philosophy and the social sciences, that is well informed on the relevant subject matter and provides novel insights into the problems that arise in resolving ethical questions in practical contexts.

The volumes are designed to assist those engaged in scholarly research by providing the core essays that all who are involved in research in that area will want to have to hand. Essays are reproduced in full with the original pagination for ease of reference and citation.

The editors are selected for their eminence in the particular area of public and professional ethics. Each volume represents the editors' selection of the most seminal essays of enduring interest in the field.

SEUMAS MILLER AND TOM CAMPBELL
Centre for Applied Philosophy and Public Ethics (CAPPE)
Australian National University
Charles Sturt University
University of Melbourne

Part VIII
Game Theory (Game Theory and Its Interpretations)

[30]

GAME THEORY AS A MODEL
FOR BUSINESS AND BUSINESS ETHICS

Robert C. Solomon

Abstract: Fifty years ago, two Princeton professors established game theory as an important new branch of applied mathematics. Game theory has become a celebrated discipline in its own right, and it now plays a prestigious role in many disciplines, including ethics, due in particular to the neo-Hobbesian thinking of David Gauthier and others. Now it is perched at the edge of business ethics. I believe that it is dangerous and demeaning. It makes us look the wrong way at business, reinforcing a destructive obsession with measurable outcomes and a false sense of competition. It falsely characterizes or insidiously advocates a style of human behavior that is utterly unacceptable. To put the matter quite crudely, a person who actually practiced the form of "rationality" advocated by game theory would be something of a monster.

We should not ask for more precision than a subject is capable of giving us. — Aristotle, (384–322 B.C.E.) *Nicomachean Ethics* Bk. 1

Not that you won or lost—but how you played the game. — Grantland Rice (1880–1954) "Alumnus Football"

After Albert Z. Carr compared doing business to playing poker in his infamous article, "Is Business Bluffing Ethical?" (*Harvard Business Review,* 1968), indignant executives and outraged business ethicists initiated what would turn out to be a long and tedious counter-offensive against the very idea that free enterprise was a kind of a "game" with its own rules, rules "different from the ethical ideals of civilized human relationships."[1] Predictably, Carr's critics emphasized the importance of integrity, honesty, hard work, trust, engagement in the community, and conscience, but their common point was that business needed a larger frame, a longer view and a stronger moral core than Carr's poker analogy suggested. (Carr himself rejected the game strategy metaphor, and is even said to have insisted that the article was tongue-in-cheek.) Many students and uncritical people in business nevertheless accept Carr's argument, in casual talk if not in theory or in practice.

Today, a somewhat broader metaphor has taken the stage and now invites our serious attention. It is not tongue-in-cheek. It does not present itself as a mere metaphor. It does not limit itself to a single, somewhat ill-reputed game such as poker. It is game theory, in general, and it has the best of credentials. Fifty years ago, two Princeton wizards (who, one might imagine, began by musing over their Friday night poker strategies) established game theory as an important new branch of applied mathematics. Game theory has become a celebrated discipline in its own right, and it now plays a prestigious role in the top business schools, in economics and sociology departments, in biology (especially ecology and evolutionary theory). More to the point, it has now made serious inroads into ethics, due in particular to the neo-Hobbesian thinking of David Gauthier and others.[2] Given its established prominence in business and economics and its appeal in ethics, it is easily understandable that it should now be perched at the edge of business ethics.

I have often said—and I admit that this is conscientiously polemical—that game theory has been a disaster in ethics, and now it threatens to become devastating to business ethics as well. It's not that the mathematical discipline itself is faulty. But formal thinking does not mix easily or comfortably with the sensitivities that are essential to ethics, and not all human activities are games, or anything like games. Out of fairness, I would want to distinguish between what I will call "refined" game theory and plain old "vulgar" game theory, especially since it is the most vulgar kind that is snapped up by most economists and too many business theorists.[3] It is not my intention to criticize the fundamentals of the theory itself, nor will I involve myself with the nuances of strategy. Rather, it is game theory as a model, or, more accurately, game theory as a *metaphor* of business activity that I want to object to, as strongly as possible. Not that I doubt that such theories sometimes apply to business activities and situations, but as a model of business as such, as a focal point and, too often, as the model of business, I believe that it is dangerous and demeaning. It makes us look the wrong way at business, reinforcing an already destructive obsession with easily measurable outcomes (namely "the bottom line") and an often false sense of competition. It represents (what some of its most avid followers would defend as) the most vulgar version of Hobbes, a version that Hobbes himself surely would not have accepted. It either falsely characterizes, or insidiously advocates, a style of human behavior that is utterly unacceptable. To put the matter quite crudely, a person who actually practiced the form of "rationality" advocated by game theory would be something of a monster. To think in terms of strategies of self-maximization, as opposed to unhesitatingly doing the right thing, is (as Bernard Williams put it, in a very different context) to have "one thought too many."[4]

Game theory, like mathematical models in physics, purports to help us to understand diverse and complex phenomena, in this case the supposedly rational behavior of that singularly abstract specimen of humanity, sometimes called "rational man" but better known as *homo economicus*. The model is "ideal"—in the standard sense of a fiction abstracted from a much more complex reality.

But such rationality is hardly an ideal as a model of human behavior in the same way that saintliness, for example, might be said to be. Or, for that matter, it

GAME THEORY AS A MODEL FOR BUSINESS ETHICS   13

is hardly an ideal as "rationality." Moreover, surely it should be noted (here briefly) that there is no subject, including sex, romance, relationships and death, on which most people are more *ir*rational than about money. Indeed, momentary reflection on peoples' savings habits, gambling compulsions, attitudes toward their jobs, the home shopping network, bargain hunting, and consumer spending in general makes this quite clear, all talk of "preferences" and "expected utilities" aside.

Moreover, game theory has distorted the very term "rationality" by co-opting and reducing its very rich meanings to one-dimensional strategic thinking. To be rational does not generally mean "to seek one's own advantage" or even, more generally still, "to seek to satisfy one's own preferences." Rationality does not simply refer to means-end ("instrumental") thinking. According to many authors, it rather refers precisely to those sorts of thinking that are not particularly self-involved, in which one does not take oneself to be a "special case" or an "exception."

Rationality, I would argue, is always culture-bound, both in its determination and its concerns. In one culture it may be rational to fear witches and in another it is rational to fear a nuclear accident. In one society rationality is determined through the use of certain procedures, in another, by appeal to a certain kind of result. In some societies, the appeal to authority, the consensus of the group, the wisdom of one's ancestors, constitutes rationality. In others, it is individual autonomy, deliberation and Baysian decision theory. Rationality, I would argue, is very much a matter of "caring about the right things," a matter of ends and not a matter of means.[5] But game theory is not merely a description of (one conception of) rationality. It takes the form of a prescription, or a rather large set of prescriptions, about how it is "rational" to behave in a number of trying and challenging circumstances. Where there is no challenge, of course, there is no "game," but—and this is important—we should note how often and how easily (in this society) a situation is wrongly viewed as a challenge when it might more rationally be viewed as an invitation to cooperative and harmonious behavior, e.g., driving in rush hour or meeting together in an academic seminar.

Game theory tells the participants in various human endeavors—especially economic endeavors—just how to play "the game." But for most people, economics is not a game. It is a means of survival, "making a living," and to think of business as a game already falsifies the seriousness as well as the locus of that activity. A game is normally something divorced or detached from ordinary concerns, real payoffs, and penalties. Business, for most of us, constitutes many of our most ordinary concerns and has all-too-real payoffs and penalties. Business is not (usually) "played" at all, and it is rarely confined to a specific "field" (however the market might sometimes be described in such spatial terms). Its participants are not, for the most part, "players" but grudging breadwinners, and the artificial urge to "maximize" one's behavior hardly describes most peoples' attitude toward their work. Consumerism may have become a primary form of entertainment for many Americans but the means by which most Americans earn the money they spend is not, for most of them, entertaining or enjoyable. (Nor, for that matter, is most of the spending itself.) Not that games by their nature must be enjoyed. But games, as games, are "played," and that suggests activity quite different from the rigors and pressures of everyday life. If some Sylvester Stallone or Hermann Kahn type argues that war is a game, I take it that what they mean is that it is something extraordinary, in which the normal rules of interaction are suspended. (The military uses the phrase "war games" for those just-practice maneuvers that are emphatically NOT real warfare and in which the usual rules of decency and fairness [more or less] obtain.) What counts as a game, and what it means to participate in a game, is a topic worthy of discussion, but such a discussion should precede, not lap at the heels of, game theory.[6]

Why would game theory appeal to business ethicists, indeed, how does it now come to fill an entire issue of one of the field's leading journals? The often-stated desire for (and current lack of) a rigorous business ethical theory and the intrinsic fascination with quasi-mathematical puzzles provides a partial answer.[7] But that business ethics—or for that matter ethics—needs a theory is by no means obvious. A more appropriate insight was anticipated by Aristotle, when he warned (in his *Nicomachean Ethics*) that we should not look for more precision in a subject than is appropriate. The problem with ethics, the subject that he was there introducing, is that it is a "sloppy" field of inquiry. I would argue that it requires, more than anything else, not a "theory" but a decent upbringing, a certain sensitivity, some compassion for human suffering—and only then some ability to calculate and measure "harms." Ethics develops with a keen sense of injustice, and not necessarily regarding one's own case, and only then might it come to involve the ability to generalize and formulate one or another conception of justice or fairness. If the practice of justice had awaited a satisfactory answer to Socrates' question, "what is justice?" we would all still be throwing rocks at one another. Ethics, first of all, requires not reflection but close attention to the nuances and intricacies of human relationships, only some of which are sometimes competitive and require strategy and tactics rather than tact, sympathy, mutual consideration and sharing. But from this short list of "preconditions" for ethics, it should be obvious that most of what counts as "ethical theory" is not of this kind at all, and many philosophers are not at all sympathetic to the idea that policy decisions, theories of justice and strategic interaction theories are meaningful only insofar as they presuppose some basic human emotional engagement. Game theory reinforces this resistance to fellow-feeling and replaces it, as in econometric theory, with cold numbers.

Ethics, they say, is the business of dispassionate reason, and, for many philosophers, the more formal the reasoning the better, the less contaminated by prejudices and bias. Feelings only interfere. The great ancestor of this position, with qualifications, is Kant, but not only Kant. Even in "moral sentiment theory," there is the "ideal observer," who is very much still with us in ethics (long after the demise of the moral sentiments themselves). Thus in business ethics, it is still considered a virtue to talk about and judge matters in which they are not

GAME THEORY AS A MODEL FOR BUSINESS ETHICS 15

themselves involved or, all too often, informed. Game theory, as formal philoso-phy *par excellence*, might be viewed as one more vehicle for avoiding engagement. Game theory, by providing the precision that ethics through most of its waffly history has lacked, allows us to avoid the messiness of real-life political feuds, long-standing animosities, coercion and exploitation. Indeed, we have all heard it argued, rather unkindly, that moral philosophers—should one add an *ad hominem*, "especially game theorists"?—are not particularly adept at dealing with real suffering, or with injustice, or with relationships, except on an ethereally abstract level. But even without such (no doubt false) accusations, it can certainly be argued that game theory, with its emphasis on precision and procedure, by-passes those nagging and controversial questions about what it is that people do or ought to care about. Does it matter that the very heart of both business and ethics gets cut out in the process?

Game Theory and Business

Game theory became a branch of economic theory with the publication of John von Neumann's and Oskar Morgenstern's treatise *Theory of Games and Economic Behavior* in the early years of World War II. It was soon seized upon by economists as a mathematical model for economic activity.[8] Even as origi-nally conceived, game theory was not restricted to "games" as such. It applied to virtually all situations in which individual interests were causally and strategi-cally interconnected, including public issues of governance and welfare and private competitions and exchanges. With the expansion of the theory as "deci-sion theory," "social choice theory," and "rationality modeling," game theoretic models of competition and cooperation came to be applied to such various so-cial and political issues as voting behavior, theories of justice and nuclear deterrence, to name but a few.[9] But game theory and its applications were from the first applied to economics and, more recently, to general business theory.

Business is, to be sure, not just a game. But the rules and strategies and con-sequently the ethics of business would seem to be amenable to precise formulation under the auspices of the mathematical theory of games. There need be no pre-sumption that business is "fun" (as in "fun and games"), nor need it be supposed that the various "players" (or "parties") are involved voluntarily. A "game," so considered, is any interaction among agents who have preferences and goals. It is not necessary that one of those goals be "to win." Not all games have winners and losers, and it is only necessary that one can be shown to be doing well or badly according to his or her own goals, and not necessarily in contrast or in opposition with others. (Although it makes sense to speak of solitudinous, one-person games, such games are arguably not relevant to any intelligible business situation.)

It is not to be assumed that all games are competitive, despite the obvious appeal and excitement of one-on-one competitive games. The more morally appealing notion of a "cooperative game" opens the possibility of cooperative strategies and mutually satisfying ("win-win") outcomes, although this notion in contemporary game theory—like so many ethical terms in technical theory—gets distorted and deflated. (A "cooperative game" is not necessarily cooperative, in the usual sense that the interests of the participants coincide.) Even if, as in classical theory, business and the market are necessarily competitive, it does not follow that business competition cannot or should not be embedded in a larger cooperative matrix. Indeed, I think that any sensible view of business, short of the pseudo-Sun-Tzu conception of "Business as War," recognizes that this must be so. In a fully affluent society where the market is perfectly efficient, the supposed competition of the market might well turn out to be nothing more than an exercise in general coordination and mutual satisfaction. Such an ideal market might give us an "ethics" in which everything is fair and everyone is (more or less) satisfied even without any of those social constraints called "morality" that would seem to form the core of an ethics.[10] But even the proponents of that ideal admit that both people and markets are "imperfect." People are often desperate, sometimes greedy. Markets are all-too-often rigged. But imperfection is hardly the problem. It is the very conception of the market that needs revision. I want to suggest that game theory gives us a false and dangerous picture of what most business activity is all about and, indeed, of what it means to be "rational."

But first, let us say what is obviously right about game theory. Business, like games, is all about *reciprocity*. The appeal of this model is obvious. If, in the simplest imaginable market situation Adam has an orange but wants an apple and Eve has an apple but wants an orange and, after a very short discussion, they decide to trade, everyone is satisfied. It is an "optimal" outcome; everyone has his first preference and no one is disappointed. But it is not just the optimal outcome that pleases us. It is the procedure, the reciprocity of the market that makes it so appealing, the fact that (after knowing not only their own interests but the interests of others) both parties agree to the outcome that each desires. No outside authority has to issue instructions or impose sanctions. So long as there is informed agreement and mutual satisfaction there need be no additional call for "morals." The picture does not change significantly if we add more people and introduce money as a mediating currency and add production to this overly simple picture of pure exchange; the basic principle of reciprocity and self-satisfaction through mutual satisfaction remains the same. Aristotle was just plain wrong insofar as he thought that all commerce is theft and exploitation (although Aristotle's early economics is much more than this).[11] Trade based on reciprocal agreements would seem to be a paradigm of mutually satisfying civilized behavior.

But this agreeable paradigm is not yet an adequate conception of business. First, on the positive side, a good deal of business—in fact, I would argue, most of business—is not so much self-interested reciprocal behavior as it is people working together, sharing values and goals, caring about the needs and interests of others. Rewards, profits and payoffs play a much more tangential role in most people's behavior in business than economists, finance managers and game theorists seem to

GAME THEORY AS A MODEL FOR BUSINESS ETHICS   17

realize. Of course, it is not hard today to find corporations—which ought to be models of cooperative behavior—which put payoffs before people and in which all relationships are strictly contractual and bottom-line oriented, but it is worth noting that most such corporations are by their own measures (and by the highly sensitive but hardly sentimental measure of the stock market) dysfunctional. Cooperation and working together require a different mind-set than mere reciprocity and rational exchange. To understand how such relationships work—not that this requires a social scientist or a philosopher to fathom—we have to appreciate the centrality of our ability to directly perceive human needs, the non-strategic structure of most human relationships, the fragility and often straightforward irrationality of the human ego, and the power of personal feelings. Reciprocity, in other words, should not be defined in game theoretical terms.

On the negative side, business is not always a mutually satisfying or agreeable exchange of goods, labor and money. Business is not only competitive but sometimes exploitative as well. The world of business is pervaded by the Hobbesian distortions of "Force and Fraud."[12] Indeed, the idea of the game as a model for business is revealing in that it is not so much the exchange that is essential but rather competition and rivalry. There are, of course, "cooperative" games, but this term does not necessarily signify cooperation in the ethically relevant sense. Truly cooperative games—that is, games in which the participants work together for shared ends and mutual benefits—have received relatively little attention in the current philosophical literature, and it is not hard to imagine why. The hard-edged competition and the paradoxes of rationality manifest themselves most obviously in competitive games. So, too, business becomes of interest to theorists in philosophy and other fields precisely when, in one sense, the market breaks down, when there is ferocious competition and strategic concerns become essential to survival. (It is worth noting that this is when economists in particular tend to praise the market as "robust.") Looking at business strictly in its competitive aspects provides an arena in which game theory seems to offer some answers, and, in desperation, we know that otherwise sensible people will even turn to psychics and the stars. But does game theory tell the skilled entrepreneur or executive anything that is not already obvious, or, more to the point, is the putative rationality of game theory precisely what the skilled entrepreneur or executive transcends?[13] The mistake is thinking that competition and strategy is what business is all about. Business, or at least most businesses, is far more about cooperation and innovation than competition. Business life consists, for the most part, of carrying out contractual and positional duties, fostering relationships between managers and employees, sales representatives and customers, procurers and suppliers, the corporation and the community. The "winning strategy" is often not a strategy at all. Not that such activities are opposed to competitive advantage, but to suppose that they are performed for the sake of competitive advantage is as thick or as sick as some of those obnoxious characters on television sit-coms, who suppose that every considerate gesture is in essence a strategy with the expectation of a pay-off.[14]

As for competition, the fact is, of course, that most games and many standard business negotiations presuppose ignorance rather than mutual knowledge. Few bargaining situations are mutually well informed. Business typically involves a certain secrecy. Knowing what your competitor is doing but not letting him know what you are doing is an enormous advantage. "The Market," accordingly, is notoriously unpredictable. Acting in the face of uncertainty (at least, the uncertainty of the market) is par for the course. And unlike the example of willing exchange, business competition does not always work for optimal and mutually satisfying outcomes. As a result, the results are often less than might be hoped for all concerned. Accordingly, most game theoretical debate these days focuses on that particularly gloomy paradigm of a non-cooperative game in which everyone (in effect) loses by being rational.

The Prisoner's Dilemma as a Paradigm for Business

That paradigm is called the "prisoner's dilemma," a competitive, non-zero-sum played by at least two persons. Credit for its formulation is usually given to A. W. Tucker, a Princeton mathematician. The prisoner's dilemma is best illustrated by the story that gives the example its name. Two men (Larry and Moe) are arrested and immediately separated by the district attorney (Curly Shirley, of course). She instructs each of them that, if he confesses (and the other does not) he will receive a greatly reduced term (let's say, one year) while the other will get the maximum (ten years). If they both confess, the D.A. will be able to convict them both (five years). What she does not tell them (but is plainly evident) is that if neither confesses, she won't have a case but can convict them on a lesser charge (2 years). What should (rationally) each do? The best outcome (that is, the least amount of time in prison for both of them) would result if neither confessed, but Larry figures that if Moe confesses and he doesn't, he's in for the long haul. Moe figures much the same way. So both confess, and what results is less than optimal. The dominant strategy, the strategy that is unequivocally rational for each of them, is such that if they both take it, the result is worse for both of them than the non-dominant, less rational strategy.

It is easy to imagine any number of business situations that fit the same model. The most obvious is two competing businessmen who must set their prices in competition with one another without knowing what the other is going to do. Each will be cautious and set a price lower than he would if he were confident that the other would set a suitably higher price. In such cases, business competition (or, more accurately, non-cooperation) is mutually disadvantageous, though it should be pointed out that this is usually to the advantage of the customer. (Thus we can understand consumer enthusiasm whenever there are price wars and, on the business side, the need for laws against collusion and price fixing.) But is this an adequate model of business? Is business made up of (in game theoretical terms) "utility maximizing" rather than "optimizing" decisions? That is, is it true that the typical business negotiation and the free market in general

GAME THEORY AS A MODEL FOR BUSINESS ETHICS 19

puts all parties in a worse-off position? (A socialist would, of course, say "yes.")
In defense of the market, the prisoner's dilemma might be taken as an atypical
"worst case scenario." Or it might be denied to be a market model at all.[15] The
obvious truth, I would argue, is that the business world involves a great many
different sorts of activities and forms of interaction, a few of which might be
imperfectly captured in the "prisoner's dilemma." But the ill-fated attempt to
capture all of business and economics (and the misleadingly singular "the market") in a single, mathematically precise model denies this obvious truth for the
sake of playing a game with strategies rather than trying to understand the actual, necessarily personal dynamics of actual business activity.

The use of such models can be particularly degrading to business. For one
thing, it is remarkable how little comment the social circumstances of the
prisoner's dilemma has received. The people who are involved in the prisoner's
dilemma are felons, co-conspirators in crime, whose goal is to minimize their
prison sentences, at each other's expense if need be. I would find it surprising,
to say the least, if most business people would or should warm up to the associations of that example. In terms of game theory itself, moreover, the prisoner's
dilemma model too often suggests a "one shot" business strategy, in which such
basic business considerations as a good reputation, dependable quality and service, established commercial and community relationships and customer loyalty
are eliminated from the picture. What sort of business would this be? It's one
that we would call "fly-by-night." There is no repeat business. There is consequently no role for any of the standard business virtues, which presuppose a
continuing community and an on-going practice, and which depend on a "sense
of honor" not just as an extraordinary but as a running assumption, a part of a
person's or a business's character or reputation. Recent theory has improved this
abysmal implicit portrait of business: at least it is generally agreed that business
involves repeating games and thus the strategy of repeated and continuing
prisoner's dilemma type games has become a topic of considerable research.[16]
The idea that business can be cooperative (without being collusive) is gaining
acceptance and the overly narrow conceptions of the goal of the games (pure
and pre-ordained self-interest) is giving rise to a much more flexible picture of
the goal-orientation of business players. For instance, it has been argued that all
of the elements of game theory and the prisoner's dilemma in particular remain
in place if, instead of self-interested goals, the players have purely altruistic
goals (for example, as administrators of two charities, competing for the same
donation dollars within a single group of supporters).[17] This means that we ought
to distinguish between what one could call *unrefined* game theoretical models—
the sort routinely and uncritically adopted by many economists—and *refined*
models, the sort that have recently been recommended by justice-minded social
planners and philosophers. The former assumes unembellished self-interest and
more or less unbridled competition while the latter presumes mutual concern,
cooperation and, where need be, arbitration. Nevertheless, it is the basic frame

and perspective of game theory that I want to challenge, and not just its (frequent) lack of refinement. Indeed, as game theory gets more sophisticated, we tend to lose sight of the problem rather than solve it. And that problem, as I see it, is how to get people to think about business and about themselves in an Aristotelian rather than a neo-Hobbesian (or even a Rawlsian) way, which the game theoretical models typically presuppose.

Objections to Game Theory

In my book, *Ethics and Excellence,* I explored seven reasons why game theory, whatever its virtues, provides a poor model for business interaction as well as, in its unrefined versions, an appalling model of human nature.[18] I, too, often tend to slip between the refined and the unrefined game theoretical models, but that, I think, is the insidiousness of the game theoretical flirtation. If my arguments serve only to force game theorists to further refine and clarify their models, I would consider my polemic worthwhile.

1. Game theory and "Rationality"

Game theory too readily equates "rationality" with prudential self-interest in the face of competition and conflict. Of course, not all games are played "against" anything (including "nature"), and, so too, not all (or even most) business activities are competitive. But though the best game theorists allude to the possibility of cooperative games and point out the parallel in competitive altruistic contexts, it is illustrative that the game-type that dominates discussion and is most often chosen as a model for business is the prisoner's dilemma in its uncompromisingly competitive and even vicious versions. The paradigm here is insidious. The "rational" approach to a problem turns out to be self-interested and the solution is the "safe" one—better not to trust the other player because he or she might not trust you either. But if games (in general) are so conceived, cooperative games turn out to be preferable only because they are the safest games. They do not eliminate competitiveness or selfishness or distrust but rather emphasize strategies that minimize these. They assure mutually satisfying as well as optimal outcomes, but without rejecting the mind-set that provoked the problem. (Thus the Hobbesian conception of society by contract is argued to be the best solution to mutual hostility and fear.)[19] What is entirely missing is any sense of shared (as opposed to merely mutual) interests and dedication to anything larger or more meaningful than one's own interests.

Nick Rescher accuses traditional game theory of begging two questions; (1) whether rationality demands this prudential, safety-first approach and, (2) much more important, whether rationality demands the cultivation of personal advantage to the exclusion of the interests of others.[20] Philosophers have taken it as "paradoxical" that rational participants in a prisoner's dilemma fail to reach their mutually preferred result. A well-known game theorist, Anatole Rapaport, writes,

GAME THEORY AS A MODEL FOR BUSINESS ETHICS   21

"the paradox is that if both players make the rational choice, . . . both lose."[21] Rescher denies the paradox: "There is in fact nothing paradoxical about this. It shows merely that the realization of a generally advantageous result may require the running of individual risks, and that the pursuit of other-disinterested prudence may produce a situation in which the general interest of the community is impaired."[22] But Rescher adds, "for these lessons we did not need to await modern game theory; the moralists of classical antiquity told us as much many years ago."[23] Indeed, they did, and this, in part, was the suspicion behind Aristotle's unsympathetic dismissal of profit-seeking commercial activity as "unnatural." But why should we, under the banner of "free enterprise," adopt as a model for business (much less for society) a self-fulfilling portrait of human nature so intrinsically unsocial and mutually so unsupportive?

2. Game Theory and Self-Interest

Game theory begins with the assumption that each player is trying to satisfy his or her own interests. Even where the assumption is so weak and so abstemious about human nature to insist only on the "interests" (not "self-interest") of the players, the notion of competitive self-interest inevitably sneaks back in. Refined game theorists insist that the notion of "interest" or "preference" here is not necessarily selfish; indeed it might include all sorts of altruistic desires, wanting to feed one's family or have money to give to the poor or to political candidates. But the slippage between this non-committal sense of "interest" and self-interest is fast and furious. One can see the slippage, for example, in John Rawls's characterization of "mutually disinterested rationality." I quote at some length:

> The assumption of mutually disinterested rationality, then, comes to this: the persons in the original position try to acknowledge principles which advance their system of ends as far as possible. They do this by attempting to win for themselves the highest index of primary social goods, since this enables them to promote their conception of the good most effectively whatever it turns out to be. The parties do not seek to confer benefits or to impose injuries on one another; they are not moved by affection or rancor. Nor do they try to gain relative to one another; they are not envious or vain. But in terms of a game, we might say: they strive for as high an absolute score as possible.[24]

The telling phrase, I think, is "attempting to win for themselves," and the problem with game theoretical thinking is that such phrases are never very far from or psychologically separable from self-interest. Indeed, even where the interests are *shared* interests, the model suggests that this is contingent rather than essential to the interests themselves. Consider, for example, acts done out of compassion, love or friendship.[25] Not that much of business is conducted in such intimate circumstances, but it could be argued that much of the recent emphasis on "dedication to the customer" and "teamwork" among employees is an effort to introduce truly shared interests into the business context. What is revealing about such interests is that they utterly resist game theoretical analysis.

Rawls tries to assure us that such efforts are "not envious or vain," but the very effort to "win for themselves the highest index" suggests that such assurances may themselves be in vain. It is curious that in the philosophical undressing that prepares no longer "encumbered" people for the "original position," they do not even know their own sex or abilities but nevertheless are left with the most ordinary and (I would argue) culturally induced emotions and motives (not to mention how much they supposedly know about game theory and the social sciences). Envy and vanity, far from being encumbrances, often appear to be primary determinants of liberal policy, indeed, of "fairness." Rawls tries to neutralize the idea of "ends," but nevertheless what emerges is difficult to defend without a relatively "thick" conception of human motivation. In the original position, Rawls argues, [people]

> do not know their conception of the good. This means that while they know that they have some rational plan of life, they do not know the details of this plan, the particular ends and interests which it is calculated to promote. How then can they decide which conceptions of justice are most to their advantage? . . . they assume that they would prefer more primary social goods rather than less. . . . from the standpoint of the original position, it is rational for the parties to suppose that they do want a larger share, since in any case they are not compelled to accept more if they do not wish to.[26]

"It is rational . . . to suppose that they do want a larger share"—this sounds a lot like "get the goods and then you can decide what to do with them." How many people in business, some of them ruthless, rationalize what can only be called their greed with the promise that, "afterward," they will engage in socially constructive, even idealistic behavior? Whereas the dominant question in business ethics, according to several illustrious theorists, is to just what extent it is possible to realistically minimize the long over-stated self-interested aspects of business.[27] Game theory does not address this concern but tends to undermine it, by stressing, despite denials, a "rational plan of life," namely the rationality of "a larger share."

3. Games and Keeping Score

In most games, we like to keep score. This is not an essential feature of games, but it does seem to be one of the most durable features of game theory. The best way to keep score is to have a dependable point system, a definite unit of worth. Not surprisingly, game theorists modeling society end up talking a great deal about money. Of course, here too the proper excuses are made, "money isn't the only or even the primary social good," "money is only a means and not an end" and so forth. But though the conversation may begin with talk about primary social goods, soon we have yet another example involving money. Economists, of course, do not apologize for this. Money-talk is their game, though they will admit (if pressed) that people do (at least occasionally) want things that money can't buy. But social theorists in general yield to the tendency to talk about money,

GAME THEORY AS A MODEL FOR BUSINESS ETHICS   23

too, if only because money is a readily measurable utility, an easily comparable measure, an apparently clear basis for comparison. Of course, even some unrefined theorists recognize that equal amounts of money do not have equal significance for different folks, and so the inescapable qualifications of marginal utility and the "utility of money" are (hesitantly) entered into the equation. But then the calculation proceeds as if all of this has been deftly settled with the simple declaration that we should "assume that these are the same." And when it's over, we can shift back to that very general talk about "primary social goods"—including such intangibles as health, freedom, self-esteem and peace of mind, as if the quantification of one carefully defined domain of the theory will extend ipso pipso to the rest.

But various ends are hard to compare (one person wants to win a downhill ski race, another wants to sleep in a hammock) and so success and "maximum utility" may be hard to measure. If we were to assign every end a monetary value, however, and rate various preferences according to their exchange value on the market, we would indeed have a single scale on which to compare and evaluate ends and means and determine maximum utility. In practice, of course, we make such interpersonal utility comparisons all the time, and one might even trace the attempted "theory" of such comparisons back to Aristotle's discussion of "proportion" in distribution among unequals in Book V of his *Ethics*.[28] But the sad fact of the matter is that, in a "capitalist" (capital-minded) society, we are all prone to that lazy reductionism in which all or at least most things are compared according to their cost, narrowly construed. More to the point, corporate finance officers do this not from intellectual sloth but according to the rules of their profession. "Cost/benefit analysis" in business tends to be exclusively about dollars. Thus the victory of the economists, and the rise of what Karl Marx called "fetishism."

4. Game Theory and Altruism

Even where self-interest is not assumed as the basis of the game and the goal of each and every player, altruism gets treated as anomalous, at best a fringe benefit not to be taken for granted but at worst an intolerable interference with the workings of the game. (Imagine an extremely generous poker player, or one who did not want to take advantage of his unusually good hands, and you get the idea.) And so we assume self-interest if not selfishness, or worse, the unrefined game theorist promotes an extreme dichotomy between self-interest and altruism, to the great disadvantage of the latter. Moritz Schlick, for example, argues:

> The unrestrained development of such [altruistic] inclinations . . . can certainly not lead to the valuable, and will not, in fact, be considered moral. To respect every desire of one's neighbor, to give in to every sympathetic impulse results, finally, neither in the highest measure of joy for the individual himself, nor indeed for the others; in such a case one no longer speaks of kindness, but of weakness.[29]

Rescher (who quotes Schlick with some sympathy) attacks this vision of pre-supposed selfishness throughout his book, insisting that it is a gross mistake to conceive of rationality in such a way that it conflicts with morality and the social good and to think of ethics in terms of "intelligent selfishness." He rejects the "prudentially safety-first-minded pursuit of personal advantage" that defines most game theory in favor of a theory of the "vicarious" sympathetic emotions. We obtain "utility" through our sympathy with others, experiencing joy at their successes, for instances, and not just from our own success. But even Rescher seems trapped in the old paradigm, which is a sign of its enduring strength. He distinguishes between "first order utility"—the satisfaction of one's own desires—and "second order utility—one's satisfaction as the result of the satisfaction of another. But the very act of ordering (and the use of the word "vicarious") shows that Rescher too can't quite take seriously the idea of truly shared—not "vicarious"—satisfaction. So, too, even cooperative games presuppose just that notion of primary individual self-interest that I want us to reject, whether or not supplemented or made possible by simultaneously satisfying the interests of others. And the concept of the virtues—that is, as opposed to the skills required to play the game—gets lost here. This is what Rescher is aiming at when he attacks utilitarianism on the grounds that it insists that "everyone counts for one and only for one," which leaves no room, according to Rescher, for relationships, kinship and other forms of affection and association. Of course, a flexible utilitarian can readily incorporate the "vicarious" sentiments and second order utility into the "happiness calculus," but Rescher denies that the utilitarian can be so flexible. But my point is that the alternative to self-interested games is not altruism, much less self-sacrifice nor even vicarious satisfaction. It is the very notion of discrete "players" with discrete interests that I want to throw into question.

5. Game Theory and Goal-Oriented Behavior

Even the "modest" assumption that our behavior is "goal-oriented" is, I think, inaccurate and prejudicial. Ned McClennen, for instance, insists that he can "avoid making any essentialist assumptions about human nature" and requires only the modest assumption that people are goal-oriented.[30] (This is not to say anything about what goals they pursue, of course, nor is it even to suggest a more general Rawlsian consensus on fundamental goals.) But although one can hardly deny that we do have many goals in life, from wanting to get to the garbage can before the dog does to wanting to win a Nobel prize, the view that our activities are essentially goal-oriented is mistaken and, sometimes, tragic. "But certainly," someone is sure to protest, "nothing is more central to the 'Aristotelian' approach that you want to defend than the notion of teleology." And, indeed, that's so. But what Aristotle had in mind by "teleology" was quite different from what we mean (and game theorists in particular mean) by "goal-oriented." For one thing, the satisfaction of desire, while certainly not irrelevant to Aristotle's teleology, is not at all what he has in mind. But a more basic concern is that when

GAME THEORY AS A MODEL FOR BUSINESS ETHICS 25

one examines Aristotle's conception of the ingredients of the good life, the virtues and our various activities, it is evident that while these involve certain standards, it is not the satisfaction of those standards that motivates us, and one would be hard pressed to identify the "goals" (in our sense) that define most of those virtues. As for all of those activities, it is not as if they are all so goal-oriented either. Friendship is part of our telos but it is not, unless the concept is stretched entirely out of shape, goal-oriented. True, Aristotle begins the *Ethics* by insisting that "every art and science has its end," but if we look at friendship, it becomes clear that "goal-orientation" is not the only meaning of "having an end." What is the goal of friendship? Indeed, on Aristotle's analysis, the mutual pursuit of goals, concretely defined, indicates something less than real friendship. So, too, I want to suggest that the game-theoretical assumption of goal-orientation is misleading as a way of thinking about most human activities, including business.[31] Business, at its best, is a worthwhile and satisfying social activity, but this is hardly the "goal" of business. Although business activity is shot through with goals, objectives and strategies, business ("busy-ness") is defined by its activities, not by its goals—much less the narrow goal summarized as "the bottom line."

6. Games and "Externalities"

As argued earlier, the notion of games in the context of decision making is too contained. It is with good reason that game theorists refer to "externalities," for it is self-containment that defines most games. The football field has carefully drawn lines around it, and only a specified number of players are allowed on the field. Poker gets played with a conscientiously non-personalized deck of cards, and every player is "in" or "out." There is no waiting on the fringe to "see how the hand goes" before joining in. Life, on the other hand, is always open-ended. There need be no fixed number of players in most business deals, and business ethics has been conscientious in its insistence that the "playing field" of corporate business is not just the boardroom but the employees and customers and entire community, "stakeholders" and not necessarily insiders. Games are closed; the market is by its very nature open. Simply adding "players" to the game won't work, not because the complications are infinite (though sometimes it seems that way) but because human contexts change as we play with them, unlike the neatly painted board on which many games are played. There are never just 52 cards in the deck and never just *n* alternatives or players in the market, and the notion of "playing" a game radically changes when not only the spectators but a multitude of mere passers-by wander onto the playing field and have their lives desperately affected by the game.

7. Games and Rules

Games as we generally conceive of them are thought to be rule-defined.[32] But business as a practice is much larger than that. The rules come after. Business ethics involves phronesis, sensitivity and imagination, not just obeying the rules. Of course there are rules (especially laws) and it is usually both unethical and imprudent to disobey them. But I think that it is essential to see business and business life first of all as a practice, not a game (which is a very specific and narrow kind of practice), in which general expectations and mutual agreements are established before there are any rules, much less laws. We get taken in by "social contract"-type thinking, when in fact it is the established practice that makes contracts possible—and rules sometimes necessary. But business has a lot longer history than business law, and, to be cryptic for lack of space, rules, regulations and laws get formulated not before but after business practices are established and, paradoxically, after the transgressions that they are designed to prohibit.

Conclusion: Game Theory and Ideology

Let me end this discussion by insisting that game theory is not just a model for business. Game theory is ideology. It is instructive. It provides the frame within which participants in the practice operate, the lenses through which they see what they are doing. "One should think of it this way." "This is how one should behave." "One should expect that this is what will happen." Some of my suspicion, accordingly, concerns how such a framework gets *used*, in defense of what policies and practices, at whose expense, to whose benefit. It is all too easy to show how a "rational" game strategy can eclipse extra-game considerations of much greater importance. The very fact that game theoreticians have felt compelled to show that their models are compatible with morals, or justice, suggests that the purview of game theory is limited, problematically focussed or outside of the realm of ethics and social philosophy. It may be neat, even elegant, but whether it is relevant to ethics or business ethics is worth serious reflection and discussion.

Some of the recent wrinkles in game theory do indeed blunt my objections, and it might even be argued that game theory suitably refined can be used to show us that we need to go beyond game theory.[33] But however captivating such paradoxes of formalism, it is a mistake to think that by solving technical problems in a theory that is already off the mark we will thereby resolve the criticism that it is indeed off the mark.[34] I am reminded of Peter Geach's infamous witticism to the effect that no amount of evidence can compensate for a conceptual error. So, too, no amount of philosophical ingenuity can compensate for what game theory excludes, namely, ethics.

Business, like most of human life, is motivated not by self-interest but by a complex of what Adam Smith called fellow-feelings and sympathy, affection and vulnerability, a sense of shame and a sense of honor, love and friendship, animosity and resentment and a hundred more emotions and attitudes. We care about what other people think of us. We care what we think of ourselves, and "doing well" (in the neo-Hobbesian, game-theoretical sense rather than the Aristotelian *eudaimonia* sense) is the dominant factor in the way we think of ourselves and the way we think of others close to us only in degenerate cases.

GAME THEORY AS A MODEL FOR BUSINESS ETHICS 27

Game theory, even where it does not presuppose pure self-interest, misses the complexity of human behavior, even economic behavior. We are not, contrary to a well-known quip by Bertrand Russell, calculating creatures. To define rationality as maximizing the chances of getting what you want is to encourage (even if it does not entail) a life devoted to personal goal orientation and strategic calculation. That makes most virtues irrational if not unintelligible. To think always in terms of getting what you want, to think strategically, is to have "one thought too many," to be, as the saying goes, "too clever by half." Such a "rational" attitude to life is itself not only irrational but something much much worse.

Notes

* Some of this article is based on my discussion of game theory in business in *Ethics and Excellence* (Oxford, 1991), which has been adapted with the permission of the publisher. Special thanks to Mark Murphy, Ken Riley, Peter Danielson, Christopher Morris, Peter Vanderschraaf and Patricia Werhane. All remaining mistakes, of course, remain my own.

[1]Albert Z. Carr, "Is Business Bluffing Ethical?" *Harvard Business Review*, January–February, 1968. Some of these responses were published in the *Harvard Business Review*, May–June, 1968.

[2]David Gauthier, *Morals by Agreement* (Oxford, 1986).

[3]"Refinement," like many more ordinary concepts, has taken on a technical meaning in game theory. I am referring to the ordinary idea of "improved and sophisticated" (as opposed to "crude and undeveloped") here.

[4]Not coincidentally, in tests of common decency (for example, the routine exercise of leaving an appropriate tip for a waitperson), economists as a group tend to do embarrassingly badly. Robert Frank, "Why Economists Make Bad Citizens" and (wth T. Gilovich and D. Regan) "Does Studying Economics Inhibit Cooperation?" *Journal of Economic Perspectives* 7, no. 2 (Spring 1993): 159–171.

[5]See my "Existentialism, Emotions, and the Cultural Limits of Rationality," *Philosophy East and West* 42, no. 4 (October 1992): 597–622.

[6]Bernard Suits, *The Grasshopper* (Toronto: University of Toronto Press, 1978).

[7]See, e.g. LaRue Tone Hosmer, "5 Years, 20 Issues, 141 Articles, and What?" *Business Ethics Quarterly* 6, no. 3 (July 1996): 325358.

[8]John von Neumann and Oscar Morgenstern, *Theory of Games and Economic Behavior*, 1944. Morgenstern was an economist. They did not invent game theory, however, as is usually supposed. Peter Vanderschraaf has argued, for example, that David Hume developed an informal version of game theory in his *Treatise of Human Nature*, part III. (This volume.)

[9]One might think of all of these as variants of cost-benefit analysis, within overlapping but different domains. Game theory could be conceived as a particular variant or, more forcefully, the formal discipline that undergirds all of them. But even broadly considered as the form of strategic interactive cost-benefit analysis, there are some serious questions of the kind I want to raise. See, e.g., David Copp, "Morality, Reason, and Management Science: The Rationale of Cost-Benefit Analysis," *Social Philosophy and Policy* 2 no. 2 (Spring 1985): 128–151.

[10]David Gauthier, *Morals by Agreement*, Chapter IV.

[11]I have argued this thesis at some length in my book, *Ethics and Excellence* (originally subtitled, "An Aristotelean Approach to Business," which is also the title of an article in *BEQ,* 1994).

[12]Hobbes, *Leviathan,* discussed as distortions of the perfect market by Gauthier, Chapter IV, p. 85. But in their uncompromising defense of free enterprise, economists and game theorists in business rarely include such qualifications.

[13]For an excellent account of the entrepreneur as one who transcends normal practices and expectations, see F. Flores, H. Dreyfus, C. Spinosa, *Disclosing New Worlds* (Cambridge: MIT Press, 1997).

[14]"George" on *Seinfeld* comes to mind, but a good deal of American comedy is based on just such absurd articulation of supposed self-interested strategies underlying normal behavior.

[15]Cf. Gauthier, *Morals by Agreement,* Chapter IV, in which he moves too far toward the other side and argues that the market "is the very antithesis of the Prisoner's Dilemma" (p. 83).

[16]Notably, by Robert Axelrod in his book, *The Evolution of Cooperation* (New York: Basic Books, 1984). The best strategy in a series of repeated game situations (that is, most business relationships) turns out to be: return trust and cooperation with trust and cooperation, breaches of trust and betrayal with breach of trust and betrayal as punishment, or "tit-for-tat." What one might do in a single encounter is rendered irrelevant (or irrational) in the light of future encounters and expected retaliation. It is a result with obvious practical implications and enormous theoretical promise (e.g., in the evolution of punishment and revenge as well as cooperation), but the basic assumptions of the problem—utility maximization and the non-cooperative stance—pertain to such sophisticated models as well as the more vulgar models, even when their conclusion is (qualified) cooperation. More recently, see Steven J. Brams, *The Theory of Moves* (Cambridge University Press, 1994), who discusses the strategy of "dynamic" games in which there are several or many moves, more or less independent of one another, a sophisticated next step beyond merely reiterated games and therefore a better model for business relationships, which are not repetitions of one and the same transaction.

[17]Derek Parfit, *Reasons and Persons* (Oxford University Press, 1984).

[18]*Ethics and Excellence,* (Oxford University Press, 1991).

[19]Here I have benefited from T. C. Schelling, *The Strategy of Conflict* (Cambridge, 1960); Edward F. McClennen, "Morality as a Public Good," a manuscript read at the Society for Business Ethics meeting in Washington, D.C., December 1988, and Bernard Suits's delightful *Grasshopper* (Toronto, 1978).

[20]Rescher, Nicholas, *Unselfishness* (University of Pittsburgh, 1975), pp. 38–39.

[21]"Escape from Paradox," *Scientific American* 217 (1967): 51.

[22]Rescher, p. 35.

[23]Ibid.

[24]John Rawls, *A Theory of Justice* (Harvard University Press, 1971), p. 144.

[25]This, I take it, is what Nietzsche means by "what is done out of love is always beyond good and evil" (*Beyond Good and Evil,* § 153), a phrase that does not have to be interpreted in the usual "immoralist" boot-in-the-face manner. Friedrich Nietzsche, *Beyond Good and Evil,* trans. Walter Kaufmann (New York: Random House, 1966), p. 90.

[26]Rawls, p. 142.

[27]See, for example, Edwin Hartman, *Organizational Ethics and the Good Life* (Oxford University Press, 1996).

[28]John Harsanyi, (rf). I am indebted to David Sherman, unpublished.

[29]Moritz Schlick, *Problems of Ethics,* trans. D. Rynin (New York: Dover, 1939), pp. 202–203.

GAME THEORY AS A MODEL FOR BUSINESS ETHICS 29

[30]Edward McClennen, "Foundational Explorations for a Normative Theory of Political Economy," in *Rationality and Dynamic Choice: Foundational Explorations* (Cambridge: Cambridge University Press, 1990).

[31]For an excellent discussion of this non–goal-oriented concept of teleology in Aristotle, see Michael Stocker in Amelie Rorty, ed., *Essays on Aristotle* (University of California Press, 1980).

[32]Ludwig Wittgenstein, *Philosophical Investigations*. See also Suits, *The Grasshopper*.

[33]Mark Murphy, in correspondence, November 1996.

[34]Jon Elster, in many books, including *Solomonic Judgments, Ulysses and the Sirens: Studies in Rationality and Irrationality,* and *Rational Choice,* brilliantly demonstrates the ways in which rationality breaks down. Nevertheless, he refuses to draw what would seem to be the obvious conclusion.

[31]

GAME THEORY AND BUSINESS ETHICS

Ken Binmore

1 Introduction

As the author of one book on the elements of game theory and another on the possible applications to ethics (Binmore [3,4,5]), I suppose it is natural that I should be asked to reply to Robert Solomon's (13) claim that "game theory has been a disaster in ethics, and now it threatens to become devastating to business ethics as well." However, I find myself somewhat at a loss as to know what to say, since the game theory he attacks is not practiced by any game theorists with whom I am familiar. At first, I thought this was because my friends and I were deemed to fall into the class of "refined" game theorists to whom Solomon is willing to grant grudging acceptance, but it turns out that their refinement lies in appealing to principles that contradict the essence of the game theoretic enterprise. My guess is therefore that the plain old "vulgar" game theory which he attacks is actually intended to be the same game theory for which John Harsanyi, John Nash, and Reinhard Selten were recently awarded the Nobel Prize. My strategy in replying will therefore have to be the same as those innocent men who are asked why they beat their wives. Instead of explaining why wife beating is a good idea, I shall have to insist that I don't beat my wife at all.

2 Solomon's Criticisms of Game Theory

After several pages of polemic, Solomon (12) reproduces seven criticisms of game theory from his book *Ethics and Excellence*. In this section I will respond to typical samples from each of these criticisms:

(1) In this criticism, he accuses game theorists of begging two questions: (a) Whether rationality demands a prudential, safety-first approach? (b) Whether rationality demands the cultivation of personal advantage to the exclusion of the interests of others? The first question perhaps relates to the misapprehension that game theory recommends the use of the maximin criterion outside zero-sum games. But even within a zero-sum game like Poker, few people would regard the enormous level of bluffing required by optional play to be either prudent or safety-first (Binmore [3]). Solomon believes that game theorists must answer the second question in the affirmative, supporting this mistaken claim with various *ad hominen* remarks about the notorious selfishness of people in my profession. But rationality as understood by game theorists is entirely neutral about the goals

of the players. For the utility theory of Von Neumann and Morgenstern to be applicable, it is only necessary that the decisions a player makes are consistent with each other.

In fact, Bergstrom (2) recently used game theory to study interaction within the family on the assumption that brothers and sisters actively care about each other's welfare. In my view, the camaraderie that Solomon rightly believes to be so important for small-group interactions inside the firm has its origins in the instinctive strategies that our species evolved for use within kin games.

(2) This criticism is largely devoted to debunking John Rawls's (9) Theory of Justice. Solomon has some excuse for classifying Anatole Rapaport and David Gauthier as game theorists, since they actually talk about games in their books. However, both fail to clear the lowest hurdle that game theorists set for their profession: both maintain that it is rational to cooperate in the one-shot Prisoners' Dilemma. But Rawls makes no pretense at being a game theorist. Behind the Rawlsian veil of ignorance, everybody is the same, and so Rawls is able to treat their predicament as a one-person decision problem. It is true that he resolves this decision problem using Von Neumann's maximum criterion, but game theorists do not endorse this idiosyncratic refusal to apply the standard methods of Bayesian decision theory. On the contrary, game theory recommends the use of maximum criterion only when two players have diametrically opposed interests. But such zero-sum games are as distant from the problem faced by the players in Rawls's original position as it is possible to get.

If Solomon wished to complain about the use of game theory behind the veil of ignorance, he would have done better to attack the widely cited ethical work of Harsanyi (6). Working independently of Rawls, he analyzed the result of using the original position to make moral judgments without appealing to unorthodox decision principles. Far from being led to Rawls' version of egalitarianism, Harsanyi concludes in favor of utilitarianism—the refutation of which was one of Rawls's (9) major aims in the Theory of Justice.

My own work criticizes both Harsanyi and Rawls for assuming that the hypothetical deal reached in the original position has the status of a binding contract (Binmore [5]). Without this assumption, the use of game-theoretic techniques leads to a conclusion much closer to Rawls than Harsanyi. If he had known of any of the literature that genuinely applies game theory to ethics, Solomon could therefore have directed his criticisms of Rawls at me. But I would be totally unmoved at game theory being criticized because its use leads to conclusions that Solomon dislikes. The principles of game theory are ethically neutral, like *modus ponens* in logic or 2 + 2 = 4 in mathematics.

It is as silly to attack game theory because it leads to ethical conclusions that you don't like as to attack logic or mathematics for the same reason. If the conclusion is wrong, the place to look for a mistake is in the assumptions from which it is deduced. For example, Harsanyi's defense of utilitarianism shouldn't be rejected because he uses orthodox decision theory, but because he can't explain why anyone should feel constrained by the terms of his hypothetical contract. Similarly, my own work is vulnerable to criticism, not I hope because the analysis is wrong, but because of the highly speculative assumptions I make about our evolutionary heritage.

(3) This criticism charges game theorists with proceeding as though people care only about money. In reply, it is only necessary to observe that it was game theorists who were largely responsible for constructing modern utility theory because it was obvious to them that it is inadequate to model people as maximizers of money.

(4) In this criticism, game theorists are taken to task for neglecting the possibility that people may be altruistic. Here he seems to forget the footnote in which he praises Axelrod's (1) game-theoretic study of the evolution of reciprocal altruism. (Although it was not Axelrod who discovered the folk theorem of repeated game theory. Nor is it true that tit-for-tat is the "best" strategy even for the indefinitely repeated Prisoners' Dilemma. Later work shows that Axelrod's claims on this front are not robust.)

(5) Here game theorists are charged again with proceeding on the assumption that people are goal-oriented, but it is not clear why Ned McClennen (7, 8) should be chosen for special mention since his theory of resolute choice is regarded as heretical by game theorists. (If McClennen were right on this subject, then Selten [10] would not be entitled to his Nobel Prize.) Let me repeat that game theorists simply assume that decisions are made consistently, and then appeal to various theorems for the conclusion that they then behave as though they were goal-oriented.

(6) This criticism would seem to apply to all mathematical modeling, since it lies in the assertion that the world is always more complicated than any specific model. His concern about the fact that it is not always clear in real-life games who should be counted among the players seems to be made in ignorance of the enormous literature within industrial organization on the entry and exit of players in games.

(7) In criticizing "social contract thinking," Solomon confuses the rules for sustaining an equilibrium in the game of life with the rules of the game of life itself. Of course established business practice should not be modeled as a game. It needs to be modeled as an equilibrium in a game. Similarly, to take up an earlier point, of course one should not model an ongoing business relationship as the one-shot Prisoners' Dilemma. But where are the game theorists who would

make such an elementary blunder? We study implicit collusion in industries controlled by only a few firms using the theory of repeated games.

3 Game Theory and Ethics

Solomon's claim that game theory has been a curse to ethics seems particularly bizarre to someone who has been seeking to gain acceptance among moral philosophers for the view that we shall never understand how and why human morality evolved until we have learned to use game theory to put some flesh on the bones of David Hume's idea that its function is to coordinate behavior on one of the many equilibria in the complicated game of life that humans play. But never has such sweet music fallen on ears so deaf! Far from game theory proving a curse to moral philosophy, it is hard to find a moral philosopher who thinks that game theory has any relevance to his subject at all. I shall therefore conclude this brief note with some propaganda about the advantages of adopting my own game-theoretic approach to ethics.

Following Singer's (11) pioneering study, it seems to me that a scientific approach has no choice but to accept that our moral systems evolved along with the human race. According to Solomon, game theorists long ago forgot Hume's emphasis on the importance of the moral sentiments, but the natural origin of our ethical intuitions takes center stage when Singer discusses their evolution in terms of three "expanding circles"—kin selection, reciprocal altruism and group selection. The first and second of these were mentioned in passing in the previous section, but it is the third that I believe to be fundamental. Human groups that find efficient, nonconfrontational ways to solve the equilibrium selection will obviously expand in size or in number when compared with groups that fall into costly disputes over which equilibrium to select. In the long run, only the former groups will therefore survive.

In my own work, I argue that nothing more than these building blocks is necessary to explain the moral intuitions that we feel so forcefully (Binmore [4, 5]). Along with the other game theorists who take this naturalistic line, I know perfectly well that my simple models don't take us very far. But we feel that the muddled platitudes of those who are unwilling to model at all take us nowhere at all. If an example is needed of the failure of traditional moral philosophy, let me recommend Solomon's (12) own *Reader's Digest* version of Aristotle's ideas. If a scientific discipline had made no progress in two thousand years, we would begin to doubt the soundness of the principles on which it was based. Perhaps we should begin to apply the same criteria to the traditional approach to ethics.

GAME THEORY AND BUSINESS ETHICS 35

Bibliography

(1) R. Axelrod. *The Evolution of Cooperation.* New York: Basic Books, 1984.

(2) T. Bergstrom. "On the evolution of altruistic ethical rules for siblings." *American Economic Review* 85 (1985).

(3) K. Binmore. *Fun and Games.* Lexington, Mass.: D. C. Heath, 1991.

(4) K. Binmore. *Playing Fair: Game Theory and the Social Contract I.* Cambridge, Mass.: MIT Press, 1994.

(5) K. Binmore. *Just Playing: Game Theory and the Social Contract II.* Cambridge, Mass.: MIT Press, 1998.

(6) J. Harsanyi. *Rational Behavior and Bargaining Equilibrium in Games and Social Situations.* Cambridge: Cambridge University Press, 1977.

(7) E. McClennen. *Rationality and Dynamic Choice.* Cambridge: Cambridge University Press, 1990.

(8) E. McClennen. "Morality as a public good." *Business Ethics Quarterly* 9, no. 1 (1999).

(9) J. Rawls. *A Theory of Justice.* Oxford: Oxford University Press, 1972.

(10) R. Selten. "Reexamination of the perfectness concept for equilibrium points in extensive-games." *International Journal of Game Theory* 4 (1975): 25–55.

(11) P. Singer. *The Expanding Circle: Ethics and Sociobiology.* New York: Farrar, Strauss and Giroux, 1980.

(12) R. Solomon. *Ethics and Excellence.* Oxford: Oxford University Press, 1991.

(13) R. Solomon. "Game theory as a model for business and business ethics." *Business Ethics Quarterly* 9, no. 1 (1999).

[32]

Game theory and the evolution of strategic thinking

Alan E. Singer
Department of Management, University of Canterbury, Christchurch, New Zealand
Tel.: +64 3 3588934; Fax: +64 3 3642020;
E-mail: aes@mang.canterbury.ac.nz

The idea that game theory could help managers to think better about strategic problems is re-interpreted, with reference to various extensions and adaptations of the theory. A conceptual model of an Ultragame is illustrated and discussed, in which the players are plurally-rational strategic-entities. Such adapted models can help managers to augment their language, their ideology and their integrity. Compared to the mathematical extensions, which have found but a few business applications, the adapted conceptual models are more directly relevant to contemporary practical business problems, such as those involving the players' boundaries and identities, not to mention their likely future problems and others' problems.

Keywords: Game theory, strategic-management, rationality, ideology, strategy

Alan E. Singer is a senior lecturer at the Department of Management, University of Canterbury. He holds a doctorate in management from Canterbury, with degrees in Mathematics (Oxford University) and Psychology (London University). He worked in the UK private sector before taking up academic appointments in New Zealand. He is author of *Strategy as Rationality* (Avebury series in philosophy) and has published over 80 academic and professional papers. He is currently on the editorial boards of *Human Systems Management* and the *Journal of Business Ethics*.

1. Introduction

It is often said that game theory can help managers to gain new insight, or to *think better* about problems of competition and business strategy [8,14,26,39]; but what does "thinking better" really mean, in contemporary management contexts? If the phrase is simply taken to mean avoiding miscalculation, or identifying an equilibrium point, then game theory and its various extensions (e.g., Supergames, Metagames, Information-dependent games, etc.) provide the appropriate analytic framework. However, if "thinking better" implies an improved understanding of the World as it now really is, or improving creativity when finding and solving important problems, then the role of game theoretic models in business strategy becomes laid open to a rather significant critique. First, the players in games of business strategy are themselves often changing their structures, their boundaries and their identities, as all types of productive entity are re-configuring in novel ways, made possible by the new communications technologies [24,44]. Secondly, while contemporary managers are undoubtedly confronting increased competition in the marketplace, they are also (often reluctantly) having to confront many social and environmental problems. In sum, formal game theory cannot be expected to yield practical solutions to many of the most important problems of contemporary "strategic" business management.

Despite the limitations, research in game theory could still help managers to "think better", especially if the theory is *adapted*, in ways to be defined shortly. As a first step, it may be noted that formal models in general (e.g., for forecasting, asset-valuation, or strategic-analysis, etc.) have often been observed to function in organizations in unorthodox ways (see Section 2) that is, ways that are disconnected from the mathematical theories that gave birth to them. In particular, the formal models of game theory, as they have become more widely known and understood, have also tended to promulgate quite distinctive assumptions about business goals, competitive behavior and the nature of rationality in management. For this reason, game theoretic models do much more than merely represent or explain strategic behavior, they also affect that behavior and slowly change it. Put differently, the models themselves are like *memes*

Table 1
Some unorthodox roles of formal models

(i)	"Political" roles include models as...
	status-symbols: when the managers who understand and operate the model acquire status and power based upon this expertise.
	pliers: when the need to estimate model parameters enables managers to extract confessions, or assumptions, from subordinates, or to squeeze them into line.
	batteries: when the participants in a detailed analysis tend to increase their psychological commitment to any resulting prescriptions (i.e., the illusion of control).
(ii)	"Soft" roles include models as...
	platforms: when models become an arena or platform for an organized discussion, or reflection.
	Socratic tutors: when models enable their users to learn, or to educate themselves, by means of structured *inquiry.* For example presentation of the Prisoners' Dilemma Game sometimes evokes questions about possibilities for cooperation.
	keys: when models become like a set of keys [47] which will "open doors for the actors and allow them to procede" [27, p. 163].
(iii)	"Ideological" roles include models as...
	rituals: when the process of model-building serves to reinforce a culture of profit-maximization (associated with *RUM*) in an organization.
	glue: when models bind or unite managers (or team members) together, behind a common set of goals, concepts and vocabulary.
	filters and switches: when a model serves to direct (or re-direct) attention towards (or away from) particular aspects of a managerial problem, such as the social and moral aspects.
	memes: when models function as units of cultural transmission. Like popular tunes, they leap from mind to mind and affect the behaviour of the "infected" entities.

(Dawkins [12]), which are the cultural equivalent of genes. The models, or memes, occupy players' minds (individually and collectively) as they are copied, spread out, or propagated through a community of thinkers, or players.

In Section 3 of the paper, various extensions and adaptations of game theory are briefly described. The "extensions" involve mathematical developments of simple game models, characterised by the fundamental assumption of Rational-Utility-Maximizing (*RUM*) players. "Adaptations", in contrast, involve extending the players' *set* of rationalities by including other distinctive forms, some of which are not captured by *RUM*. (For fuller accounts of but a few of the *elusive* forms of rationality see [2,10,17,22,35,38, 40].) Examples of adaptations include the operationalized version of Metagames [26] and Hypergames [4], as well as the conceptual model of an Ultragame [45,48,50], elaborated in Section 3. Section 4 of the paper then discusses various ways of comparing and evaluating the extensions and adaptations. Finally, by invoking the conceptual framework of Strategy-as-Rationality [44,49], this meta-theoretic treatment of games and their rationalities is placed at the core of *strategic management* theory and practice.

2. Roles of mathematical models

Several studies have identified unorthodox roles of formal (quantitative or mathematical) models in organizations [16,18,36]. These roles can be classified (Table 1) as (i) relating to the internal politics of organizations, such as conferring power to individuals based upon their expertise with the model, (ii) soft-OR applications, in which adapted models function as problem-structuring methodologies, and (iii) ideological roles, in which formal models come to symbolize, promulgate, or propagate particular assumptions and beliefs about the organization and its strategic problems. Each of the above "roles" is quite plainly *social*, as well as analytic and cognitive. Indeed, it has increasingly become recognized by management scientists [11,18,27,36] that the building and validating of *all* formal mathematical models are "not only cognitive activities, but also social activities" [27, p. 162]. The present paper explores this social dimension, in the special case of game theory: its politics, its formulations and its ideologies.

With game theory, the consequences of ignoring the social dimension of model-validation and model-use, whilst attending to the traditional mathematics of optimization, can indeed be rather serious. Fifteen years ago, Davis and Hersh [11] suggested that mathematical modellers often "deliberately force... social aspects of the universe" into the "delightful (mathematical) patterns they have wrought"; implying that they force out the more elusive social, ideological and moral aspects of the system being modelled. Later, Etzion [17] made a rather similar point, in his book, *The Moral Dimension*. He noted that formal economic theories, based upon *RUM* players and agents, often "miseducate" students of business management and tend to co-produce a future society or social-system with all the "wrong" characteristics. For example, the students (and the society) become more comfortable with, or de-sensitized to the corresponding language of threat, fear, predation, opportunism and guile (all in the name of fiduciary duty); but they remain relatively impatient, careless or ignorant about words such as fairness, justice, dignity and moral-rights.

It is not only neo-classical and evolutionary economics, with their corresponding perspectives on strategic management [44,56], that have successfully propogated the seductive language of Jungle-Warfare, throughout many business and political communities: in his book *Darwin's Dangerous Idea*, the philosopher Daniel Dennett has specifically warned of the risks associated with "doing good work in Evolutionary Ethics", also based upon game theoretic models, whilst nonetheless remaining "dismayingly heedless of the misuses to which (these models) might be put, by ideologues of one persuasion or another" [13, p. 491].

2.1. Models as memes

Formal models quickly "leap from mind to mind", like memes, in effect generating copies of themselves, changing or infecting individual and collective minds and slowly influencing the *Zeitgeist*. Accordingly, the general characteristics of memes become noteworthy. First, like genes, memes help themselves: once they have been created, they tend to disable any opposing or hostile forces in their environment. This dynamic was clearly illustrated in the success of the Tit-for-Tat algorithm (a meme) in Axelrod's evolutionary competition [1]. In the case of game models (like the Prisoners' Dilemma Game viewed as a meme), this "disabling" capability has historically taken on the form of *RUM*-capturing: the many attempts (some Nobel-prize winning) to disable our more traditional notions

of morality and sociality, by capturing them in terms of the players' interests and utilities.

Secondly, successful memes (like genes) are *not* necessarily advantageous to the society or total system that hosts them. As Darwin himself wrote "I cannot persuade myself that a beneficient and omnipotent God would have designedly created the *Ichneumonidae* (a type of wasp) with the express intention of their feeding within the living bodies of caterpillars". Put differently, some of the genes (or memes) that are generously hosted by a system (or culture) can turn out to be highly destructive. In this sense, there are good memes and bad memes [13].

Is game theory "good" or "bad"? Those who see something distinctive and elusive (i.e., not "captured") in their notions of morality, sociality and ethics; something that cannot be adequately represented or expressed in terms of mere interests, preferences and desires, must also see something correspondingly "bad" about game theory... its ideological overtones, with its potentially corrosive social impact. More constructively, despite the occasional claims, by economists, of the theory's capability for generating "good advice" [7, p. 215] for managers and strategists, it would now seem that it is also capable of improvement. Like other memes, game theoretic models might also be purposefully adapted, or consciously re-designed, by deliberate and persistent human intervention.

3. Adaptations

During their 50 year history, the so-called "simple" game models [26] have been extended, in various ways (Fig. 1 and Table 2). An "extension" of a formal model is a mathematical development which yields a deeper or more comprehensive analysis. Such extensions characteristically retain the implicit assumption of *RUM* players[1]. This means, as Von Neumann himself put it, that "the behavior (of each of the players) is (assumed to be) motivated by the same selfish interests as the behavior of the first player" [64, p. 13]. Examples of this types of formal extension include Supergames [1,29,30], Games-with-imperfect-information [23], Metagames [26] and Psychological,

---

[1] Various distinctive forms of rationality are special cases of *RUM*, such as the *extensive* form [5] in which the objects-of-choice are forecasts based upon extrapolated of historical data. Many other forms such as *bounded*, *sympathy*, could be captured as *RUM*.

Table 2
Extensions of games, with some properties

Model m	Decision-function rationality is ...	Objects-of-choice are ...	Type of prescription	Rigour-relevance	Purpose(s)	Players are homo ...	Decision error is to ...
m₁ Simple game (normal or extensive form)	*RUM* (strategic)	given and probabilistic	Choose a pure or mixed or probabilistic strategy, and/or make side-agreements.	High rigour.	Improve under-standing, provide insight, prescribe, guide and hypothesise.	*economicus*	Choose a dominated strategy, etc.
m₂ Supergame	*RUM* (evolutionary)						miscalculate
m₃ Imp-info-game	*RUM* (with Bayesian revision)						
m₄ Metagame (1) (1971)	*RUM* (meta-rationality₁)	constructed algorithmically from the given OOCs	Choose a metastrategy or conditional strategy, etc.	Hardly ever used as technique.	To uncover the objectively rational behaviour in a game.		
m₅ Info-dependent or psychological games	*RUM* (psychic utility)	given, incorporating psychological states	As in m₁-m₃.		To capture hopes, fears, disappointments, etc.		

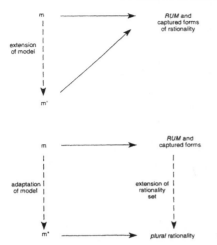

Fig. 1. Extensions vs. adaptations of formal models.

or information-dependent games [19,20]. These are labelled m_1 to m_5 in Table 2, where some of their more salient properties are listed.

In contrast with extensions, the term "adaptation of a formal model", as used here, refers to developments of the model, or its operationalized methodology, that incorporate, or sweep-in, some other distinctive forms of rationality. These could include the elusive forms [2,10,17,22,35,38,40] that may not necessarily be captured, or reducible to *RUM*. When a model is adapted, in this sense, its image under the mapping decision-function-rationality [43,47] becomes extended, but not necessarily the pure mathematics of the model itself (Fig. 1). Examples of such "adaptations" of simple games include Metagames in their operational form [26], Hypergames as a "methodique" [4] and Ultragames (described below). These adaptations are labelled m_6 to m_9 in Table 3.

3.1. The Ultragame model

The conceptual model of an Ultragame [45,48,50] is the result of pursuing the process of adaptation of game models, to its ultimate conclusion. An Ultragame (m_8 and m_9 in Table 3) simply sweeps in *all* the distinctive forms of rationality, the entire rationality-set, into a model[2] of strategic interaction

---

[2]More formally, we could write: $\mathcal{D}(m_8) = \mathbb{R}$ where $\mathcal{D}$ is the mapping decision-function-rationality [53] and m_8 is an Ultragame model and $\mathbb{R}$ is the rationality-set.

amongst multiple types of entity, based upon their *plural*-rationality. It is implicitly assumed that each player is not only engaged in a competitive battle to further its "selfish interests", or utilities, even when broadly defined; but it is also engaged in a search for success, with reference to *plural*-rationality. Put differently, all of the players in an Ultragame are assumed to have significant concerns for society, morality, ecology and autonomy that mediate their behavior, but that cannot be fully captured as preferences over a set of well-defined strategic alternatives.

Despite its incomplete formal exposition, the conceptual model of an Ultragame can readily be made operational as a structured *inquiry*, or framework for strategic thinking [55]. This can be used in practice to support internal strategic analysis, when players direct questions at themselves, or for understanding the behavior of other entities, as in traditional business "competitor" analysis methodologies [55]. Various questions, in ordinary, natural-language, flow directly from each distinctive form of rationality. For example, there are questions rooted in the *cognitive* and *instrumental* forms of rationality, but associated with simple-games, such as: "What are the competitors' expectations about our behavior? What are its internal incentive structures?" (e.g., [42]), but there are other questions, based upon the more *elusive* forms of rationality, such as: "Does the entity... have a history or policy of treating others fairly? ... avoiding or minimising harm? ... preserving traditions? ... contributing to the development of institutions that symbolise a good life with others? ... protecting the rights of others? ... fostering autonomy and positive freedom?

There are many people who think that contemporary corporate managers and network participants should be asking *all* of these questions, then seeking or designing some answers; not to mention openly discussing the questions whilst encouraging others to do so. Indeed, it is the primary purpose of the Ultragames model to re-direct the players' attention accordingly (cf. Table 2).

3.2. Synergistic design

A further adaptation of game theory, an Ultragame (2) [58] also incorporates the idea of *synergies* amongst the distinctive forms of rationality[3]. In this adaptation, each strategic-entity is re-conceptualized

---

[3]If $\mathbb{Y}$ is the set of such synergies, we could write: $\mathcal{D}(m_9) = \mathbb{R} \cup \mathbb{Y}$.

Table 3
Adaptations of games, with some properties

Model m	Decision-function rationality is...	Objects-of-choice are...	Type of prescription	Rigour-relevance	Purpose(s)	Players are homo...	Decision error is to...
m_6 Metagame (1987)	meta-rationality$_1$ with belief-forms	actions (given or generated) perceived as means of control of issues	Inquiry, incorporating promises, fears, etc.	Moderate rigour, used as tool and technique.	Problem-structuring, facilitating agreements, understanding conflict, arming oneself, exploring scenarios.	economicus and cogitans	Overlook possible outcome scenarios.
m_7 Hypergame	RUM with belief-forms	perceived hypothesised (assumed)	As for (meta-) game but with reconsideration of the identity of other players and their preferences.				Misperceive other players' perceived game.
m_8 Ultragame (1)	plural-rationality	vaguely perceived, partially defined, constructed, symbolic, hyper-real	Inquiry based upon plural-rationality.	Low rigour. Relevant to problem-owner, other's problems and future problems.	Redirect attention, propogate ideology, re-make players.	economicus and cogitans and civicus	Poor choice of rationality as evaluated by meta-criteria.
m_9 Ultragame (2)	hyper-rationality	designed strategies	Engage in optimal design, with synergies.		As above. Motivate synergies and optimal design.	creans and designans	Failure to design synergistic alternatives.

as being *hyper*-rational, in the special sense of the word used recently in Sociology (see Glossary). Hyper-rational entities seek to implant synergies amongst their own plural forms of rationality [33, 48]. Additional questions for strategic analysis follow quite naturally from various forms of rationality-synergy [48,49], for example:

"Does the entity (or player)...

... apply scientific knowledge to *increase* the utilization of its lower-level practical skills?" (i.e., the theoretical and practical Weberian forms.)

... forge links with benevolent institutions in ways that *strengthen* its sense of identity?" (i.e., the contextual and expressive forms.)

... creatively seek new ways of producing wealth for exchange, that *also* promote social justice, further democratic aims and *also* help to restore vital ecosystems." (i.e., the deliberative and *RUM* forms.)

There are indeed a great many people who now think that managers should be asking precisely *these* sorts of questions, then actively seeking or designing some positive answers, much more often [15,24,25, 52]. Yet, neither simple game theory nor its extensions can possibly help to cultivate or propagate this type of strategic thinking.

3.3. Illustration

Despite the prevailing competitive ideology, associated with extended games, some contemporary strategic-entities already behave as if they were players in an Ultragame, but not an extended game. For example, in 1992, the famous clothing company Levi Strauss reportedly broke off its relationship with some of its international garment suppliers, because the suppliers' business practices were deemed to be socially or environmentally unacceptable. The company then documented its "Business-partner terms of engagement" that set out some hard *questions* to be asked about suppliers, thus encouraging all players to adopt more socially responsible business practices. In this episode, Levi Strauss were *not* searching for some optimal price-quality vector amongst some given alternatives. Like many other business players, they had committed themselves to a process of persuasion, assistance and co-operative re-design.

In this socially responsible business practice of active "partner engagement", or persuasion (with words

as well as money), in which dialogue and morality play a distinctive role in bringing about creative change, can be modelled as an Ultragame. Yet it cannot be fully captured as an extended games, nor the "supplier as a competitor" conceptual model of business strategy (e.g., [42]). The latter models completely fail to capture the spirit and rationale of the more progressive "partner engagement" doctrine.

This contrast between the Simple game model and an Ultragame is amplified in Figs 2 and 3. In the figures, player 1 is a supplier company (a workshop, or sweatshop) located in a less-developed country. Its owner-managers (not to mention the employees) can perceive an alternative to the *status quo*: to become a progressive business. However, this would require some further investment, leading to a higher unit cost, at least in the short term. These costs could be passed on, as a higher supply price. The *status quo* choice is simply to continue as an oppressive employer, paying very low wages for long hours; but enjoying relatively low unit cost. Player 1's preference then depends upon what player 2, the overseas buyer, is expected to do. Player 2 might prefer to renew the contract, or go elsewhere. When the strategic problem is thus *formulated*, as a Simple game, the rankings for both players are as shown in the matrix (Fig. 2).

With this formulation, the calculated (*RUM*) solution is to close the deal at the lower price. When implemented in the real world, this solution helps perpetuate and reinforce the *habits of oppression*. Casual observation of many global sourcing policies readily confirms that this is not such a rare outcome. Indeed... and this is a the major point of the present paper... the outcome is rather inevitable, so long as one persists in *formulating* strategic business problems as games of interests. Therefore, from a human systems perspective, this formulation is itself a major part of the *problem*.

The Ultragame model now offers an explicit alternative formulation (Fig. 3). Rather than calculate joint interests, Ultragame players are engaging in inquiry, persuasion, reflection and creative re-design of their strategic possibilities. This process continues until the strategic problem is settled, resolved, or dissolved [47, 51,58]. More specifically, player 1, the supplier, asks some hard questions about player 2 (Q in the figure) and about itself (Q'). Some specific examples are:

Q1. Does this entity (i.e., buyer and self) have a reputation or policy emphasizing fairness in the treatment of stakeholders?

PLAYER 2
(Buyer)

	give contract to supplier.	find another supplier.
progressive (higher cost & price)	$1^=, 4$	$3, 2^=$
oppressive (lower cost & price)	$1^=, 1$	$4, 2^=$

PLAYER 1
(Supplier)

RANKINGS
(1 is best, 4 is worst)

PLAYER 1
1* becomes progressive and gets contract.
1* remains oppressive and gets contract.
3   becomes progressive but loses contract
    and is consoled by conscience.
4   loses contract, remains oppressive.

PLAYER 2
1   buyer gets low-price supply.
2   buyer finds another cheaper
    supplier but incurs costs of search.
4   buyer gets high-price supply.

FORMULATION: Matrix of ranked interests
OUTCOME: Deal closed, oppression
        perpetuated.

Fig. 2. A sourcing decision as a simple game.

Q2. Are the entity's routine practices in line with its expressed values?

Q3. Does the entity utilize experience at all levels of operation in a process of continual improvement and re-design? etc.

At the same time, player 2 (the buyer) seeks answers to another set of questions as they apply to player 1 (q in Fig. 3) and to itself (q'), as follows:

q1. Does the entity have programs in place to develop its internal capabilities (e.g., training, education, etc.)?

q2. Is there a pattern over time in this supplier's decisions? (e.g., delays, quality problems, poor treatment of staff, broken agreements, etc.)

q3. Is our own situation (e.g., cashflow problems) unduly influencing our current dealings with the supplier? (e.g., inclining us to overlook the bad working conditions, etc.).

All of these questions flow from considerations of *plural* rationality and *hyper* rationality (in the synergy-seeking sense). That is, entities ask whether each particular form of rationality and form of synergy is manifest in all of the other entities within the system being modelled. When this type of conceptual modelling occurs amongst multiple players, the outcome in the real world tends towards increased levels of trust and openness, as well as health, or competitive fitness [58]. Put differently, the adapted conceptual model, with the re-formulation of the strategic problem as an Ultragame, is itself a *solution* [68].

4. Meta-modelling

Despite the likely outcome of choosing Ultragames as a method of strategic analysis, they are not universally preferred. Accordingly, of the various models listed in Tables 2 and 3 one could ask the meta-modelling question: "Which model is best?" The column headings of the tables then provide a framework for structuring an evaluation of the alternative models, as follows.

4.1. Rigour-relevance

All of the extensions of simple games (m_1 to m_5 in Table 1) are mathematically rigorous, but, for var-

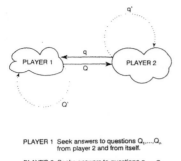

PLAYER 1 Seek answers to questions $Q_1,....,Q_n$ from player 2 and from itself.

PLAYER 2 Seeks answers to questions $q_1,....,q_n$ from player 1 and from itself.

FORMULATION & SOLUTION

Structured inquiry, constructive engagement, creative and synergistic design.

OUTCOME : increased level of openness, trust, autonomy, quality.

Fig. 3. Sourcing policy as an Ultragame.

ious reasons [7] they are hardly ever used to solve real managerial problems. (However, almost 50 years after the original work, applications have been found to problems such as the setting of "fair" user-pays fees for privatised airport runway facilities.) In contrast, the soft-OR adaptations (m_6 and m_7 in Table 3) have been used in practice to facilitate problem-solving in a variety of organizations [46]. Ultragames (m_8 and m_9) now occupy a rather special position on the rigour-relevance spectrum [41]. They are plainly conceptual rather than mathematical, but they are particularly relevant to problems that the players themselves may not even consciously perceive. These include problems associated with the players' integrity, ideology and language, as well as future problems and others' problems.

4.2. The purposes

The mathematical extensions of game theory were developed partly out of intrinsic curiosity [11], but also to yield potentially useful insights into utility-maximizing behavior. They have been used to prescribe action, accordingly (e.g., find an equilibrium point). In addition, the models have yielded many testable experimental hypotheses [9]. In contrast, the adaptations of game theory were designed in order to function as *platforms, tutors* and *keys* (Table 1), to "open doors" [27, p. 163], to explore scenarios, or to prepare for negotiations. The purpose of Ultra-

games is much more fundamental: it is to function as a *switch* (Table 1) that re-directs the players' attention away from their immediate interests and desires, but towards the more elusive forms of rationality and the task of creative re-design.

4.3. The players

In extended games, the players are conceptualized as utility maximizing *homo economicus*. They have consistent preferences amongst given well-defined objects-of-choice (moves or strategies). In the soft-OR adaptations, however, the players are *homo economicus* AND *homo cogitans*. The strategic alternatives are constructed percepts, whilst beliefs are accessed and revised as the game is played (i.e., the belief-oriented, or cognitive forms of rationality are swept into the model). In Ultragames, the players also become *homo civicus* [15]; that is, they are mindful of the elusive forms of rationality and the importance of remaining open to persuasion by social dialogue and reflective deliberation. The objects-of-choice in the game might be partly defined, partly constructed, or vaguely perceived. For example, they could be hyper-real symbols and signs [21], or prototypes of synergistic designs, envisioned and experienced in virtual worlds. In the latter case, the players have also become *homo creans* (creator) AND *homo designans* (designer) [48,52,57].

4.4. Decision-errors

In extensions of games, an error takes the form of a miscalculation, or a player's choice of a dominated strategy. For example, in the one-off, 2-player Prisoners' Dilemma Game, "co-operate" is sometimes called an "error", because it is dominated by "defect". In games of imperfect information, errors are normally associated with miscalculations involving probabilities. (In the metatheory, these are sometimes interpreted in misapplications of players' cognitive heuristics.) In psychological games, errors can also involve the overlooking of some of the outcome-related influences on the psychic-utilities of the players [63]. In metagame and hypergame analysis, the notion of "error" is further expanded to include the overlooking of important possibilities, the mis-construing the other players' perceived games, or even wrongly identifying the other players [26,36].

An error in an Ultragame is much more fundamental: it is a *poor choice of rationalities* by the players

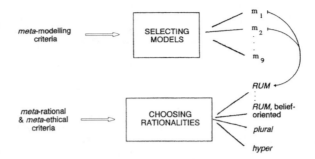

Fig. 4. Selecting game-models as choosing rationalities.

(Fig. 4). In this context, "poor" refers to evaluative meta-rational criteria, such as *globality, universalizability* and *self-support* [46,51]. Ultragame players can make errors-of-omission, when they ignore the elusive forms of rationality, or when they fail to design and implant rationality-synergies. It is becoming increasingly apparent that this type of "error", when it becomes widespread in a human system, leads to increased levels of disparity, resentment, frustration and oppression.

5. Implications for managers

The meta-analysis of game models, with their rationalities, can be placed at the heart of *Strategic Management* theory and practice, simply by invoking the conceptual framework of Strategy-as-Rationality [44,49]. This framework consists of (i) a strategy-*set* whose elements are the major concepts and components of theories of Strategic Management, (ii) an entity-*set* whose elements are the multiple types of player, or strategic-entity (e.g., individual, firm, network, virtual-corporation, etc.), and (iii) the rationality-*set*. "Strategy-as-Rationality" then sets out an isomorphic correspondence between the strategy-set and the rationality-set. The framework extends the "individual metaphor" for the firm, widely employed in the general theory of strategic management [3]. (It is noteworthy that objections to the metaphor have been described elsewhere as "roadblocks in the path of *inquiry*" [38].)

When the Ultragame model is placed within the framework of Strategy-as-Rationality, it carries some rather fundamental implications for managerial policies and practices. In addition to the methodology of inquiry (set out in the previous section), there are other prescriptions concerning (i) the enrichment of the language of Strategic Management, (ii) the propogation of an augmented ideology, and (iii) the possibility of attaining individual and collective integrity.

5.1. Enriched language

The problem of choosing models, as depicted in Fig. 4, corresponds (*via* the isomorphism in the framework) to a choice of concepts in strategic-thinking, as well as language for the strategy-discourse (Fig. 5). Thus, for example, the choice of the *RUM*-captured forms of rationality, with the extended (but not adapted) game models, corresponds with the deployment of the traditional language of economic competition. Words like threat, fear, predation, sanctions, monitoring and control, then become the norm [42]. In comparison, the (meta-rational and meta-modelling) choice of *plural* and *hyper* forms of rationality, with the corresponding Ultragame model, leads quickly to an enriched discourse with an augmented vocabulary. This includes words like coexistence (*Kyosei* in Japanese), sociality, civility, openness, creativity and synergistic design [52,56]. Many people think that such words should be heard much more often, in contemporary business and politics, at all levels.

5.2. Ideological transition

The traditional language of Competitive Strategy is often associated with the relentless pursuit of essentially selfish interests, by the stronger and more powerful players. For many people this has now come to symbolise a negation of freedom: unacceptable levels of subjugation, disempowerment and marginalization. They have slowly become trapped within the

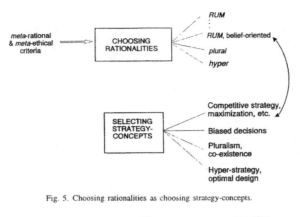

Fig. 5. Choosing rationalities as choosing strategy-concepts.

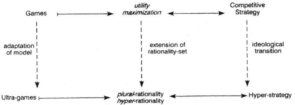

Fig. 6. Adaptations and transitions.

"descending iron cage" that Max Weber associated quite directy with instrumental or calculated forms of rationality. Put differently, they have become victims of the economization of society (G. Ritzer calls this "McDonaldization").

It is now possible that new models like Ultragames, with other, similar techniques [47,51,57] could take on the role of *keys* (cf. Table 1) enabling all types of entity to prise open the doors of this cage. To amplify and communicate this point, the three notions discussed so far: adaptation of models, extensions of the rationality-set, and augmentation of language, can be presented together as a unified schema (Fig. 6). As simple game models are adapted, becoming more like Ultragames, their decision-function-rationalities become extended and the corresponding language of Management becomes augmented and enriched. As the adapted models and the augmented language spread throughout individual and collective minds, the ideology of Strategic Management is slowly transformed, becoming much more like Business Ethics [25,46,53].

5.3. Integrity

The notion of ideological transition (the right hand side of Fig. 6) can also be expressed in much more personal and practical terms, literally closer to home. The ideology of economic competition, competitive strategy and utility maximization (the top of Fig. 6) has encouraged countless individuals to strongly *differentiate* their work life from their personal or family life. When these people enter an office, or a factory, they become fighters, warriors, or slaves; but when they physically leave the workspace, they quickly transform themselves into discussants, mentors, friends, or lovers. Despite the growth of working at home (and in transit) many continue to defend this way of life, i.e., the principle of role-differentiation.

Strategy-as-rationality fosters an alternative principle: role-*integration*. The ideology of Ultragames, with plural-rationality and hyper-strategy (bottom of Fig. 6) seeks to trap all entities, including individual managers themselves, into becoming "integrated and balanced persons", at all times [59, p. 100]. This forced re-integration of personal and managerial (or productive) life-roles seems rather timely. It is especially well-suited to the many new forms of production now made possible by technological advance (e.g., the virtual firm or network), not to mention the many new types of family.

6. Conclusion

The idea that game theory can help managers to "think better" about their strategic problems has now been given a much wider interpretation. Traditional game theory and its extensions have certainly yielded many mathematical insights, with some testable hypotheses. The methodologies of metagames and hypergames have helped managers to explore scenarios, or to arm themselves more thoroughly for negotiations; but, when they are re-armed with the concept of an Ultragame, managers quickly become capable of thinking better and talking better about their strategic problems, others' problems and future problems. In this way, the adaptations of game theory could now be used as platforms, for designing, discussing and reflecting upon new strategies and structures for living and working together, for the common good. Put differently [13, p. 510] adapted game theory could become one of "the mind tools we need to design and redesign ourselves, ever searching for better solutions to the problems we create for ourselves and others".

References

[1]   R. Axelrod, *The Evolution of Cooperation*, Basic Books, New York, 1984.

[2]   K. Baier, *The Rational and Moral Order: the Social Roots of Reason and Morality*, Open Court Publishing, LaSalle, IL, 1995.

[3]   J.B. Barney, Beyond individual metaphors in understanding how firms behave: a comment on game theory and prospect theory models of firm behavior, in: *Fundamental Issues in Strategy: A Research Agenda*, R. Rumelt, D. Schendel and D. Teece, eds, HBS Press, Boston, MA, 1994, pp. 55–70.

[4]   P.G. Bennett and C.S. Huxham, Hypergames and what they do: a 'soft OR' approach, *JORS* 33 (1982), 41–50.

[5]   K. Binmore, Modelling rational players, *Economics & Philosophy* 3 (1987), 179–214.

[6]   P. Bourgine, *Homo oeconomicus* is also *homo cogitans*, *Theory & Decision* 27 (1989), 1–6.

[7]   C.F. Camerer, Does strategy research need game theory?, in: R. Rumelt et al., eds, 1994, *op cit.*, pp. 195–220.

[8]   K. Chatterjee and G.L. Lilien, Game theory in marketing science, uses and limitations, *Int. Jnl. of Research in Mktg.* 3 (1986), 79–93.

[9]   A. Colman, *Game Theory and Experimental Games*, Pergamon Press, 1982.

[10] A. Cudd, Game theory and the history of ideas about rationality, *Economics & Philosophy* 9 (1993), 101–133.

[11] P.J. Davis and R. Hersch, *The Mathematical Experience*, Birkhauser, Boston, 1981.

[12] R. Dawkins, *The Selfish Gene*, OUP, Oxford, 1976.

[13] D. Dennett, *Darwin's Dangerous Idea*, Allen Lane, 1995.

[14] C.A. Di Benedetto, Modelling rationality in marketing decision making with game theory, *Jnl. Acad. Mkt. Sci.* 15(4) (1987), 22–32.

[15] J.S. Dryzek, Democracy and environmental policy instruments, in: *Markets, the State and the Environment: Towards Integration*, R. Eckersley, ed., MacMillan, Melbourne, 1995.

[16] A. Eerola, The role of general purpose forecasts in companies' strategic decision making, Paper presented at *9th ISF*, Vancouver, 1989.

[17] A. Etzioni, *The Moral Dimension: Towards a New Economics*, Free Press, New York, 1988.

[18] B. Fischoff and B. Goiten, The informal use of formal models, *Acad. Mgmnt. Rev.* 9(3) (1984), 505–512.

[19] J. Geanakoplos and D. Schmeidler, Information-dependent games: sequential rationality, *Games & Economic Behavior* 1 (1989), 60–79.

[20] I. Gilboa and D. Schmeidler, Information-dependent games: can common sense be common knowledge?, *Econ. Lett.* 27 (1988), 215–221.

[21] R. Goldman and S. Sapson, Advertising in the age of hypersignification, *Theory, Culture and Society* 11 (1994), 23–54.

[22] S. Hargreaves-Heap, *Rationality in Economics*, Blackwell, Oxford, 1989.

[23] J.C. Harsanyi, Games with incomplete information played by Bayesian players. III. The basic probability distribution of the game, *Management Science* 14 (1968), 486–502.

[24] P. Hawken, *The Ecology of Commerce*, Weisenfeld & Nicolson, London, 1993.

[25] L. Hosmer, Strategic planning as if ethics mattered, *Strategic Management Journal* (Summer Special Issue) 15 (1994), 17–34.

[26] N. Howard, *Paradoxes of Rationality: Theory of Games and Political Behavior*, MIT Press, Cambridge, MA, 1971.

[27] M. Landry and M. Oral, In search of a valid view of model validation for operations research, *EJOR* 66(2) (1993), 161–167.

[28] I. Levi, *Hard Choices: Decision Making Under Unresolved Conflict*, CUP, Cambridge, MA, 1986.

[29] D. Luce and H. Raiffa, *Games and Decisions: Introduction and Critical Survey*, Wiley & Sons, New York, 1957.

[30] B. Mor and Z. Maoz, Learning, preference change and the evolution of enduring rivalries, in: *The Dynamics of Enduring Rivalries*, P. Diehl, ed., Urbana, U. Illinois Press (forthcoming).

[31] M. Oral and O. Kettani, The facets of modelling and validation in Operational Research, *EJOR* 66(2) (1993), 216–234.

[32] M. Porter, *Competitive Strategy*, Free Press, New York, 1980.

[33] G. Ritzer and T. Le Moyne, Hyperrationality: an extension of Weberian and Neo-Weberian theory, in: G. Ritzer, *Metatheorizing in Sociology*, Lexington Books, MA, 1991.

[34] R. Rorty, *Consequences of Pragmatism*, Univ. Minnesota Press, Minneapolis, 1982.

[35] R. Rorty, Science as solidarity, in: *The Rhetoric of Human Science*, J. Nelson, A. Megill and D. McClosky, eds, Univ. Wisconsin Press, Madison, 1986.

[36] J. Rosenhead, ed., *Rational Analysis for a Problematic World*, Wiley, Chichester, 1989.

[37] B. Roy, Decision science or decision-aid science?, *EJOR* **66** (1993), 184–203.

[38] M. Sagoff, *The Economy of the Earth*, Cambridge University Press, 1988.

[39] G. Saloner, Game theory and strategic management: contributions, applications and limitations, in: R. Rumelt et al., eds, *op cit.*, 1994.

[40] F. Schick, *Having Reasons: an Essay on Rationality & Sociality*, Princeton University Press, 1984.

[41] A. Sen, Rational fools: a critique of the behavioral foundations of economic theory, *Philosophy and Public Affairs* **6** (1977), 317–344.

[42] P. Shrivastava and H. Scott, Corporate self-greenewal: strategic responses to environmentalism, *Business Strategy and the Environment* **1**(3) (1992), 9–21.

[43] A.E. Singer, Meta-rationality and strategy, *OMEGA* **19**(2) (1991), 101–110.

[44] A.E. Singer, Strategy as rationality, *Human Systems Management* **11**(1) (1992), 7–21.

[45] A.E. Singer, Plural rationality and strategic intelligence, in: *Global Perspectives on Competitive Intelligence*, J. Prescott and P. Gibbons, eds, SCIP, Alexandria, Virginia, 1993.

[46] A.E. Singer, Strategy as moral philosophy, *Strategic Management Journal* **15** (1994), 191–213.

[47] A.E. Singer, DCF without forecasts, *OMEGA* **22**(3) (1994), 221–35.

[48] A.E. Singer, Competitiveness as hyper-strategy, *Human Systems Management* **14**(2) (1995), 163–178.

[49] A.E. Singer, *Strategy as Rationality: Redirecting Strategic Thought and Action*, Avebury Series in Philosophy, Avebury, Aldershot, 1996.

[50] A.E. Singer, Metatheory, Hyperstrategy and Ultragames, in: *Management, Marketing and the Competitive Process*, P.E. Earl, ed., Edward Elgar, Aldershot, 1996.

[51] A.E. Singer, Strategic thinking without boundaries: Meta-decisions and transitions, *Systems Practice* **9**(5) (1996).

[52] A.E. Singer, Optimality and strategy, *Int. J. Oper. Quant. Management* (forthcoming).

[53] A.E. Singer and M. Singer, Management science and business ethics, *Journal of Business Ethics* (forthcoming).

[54] J. von Neumann, On the theory of games of strategy, in: *Contributions to the Theory of Games*, Vol. IV, A. Tucker and R. Luce, eds, 1959 (first edn. 1928), pp. 13–42..

[55] B. Walliser, Instrumental rationality and cognitive rationality, *Theory and Decision* **27** (1989), 7–36.

[56] R. Whittington, *What is Strategy and Does it Matter?*, Routledge, London, 1993.

[57] M. Zeleny, Tradeoffs-free management *via* de-novo programming, *Int. J. Oper. Quant. Management* **1** (1995), 3–13.

[58] M. Zeleny, In search of cognitive equilibrium: beauty, quality and harmony, *Journal of Multicriteria Decision Analysis* **3**(3) (1994), 3–13.

Glossary

Metagame

A metagame is the game that would exist if one of the players in a simple game chose his strategy after the others, in full knowledge of their choices.

Hypergame

A hypergame is a game-like model of conflict in which each 'Player' can have a distinctive perception of what the 'game' is. Specifically, Player 1 might think that Player 2 has a particular set of preferences for the outcomes of a simple game, but these could differ from player 2's actual preferences; and vice versa.

Ultragame (1)

A conceptual model of strategic interaction amongst multiple types of strategic entity, in which each entity is *plurally*-rational (see Section 3).

Ultragame (2)

A conceptual model of strategic interaction amongst many strategic entities, in which each entity is *hyper*-rational (in the synergy-seeking sense described below).

Meta-rationality₁

The philosphical and mathematical arguments and criteria that have been used to classify, evaluate and inter-relate the distinctive forms of rationality in the rationality-set, or to place them relative to each other.

Meta-rationality₂

This is utility-maximization in the special context of a *metagame*, where the objects of choice are the conditional strategies. (If player 1 chooses this, then player 2 prefers that.)

Plural-rationality

The rationality-set, whose elements are the many distinctive forms of rationality defined within the broad spectrum of the social sciences, including economics and philosophy.

Hyper-rationality

A hyper-rational entity (in the sense used throughout the paper) is one that seeks out, creates, designs and achieves synergies amongst the distinctive forms of rationality. This usage of the term "hyper-rational" (which differs from the better-known Economic usage of extreme-calculatedness [3,13], or strong-intrumental rationality [5,46,55]) owes its origin to a recent study of the Japanese industrial system by sociologists G. Ritzer and T. LeMoyne [43], who identified synergies amongst the Neo-Weberian forms of rationality in that system (*practical, substantive-value*, etc.). The concept readily generalizes to the entire rationality-set and entity-set [58].

Part IX
Trust (Trustworthiness
and Trust-Building)

[33]

TRUST, MORALITY AND INTERNATIONAL BUSINESS

George G. Brenkert

Abstract: This paper argues that trust is one of the crucial bases for an international business morality. To defend this claim, it identifies three prominent senses of trust in the current literature and defends one of them, viz., what I term the "Attitudinal view." Three different contexts in which such trust plays a role in business relationships are then described, as well as the conditions for the specific kinds of Attitudinal trust which appear in those contexts. Difficulties for the international development of these forms of trust are briefly characterized and some of the possible responses are noted. Finally, the paper identifies morally important features of trust and some of their implications for an international business morality.

I. Introduction

The expanding globalization of business has brought with it the increased importance of an international business ethics. We need answers to a multitude of questions concerning an international business community in which commerce would occur in accordance with justified moral standards. This ethics would tell us when workers in developing nations were being exploited, which dangerous products should not be shipped across national borders to be sold, and when the offer of cash or gifts amounted to bribes or were being extorted by members of another society. It would speak to the managers of multinationals about transfer pricing, the use of child labor, and attempts to economically develop people living in tribal conditions. It would provide moral guidance for those considering the development of large industrial plants, electrical plants, dams, etc., in developing nations.

However, if we are to speak productively of an international business ethics, we must seek an ethics that can be a morality.[1] By this I mean, among other things, an ethics whose rules, principles and values are capable of being taught and communicated to others; one for which there are forces that lead to its renewal; and one that will be stable across different societies. An important part, then, of defending an international business ethics is the identification of its practical conditions. Such an exercise would serve two important purposes.

First, it may serve as a response to those realists who claim that an international business ethics is impossible because it lacks the necessary basis (cf. Donaldson, 1989). Without an appropriate practical basis, realists contend that ethical theories amount to little more than finely spun fantasies. They may entertain and impress, but they cannot do the work of an actual morality.

Second, most current accounts of an international business ethics, which provide rules, principles, and guidelines claimed to be internationally applicable, fail to provide an account of their own background or structural conditions.[2] These conditions concern the circumstances under which an international business ethics might be adopted and maintained as a working morality. In this sense they are abstract and of doubtful efficacy. Business ethicists and philosophers have too often treated these as "simply" practical, mean and dirty conditions not worthy of philosophical consideration—something in the manner that Plato treated mud and hair when it came to the Forms.

The following paper maintains that trust is one of the important background bases of an international business ethics. Though the role of trust has been examined recently from a number of directions, e.g., its role in the production of national prosperity (Fukuyama, 1995); in competitive advantage (Barney and Hansen; Jones); and even as part of morality itself (Hosmer, 1995), it has not, as far as I know, been considered in the role of providing a basic condition for an international business morality. To do so carries important and interesting implications for an international business ethics. As such, a central aim of this paper is to spell out the conditions surrounding trust and an international business morality. More generally, this paper is an exploration of the relation of trust and morality on the international level between commercial agents.

Accordingly, this paper begins by briefly identifying several different senses of trust that are invoked in the literature relevant to international business and ethics. It argues that only one of these senses of trust is appropriate for issues of business ethics. Next it identifies three morally crucial contexts in which trust plays different roles in business relationships. These different kinds of trusting relationships are essential to moral business. Trust, in this sense, is a necessary condition for an international business morality. This is not surprising. In the international, as well as the national and local, setting "...conditions of trust sustain the *contexts* in which moral principles achieve their concrete embodiment" (King, 1988: 475).

I then specify several conditions for each kind of trust and note some difficulties which arise for the development of trust within international contexts. These difficulties must be met by a variety of responses, which are only briefly referred to here. The paper proceeds to identify morally important features of trust and some of the implications of these features for an international business morality. This leads to a final suggestion that by focusing on trust an international business ethics might be developed from the bottom up, rather than imposed by business ethicists from the top down. This might have welcome implications both for business and an international business ethics.

II. The Nature of Trust

At the outset it is appropriate to note several different understandings of trust which have been used in the literature. They may be characterized as the Attitudinal, Predictability, and Voluntarist senses of "trust."

The Attitudinal understanding of "trust" is used in a wide variety of discussions. It is captured by such statements as the following: "Trust is the mutual confidence that no party to an exchange will exploit another's vulnerabilities" (Sable, 1993: 1133); and trust is "a relatively informed attitude or propensity to allow oneself and perhaps others to be vulnerable to harm in the interest of some perceived greater good" (Michalos, 1990: 619). Finally, trust has also been conceptualized as "the willingness of a party to be vulnerable to the actions of another party based on the expectation that the other will perform a particular action important to the trustor, irrespective of the ability to monitor or control that other party" (Mayer, Davis, Schoorman, 1995: 712). On this Attitudinal View, trust is not simply a belief or cognitive state. Rather it involves an attitude, disposition, or inclination to act in certain ways in light of various beliefs one has both about oneself and others. Typically these beliefs concern one's own vulnerability and the restraint the trusted agent is prepared to exercise not to take advantage of that vulnerability.

The Predictability View claims that "trust" is to be interpreted as "the extent to which one person can expect predictability in the other's behavior in terms of what is 'normally' expected of a person acting in good faith" (Gabarro, 1978: 294). Similarly, Gordon Tullock has suggested that "trust" means "being able to predict accurately the behavior of the person trusted" (Held, 156; emphasis deleted).[3] Finally, Dasgupta uses "trust" in "the sense of correct expectations about the *actions* of other people that have a bearing on one's own choice of action when that action must be chosen before one can *monitor* the actions of those others" (Dasgupta, 1988: 51).

On this view, trust is simply a belief that one person has about another. Sometimes this is formulated in terms of an ability to predict certain behaviors. At other times, it is developed in terms of expectations one might have about the predictability of others' behavior. Of course, expectations might be viewed as a kind of attitude or disposition one has. But the emphasis here is on the predictability of the behavior of someone else. When Dasgupta speaks of the correct expectations about the actions of others, there appears to be little emphasis on attitudes or dispositions. This is compatible with beliefs that one party has about the actions of other parties.

The Voluntarist sense of "trust" is less frequently held, but has received prominent defense. It is found in such statements as: "To trust another is to voluntarily make oneself vulnerable with respect to some good, having been led to believe by the other's actions toward one that no loss or harm will come to one as a result" (Thomas, 1989: 181). Annette Baier suggests that "trust...is letting other persons (natural or artificial, such as firms, nations, etc.) take care of something the truster cares about, where such 'caring for' involves some exercise of discretionary powers" (Baier, 1995: 105). Baier notes that this model of trust is based on an "entrusting" view from Locke (Baier, 1995: 101). Similarly, D. O. Thomas has claimed that "trust involves commissioning a person to do something, investing them with a charge or a responsibility" (Thomas, 1987: 91).

On the Voluntarist view, trust involves various actions voluntarily or freely undertaken whereby one places oneself, or what one cares about, within the powers of another who, but for their good will, might impose harm upon oneself or those things one values. Trust here consists not in a prediction or an attitude that one person has towards others, but rather in the voluntary action of placing oneself in the hands of another. Baier maintains that such an account of trust is desirable since it may be applied not simply to articulate and equal adults, but may also be applied to individuals who exist in relations in which there are significant power disparities. Accordingly, this voluntarist account supposedly may also account for cases in which subordinates trust superiors and infants or children trust adults, even though those doing the trusting have few beliefs, expectations or informed attitudes towards their superiors or adults. Indeed, proponents of this view may emphasize that some form of trust must be innate, since people (adults or children) may spontaneously and freely trust another being without any reflections on or judgments about the other (Baier, 1995: 107). It is the commitment, conveyance or bestowing, i.e., the entrusting, of oneself to another that is the focus of this view. In short, the Voluntarist view focuses on the action that takes place in trust; the Attitudinal view looks to the dispositions or attitudes to behave in certain ways; and the Predictability view concentrates on the predictions one has about the behavior of those who are trusted.

Now since we are interested in a notion of trust which can capture our concerns for an international business ethics, I contend that we should reject the Predictability and Voluntarist views of trust.[4]

The Predictability view is inappropriate for several reasons. First, a business or an individual may be able to predict the behavior of another firm, and undertake with it various mutual activities or exchanges, but still not trust the other firm (cf. Thomas, 1989: 178f). Just because we can accurately predict that firm XYZ will share a particular technology with our firm, it does not follow that we thereby trust XYZ either in their performance of that act or more generally. We may. We may not. Second, questions of trust frequently arise in contexts when we cannot accurately or definitely predict the behavior of others, rather than in those contexts when we can. If I can accurately predict your behavior, it would seem that there is no need for me to trust you. On the other hand, if I cannot predict your behavior and do not have the means to ensure that your behavior must take certain forms, then I might seek to defend myself against you, flee from you, or (possibly) trust you. In short, trust involves some form of uncertainty or risk in the attitudes and behavior of one party towards another party. Third, suppose that one agent could roughly predict the behavior of another agent. This may serve as one reason, among others, for the former to trust the latter. But then the predictability is a *reason* for trusting, rather than the trust itself.

Accordingly, predictability and trust are two different things. This does not imply that predictability is not important in the determination of whether to trust. It does mean that predictability cannot be equated with, or is not sufficient for, trust as it may be sought in business relations. Further, it may not, on some occasions, even be necessary. There may be situations in which one person cannot accurately predict another person's behavior, but may still trust the other person for different reasons. Accordingly, we will have to consider below what role predictability may play in the justification, development and maintenance of trust. Finally, none of the preceding is to say that we do not use the word "trust" in the manner which the Predictability view suggests. We might say, for example, that we trust that Indian visitors to our home will like a curry meal. There may be little doubt in our minds about this. They haven't had any curry for weeks. We know that they eat curry in India. We confidently predict that they will enjoy this curry meal. To speak of trust in such circumstances is simply to speak of a prediction one believes one is entitled to make on the basis of some body of information. My argument above is not that we may not speak in this way. Rather, it is that this view of trust is less relevant than the Attitudinal view for discussions of (international) business for the above reasons. It is not the Predictability view that exercises people when they seek to trust their business associates.

It is also mistaken for present purposes to adopt the Voluntarist view of trust. Trust is not simply letting someone else take care of something one cares about, since a business might do this and still be able to monitor and oversee each aspect of that person's caring (contra Baier). Further, trust is more than simply voluntarily making oneself vulnerable to another with respect to some good (albeit on the basis of a belief, due to the other's actions toward one, that no loss or harm will come to one as a result), since I might let someone take care of something I care about but do this out of a sense of obligation, fear, or social embarrassment of doing anything else, while, at the same time, remaining quite worried about the results. In addition, though the action of placing oneself, or what one cares about, in the hands of others is an important part of trust, this seems only a part of a broader understanding of trust that encompasses one's ongoing preparedness to do so. This broader attitude or disposition involves various beliefs, values and expectations which are part and parcel of the trust one may be willing to extend to another person or firm. Finally, the Voluntarist view of trust is an account which is more designed to capture the nature of trusting relations between individuals rather than organizations, and between a wide variety of individuals, e.g., infants, children, and parents, rather than participants in the marketplace. As such, it is encompasses instances of trust in which trust does not need to be won, but simply exists in some innate fashion (Baier, 1995: 107). Again, though we may be willing to speak of trust in such circumstances, this kind of trust is less relevant to the trust that businesses seek between themselves when they do international business.

Accordingly, if we are to consider the role of trust for an international business ethics, we should adopt the Attitudinal sense of "trust."[5] However, the nature of this form of trust needs further specification.

III. Trust and Morality

There are several important characteristics of this form of trust which influence the role it can play in an international business ethics.

First, trust is not a principle, let alone a moral principle, but an attitude or disposition to behave and respond in certain ways, viz., to accept certain risks of harm or injury from another agent on the basis of a belief (for which there is some degree of uncertainty) that the other does not intend to do harm to one (or those one cares about), even though he/she could (cf. Solomon, 1992: 213).[6] It is not surprising, then, that Rawls calls trust a natural attitude (Rawls, 1972: 497). Solomon calls trust a business virtue, due to its dispositional nature and because it involves acting in admirable ways (Solomon, 1992: 107f).

Held denies that trust is, as such, a virtue. Her reason is that trust may be misguided, misplaced or foolish (Held, 1984: 65). However, this reasoning would have the unfortunate consequence of excluding not only trust, but other dispositions such as courage and loyalty, from being virtues. But surely courage and loyalty, as well as trust, are virtues even when they are misdirected. We must simply allow, in response to Held, that there may be courageous enemies, employees loyal to corrupt bosses, and managers who foolishly trust those who deceive them. Nevertheless, we speak intelligibly of the courage, loyalty and trust of these individuals. Depending upon the context, these ordinarily exemplary ways of getting along with other people may lead to harm, and destruction of social harmony (cf. Solomon, 1992: 108; 192). What this points out is that trust is not necessarily the same thing as morality or moral action. Though trust is essential for moral (as this notion contrasts with nonmoral) relations, this does not imply that all instances of trust are themselves moral (as opposed to immoral) occasions.

Second, trust involves a commonality of values or aims (real or perceived) in terms of which the trust relationship is built. This commonality need not be complete or even extensive. People with very different values can trust each other. Still, there must be some common aims or values in light of which the trust relationship is established and maintained. Such values might include those of consistency, non-maleficence, certain forms of expertise, as well as appreciation of similar activities and forms of success. In short, both moral and nonmoral values and aims might be part of this commonality. The role of these common values and aims is to foster the development of trusting attitudes inasmuch as they may give one reasons to believe that the trusted party will not act contrary to, or harm, vulnerable interests one deems important. Such reasons may take the form of various explicit expectations or predictions of the other's future behavior. They may also take more implicit intuitive forms of confidence in the trusted individual. Her wants are compatible with ours; they value the same things

INTERNATIONAL BUSINESS   299

we do; we enjoy a strong sense of mutual sympathy. In these situations, we may trust each other, not because we are thinking about predicting future behaviors, but because we are responding to present mutual connections.

Due to these common values or aims there is, then, a form of mutuality in any trusting relationship. Unfortunately, this mutuality is confused by some with the view that trust involves a mutual confidence in each other (cf. Sabel; Barney and Hansen). But this latter form of mutuality, i.e., "mutual confidence," is not necessary for trust, since one agent may trust another, without that trust being reciprocated. Thus, Barney and Hansen are mistaken to adopt Sabel's view that "trust is the *mutual* confidence that no party to an exchange will exploit another's vulnerabilities" (Barney and Hansen, 1994: 176; my emphasis). Nevertheless, even when only one member of a dyad trusts the other, if there were not some common values or aims there would not be trust.

This mutuality of values may also explain why the trust people have in each other is not simply an economic calculation. When people trust, in light of shared values, their trust involves a mutual affirmation or identification with the agent trusted through these common values or aims. As such, their trust grows out of this mutuality of values, rather than an economic calculation.[7] It is not surprising, then, that others have noted that, when one trusts, the loss that one may suffer through harm from the trust not being fulfilled is greater than the gain one might obtain by not trusting. This is an expression of the fact that the trust involved is not simply an instance of economic rationality (Hosmer, 1995: 381).[8] However, one might also anticipate that the gain one (or both individuals) will receive if the trust is kept is greater than if there had been no trust at all. We need not deny that there may be some economic (or other) gain through trust.

Third, trust may involve judgment in at least two ways. On the one hand, one may make certain judgments about the trustworthiness of someone else. And this may play an important role in entering a trusting relation with that other individual or firm.[9] On the other hand, trust involves allowing some discretion on the part of the person or agent trusted. Thus, Baier comments that "...to trust is to give discretionary powers to the trusted, to let the trusted decide how, on a given matter, one's welfare is best advanced, to delay the account for a while, to be willing to wait to see how the trusted has advanced one's welfare" (Baier, 1995: 136).[10] That is, each member of the relation is granted some leeway to make various judgments and decisions which are not themselves prescribed by a contract or other set of rules. Rather, the good will and intentions of each member are assumed. It is assumed that they will competently make certain judgments as to what is to be done for the well-being of both parties in the relationship.

Fourth, trust must be distinguished from trustworthiness. Trust is an attitude or disposition to place oneself under certain circumstances in a situation where one is vulnerable to harm which may come from others on whose good will one depends. As an attitude or disposition, trust tends to be open-ended; it need not be specific to a particular, single situation. Hence, it tends to concern longer-term relationships than simply brief, limited ones. The temporal extendedness of trust variously depends upon a number of factors, including the mutuality of the interests that bring those that trust together, the degree and kind of trust, the non-violation of vulnerabilities, and the continuing fulfillment of the conditions of trust.

Trustworthiness, however, is not an attitude, but the evaluative appraisal that an individual is worthy of trust, i.e., that another person might reasonably place his or her trust in that individual. As such, trustworthiness cannot be equated with an individual (or firm) being one that others ought to trust (cf. Horsburgh, 1962: 28) or with simply not being opportunistic (Jones, 1995: 421). The fact that a person or business is trustworthy does not imply that others ought to trust them, since other firms or people may have no reasons to form a relationship with them at all. Further, if "opportunism" is understood as "pursuing self-interest with guile," then a person might not be opportunistic and still not trustworthy. This might occur when a person wished only the best for someone else, but could not be considered trustworthy because he was incompetent, not able to keep promises, or unwilling to listen to what others really wanted. Instead, one's trustworthiness betokens the reasonableness with which others might trust one.

Accordingly, trustworthiness relates both to the qualities of the person or organization to be trusted, as well as to those doing the trusting. Relevant conditions regarding the former are discussed below. With regard to the latter, to make appropriate determinations they must have a certain amount of knowledge about the other person and the circumstances within which the question of trust arises. The limiting case of such trust, when an individual has virtually no knowledge of another, is what we call "blind trust." More generally, one's preparedness to consider another person or organization trustworthy will depend on the level of confidence one has that the trusted individual will not harm one's interests, the degree of vulnerability to which one is prepared to expose oneself and the value one places upon the interest which is vulnerable. Thus, I will look for greater trustworthiness in a person who asks to borrow my car or for me to disclose my inner most secrets, than from a person who asks to borrow my pen or what television programs I have been watching. This analysis also implies that one firm (e.g., a disreputable firm) may judge another firm not to be trustworthy ("They won't engage in shenanigans with us"), while a different firm (e.g., a reputable one) might judge the same firm to be trustworthy ("They have high standards"). To the extent, then, that a firm may be said to be trustworthy, it has particular qualities which render it worthy of trust by specific others. This means, we have seen, that it will not violate their vulnerabilities in certain risky situations. To this extent, then, trustworthiness too is a virtue. However, just because an individual person or firm is trustworthy it does not follow that that individual trusts others. There might be cases where it is possible to trust a firm which is trustworthy, but that firm be unable to reciprocate such trust.

Fifth, the conflicted relation of trust to morality deserves notice. On the one hand, trust is widely accepted as an important value. Part of the importance of trust is that it is valued by individuals and cultures around the globe even though

INTERNATIONAL BUSINESS 301

they are divided on a variety of other values and principles. For example, Puffer and McCarthy note that "maintaining trust" is one value which both Americans and Russians share and on which they can build mutual relationships (Puffer and McCarthy, 1995: 35). In contrast, they claim, "maximizing profits" though viewed as ethical in the U.S. is considered unethical in Russia, whereas "price fixing" is deemed to be unethical in the U.S. but ethical in Russia (Puffer and McCarthy, 1995: 35). However, "maintaining trust" is ethically esteemed by both societies. This result may well be replicated with other countries (e.g., Japan). Thus, trust may constitute a common value to which people and organizations across different cultures may (and must) appeal.

This is not to say, however, that certain instances of trust may not serve immoral ends. When some are able, because they trust each other, to engage in an enterprise that dumps toxic chemicals in the ocean, overbills a government, colludes against other firms, or misappropriates funds intended for villages affected by their manufacturing plants, then immoral ends are served. Accordingly, Baier comments that "there are immoral as well as moral trust relationships, and trust-busting can be a morally proper goal" (Baier, 1995: 95). Consequently, trust is not an unconditional value. Its value in particular instances depends upon the context within which it is exercised. If trust is employed concerning morally worthy projects, then such trust is valuable. On the other hand, when it is formed around morally unworthy projects trust may lack moral value. Without a good will, as Kant might say, trust can be extremely bad or harmful. What this implies is that trust cannot be a sufficient condition for moral business relations, though it is a necessary condition. As we shall see below, trust involves various forms of interaction which are essential to moral systems and upon which a business ethics may draw. Consequently, it is mistaken to think that trust has no relation to morality or ethics at all because it does not guarantee moral action. People may dispute over whether a glass of water filled to the middle is half empty or half full, but it would be hasty for those who decide it is half empty to proceed to conclude that there is no water in the glass at all.

Still, it would appear that trust is not simply something of instrumental value, but also of intrinsic value. Trust is like courage in that even when it occurs in conjunction with immoral ends we can appreciate the value of the trusting (or the courage) itself. Trust, in this sense, is a kind of attitude and behavior which is distinguishable from instances in which people are unable or unwilling ever to render themselves vulnerable to others, as well as those who recklessly place themselves in the hands of others. The former end up recluses, isolated from others. In the latter case, when people simply place themselves in the hands of others whom everyone else can see are utterly untrustworthy, what might be a valuable form of trusting behavior may be viewed as simply a case of foolhardiness and recklessness.

It follows that the tendency of Jones, Hosmer and others to equate trust and morality must also be rejected. A firm which contracts with suppliers on the basis of mutual trust and cooperation need not be a moral firm (cf. Jones, 1995:

422). Similarly, Hosmer's recent definition of trust as "the expectation by one person, group, or firm of ethically justifiable behavior...on the part of the other person, group, or firm in a joint endeavor or economic exchange" must also be rejected (Hosmer, 1995: 399). First, this moralization of trust excludes by definition what we know otherwise about trust, i.e., that trust may undermine morality (cf. Hosmer, 1995: 399). Though trust in another person or institution may be important, such trust may also be the basis for immoral behavior. Presumably even thieves may trust each other.

Further, moralized accounts of trust do not allow for situations in which one person or group trusts a second person or group, which has not, however, accepted any duty toward the first person's or group's interests or rights (cf. Hosmer, 1995: 393). And yet surely this may happen when the people of a community trust a multinational company (MNC) which has established a manufacturing plant in their community, but which is not prepared to accept the broad implications of the trust which those individuals have placed on it. Accordingly, trust does not characterize the mutual relationship, i.e., "the mutual confidence," of those who trust, but rather the individuals engaged in that relationship. And, it may pertain to only one of the members of a relationship involving trust.

Finally, the role that trust plays within a competitive system such as the marketplace is different from the role it plays in ordinary life. This means that trust plays a different role in business ethics than in everyday ethics. For example, Horsburgh claims that, in ordinary life, anything which tends to give strong support to other moral agents will often be obligatory. Now though there is no *prima facie* obligation to trust one another, since trust is one of the most important ways in which one individual can give moral support to another, it is often one's duty to trust others, including those whose past conduct makes it seem probable that one's trust will be abused (Horsburgh, 1960: 354). However, this duty does not seem appropriate in the marketplace. Individuals do not have an obligation to trust the businesses or corporations they deal with in the market in order to give them moral support. And corporations don't have an obligation to trust unspecified others as a means whereby to help support them. They may have some obligation to be trustworthy, particularly with regard to stakeholders, however it is not obvious that they have obligations to engage in trust relations with other individuals simply on the basis that it might help them.

In fact, there appears to be some tension between market competition and trust. When we engage in tough competition I try to figure out your weaknesses and attempt to exploit them. Within the rules of the market, this is legitimate. However, I must also be able to trust that you will not exploit certain other weaknesses or vulnerabilities I have (e.g., you won't shoot me to get my customers). Thus, Gambetta comments that "even to compete, in a mutually non-destructive way, one needs at some level to *trust* one's competitors to comply with certain rules" (Gambetta, 1988: 215). But there is always a risk here that a highly competitive firm will take advantage of certain vulnerabilities which no one else has exploited before and concerning which the law is silent, and morality unclear.

Thus, we may fear that trust and competition conflict and that competition may undo trust. This is not necessarily the case, as we will see. In the next section, I shall adopt the view some have defended that trust of others may provide certain firms a competitive advantage over others. However, within the market, trust will require special efforts and commitments which it does not necessarily require in ordinary life.

Thus, we must look closely at the role trust plays in the marketplace, as well as in an efficacious and stable international business morality. It is clear from the preceding that trust is both important to business morality and, at the same time, at odds with certain aspects of the competitive marketplace.

IV. Trust Within the Business Context

We may portray the role of trust within business by distinguishing three different forms of trust. These are distinguished in terms of the particular contexts in which trust plays a role. Accordingly, we may distinguish Basic Trust, Guarded Trust and Extended Trust. A complete account of trust and of business ethics needs to address these forms of trust.[11]

Basic trust is the trust that individual agents have that other moral agents, with whom they have only impersonal, systematic relations, will act in certain kinds of standard ways not to take advantage of their vulnerabilities. This is a general form of trust which might be said to be "coextensive with the very existence of a social order" such as the market or morality itself (Gellner, 1988: 142; Thomas, 1978: 90). Sable speaks of such trust as being a precondition of social life (Sabel, 1993: 1136). Thus, DeGeorge comments that "if there were not some minimum level of trust between buyer and seller on the international level, just as on the national level, business transactions would prove impossible" (DeGeorge, 1993: 21). And Baier says that "...as anything more than a law within, [morality] itself requires trust in order to thrive..." (Baier, 1986: 232). Accordingly, trust is a background condition, or part of the background environment (Dasgupta, 1988: 49; DeGeorge, 1993; Brenkert, 1994). In this sense of trust, we must trust strangers. Hence this is an underlying, impersonal, and systematic form of trust.

So understood, basic trust differs from the "goodwill trust" that Sako identifies. "Goodwill trust" holds between specific individuals and requires that a person be "dependable and can be credited with high discretion, as he can be expected to take initiatives while refraining from unfair advantage taking" (Sako, 1991: 452-3). Basic trust is a background form of trust for this more specialized case of trust. If we did not regularly trust in this basic manner, but distrusted each other or doubted each other's sincerity, cooperation and good intentions, more elaborate forms of trust would be difficult if not impossible. It is in this sense then that H. B. Acton is said to have held that "trust and mutual confidence are the norm in social life, and that deception and wrong-doing are to be regarded as abnormalities" (Thomas, 1978: 90). This does not mean that social life cannot tolerate distrust. However, as D. O. Thomas argues, "the more violations of trust there are and the greater the reluctance to trust, the more impoverished does social life become and the fewer the benefits that men derive from it" (Thomas, 1978: 92). Basic trust need not be, and most generally is not, articulated or made explicit. However, when it is violated, those involved are made painfully aware that they had indeed trusted that the violator would not act in the way in which he/she did. Basic trust within the market system assumes that others will play by recognized, generally accepted rules, customs or standards, not that they won't use those rules and their abilities to try to get an advantage over one's firm.

Guarded trust is necessary when agents invoke various explicit contracts to protect their vulnerabilities and specify penalties for injury to those vulnerabilities and their interests. Trust is required here to maintain the relation in the face of unclarities in contracts. "In fact no contract, even if it is scrutinized by sharp lawyers, can detail every eventuality, if for no other reason than that no language can cope with unlimited refinement in distinguishing continuities. Trust covers expectations about what others will do or have done…in circumstances that are not explicitly covered in the agreement" (Dasgupta, 1988: 52-53). Thus, guarded trust makes contracts possible. As such, it is singularly important for business. Sako refers to this as contractual trust, i.e., when each partner adheres to agreements and keeps promises (Sako, 1991, 1992). However, "guarded trust" does not require, as does Sako's contractual trust, that those who engage in this form of trust are involved in "upholding a universalistic ethical standard, namely that of keeping promises" (Sako, 1991: 451). Of course, they might be doing this. On the other hand, they might be appealing to some other moral standard(s) or simply to some nonmoral values or aims which motivate and justify their maintenance of the contract. Sako's view overly moralizes this form of trust. Barney and Hansen refer to this trust as "Semi-strong form trust." When significant exchange vulnerabilities exist, but the parties can protect themselves through various governance devices, semi-strong trust can exist (Barney and Hansen, 1994: 177). Both market based and contractual governance devices are relevant to guarded trust (Barney and Hansen, 1994: 178).

In contrast to basic trust, guarded trust holds only between those firms and individuals who set up specific contracts and monitoring practices. Hence it is limited in time. In addition, the monitoring devices and restricted range of guarded trust limit the flexibility of the partners and involve various transaction costs. Do such contracts, monitoring devices and sanctions render guarded trust irrelevant? Some have claimed that trust is incompatible with sanctions, contracts, etc. D. O. Thomas says that "…trusting someone to do something does, logically, exclude sanctions…" (Thomas, 1978: 91). Accordingly, he claims that "the risks we run [with trusting] are those that come from denying ourselves the use of sanctions and from sacrificing the benefits that come from the kind of conformity that sanctions can produce" (Thomas, 1978: 100).

This view is, however, mistaken. Trust may involve sanctions in various ways. For example, I may trust my friend to do something, understanding that if he breaks my trust other people will be prepared to condemn him, reluctant to accept him as a friend, or to trust his word. These are real sanctions in the background of our trust. These are compatible with trust since they do not remove all uncertainty or my vulnerabilities. Still, they provide a context within which I may trust. In business contexts, this background framework may further include legal sanctions and standards formulated by trade associations which together may promote long-term relations in which trust might develop (Arrighetti, Bachmann and Deakin, 1997). What would be incompatible with trust would be an individual or a firm surrounding the performance of an action by another firm it claimed to trust with a complete, detailed and significant set of sanctions, e.g., the firm claims to trust another firm with some confidential information, but clearly indicates that others will monitor each step of its use of that information and that any misuse will result in significant monetary penalties.

In their recent article on integrated social contracts theory, Donaldson and Dunfee refer to a macro negotiation process which occurs prior to reaching agreement on the micro social contracts which spell out the ethical details of how particular business communities ought to act. They maintain that such negotiation must occur against a backdrop of ethical rules or norms (Donaldson and Dunfee, 1994: 260). Part of the point of this section is that, though such rules or norms are important, an element of guarded trust is also crucial to such negotiations and to the viability of the ensuing contracts.

Extended trust involves firms and individuals acting to trust one another beyond basic and guarded forms of trust. It develops within special relations which involve trusting other firms and individuals when contracts, and monitoring devices are not in place or have been significantly reduced. It is in this sense of trust that we are taught as children not to trust strangers, but only certain special individuals. Extended trust requires that firms and individuals expose their vulnerabilities to one another when there is clear uncertainty and risk that harm could come to the firm, or individuals in the firm, from those who are trusted. It is part of an ongoing relationship which is not necessarily temporally limited to a particular contract, but arises out of the value structures of the firms which permit this greater exposure of each firm's vulnerabilities to the other firm so as to create a relation which is mutually desired. To the extent that firms and individuals can trust in this manner they will be able to act with greater flexibility and freedom in their relations with those whom they so trust (cf. Barney and Hansen, 1994; Jones, 1995). This relation may exist not only between firms, but also between firms and their stakeholders (e.g., employees, stockholders, and members of the community). Jones and Sako have both called attention to this broader role for trust. Sako calls it "goodwill trust." However, Sako's "goodwill trust" involves the expectation that one's trusted partner is "committed to take initiatives (or exercise discretion) to exploit new opportunities over and above what was explicitly promised" (Sako, 1991: 453). Extended trust does not. Extended trust is compatible with such an expectation, but does not require it. Business firms might share a relation of extended trust but not expect each other to "exploit new opportunities." They may also be content to do business outside the limits of guarded trust. Extended trust, then, differs from guarded trust in the lack of monitoring devices, formal contracts and special sanctions that are required for guarded trust, as well as in its dependence on the value structures of the participants which permit greater openness to each other through their restriction of their self-interested actions (cf. Barney and Hansen, 1994). Those who trust in this extended fashion may well go on to engage in special initiatives. But firms may also engage in extended trust relations with each other without each partner doing so. It would be sufficient that they engage in various forms of exchange and interchange within a present set of activities, which lack the protections of contracts, etc.

Accordingly, basic trust and guarded trust are important for sustaining the social, economic and moral systems within which business acts. Without these forms of trust, these systems would collapse. Extended trust is important for the flexibility and independence which it may afford particular businesses which can engage in it as well as for the morally richer relationships which it permits. In addition, one might maintain that if there is extended trust between a firm and its subsidiaries, then the subsidiary will be allowed to make a wider range of decisions involving product differentiation, etc. which permits a fuller moral agency of the subsidiary. If we assume that, all things being equal, a person or group which is accorded full moral agency will respond favorably, then we might expect not only a higher level of morality, but also greater efficiency from such a unit (cf. Horng, 1993). Consequently, a business ethics which does not take these forms of trust into account or provide for their development cannot be complete or a sustainable business ethics. However, since trust may also be involved in nefarious relationships, we must now look more closely at trust within the context of an international business morality.

V. Trust and International Business

Different conditions are required to produce each of the preceding forms of trust. By considering these conditions, we may also see the problems which trust within an international business context faces. We can also identify difficulties which an international business ethics must confront.

Basic trust rests upon two underlying conditions: a) the commonality of motives associated with mutual acceptance of common basic norms, values and customs; and b) the consistency of behavior of those acting on those motives. Individuals tend to trust each other the greater the similarity and mutuality of their motives, values and ends. Accordingly, basic trust rests on several assumptions: that others do not have motives to harm them; that if they do have such motives, they have other overriding motives which keep the former in check; or, finally, that if they have motives which may lead to their harm, these motives are exercised within certain widely recognized and accepted forms of behavior such that they may be anticipated or avoided. Consequently, if one business simply outcompetes another business, this is not a reason to abandon one's basic trust in the market system or in other individuals more generally.

The consistency of the behavior of others is also crucial for basic trust. Obviously, in cases of trust, there is uncertainty by the nature of the case. However, if an individual or firm acted simply arbitrarily or inconsistently, it would not be one that would readily be trusted.[12] It is for this reason that reputation is also so important in establishing the trustworthiness of a firm or individual (Dasgupta, 1988).

Guarded trust requires both of the preceding two conditions regarding common motives and consistency of behavior, as well as knowledge of the competence of the other party, i.e., that the other party is capable of carrying out the contract. If a firm is prepared to commit itself to doing certain things, but is perceived not to be able or competent to do those things, then trust is less likely in such cases. Such competence might include categories which Gabarro has identified: a) functional or specific competence: competence in the specialized knowledge and skills required to do a particular job; and b) interpersonal competence: people skills and knowing how to work with people (Gabarro, 1978).

Finally, extended trust requires the preceding three conditions (common motives, consistency of behavior and acknowledged competence) as well as a fourth condition, openness. Individuals or firms may engage in extended trust depending upon whether each is prepared to open up to the other so as to reveal private or confidential information. Openness may also involve being physically available to the other, e.g., opening the doors of one's plant to the trusted partner. Finally, openness may involve leveling with another, as well as not creating or permitting misleading expectations to be generated in the other (cf. Gabarro, 1978).

Thus, as we move from simpler to more complex forms of trust, the conditions required for earlier forms of trust are added to those required for later forms of trust. Extended trust, the most developed form of trust, requires commonality of motives (or ends), consistency of behavior, acknowledged competence, and openness.

It is immediately obvious that the creation of morally worthy trust within international contexts faces special problems that it does not face on the national level. A partial list of obstacles include the following:

Values and motives may differ dramatically. For example, attitudes towards and evaluations of individualism, uncertainty, and aggressive competition may impede trusting relationships (cf. Hofstede, 1979).[13] It is not surprising then that it is frequently claimed that trust is more likely developed in circumstances where there is a common history, belief in the same god, and dedication to the same political ends (Sabel, 1993: 1135). Thus Shell comments that "similarity of backgrounds and tastes also helps smooth the way to trusting relations" (Shell, 1991: 258). And Baier agrees that "awareness of what is customary...affects one's ability to trust" (Baier, 1986: 245). Since it is not possible internationally, to rely on joint customs, traditions, language, or histories, much of the common basis upon which trust may develop within a national culture is missing. In addition, similar institutions and social structures such as those regarding property also help in the production of trust. But where there exist significant differences, for example, over intellectual property, obstacles to trust will again be perceived.

Ethnocentric and egocentric tendencies will also impede trusting relations internationally. For example, the tendency of an egocentric fairness bias, "which is a tendency for people to see arrangements that favour themselves over others as fairer than arrangements that favour others" will acerbate other ethnocentric biases (Michalos, 1990: 624; Messick et al., 1985).[14] Michalos notes studies which show that "most people think most [other] people are not as nice as they are themselves and, therefore, cannot be trusted to behave as well" (Michalos, 1990: 627). These tendencies will be particularly acute internationally, where people look, talk, and behave differently.

Due to past colonialism and imperialism, past histories may stand in the way of trusting relationships. Further, due to racism (or suspicions of racism) trusting relations will also be hampered. Similarly, different economic histories of capitalism, socialism, and communism will also play a role in restricting such trusting relations between various MNCs and Third World Nations. Further, some cultures may have different tolerances for inconsistency or standards for competence and different time frames within which performance of various activities may be expected.

Finally, individuals in some cultural contexts might find it more difficult to be open in the same manner as those from other cultures. Their concern might not be with openness so much as not hurting another's feelings or with, perhaps, saving face and not embarrassing themselves or others. When circumstances exist in which these different responses arise, the trust between partners might be jeopardized. One member of the relation might feel that he or she can never "really" know what the others are thinking, because they will not speak their minds. Similarly, if Fukuyama is correct, the social structures within societies differ with respect to the extensiveness of trust which members of those societies may "naturally" engage in (Fukuyama, 1995). These differences will also inhibit the development of trusting relations both within certain societies and between societies.

In short, the obstacles to trust within an international market are substantial. Further, these are also obstacles to the ready acceptance of, and adherence to, systems of international business ethics. Suppose, for instance, that we invoke our earlier distinction between ethics, as a theoretical statement of principles, rules, values and ideals by which individuals, business and countries ought to live and act, and morality which (for present purposes) we may take to be an embedded or lived form of an ethics. A morality, then, is an embodied or lived ethics. As such, an embodied ethics must be capable of being taught and communicated to others; it must not be radically inconsistent; it must have forces which lead to its renewal; it must be something that can be stable. If we are to speak of an international business ethics, then surely we seek an ethics that can be a morality. But to speak of such an ethics as being a morality, we must seek to identify the conditions for this transformation of the theoretical into the practical.[15] Trust, as we have seen, is one of these conditions.

Hence, any international business ethics which does not give significant place to the commonality of values or motives, consistency of behavior, reputation, competency determinations and openness will be an ethics which does not allow for basic conditions which promote its own stability and efficacy as a morality. It is these factors which the preceding identifies as necessary conditions for the various forms of trust. And these forms of trust are crucial as background or supporting conditions for the development and maintenance of morality. Without them an international business ethics will not become a morality.

Now the obstacles to trust can be met only gradually and incrementally. The instruction of managers and participants in international business in ethics will be important (Noreen, 1988), but clearly not be sufficient. Instead, a complicated pattern of interaction among individuals, firms, industries, international organizations, and governmental structures and mechanisms will be required to overcome the obstacles briefly noted above. They will require various trust enhancing mechanisms including the law, trade associations, various third parties, and the like (Arrighetti, Bachmann, Deakin, 1997). Periods of adjustment with gradual increments of trust formation are obviously required. This will involve confidence building measures (Bluhm, 1987). For example, extended trust might be enhanced by an exchange of personnel at home and abroad so that all sides may keep in touch and different interpretations or understandings are recognized. Guarded trust will be enhanced through various market-based and contractual governance devices (Barney and Hansen, 1994). Basic trust will be enhanced by other background institutions, frequency of contact, etc. Accordingly, we must look to both informal and formal means to overcome obstacles to trust.

What this suggests is a shift in the practical basis for business morality as we move from the national to the international arena. We move from a basis which includes common histories, customs, languages, etc. to more external and formal mechanisms (Sellerberg, 1982). On this view, personal relations continue to be crucial for international trust, since it is the individuals from different businesses and different cultures who gain knowledge of and form trust with each other. It is for this reason that business executives travel with the presidents, prime ministers and commerce secretaries of their national states. "Face-to-face interaction with very senior people...[overseas and in the company of national leaders] sends a powerful symbolic message. It helps establish trust."[16] This implies the importance of the time and circumstances to allow such relations to develop. Still, inter- and intra-institutional structures are required to support and sustain such personal trust, and to transform it into the organizational trust which could support an international business morality (Dodgson, 1993; Zucker, 1986).

VI. Morally Relevant Features of Trust

Finally, though specific cases of trust are not necessarily moral, the fact that firms and people can and do trust in the preceding ways means that something morally important happens in trust. This 'something' is the fact that trust goes beyond simple self-seeking behavior. This is not to deny that individuals and firms form various relations involving trust for self-interested reasons. Obviously they do. However, it does not follow from this, when these relations include the different forms of trust distinguished above, that these forms of trust can be understood *simply* in terms of self-interest. They cannot. Self-interest may be the occasion for seeking or desiring relations with some other person or firm which require trust. Further, one's self-interests may also be met through those trusting relations. But, again, this does not imply that such trust does not include features important for morality. It is an overly rigorous, if not misguided, morality which demands that self-interest and morality be wholly separate. Still, self-interest does not itself provide an account of the nature or justification of the trust that they may develop between individuals and firms. For this, we have seen that (depending upon the kind of trust) we must look to one's preparedness to refrain from taking advantage of another's vulnerabilities or weaknesses, the consistency of one's behavior, the appropriateness of one's competencies and one's readiness to be open regarding knowledge of one's self or firm to others. All these conditions may restrict action on behalf of one's self-interests. Further, social (and industry) norms and expectations, which are part of the commonality of values and beliefs crucial to trust, play a role in constituting forms of behavior, as well as individuals and firms themselves, which are not simply self-seeking. Finally, in trust there is a consideration of the interests of others, beyond one's own present interests. There are, that is, various inherent aspects of trust that might be exploited to promote moral forms of trust. I wish to explore these in the following.

First, to the extent people mutually and consciously trust each other (for example, especially in guarded and extended trust), they must be in communication with, and have a mutual understanding of, each other. They must seek and share knowledge about each other as well as make judgments about the fitness of each other. As we have seen, this mutual understanding involves knowing and assessing each other's motives, consistency, competency and openness. Such knowledge of others (and oneself) has, traditionally, been held to be important for morality.

Second, trust involves a morally significant exposure of oneself to others in the sense that one permits the exposure of one's vulnerabilities to others. With mutual trust there is a sharing of one's vulnerabilities. In this manner a dependence (possibly a mutual dependence) is developed whereby one is expected not only not to harm the other but also to act in ways which promote the well-being of the other. The fact that trust exposes one's vulnerabilities to others and creates certain expectations about the future behavior of those who trust may open firms and individuals up to other more obviously moral relations. For example, to the extent that one trusts others one treats them "as being able and willing to act in accord with the rules without inducement or threats" (Thomas, 1978: 92). Accordingly, Thomas has claimed that trust is involved in respecting the moral dignity of each person. As such, trust creates a potential for morality between those who share in the trust.

Third, trust involves the restriction of self-interested behavior; the interests of the other are not harmed, and may be promoted, even though doing so might not be in one's immediate self-interest. This may involve various preventative forms of behavior as well. For example, to the extent that individuals share such a relation they do not manipulate each other "...by deliberately raising false expectations in them about how one will respond to something one wants them to do" (Baier, 1995: 134).[17] Similarly, they "...take due care not to lead others to form reasonable but false expectations about what one will do, where they would face significant loss if they relied on such false expectations" (Baier, 1995: 134). Finally, they "...take steps to prevent any loss that others would face through reliance on expectations about one's future behavior, expectations that one has either intentionally or negligently led them to form" (Baier, 1995: 134). In short, those engaged in trust relations avoid certain standard negotiating tactics which result in zero-sum games with one's negotiating partner.

Fourth, mutual trust involves a reciprocity between members of the trusting relation which fosters their autonomy. Guarded and extended trust relationships usually only develop slowly, after initial experiences and probing of each other's intentions and reliability. When the other responds positively and in a trusting manner, one may oneself (further) respond in a positive and trusting manner. As such relationships develop, particularly extended ones, it may be that something one does may give the other a one-sided benefit, which one then trusts he or she will not take advantage of. It may even occur that the trust one has bestowed on another is not fulfilled, or not fulfilled in the manner expected. This need not result, however, in a "tit for tat" response, if the trust relationship is healthy and firm. Indeed, when there is trust between individuals, each person will allow the other a wider range of decisions and actions than when distrust characterizes their relationships. If we may then assume that morality is bound up with some form of autonomy or self-determination, trust will promote the realization of this basic condition for morality. In this way, trust is not indifferent to morality, but is positively linked with it. This is in harmony with the connection Horsburgh draws between trust and moral agency in his view that for a person to be a moral agent he or she cannot hold an attitude of systematic and pervasive distrust toward all other people (Horsburgh, 1960: 354).

Hence, at least four morally significant phenomena are inherently linked with trust: a) communication of self-understanding to others; b) the voluntary exposure of one's vulnerabilities to others; c) voluntary restriction of self-interested behavior; and d) a reciprocity which fosters autonomy. These inherent features of trust are central to the institution of morality as well and, hence, link these two concepts.

It is in this sense, perhaps, that we should understand Gewirth's claim that "a principle of mutual trust" is "the moral principle which is at the basis of a civilized society" (Gewirth, 1982: 185). I think that Gewirth clearly overstates the moral nature of trust. Trust may also exist, as we have seen, between corrupt parties. Further, Gewirth is mistaken to link the principle of mutual trust with that of "mutual respect for certain basic rights" (Gewirth, 1982: 185). We may speak about such moral relations without necessarily introducing the notion of rights. Gewirth's view moves the notion of trust from one concerning relations to one concerning rights, rules and obligations. Feminists might object that this replaces a care based ethic with a rule based ethic. However, in the sense developed in the preceding paragraphs, Gewirth's reference to the basic importance of trust is surely correct.

This account of trust has a wide range of implications for international business ethics as currently pursued. I will mention only a few.

A. Donaldson and Dunfee have recently proposed a structure of hypernorms, a macro-social contract, micro-social contracts and priority rules to constitute an international business ethics. Their priority rules are to adjudicate disputes between ethical norms within micro-social contracts which are in accord with the universal hypernorms. One of these rules is that "the more extensive or more global the community which is the source of the norm, the greater the priority which should be given to the norm" (Donaldson and Dunfee, 1994: 269). I suggest that though this may sound acceptable to those coming from large countries, it will be much less acceptable to those coming from small countries. I submit that it would raise suspicion and questions of trust within the relations of members of the different communities. Such a priority rule would increase the vulnerabilities of those in smaller countries and raise questions about the concern of others for their well-being.

B. In *Competing with Integrity* DeGeorge proposes that firms of integrity have obligations to go beyond a moral minimum to fulfill various positive obligations and ethical ideals (DeGeorge, 1993). These include fulfilling various obligations to be charitable, promote the working conditions of their employees, etc. Such activities will be enhanced, if not made possible, to the extent that trusting relationships are developed between the firm and those who are to be the recipients of these activities. Indeed, such trusting relationships may be involved in differentiating paternalistic behavior on the part of the firm from behavior which is received as genuinely helpful. Thus, the greater the level of trust, the more likely that firms will be able, in DeGeorge's fashion, to engage in the full range of activities whereby they are businesses of integrity, rather than businesses simply meeting some minimal standards.

C. The nature and extent of moral guidelines that an international business ethics requires will depend upon the extent and levels of trust which are generated among the participants in a particular moral arena. Thus, the greater the level and extent of trust, the more it will be morally acceptable to leave ethical determinations to those businesses, their subsidiaries and the communities involved. On the other hand, interactions between members of societies with low levels of trust may be expected to produce greater moral dissonance than those in which the levels of trust are high. Such moral dissonance may require the greater moral guidance of explicit rules, principles and guidelines, as well as protections from various monitoring agencies.[18]

D. Finally, though trust cannot be the sole foundation for an international business ethics, the inherent features of trust noted above as morally significant might serve not only as (part of the) practical and effective basis for an ethics, but also for (part of) the basis upon which the norms of an international business ethics might themselves be developed and justified. The moral test of such norms would not be their coincidence with hypernorms (Donaldson and Dunfee) or their survival of awareness by others of what the trusting relationships are built upon (Baier). Instead, it would be based upon the extent and level of the trusting relationships from which such norms were derived. Thus, those ethical norms that derive from a broad range of trusting relationships (i.e., basic, guarded and extended trusting relationships) which are also extensively held (i.e., across all the communities and individuals affected) would have a *prima facie* moral acceptability to them. This might be part of a bottom-up ethics, rather than a top-down ethics. It would be an ethics with a strong endogamous component, rather than one fundamentally exogamous. Such an ethics would not begin with hypothetical contracts or postulated hypernorms. Instead, it would begin with the urgent need of individuals and firms to do business with each other, with communities and governments, and the trust which is necessary to these relationships. Out of these bilateral and multilateral relationships of various organizations and institutions would develop the effective morality from which an international business ethics might be abstracted. This can be viewed as an elaboration on the comment by Luhmann that "the necessity of trust can be regarded as the correct and appropriate starting point for the derivation of rules for proper conduct" (Luhmann, 1979: 4). This view is also in accord with Baier's comments that

> morality is a proliferating succession of responses, individual and collective, to those primitive responses to the risky adventure of interdependence. Morality then becomes a bootstrap operation. It starts from natural responses to aspects of our relations to others, aspects that are naturally feared or welcomed. These responses all involve risk and uncertainty; and moral training and criticism responds in ways which, if effective, decrease risk of evils of a variety of related sorts, and increase the chances of a family of goods but always at the cost of new risk. (Baier, 1985: 222-3)

Though Baier does not mention trust in this or the surrounding passages, clearly trust will play a significant role in the bottom-up, bootstrapping operation she has in mind for morality.

Т̣his is not to say that the ethical environment within these organizations and institutions would not have to be strongly supported by those at the top. It is also not to say that there would not need to be strong international monitoring organizations which would work to foster international business morality. In this sense, morality within organizations requires strong "top-down" ethical support. However, the preceding is to say that the norms which might be supported and imposed in those cases would arise out of the characteristics of the trusting relations which these organizations develop, rather than be derived from various philosophical constructions such as hypernorms and hypothetical contracts. Such a morality would have an inductive, rather than a deductive, nature.

314   BUSINESS ETHICS QUARTERLY

VII. Conclusion

Trust has been both oversold and underbilled in current discussions of international business ethics. Its value extends beyond the prudential or self-interested value for individuals and firms which has been frequently portrayed. However, it is too much to identify trust with morality itself. Those who trust might still harm others. Thus, trust is not the final solution to moral questions.

In seeking its proper place in international business ethics, I have argued that the Attitudinal view of trust, rather than the Predictability or Voluntarist views, is the proper one. In its Attitudinal form, trust plays a crucial role in three crucial kinds of instances: basic trust, guarded trust and extended trust. Each of these kinds of trust requires various conditions to foster or develop. Thus, basic trust requires conditions surrounding the commonality of motives and consistency of behavior of individuals or firms. Guarded trust requires conditions concerning motives, consistency and competence. And Extended trust requires conditions involving motives, consistency, competence and openness.

However, given the international setting within which these conditions must be fulfilled, various obstacles arise which don't arise (or do so to a much lesser degree) within a particular culture or society, e.g., problems of knowledge and interpretation of the motives and values of others, differences of motives and values, egocentric and ethnocentric tendencies, etc. This is the truth to the realist challenge. It poses genuine difficulties for an international business morality. These obstacles will have to be met with a variety of formal and informal mechanisms about which it is difficult to generalize. Still, out of the nature of trust we can draw certain conditions for morally worthy trust. If these conditions were broadly extended we might have part of a basis for an international business ethics which would arise from the bottom up, rather than be imposed top down.[19]

Notes

[1] Some people (including myself, on occasion) use the terms "ethics" and "morality" interchangeably. I am not doing so (obviously) in the present context. In this paper, I use "ethics" to refer to the theoretical study of moral values, standards and ideals by which people ought to live. "Morality" is used here to refer to the moral values or standards a society (or a person) lives by (whether justifiedly or not), rather than the theoretical investigation of them. Sometimes these "lived" values and standards are referred to as a person's "ethics." But in this context I do not follow this practice. Instead, I separate the two in order to emphasize that we need to develop a theoretical account (i.e., an ethics) of the values and standards by which people could actually morally live (i.e., a morality), rather than simply spin out fine theories which might not actually contain standards and values by which people or business could actually live and operate.

[2] Richard DeGeorge devotes a significant part of his book, *Competing With Integrity,* to a discussion of background conditions (DeGeorge, 1993).

[3] This is Held's statement of Tullock's views. I believe it to be an accurate statement (cf. Tullock, 1967).

INTERNATIONAL BUSINESS 315

[4] As I indicate, my argument that we should reject these two views of trust is aimed at the identification of a notion of trust that will be useful in international business ethics. However, I believe that the Attitudinal View of trust I defend is also the most useful and justified for any business context, not simply international ones.

[5] Hereafter, instead of speaking of "attitudinal trust," I will simply refer to "trust," by which I will understand its attitudinal variety.

[6] To the extent that one's belief that the other will not harm one is strongly held either on the basis of much evidence (though not conclusive evidence), or is held such that contrary evidence will not shake it, trust involves a confidence in the other. In those cases when weaker reason or evidence for the benignity of the other's behavior leads to weaker confidence, such trust as remains becomes a reliance on the other. (When there is little rational evidence of the other's benign disposition, we might speak of "blind trust.") Thus, confidence and reliance are not so much different criteria of trust, as markers of the grounds for the attitude or disposition one has towards the other (cf. Horsburgh, 1962: 28). As such, trust is not the same as reliance since, as Baier points out, "we may rely on our fellows' fear of the newly appointed security guards in shops to deter them from injecting poison into the food on the shelves, once we have ceased to trust them" (Baier, 1986: 234). L. Thomas also contends that trust and reliance are different. I may rely on someone I don't trust (cf. Thomas, 1989).

[7] Ken Alpern has urged on me the importance for trust of the notion of the affirmation of the other.

[8] Hosmer is drawing on Deutsch, 1958. See Luhmann: "Trust therefore always bears upon a critical alternative, in which the harm resulting from a breach of trust may be greater than the benefit to be gained from the trust proving warranted" (Luhmann, 1979: 24).

[9] What of the "trust" of an infant for a parent? If only those who are aware of the risks may trust, then infants cannot trust. Instead, the infant depends on its parents. D. O. Thomas notes that in learning whom to trust "we need to make judgments on our own account and doing this is not simply a matter of applying current rules and principles" (Thomas, 1978: 94).

[10] Cf. Baier, 1986: 237, 240, 253.

[11] Others also draw distinctions among different forms of trust. Among such accounts are: Barney and Hansen (1994) and L. Thomas (1989). I believe that my account is importantly different from each of these accounts and serves different purposes than those authors sought to address in their accounts.

[12] Gabarro explicitly notes the condition of consistency of behavior. He interprets it in the related senses of reliability and predictability (Gabarro, 1978).

[13] Hofstede measures the value differences between cultures in terms of a Power Distance Index, an Uncertainty Index, an Individualism Index and a Masculinity Index (Hofstede, 1979).

[14] In Liebrand et al., they show that 'these fairness biases have transcultural generality' (Liebrand et al., 1986: 602).

[15] Brandt raises the question of what makes a moral code effective in a society (Brandt, 1979: 180).

[16] The quotation is from Robert Bontempo, Associate Professor of International Management at Columbia University Business School. He was cited by Alex Markels, Joann S. Lublin and Phil Kuntz, in "Why Executives Tour World With Politicians," *The Wall Street Journal* (April 4, 1996), B1.

[17] I cite this and the following two passages from Baier, who is rephrasing the work of Thomas Scanlon on promises and the expectations that promises may set up in others (cf. Scanlon, 1990).

[18] Jones suggests the competitive disadvantage that may flow from a "cultural tradition of opportunism or of expensively constrained opportunism" such as that of the U.S. in contrast with other less opportunistic world cultures or nations (Jones, 1995: 431).

316   BUSINESS ETHICS QUARTERLY

[19] I am indebted to the comments of Ken Alpern, Reinhard Bachmann, Robbin Derry, John Dienhart, Darryl Koehn, Christel Lane and Pat Werhane on earlier versions of this paper.

Bibliography

Arrighetti, A., Bachmann, R., Deakin, S. 1997. 'Contract Law, Social Norms and Inter-firm Cooperation.' *Cambridge Journal of Economics* (forthcoming).

Baier, A. 1985. *Postures of the Mind.* Minneapolis: University of Minnesota Press.

_____. 1986. 'Trust and Antitrust.' *Ethics,* 96: 231-260.

_____. 1995. *Moral Prejudices.* Cambridge: Harvard University Press.

Barney, J. B. and Hansen, M. H. 1994. 'Trustworthiness as a Source of Competitive Advantage.' *Strategic Management Journal,* 15: 175-190.

Bluhm L. H. 1987. 'Trust, Terrorism, and Technology.' *Journal of Business Ethics,* 6: 333-341.

Brandt, R. B. 1979. *A Theory of the Good and the Right.* Oxford: Clarendon Press.

Brenkert, G. 1994. 'The Importance of the Structural Features of Moral Systems for International Business Ethics.' *Proceedings of the Fifth Annual Meeting of the International Association For Business and Society,* pp. 101-106.

Dasgupta, P. 1988. 'Trust as a Commodity.' In D. Gambetta (ed.), *Trust.* Oxford: Basil Blackwell.

DeGeorge, R. 1993. *Competing With Integrity In International Business.* New York: Oxford University Press.

Deutsch, M. 1958. 'Trust and Suspicion.' *Journal of Conflict Resolution,* 2: 265-279.

Dodgson, M. 1993. 'Learning, Trust and Technological Collaboration.' *Human Relations,* 46: 77-95.

Donaldson, T. and Dunfee, T. W. 1994. 'Towards A Unified Conception of Business Ethics: Integrative Social Contracts Theory.' *Academy of Management Review,* 19 (2): 252-284.

Fukuyama, F. 1995. *Trust: The Social Virtues and The Creation of Prosperity.* New York: Macmillan.

Gabarro, J. J. 1978. 'The Development of Trust, Influence and Expectations.' *Interpersonal Behavior.* Englewood Cliffs, NJ: Prentice-Hall.

Gambetta, D. 1988. 'Can We Trust Trust?' In D. Gambetta, D. (ed.), *Trust.* Oxford: Basil Blackwell.

Gellner, E. 1988. 'Trust, Cohesion and the Social Order.' In D. Gambetta (ed.), *Trust.* Oxford: Basil Blackwell.

Gewirth, A. 1982. 'Human Rights and the Prevention of Cancer.' In A. Gewirth, (ed.), *Human Rights.* Chicago: University of Chicago Press.

Held, V. 1968. 'On the Meaning of Trust.' *Ethics,* 78: 15-159.

_____. 1984. *Rights and Goods.* New York: The Free Press.

Hofstede, G. 1979. 'Value Systems in Forty Countries: Interpretation Validation and Consequences for Theory.' In L. H. Eckensberger, W. J. Lonner, and Y. H. Poortinga (eds.), *Cross-Cultural Contributions to Psychology.* Lisse: Swes & Zeiliner, B. V., pp. 389-407.

Horng, C. 1993. 'Cultural Differences, Trust and Their Relationships to Business Strategy and Control.' *Advances in International Comparative Management,* 8: 175-197.

Horsburgh, H. J. N. 1960. 'The Ethics of Trust.' *Philosophical Quarterly,* 10: 343-354.

Hosmer, L. T. 1995. 'Trust: The Connecting Link Between Organizational Theory and Philosophical Ethics.' *Academy of Management Review,* 20: 379-403.

Jones, T. M. 1995. 'Instrumental Stakeholder Theory: A Synthesis of Ethics and Economics.' *Academy of Management Review,* 20: 404-437.

King, J. B 1988. 'Prisoner's Paradoxes.' *Journal of Business Ethics,* 7: 475-487.

Liebrand, W. B. G., Jansen, R. W. T. L., Rijken, V. M. and Suhre, C. J. M. 1986. 'Might Over Morality: Social Values and the Perception of Other Players in Experimental Games.' *Journal of Experimental Social Psychology,* 22: 203-215.

Luhmann, N. 1979. *Trust and Power.* Chichester: John Wiley & Sons.

Markels, A., Lublin, J. S. and Kuntz, P. 1996. 'Why Executives Tour World with Politicians.' *The Wall Street Journal,* April 4: B1.

Mayer, R. C., Davis, J. H. and Schoorman, F. D. 1995. "An Integrative Model of Organizational Trust," *Academy of Management Review* 20(3): 709-734.

Messick, D. M., Bloom, S., Boldizar, J. P. and Samuelson, C. D. 1985. 'Why We Are Fairer than Others.' *Journal of Business Ethics,* 9: 619-638.

Noreen, E. 1988. 'The Economics of Ethics: A New Perspective on Agency Theory.' *Accounting, Organizations and Society,* 13: 359-369.

Puffer, S. M. and McCarthy, D. J. 1995. 'Finding the Common Ground in Russian and American Business Ethics.' *California Management Review,* 37: 29-46.

Rawls, J. 1971. *A Theory of Justice.* Cambridge : Harvard University Press.

Sable, C. F. 1993. 'Studied Trust: Building New Forms of Cooperation in a Volatile Economy.' *Human Relations,* 9: 1133-1170.

Sako, M. 1991. 'The Role of "Trust" in Japanese Buyer-Supplier Relationships.' *Ricerche Economiche,* 45: 449-474.

―――――. 1992. *Prices, quality and trust.* Cambridge: Cambridge University Press.

Scanlon, T. 1990. 'Promises and Practices.' *Philosophy & Public Affairs,* 19: 199-226.

Sellerberg, A.-M. 1982. 'On Modern Confidence.' *Acta Sociologica,* 25: 39-48.

Shell, G. R. 1991. 'Opportunism and Trust in the Negotiation of Commercial Contracts: Toward a New Cause of Action.' *Vanderbilt Law Review,* 44: 221-282.

Solomon, R. C. 1992. *Ethics and Excellence.* New York: Oxford University Press.

Thomas, D. O. 1978. 'The Duty to Trust.' *Proceedings of the Aristotelian Society,* 79: 89-101.

Thomas, L. 1989. *Living Morally.* Philadelphia: Temple University Press.

Tullock, G. 1967. 'The Prisoner's Dilemma and Mutual Trust.' *Ethics,* 77: 229-235.

Zucker, L. 1986. 'Production of Trust: Institutional Sources of Economic Structure, 1840-1920.' *Research in Organizational Behavior,* 8: 53-111.

[34]

TRUSTWORTHINESS AS A SOURCE OF COMPETITIVE ADVANTAGE

JAY B. BARNEY
Fisher College of Business, The Ohio State University, Columbus, Ohio, U.S.A.

MARK H. HANSEN
College of Business Administration, Texas A & M University, College Station, Texas, U.S.A.

Three types of trust in economic exchanges are identified: weak form trust, semi-strong form trust, and strong form trust. It is shown that weak form trust can only be a source of competitive advantage when competitors invest in unnecessary and expensive governance mechanisms. Semi-strong form trust can be a source of competitive advantage when competitors have differential exchange governance skills and abilities, and when these skills and abilities are costly to imitate. The conditions under which strong form trust can be a source of competitive advantage are also identified. Implications of this analysis for theoretical and empirical work in strategic management are discussed.

Significant differences in assumption and method exist between behaviorally oriented and economically oriented organizational scholars (Donaldson, 1990; Barney, 1990). While these differences manifest themselves in a wide variety of research contexts, no where are they more obvious than in research on the role of trust in economic exchanges.

On the one hand, behaviorally oriented researchers often criticize economic models that assume exchange partners are inherently untrustworthy (Mahoney, Huff, and Huff, 1993) and constantly tempted to behave in opportunistic ways (Donaldson, 1990). These scholars are dissatisfied with economic analyses that suggest trust will only emerge in an exchange when parties to that exchange erect legal and contractual protections (called governance mechanisms) which make it in their self-interest to behave in a trustworthy manner (Williamson, 1975). This rational, calculative, economic approach to trust, many behavioral scholars argue, is empirically

Key words: Trust, competitive advantage, resource-based view of the firm, organizational economics, transaction cost economics

incorrect (since most exchange partners are, in fact, trustworthy), socially inefficient (since it leads to an overinvestment in unnecessary governance), and morally bankrupt (Etzioni, 1988). A more reasonable approach, it is argued, would adopt the assumption that most exchange partners are trustworthy, that they behave as stewards over the resources they have under their control (Donaldson and Davis, 1991), and thus that trust in exchange relationships—even without legal and contractual governance protections—will be common.

On the other hand, more economically oriented scholars respond by observing that, at the very least, it is difficult to distinguish between exchange partners that are actually trustworthy and those that only claim to be trustworthy (Arrow, 1974; Williamson, 1985). Since one cannot reliably distinguish between these types of exchange partners, legal and contractual protections are a rational and effective means of assuring efficient exchange. Trust, many economists would argue, is in fact common in exchange relationships, precisely because of the constant threat of opportunistic behavior, linked with governance (Hill, 1990). Behavioral assertions that most

176   *J.B. Barney and M.H. Hansen*

exchange partners are inherently trustworthy and
that legal or contractual governance is thus
unnecessary are, at best, naive, and at worst,
foolish.

These debates about the role of trust in
exchange relationsips are interesting, in their
own right, but they are not terribly relevant for
strategic management research. Much of this
research focuses on understanding sources of
competitive advantage for firms (Rumelt, Schendel, and Teece, 1991; Bowman, 1974). The effort
to understand sources of competitive advantage
leads strategy researchers to study differences
between firms that enable some firms to conceive
of and implement valuable strategies that other
firms can either not conceive of and/or cannot
implement (Barney, 1991). Debates between
behavioral and economically oriented researchers
about how trustworthy individuals or firms are
fail to point to these kinds of differences.
Moreover, while the behavioral and economic
approaches suggest very different processes
through which trust emerges in economic
exchanges, both these approaches assert that
trust in economic exchanges will be very common.
Such common attributes of exchange relationships
cannot be sources of competitive advantage for
individual firms (Barney, 1991). To be a source
of competitive advantage, trust must be available
to only a few firms in their exchange relationships,
not to most firms in most exchange relationships
(Peteraf, 1993).

The purpose of this paper is to understand the
conditions under which trust and trustworthiness
in exchange relationships can, in fact, be a source
of competitive advantage for firms. The paper
begins by defining trust, trustworthiness, and the
closely related concept of opportunism. Next,
three types of trust in exchange relationships are
defined and described: weak form trust, semi-
strong form trust, and strong form trust.[1] Then,
the conditions under which these different types
of trust will, and will not, be sources of
competitive advantage for firms are discussed.
The paper concludes with a discussion of some
of the empirical and theoretical implications of
the analysis.

---
[1] With apologies to Gene Fama (1970).

DEFINING TRUST AND TRUSTWORTHINESS

Numerous definitions of trust and trustworthiness
have been presented in the literature (Bradach
and Eccles, 1989; Gambetta, 1988; Lewicki and
Bunker, 1994). For purposes of this discussion,
Sabel's (1993: 1133) definition of trust has been
adopted: trust is the mutual confidence that no
party to an exchange will exploit another's
vulnerabilities.

Parties to an exchange can be vulnerable in
several different ways. For example, when parties
to an exchange find it very costly to evaluate
accurately the quality of the resources or assets
others assert they will bring to an exchange,
these economic actors are subject to adverse
selection vulnerabilities (Akerlof, 1970). When
parties to an exchange find it very costly to
evaluate accurately the quality of the resources
or assets others are actually offering in exchange,
these economic actors are subject to moral hazard
vulnerabilities (Holmstrom, 1979). Also, when
parties to an exchange make large, asymmetric
transaction-specific investments in an exchange,
they are subject to hold-up vulnerabilities (Klein,
Crawford, and Alchian, 1978). According to
Sabel, when parties to an exchange trust each
other, they share a mutual confidence that others
will not exploit any adverse selection, moral
hazard, hold-up, or any other vulnerabilities that
might exist in a particular exchange.

A definition of trustworthiness follows directly
from Sabel's definition of trust. As the word itself
implies, an exchange partner is trustworthy when
it is worthy of the trust of others. An exchange
partner worthy of trust is one that will not exploit
other's exchange vulnerabilities. Notice that while
trust is an attribute of a relationship between
exchange partners, trustworthiness is an attribute
of individual exchange partners.

In many ways, opportunism is the opposite of
trust. A firm's actions are opportunistic to the
extent that they take advantage of another's
exchange vulnerabilities. Williamson (1979)
emphasizes firms exploiting hold-up vulnerabilities of exchange partners, caused by asymmetric
transaction-specific investment. However, the
exploitation of other exchange vulnerabilities,
including adverse selection and moral hazard
vulnerabilities, can also be opportunistic in
nature.

TYPES OF TRUST

While trust is the mutual confidence that one's vulnerabilities will not be exploited in an exchange, different types of trust can exist in different economic exchanges. These different types of trust reflect different reasons parties to an exchange can have the confidence that their vulnerabilities will not be exploited. At least three types of trust can be identified: weak from trust, semi-strong form trust, and strong form trust.

Weak form trust: Limited opportunities for opportunism

One reason that exchange partners can have the mutual confidence that others will not exploit their vulnerabilities is that they have no significant vulnerabilities, at least in a particular exchange. If there are no vulnerabilities, from adverse selection, moral hazard, hold-up, or other sources, then the trustworthiness of exchange partners will be high, and trust will be the norm in the exchange.

This type of trust can be called weak form trust because its existence does not depend on the erection of contractual or other forms of exchange governance. Nor does its existence depend on commitments by parties to an exchange to trustworthy standards of behavior. Rather, trust emerges in this type of exchange because there are limited opportunities for opportunism. Parties to an exchange, in this weak form context, will gain all the benefits of being able to trust their exchange partners without substantial governance or other costs.

Of course, weak form trust is likely to emerge in only very specific kinds of exchanges, i.e., exchanges where there are limited vulnerabilities. In general, whenever the quality of goods or services that are being exchanged can be evaluated at low cost, and whenever exchange partners do not need to make transaction-specific investments to obtain gains from an exchange, vulnerabilities in that exchange will be limited, and weak form trust will be common. Easy-to-evaluate quality effectively eliminates adverse selection and moral hazard vulnerabilities; no transaction-specific investments effectively eliminate hold-up vulnerabilities. Without vulnerabilities, opportunistic behavior is unlikely, and weak form trustworthiness will exist.

In this sense, weak form trust is clearly endogenous; i.e., it emerges out of a very specific exchange structure. Of course, this exchange structure can change and evolve over time. If an exchange evolves such that the cost of evaluating the quality of the goods or services in an exchange increases, then adverse selection and/ or moral hazard vulnerabilities may emerge, making weak form trust no longer possible. Also, if transaction-specific investments develop over time in an exchange, then hold-up vulnerabilities may emerge, and weak form trust will no longer exist.

Given this analysis, an important question becomes: how often will weak form trustworthiness exist? While, ultimately, this is an empirical question, it seems likely that weak form trust will be the norm in highly competitive commodity markets (Williamson, 1975). Examples of such markets include the market for crude oil and the market for soy beans. In all these markets, it is relatively easy for buyers and sellers to evaluate the quality of the goods or services they are receiving (limited adverse selection and moral hazard vulnerabilities). Moreover, in all these markets, there are large numbers of equally qualified buyers and sellers. Thus, firms do not have to make transaction-specific investments to trade with any one firm. Since parties to exchanges in these kinds of markets are not subject to significant exchange vulnerabilities, weak form trustworthiness is usually the norm.

Of course, that a market was once a highly competitive commodity market does not mean that it will always be a highly competitive commodity market. The cost of evaluating the quality of goods or services can increase, the number of buyers or suppliers can fall, and significant exchange vulnerabilities can develop. In this new exchange context, exchange partners cannot rely on the emergence of weak form trust, although other types of trust may develop.

Semi-strong form trust: Trust through governance

When significant exchange vulnerabilities exist (due to adverse selection, moral hazard, hold-up, or other sources), trust can still emerge, if parties to an exchange are protected through various governance devices. Governance devices impose costs of various kinds on parties to an exchange that behave opportunistically. If the appropriate governance devices are in place, the cost of opportunistic behavior will be greater than its benefit, and it will be in the rational self-interest of exchange partners to behave in a trustworthy way (Hill, 1990). In this context, parties to an exchange will have the mutual confidence that their vulnerabilities will not be exploited because it would be irrational to do so. This type of trust can be called semi-strong form trust, and is the type of trust emphasized in most economic models of exchange (Hill, 1990).

A wide range of governance devices have been described in the literature. Economists have tended to focus on market-based and contractual governance devices. One market-based governance device is the market for reputations (Klein *et al.*, 1978). Firms or individuals that develop a reputation for behaving opportunistically will often be excluded from future economic exchanges where exchange vulnerabilities are significant. The cost of these opportunities foregone can be substantial, and the avoidance of these costs can lead exchange partners to be trustworthy in current exchanges, albeit in a semi-strong way. Examples of more contractual forms of governance include complete contingent claims contracts, sequential contracting, strategic alliances, and hierarchical governance (Williamson, 1985; Hennart, 1988; Kogut, 1988). Contractual governance devices explicitly define what constitutes opportunistic behavior in a particular exchange, and specify the economic costs that will be imposed on offending parties (Williamson, 1979).

Recently, this economic focus on market-based and contractual governance devices has been criticized as being badly under socialized (Granovetter, 1985). Several authors have suggested that a variety of social costs can also be imposed on exchange partners that behave in opportunistic ways. For example, a firm that gains a reputation as a 'cheater' may bear substantial economic opportunity costs (Klein *et al.*, 1978), but it may also lose its social legitimacy (DiMaggio and Powell, 1983). Also, Granovetter (1985) has argued that exchange partners, be they individuals or firms, that are deeply embedded in social networks put those networks of relations at risk when they engage in opportunistic behavior. The imposition of these social costs

also acts to reduce the threat of opportunistic behavior.

One implication of including governance devices that impose social costs on opportunistic exchange partners, instead of just economic costs, is the expectation that opportunistic behavior will be unusual, even in settings where few market-based or contractual governance devices are in place, as long as these more social forms of governance exist (Granovetter, 1985). Even some economists are beginning to recognize the importance of these more socially oriented forms of governance (Williamson, 1991). However, while this more social approach to governance broadens the range of governance devices that should be studied, the trust that emerges among parties to an exchange with these social governance mechanisms in place is of the same type as the trust that emerges with only economic governance devices in place. In both cases, trust emerges because rational actors find it in their self-interest, for both economic and social reasons, not to behave opportunistically. Put another way, neither economic nor behavioral scholars would generally predict the emergence of trust in exchanges where significant vulnerabilities exist, and in which there are no market-based, contractual, or social forms of governance.[2] With governance in place, however, trust—of the semi-strong variety—may emerge, despite the existence of significant exchange vulnerabilities.

Like weak form trust, semi-strong form trust is endogenous; i.e., it emerges out of the structure of a particular exchange. However, unlike weak form trust, the structure of that exchange is modified, in the semi-strong case, through the use of governance devices of various types. If parties to an exchange create and/or exploit the correct governance devices, then opportunistic behavior in that exchange will be unlikely, and trust—albeit of the semi-strong variety—will exist.

Of course, the creation and exploitation of different forms of governance is not costless. The costs of market-based and contractual forms

---

[2] Granovetter (1985) would probably argue that relatively few economic exchanges are not embedded in some broader network of social relations. This, of course, is ultimately an empirical question. However, Granovetter's theory suggests that without some mechanism to impose social costs on those that behave opportunistically, social governance will not generate trust in a relationship.

of governance are well documented (Williamson, 1985). While social forms of governance have fewer direct costs associated with them, they are nevertheless costly, in the sense that the use of these forms of governance requires one only to engage in exchanges where potential partners are embedded in specific broader social networks of relations. This limitation on potential exchange partners is an opportunity cost of using social forms of governance.

Traditional transactions cost logic suggests that rational economic actors will insist on just that level of governance necessary to ensure the semi-strong trustworthiness of exchange partners. If existing social forms of governance cannot assure the emergence of semi-strong trustworthiness, then additional, and costly, legalistic and contractual forms of governance (including, perhaps, complete contingent claims contracts and sequential contracting) will need to be created. If this level of governance is not sufficient, more elaborate and costly intermediate market forms may be erected (e.g., strategic alliances). If even this level of governance is not sufficient, then even more costly hierarchical forms of governance may be erected (Williamson, 1975, 1979). There may even be some exchanges where hierarchical governance is not sufficient to create semi-strong form trust (Grossman and Hart, 1986).

One implication of this analysis is that there may be some potentially valuable exchanges that cannot be pursued. Whenever the cost of governance needed to generate semi-strong form trust is greater than the expected gains from trade, and exchange with semi-strong trustworthy partners will not be pursued. This can happen in at least two ways. First, the expected gains from trade may be relatively small, in which case even modest investments in governance mechanisms may not pay off. Second, the expected gains from trade may be very large, but so may be the exchange vulnerabilities in that trade. In this type of exchange, the high cost of governance may still be greater than the expected value of exchange, even if that expected value is large. Indeed, as Grossman and Hart (1986) suggest, there may be some exchanges where no governance devices will create semi-strong form trust (i.e., where the cost of governance is infinitely high). If the only types of trust that can exist in economic exchanges are of the weak and semi-strong types, then these

valuable, but costly to govern, exchanges may have to remain unexploited.

Strong form trust: Hard-core trustworthiness

In weak form trust, trust is possible because exchange vulnerabilities do not exist. In the semi-strong case, trust is possible, despite exchange vulnerabilities, because of the significant social and economic costs imposed by governance mechanisms on the opportunistic behavior of exchange partners. In strong form trust, trust emerges in the face of significant exchange vulnerabilities, independent of whether or not elaborate social and economic governance mechanisms exist, because opportunistic behavior would violate values, principles, and standards of behavior that have been internalized by parties to an exchange.

Strong form trust could also be called principled trust, since trustworthy behavior emerges in response to sets of principles and standards that guide the behavior of exchange partners. Frank (1988) might call strong form trust 'hard-core trust'. Hard-core trustworthy exchange partners are trustworthy, independent of whether or not exchange vulnerabilities exist and independent of whether or not governance mechanisms exist. Rather, hard-core trustworthy exchange partners are trustworthy because that is who, or what, they are. This type of trust is, perhaps, closest to the type of trust emphasized by more behavioral scholars (Mahoney et al., 1993).[3]

In this sense, strong form trustworthiness is clearly exogenous to a particular exchange structure. Strong form trust does not emerge from the structure of an exchange, but rather, reflects the values, principles, and standards that partners bring to an exchange. Those values, principles, and standards may reflect an exchange partner's unique history, its culture, or the personal beliefs and values of critical individuals associated with it (Arthur, 1989; Barney, 1986; Dierickx and Cool, 1989).

---

[3] In principle, some level of compensation will always exist where strong form trustworthy exchange partners will abandon their values, principles, and standards of behavior, and act in opportunistic ways. This level of compensation might be called the 'Faustian' price. However, this level of compensation is *much* higher for a strong form trustworthy exchange partner, compared to a semi-strong form trustworthy exchange partner.

180   *J.B. Barney and M.H. Hansen*

The strong form trustworthiness of individuals

While the existence of strong form trustworthiness is, ultimately, an empirical question, research from a variety of disciplines can be helpful in answering the existence question. If exchange partners are individuals, then research in developmental psychology suggests that strong form trustworthiness can exist in at least some people.

Developmental psychologists have studied the stages of moral development in children and young adults (Kohlberg, 1969, 1971). These stages are summarized in Table 1.[4] When children are very young (small babies), they are able to make very few, if any, moral choices. In this stage, decision making and behavior are essentially amoral. However, as children mature, they often have to decide whether or not to conform their choices and behaviors to a set of values, principles, and standards.[5] In the conventional morality stage (Kohlberg, 1969), children conform their choices and behaviors to a set of values, principles, and standards in order to avoid the costs imposed on them by others for failing to do so. In this stage, children are moral because the costs of being caught violating principles and standards (i.e., punishment) are too high. In the post conventional morality stage, choices and behaviors conform to a set of values, principles, and standards because they are internalized by individuals. While external costs could still be imposed on choices and behaviors that do not conform to these principles and standards, avoiding these costs is not the primary motivation for moral behavior. Rather, the primary motivation for such behavior is to avoid internally imposed costs, including a sense of personal failure, guilt, and so forth.

Some obvious parallels exist between the types of trust and trustworthiness identified here, and the stages of moral development identified in developmental psychology. These parallels are identified in Table 1. The amoral stage in the moral development literature is analogous to weak form trustworthiness. Just as young children cannot violate moral standards when they are unable to make moral choices, individuals in exchange relationships cannot act opportunistically when there are no opportunities to do so. Conventional morality is analogous to semi-strong form trustworthiness. In conventional morality, individuals make choices to conform their behavior to a set of principles and standards in order to avoid the cost of failing to do so; in semi-strong form trust, opportunistic behavior is avoided because of the economic and social costs imposed on such behavior by governance mechanisms. Finally, post conventional morality is analogous to strong form trustworthiness. In both cases, choices and behavior conform to a set of principles and standards because those principles and standards have been internalized. While external costs may be imposed on individuals that violate these principles and standards, avoiding these external costs is not the primary reason choices and behavior conform to them. Rather, the avoidance of internally imposed costs—including a sense of personal failure and guilt—provide the primary motivation for this type of principled behavior.

Psychologists have shown that postconventional morality is not uncommon (Kohlberg, 1971). While some people never mature beyond the amoral or conventional morality stages, many have sets of values, principles, and standards that they use to guide their choices and behaviors. In order for postconventional morality to lead to strong form trustworthiness, all that is additionally required is that some of these values, principles, and standards suggest that exploiting an exchange partners vulnerabilities is inappropriate.

The strong form trustworthiness of firms

At the individual level, the existence of strong form trustworthiness in at least some people seems plausible. However, that individuals—as exchange partners—can be strong form trustworthy does not necessarily imply that firms—as exchange partners—can be strong form trustworthy. Firms, as exchange partners, can be strong form trustworthy for at least two reasons. Either a firm may possess a culture and associated control systems that reward strong form trustworthy behavior, or the specific individuals involved in a particular exchange may, themselves, be strong form trustworthy.

Zucker (1987) has shown that firm founders

---

[4] This is a simplification of the actual typology developed by Kohlberg (1969, 1971). However, it is consistent with Kohlberg's findings.
[5] These values, standards, and principles are normally taken from a child's parents or other caregivers (Kohlberg, 1969).

Table 1. Parallels between stages of moral development and types of trust

Stages in moral development	Types of trust and trustworthiness
Amoral stage When there are no moral choices to be made	*Weak form trust* Limited opportunities for opportunism
Conventional morality Decisions and behaviors conform to standards in order to avoid the cost of being caught violating standards	*Semi-strong form trust* Trust emerges in response to social and economic governance mechanisms that impose costs on opportunistic behavior
Postconventional morality Decisions and behaviors conform to standards because they have been internalized as principles and values	*Strong form trust* An exchange partner behaves in a trustworthy manner because to do otherwise would be to violate values, standards, and principles of behavior

can have a very strong impact on the culture and other institutional attributes of firms. This impact can continue, even if these individuals have been dead for many years. Others, besides founders, can also have these strong cultural and institutional effects. For example, transformational leaders (Tichy and Devanna, 1986) can have the effect of re-creating a firm's culture and fundamentally changing other of its institutional attributes.

If these influential individuals were themselves strong form trustworthy, they may have created an organizational culture characterized by strong form trustworthy values and beliefs. These strong form trustworthy values and beliefs may also be supported and reinforced by internal reward and compensation systems, together with decision-making mechanisms that reflect strong form trustworthy standards. A firm with these cultural and institutional mechanisms in place will often behave in a strong form trustworthy manner in exchange relationships.

Notice that, if a firm has a strong form trustworthy culture and associated control mechanisms, it is not necessary for each individual in a firm to be strong form trustworthy. Rather, all that is required is that individuals in a firm be at least self-interested in their behavior. In this situation, individuals in a firm will find it in their self-interest to behave in a strong form trustworthy way, when representing the firm, for failure to do so would lead them to be subject to a variety of social and economic sanctions. Individuals who are unable to conform themselves

to a firm's strong form trustworthy standards have several options, including, for example, finding positions in the firm where trustworthiness issues are not likely to arise, or changing firms.

Of course, that a firm once had a culture, and associated internal control mechanisms, that encouraged strong form trustworthiness does not mean that it will always have these attributes. Cultures can evolve, control mechanisms can change, and a firm may no longer have the attributes to qualify as strong form trustworthy. However, even when firms do not have strong form trustworthiness cultures, it still may be possible for some of the exchanges in which a firm engages to be characterized by strong form trust.

Exchanges between firms are, more often then not, actually exchanges between small groups of individuals in different firms. For example, when an automobile company signs a supply agreement with a supplier, the two groups of individuals most directly involved in this agreement are the purchasing people, in the automobile company, and the sales people, in the supply company. When two firms agree to form an equity joint venture, several groups of people are directly involved, including those in each parent firm that are assigned the responsibility to interact with the joint venture, and those that work in the joint venture itself.

While the firms in these exchanges may not have strong form trustworthy cultures, the specific individuals that are most directly involved in these exchanges may, themselves, be strong form trustworthy. Exchanges between strong form trustworthy individuals in different firms can lead to strong form trust, even though the firms, themselves, may not be strong form trustworthy.[6]

TRUST AND COMPETITIVE ADVANTAGE

Trust can emerge in economic exchanges in any of the three ways discussed. However, these three types of trust are not equally likely to be sources of competitive advantage. A strategic analysis of trust and trustworthiness focuses attention on the conditions under which a particular type of trust will be a source of competitive advantage.

Weak form trust and competitive advantage

The exchange attributes that make weak form trust possible suggest that weak form trust will usually not be a source of competitive advantage. As suggested earlier, weak form trust is most likely to emerge in highly competitive commodity markets. It is well known that exchange partners in highly competitive commodity markets can expect to gain few, if any, competitive advantages (Porter, 1980). In particular, while those participating in these markets will be able to rely on the existence of weak form trust in their exchange relationships, the advantages of weak form trust will accrue to all exchange partners in these markets equally, thereby giving no one of them a competitive advantage.

Indeed, one of the few ways those trading in these markets can expect to gain advantages from weak form trust is if some competitors fail to rely on weak form trust and, indeed, invest in unnecessary and costly governance devices to create semi-strong form trust. Both those that rely on weak form and semi-strong form trust, in these highly competitive commodity markets,

---

[6] Conflicts between individual and firm values, in this context, act as a constraint on the ability of strong form trustworthy individuals to engage in strong form trust exchanges. However, strong form trustworthy individuals can be expected to engage in a variety of activities to neutralize the non-strong form trustworthy effects of the firm within which they operate. Moreover, the firm has strong incentives to let the strong form trustworthy individuals continue in strong form trust exchanges, since it gains all the advantages of these exchanges.

can expect trust to exist in their exchange relationships. However, those that invest in governance to generate semi-strong form trust will have higher costs, compared to those that rely on weak form trust. Over time, those that have invested in unnecessary (and costly) governance will either abandon those governance devices or suffer from competitive disadvantages.

Put differently, the cost advantage of those that rely on weak form trust over those that rely on semi-strong form trust, in these highly competitive conditions, is a measure of the economic value of weak form trust. However, if numerous competitors are all able to obtain this value at the same low cost, then it will not be a source of competitive advantage to any one of them (Barney, 1991).

Semi-strong form trust and competitive advantage

Semi-strong form trust in exchange relationships is economically valuable, in the sense that its creation assures parties to an exchange that their vulnerabilities will not be exploited. However, the ability to create semi-strong form trust in economic exchanges depends on several important governance skills and abilities that parties to an exchange must possess. For example, for semi-strong form trust to emerge, exchange partners must be able accurately to anticipate sources and levels of opportunistic threat in the exchanges in which they may participate. Also, to create semi-strong form trust, exchange partners must be able to rely on existing social governance mechanisms and/or to conceive of, implement, and manage the appropriate market-based and contractual governance mechanisms. Only if exchange partners can accomplish these tasks will the 'right' types of governance be chosen to create semi-strong form trust, and will the value of semi-strong form trust be realized.

However, for semi-strong form trust to be a source of competitive advantage, there must be heterogeneity in the exchange governance skills and abilities of competing firms (Barney, 1991). If most competing firms or individuals have similar governance skills and abilities, they will all be equally able to create the conditions under which semi-strong form trust will emerge in their exchange relationships. Moreover, the cost of creating semi-strong form trust will also not vary dramatically across these equally skilled competitors. Since these competitors do not vary in their exchange governance skills, no one of them will be able to gain a competitive advantage based on the semi-strong form trust that they are able to create with these skills.[7]

Of course, there is no reason to believe, *a priori*, that competing exchange partners will be equally skilled or able in creating the conditions necessary for semi-strong form trust. For example, some exchange partners may have developed a high degree of skill in managing, say, intermediate market forms of governance (e.g., equity joint ventures). These highly skilled actors may be able to create semi-strong form trust using these intermediate market forms of governance in economic exchanges where less skilled actors may be forced to use hierarchical forms of governance. If intermediate market forms of governance are, in fact, less costly than hierarchical forms of governance, those that obtain semi-strong form trust through intermediate market forms will have a competitive advantage over those that must obtain trust in that exchange through hierarchical forms of governance. Similar reasoning could apply to those that are highly skilled in managing contractual forms of governance (e.g., complete contingent claims contracts) compared to those that are only able to use more costly intermediate market forms of governance or hierarchical forms of governance.

Heterogeneity in the skills and ability to create semi-strong form trust in an exchange may also reflect important social differences among competing exchange partners. For example, if a particular firm is contemplating an exchange with another firm, where that relationship is deeply embedded in a large complex network of social relations, these firms may be able to rely on (relatively inexpensive) social governance mechanisms to develop semi-strong form trust. On the other hand, if a competing firm is anticipating a similar exchange that is not deeply

embedded in this broader social network of relations, parties to this exchange may have to rely on (more costly) economic forms of governance to ensure semi-strong form trust. The firm that can rely on social governance to generate semi-strong form trust will have a cost-based competitive advantage over the firm that must rely on economic governance to generate semi-strong form trust.

Heterogeneity in governance skills and abilities is an important explanation of variance in a wide variety of different economic exchanges. Compare, for example, the exchanges between Toyota and its suppliers, on the one hand, and General Motors and its suppliers (Dyer and Ouchi, 1993; Womack, Jones, and Roos, 1990), on the other. Toyota's supply relationships are deeply embedded in long-standing networks of social and economic relationships. These social governance mechanisms have enabled both Toyota and its suppliers to engage in very vulnerable exchanges (due to high transaction-specific investments that lead to a high risk of hold-up) with substantially less contractual or other forms of governance than is the case at General Motors (GM). Without the ability to rely on social embeddedness to constrain the opportunistic behavior of its suppliers, GM has had to reduce the threat of opportunism by reducing the level of transaction-specific investment in its suppliers (i.e., by having multiple competing suppliers), by insisting on elaborate contractual protections, or by vertically integrating the supply relationship (Dyer and Ouchi, 1993; Womack *et al.*, 1990). Overall, the cost of creating semi-strong form trust at Toyota has been substantially lower than the cost of creating semi-strong form trust at GM.[8]

Of course, if several competitors all possess these special governance skills and abilities to approximately the same level, then they will not be a source of competitive advantage for any one of them, even if there are some competitors that do not possess these skills. However, as long as the number of competitors that have these special governance skills and abilities is less than what is required to generate perfect competition dynamics, then they can be a source

---

[7] Competing exchange partners do not have to erect the same governance mechanisms for semi-strong trust to generate competitive parity. Rather, all that is required is that competing exchange partners erect functionally equivalent governance devices (i.e., governance devices that generate the same level of semi-strong form trust) and that these governance devices are about equally costly. These arguments also apply to *bundles* of governance devices to create semi-strong form trust.

[8] Obviously, there may be some strong form trustworthiness attributes to Toyota's relationships with its suppliers that do not exist between GM and its suppliers.

of competitive advantage for those that possess them (Barney, 1991).

Moreover, if these skills and abilities can rapidly diffuse among competitors, they will be the source of only temporary competitive advantages. However, it seems likely that these skills and abilities will not rapidly diffuse through most populations. For example, the ability to rely on social governance mechanisms in different exchanges depends upon the structure of the network of relations within which an exchange is embedded. Those networks of relations, in turn, are developed over long perods of time, and are unique to a particular point in history. Such path-dependent (Arthur, 1989) phenomena are subject to time compression diseconomies (Dierickx and Cool, 1989), and thus costly to imitate. The development of special governance skills is also path dependent. Moreover, these skills are often socially complex, and thus costly to imitate (Barney, 1991).

Whenever exchange partners possess rare and costly-to-imitate governance skills and abilities, they may be able to use those abilities to gain competitive advantages in creating semi-strong form trust. On the other hand, when competing exchange partners possess similar governance skills and abilities, the creation of semi-strong trust will generate only competitive parity.

Strong form trust and competitive advantage

For strong form trustworthiness to be economically valuable, all those with a significant stake in an exchange must be strong form trustworthy. If one or more parties to an exchange may behave opportunistically in that exchange, then all parties to that exchange will need to invest in a variety of social and economic governance mechanisms to insure semi-strong form trust. Any potential economic advantages of being strong form trustworthy are irrelevant when semi-strong form governance protections are erected and exploited, since strong form trustworthy parties are forced to behave as if they were only semi-strong form trustworthy.

Economic opportunities in strong form trust exchanges

On the other hand, if all those with a significant stake in an exchange are strong form trustworthy, some important and valuable economic opportunities may exist. These opportunities reflect either the governance cost advantages that strong form trust exchanges may enjoy over semi-strong form trust exchanges and/or the ability that strong form trustworthy exchange partners may have to explore exchange options not available to semi-strong form trustworthy exchange partners.

When two or more strong form trustworthy individuals or firms engage in an exchange, they can all be assured that any vulnerabilities that might exist in this exchange will not be exploited by their partners. Moreover, this assurance comes with no additional investment in social or economic forms of governance. As long as the cost of developing and maintaining strong form trustworthiness in an individual or firm, plus cost of discovering strong form trustworthy partners, is less than the cost of exploiting or creating semi-strong form governance devices, those engaging in a strong form trustworthy context will gain a cost advantage over those exchanging in a semi-strong trustworthy context.

Consider, for example, several competing firms looking to purchase raw materials from a set of suppliers. Suppose that a small number of these buyers and sellers are strong form trustworthy, and that there are some significant exchange vulnerabilities in this raw materials purchase. In order to complete this purchase, those purchasing from semi-strong suppliers will need to rely on and/or erect a variety of social or economic governance devices. While these governance devices are costly, their existence will enable firms to purchase the raw material in question. On the other hand, strong form trustworthy buyers purchasing from strong form trustworthy suppliers will not have to rely on or erect social or economic forms of governance in order to complete their purchase of the raw material. As long as the cost of developing and maintaining strong form trustworthiness, plus the cost of discovering strong form trustworthy exchange partners, is less than the cost of relying on or erecting social or economic governance devices, the firms purchasing raw materials in a strong form trust exchange will have a cost advantage over those firms purchasing raw materials in a semi-strong trust exchange.[9]

---

[9] While ultimately an empirical question, it seems likely that the cost of creating and maintaining strong form

Perhaps even more important than this governance cost advantage, those engaging in strong form trust exchanges may be able to exploit exchange opportunities that are not available to those who are only able to engage in semi-strong form trust exchanges. It has already been suggested that valuable semi-strong form exchanges will not be pursued when the cost of governance needed to generate semi-strong form trust is greater than the expected gains from trade. This can happen when the expected gains from trade are small (but modest vulnerabilities in this exchange require modest levels of expensive governance) or when the expected gains from trade are substantial (but very large vulnerabilities in this exchange require very substantial levels of costly governance). While semi-strong form trust exchanges will not be pursued in these situations, it may be possible to pursue strong form trust exchanges. In this sense, strong form trustworthiness may increase the set of exchange opportunities available to an individual or firm, compared to those who are only semi-strong form trustworthy (Zajac and Olsen, 1993; Ring and Van de Ven, 1994).

Consider, for example, several competing firms looking to cooperate with one or more of several other firms in the development and exploitation of a new, and sophisticated, technology. Suppose that only a small number of these two sets of firms are strong form trustworthy, that the technology in question has significant economic potential, but that there are enormous exchange vulnerabilities in the technology development process. Semi-strong form trustworthy firms, in this setting, will need to invest in substantial amounts of costly governance to try to create semi-strong form trust. It may even be the case that no form of governance will create semi-strong form trust (Grossman and Hart, 1986). The potential economic return that could be obtained from this exchange will need to be reduced by an amount equal to the present value

of the cost of governing this exchange. Moreover, the present value of this exchange will also have to be discounted by any residual threat of opportunism. The reduced value of this exchange could lead semi-strong form trustworthy firms to decide not to pursue it, even though substantial economic value may exist.

On the other hand, exchanges of this sort between strong form trustworthy firms are burdened neither by the high cost of governance nor any residual threat of opportunism. Strong form trustworthy firms will be able to pursue these valuable, but highly vulnerable exchanges, while semi-strong form trustworthy firms will be unable to pursue them. This may represent a substantial opportunity cost for semi-strong form trustworthy exchange partners, and a source of competitive advantage for strong form trustworthy exchange partners.[10]

Traditional transactions cost logic suggests that, when faced with these valuable but highly vulnerable exchanges, exchange partners will opt for hierarchical forms of governance and use managerial fiat as a way to manage trustworthiness problems (Williamson, 1985). However, hierarchical governance is not always a solution to these problems. First, there may be important legal and political restrictions on the use of hierarchical governance. For example, one cannot acquire a direct competitor if such actions lead to unacceptably high levels of industry concentration. Also, firms may be required, for political reasons, to maintain market or intermediate market relationships with an exchange partner (e.g., when entering into a new country market).

Second, as Grossman and Hart (1986) suggest, hierarchical governance does not necessarily 'solve' opportunism problems. Rather it simply shifts those problems from a market or intermediate market context to inside the boundaries of the firm. Where, in market-based exchanges, firms face the threat of opportunism in exchanges with other firms, bringing these transactions within the boundaries of a firm can simply lead to division facing the threat of opportunism in

---

trustworthiness, plus the cost of discovering strong form trustworthy exchange partners, will often be less than the cost of relying on or erecting semi-strong governance devices. The cost of creating and maintaining strong form trustworthiness can be spread across numerous economic exchanges, thus reducing the per exchange cost. The cost of discovering strong form trustworthy exchange partners can be reduced through the discovery and signalling mechanisms described below.

---

[10] As previously, it seems likely that the cost of creating and maintaining strong form trustworthiness, plus the cost of discovering strong form trustworthy exchange partners, will be less than the opportunity cost of relying only on semi-strong form trust governance devices.

186   *J.B. Barney and M.H. Hansen*

exchanges with other divisions. Put differently, hierarchical governance does not automatically create strong form trust exchange (Ouchi, 1980).

Where hierarchical governance may not always be a solution to the threat of opportunism, exchanges between strong form trustworthy exchange partners—whether those exchanges are within the boundary of a single firm or not—will, in general, create strong form trust. Strong form trustworthy individuals or firms will often be able to gain governance cost advantages over semi-strong form trustworthy individuals or firms. Moreover, strong form trustworthy individuals or firms will often be able to engage in economic exchanges that cannot be pursued by semi-strong form trustworthy exchange partners. Put differently, the level of vulnerability in some economic exchanges may be greater than the ability of any standard governance devices to protect against the threat of opportunism. The only way to pursue these exchanges is through strong form trustworthiness.

Of course, if most competitors are strong form trustworthy, and engage in exchanges with others that are also strong form trustworthy, then the advantages of strong form trustworthiness would only be a source of competitive parity, and not competitive advantage. However, while the number of strong form trustworthy exchange partners in a particular segment of the economy is ultimately an empirical question, it seems like a reasonable guess that strong form trustworthiness in at least some segments of the economy is probably rare, and thus (assuming exchanges with other strong form trustworthy exchange partners are developed) at least a source of temporary competitive advantage for strong form trustworthy individuals and firms.

Locating strong form trustworthy exchange partners

Given the important competitive advantages that may attend exchanges between strong form trustworthy exchange partners, an important question becomes: how can strong form trustworthy exchange partners recognize each other? This process is problematic, since exchange partners that are not strong form trustworthy have a strong incentive to assert that they are. If a strong form trustworthy individual or firm believes that an exchange partner is strong form

trustworthy, even though this partner is not, then that strong form trustworthy individual or firm will be willing to engage in a highly vulnerable exchange without social or economic governance devices. Without these devices in place, the untrustworthy exchange partner could exploit the strong form trustworthy partner's exchange vulnerabilities with impunity. Thus, simple assertions that one is strong form trustworthy are not sufficient justification for assuming that an exchange partner is, in fact, strong form trustworthy.

Of course, a simple solution to this adverse selection problem would be to observe directly whether or not a potential exchange partner is stong form trustworthy, and respond appropriately. Unfortunately, the individual and organizational attributes that create strong form trustworthiness are difficult to observe directly. At an individual level, the values, principles, and standards around which strong form trustworthy individuals organize their lives are clearly not directly observable. At the firm level, an organization's culture, and associated control systems, may be difficult to observe, and their implications for individual behavior ambiguous—at least to those not deeply embedded in this culture and control system. Moreover, if the development of strong form trust depends on the strong form trustworthiness of small groups of people in a larger organization, evaluating the individual values, principles, and standards of these people remains difficult.

Even with these challenges, strong form trustworthy exchange partners can still be found. It will often be the case, for example, that exchange partners will begin a relationship assuming that others are at least semi-strong form trustworthy. As this relationship evolves overtime, parties to an exchange may be able to gain sufficient information to judge accurately whether or not others are strong form trustworthy. If two or more parties to an exchange discover that they are strong form trustworthy, any subsequent exchanges between these parties can generate strong form trust, and these exchange partners will subsequently obtain all the advantages of strong form trustworthiness. On the other hand, if experience shows that an exchange partner is only semi-strong form trustworthy, then future exchanges with this partner will continue with semi-strong form trust generating governance mechanism in place.

Notice that this process of discovering strong form trustworthy exchange partners assumes that one's trustworthiness type does not automatically change as a result of experience in a semi-strong form trust relationship. If the creation of semi-strong trust exchanges inevitably led exchange partners to become strong form trustworthy, then all exchanges would inevitably be characterized by strong form trust, and strong form trustworthiness would not be a source of competitive advantage to any individual or firm. Rather than changing an exchange partner's trustworthiness type, the creation of a semi-strong form trust exchange creates an opportunity for exchange partners to observe more directly another's trustworthiness type. While it is certainly true that an exchange partner's trustworthiness type may evolve over the long run, the historical, path-dependent, socially complex, and causally ambiguous nature of strong form trustworthiness makes it unlikely that semi-strong form trustworthy firms will be able to become strong form trustworthy in the short and medium term.

This search for potential strong form trustworthy exchange partners can be shortened through the use of signals of strong form trustworthiness (Spence, 1973). Signals of strong form trustworthiness must have two properties: (1) they must be correlated with the underlying (but costly to observe) actual level of strong form trustworthiness in a potential exchange partner; and (2) they must be less costly to exchange partners that are actually strong form trustworthy than they are to exchange partners that only claim they are strong form trustworthy (Spence, 1973).

Several behaviors by exchange partners qualify as signals for strong form trustworthiness. For example, a reputation for being strong form trustworthy is a signal of strong form trustworthiness.[11] Gaining a reputation as a strong form trustworthy exchange partner occurs, over time, as an exchange partner confronts situations where opportunistic behavior is possible, but chooses not to engage in opportunistic activities. There

are no opportunity costs associated with a strong form trustworthy individual or firm not behaving opportunistically, since such behavior is not in this kind of exchange partner's opportunity set. On the other hand, a nonstrong form trustworthy exchange partner will have to absorb opportunity costs each time they decide not to behave in an opportunistic way. These opportunity costs make it more costly for an exchange partner that is not strong form trustworthy to develop a reputation as strong form trustworthy, compared to an exchange partner that is actually strong form trustworthy.

While a reputation for being strong form trustworthy is a signal of strong form trustworthiness, it is noisy. In particular, this reputation cannot distinguish between those exchange partners that are actually strong form trustworthy, and those that are not strong form trustworthy, but have yet to engage in an exchange where returns to opportunistic behavior are large enough to motivate opportunistic behavior. While a reputation for being strong form trustworthy does eliminate those exchange partners who have acted opportunistically, it does not eliminate those exchange partners who might act opportunistically, given the right incentives.

Another signal of strong form trustworthiness is being open to outside auditing of the exchange relationship. This is less costly to strong form trustworthy exchange partners, compared to those that are not strong form trustworthy, since trustworthy exchange partners were not going to behave opportunistically anyway. One would expect to see strong form trustworthy firms and individuals to be very open to outside auditors, perhaps even paying the cost of outside auditors chosen by potential exchange partners.

A third signal of strong form trustworthiness might be to make unilateral transaction-specific investments in an exchange before that exchange is actually in place. Gulati, Khana, and Nohria (1994) have found, for example, that it is not uncommon for firms with a strong track record of successfully engaging in joint ventures to sign long-term third-party supply contracts that are only valuable if a particular joint venture actually goes forward—before that joint venture agreement is complete. Such unilateral transaction-specific investments are less costly to strong form trustworthy firms, since they were not going to behave in an opportunistic manner in developing

---

[11] Note that having a reputation for being strong form trustworthy is not the same as not having a reputation for being opportunistic. A potential exchange partner may not have a reputation for being opportunistic (i.e., they may not be known as a 'cheater') but still not have a reputation for being strong form trustworthy (i.e., they may not be known as 'hard-core' trustworthy).

188   *J.B. Barney and M.H. Hansen*

this joint venture anyway. These investments foreclose opportunistic opportunities for firms that are not strong form trustworthy, and thus represent significant opportunity costs to these firms. If all those involved in an exchange independently make these kinds of unilateral transaction-specific investments, then others in these exchanges can conclude, with some reliability, that they are strong form trustworthy.

If strong form trustworthiness is relatively rare among a set of competitors, and if two or more strong form trustworthy exchange partners are able to engage in trade, then these strong form trustworthy individuals or firms will gain at least a temporary competitive advantage over individuals or firms that are not strong form trustworthy. For this competitive advantage to remain, however, the individual and organizational attributes that make strong form trustworthiness possible must also be costly to imitate and immune from rapid diffusion. Fortunately, the individual and organizational attributes that make strong form trustworthiness possible (i.e., individual values, principles, and standards; an organization's culture and associated control system) reflect an exchange partner's unique path through history (path dependence) and are socially complex. As was suggested earlier, these types of individual and organizational attributes are usually immune from imitation and rapid diffusion among competitors (Barney, 1991; Arthur, 1989; Dierickx and Cool, 1989).[12]

DISCUSSION

Trust, in economic exchanges, can be a source of competitive advantage. However, trust in these exchanges is not always a source of competitive advantage. Weak form trust is only a competitive advantage when competitors invest in unnecessary and costly semi-strong form

governance mechanisms. Semi-strong form trust is only a source of competitive advantage when a small number of competitors have special skills and abilities in conceiving of and implementing social and economic governance devices, and when those skills and abilities are immune from low-cost imitation. Strong form trust is a source of competitive advantage when two or more strong form trustworthy individuals or firms engage in an exchange, when strong form trustworthiness is relatively rare among a set of competitors, and when the individual and organizational attributes that lead to strong form trustworthiness are immune from low-cost imitation.

This analysis has important implications for research in organization theory and strategic management. For example, these ideas can be seen as an extension of transactions cost theory— an extension that makes this form of analysis strategically more relevant. Where transactions cost economics implicitly assumes that the skills and abilities needed to conceive of and implement governance mechanisms are constant across individuals and firms (Williamson, 1985), this approach suggests that these skills and abilities may vary in some strategicially important ways. Also, where transactions cost theory assumes either that all potential exchange partners are equally likely to behave opportunistically or that one cannot distinguish between those that will behave opportunistically and those that will not behave opportunistically (Williamson, 1985), this analysis suggests that potential exchange partners' opportunistic tendencies may vary, and that these differences can be discovered. Discovery of exchange partners that will not engage in opportunistic behavior enables firms to gain all the advantages of trade, without the cost of governance.

Thus, consistent with many of the more behaviorally oriented organizational scholars cited earlier, the approach in this paper rejects both the assumption that all exchange partners are likely to engage in opportunistic behavior and the assumption that it is not possible to know how opportunistic a particular exchange partner is likely to be. However, these transactions cost assumptions are not replaced by equally extreme, if opposite, assumptions that most exchange partners are trustworthy most of the time. Rather, the approach adopted here is

---

[12] Given the challenge of discovering strong form trustworthy exchange partners, these relationships are likely to be relatively stable over time. Indeed, it may well be the case that exchanges between strong form trustworthy partners may continue, even though they have limited potential for generating current economic value (Ring and Van de Ven, 1994). In this setting, the challenge facing exchange partners is to discover new ways to generate economic value with older, stable, relationships. Even when this cannot be done, economically nonviable exchanges may continue for some time because of the close relationships between partners.

that the trustworthiness of exchange partners can vary, and that how trustworthy an exchange partner is can be discovered. The adoption of this approach leads to the conclusion that, in some circumstances, trust can be a source of competitive advantage—a conclusion that is not possible if it is assumed that most exchange partners are either untrustworthy or that most exchange partners are trustworthy.

This analysis also points to two important exchange processes that have not received sufficient attention in the organizations and strategy literatures. First, the argument suggests that semi-strong form trust can be a source of competitive advantage if competing exchange partners vary in their skills and abilities in conceiving of and implementing governance mechanisms. What these specific skills and abilities might be, and why they might develop in some economic actors and not others, are unexplored issues in this paper. Casual observation suggests that, for example, some firms seem to be better at managing certain kinds of governance devices than others. Corning seems to be able to manage joint ventures more effectively than, say, TRW (Sherman, 1992). Toyota seems to be able to manage complex supply relationships more effectively than GM (Dyer and Ouchi, 1993; Womack *et al.*, 1990). How these different skills and abilities evolve, and their competitive implications, are important research questions. In this context, comparative research on semi-strong form governance in different industries and different countries is likely to be very important (Dyer and Ouchi, 1993).

Second, the argument suggests that strong form trustworthy exchange partners may be able to discover other strong form trustworthy exchange partners. Once discovered, these kinds of exchange partners can gain important competitive advantages from working with each other. However, much more empirical work needs to focus on the process through which strong form trustworthiness evolves in an economic actor. Such empirical work will establish whether or not strong form trustworthiness is a relatively stable attribute of economic actors, and whether or not this attribute can be imitated at low cost. Also, empirical research needs to focus on the process of searching for strong form trustworthy exchange partners. In particular, the role of

signals of strong form trustworthiness deserves special empirical attention. In this context, it may be helpful to compare the decisions and behaviors of firms that have been able to develop many strong form trustworthy exchanges (e.g., Corning) with the decisions and behaviors of firms that have been unable to develop these strong form trustworthy exchanges.

By examining the competitive implications of different types of trust in economic exchanges, it becomes clear that extreme assumptions about potential exchange partners—that most are trustworthy and that most are opportunistic—are overly simplistic. Rather, the trustworthiness of exchange partners may vary, and in that variance the possibility of competitive advantage may exist.

ACKNOWLEDGEMENTS

Comments and suggestions from Ed Zajac, Kathleen Conner, and Peter Ring were important in the development of this paper. Useful feedback was received from workshops at The Kellogg School (Northwestern), Emory University, the 1994 Texas Conference on Organizations, the University of Tennessee, and from participants at the 1994 Strategic Management Society meeting, held at HEC, near Paris, France. Andy Van de Ven is amazed that the first author finally understood the work of John R. Commons.

REFERENCES

Akerlof, G. A. (1970). 'The market for "lemons": Quality uncertainty and the market mechanism,' *Quarterly Journal of Economics*, 84, pp. 488–500.
Arrow, K. J. (1974) *The Limits of Organization*. Norton, New York.
Arthur, W. B. (1989). 'Competing technologies, increasing returns, and lock-in by historical events,' *Economic Journal*, 99, pp. 116–131.
Bradach, J. L. and R. G. Eccles (1989). 'Price, authority, and trust', *Annual Review of Sociology*, 15, pp. 97–118.
Barney, J. B. (1986). 'Organizational culture: Can it be a source of sustained competitive advantage?', *Academy of Management Review*, 11, pp. 656–665.
Barney, J. B. (1990). 'The debate between traditional management theory and organizational economics: Substantive differences or intergroup conflict?', *Academy of Management Review*, 15, pp. 382–393.
Barney, J. B. (1991). 'Firm resources and sustained

190   J.B. Barney and M.H. Hansen

competitive advantage?', *Journal of Management*, **17**, pp. 99–120.

Bowman, E. H. (1974), 'Epistemology, corporate strategy and academe', *Sloan Management Review*, **15**, pp. 35–50.

Dierickx, I. and K. Cool. (1989). 'Asset stock accumulation and sustainability of competitive advantage', *Management Science*, **35**, pp. 1504–1511.

DiMaggio, P. and W. Powell (1983). 'The iron cage revisited: Institutional isomorphism and collective rationality in organizational fields', *American Sociological Review*, **48**, pp. 147–160.

Donaldson, L. (1990). 'A rational basis for criticisms of organizational economics: A reply to Barney', *Academy of Management Review*, **15**, pp. 394–401.

Donaldson, L. and J. H. Davis (1991). 'Stewardship theory or agency theory: CEO governance and shareholder returns', *Australian Journal of Management*, **16** (1), pp. 49–64.

Dyer, J. H. and W. G. Ouchi (1993), 'Japanese-style partnerships: Giving companies a competitive edge', *Sloan Management Review*, **35**, pp. 51–63.

Etzioni, E. (1988). *The Moral Dimension: Toward a New Economics*. Free Press, New York.

Fama, E. (1970). 'Efficient capital markets: A review of theory and empirical work', *Journal of Finance*, **25**, pp. 383–417.

Frank, R. H. (1988). *Passions Within Reason*. Norton, New York.

Gambetta, D. (1988). *Trust: Making and Breaking Cooperative Relations*. Basil Blackwell, New York.

Granovetter, M. (1985). 'Economic action and social structure: The problem of embeddedness', *American Journal of Sociology*, **91**(3), pp. 481–510.

Grossman, S. J. and O. Hart. (1986). 'The costs and benefits of ownership: A theory of vertical and lateral integration', *Journal of Political Economy*, **94**, pp. 691–719.

Gulati, R., T. Khana and N. Nohria. (1994). 'Unilateral commitments and the importance of process in alliances', *Sloan Management Review*, **35** (3), pp. 61–69.

Hennart, J.-F. (1988) 'A transaction costs theory of equity joint ventures', *Strategic Management Journal*, **9** (4), pp. 361–374.

Hill, C. W. L. (1990), 'Cooperation, opportunism, and the invisible hand: Implications for transactions cost theory', *Academy of Management Review*, **15** (3), pp. 500–513.

Holmstrom, B. (1979). 'Moral hazard and observability', *Bell Journal of Economics*, **10**, pp. 74–91.

Klein, B., R. A. Crawford and A. A. Alchian (1978). 'Vertical integration, appropriable rents, and the competitive contracting process', *Journal of Law and Economics*, **21**, pp. 297–326.

Kogut, B. (1988). 'Joint ventures: Theoretical and empirical perspectives', *Strategic Management Journal*, **9**(4), pp. 319–332.

Kohlberg, L. (1969). 'Stage and sequence: The cognitive-developmental approach to socialization'. In D. A. Goslin (ed.), *Handbook of Socialization*. Rand McNally, New York, pp. 347–480.

Kohlberg, L. (1971). 'From is to ought'. In T. Mischel (ed.), *Cognitive Development and Epistemology*. Academic Press, New York, pp. 151–236.

Lewicki, R. J. and B. B. Bunker (1994). 'Trust in relationships: A model of trust development and decline'. Working paper, Department of Management and Human Resources, Ohio State University.

Mahoney, J. T., A. S. Huff and J. O. Huff, (1993). 'Toward a new social contract theory in organization science'. Working paper 93-0136, Department of Management, University of Illinois at Urbana-Champaign.

Ouchi, W. G. (1980). 'Markets, bureaucracies, and clans', *Administrative Science Quarterly*, **25**, pp. 121–141.

Peteraf, M. A. (1993). 'The cornerstones of competitive advantages: A resource-based view', *Strategic Management Journal*, **14**(3), pp. 179–192.

Porter, M. (1980). *Competitive Strategy*. Free Press, New York.

Ring, P. and A. Van de Ven (1994). 'Developmental processes of cooperative interorganizational relationships', *Academy of Management Review*, **19**, pp. 90–118.

Rumelt, R., D. Schendel and D. Teece (1991). 'Strategic management and economics', *Strategic Management Journal*, Winter Special Issue, **12**, pp. 5–29.

Sabel, C. F. (1993). 'Studied trust: Building new forms of cooperation in a volatile economy', *Human Relations*, **46** (9), pp. 1133–1170.

Sherman, S. (September 21, 1992). 'Are strategic alliances working?', *Fortune*, pp. 77–78.

Spence, A. M. (1973). *Market Signalling: Information Transfer in Hiring and Related Processes*. Harvard University Press, Cambridge, MA.

Tichy, N. M. and M. A. Devanna (1986). *The Transformational Leader*. Wiley, New York.

Williamson, O. E. (1975). *Markets and Hierarchies: Analysis and Antitrust Implications*. Free Press, New York.

Williamson, O. E. (1979). 'Transaction-cost economics: The governance of contractual relations', *Journal of Law and Economics*, **22**, pp. 233–261.

Williamson, O. E. (1985). *The Economic Institutions of Capitalism*. Free Press, New York.

Williamson, O. E. (1991). 'Comparative economic organization: The analysis of discrete structural alternatives', *Administrative Science Quarterly*, **36**, pp. 269–296.

Womack, J. P., D. T. Jones and D. Roos. (1990). *The Machine that Changed the World*. Harper Perennial, New York.

Zajac, E. and C. P. Olsen (1993). 'From transaction cost to transaction value analysis: Implications for the study of interorganizational strategies', *Journal of Management Studies*, **30**, pp. 131–145.

Zucker, L. G. (1987). 'Institutional theories of organization', *Annual Review of Sociology*, **13**, pp. 443–464.

[35]

SOCIAL CONTRACTING AS A TRUST-BUILDING PROCESS OF NETWORK GOVERNANCE

Jerry M. Calton and Lawrence J. Lad

Abstract: Social contracting has a long and important place in the history of political philosophy (Hardin, 1991; Waldron, 1989) and as a theory of justice (Baynes, 1989; Rawls, 1971). More recently, it has been developed into an individual rights-based theory of organizations (Keeley, 1980, 1988), and as a way to integrate ethics and moral legitimacy into corporate strategy and action (Donaldson, 1982; Freeman & Gilbert, 1988). Currently, it is being proposed as an integrative theory of economic ethics (Donaldson & Dunfee, forthcoming). This paper will extend the Donaldson and Dunfee approach by arguing that *social contracting can best be understood and applied in organizational settings if it is perceived and treated as a network governance process*. This insight can benefit management scholars and practitioners alike, since it calls attention to the processes by which trust is created and sustained in on-going contractual relationships. It also strongly suggests that a new approach to applying managerial discretion, as *moral agency*, is needed to realize the full competitive and ethical potential of emerging network forms.

Social Contracting as an Integrative Theory of Economic Ethics

Donaldson & Dunfee argue that traditional ethical theories fail to provide precise normative guidelines for business decision-makers, who must cope with a wide variety of organizational contexts and overlapping, often conflicting, contractual obligations. They criticize utilitarianism, deontological approaches such as neoKantianism, and even the stakeholder model for their "high degree of generality and relatively low recognition of community diversity" (forthcoming, p.2). Application of the utilitarian moral consequences test requires the business decision-maker to choose among potential alternative actions by predicting, weighing, and maximizing hypothetical aggregate benefits among all affected parties. The deontological approach calls upon the decision-maker to recognize, internalize, and apply universal ethical rules (e.g., Kant's categorical imperative) so that "right actions" will be grounded on fundamental moral principles, rather than upon consequentialist conjecture or expediency. Donaldson & Dunfee concede that the stakeholder model offers managers "convenient rules of thumb for mapping moral obligations..." (forthcoming: 4). However, the call for managers to trace "stakeholder maps" so that all stakeholders of the firm can be recognized and treated "fairly" is not enough.

For Donaldson & Dunfee (forthcoming: 4), the shortcomings of stakeholder theory include:

(1) It is "mute with respect to community standards."

(2) It "leaves unresolved problems of stakeholders who have conflicting interests and questions of who should be counted as stakeholders."

(3) It "lacks a normative foundation both for assessing the ethical validity of the interests asserted by particular groups of stakeholders, as well as for identifying and prioritizing the rights and duties of affected stakeholders."

(4) It "lacks the normative sophistication necessary for making precise moral distinctions in moral dilemmas."

The Donaldson & Dunfee "integrative social contracts theory" of economic ethics begins with the assertion that

> all rational humans aware of the bounded nature of their own rationality would consent to a hypothetical social contract, i.e., a "macro social contract," that would preserve for individual economic communities significant moral free space in which to generate their own norms of economic conduct, i.e., actual "micro social contracts" (forthcoming: 5).

They seek to explain the diversity in community-based ethical norms, while avoiding the easy trap of moral relativism. Economic institutions, including markets and organizational or inter-organizational arrangements, are "artifacts" of human designs and purposes. Moral free space at the micro contracting level is necessary to accommodate the artifactual (and hence various) nature of institutional arrangements and contractual relationships in different economic communities (or organizations). The diversity of artifactual arrangements in economic activity accounts for the boundedness of moral rationality. The limits of bounded moral rationality force economic actors to engage in a micro contracting process to craft ethical decision rules that can govern the terms of their interaction (forthcoming: 7-8).

For Donaldson & Dunfee (forthcoming: 5-6), the possibility of moral relativism in the micro social contracting process is tempered by implicit requirements of the macro social contract:

(1) All micro social contracts must be based on mutual consent of the contracting parties.

(2) Micro social contracts cannot violate independently authoritative "hypernorms," such as the universally held belief that killing or abusing children is wrong.

(3) When the ethical norms of different communities come into conflict, a set of "priority rules" will determine which norm is authoritative.

A panoramic, longitudinal perspective on this complex, interactive process of evolution in community-based artifactual arrangements and associated ethical decision rules would reveal a shimmering, many-layered web within which contracting parties interacted according to their respective "ethics of games." No comprehensive theory of the ethics of games is possible, since "game ethics must be contoured to fit the different sets of rules and the goals of different games or forms of games" (Donaldson & Dunfee, forthcoming: 9).

Social Contracting in the Context of Network Theory

Nitin Nohria, co-editor of a recent book on network theory, noted that a network perspective pushes for comparisons in terms of variables and measures that reflect the overall structure of relationships in the organization, eschewing variables and measures that are generalizations of the pattern of dyadic interactions in the organization (Nohria, 1992: 8).

He went on to assert that operationalizing the network perspective required more than "adopting a new metaphysical image of organizations or bolting a few network variables onto traditional analytical perspectives." Rather, it meant "adopting a different intellectual lens and discipline, gathering different kinds of data, learning new analytical and methodological techniques, and seeking explanations that are quite different from conventional ones" (1992: 8).

Broadly defined, a network is the "structure of ties among the actors of a social system" (Nohria & Eccles, 1992: 288). Using this broader definition, markets and hierarchies may be subsumed into network forms (see Bradach & Eccles, 1989). To the extent that market exchanges take place within a long-term relationship between loyal, repeat customers and conscientious providers of a good or service, a rudimentary network can be said to exist. From the above definition, a hierarchy also can be seen as a kind of network, albeit spiritually stunted and excessively "rational" in form and function. The "informal organization" that often emerges to overcome the social frigidity, information constipation, and routinized lethargy in hierarchies is closer to what we typically think of as a network form. It has been defined as an "informal structure, based on instrumental and trust relations across formal boundaries, [that can]... facilitate the pursuit of organizational objectives" (DiMaggio, 1992: 131). Thus, *a network can be defined more narrowly as a "new ideal type of organization that is radically different from the Weberian bureaucracy... and is characterized by relations that are based on neither hierarchical authority nor market transactions"* (Nohria & Eccles, 1992: 288). Proponents of this narrower definition argue that such networks facilitate the generation of flexible, adaptive learning capabilities that are well suited to competitive survival in a "turbulent" environment (Alter & Hage, 1993; Handy, 1990; Powell, 1990; Quinn, 1992; Snow, Miles & Coleman, 1992). Thus, Ouchi's (1980) "clan" and Burns & Stalker's (1961) "organic" (as opposed to a "mechanistic" or hierarchical) organizational forms are networks. Other examples of this proliferating "web of enterprise" (Reich, 1992) include: durable TQM linkages among assemblers, suppliers, and customers (Schonenberger,1992); cross-functional product development teams (Jaikumar, 1986); multinational enterprises (Bartlett & Ghoshal, 1989); international strategic alliances (Contractor & Lorange, 1988); public-private social problem-solving alliances (Austrom & Lad, 1989; Hood, Logsdon & Thompson, 1993); Japanese *keiretsu* (Gerlach & Lincoln, 1992); and even the "virtual corporation" (Davidow & Malone, 1992), composed of a business core, surrounded by a transitory web of project-specific service providers. It is important to note from these examples that networks can take on either organizational or interorganizational configurations.

In developing the argument that social contracting can best be understood and applied in organizational settings as a network governance process, this paper will apply the narrower definition of networks as an emerging alternative to market transactions and hierarchical governance. The network perspective can transform not only the way we think about organizational relationships, but also our understanding of the manner in which ethical guidelines and decision processes are (or should be) shaped and enforced within organizational contexts. Social contracting within networks is, essentially, an interactive, participant-driven, developmental trust-building process. This paper will show that social contracting works to create and sustain a durable, resilient basis for effective and efficient organizational interaction by minimizing the moral hazard of participant opportunism.

Network relationships overlay (and may even be supplanting) simple, dyadic (two-party) market transactions and bilateral relationships within hierarchies. To the extent that trust is the essential glue and lubricant for long-term, value-creating organizational interactions, effective network governance would seem to hold the key, not only for ethical, socially responsible business performance, but also for business survival in the ever more turbulent competitive environment.

To develop the above argument further, this paper will point to some analytical limitations in dyadic interaction-based contractual theories of the firm. It will then show how social contracting as network governance can resolve some of the practical and conceptual difficulties with stakeholder theory, raised by Donaldson & Dunfee, among others (see also Calton, 1993; Goodpaster, 1991; Michael & Savage, 1993). Finally, the paper will offer some core propositions about social contracting as a trust-building process of network governance. These propositions will build upon the argument that trust is the essential ingredient for sustaining learning-based, value-creating interactions within organizational and interorganizational networks. Further development and testing of these propositions can help in reframing the theory of the firm into a more comprehensive and integrative "theory of the firm in society" (see Wood, 1992). These propositions also can suggest to business practitioners a new approach to exercising managerial discretion as "moral agency" in facilitating trust-based network interactions.

Limitations of Dyadic Interaction-based Contractual Theories of the Firm

In neoclassical economic theory, efficient, "arms-length" transactions between two contracting parties are the rule. The firm is treated as a "black box" that validates the model's presumption of utility (or profit)-maximizing behavior in the marketplace. Regarding simple, dyadic (one-time, two-party) transactions to be the market norm, this theory failed to consider the wide range of potential contractual agreements associated with different transactional or interaction patterns (See Macneil, 1981, below).

In agency theory, the firm is conceived as a contractual microcosm of the marketplace. Jensen & Meckling (1976: 311) replaced the "black box" with the notion of the firm as a "legal fiction which serves as the nexus of contracting relationships." They depicted the behavior of the firm as "like the behavior of a market, i.e., the outcome of a complex equilibrium process." However, they excluded from their analysis the complex set of multilateral, on-going, network-like interrelationships within this nexus of contracts. They focused, instead, on bilateral interactions between manager-agents and owner-principals. They did so to "retain the notion of maximizing behavior of all individuals..." (1976: 307). This inclusive claim is misleading in that agency theory confines its analysis to behavior that can be modelled as dyadic interactions between selfishly rational individuals. This economizing trick allows agency theorists to concentrate on the design of optimal "equilibrium contracts" that can minimize the "agency costs" associated with managerial "shirking" or other forms of agent opportunism that create moral hazards in bilateral transactions. Jensen & Meckling hypothesized that such costs could be minimized by "inducing an 'agent' to behave as if he were maximizing the 'principal's' welfare..." (1976: 309).

All potentially conflicting (and hence non-maximizing) interests, goals, or "stakes" are anathema to the agency theory of the firm. If the firm is to be regarded as an efficiency-driven microcosm of "market equilibrium" processes, managerial discretion must be bound to the objective function of maximizing ownership interests. To preserve this restrictive assumption, non-owner participants in the more complex nexus of multilateral contracts are banished to the outer darkness. Enlightenment as to the nature and significance of the wider range of contractual relations within the nexus had to await development of a "rich theory of organizations." The authors left that thorny subject to "another paper" (Jensen & Meckling, 1976: 309-310).

Macneil's (1981) "rich" classification links transaction patterns associated with markets and hierarchies (internal organizations) to different types of contracts. The distinction between explicit and implicit (psychological or socially embedded) contracts will be added to lend further "richness" to Macneil's classification. This typology of contracts is useful in exploring and contrasting different approaches to governance in hierarchies and networks. This paper will point to the common social contracting elements in the governance of organizational and interorganizational networks, in contrast to the more conventional pattern of hierarchical governance that has been elaborated in the institutional economics writings of Oliver Williamson.

According to Macneil, *"discrete"* and *"recurrent"* contracts are associated with arms-length market exchanges. Since the terms and conditions of exchange are certain, clearly understood, and agreed upon by both parties, neither one-time (discrete contract-based) market exchanges nor a series of identical (recurrent contract-based) market exchanges require governance mechanisms to resolve potential conflicts or unanswered questions.

Relational contracts define the "rules of the game" by which on-going organizational interactions are governed. An *explicit relational contract*, such as a corporate charter, partnership agreement, or marriage vow, defines the initial set of formal rights and obligations associated with an on-going, open-ended contractual relationship. However, many of the "rules of the game" that come to govern this relationship will evolve in the form of implicit, mutually accepted understandings, shared values, and unfolding institutional arrangements. *Implicit relational contracts* are enacted over time within a pattern of participant interactions. This evolving expression of the micro social contracting process is gradually "embedded" (Granovetter, 1985) in a shared culture that defines and shapes the "negotiated order" of organizational (and interorganizational) networks. (See Nathan & Mitroff, 1991, on negotiated order theory, which can usefully be integrated into the social contracting process model for network governance.)

Oliver Williamson (1985, 1991) has discussed relational contracting primarily in the context of hierarchical governance processes. Williamson puts an institutional twist on Coase's (1937) "transaction cost" explanation of why some exchanges are less costly within hierarchies than in the external marketplace. Recently, Williamson (1991: 274) argued that the "implicit contract law of internal organization is forbearance." Professional managers, as agents of the board of directors, must have discretionary authority within the hierarchy to resolve by "fiat" the complex problems that arise from the interaction of participants (i.e., stakeholders) within the nexus of explicit and implicit relational contracts. For Williamson, managerial discretion gives internal organizations the "elastic and adaptive" capabilities needed to cope with the problems of "bounded rationality." Among these problems (which impair the efficiency of external market transactions) are environmental uncertainty, the threat of opportunistic behavior, and "asset specificity." This latter condition refers to the difficulty of finding alternative productive uses in the external market for assets (such as specialized skills or technologies) invested or developed in the firm.

According to Williamson, managerial discretion within the hierarchy is constrained primarily by the board's fiduciary duty to act as a trustee of shareholder interests. Only shareholder interests should be represented on the board of directors because it is not possible to design explicit governance safeguards that can "efficiently" reconcile multiple, often conflicting, stakeholder claims. When managerial activism strays beyond the "zone of acceptance" (Williamson, 1991: 275), participant protests (voice) and threats to exit the nexus define the limits of stakeholder forbearance. The forbearance rule isolates the internal governance process from external pressures. Manager-agents and director-trustees are required to act in a manner consistent with the "business judgment rule." In the absence of evidence of bad faith or some other corrupt (i.e., opportunistic) motive, neither agents nor trustees can be held legally accountable for errors in business judgment. If business judgment is defined narrowly as pursuing an objective function of profit-maximization within constraints imposed by participant protests and threats of exit, non-shareholder stakeholders of the firm are restricted to tenuous, indirect means for participating in the hierarchical governance process (see also, Williamson, 1984).

Social Contracting as Network Governance:
Toward a Resolution of the "Stakeholder Paradox"

Kenneth Goodpaster (1991) neatly posed the paradox that has rendered the stakeholder model so problematic as a conceptual framework for guiding ethical decision-making in organizational settings. He points out that "stakeholder analysis," the charting of stakeholder relationships within the nexus of contracts that comprise the firm, is not difficult. It is a descriptive rather than an ethical decision-making process. Freeman (1984: 46) defines stakeholders as "any group or individual who can affect or is affected by the achievement of the organization's objectives." However, as noted by Donaldson & Dunfee and others (see above), this information provides the manager with little or no guidance as to the legitimacy of stakeholder claims; nor does it help the manager prioritize conflicting claims in the effort to craft a strategy that treats all stakeholders fairly.

Goodpaster (1991: 57-61) suggests that the paradox arises from two different approaches to "stakeholder synthesis." This is the decision-making process by which managers craft an organizational response to stakeholder claims. If non-owner stakeholders are treated "strategically" as actual or potential external constraints that must be manipulated or placated to accomplish organizational objectives, then managerial agents of shareholder interests are engaged in "business without ethics." However, if managerial agents genuinely try to fulfill their "multi-fiduciary" responsibilities to all of the firm's stakeholders, they may be accused of practicing "ethics without business" (1991: 61-63). The managerial effort to reconcile conflicting multi-fiduciary duties would push the agent, necessarily, toward diluting his or her primary fiduciary responsibility to maximize profit for the ownership interest. Stated formally, the stakeholder paradox is that

> it seems essential, yet in some way illegitimate, to orient corporate decisions by ethical values that go beyond strategic stakeholder considerations to multi-fiduciary ones (1991: 63).

Goodpaster proposed a resolution of this paradox by separating the agent's *fiduciary* responsibility to shareholders from his or her *ethical* responsibility to minimize harm to other stakeholders affected by corporate actions. He drew this distinction because he felt that the multi-fiduciary approach to stakeholder synthesis

> represents nothing less than the conversion of the modern private corporation into a public institution and probably calls for a corresponding restructuring of corporate governance (e.g., representatives of each stakeholder group on the board of directors)" (1991: 66).

Goodpaster's resolution of the stakeholder paradox has the advantage of a certain neatness. It seeks to incorporate, by informal and unilateral managerial means, the ethical claims of non-owner stakeholders into the hierarchical governance process. However, this neatness is achieved at the expense of a conceptual dependence on the heroic exercise of managerial discretion. Since Goodpaster didn't explore the *process* by which non-owner stakes can be identified, legitimated, balanced, and adjudicated within the nexus of explicit and implicit relational contracts, stakeholder theory remains an ethical "black box."

Social contracting as a network governance process offers a more promising (and more complex) resolution of the stakeholder paradox. The governance of relational contracts is not confined to hierarchical contexts. Quasi-public corporate ownership and governance via multi-stakeholder boards is not the only (or even the most likely or attractive) alternative to the hierarchical governance of privately-owned corporations. There is more to governance than has been dreamed of in the deliberations of corporate boards. A closer look at the longitudinal pattern of interaction among network participants, expressed in the articulation of explicit and implicit relational contracting "rules of the game," can help in determining which stakeholders have "legitimate" claims and in showing how their stakes are defined, prioritized, and balanced within the governance process. The stakeholder theory of the firm cannot be fully developed and made operational until the firm is reinvented as a network of initially autonomous, yet interdependent, stakeholders, bound together by "reciprocal stakes" (Evan & Freeman: 1993) in their cooperative enterprise.

Micro social contracting is a process by which participants in a network define themselves and the meaning of their collective enterprise through the interactive pattern of joint rule-making that governs the common effort. To the extent that implicit relational contracts are drafted and socially embedded in an evolving pattern of participant interaction, the hierarchically-defined boundary between the "firm" and its environment begins to dissolve. The governance of a stakeholder-based firm (which includes participants, such as customers and suppliers, nominally located in the "external" environment) should not be all that different from the process by which initially autonomous participants come together to grapple with a complex, multi-dimensional, shared problem that defines the boundaries of an "interorganizational field" or "problem domain" (Wood & Gray, 1991). *Stakeholder management and the process governing collaborative interaction among participants in an interorganizational field can best be understood as related forms of network governance, operating at different levels of aggregation and complexity.*

The Wood & Gray (1991) integrative framework for developing a comprehensive theory of interorganizational collaboration, based on *preconditions, processes,* and *outcomes,* can be extended to enhance our understanding of the emergence of this more integrative and comprehensive form of network governance. Network governance, driven by a micro social contracting process to create a more durable and resilient form of participant trust, will resolve the stakeholder paradox by placing ethical decision-making at the core of a new approach to managerial discretion. This preconditions, processes, and outcomes framework will be subsumed within a discussion of some core propositions about micro social contracting as a network governance process.

A description of the preconditions and processes by which network participants in organizational and interorganizational fields are learning how to interact to solve shared problems necessarily requires a normative consideration of how these complex, interdependent interactions can be governed more fairly and effectively. Thus, description and normative prescription are inextricably intertwined in developing propositions about micro social contracting processes for governing emergent network forms.

Core Propositions About Social Contracting as a Trust-Building Process of Network Governance

Proposition #1: A precondition of growing environmental turbulence   or cognitive complexity is promoting more widespread and formal   application of the micro social contracting process for defining and   addressing collective, network-based problems.

Participants in organizational and inter-organizational problem domains share the need to learn how to collectively manage what this paper will characterize as "messes." These shared messes are complex, open-ended, multi-faceted, interdependent problems that must be addressed collectively over time. Messes do not lend themselves to simple, one-time, dyadic solutions. Separate interests cannot be served unless all cooperate to solve the shared problem. This is the "high stakes/high interdependence" state that Logsdon (1991) has identified as the primary precondition for successful interorganizational collaboration. In like manner, Freeman & Evan (1990) ground their "fair contracting" approach to corporate governance on the need to manage "multilateral interdependence" among stakeholder interests. A similar precondition drives Aoki's (1984) "cooperative game theory of the firm," to be discussed below.

Aram (1989) has characterized the principal problem associated with collectively managing messes as the "paradox of interdependent relations." This paradox arises because "short-term individual rationality... result[s] in deficient collective action" when such messes are addressed at different levels of aggregation (1989: 267). Behaviors and decisions that seem rational at the individual, group, or firm level may seem irrational when the unit of analysis and decision-making is the industry, community, country, or international system.

Poor corporate social performance typically arises from this discontinuity between individual and collective rationality. When managerial decisions and accountability systems are based on neoclassical economic and organizational (i.e., agency and institutional) theories that decompose into a presumption of individual rationality and a unitary objective function (goal set) for the firm, a small subset of interests within the nexus of contracts typically will prevail. These static equilibrium, dyadic transaction-based theories treat other interests as (at worst) non-existent or (at best) as peripheral external constraints upon managerial discretion.

One example of a "messy" collective problem, to be discussed more fully below, must suffice. In the Pacific Northwest, "clear-cutting" of timber on private and public lands has been the standard industry practice. Its adherents in the timber industry defend clear cutting on the grounds that it is more "cost-effective" and that it "maximizes yields." However, the cost "savings" from clear-cut harvesting and monoculture reforestation practices may well be negated by the "social costs" borne by non-industry stakeholder interests. These losses can range from a decrease in ecological "biodiversity," and the despoliation of a favorite hiking route, to the degradation of stream quality due to soil erosion from water runoff in massively deforested areas. Until recently, the typical timber industry practice has been to maximize yields for the primary economic stakeholders, subject to minimal compliance with (weakly enforced) state and federal government regulations.

Proposition #2: Networks are the evolving organizational expression of implicit (and occasionally explicit) relational social contracts among autonomous, interdependent entities.

Donaldson & Dunfee (see above) argue that human society, as a whole, is governed by an implicit macro social contract that defines fundamental individual rights, as well as the basic conditions under which the micro social contracting process is conducted in different communities. Keeley (1988: 17) defines individual rights as "claims justified within a system of rules" objectified in the social contract. Freeman and Evan (1990: 352) argue that the individual "right to bargain" is implicit in the stakeholder theory of the firm. This right is more fundamental than the "efficient transaction" reified in neoclassical economic, agency, and institutional theories of the firm. It precedes transactions, and it animates the subsequent collective forging of the nexus of implicit and explicit relational contracts among social actors. Relational contracts are forged because individual ends can rarely be accomplished in a hypothetical "state of nature" where social networks are absent. This "right to bargain" drives the interaction and legitimizes the voice of autonomous, interdependent participants within both (a) the firm as a network, and (b) interorganizational networks within which the firm is one of the players.

Proposition #3: The micro social contracting process in networks is a collective effort at sense-making, rule-building, and problem-solving.

Wood & Gray (1991: 146) define collaboration as a phenomenon that occurs "when a group of autonomous stakeholders in a problem domain engage in an interactive process, using shared rules, norms, and structures to act on or decide on issues related to that domain." This definition of collaboration is an equally apt characterization of social contracting as a collective process that strives toward a "social (or cognitive) construction of reality" (Argyris & Schon, 1978; Fiske & Taylor, 1991). Powell (1990: 301) has identified the central problem in network formation as the search for a distinctive "logic of collective action that enables cooperation to be sustained over the long run." To the extent that social (and economic) institutions and values are human artifacts, some "negotiated order" (Nathan & Mitroff, 1991) must be constructed to make sense out of the unfolding of artifactual events. Thus, micro social contracting is a collective process for defining and enforcing community-based ethical "rules of the game."

This focus on iterative collective learning suggests a new way of looking at networks as sense-making processes. Networks demonstrate a self-renewing, self-regulating, flowing, process-driven quality that Jantsch (1980: 7)) has characterized as *autopoesis*: "the characteristic of living systems to continuously renew themselves and to regulate this process in such a way that the integrity of their structure is maintained."

Margaret Wheatley (1992) has drawn metaphoric insights from quantum physics and the mathematics of chaos theory that illuminate the dynamics of network governance. From the realm of "quantum leaps" and "strange attractors" she finds evidence that "*disorder* can be a source of *order*, and that growth is found in disequilibrium, not in balance." As the environment becomes more complex, new information is introduced into the system as a form of disorder. If the system fails to accommodate this new information, the disturbance will grow in strength until the existing system is destroyed. However, disintegration can be a force for rebirth, rather than extinction: "In most cases the system can *reconfigure itself to a higher level of complexity*, one better able to deal with the demands of its environment" (1992: 339). Wheatley argues that current and future conditions call for fluid, permeable, "self-designing" forms. Structures and processes intermingle and flow, moving from disorder toward order:

> It is not that we are moving toward disorder when we dissolve current structures and speak of worlds without boundaries. Rather, we are engaged in a fundamentally new relationship with order, order that is identified in processes that only temporarily manifest in structures (1992: 341).

This paper goes beyond Wheatley's arresting imagery of new systems of order rising, unbidden, out of chaos on the wings of butterflies. It stresses the role of a dialogue-driven, learning-based micro social contracting process that defines and enforces the rules of the unfolding negotiated order within which the on-going, interactive game of social action is played.

Proposition #4: Network sustainability depends on the creation and maintenance of a social context of mutual trust among participants in the collective learning, problem-solving process.

If participants in relational contract-based negotiated orders are to take concerted action to clean up or collectively manage "messes," all must learn how to work together. Wood & Gray (1991: 159-160) use the Belenky, et al. (1986) image of a supportive network of women as "connected knowers" to suggest the manner in which collaborative alliances can achieve "shared responsiveness" in solving "messy" problems. In like manner, Aoki's (1984) "cooperative game theory of the firm" holds that participants (employees, managers, suppliers, etc.) can create value only to the extent that they work together, mobilizing their firm-specific, invisible "learning assets" to solve problems created by opportunities or threats thrown up by the turbulent environment. Aoki (1990b) contrasts his "J-model" of the Japanese firm, which stresses horizontal information-sharing and network-like interactive problem-solving, with the threatened hierarchical U.S. "A-model" of the firm. Alter & Hage (1993: 7-8) argue that the Japanese firm's superior learning capabilities give it the "adaptive efficiency" needed to cope with "cognitive complexity" in the emerging "post-industrial" order. Clegg (1990: 184-207) also cast the Japanese firm as the prototype of the flexible "post-modern" organization. The recent movement in U.S. firms toward organizational transformation via "cultural" (i.e., clan) management, employee participation and empowerment, total quality management, and "capability-based" strategies is largely a response to the Japanese competitive challenge and example. This apparent trend toward convergence between Japanese and Western organizational forms prompted Aoki (1990b: 23) to speculate that "the J-model and the agency model represent only prototypes to be absorbed into a more general hybrid model of the firm."

Network-building to promote cooperative learning arises from a condition of reciprocity or multilateral interdependence (i.e., reciprocal stakes) in social problem-solving. Network participants depend on each other to come up with a common understanding of the problem, while all continue contributing their specialized information assets to the common learning pool. Mistrust, created by the perception or reality of participant opportunism, can diminish the voluntary commitment of participants, thereby impairing the effectiveness or viability of learning networks. Mistrust can also raise significantly the cost of enforcing "credible commitments" (Williamson, 1985) within the nexus of implicit and explicit relational contracts. Some economists have recognized this problem (Arrow, 1973; Hardin, 1968; Noreen, 1988). However, trust remains an exogenous variable in the economic model of organizations. Williamson's (1991) presumption of participant "forbearance" of managerial discretion within a hierarchy is no more adequate as a treatment of trust-building processes within networks.

Trust is a mutually constructed, jointly shared state of mind that enables social actors to continue working cooperatively in the absence of formal, explicit governance mechanisms that safeguard against malfeasance or participant opportunism. Network theorists stress the critical role of trust in sustaining value-creating, learning-based network interactions. Micro social contracting, trust-building, and network formation/maintenance are virtually synonymous interaction-driven developmental processes. Nohria and Eccles (1992: 292) argue that "the basic building blocks of all social organization are the repeated interactions among two or more members that take place in different settings." Kogut, Shan, and Walker (1992: 349) argue that the pattern of participant interaction is "nested within the changing structure of [the] network as determined by the history of prior cooperation." Participants behave in a non-opportunistic manner, not because they want to build a general reputation for fair dealing, but because they want to maintain the trust of others in the network. The continuing history of this interaction produces the "emotional energy," "sympathy," or "chemistry" that motivates participants to engage in future interaction. The history of past interactions also spells out the repertoire of future interaction patterns (Nohria, 1992: 242). Thus, trust is a mutual, relationship-based affection built up and sustained by a history of non-opportunistic interactions.

Axelrod (1984) has demonstrated the effectiveness of a "tit-for-tat" process for incrementally strengthening and reinforcing trust within a nexus of relational contracts. When one trusting act is reciprocated by another, gradually a durable basis for cooperation can be erected. Axelrod offered this advice to the manager who wished to nurture a cooperative system:

> Increase the durability and frequency of interaction in order to heighten awareness of the present value of future cooperation [enlarge the shadow of the future] (quoted by Aram, 1989: 277).

SOCIAL CONTRACTS AND NETWORK GOVERNANCE 283

Granovetter (1992: 42-43) contrasts the calm, network-sustaining behavior of a family with the panic of a mob of strangers during a theater fire. Strangers, as atomistic individuals, have no assurance that others will not stampede, even though all would benefit by cooperating and exiting calmly. Family members, trusting others in the group to behave selflessly, are more likely to survive because they base their cooperative actions on behavioral expectations "embedded" in a history of trust.

Proposition #5: The maintenance of trust among network participants requires an equitable resolution of the problem of unequal power within relational contracts.

Neoclassical economic theory and "efficient contracting" (i.e., agency and institutional) theory accept the power balance within a nexus of contracts as a given. These theories simply assume that bilateral power is a precondition of voluntary contracting and that power-seeking is not a relevant goal in an efficient universe. However, Macneil (1981: 1052-1059) notes that bilateral power is more typical of simple, dyadic transactions and voluntary discrete contracts. Unilateral power (particularly in the form of discretionary authority) exists and can change over time within the exchange structure of relational contracts. Macneil (1981: 1059-1063) concludes that restraints upon unilateral power must be embedded in relational contracts. Perrow (1986) also criticizes agency theory for turning a blind eye to the power asymmetry within the employment relationship:

> Once unequal power is entertained, it becomes obvious that, given self-interested behavior, the boss has more occasions for cheating on employees than the reverse.... Agency theory appears to be ideologically incapable of keeping an eye on both ends of the contract.... [Indeed, agency theory] may be designed to distract us from the existence of power differences (1986: 14-15).

Hill & Jones have responded to the above criticism by offering a "stakeholder-agency theory" that recognizes the existence of "power differentials [in] the stakeholder-agent equation" (1992: 132). Managers, exercising exclusive "control over the decision-making apparatus of the firm," may exploit the resulting situation of "unequal dependence" within the nexus of explicit and implicit contracts (1992: 134). Hill & Jones point to "institutional structures that have evolved [to] serve the function of monitoring and enforcing the terms of implicit contracts." They use the term "institutional" rather than "governance" structures because the latter term is typically associated with oversight by trustees on a board of directors. Hill and Jones prefer to focus on the "institutions that have evolved to represent and further the interests of stakeholders," such as trade unions, consumer unions, and other special interest groups (1992: 140). These groups have worked to reduce the "information asymmetry" existing between managers and stakeholders. They have acted in the political arena to improve the external legal/regulatory protection of employee, consumer, community, and other stakeholder rights. Stakeholder groups also have exercised their right of "voice" and the threat of "exit" as negotiating weapons to redress the imbalance of power within the nexus of relational contracts (1992: 141-142).

The Hill & Jones treatment of the "institutional evolution" of stakeholder safeguards recognizes the need for (but does not develop) the emerging pattern of collaborative network governance. This new approach to governance is needed to reach and sustain the state of "organizational equilibrium" postulated in Aoki's (1984) cooperative game theory of the firm. Hill & Jones define this as

> a state in which no one group of stakeholders can increase its utility without risking a higher expected loss of utility owing to the possible withdrawal of co-operation by the other stakeholders" (1992: 145).

The network governance process needed to approach "organizational equilibrium" does not presuppose a utopian, conflict-free political vacuum. The process of defining and enforcing the "rules of the game" within a "negotiated order" arises out of a pluralistic struggle to achieve a "just" equilibrium of power and distribution of gains. Consensus over what is just does not preclude a struggle to achieve that consensus. This is as true of interorganizational domains as it is of stakeholder-based firms. Gray and Wood (1991: 10-11) note the need to illuminate the "power dynamics" that influence the shaping of questions, the formation of rules, and the distribution of gains within a network of interorganizational stakeholders.

Proposition #6: A consent-based, dialogue-driven, micro social contracting process of collaborative governance is needed to promote and preserve conditions of mutual trust within networks.

The presumption of mutual, voluntary consent is fundamental to the process by which competent parties enter into valid contractual relationships (Ring, 1992: 286). Donaldson and Dunfee (see above) argue that mutual consent among participants in the micro social contracting process is an implicit fundamental requirement of the macro social contract.

Hirschman's (1970) "exit, voice, and loyalty" framework identifies options open to parties in the governance of relational contracts. Loyalty (or voluntary organizational commitment) cannot be sustained if any party in the relationship lacks the option to voice disagreement over how contract terms are being defined or applied. The contract is hardly voluntary if a viable option to exit the relationship does not exist. Keeley (1988: 13-15) has argued that the failure of a party to exit does not necessarily imply consent to continuation of the relationship. A power differential among participants within the nexus of contracts, or an inequitable distribution of the costs of exit (borne primarily by the weaker participant) may create the conditions of a coercive (and therefore invalid or illegitimate) contractual relationship.

Keeley's individual rights-based argument is reinforced by the condition of reciprocity or mutual dependence within learning-based networks. Trust is the primary glue and lubricant of voluntary participation in joint problem-solving. However, neither blind loyalty (i.e., unquestioning forbearance of managerial discretion) nor the exit option are adequate to nurture and sustain trusting relationships within a network. Interactive collaborative processes are needed to

SOCIAL CONTRACTS AND NETWORK GOVERNANCE   285

give participants a formal opportunity to exercise their right to "voice" in defining and enforcing the contractual "rules of the game." This is necessary to validate Aoki's (1984, 1990a, 1990b) argument that the "cooperative game" to create value (or information rents) within the firm cannot be sustained unless participants trust that the power and proceeds of collective problem-solving will be shared equitably. The right to exercise "voice" is inherent in the Freeman & Evan (1990) call for "fair contracting" among stakeholders of the firm. Lewin & Mitchell (1992: 107) note that emerging employee voice mechanisms in U.S. firms include grievance systems, suggestion systems, quality circles, and "other high involvement-participation work systems."

Adler (1993: 107) has called attention to the success of self-regulating work teams at NUMMI, the GM-Toyota automotive joint venture in California. He cited the views of one local UAW official on the need for "voice" and power-sharing in a collaborative governance system:

> If managers want to motivate workers to contribute and learn, they have to give
> up some of their power. If managers want workers to trust them, we need to be
> 50-50 in making the decision. Don't just make the decision and say, 'Trust me'."

A similar approach to collaborative network governance is notable in Wood & Gray's (1991: 159) observation that interorganizational collaboration aspires toward "shared control or joint governance... [of] actions taken that influence the [problem] domain." Alter & Hage (1993: 77) also make the normative declaration that network governance should be "non-hierarchical and self-regulating."

External regulatory pressure and the growing recognition that simple, dyadic transactions cannot grapple with the multilateral dimensions of shared "messes" are driving recent experiments in collaborative network governance. To return to the example of forestry management practices introduced above, a new, collaborative governance process is being tried in the Pacific Northwest. In response to the growing political and legal controversy over the negative, interdependent effects of "efficient" logging practices, the Washington State Forestry Practices Board has mandated a "watershed analysis" for public and privately-held timber holdings in the state's 400 watershed basins. This new approach to governance is being applied initially in developing new logging guidelines for the Tolt River Basin, north of Seattle. Weyerhauser forestry managers are required to work with state agencies, the Seattle Water Department, and representatives of Native American tribes and environmental groups in developing these guidelines. These guidelines are to be based on the special conditions of each watershed basin, with particular emphasis on remediating the damage caused by previous logging practices and on minimizing such damage in the future. Previous logging practices have promoted soil erosion from excessive water runoff, thereby causing silting of the river channel. This has caused flooding of farms and towns along the lower Tolt, unacceptable water turbidity for the Water Department, and drastically curtailed fish runs. The summer steelhead species on the Tolt and its tributaries is approaching extinction. Weyerhauser executives were driven to participate in the watershed analysis process to avoid entanglement with the Endangered Species Act.

Judy Turpin of the Washington Environmental Council characterized Weyerhauser's attitude as "Y'all come." Stakeholders of the Tolt River watershed (identified by a previous pattern of adversarial interactions and legitimized by the regulatory mandate to clean up the shared mess) met in a Weyerhauser office, dubbed the "War Room" by some participants. They studied the results of a joint assessment of the river basin's condition and hammered out new consensus-based logging guidelines. Participants finally agreed upon a 70-foot buffer of trees on each side of the Tolt and its tributaries. This was three times wider than the new state regulation, which had ended, six years previously, the industry practice of cutting to the river bank. Some participants wanted even more stringent limits against logging the upper Tolt basin. The final compromise was achieved because all participants had developed a level of trust and understanding of other points of view as they searched for a shared solution to a common "messy" problem.

John Larkoski, the Weyerhauser forester who headed the Tolt basin watershed analysis team, confessed that involving outsiders in management decisions was "a little scary" for the company. However, the process for reaching a voluntary consensus, by giving "voice" to network participants within a collaborative governance framework, avoided extended adversarial proceedings. If voluntary consensus had not been won, disgruntled stakeholders had the option of voicing complaints through an external outlet. They could propose alternative "rules of the game" to the state Department of Natural Resources and call for a time-consuming, costly environmental impact statement.

By internalizing multiple stakeholder voices within the governance process, Weyerhauser executives redressed the balance of power within the nexus of relational contracts and muted a potential adversarial cacophony of external stakeholder voices. An effective multilateral outcome, based on "fair contracting" within the interorganizational network, was achieved. Moreover, this new approach to collaborative network governance will serve as the model for resolving similar "messes" in future watershed analyses elsewhere in the state. (See Pryne, 1993, inclusive, for the above case example. For a discussion of the emergence of this new pattern of collaborative governance in public utility resource planning, see Cohen & Townsley, 1990; Ellis, 1989.)

Proposition #7: Facilitation of the trust-building process and of collaborative governance within networks requires the recasting of managerial discretion into a new form of "moral agency."

Wood (1991) has identified managerial discretion as the individual-level principle of corporate social performance. However, she noted that the Social Issues in Management field "has not built a concept of discretion, or discretionary social responsibility, that is related to the standard concept of managerial discretion" (1991: 698-699). The concept of "moral agency," as it is (or could be) applied by managers within a participative micro social contracting process-as-dialogue, is a promising new way to think about managerial discretion.

SOCIAL CONTRACTS AND NETWORK GOVERNANCE   287

Freeman & Evan (1990: 349) point out that the standard approach to enacting managerial discretion has been for managers, as agents, to treat their relationship to each stakeholder group as a separate bilateral contract. This hierarchical governance game encourages managers to preserve their position of autonomy and control by playing one stakeholder group against the other. Managers prefer to ignore the complex reality of multilateral, interdependent contractual relations within the nexus. Wood & Gray (1991: 160) make a similar point in the context of interorganizational collaboration. They suggest the need to reconceptualize agency in problem-solving networks in terms of the managerial role of "convenor" — as someone contributing to "fusion and acceptance" among participants, rather that seeking separation and control.

Gilligan's (1982, 1988) frame-breaking distinction between the "ethic of care" and the "ethic of justice" is very suggestive of the nature and scope of this new conception of moral agency within relational networks. Of related interest is Gilligan's argument, further developed by others (see Belenky, et al., 1986) that the development of human personality, associated with the articulation and internalization of a sense of moral order, is expressed in different ethical "voices." Gilligan and her adherents argue that these moral voices reflect different "ethic of care" and "ethic of justice" perspectives. Moreover, they argue, these perspectives arise out of different learning processes: "separate" and "connected" knowing. While Gilligan, et al. argue that these different ethical perspectives, voices, and learning processes tend to be gender-based, this paper will submit that "moral agency," the new conception of managerial discretion within a network governance process, need not be gender-specific. However, the possibility that male managers could learn from women's "ways of knowing" is not ruled out.

The "ethic of justice" reinforces the conventional notion of the ethical decision-maker as an autonomous (prototypically male) moral actor. His challenge is to resolve an ethical dilemma by applying universal ethical norms, derived from a consideration of the respective individual rights of the contending parties. The "ethic of justice" is consistent with the traditional business ethics approach to introducing the moral dimension into managerial decision-making. This has involved attempts at elevating managerial discretion, without transforming it. This approach recalls the "mirror of the prince" literature of the late Middle Ages and early Renaissance periods. During these earlier times of turbulence and institutional flux, clerics penned earnest moral tracts for young potentates-to-be, advising them on how they could serve as "good" sovereigns. The ultimate political embodiment of this approach to moral agency is the philosopher king or the benevolent despot. Corporate managers are called upon to assume the throne and scepter of King Solomon, disseminating "justice" to a contentious multitude of stakeholders with a fair and even hand. Recent refinements to this approach include the "stakeholder value matrix" (Brenner & Cochran, 1991) and other conceptual devices designed to help managers screen and prioritize stakeholder claims as they proceed down the "road to Jerusalem" (see Michael & Savage, 1993). While these "ethical decision-making tools" can be useful in sorting out stakeholder claims, they can never be fully or effectively implemented as long as they are treated, implicitly, as morally uplifting adjuncts to hierarchical governance. The SIM/BE field needs to replace its preoccupation with the moral potential of "rational actors" (Allison, 1971) with a new conception of moral agency that assigns managers a creative, facilitative role within a collaborative, dialogue-driven process of network governance.

The "ethic of care" is concerned with the definition of self and managerial roles in terms of responsibilities and relationships with others. It is expressed in acts and "conversations" (including gossip among friends) that sustain trust-based, mutually supportive relationships within a social network. Heimer (1992) has applied the care perspective to recast the discretionary responsibilities of managers within a network. She notes that "fair" treatment requires the manager-as-agent to apply *universal* rules of justice in balancing stakeholder interests. This is consistent with the hierarchical governance process. However, the maintenance of trust-based network relationships calls for a more *particularist* application of discretion as an expression of the agent's responsibility to serve the interests of network participants. Trusted long-term customers, employees, and suppliers expect special consideration, not standard procedural responses. The process of "connected knowing," within which network participants jointly seek ways to respond to shared problems, can guide the agent's particular exercise of discretionary responsibility. The agent must work out his/her particular response to stakeholder (as well as common network) needs in the context of a relationship of trust, built and nurtured over time in a social contracting dialogue of mutual discovery and joint rule-making.

The Saturn Corporation, an autonomous division of General Motors, has adopted a collaborative governance process and an ethic of care perspective. When customer complaints revealed that the aluminum engines in 1,800 Saturn cars had been damaged by a caustic mix of antifreeze installed at the factory, company managers entered into a dialogue with employees, dealers, suppliers, and customers. Saturn's "living constitution," a precedent-shattering explicit relational employment contract signed in 1985, stipulates that labor and management "team members" should have joint decision-making responsibility at every organizational level. The "70 percent comfortable rule" is applied to avoid gridlock. Dissenters from a team decision are required to offer a positive alternative. No decision is implemented until all team members are at least 70 percent comfortable with it. Saturn's "partnership agreements" with dealers and "loose operating agreements" with suppliers also include formal and informal voice mechanisms for sharing information, articulating differences, and solving shared problems. All of these avenues for promoting a collaborative exchange of views are designed to help all parties get "close to the customer."

From the dialogue over the effects of the caustic batch of antifreeze emerged a joint decision to voluntarily recall and replace affected units. Customers were offered new cars, often with more features, to avoid the inconvenience of waiting for installation of a new engine and cooling system. The supplier, Texaco, was not dropped and sued for damages. Rather, Texaco was asked to contribute to the cost of redressing harm to customers, and to develop control procedures that would prevent a repetition of the incident. The resolution of this incident was based neither upon the "rule book," nor upon the unilateral application of managerial discretion. It was a joint decision, consistent with the Saturn philosophy:

SOCIAL CONTRACTS AND NETWORK GOVERNANCE 289

> We, the Saturn Team, in concert with the UAW and General Motors, believe that meeting the needs of Customers, Saturn Members, Suppliers, Retailers and Neighbors is fundamental to fulfilling our mission.

All members of the Saturn network learned from the experience, and the company reaped invaluable press coverage and advertising copy from the "special" way its customers were treated. By taking actions within the network to build and sustain trust, in a manner consistent with an "ethic of care," Saturn garnered a very real competitive advantage. (See Calton & Lad, 1993: 86-87 on Saturn's collaborative network governance philosophy and practices.)

Lyons (1988: 21-22) has compared the discrete moral act, associated with the ethic of justice, with an alternative moral perspective, expressed as a "sense of connectedness." The ethic of care becomes a "'type of consciousness' which, although rooted in time, is not bound by the single moment." Lyons cited the work of the novelist, Iris Murdoch, in suggesting the limits of treating moral decisions as the creation of a rational actor, who exercises moral choice in the "quick flash of the choosing will." For Murdoch, moral choice is:

> as often a mysterious matter, because, what we really are seems much more like an obscure system of energy out of which choices and visible acts of will emerge at intervals in ways that are often unclear and often dependent on the condition of the system in between moments of choice (quoted in Lyons, 1988: 22)

Gilligan (1988: 18) and Belenky, et al. (1986: 133-152) agree that an integrative perspective on moral agency and ethical decision-making must incorporate both justice and care perspectives. The preconditions of environmental turbulence and growing cognitive complexity suggest that network forms and processes will continue to proliferate at both organizational and interorganizational levels. A contingency-based approach to ethical decision-making requires further exploration of the relational care perspective on moral agency, so that managerial discretion can be applied more appropriately in the network governance process.

Wheatley's views on "autopoeitic" or self-renewing network forms are suggestive of the new, facilitative, non-hierarchical approach to exercising managerial discretion. She cites Jantsch on the inherent orderliness of flowing organizational processes: "In life, the issue is not control, but dynamic connectedness" (1980: 196. Cited in Wheatley, 1992: 341). She notes the emergence of informal leadership in team problem-solving efforts:

> They emerge from the group, not from self-assertion, but because they make sense, given what the group needs to thrive and what individuals need in order to grow (Wheatley, 1992: 340).

As agents of multiple stakeholders within networks, managers have a special facilitative role to play in this learning-based, micro social contracting dialogue.

An approach to crafting ethical decision rules within a collective process of moral discourse has also been proposed by Jennings (1991). Managers, as they seek to become moral agents within collaborative networks, could benefit from his message about the importance of achieving "consensus with a democratic face." Jennings defines morality as a "socially embedded practice...." Thus,

achieving consensus on ethical decision rules for the community "requires placing moral agents in a practice informed by a *common sense* of what their
problems are, and a practice that transforms the consciousness of moral agents
from particularistic self-concern into a *sense of what they have in common*"
(1991: 448). Jennings concluded that

> consensus has its strongest moral claim on us, not just when it produces a
> conclusion of belief that is justified or socially useful, but by dint of a kind of
> space for moral agency and participation out of which consensus develops.
> Consensus in the strongest sense of the term happens only when it is seen as a
> common good to be created, and thus the creation of consensus becomes a special
> civic intention shared by the participants in a moral dialogue (1991: 461).

Mutual trust arises out of a social learning process that jointly creates moral
order and promotes voluntary adherance to internalized "clan" rules. By facilitating dialogue among stakeholders and convergence toward rule-based consensus, network managers could exercise ethical responsibility in acting out their
new role as moral agents. By "walking the walk, and talking the talk" in dealing
with multiple stakeholders, they could enact Desjardin's (1990) vision of a
"virtue-based CSR, building on Aristotle's dictum that 'we become just by doing
just actions'" (quoted in Klonoski, 1991: 16).

Conclusion: Opportunities and Outcomes in Emergent Network Governance Processes

Successful outcomes in the cognitive construction of reality reflect the appropriateness with which the micro social contracting process responds to collectively recognized preconditions. If we accept the widely-held presumption of
growing environmental turbulence and cognitive complexity, then collaborative
network governance processes are an appropriate response. Hierarchical governance structures and processes appear too constraining and inflexible to accommodate such turbulence and complexity. This novel organizational and
interorganizational response can vary in scope and complexity according to the
size of the "mess" in need of collective management. It works to resolve the
"paradox of interdependent relations" (Aram, 1989) by substituting systems
based on individual rationality with a dialogue-driven process that searches for
a higher order of shared collective rationality.

A social contracting theory of the firm in society cannot simply subsume other
contractual theories built on core presumptions about selfishly rational individual behavior and "efficient" bilateral transactions. Perrow has challenged the
notion that social systems must channel or control an inherently opportunistic
human nature. He argues that human nature is signified by a "lack of instinctual
responses." Human behavior is an adaptive, learned (and learning) response:

> If so, the setting in which interactions or contracts occur is the most important
> thing to consider in explaining behavior. Some settings, or organizational struc-
> tures... will promote self-interested behavior, others will promote other-regard-
> ing behavior, and still others will be neutral (1986: 13-14).

SOCIAL CONTRACTS AND NETWORK GOVERNANCE 291

A new social contracting theory of the firm in society, then, must explore the collective effort to design institutional settings that offer the greatest prospect for validating each participant's right to a justly-earned place in the "good society." This paper has called attention to the need for a wider recognition of the social contracting origin of the firm as a stakeholder-based network, and for further development and legitimization of mechanisms to give "voice" to stakeholder participants in organizational and interorganizational settings. If more business managers were to seriously consider and begin exercising the proposed new approach to moral agency, a productive dialogue with network stakeholders could facilitate the collective search for solutions to this troubled world's abundance of shared "messes."

A theoretical and empirical investigation of the design and governance of nested network forms can transform, as it integrates, the concept of corporate social performance and ethical decision-making. Since the normative and descriptive dimensions of emergent network relationships are inextricably intertwined, there is room for both "critical" and "positivist" contributions to this investigation. The converging forces of "disorder" have created an opportunity for cognitive leadership. Fortunately, the SIM/BE field is developing the conceptual tools that can empower us to become involved in "real world" efforts to define and enact "negotiated orders" that bind and enrich us all, one step at a time.

Bibliography

Adler, P. 1993. "Time-and-Motion Regained." *Harvard Business Review*, 71(1): 97-108.

Alter, C., & Hage, J. 1993. *Organizations Working Together*. Newbury Park, CA: Sage Publications, Inc.

Allison, G. 1971. *Essence of Decision: Explaining the Cuban Missile Crisis*. Boston: Little, Brown.

Aoki, M. 1984. *The Cooperative Game Theory of the Firm*. London: Oxford University Press.

Aoki, M. 1990a. "The Participatory Generation of Information Rents and the Theory of the Firm." In M. Aoki, B. Gustafsson & O. Williamson (Eds.), *The Firm as a Nexus of Treaties*: 26-52. London: Sage Publications.

Aoki, M. 1990b. "Toward an Economic Model of the Japanese Firm." *Journal of Economic Literature*, 28(1): 1-27.

Aram, J. 1989. "The Paradox of Interdependent Relations in the Field of Social Issues in Management." *Academy of Management Journal*, 14(2): 266-283.

Argyris, C., & Schon. 1978. *Organizational Learning: A Theory of Action Perspective*. Reading, MA: Addison-Wesley Publishing Company.

Arrow, K. 1973. "Social Responsibility and Economic Efficiency." *Public Policy*, 21: 303-317.

Austrom, D., & Lad, L. 1989. "Issues Management Alliances: New Responses, New Values, and New Logics." In J. Post (Ed.), *Research in Corporate Social Performance and Policy*: 233-255. Greenwich, CT: JAI Press.

292   BUSINESS ETHICS QUARTERLY

Bartlett, C., & Ghoshal, S. 1989. *Managing Across Borders: The Transnational Solution*. Boston: Harvard Business School Press.

Baynes, K. 1989. "Kant on Property Rights and the Social Contract." *The Monist*, 72(3) 433-453.

Belenky, M., Clinchy, B., Goldberger, N., & Tarule, J. 1986. *Women's Ways of Knowing: The Development of Self, Voice, and Mind*. New York: Basic Books.

Bradach, J., & Eccles, R. 1989. "Price, Authority, and Trust: From Ideal Types to Plural Forms." *Annual Review of Sociology*, 97-118.

Brenner, S., & Cochran, P. 1991. "The Stakeholder Theory of the Firm: Implications for Business and Society Research." In J. Mahon (Ed.), *Proceedings of the Second Annual Meeting of the International Association for Business and Society*: 449-467.

Burns, T., & Stalker, G. 1961. *The Management of Innovation*. London: Tavistock.

Calton, J. 1993. "What is at Stake in the Stakeholder Model?" In D. Ludwig, (Ed.), *Business & Society in a Changing World Order*. Lewiston, NY: Edwin Mellen Press, pp. 101-127.

Calton, J., & Lad, L. 1993. "Collaborative Governance: The Firm, the Interorganizational Field, and 'Negotiated Order.'" In J. Pasquero and D. Collins (Eds.), *Proceedings of the Fourth Annual Meeting of the International Association for Business and Society*: 84-89.

Clegg, S. 1990. *Modern Organizations: Organizational Studies in the Postmodern World*. London: Sage Publications, Inc.

Coase, R. 1937. "The Nature of the Firm." *Economica*, 4: 386-405.

Cohen, A., and Townsley, M. 1990. "Perspectives on Collaboration as Replacement for Confrontation," *Public Utilities Fortnightly*, March 1, pp. 9-13.

Contractor, F., & Lorange, P. 1988. *Cooperative Strategies in International Business*. Lexington, MA: D.C. Heath & Co.

Davidow, W., & Malone, M. 1992. *The Virtual Corporation: Structuring and Revitalizing the Corporation for the 21st Century*. New York: Harper Collins Publishers.

Desjardin, J. 1990. "Virtue and Business Ethics." In J. Desjardins & J. McCall (Eds.), *Contemporary Issues in Business Ethics*: 54-59. Belmont, CA: Wadsworth Publishing Co.

DiMaggio. P. 1992. "Nadel's Paradox Revisited: Relational and Cultural Aspects of Organizational Structure." In N. Nohria & R. Eccles (Eds.), *Networks and Organizations: Structure, Form, and Action*: 118-142. Boston: Harvard Business School Press.

Donaldson, T. 1982. *Corporations and Morality*. Englewood Cliffs, NJ: Prentice-Hall.

Donaldson, T., & Dunfee, T. Forthcoming. "Integrative Social Contracts Theory: A Communitarian Conception of Economic Ethics." *Economics and Philosophy*.

Ellis, W. B. 1989. "The Collaborative Process in Utility Resource Planning," *Public Utilities Fortnightly*, June 22, pp. 9-11.

Evan, W., & Freeman, E. 1993. "A Stakeholder Theory of the Modern Corporation: Kantian Capitalism." In T. Beauchamp & N. Bowie (Eds.), *Ethical Theory and Business* (4th ed.): 75-93. Englewood Cliffs, NJ: Prentice-Hall.

Fiske, S., & Taylor, S. 1991. *Social Cognition* (2nd ed.). New York: McGraw-Hill.

Freeman, E. 1984. *Strategic Management: A Stakeholder Approach*. Boston: Pitman

Freeman, E., & Evan, W. 1990. "Corporate Governance: A Stakeholder Interpretation." *Journal of Behavioral Economics*, 19(4): 337-359.

Freeman, E., & Gilbert, D., Jr. 1988. *Corporate Strategy and the Search for Ethics*. Englewood Cliffs, NJ: Prentice-Hall.

Gerlach, M., & Lincoln, J. 1992. "The Organization of Business Networks in the United States and Japan." In N. Nohria & R. Eccles (Eds.), *Networks and Organizations: Structure, Form, and Action*: 491-520. Boston: Harvard Business School Press.

Gilligan, C. 1982. *In a Different Voice*. Cambridge: Harvard University Press.

Gilligan, C. 1988. "Remapping the Moral Domain: New Images of Self in Relationship." In C. Gilligan, J. Ward, & J. Taylor, with Bardige, B. (Eds.), *Mapping the Moral Domain: A Contribution of Women's Thinking to Psychological Theory and Education*: 3-19. Cambridge, MA: Harvard University Press.

Goodpaster, K. 1991. "Business Ethics and Stakeholder Analysis." *Business Ethics Quarterly*, 1: 53-73

Granovetter, M. 1985. "Economic Action and Social Structure: The Problem of Embeddedness." *American Journal of Sociology*, 91: 481-510.

Granovetter, M. 1992. "Problems of Explanation in Economic Sociology." In N. Nohria & R. Eccles (Eds.), *Networks and Organizations: Structure, Form, and Action*: 25-56. Boston: Harvard Business School Press.

Gray, B., & Wood, D. 1991. "Collaborative Alliances: Moving from Practice to Theory." *Journal of Applied Behavioral Science*, 27(1): 3-21.

Handy, C. 1990. *The Age of Unreason*. Boston: Harvard Business School Press.

Hardin, G. 1968. "The Tragedy of the Commons." *Science*. 162: 1243-1248.

Hardin, R. 1991. "Hobbesian Political Order — Reading Hobbes in Other Words: Contractarian, Utilitarian, Game Theorist." *Political Theory*, 19(2): 156-180.

Heimer, C. 1992. "Doing Your Job and Helping Your Friends: Universalistic Norms about Obligations to Particular Others in Networks." In N. Nohria & R. Eccles (Eds.), *Networks and Organizations: Structure, Form, and Action*:143-164. Boston: Harvard Business School Press.

Hill, C., & Jones, T. 1992. "Stakeholder-Agency Theory." *Journal of Management Studies*, 29(2):131-154.

Hirschman, A. 1970. *Exit, Voice, and Loyalty: Responses to Decline in Firms, Organizations, and States*. Cambridge, MA: Harvard University Press.

Hood, J., Logsdon, J., and Thompson, J. 1993. "Collaboration for Social Problem-Solving: A Process Model." *Business & Society*, 32(1): 1-17.

Jaikumar, R. 1986. "Post-Industrial Manufacturing." *Harvard Business Review*, 64(6), Nov.-Dec.: 69-76.

Jantsch, E. 1980. *The Self-Organizing Universe*. Oxford: Pergamon Press.

Jennings, B. 1991. "Possibilities of Consensus: Toward Democratic Moral Discourse." *Journal of Medicine and Philosophy*, 16(4): 447-463.

Jensen, M., & Meckling, W. 1976. "Theory of the Firm: Managerial Behavior, Agency Costs and Ownership Structure." *Journal of Financial Economics*, 3: 305-360.

294   BUSINESS ETHICS QUARTERLY

Keeley, M. 1980. "Organizational Analogy: A Comparison of Organismic and Social Contract Models." *Administrative Science Quarterly*, 25: 337-362.

Keeley, M. 1988. *A Social-Contract Theory of Organizations*. Notre Dame, IN: University of Notre Dame Press.

Klonoski, R. 1991. "Foundational Considerations in the Corporate Social Responsibility Debate." *Business Horizons*, 34(4): 9-18.

Kogut, B., Shan, W., and Walker, G. 1992. "The Make or Cooperate Decision in the Context of an Industry Network." In N. Nohria & R. Eccles (Eds.), *Networks and Organizations: Structure, Form, and Action*:348-365. Boston: Harvard Business School Press.

Lewin, D., & Mitchell, D. 1992. "Systems of Employee Voice: Theoretical and Empirical Perspectives." *California Management Review*, 34(3): 95-111.

Lyons, N. P. 1988. "Two Perspectives: On Self, Relationships, and Morality." In C. Gilligan, J. Ward, & J. Taylor, with Bardige, B. (Eds.), *Mapping the Moral Domain: A Contribution of Women's Thinking to Psychological Theory and Education*: 21-48. Cambridge, MA: Harvard University Press.

Logsdon, J. 1991. "Interests and Interdependence in the Formation of Social Problem-Solving Collaborations." *Journal of Applied Behavioral Science*, 27(1): 23-37.

Macneil, I. 1981. "Economic Analysis of Contractual Relations: Its Shortfalls and the Need for a 'Rich' Classificatory Apparatus." *Northwestern University Law Review*, 75: 1018-1063.

Michael, E., & Savage, G. 1993. "On the Road to Jerusalem: Exploring the Ethical Ground for Stakeholder Management." In J. Pasquero & D. Colins, (Eds.). *Proceedings of the Fourth Annual Meeting of the International Association for Business & Society*: 418-428.

Nathan, M., & Mitroff, I. 1991. "The Use of Negotiated Order Theory as a Tool for the Analysis and Development of an Interorganizational Field." *Journal of Applied Behavioral Science*, 27(2): 163-180.

Nisbett, R., & Ross, L. 1980. *Human Inference: Strategies and Shortcomings of Social Judgment*. Englewood Cliffs, NJ: Prentice-Hall.

Nohria, N. 1992. "Is a Network Perspective a Useful Way of Studying Organizations?" In N. Nohria & R. Eccles (Eds.). *Networks and Organizations: Structure, Form, and Action*: 1-22. Boston: Harvard Business School Press.

Nohria, N., & Eccles, R. 1992. "Face to Face: Making Network Organizations Work." In N. Nohria & R. Eccles (Eds.). *Networks and Organizations: Structure, Form, and Action*: 288-308. Boston: Harvard Business School Press.

Noreen, E. 1988. "The Economics of Ethics: A New Perspective on Agency Theory." *Accounting, Organizations and Society*, 13(4): 359-369.

Ouchi, W. 1980. "Markets, Bureaucracies, and Clans." *Administrative Science Quarterly*, 25: 129-141.

Peters, T. 1986. *Thriving on Chaos: Handbook for a Management Revolution*. New York: Free Press.

Perrow, C. 1986. "Economic Theories of Organizations." *Theory and Society*, 15: 11-45.

Powell, W. 1990. "Neither Market nor Hierarchy: Network Forms of Organization." *Research in Organizational Behavior*, 12: 295-336.

Pryne, E. 1993. "A New Horizon for the Tolt Basin; Watershed Analysis Helps Teams See Forest for the Trees," *Seattle Times*, December 6: B-1, B2.

Quinn, J. B. 1992. *Intelligent Enterprise: A Knowledge and Service Based Paradigm for Industry.* New York: Free Press.

Rawls, J. 1971. *A Theory of Justice.* Cambridge, MA: Belknap Press.

Reich, R. 1992. *The Work of Nations.* New York: Vintage Books.

Ring, P. 1992. "The Role of Trust in the Design and Management of Business Organizations." In S. Waddock (Ed.). *Proceedings of the Third Annual Meeting of the International Association for Business & Society*: 284-292.

Schonberger, R. 1992. "Total Quality Management cuts a Broad Swath through Manufacturing and Beyond." *Organizational Dynamics*, 20(4): 16-27.

Snow, C., Miles, R., & Coleman, H. 1992. "Managing 21st Century Network Organizations." *Organizational Dynamics*, 20(3): 5-19.

Waldron, J. 1989. "John Locke: Social Contract versus Political Anthropology." *Review of Politics*, 57(1): 3-27.

Wheatley, M. 1992. "Searching for Order in an Orderly World: A Poetic for Post-Machine-Age Managers." *Journal of Management Inquiry*, 1(4): 337-342.

Williamson, O. 1984. "Corporate Governance." *Yale Law Journal*, 93: 1197-1230.

Williamson, O. 1985. *The Economic Institutions of Capitalism: Firms, Markets, and Relational Contracting.* New York: Free Press.

Williamson, O. 1991. "Comparative Economic Organization: The Analysis of Discrete Structural Alternatives." *Administrative Science Quarterly*, 36: 269-296.

Wood, D. 1991. Corporate Social Performance Revisited. *Academy of Management Review*, 16: 691-718.

Wood, D. 1992. *Discovering the Structure of Corporate Social Performance.* Chairperson's address to the Social Issues in Management division of the Academy of Management, Las Vegas.

Wood, D., & Gray, B. 1991. "Toward a Comprehensive Theory of Collaboration." *Journal of Applied Behavioral Science*, 27(2): 139-162.

[36]

TRUST: THE CONNECTING LINK BETWEEN ORGANIZATIONAL THEORY AND PHILOSOPHICAL ETHICS

LARUE TONE HOSMER
University of Michigan

Numerous researchers have proposed that trust is essential for understanding interpersonal and group behavior, managerial effectiveness, economic exchange and social or political stability, yet according to a majority of these scholars, this concept has never been precisely defined. This article reviews definitions from various approaches within organizational theory, examines the consistencies and differences, and proposes that trust is based upon an underlying assumption of an implicit moral duty. This moral duty—an anomaly in much of organizational theory—has made a precise definition problematic. Trust also is examined from philosophical ethics, and a synthesis of the organizational and philosophical definitions that emphasizes an explicit sense of moral duty and is based upon accepted ethical principles of analysis is proposed. This new definition has the potential to combine research from the two fields of study in important areas of inquiry.

Many economists, psychologists, sociologists, and management theorists appear united on the importance of trust in the conduct of human affairs. Blau (1964: 99) described trust as "essential for stable social relationships." Weber (Eisenstadt 1968: 114) claimed that the exchange of goods "is possible only on the basis of far-reaching personal confidence and trust." Rotter, Chance, and Phares (1972: 40) argued that "a generalized expectancy of trust or distrust can be an important determinant of behavior." Golembiewski and McConkie (1975: 131) stated that, "There is no single variable which so thoroughly influences interpersonal and group behavior as does trust." Hirsch (1978: 78) reemphasized its importance for exchange when he explained that trust was a "public good, necessary for the success of economic transactions." Bok (1978: 26) went even further and claimed that "when trust is destroyed, societies falter and collapse." Lewis and Weigert (1985: 968) agreed, adding that trust was "indispensable in social relationships." Zucker (1986: 56) followed with the statement that trust was "vital for the maintenance of cooperation in society and necessary as grounds for even the most routine, everyday interactions."

Trust is viewed as an important concept by academic researchers and by business practitioners and consultants as well. (See, for example,

Bartolome, 1989; Belasco, 1989; Bennis, 1989; Clawson, 1989; Covey, 1989; Horton & Reid, 1991; and Watson, 1991.) All stressed the critical importance of building trusting relationships in management.

There appears to be widespread agreement on the importance of trust in human conduct, but unfortunately there also appears to be equally widespread lack of agreement on a suitable definition of the concept. Golembiewski and McConkie (1975: 131), for example, summarized their disappointment with much of the earlier work when they expressed the belief that the study of trust was essentially "a paradox." "Diverse conceptualizations of interpersonal trust coexist," they explained, "with intense convictions that the various somethings described are central in all of human life." Luhmann (1980: 8) followed with the complaint that "there is a regrettably sparse literature which has trust as its main theme within sociology," and added that work outside that field seemed "theoretically unintegrated and incomplete." Barber (1983: 7) agreed, saying "in both serious social thought and everyday discourse it is assumed that the meaning of trust, and of its many apparent synonyms, is so well known that it can be left undefined or to contextual implications." Zucker (1986: 58) also criticized much that had been done previously and explained that "recognition of the importance of trust has led to concern with defining the concept, but the definitions proposed unfortunately have little in common." Shapiro (1987: 624) expanded on this last point, saying "the conceptualization [of trust] has received considerable attention in recent years, resulting in a confusing potpourri of definitions applied to a host of units and levels of analysis." Bluhm (1987: 334) followed with his belief that "trust mechanisms have not received the analytical attention they deserve," but noted that "the lack of conceptual clarity has not inhibited the wide use of the concept." Reichmann (1989: 185) agreed, attesting to the "considerable uncertainty about what trust is and how precisely it falters." Butler (1991: 647) believed that it would be more useful to study the conditions or determinants of trust than to attempt further definition of what he called "the global attitude" of the concept. "Currently," he wrote, "there is no agreement as to what these trust conditions are, and there is no instrument for measuring an exhaustive set of them." Ring and Van de Ven (1992: 485) followed through on this pragmatic approach when they wrote, "The implications of trusting behavior in designing governance mechanisms are generally ignored."

PURPOSE OF THE ARTICLE

A current review of the literature on trust, however, does not seem to warrant those discouraging views. Certainly there is no agreement on a single definition of the concept, and certainly many researchers have taken multiple paths in attempting to reach such a definition. But the earlier work has not been wasted. Each of the proposed definitions seems to this author to add insight and understanding. Each—again to this author—seems to provide dimensions and boundaries to what admittedly is a hazy and diffuse topic. These definitions seem to be based, at least in part, upon an underlying assumption of a moral duty with a strong ethical component owed by the trusted person to the trusting individuals. Perhaps it is the presence of this implied moral duty—an anomaly in much of organizational theory—that has made a precise definition of the concept of trust so difficult. Perhaps if we make that moral duty explicit rather than implicit, and compare the organizational theory definitions of trust with those from moral philosophy, it will be possible to synthesize the "global" definition of trust that Butler felt was needed but difficult to attain. In any event, such an effort would seem worthwhile. Such a definition, if accepted, would provide a connecting link between the two fields of study and bring issues of what is "right," what is "just," and what is "fair"—the topic of philosophical ethics—into the mainstream of organizational theory and management practice. Such a definition, again if accepted, would also bring issues of what is "efficient," what is "effective," and what is "practical"—the essence of organizational theory—into the mainstream of moral philosophy. Both changes are badly needed, in my view.

In attempting to synthesize the prior writings on trust, particularly those from organizational theory, it is necessary to remember that most of the early researchers were attempting to use the concept in different contexts. It would seem critical to recognize those contexts. Indeed, Husted (1989: 23) argued that "the definition of trust is problematic because there is such a wide variety of approaches to the concept." This article will briefly review the various definitions of trust that have been proposed within the approaches or contexts of (a) individual expectations, (b) interpersonal relationships, (c) economic exchanges, (d) social structures, and (e) ethical principles. I assume that the definitions of trust derived from the ethical principles of moral philosophy will be less familiar to readers of the *Academy of Management Review* than the definitions cited in the other contexts, so the philosophical literature will be examined in somewhat greater detail, with a summary (Table 2) of the major sources.

TRUST AS INDIVIDUAL EXPECTATIONS

Trust as an individual's optimistic expectation about the outcome of an event is one of the earliest—but not necessarily one of the least sophisticated—academic definitions of the concept. Deutsch (1958) believed that trust was the nonrational choice of a person faced with an uncertain event in which the expected loss was greater than the expected gain. Why was the loss necessarily greater than the gain? If the reverse were true, then trust would be simple economic rationality. Consequently, Deutsch stressed the vulnerability aspects of the concept. The trusting person, he wrote, "perceives that he will be worse off if he trusts and his trust is not fulfilled than if he does not trust" (1958: 266). Trust, therefore, was seen as the nonrational expectation of the outcome of an uncertain event, given conditions of personal vulnerability. A synonym would seem to be "confidence," though Deutsch never made that explicit claim.

Zand (1972) also emphasized the vulnerability aspect of trust, but he divided trust into personal behavior and individual expectations. The behavior was the giving up of control, which he termed the "decision to trust." This decision was guided by the nature of the problem (or the degree of vulnerability) and by the expectations of the outcome or, more formally, "the hypothesized consequences of high trust versus low trust" (1972: 232). Again confidence was implicitly synonymous with trust, but the important additive for Zand was the giving up of control over the outcome. At this point, trust was now an individual decision, based upon optimistic expectations or confidence about the outcome of an uncertain event, given personal vulnerability and the lack of personal control over the actions of others.

Golembiewski and McConkie (1975: 133) expanded on the equation of trust and confidence. Trust, they wrote, "implies reliance on, or confidence in, some event, process or person." This reliance remained nonrational in any strict economic sense; it was, the authors believed, subjective, being based upon personal perceptions and experiences. It was not, however, a duality as proposed by Zand (1972); instead it was now seen as a continuum, with the degree of trust equal to the amount of hope for a positive outcome. Trust, they concluded, is "strongly linked to confidence in, and overall optimism about, desirable events taking place" (1975: 134).

Barber (1983: 9–10), who provided an excellent summary of some of the earliest works on the concept, agreed that trust was a set of optimistic expectations on the part of an individual, but shifted the focus of those expectations from the outcome of a single uncertain event to three conditions and/or assumptions that determined that outcome:

1. Expectation of the persistence and fulfillment of the natural (and existing) social order in which the individual found himself or herself. Here Barber quoted Nicholas Luhman (1980: 4), who claimed that the world presented itself to any thoughtful person as "unmanageable complexity," and that trust reduced this complexity with "cognitive, emotional, and moral expectations that some things will remain as they are or ought to be." In short, part of trust was the personal expectation that the world would continue without discontinuous change.

2. Expectation of technically competent role performances from those involved with the individual. Many of the earlier writers on trust (e.g., Gabarro, 1978; Jennings, 1971; Luhmann, 1980) were concerned about the connection between trust and competence. Could you trust a noncompetent physician or attorney? was a question that was frequently asked without a satisfactory answer. The difficulty, of course, was that most people were unable to critically evaluate the competence of specialists. Barber avoided this conundrum with his expectation of technically competent role performance.

3. Expectation of morally correct role performance from those associated with the individual. Many of the earlier writers on trust also tended to equate the concept with fiduciary duties and responsibilities, but they

did not define those terms. Barber avoided this problem by stating that the fiduciary duty of professionals, in certain situations, was to place the interests of the individual who is trusting before the interests of the professional who is trusted.

Barber (1983) added greatly to the "personal expectations" literature on trust. He moved toward an interpersonal definition—his concept required a person who was trusting and a second person who was worthy of that trust—but trust remained basically the optimistic expectations of a single individual relative to the eventual outcome of an uncertain event. Remember, however, Barber's simple definition of fiduciary duty: placing the interests of others before the interests of the person being trusted. It is found, in some form, in each of the behavioral and ethical contexts in which trust has been defined.

TRUST AS INTERPERSONAL RELATIONS

Zand (1972) expanded his first definition of trust from the confident expectations of a single individual to approach the dependent interactions of a dyad. Trust, he suggested, was the willingness of one person to increase his or her vulnerability to the actions of another person whose behavior he or she could not control. In this case, as with Barber, we see trust as dependence as well as confidence. The decision to trust was still made by one person, but the "hypothesized consequences" of that decision were now dependent upon the actions of others. Trust, Zand believed, went beyond expectations of outcome under conditions of uncertainty to expectations of behavior under conditions of vulnerability. Trust, he wrote, became the "conscious regulation of one's dependence on another that will vary with the task, the situation, and the person" (1972: 230). Rotter (1967: 650) had earlier emphasized the dependence argument with his definition that "interpersonal trust [was] an expectancy held by an individual or a group that the word, promise, verbal or written statement of another individual or group [could] be relied upon."

Michalos (1990: 620) accepted the vulnerability and dependence components, but added the notion of an ultimate net good: "It is enough to think of trust as a relatively informed attitude or propensity to allow oneself and perhaps others to be vulnerable to harm in the interests of some perceived greater good." This perceived greater good, it could be assumed, might be on the interpersonal, organizational, or even social level; it was not necessarily a direct personal benefit to the trusting individual.

Gambetta (1988: 217) also accepted the vulnerable and dependent conditions of trust, but substituted the goal of interpersonal cooperation for that of an ultimate net good. Trust, he wrote, was "the probability that a person with whom we are in contact will perform an action that is beneficial or at least not detrimental is high enough for us to consider engaging in some form of cooperation with him." Carnevale, Pruitt, and

384 *Academy of Management Review* April

Carrington (1982: 13) had earlier defined trust as "a concomitant expectation that the other [in a dyad] will reciprocate" and had declared this expectation essential for "the goal of achieving mutual cooperation." Meeker (1983: 231), who also stressed the importance of willing cooperation in her definition of trust, maintained that "the trusting person expects helpful or cooperative behavior from the other." Deutsch, quoted in Lewis and Weigert (1985: 975), had gone even further when he termed trust as the equivalent of "cooperative behavior," though only in the specific context of game theory. The goals of an ultimate net benefit and/or willing interpersonal cooperation are clearly associated with the concept of trust in the behavioral literature.

Butler and Cantrell (1984) followed through on the interpersonal nature of trust as a condition for cooperation, but added the complicating factor of inequality in position. They examined two earlier works that dealt with superior/subordinate relationships in management. Jennings (1971) had looked at the career paths of executives and found that trust by the superior was an essential condition for the eventual promotion of a subordinate. He then defined trust in terms of four general dimensions. Gabarro (1978), in contrast, examined the actions of newly appointed presidents in underperforming companies and found that trust by the subordinate was an essential condition for effective action by the superior. Here trust was defined on nine dimensions. Butler and Cantrell synthesized the two earlier works and proposed five specific components of trust, or characteristics of the people. It was expected that the degree of each would differ depending upon the position (superior or subordinate) of the person:

1. Integrity—the reputation for honesty and truthfulness on the part of the trusted individual.
2. Competence—the technical knowledge and interpersonal skill needed to perform the job.
3. Consistency—the reliability, predictability, and good judgment in handling situations.
4. Loyalty—benevolence, or the willingness to protect, support, and encourage others.
5. Openness—mental accessibility, or the willingness to share ideas and information freely with others.

Here we have four moral values—integrity, consistency, loyalty, and openness—among the five terms in one behavioral definition of trust. Normative philosophy can supply precise definitions and ethical justifications—why each can be expected to lead to a "good" society—for each of those terms. Let me here anticipate just a bit the later argument of this article. A synthesis of the definitions of trust from both organizational theory and normative philosophy should have the potential of providing greater precision and greater justification than a definition from organizational theory alone, and the same synthesis should have greater relevance to managerial issues than a definition from normative philosophy alone.

Butler (1991) in a later work made the loyalty dimension or determinant of trust much more precise when he changed from a proposed attitude of general benevolence to an implicit promise from one individual in the dyad not to bring harm to the other. This followed Rempel and Holmes (1986), who had analyzed trust in personal rather than managerial relationships and concluded that predictability, reliability, and responsiveness (i.e., caring for the welfare of the other person) were equally important. Ring and Van de Ven (1992: 488) went further and termed trust a mixture of two aspects: "(1) confidence or predictability in one's expectations (Zucker, 1986) and (2) confidence in the other's goodwill (Friedman, 1991)." Again, as in Barber (1983), we find moral values, particularly benevolence (the duty to care for the protection of others) and good will (the intent to look after the interests of others) in behavioral definitions of trust.

Butler (1991: 647) concluded in his later work that "the literature on trust has converged on the beliefs that (a) trust is an important aspect of interpersonal relationships, (b) trust is essential to the development of managerial careers, and (c) trust in a specific person is more relevant in terms of predicting outcomes than is the global attitude of trust in generalized others." The interpersonal literature on trust in management appeared to be focusing on superior/subordinate relationships and the personal characteristics of specific individuals within those relationships. The institutional economics literature on *distrust* in management, however, was definitely expanding to include principal/agent relationships, economic transactions, and the personal characteristics of very generalized others.

ECONOMIC TRANSACTIONS

In one sense economic transactions can be seen as just a specialized form of interpersonal behavior, but it is necessary to remember that in Williamson (1975) the terms "principal" and "agent" could refer to individuals, to groups, or to firms. Consequently the transactions could be on an individual-to-individual, group-to-group, or firm-to-firm basis, or on the basis of any combination of those units. This was a considerable expansion of the concept of trust, or more properly distrust, because the concept is most often viewed from the negative or pessimistic side in economic exchange theory. At this point the theory was focusing on a principal versus his or her agents, or on a corporation versus its stakeholders (Freeman, 1984), rather than on one individual anticipating the outcome of an event or the behavior of a person.

One of the central assumptions of transaction cost economics is the belief that the agent in any principal/agent relationship is not to be trusted, and that the risk of opportunism is high. *Opportunism* was defined, in a famous phrase from Williamson, as "self-interest seeking with guile" (1985: 47). It included, according to Hill (1990), not only the more blatant forms of cheating, but also the less obvious but clearly calculated methods of misleading, distorting, disguising, and confusing.

Williamson's argument was that cheating in all of these nefarious forms was not endemic—indeed in one of his earlier works (1975: 109) he admitted that business managers often do act on the basis of trust—but that the difficulty in identifying trustworthy agents was so great that organizations had to structure themselves as if all agents could not be trusted. In a market that meant principals had to negotiate and monitor detailed contracts to protect against opportunistic behavior. In a hierarchy that meant principals had to establish and review stringent controls for the same purpose. These contracts and controls, termed *substitutes for trust*, were needed only because untrustworthy agents could not be clearly identified. Transaction costs were, of course, incurred with both markets and hierarchies, and Williamson suggested that differences in the costs of contracts versus the costs of controls determined the strategic options and structural formats of the firm.

Hill (1990) proposed that it was possible to reduce these transaction costs through a reputation for nonopportunistic behavior. Although we do not and cannot know the distribution of opportunistic versus cooperative actors in any given population, he explained, we do have selection mechanisms to identify those more likely to cooperate. Each firm, in Hill's view, was surrounded by a system of markets, including debt and equity capital markets, material and labor input markets, and goods and services output markets. Opportunistic actions within a single market, he continued, might yield short-term benefits, but there would be a long-term cost in the sense of a lack of trust that might inhibit future acquisitions of cost-reducing and/or quality-enhancing assets. "Reputation has an economic value" (1990: 505), he concluded; it played an important part in determining the willingness of others to enter into an exchange with a given actor. Reputation, of course, is the result of trustworthy behavior, and trust in this sense is—though Hill does not offer this specific definition or, for that matter, any definition—the economically rational decision to do exactly what you have contracted to do or promised to do because otherwise you would suffer an eventual loss in reputation and, hence, in contracting opportunities.

Bromily and Cummings (1992: 4) argued that trust could reduce transaction costs, and they went on to provide a specific definition of the concept. "Trust," they wrote, "is the expectation that another individual or group will (1) make a good faith effort to behave in accordance with any commitments, both explicit or implicit; (2) be honest in whatever negotiations preceded those commitments; and (3) not take excessive advantage of others even when the opportunity [to renegotiate] is available." This definition, obviously, was the opposite of self-interest seeking with guile. It did, however, create additional definitional problems: What does it mean to "be honest in negotiations"? How far are we permitted to go before we start to "take excessive advantage" of others? Despite these admittedly imprecise terms, the authors claimed that "the degree to which an individual can be trusted can be ascertained with at least a modest level of accuracy" (1992: 5).

Higher levels of trust, Bromily and Cummings continued in the same article, not only reduced the cost of monitoring performance, but also eliminated the need for installing control systems that were based on short-term financial results and that in turn could—and here the authors referred to Hoskisson and Hitt (1988)—have the undesirable side effects of reducing innovation and cooperation.

Empirical support for the connection of trust with cooperation comes from game theory. *Trust* was at one time defined (Deutsch, quoted in Lewis & Weigert, 1985: 975) as "cooperative behavior in the prisoner's dilemma game" but, as is well known, in a game with a finite number of plays the trusting actor with a strategy of unconditional cooperation will always lose to a nontrusting player with a strategy of unconditional competition. This definition, reasonable on the surface, repeated the earlier association of trust with optimistic expectations about the outcomes of uncertain events, which in a "win-lose" economic contest could easily become confused with naivete, altruism, or stupidity.

Friedland (1990), however, disassociated trust from naivete, altruism, or stupidity. She found that in games with an infinite number of plays— which are, after all, much more representative of "real-world" situations—a matching or "tit-for-tat" strategy consisting of the systematic reciprocation of competitive and cooperative behaviors might not win outright but would substantially reduce the chance of loss. It would reduce the chance of loss, Friedland explained, because the tit-for-tat strategy would elicit more cooperation from adversaries than strategies of unconditional cooperation or of unconditional competition. Friedland, in short, clearly brought rational self-interest back into the concept of trust.

Friedland explained the results she cited by saying that a strategy of unconditional cooperation invited exploitation by casting the strategist as fair but weak. Unconditional competition invited retribution by casting the strategist as strong but unfair. The matching strategy, however, elicited in the other player a feeling of control over the strategist's behavior. The adversary came to believe that he or she could cooperate for mutual gain without risking exploitation. "Specifically," Friedland concluded, "trust is most typically promoted when a party to an interaction shows a genuine responsiveness to the needs of its partner" (1990: 317). Even in economic transaction analysis this sense of concern for others informs a scholarly definition of the concept of trust.

Bradach and Eccles (1989) proposed approximately the same definition. They argued that markets and hierarchies were not mutually exclusive means of governing economic transactions, but that price, authority, and trust were independent methods that could be combined in a variety of ways. Trust did not replace the market or the hierarchy, they said; instead, it complemented and strengthened the other methods. They agreed with Gambetta (1988: 217) that trust was "the probability that one economic actor will make decisions and take actions that will be beneficial or at the least not detrimental to another," and that, consequently, cooperation would be a more valid strategy than competition. Bradach and Eccles, however, differed with Hill, Bromily and Cummings, Friedland, and Gambetta because they viewed the sources of trust as social norms and interpersonal relationships, rather than rational computations of self-interest. This leads to the familiar "embeddedness" argument that trust is part of our formal and informal social structures.

SOCIAL STRUCTURES

Weber (Eisenstadt, quoted in Bluhm, 1987: 334) was the first to observe that formal social mechanisms, such as the legal system, were designed to "guarantee or secure trustworthy conduct." The process of economic development tended, he believed, to shift the focus of trust from a personal relationship to a social mechanism. This shift, if true, would help to explain the varying definitions of trust; the concept would differ depending upon the stage of economic development reached by a given society.

Coleman (1984: 85) followed with the observation that both the functioning of economic institutions and the theory of that functioning assumed a foundation of trust. He did not define trust except to say that it was a "relation between two actors" and that "one actor's placement of trust in a second may be conditional upon that of a third." That is, one person's trust in a second person may be conditional upon trust in a third person to enforce the earlier contract or agreement. Trust in the third person, of course, may then be conditional upon trust in a fourth to oversee the third, and in a fifth to review the actions of the fourth, and so on. This created for Coleman (1984: 85) a "social organization of trust" that— and here he used the analogy of electrical grids or networks—could fail at the weakest spot in the grid or the most susceptible person in the organization with disastrous consequences for society.

Granovetter (1985) put both Weber and Coleman on much more solid academic footing. He started from Williamson's (1985) position that economic man or woman was a more subtle and devious creature than the usual self-interest seeking assumption typically conceded. In an amusing passage he enlarged on Williamson's point that agents who were skilled at dissembling realized transactional advantages; he noted this was the same message delivered by Leo Durocher—"Nice guys finish last"—in less exact but more memorable terms. In short, Granovetter objected to the "peculiar assumption of modern economic theory that one's economic interest is pursued only by comparatively gentlemanly means" (1985: 488).

Most economists, Granovetter said, believed that this non-gentlemanly malfeasance could be avoided by market contracts and hierarchical controls. Other economists, he admitted, cited the existence of a "generalized morality" (Arrow, 1974: 26), which was an implicit agree-

ment among members of a given society to respect certain kinds of rights
for others.

Granovetter (1985) rejected both institutional arrangements and generalized morality as a basis for trust and, instead, argued that economic
behavior was embedded in informal social relationships and the obligations inherent in those relationships. In short, he said that trust in the past
led to trust in the future. That is, if a person found that a group of people
with whom he or she had conducted economic transactions in the past
had acted according to the informal or "embedded" obligations of the
society in the past, he or she would be more likely to trust those group
members in the future. This could, Granovetter admitted, lead to even
greater opportunities for malfeasance if that trust was broken because the
informal nature of the social obligation concept provided no enforcement
procedure.

Lewis and Weigert (1985: 968) reinforced the belief that trust was a
"collective attribute" based upon the relationships between people that
existed in a social system. They argued that trusting behavior could be
motivated either by strong positive affect for the object of trust (emotional
trust) or by good rational reasons for the awarding of trust (cognitive trust)
but more usually by some combination of both. Trust, they concluded,
was essentially social and normative rather than individual and calculative and, therefore, required prior social relationships to exist.

Zucker (1986: 54) explicitly stated that trust was a set of social expectations shared by everyone involved in an economic exchange. It included broad social rules, such as what was a "fair" rate of interest for a
given situation, and legitimate social processes, such as who had the
"right" to determine that rate of interest for that situation. These were the
background expectations, or common understandings "taken for granted"
as part of a "world known in common" among members of a society. They
resulted, Zucker argued, from three sources:

1. *Process based*—trust was tied to a record of past operations. Here,
   exchanges usually were limited to those whose exchange histories
   were known, and respected
2. *Person based*—trust was tied to similarities between people. Here,
   exchanges were limited to those with a common cultural system, with
   shared background expectations
3. *Institution based*—trust was tied to formal mechanisms such as pro-
   fessionalism or third-party insurance. Here exchanges were limited to
   those with access to those guarantees.

Shapiro (1987), however, rejected the argument that trust could be
institution based. Despite the ethics codes, practice standards, and regulatory statutes in which the common expectations were embedded, she
wrote, the temptations to lie, to steal, and to misrepresent the safety and
security of institution-based guarantees continued to exist. She asked the
obvious question: Who guards the guardians? Who would ensure that the
professionals and third-party guarantors would follow the rules of fiduciary disinterestedness? She concluded that "in complex societies in

which agency relationships are indispensable, opportunities for agent abuse sometimes irresistible, and the ability to specify and enforce substantive norms governing the outcomes of agency action nearly impossible, a spiraling evolution of procedural norms, structural constraints, and insurance-like arrangements seems inevitable" (Shapiro, 1987: 649).

Reichman (1989: 188) reached the same conclusion following an examination of fiduciary relationships in capital markets. Role conflicts exist, she wrote, and have not been resolved. She included a memorable quote from Stevens (1987) to show the difficulty of relying upon legal constraints and regulatory procedures: "In the pretzel logic of insider trading laws, gaining secret information from insiders such as lawyers, bankers or arbs is illegal; uncovering it on your own is ingenious. The former makes you a criminal; the latter makes you rich."

CONCLUSIONS FROM THE ORGANIZATIONAL THEORY LITERATURE

Scholars from a wide range of disciplines have looked at trust in a number of different contexts (see Table 1) and, despite the claims that little has been done or that no agreement can be found, have reached a number of similar conclusions:

1. Trust is generally expressed as an optimistic expectation on the part of an individual about the outcome of an event or the behavior of a person. The trusting individual is always thought to expect the best. This is perhaps not immediately obvious in the contexts of economic transactions and social structures, where conditions of distrust are predominant. In such cases, it is assumed that prudent individuals expect the worst, and protect themselves against that outcome or behavior by means of market contracts, hierarchical controls, legal requirements, and informal obligations. But trust is the opposite of those untrustworthy assumptions; it remains an optimistic expectation when viewed in positive rather than negative terms.

2. Trust generally occurs under conditions of vulnerability to the interests of the individual and dependence upon the behavior of other people. An essential part of the definition of trust is the expectation that the loss if trust is broken will be much greater than the gain when trust is maintained; otherwise, the decision to trust would be simple economic rationality. Also integral to the definition is the belief that probability that the trust will be broken is both unknown and outside the control of the trusting individual; otherwise, the decision would again be simple economic rationality, though this time adjusted for a known degree of risk. Why, then, would any rational individual trust another person, group, or firm and thus become vulnerable to greater harm than good and dependent upon the uncertain actions of others? Perhaps there is little choice, for the reasons that follow.

3. Trust is generally associated with willing, not forced, cooperation and with the benefits resulting from that cooperation. Except within the context of individual actions, where trust is viewed as a means for dealing with complexity by eliminating unlikely scenarios and alternatives, the objective of trust is usually expressed as an attempt to increase or facilitate cooperation and/or the potential for joint benefits.

TABLE 1
Comparison of the Behavioral Definitions of Trust

Individual actions	Optimistic expectations of the outcome of an uncertain event under conditions of personal vulnerability.
Assumption	Nonrational behavior based upon past experiences and future forecasts.
Goal/intent	Gain the ability to deal with complexity by eliminating many scenarios and alternatives.
Moral content	Interests of trusting person should be placed ahead of those of the trusted person.
Interpersonal relationships	Optimistic expectations of the behavior of a second person under conditions of personal vulnerability and dependence.
Assumption	Nonrational behavior, based upon characteristics and traits of both individuals.
Goal/intent	Improve cooperation between individuals within a group or an organization.
Moral content	An implicit promise from one person not to bring harm to the other.
Economic transactions	Optimistic expectations of the behavior of a stakeholder of the firm under conditions of organizational vulnerability and dependence.
Assumption	Economically rational behavior, constrained by contracts and controls.
Goal/intent	Improve cooperation by the stakeholder within manager/stakeholder relationships.
Moral content	A genuine responsiveness to the needs of the other party in an economic exchange.
Social structures	Optimistic expectations of the behavior of managers and professionals under conditions of social vulnerability.
Assumption	Socially rational behavior, directed by formal requirements and informal obligations.
Goal/intent	Increase cooperation between diverse elements of society.
Moral content	Informal rules have a normative content with "fair" standards and a "right" to act.

Cooperation and ultimate benefits are particularly relevant regarding stakeholders—the suppliers, distributors, creditors, owners, employees, and managers—of a business firm. Cooperation between those groups is obviously important to improve performance and is acknowledged to be so by transactional cost economists, but the argument made by these scholars is that cooperation cannot be assumed through trust, but must be enforced through contracts and controls.

4. Trust is generally difficult to enforce. Except for the contexts of individual actions and interpersonal relationships where loss of control is frankly acknowledged but contracts and hierarchies are not considered as a means of regaining that control, the major emphasis of much of the literature on trust has been placed upon enforcement

procedures. Market contracts, hierarchical controls, legal requirements, and "embedded" obligations are all considered, recommended,
yet ultimately found wanting. In economic exchange analysis it is
thought that contracts and controls are expensive substitutes for trust
and have the undesirable side effect of reducing innovative and cooperative behaviors. In social structure analysis it is acknowledged that
the legal requirements and professional obligations are ineffective
because of the presence of severe conflicts of interest and the lack of
effective oversight procedures.

5. Trust is generally accompanied by an assumption of an acknowledged
   or accepted duty to protect the rights and interests of others. An expectation of generous or helpful or, at the very least, nonharmful behavior on the part of the trusted person, group, or firm is a continual
   undercurrent in discussions of trust in all four of the approaches of
   organizational theory:
   - Barber (1983) talked specifically about the need to place the interests
     of the trusting person ahead of those of the trusted person.
   - Meeker (1983) said that the trusting person expected helpful behavior
     from the trusted person.
   - Butler and Cantrell (1984) suggested that four moral values—
     integrity, consistency, loyalty, and openness—were essential com-
     ponents in any definition of trust.
   - Zucker (1986) believed that trust was based upon "fair" social rules
     and generally accepted "rights" for each of the participants in an
     exchange.
   - Rempel and Holmes (1986) suggested that caring for the trusting
     person's welfare was an essential element in the concept of trust.
   - Gambetta (1988) stated that trust was the probability that one eco-
     nomic actor would make decisions or take actions that would be
     beneficial or, at the very least, not be detrimental to the other.
   - Friedland (1990) thought that trust had to include a genuine respon-
     siveness to the needs of the other party.
   - Butler (1991) said that trust included an implicit promise from one
     individual not to bring harm to the other.
   - Ring and Van de Ven (1992) concluded that confidence in the other's
     goodwill was fully as important as confidence in the other's behav-
     ior.

These voluntarily accepted duties clearly go beyond a negative promise not to harm the interests of the other party; they seem to provide a
positive guarantee that the rights and interests of the other party will be
included in the final outcome. Behavior that protects the rights and interests of others is, of course, directly contrary to neoclassical economic
theory, yet this belief in consideration, kindness, or even compassion is
present in all of the approaches explored, just below the level of explicit
inclusion in the proposed definitions.

If we attempt to draw the essentials from each of the approaches in
which the concept of trust has been used in the literature of organizational
theory and its related disciplines, with a synthesis of the five major similarities listed above, we could propose the definition:

> *Trust* is the optimistic expectation by one person, group, or
> firm of the behavior of another person, group, or firm in a

> common endeavor or economic exchange, under conditions of
> vulnerability and dependence on the part of the trusting party,
> for the purpose of facilitating cooperation between both par-
> ties that will result in an ultimate joint gain but, given the lack
> of effective contractural, hierarchical, legal, or social enforce-
> ment methods, with reliance upon a voluntarily accepted duty
> by the trusted party to protect the rights and interests of all
> others engaged in the endeavor or exchange.

It is relatively easy to argue that this is not an acceptable definition.
What exactly is an optimistic expectation? How vulnerable to harm and
how dependent upon the behavior of others does the trusting party have
to be? Do both parties have to agree that cooperation is the goal, or can
one be thinking more independent thoughts? What happens if the ultimate joint gain is not realized; is the trust automatically abrogated? Do
we have to confirm the lack of effective market contracts, hierarchical
controls, legal requirements, and social obligations in each instance of
trust, or can we assume that these are inoperable? It is possible to avoid
most, if not all, of these problems of imprecision with a simpler and much
shorter definition:

> Trust is the reliance by one person, group, or firm upon a
> voluntarily accepted duty on the part of another person,
> group, or firm to recognize and protect the rights and interests
> of all others engaged in a joint endeavor or economic ex-
> change.

A reliance by one person, group, or firm upon a voluntarily accepted
duty on the part of another person, group, or firm to recognize and protect
the rights and interests of all others engaged in a joint endeavor or economic exchange automatically leaves the first party vulnerable to extensive harm and dependent upon the uncertain behavior of the other person, group, or firm if the trust is broken. The reliance must be for the
purpose of improving cooperation and achieving benefits; no rational
person would increase his or her vulnerability and dependence in order to
expand conflict and multiply losses. The lack of effective enforcement
procedures is a given, once the reliance is on behavior that recognizes
and protects the rights and interests of others; such behavior that necessarily combines self-interest and other interest to a degree that satisfies
the accepted or acknowledged duty cannot presently be measured and,
therefore, cannot presently be controlled.

In brief, the proposed definition of trust has the advantages of being
simple, short, and direct. It is certainly parsimonious. The question that
remains is whether or not it is useful, and that depends upon whether we
can sufficiently define the voluntarily accepted duty of recognizing and
protecting the rights and interests of others. What does it mean to recognize and protect another's rights? There is no agreement in organizational
theory that the trusted person has to put the rights and interests of the

394   *Academy of Management Review*   April

trusting person ahead of his or her own, even though this was specifically suggested by Barber (1983). Instead, the agreement seems to stop well short of that rigid "no self-interest" rule, with general admonitions to be "helpful," to be "honest," to be "consistent," to be "loyal," to be "fair," to be "beneficial," to be "responsive," to be "nonharmful," and to evidence "good will." This means that the trusted person has to combine the rights and interests of the trusting party with his or her own, not substitute those rights and interests for his or her own, but there are no rules as to exactly how this is to be done, nor any standards as to what percentages or ratios among the different rights and interests can be considered to be "helpful," "honest," and "consistent," or "right" and "just" and "fair." How disinterested does a trusted person have to be to recognize and protect the rights and interests of trusting others? The literature of organizational theory does not tell us. Here we have to look to normative philosophy for help, for voluntary disinterestedness is a moral duty, owed by the "good" man or woman to others for the prevention of unwarranted harm, and "right" and "just" and "fair" are ethical terms, subject to definition by philosophical, not behavioral, standards.

TRUST IN NORMATIVE PHILOSOPHY

Most normative or moral philosophers have not written extensively about trust. The classical ethicists—Socrates, Plato, Aristotle, St. Augustine, St. Thomas Aquinas, Hobbes, Locke, Rousseau, Mill, Kant, Smith, Jefferson, Ross, Rawls, and Nozick—scarcely mention the term except occasionally as an aside or observation. The *Encyclopedia of Ethics* (1992) devotes less than 2 of its 600 pages to a discussion of the topic, and then cites only minor passages from Aristotle and Locke. Baier (1986: 232), who conducted her own survey of the philosophical literature on trust, was surprised at this lack of attention. "There has been a strange silence on the topic in the tradition of moral philosophy with which I am familiar [that is, in Western rather than Eastern thought and practice]," she said.

This "strange silence" is perhaps understandable when we consider the goal of Western moral philosophy. The goal has been to find the "first principle," or the ideal rule upon which all other rules could be based, that would lead to a "good" society. A "good" society has been defined (Rawls, 1967) as one in which the members willingly cooperate for the ultimate benefit of all.

The "willing cooperation" and the "ultimate benefit" together show that there is an obvious association between the definition of trust in organizational theory and the concept of the "good" society in moral philosophy. However, the search for the ideal decision rule has always been the crucial topic in moral philosophy, not the analysis of human behavior that might result from the use of that decision rule. Western moral philosophy, until recently, has been almost totally theoretical, with few applied concepts. Trust, consequently, was pushed to the background of normative ethics; it remained a result of proper actions, not a part of proper actions.

The ideal decision rule has not been found, of course. Instead there are now believed to be a number of alternative decision rules (Hosmer, 1991) that provide different perspectives or views of moral problems and that are applied in sequence to gain understanding and insight. This is the approach to business ethics that Dunfee (1991) termed "ecumenical." Ten of these first principles or decision rules are summarized in Table 2.

Each of the first principles or decision rules or alternative perspectives from the classical ethicists asserts that a "good" man or woman should act not for his or her short-term self gain only, but for a mixture of that gain together with his or her vision of the future (Protagoras), his or her sense of self-worth (Aristotle), his or her goal of community (St. Augustine), his or her fear of retribution (Hobbes), his or her calculation of social benefit (Mill), his or her understanding of universal duty (Kant), or his or her recognition of individual rights (Jefferson). This listing could easily be extended to the distributive justice of Rawls and the contributive liberty of Nozick, as shown in Table 2. The only exception to the denial of primary self-interest is the economic efficiency of Adam Smith, who believed that the good man or woman should act for his or her short-term self gain, but that those individual actions would lead, through the invisible hand of market forces, toward an ultimate net benefit for society.

Each of these first principles or decision rules or alternative perspectives provides, then, a means of limiting or constraining the self-interests of the decision maker. They do not eliminate that self-interest, for that would be mere altruism. What they do, as stated in a recent and very pragmatic article by Magee and Nayak (1994: 67), is to take the valid self-interest of others into account. "When all interested parties cannot participate in making a decision—which is often the case—the decision maker must take the legitimate interests of all constituents into account, whether they are there to argue their interests or not." It is both difficult and presumptuous to attempt to do this—take the legitimate interests of *all* constituents into account—by merely placing one's self in the position of each of those constituent groups and attempting to envisage their true self-interests. There are too many groups, and their interests are too varied and private. The normative rules or first principles of moral philosophy were developed to replace that admittedly awkward reasoning method.

All of these normative rules, designed to take the legitimate interests of others into account, were assumed by moral philosophers to encourage greater trust among and improve cooperation between the diverse elements of society and, consequently, result in "good" (in the widest possible sense of that term) for the society rather than the individual. Aristotle, for example, proposed that the warriors, merchants, and statesmen of Athens should follow the 14 precepts of Nicomachean Ethics (be courageous, be temperate, be gentle, be truthful, be honest, be proud, and so

396   *Academy of Management Review*   April

TABLE 2
Brief Summaries of Ten Ethical Principles[a]

Self-interests (Protagoras and others). If we would all look after our own self-interests, without forcefully interfering with the rights of others, then society as a whole will be better off because it will be as free and productive as possible. Over the short term this would seem to be a simple recipe for selfishness; over the long term, however, it creates a much more meaningful guide for action because our long-term interests are usually very different from our short-term desires. The principle, then, can be expressed as "Never take any action that is not in the long-term self-interests of yourself and the organization to which you belong."

Personal virtues (Plato and Aristotle). The lack of forceful interference with the rights of others is not enough. As we each pursue our own self-interests, even those that are good only over the long term, we have to adopt a set of standards for our "fair" and courteous treatment of one another. We have to be honest, open, and truthful, for example, to eliminate distrust, and we should live temperately so as not to incite envy. In short, we should be proud of our actions and of our lives. The principle, then, can be expressed as "Never take any action that is not honest, open, and truthful, and which you would not be proud to see reported widely in national newspapers and on network television."

Religious injunctions (St. Augustine). Honesty, truthfulness, and temperance are not enough; we also have to have some degree of compassion and kindness toward others to form a truly "good" society. That compassion and kindness is best expressed in the Golden Rule, which is not limited to the Judeo-Christian tradition but is part of almost all of the world's religions. Reciprocity—"Do unto others as you would have them do unto you"—and compassion together build a sense of community. The principle, then, can be expressed as "Never take any action that is not kind, and that does not build a sense of community, a sense of all of us working together for a commonly accepted goal."

Government requirements (Hobbes and Locke). Compassion and kindness would be ideal if everyone would be compassionate and kind, but everyone won't be. People compete for property and for position, and some people will always take advantage of others. In order to restrain that competition and maintain peace within our society, we all have to agree to obey some basic rules from a central authority that has the power to enforce those rules. In a democratic nation, we think of that authority as the government and of those rules as the law. The principle, then, can be expressed as "Never take any action that violates the law, for the law represents the minimal moral standards of our society."

Utilitarian benefits (Bentham and Mill). Common obedience to basic rules would work if the people associated with the central authority did not have self-interests of their own. They do. Consequently, we need a means of evaluating the laws of the government, and that same means can be used to evaluate the justice of our own actions. A law or an act is "right" if it leads to greater net social benefits than social harms. This is the principle that is often summarized as the *greatest good for the greatest number.* A more accurate way of expressing the principle is "Never take any action that does not result in greater good than harm for the society of which you are a part."

TABLE 2 (continued)

Universal rules (Kant). Net social benefit is elegant in theory, but the theory does not say anything about how we should measure either the benefits or the harms—what is your life or health or well-being worth?—nor how we should distribute those benefits and allocate those harms. What we need is a rule to eliminate the self-interest of the person who decides, and that rule must be applicable to everyone. This principle, then, can be expressed as "Never take any action that you would not be willing to see others, faced with the same or a closely similar situation, also be encouraged to take."

Individual rights (Rousseau and Jefferson). Eliminating self-interest on the part of the decision maker isn't really possible, given what people actually are like. They are self-interested. Consequently, we need a list of agreed-upon rights for everyone that will be upheld by everyone. These rights would certainly include guarantees against arbitrary actions of the government and would ensure freedom of speech, of assembly, of religion, etc., and would provide security against seizure of property, interference with privacy, or deprivation of liberty without due process. The principle, then, can be expressed as "Never take any action that abridges the agreed-upon rights of others."

Economic efficiency (Adam Smith). Basic rights are meaningless without the essentials of food, clothing, and shelter. Therefore, we should maximize the output of the needed goods and services by setting marginal revenues equal to marginal costs. At this point, the economic system will be operating as efficiently as possible, and we can reach a condition known as "Pareto Optimality," in which it is impossible to make any one person better off without harming someone else. The principle, then, is "Always act to maximize profits subject to legal and market constraints and with full recognition of external costs, for maximum profits under those conditions are the sign of the most efficient production."

Distributive justice (Rawls). The problem with the economic efficiency argument is that the market distributes the output of needed goods and services unjustly, for it excludes those who are poor, uneducated, or unemployed. We need a rule to ensure that those people are not left out. If we did not know who among us would be rich and who poor, who educated and who uneducated, then any rule that we made for the distribution of the output goods and services could be considered just. It can be argued that under those conditions—known as the "Social Contract"—the only agreement we could make would be that the poor and uneducated and unemployed should not be made worse off. The principle, then, is "Never take any action in which the least among us are harmed in some way."

Contributing liberty (Nozick). Perhaps liberty—the freedom to follow one's own self-interests within the constraints of the law and the market—is more important than justice—the right to be included in the overall distribution of goods and services. If so, then the only agreement that would be made under the conditions of the Social Contract—in which people do not know who would be rich or poor, who active or slothful—would be that no one should interfere with the self-development of others, for personal self-development will eventually contribute to society. The principle, then, is "Never take any action that will interfere with the rights of others for self-development and self-fulfillment."

^a Derived from Hosmer (1994).

398   *Academy of Management Review*   April

on) to reduce the conflict and increase the trust and cooperation between those ruling groups in Athenian society. St. Augustine, in a further example, proposed that members of his City of God should act for the community rather than for the person; his argument implied that nonrational faith in God led (he doesn't quite say this, but comes very close) to a nonrational trust in humanity, culminating in an ultimate degree of cooperation and "good." Hobbes, in a last example, proposed that men and women should always obey the laws of a central authority—the Leviathan—because otherwise continual strife would result in a society with no trust, no cooperation, no science or industry, and "the life of man: solitary, poor, nasty, brutish, and short" (Hobbes, 1936: 85).

Baier (1986: 234) agreed that cooperation was the major theme of moral philosophy, and that trust was essential to gain cooperation, but then asked the important question: What was the difference between trusting others and merely relying upon them? She answered by saying that it was reliance upon their good will as distinct from their regular habits. "Trust," she concluded, "is reliance upon another's good will." It is instructive that Baier (1986), from philosophical ethics, and Ring and Van de Ven (1992), from organizational theory, have come independently to almost identical definitions of the concept of trust.

"Good will" is the most precisely defined concept in normative or moral philosophy. It is the topic of Kant's *Groundwork for the Metaphysics of Morals* (1964: 1), which opens with the statement: "Nothing can possibly be conceived in the world, or even out of it, which can be called good without qualification except a good will." Kant then showed logically that the only will that could be called "good" without qualification was the will that followed the universal law that if it was right for one person to take a given action then it must be right for all others to be encouraged to take that same action. This is the first formulation of the Categorical Imperative. The second formulation—which Kant proved has exactly the same meaning—is that we should all treat other people as ends in themselves, individuals worthy of dignity and respect, and never as means to our own ends.

Professor Baier is very evidently a Kantian, and she defined trust in terms of that universalist or duty principle. Others might prefer Bentham and Mill and make use of the utilitarian or outcome principle. Still others might follow the widely separated in time but closely similar in concept Hobbes, Locke, Rawls, and Nozick and be social contractarians. A defiant few still hold to the vision of Protagoras, the virtue of Aristotle, or the compassion of St. Augustine. A growing number are ecumenicists, as explained previously, and attempt to find insights rather than rules by applying all 10 of the basic ethical principles. Any of these approaches will, it is the essential claim of normative or moral philosophy, ensure the *proper* mixture of other-interested and self-interested behavior on the part of all who employ that approach, which will lead in turn to trust between individuals and cooperation within society. Trust is therefore a result of "proper" decisions and actions, and proper decisions and actions are those that follow the ethical principles of analysis. We can, then, derive the following definition of trust from the essential goal—the "good" society—of moral philosophy:

> *Trust* is the result of "right," "just," and "fair" behavior—that is, morally correct decisions and actions based upon the ethical principles of analysis—that recognizes and protects the rights and interests of others within society.

Trust in philosophic ethics is the *result* of a given decision or action that recognizes and protects the rights and interests of other people through an application of the ethical principles of analysis. These principles focus on what is "good" for the society rather than on what is "good" for the individual. If we focus on what is "good" for a society composed of individuals, we will automatically recognize and protect the rights and interests of all others within that society. Trust in organizational theory is the *expectation* of a similar behavior that recognizes and protects the interests of other people in order to increase willing cooperation and expand ultimate benefits within a joint endeavor or economic exchange. We can, then, synthesize a single definition of trust from the two intellectual traditions:

> *Trust* is the expectation by one person, group, or firm of ethically justifiable behavior—that is, morally correct decisions and actions based upon ethical principles of analysis—on the part of the other person, group, or firm in a joint endeavor or economic exchange.

PROPOSALS FOR EMPIRICAL RESEARCH

Ethically justifiable behavior, to repeat the argument for emphasis, consists of morally correct decisions and actions in which the interests of the society take the degree of precedence that is "right," that is "just," and that is "fair" over the interests of the individual. It is behavior that is "good" for society according to the ethical principles of normative philosophy, not according to the moral standards of a given group or culture. It should, according to the underlying assumptions of both organizational theory and normative philosophy, result in greater cooperation among the participants in a dyad, the stakeholders of a firm, or the citizens of a society.

If we make the next assumption, that greater cooperation among the participants in a dyad, the stakeholders of a firm, or the citizens of a society leads to improved performance by that dyad, firm, or society, then we have obvious opportunities for joint empirical research. There will be problems in measuring performance, of course, though those problems have been extensively discussed in the literature. There also will be difficulties in measuring the degree of other-interest versus self-interest in the original set of decisions or actions that generate trust, but let me suggest that a panel of applied ethicists would arrive at a surprisingly narrow distribution of the "proper" points along that spectrum in most moral problems of management so that deviations from what is "right" and "just" and "fair" can be measured.

"Why be moral?" is the most critical issue in normative philosophy. Why should a rational man or woman be concerned with the rights and interests of others? This a question that has troubled ethicists for centuries. (See, for example, "The Ring of Gyges," in Plato's *Dialogues* or "Why Should a Man Keep Contracts?") in Locke's *Concerning Human Understanding*. If researchers can show empirically that there is a connection—through trust—between the moral duty of managers and the output performance of organizations there would be an obvious impact upon philosophical ethics and—I would like to think—upon organizational theory as well. The intent of this article is to show, theoretically, that such a connection does indeed exist.

REFERENCES

Aquinas, Saint Thomas. 1965. Summa theologica. In A. Pagis (Ed.), *Introduction to St. Thomas Aquinas.* New York: McGraw Hill.

Aristotle. 1947. Nichomachean ethics. In R. McKeon (Ed), *Introduction to Aristotle.* New York: Random House.

Arrow, K. J. 1974. *The limits of organization.* New York: Norton.

Augustine, Saint. 1977. *The city of God* (D Marcus, Trans.). New York: Random House.

Baier, A. 1986. Trust and antitrust. *Ethics,* 96: 231–260.

Barber, B. 1983. *The logic and limits of trust.* New Brunswick, NJ: Rutgers University Press.

Bartolme, F. 1989. Nobody trusts the bosses completely—now what? *Harvard Business Review,* 67(2): 135–142.

Belasco, J. 1989. What went wrong? *Executive Excellence,* 6(4): 13–14.

Bennis, W. 1989. Why leaders can't lead. *Training and Development Journal,* 43(4): 35–39.

Bentham, J. 1948. *An introduction to the principles of morals and legislation.* Oxford: Basil Blackwell.

Blau, P. M. 1964. *Exchange and power in social life.* New York: Wiley.

Bluhm, L. H. 1987. Trust, terrorism and technology. *Journal of Business Ethics,* 6: 333–342.

Bok, S. 1978. *Lying: Moral choice in public and private life.* New York: Pantheon Books.

Bradach, J. L., & Eccles, R. G. 1989. Price, authority and trust: From ideal types to plural forms. *Annual Review of Sociology,* 15: 97–118.

Bromily, P., & Cummings, L. L. 1992. *Transaction costs in organizations with trust.* Working paper No. 28, Strategic Management Research Center, University of Minnesota, Minneapolis.

Butler, J. K. 1991. Toward understanding and measuring conditions of trust: Evolution of a conditions of trust inventory. *Journal of Management,* 17: 643–663.

Butler, J. K., & Cantrell, R. S. 1984. A behavioral decision theory approach to modeling dyadic trust in superiors and subordinates. *Psychological Reports,* 55: 19–28.

Carnevale, P. J. D., Pruitt, D. G., & Carrington, P. J. 1982. Effects of future dependence, liking and repeated requests for help on helping behavior. *Social Psychology Quarterly,* 45: 9–14.

Clawson, J. 1989. You can't manage them if they don't trust you. *Executive Excellence,* 6(4): 10–11.

Coleman, J. S. 1984. Introducing social structure into economic analysis. *American Economic Review,* 74: 84–88.

Covey, S. 1989. Seven chronic problems. *Executive Excellence,* 6(2): 3–6.

Deutsch, M. 1958. Trust and suspicion. *Journal of Conflict Resolution,* 2: 265–279.

Dunfee, T. W. 1991. Business ethics and extant social contracts. *Business Ethics Quarterly,* 1: 23–51.

Eisenstadt, S. N. 1968. *Max Weber on charisma and institution building.* Chicago: Chicago University Press.

Encyclopedia of ethics. 1992. New York: Garland.

Freeman, R. 1984. *Strategic management: A stakeholder approach.* Marshfield, MA: Pitman.

Friedland, N. 1990. Attribution of control as a determinant of cooperation in exchange interactions. *Journal of Applied Social Psychology,* 20: 303–320.

Gabarro, J. J. 1978. The development of trust, influence and expectations. In A. G. Athos & J. J. Gabarro (Eds.), *Interpersonal behaviors: Communication and understanding in relationships:* 290–303. Englewood Cliffs, NJ: Prentice Hall.

Gambetta, D. 1988. Can we trust trust? In D. Gambetta (Ed.), *Trust: Making and breaking cooperative relations:* 213–238. New York: Basil Blackwell.

Golembiewski, R. T., & McConkie, M. 1975. The centrality of interpersonal trust in group processes. In C. L. Cooper (Ed.), *Theories of group processes:* 131–185. New York: Wiley.

Granovetter, M. 1985. Economic action and social structure: The problem of embeddedness. *American Journal of Sociology,* 91: 481–510.

Hill, C. W. L. 1990. Cooperation, opportunism, and the invisible hand: Implications for transaction cost theory. *Academy of Management Review,* 15: 500–513.

Hirsch, F. 1978. *Social limits to growth.* Cambridge, MA: Harvard University Press.

Hobbes, T. 1973. *Leviathan.* New York: Dutton. (Original work published 1936)

Horton, T. R., & Reid, P. C. 1991. *Beyond the trust gap: Forging a new partnership between managers and their employees.* Homewood, IL: Business One Irwin.

Hoskisson, R. E., & Hitt, M. A. 1988. Strategic control systems and relative R&D investment in large multiproduct firms. *Strategic Management Journal,* 9: 605–621.

Hosmer, L. T. 1991. *The ethics of management* (2nd ed.). Homewood, IL: Irwin.

Hosmer, L. T. 1994. *Moral leadership in business.* Homewood, IL: Irwin.

Husted, B. W. 1989. Trust in business relations: Directions for empirical research. *Business and Professional Ethics Journal,* 8(2): 23–40.

Jefferson, T. L. 1939. In S. Padover (Ed.), *Writings on democracy.* Westport, CT: Greenwood Press.

Jennings, E. E. 1971. *Routes to the executive suite.* New York: McGraw-Hill.

Kant, I. 1964. *Groundwork for the metaphysics of morals.* New York: Harper & Row.

Lewis, J. D., & Weigert, A. 1985. Trust as social reality. *Social Forces,* 63: 967–985.

Locke, J. 1952. *The second treatise of government.* Indianapolis, IN: Bobbs-Merrill.

Locke, J. 1959. *An essay concerning human understanding.* New York: Dover.

Luhmann, N. 1980. *Trust and power.* New York: Wiley.

Luhmann, N. 1988. Familiarity, confidence, trust: Problems and alternatives. In D. Gambetta
    (Ed.), *Trust: Making and breaking cooperative relations:* 94–108. New York: Basil Black-
    well.

Magee, J. F., & Nayiak, P.R. 1994. Leaders' perspectives on business ethics: An interim
    report. *Prism,* 1st Quarter: 65–77.

Meeker, B. F. 1983. Cooperative orientation, trust, and reciprocity. *Human Relations,* 37:
    225–243.

Michalos, A. 1990. The impact of trust on business, international security, and the quality of
    life. *Journal of Business Ethics,* 9: 619–638.

Mill, J. S. 1951. *Utilitarianism.* New York: Hutton.

Nozick, R. 1974. *Anarchy, state and utopia.* New York: Basic Books.

Plato. 1955. *Republic* (B. Jowett, Trans.). New York: Random House.

Plato. 1987. *Dialogues* [of Socrates]. (B. Jowett, Trans.). New York: Random House.

Protagoras. 1968. Man is the measure. In J. M. Robinson (Ed.), *An introduction to early Greek
    philosophy.* New York: Houghton-Mifflin.

Rawls, J. 1967. *A theory of justice.* Cambridge, MA: Harvard University Press.

Reichman, N. 1989. Breaking confidences: Organizational influences on insider trading.
    Sociological Quarterly, 30: 185–204.

Rempel, J. K., & Holmes, J. G. 1986. How do I trust thee? *Psychology Today,* 20(2): 28–34.

Ring, P. S., & Van de Ven, A. H. 1992. Structuring cooperative relationships between orga-
    nizations. *Strategic Management Journal,* 13: 483–498.

Ross, W. D. 1930. *The right and the good.* Oxford, England: Clarendon Press.

Rotter, J. B. 1967. A new scale for the measurement of trust. *Journal of Personality,* 35:
    651–665.

Rotter, J. B., Chance, J. E., & Phares, E. J. 1972. *Applications of a social learning theory of
    personality.* New York: Holt, Rinehart and Winston.

Rousseau, J-J. 1967. Du contract social ou principes du droit politique. [The social contract
    and the principles of law]. In *Oerves Completes,* vol. 2: 518–525. Paris: Editions due
    Seuil.

Shapiro, S. 1987. The social control of impersonal trust. *American Journal of Sociology,* 93:
    623–658.

Smith, A. 1952. *An inquiry into the nature and causes of the wealth of nations.* Chicago:
    Benton.

Stevens, M. 1987. *The insiders.* New York: Putnam.

Watson, C. 1991. Doing what's right and doing well in business. *Business Forum,* 16(2):
    28–30.

Williamson, O. E. 1975. *Markets and hierarchies: Analysis and antitrust implications.* New
    York: Free Press.

Williamson, O. E. 1985. *The economic institutions of capitalism.* New York: Free Press.

Zand, D. E. 1972. Trust and managerial problem solving. *Administrative Science Quarterly,* 17: 229–239.

Zucker, L. G. 1986. Production of trust: Institutional sources of economic structure, 1840–1920. In B. M. Staw & L. L. Cummings (Eds.), *Research in organizational behavior,* vol. 8: 53–111. Greenwich, CT: JAI Press.

LaRue Tone Hosmer received his D.B.A. from Harvard University. He is currently professor of corporate strategy and managerial ethics at the School of Business Administration of the University of Michigan. His current research focuses on the relationship between ethical management and organizational performance.

Part X
Lobbying (Lobbying and Corporate Citizenship)

[37]

ETHICAL STANDARDS FOR BUSINESS LOBBYING: SOME PRACTICAL SUGGESTIONS

J. Brooke Hamilton, III
David Hoch

Abstract: Rather than being inherently evil, business lobbying is a socially responsible activity which needs to be restrained by ethical standards. To be effective in a business environment, traditional ethical standards need to be translated into language which business persons can speak comfortably. Economical explanations must also be available to explain why ethical standards are appropriate in business. Eight such standards and their validating arguments are proposed with examples showing their use. Internal dialogues regarding the ethics of lobbying objectives and tactics will plausibly occur only in businesses which recognize social responsibility mandates. Public interest stakeholders could hasten this recognition by making use of information made available by the Lobbying Disclosure Act of 1995 to institute external dialogues regarding lobbying by specific businesses and industry groups. Given practical ethical standards and the information on business lobbying provided by the law, the press, corporate activists, consumers, pension fund managers and the public can apply pressure for ethical lobbying practices.

Introduction

Most business activities in the political realm are perceived to be greedy and self-interested attempts to extend the influence of the board room into governmental policy making at all levels. The famous "Harry and Louise" campaign of the independent health insurance industry, credited with doing much to raise public doubts about the Clinton health care reform plan, the recent activities of the tobacco industry in California to subvert the spending of dedicated tax money on anti-smoking campaigns and the lobbying of timber interests to eviscerate environmental protections through the Timber Salvage Act (Timber) are recently publicized examples of business political activity. Political candidates and public and environmental interest groups have criticized the effectiveness of business lobbying coupled with campaign contributions. The charge is that well-financed business lobbying has captured the political process and prevented other legitimate voices from being heard in the debate on public issues (Birnbaum, 1993). Large corporations and industry trade groups, with their deep pockets, are seen as having undue influence and various reforms have been proposed to correct the situation (Weber, 1996). As Christopher Stone asked,

"Exactly what is it about corporations, and exactly what is it about the institutions we have available to control them, that so often seems to leave the one so frustratingly outside the grasp of the other (1975)?"

Much discussion is taking place regarding structural changes in the financing and organizing of political campaigns and parties to correct business abuses of the political system.   In the spirit of Stone's advocacy of social controls in addition to legal structures (1975), this paper proposes practical steps to creating an ethical dialogue on the form and content of business lobbying. The application of ethical standards to business lobbying should benefit both commercial and public interests.

The argument begins with the proposition that, rather than being inherently evil, business lobbying is a socially responsible activity. The promotion of the public interest and self-interest through lobbying, however, needs to be restrained by ethical standards. What is needed are some practical standards that could actually function in internal and external dialogues on lobbying objectives and tactics. We propose eight such standards, using examples from environmental issues to show how the standards can be used to evaluate business lobbying.

Is there any realistic hope that such dialogues will actually occur? Yes, because of new social mandates on business, coupled with new information made available by the Lobbying Disclosure Act of 1995 (Lobbying). Given practical ethical standards and information on lobbying provided by the law, the press can conduct an external discussion of business lobbying, corporate activists can use shareholder resolutions to pressure for internal dialogue, consumers can make choices of products and services, pension fund managers can apply pressure for ethical lobbying practices and the informed public can indicate its doubts about the legitimacy of unethical business lobbying. Thus this paper suggests both ethical standards and groups who can encourage business to use these standards to evaluate their lobbying activities.

Lobbying as a Socially Responsible Activity for Businesses

In discussing corporate political involvement, it is necessary to dispel the belief that such activity is inherently unethical because it promotes self-interest through concentrated corporate power, and to abandon the view that ethical corporations should passively accept laws passed by "the will of the people" through democratically elected representatives. To the contrary, in order to fulfill their social responsibilities (as well as promote their self-interest), corporations ought to lobby.

An examination of criteria proposed for deciding what socially responsible actions a corporation should undertake (Pava & Krausz, 1995 and Wood, 1994), suggests that lobbying is not only a right but an obligation. Pava and Krausz indicate that corporations or industry groups should undertake socially responsible or responsive activities when they possess "local knowledge" of a problem, have some "level of responsibility" to act, can point to a "shared consensus among corporate stakeholders" in favor of involvement, and that these three criteria have some "relationship to financial performance" of the corporation.

An application of the Pava & Krausz criteria to business lobbying as a socially responsible activity indicates that it can be legitimate. Corporations and industry groups may have relevant 'local knowledge' of a social problem and how to remediate it, ethically obliging them to engage in the political process. Timber companies, for example, with their knowledge of timber management, should be engaged in the debate over how best to manage private and public forests. If a corporation or industry has some level of responsibility for having created a problem whose solution requires public policy decision making at the state or national level, that corporation or industry should contribute to the public policy debate as well as to the implementation of the decisions. If logging has contributed to the degradation of stream bed habitat which threatens the salmon, the timber industry should be contributing to the debate regarding effective conservation practices. There may be stakeholder consensus that the corporation should promote certain values or policies in the political arena through lobbying, and corporations and industry groups often have the resources to carry out these activities.

Wood's principle of public responsibility states that businesses are responsible for outcomes related to their primary and secondary areas of involvement with society, so corporations involved in the timber and lumber businesses should be involved in the molding of public policy governing the forests. But she also maintains that society grants legitimacy and power to businesses and those who wield it irresponsibly tend to lose it. Thus corporations which seek to influence the making of public policy must do so in legitimate ways or society may withdraw the franchise of businesses to influence the legislative and regulatory processes. Hiring of government officials by businesses was seen to be an illegitimate way to gain government contracts and revolving door legislation outlawed this practice at the federal level. Wood's principle of managerial responsibility suggests that individual business persons who believe in the correctness of their cause should take action by lobbying to support it.

Stakeholder theory also provides grounds for arguing for the legitimacy of business lobbying. Corporations have a duty to represent their stakeholders in the political arena. Critics often label this representation as self-interested greed, but it can be legitimate for corporate officers to promote their interests and those of their stakeholders. Corporate lobbying is necessary to represent the interests of the customers in quality goods and services at realistic prices; the interests of workers to have jobs and incomes; the interests of communities to have a tax base; and the interests of stockholders who have a reasonable desire for profits. Thus timber companies argue that stream bed buffers confiscate their resources for public benefit without compensation; that access to federal timber promotes lower cost housing for consumers; and that loggers, millworkers and their communities will suffer greatly if old growth forests are completely closed to cutting. The fact that their interests conflict with other important interests does not necessarily make them illegitimately self-serving. Corporations are in a unique position to promote their stakeholders' interests and have a duty to do so.

Lobbying for the Public Interest or Self Interest: the Need for Ethical Standards

This claim that corporations can legitimately lobby on behalf of the interests of their stakeholders seems to run contrary to the proposal that in order to act as responsible citizens, businesses should regard political activity as different from the pursuit of private interests. Weber (1996) suggests that corporate political activity ". . .

should, perhaps, be understood as a different type of activity, . . . to be governed by different goals and standards." These goals and standards involve the pursuit of public rather than private goods. What we are suggesting, however, is that the standards for evaluating lobbying are better understood not by a "public interest versus private interest" distinction but as the ethical standards and value claims that determine what is legitimate in both public and private goods. Just as individuals may legitimately act as consumers to promote their private good or as citizens to promote the public good (Sagoff, 1986), so businesses can legitimately promote their private goods and the public good. The decision as to when the public good requires subordination of one's private good, either for an individual or a business, is determined by ethical standards.

The role played by ethical standards can be made clearer by distinguishing among lobbying for the public interest, lobbying for legitimate self-interest and lobbying for illegitimate or selfish self-interest. The public interest involves the good of the whole of society, including all interest-bearing or intrinsically valuable entities such as persons, trees and endangered species, and including the good of future generations as well as the present (and perhaps even a measure of respect for the past). But what constitutes the public interest, how it should be distributed among the various interest-bearing entities, and which of the entities have intrinsic as well as instrumental value are matters that are subject to different interpretations (Hoch, 1995). Environmentalists may see the public interest as requiring more wildlife refuges and less energy production or more redwoods and fewer or different jobs for loggers and mill hands. Businesses and their stakeholder constituents on the other hand may see the public interest as including responsible access to energy reserves and less pristine wilderness or as fewer redwoods and more jobs for loggers and millworkers. Though they may disagree, environmentalists and businesses are conducting a legitimate debate over what constitutes the public interest. Thus lobbying on environmental issues (as well as other issues) is public interest lobbying insofar as it advances a conception of the public good. Environmentalists may engage in this activity more often than businesses but businesses engage in this type of lobbying also.

Arguments in support of a conception of what is in the public interest are based on ethical principles—notions like utility, respect for persons and other intrinsically valuable entities, rights and justice—and on perceptions of what is more and less valuable. Thus it is important for those carrying on a debate over what constitutes the public interest be able to recognize and evaluate the ethical or value claims that are being made. It is this dialogue over what really is in the public interest that makes representative democracy so creative.

Much of business lobbying, rather than being in the public interest, is "special interest" lobbying which seeks to gain an advantage for a particular business or industry group or its stakeholders. The fact that this political activity is self-interested does not make it inherently wrong. Special advantages for one business do not necessarily come at the expense of others or at the expense of the general welfare and may in fact promote the interests of others and of the common good. The Timber Salvage Rider was advanced by the timber and mill interests as just such a proposal that would increase wealth for all by harvesting downed and damaged timber in national forests. Whether the claim was true or was ignoring the costs to taxpayers of providing access was a matter of great controversy.

ETHICAL STANDARDS FOR BUSINESS LOBBYING   121

Self-interested lobbying for the transfer of wealth from one business or industry group to another or from the public interest to a private interest may be legitimate if all sides present their case and a decision is made through democratic processes on the basis of maximizing benefits, respecting rights and insuring a just distribution. The redistribution of wealth argued for in the Timber Salvage Rider would have to be evaluated based on its balance of benefits over harms, its respect for the rights of others affected and the fairness of its distribution of benefits and burdens among the timber interests, the taxpayers, the salmon industry, the wildlife and others. That is, the objectives and tactics in lobbying for this act would have to be evaluated on ethical grounds to see if they were legitimately or illegitimately self-serving.

Self-interested lobbying becomes illegitimate, however, when the objectives or tactics allow corporations or industry groups to profit at the expense of others or at the expense of the general good without due consideration for the benefits and costs to and rights of others. In other words, self-interested lobbying becomes selfish lobbying when it violates the ethical norms which society has established to govern commerce among its members. Lobbying for entry into the Gulf War which would put countless young men and women and the U. S. Treasury in harms way in order to promote the sales of a company's pallets and paper cartons is a clear example of such illegitimate self-interested lobbying (Lee, 1991).

It is also important to note that arguments about what constitutes the public interest may either be combined with arguments for self-interest or difficult to distinguish from the promotion of self-interest. When environmentalists lobby against clearcutting because they do not like to see its effects as they drive by logged over woodlands, are they arguing for the preservation of an aesthetic which is in the public interest or in their private interest, or both? When businesses lobby against government regulations which restrict their profits by arguing that the cost of regulations and the loss of creativity are contrary to the public interest, are they in fact advancing their private or the public interest? The important question in both cases is not whether the interests are public or private but whether they are legitimate.

Thus rather than trying to distinguish self-interested political activity from public interested activity in order to determine what businesses may legitimately do, it seems clearer to suggest that both types of political activity be subjected to ethical scrutiny, public interest lobbying to determine by ethical argument what really is in the interest of the public and self-interested lobbying to determine if it shows an ethical regard for the legitimate interests of others and for the common good.

On this analysis, the problem with the political action by businesses arises when the players engaged in the democratic process come to see politics as an arena for self-interested action unrestrained by ethical considerations. Individual parties to the process do not and, in their view, should not restrain their actions because (1) that would put them at a competitive disadvantage to unrestrained actors, and (2) the contending of all self-interested forces in the process will bring about a compromise which is socially beneficial, and therefore ethical. Politics, like the processes of criminal law (Shaffer & Shaffer, 1991), has come to be viewed as a system in which the clash of amoral actions produces a moral result. Economists similarly have argued that the market's invisible hand molds a common good out of the self-interested search for individual gain. Sharing Milton Friedman's vision (1970) of a corporation bound only by law and social norms, corporate managers hold that the law allows lobbying and that political ethics free everyone to pursue their own interests.

This lack of ethical restraint extends not only to the objectives to be gained by lobbying but to the tactics used as well. Adopting an "all is fair in love and war" mentality, contestants in the influence game see winning as the ultimate validation of tactics, with little concern paid to the damage these tactics may do to democratic institutions and ultimately to society.

Justice and the good of the society, however, are not the products of conflicting political amoralities. Institutional democracy works best when its players are restrained by ethical concern for the fate of other participants and for the viability of the institutions in which they contend. Game theory research (Dixit & Nalebuff, 1991) and critiques of self-maximizing economics (Werhane, 1991) have shown that in a world with scarce benefits and a superfluity of burdens, cooperation and ethical competition produce better results for all.

Ethical Standards for Lobbying Activity

If the proposition that ethical principles have a place in politics is accepted, how can moral restraints be effectively integrated into corporate political behavior? The first step is to provide ethical standards for lobbying that can stimulate dialogue within the corporation. The second is to provide these standards and information on company activities to interested stakeholders outside of management so that they can engage managers in a public dialogue about the ethics of the company's lobbying activities. While by no means a complete remedy, these two steps provide a practical antidote to the amoral view of political activities which many businesses have assumed. We are fortunate to be at a point in the development of the study of business ethics and federal lobbying legislation that make both steps are possible.

Applying principles of ethical conduct to corporate lobbying activities requires a translation of these theories into a vocabulary that can be spoken in the board room (Waters, 1978) without the embarrassed silence that would attend the use of technical terms like 'deontology' or 'universalizing maxims.' What is needed are some easily remembered shorthand versions of ethics concepts (Nash, 1981) which can be used by managers along with "return on investment" and "product life-cycle." Given appropriate translation, utilitarianism, Kant's three principles, rights and justice considerations, social contract theories, and character ethics could all be utilized to evaluate the objectives and tactics of business lobbying. These ethical theories, when operationalized for business, yield the following rules:

1. Maximize good and minimize harm for those affected.
2. Don't make exceptions for yourself.
3. Let others make their own choices.
4. Use the publicity test.
5. Respect human rights.
6. Insure a fair distribution of benefits and burdens.
7. Honor the social contract.
8. Act in accordance with your character and the company's reputation.

ETHICAL STANDARDS FOR BUSINESS LOBBYING 123

In evaluating lobbying objectives and tactics, all eight rules should be considered. No one rule can screen for all aspects of what makes an action ethical (Velasquez, 1992; Boatright, 1993). Each offers a different insight into the complexities of a situation, highlighting the importance of good outcomes, of holding everyone to the same standard, of respecting others' choices or rights, of justifying inequalities, and of recognizing the importance of society and character. One rule will often provide a corrective for another: the emphasis on good outcomes for the majority needs to be tempered by concern for the needs and rights of individuals, and vice-versa. In most instances the rules all yield a similar judgment.

There are instances, however, in which the rules conflict. An action which maximizes happiness may deny choice to some or unfairly distribute benefits and burdens. When the rules conflict there is no super-rule to determine which will have priority. Individuals and institutions must recognize the conflict and continue the ethical dialogue with others who are affected (Bowen and Clark, 1993). Ultimately, those acting must choose the values or principles they think most important to uphold in that situation. At the least, conflicts at this level will be principled and the choices grounded on ethical principles.

In order to give these principles credibility in a business discussion, it is not enough to indicate that they are translations of traditional ethical principles developed within the philosophical and religious traditions of Western culture. Captivated as they are by the siren song of amorality not only in politics but in business (Carr, 1968), business persons may challenge the relevance of any ethical principles to their activities. Thus it is essential that these translated principles be accompanied by a brief argument for their validity. When challenged as to why "happiness should be maximized" or "the choices of others respected" in business or politics, a proponent of ethical restraints must have a compact explanation of why these principles are applicable.

While not proving the validity of the principles in an absolute sense, these explanations show how the principles follow from some fundamental values which most business persons share, though they may have never realized their connection to rules of ethics for business. The recognition, for example, that everyone wants to be happy and that all persons have equal value makes it legitimate to act to create the most happiness and the least unhappiness for all those who are affected. Those who reject values such as the intrinsic equality of persons will remain unconvinced of the validity of the rules, though they should recognize that this rejection places them at odds with the rest of society.

Applying Ethical Standards to Lobbying

The utilitarian approach, based as it is on balancing costs and benefits, is most akin to decision making approaches which businesses already employ. It requires that the action chosen *maximizes good and minimizes harm for all those affected*. This rule makes it legitimate to consider the good of others as well as the good of the individual corporation and its inside stakeholders. If all those affected are equally valuable and they all want happiness, then the ethical alternative is the one that maximizes happiness.

A corporate officer devising a lobbying strategy for the Timber Salvage Act, therefore, should ask what position would produce the greatest good for the greatest number. The good outcomes for external stakeholders who will be affected by the law (citizens, salmon, commercial fishers, etc) should be calculated as well as for the corporate stakeholders (stockholders, loggers, communities). Long-term as well as short-term consequences need to be considered. It is legitimate to argue for a transfer of benefits from others to corporate stakeholders as long as the transfer does not decrease the amount of good being produced or harm being avoided. To argue for a policy which benefits internal stakeholders (through timber harvesting) but produces an overall loss (through environmental degradation) would not be ethical. Setting a value in these calculations on the recreational uses of resources can be a straight forward process of determining what people would likely pay for such usage. Setting a value on a given level of species diversity or assigning a value to old growth forests which some claim to have intrinsic rather than instrumental value are processes over which ethical individuals can disagree. If the alternative which produces the greatest company benefits is unethical on a cost/benefit basis, then management should exercise moral imagination to determine other uses for company resources that will increase, rather than decrease, the overall good. Harvesting genuinely diseased or dying timber, for example, might increase the overall good if environmental safeguards were respected. Likewise the tactics used must pass utilitarian muster. The use of advertising to raise the anxiety level of a large block of older voters in order to benefit internal corporate stakeholders would be difficult to justify.

Kant's first principle, which requires universalizability, can be operationalized as *Don't make exceptions for yourself.* If all moral actors are equal, why should it be ethical for one company to do something that it is unethical for others to do? Why should Company A consider it ethical to harm the fisheries industry by suspending environmental protections when it would oppose another company doing the same to it? If a tactic used by one corporation, such as purchasing "grass roots" mailings to legislators, would destroy the usefulness of grass roots responses as a gauge of public sentiment, if the tactic were used by all political organizations, then it is unethical.

Kant's third principle to act as a universal legislator is often translated as the *publicity test.* What would be the reaction if a description of the company's lobbying activities were to appear in the Wall Street Journal? If the society is made up largely of ethical individuals, then their collective judgement regarding the rightness or wrongness of a course of action should carry some weight.

Human rights are the minimum liberties or welfare which persons must have access to in order to live a life which expresses their value. Recognizing the rights of all those involved is seen to be legitimate when a person recognizes the value in his/her life and the essential similarity of himself/herself to others. To apply the rights principle in regard to lobbying, one should ask *whether the substance or tactics in question infringe upon or promote basic rights.* Especially in regards to environmental issues, arguments have been made to extend the notion of rights to animals and other interest-bearing entities (Hoch, 1995).

Justice has to do with a *fair distribution of benefits and burdens.* Do those who receive the benefits also share the burdens, and do those who shoulder the burdens

ETHICAL STANDARDS FOR BUSINESS LOBBYING 125

also share the benefits? The initial assumption is that if everyone is equal, then everyone deserves equal shares. When various stakeholders deserve unequal shares, because of their contributions, sacrifices, needs, or effort expended, then an unequal distribution of benefits and burdens can be made based on these inequalities. Justice requires an explanation of why the unequal distribution is fair. Does the Timber Salvage Act give all of the benefits to the timber interests and leave all of the burdens to the environment and others dependent upon it? If so, why this is fair? Do bundled campaign contributions give more access to business lobbyists than to ordinary citizens? If so, why is this inequality fair?

Other ethical questions about the substance or tactics of corporate lobbying could also be raised on the basis of an implied social contract regarding the conditions necessary to preserve society for the good of all and how lobbying conforms with or affects the moral character of the corporation and its directors and managers. Questions regarding professional character might be couched in Aristotelian terms (Solomon, 1992) or in the Buddhist context of "right livelihood," a moral guide which proscribes work that causes harm (Whitmyer,1994).

The application of these ethical principles should temper corporate lobbying and mitigate the undertaking of self-interested acts that harm others, but cannot guarantee that all parties to public policy disputes will agree upon an optimal course of action. Individuals with differing perceptions and values may also differ in their choice of optimal conduct and willingness to honor it. The dialogue would be greatly enhanced, however, if all parties recognized ethical principles as legitimate guides to political behavior, for by taking ethics seriously, they would exercise moral imagination in trying to resolve disagreements.

Encouraging an Ethical Dialogue

No matter how well designed for use in a business context, expecting ethical standards to be included in corporate lobbying strategy may seem hopelessly naive. Why should companies initiate ethics discussions regarding lobbying when they have rarely done so in the past? One factor that may dispose businesses to consider ethical restraints on their lobbying activity is the increasing concern of society as a whole and consumers and stockholders in particular, that business operate in an ethically responsible manner. No longer are businesses mandated simply to increase the wealth of the society by producing better quality goods and services at lower prices and providing profits for their stockholders (DeGeorge, 1990). Businesses are expected to carry on these activities in ways which respect the basic moral standards of society. The recent discussions by politicians, the media and even the business press, of the perceived unfairness of corporate downsizing is just one example of this willingness to hold business accountable.

Another tangible incentive for ethical self-restraint is the increased availability of information regarding business' lobbying that will result from Congress's recently passed Lobbying Disclosure Act of 1995. The law does not require corporations to disclose their position on legislation, but does require lobbyists to reveal what issues they are working on, thus providing more complete profiles of corporate lobbying activities.

This information, combined with legal access to information from public corporations, can provide the catalyst for public dialogue on the ethics of specific corporate lobbying activities. Press accounts of ethically questionable lobbying will allow stock market reaction to shareholder perceptions of unethical corporate activity. Research has shown that investors tend to react negatively to companies that are cited in the press for unethical behavior (Rao and Hamilton, 1996), so press accounts of questionable lobbying activities should encourage managers to scrutinize the ethics of a lobbying program before launching it. Consumers whose choice of products and services are influenced by the ethical behavior of corporations would also be interested in this information. Large institutional investors such as state government employee and labor union pension funds, who represent socially aware constituencies and have a great deal of influence over the price of individual stocks because of the size of their holdings, could use the information to encourage more responsible lobbying.

An example of the effects of published information about lobbying activities was provided in the debate leading up to the U.S. involvement in the Persian Gulf War. Reporter Gary Lee of *the Washington Post* quoted an official of the National Wooden Pallet and Container Association as suggesting that their group was supporting a tough policy in the Persian Gulf because "War, though hell on the military and others, is good for the business of making pallets . . . .". With no characterization of their conduct as ethical or unethical, Lee also quoted an official of the Composite Can and Tube Institute that their members supported the use of force in the gulf because ". . . they do quite a business in wartime." (Lee, 1991) The ethical dialogue that followed in the *Post's* letters to the editor was an indication of public reaction to information about corporate lobbying activities which so clearly violated basic ethical standards.

Outside of the press, the most potentially effective forum for encouraging public dialogue on the ethics of corporate lobbing is the corporate shareholder meeting. Armed by the shareholder proxy proposal rule with access to corporate proxy mailings and a place on the agenda at annual meetings, corporate social responsibility groups can use the information to file shareholder resolutions regarding the corporation's lobbying activities. These resolutions can call for the management to report to the shareholders on the lobbying objectives and tactics or, given information about questionable lobbying efforts, to justify or halt these efforts. Though opposed by management and doomed to failure in voting by shareholders, these resolutions can have powerful effects on the actions of a corporation. The resolutions inform fellow equity holders of the social implications of corporate actions, embarrass the management into changing their policies in return for withdrawal of the resolution and are effective in gaining media attention for issues that might not normally gain exposure (Hoch and Hamilton, 1994). These resolutions have affected the policies of individual companies on South African operations, affirmative action and hiring practices and the use of animals in product testing. What is needed is for shareholder groups to focus on lobbying as an area of concern and to adopt the standards proposed above to evaluate the activities of particular corporations. Being called to account for their lobbying on the basis of maximizing benefits, respecting others, protecting rights, fairly distributing benefits and burdens, respecting the social contract and acting consistent with character and reputation will reinforce the use of these ethical standards within the corporation.

ETHICAL STANDARDS FOR BUSINESS LOBBYING   127

Providing ethical standards for corporations to evaluate their lobbying activities is not in and of itself sufficient. An ongoing dialogue among outside and inside stakeholders is a much needed corrective to the perspective of the participants. As one reviewer of this paper suggested, "Disparity of power and social location often affect the way in which terms like 'fair' and 'respect' and 'social contract' are understood. They are seen one way by those who are privileged and powerful and another way by those who are marginalized." A recent *New Yorker* cartoon made the same point. One upscale restaurant customer is heard saying to another: "I understand Steve Forbes' flat tax will be hard on the poor, and I can live with that." Subjecting past or proposed lobbying actions to the scrutiny of an ethical dialogue among all those who are affected will quickly expose such limitations of perspective (Bowen & Clark, 1993).

What outcome could be expected from carrying on a dialogue regarding the ethics of business lobbying? Will the lion lie down with the lamb, disagreements cease, corporations accept the views and values of environmentalists or other social critics of business? Such outcomes are unlikely. Even within the restraints imposed by ethics, people of good will can have serious and long standing differences over what is the ethical course of action to pursue. Interpretations of the facts will differ and choices of which ethical principles should be dominant or of which values are more important will sometimes prevent agreement. Corporations may still see forest resources primarily in terms of their instrumental value for lumber, jobs, recreation, and aesthetics whereas environmentalists see ancient trees as having intrinsic value which must be respected in and of itself (Sagoff, 1991).

Disagreements over the objectives and tactics of lobbying, however, can take place within the context of ethical restraints. Corporations should be encouraged by public awareness to engage in more public interest lobbying and to avoid self-interested lobbying which is illegitimate on ethical grounds. The question "Have you no sense of decency, sir, at long last? Have you left no sense of decency?" will again become a criticism rather than a compliment among political operatives (Reeves, 1982).

An understanding by key corporate constituencies of the relevant ethical standards and of the disclosure law's potential could be a catalyst for this new dialogue regarding lobbying. What is required is a more inclusive understanding of the dialectic of law, ethics and public opinion. Just as corporations do not passively accept the imposition of law, the public should not passively accept the substance and tactics of corporate lobbying. With the new information made possible by disclosure, increased public pressure can convince corporations to exercise restraint. Ethics will provide the common language. There is no proof yet that this dialogue will occur, but recognizing the need for it may be the best hope for promoting ethical lobbying by business.

Bibliography

Birnbaum, Jeffrey H. *The Lobbyists: How Influence Peddlers Work Their Ways in Washington.* Times Books, New York. 1993.

Boatright, John R. *Ethics and the Conduct of Business.* Prentice Hall, Englewood Cliffs, New Jersey. 1993.

Bowen, Michael & Power, F. Clark. "The Moral Manager: Communicative Ethics and the *Exxon Valdez* Disaster," *Business Ethics Quarterly*, Vol. 3, No. 2 (April) pp. 97-115. 1993.

Carr, Albert Z.   "Is Business Bluffing Ethical?," *Harvard Business Review*, 46 (January/February) pp. 143-155. 1968.

DeGeorge, Richard T. *Business Ethics*. Third Edition. Macmillan, New York. 1990.

Dixit, Avinash & Nalebuff, Barry. *Thinking Strategically*. Norton, New York. 1991.

Friedman, Milton. "The Social Responsibility of Business is to Increase Its Profits," *New York Times Magazine* 33 (September 13, 1970). 1970.

Hoch, David. "There Ought to be a Law: Dolphins Are Ethical Stakeholders Who Should Not Be Captured for Fun and Profit," *Journal of Legal Studies in Business*, Vol. 4, No.1, pp. 123-145. 1995.

Hoch, David & Hamilton, J. Brooke III. "Do Shareholder Resolutions Influence Corporate Ethics?," *Southeastern Journal of Legal Studies in Business*, Vol. 3, No. 1 (Spring,), pp. 1-18. 1994.

Lee, Gary. "Even in War, Somebody's Got to Read the Legislative Fine Print," *The Washington Post National Weekly Edition*, (February 4-10), p. 15. 1991.

Lobbying Disclosure Act of 1995, P.L. 104-65, 109 Stat. 691, Approved Dec. 19, 1995.

Nash, Laura L. "Ethics Without the Sermon," *Harvard Business Review*, (November-December) pp. 79-90. 1981.

Pava, M. L. & Krausz, J. "Criteria for Evaluating the Legitimacy of Corporate Social Responsibility Projects," National Conference on Ethical Issues in Finance, University of Florida (January). 1995.

Rao, Spuma and Hamilton, J. Brooke III. "The Effect of Published Reports of Unethical Conduct on Stock Price," *The Journal of Business Ethics*, 15: 1321-1330. 1996.

Reeves, Thomas C.   *The Life and Times of Joe McCarthy: A Biography*. Stein and Day, New York, N.Y. pp. 630-631. 1982.

Sagoff, Mark. "At the Shrine of Our Lady of Fatima, or Why Political Questions Are Not All Economic," in VanDeVeer, Donald and Pierce, Christine (eds.), *People, Penguins, and Plastic Trees: Issues in Environmental Ethics*.   Wadsworth Publishing Company, Belmont, CA. 1986.

Sagoff, Mark. "Zuckerman's Dilemma: A Plea for Environmental Ethics," *Hastings Center Report*, Vol. 21, No. 5 (September-October), pp. 32-40. 1991.

Shaffer, T.L. and Shaffer, M. *American Lawyers and Their Communities: Ethics in the Legal Profession*, University of Notre Dame Press, Notre Dame Indiana. 1991.

Solomon, Robert C. *Ethics and Excellence: Cooperation and Integrity in Business*, Oxford University Press, New York. 1992.

Stone, Christopher D. *Where the Law Ends: The Social Control of Corporate Behavior*, Harper & Row, New York, N.Y. 1975.

Timber Salvage Act, formally cited as: Emergency Supplemental Appropriations for Additional Disaster Assistance, for Anti-Terrorism Initiatives, for Assistance in the Recovery From the Tragedy that Occurred at Oklahoma City, and Rescissions Act, 1995, P.L. 104-119, 109 Stat. 194, Approved July 22, 1995.

Velasquez, Manuel G. *Business Ethics: Concepts and Cases, Third Edition*. Prentice Hall, Englewood Cliffs, New Jersey. 1992.

ETHICAL STANDARDS FOR BUSINESS LOBBYING 129

Waters, J. A. "Catch 20.5: Corporate Morality as an Organizational Phenomenon," *Organizational Dynamics*, Spring. 1978.

Weber, Leonard J. "Citizenship and Democracy: The Ethics of Corporate Lobbying," *Business Ethics Quarterly*, Vol. 6, No. 2 (April), pp. 253-259. 1996.

Werhane, Patricia. *Adam Smith and His Legacy for Modern Capitalism*, Oxford University Press, New York. 1991.

Whitmyer, C. "Using Mindfulness to Find Meaningful Work," in Claude Whitmyer (ed.), *Mindfulness and Meaningful Work: Explorations in Right Livelihood*, pp. 251-267, Parallax Press, Berkeley, California. 1994.

Wood, Donna J. *Business and Society, 2nd Edition*, Harper Collins, New York. 1994.

[38]

CITIZENSHIP AND DEMOCRACY: THE ETHICS OF CORPORATE LOBBYING

Leonard J. Weber

**The Lobbyists: How Influence Peddlers
Work Their Way in Washington**

Jeffrey H. Birnbaum

New York: Times Books, 1993

While government relations is an important dimension of business activity, there is little discussion in the business ethics and corporate social responsibility literature regarding the goals and methods of business efforts to influence public policy decisions. Most business ethics texts and anthologies do not include the topic at all. Most "business and society" texts *describe* corporate political activity, but do not include any significant discussion of ethical guidelines to be followed.

There has been a growing interest in American society in recent years in government ethics, in clarifying and articulating standards of behavior for government officials and candidates for elective office. At all levels of government, ethics laws are becoming more detailed and mechanisms are being put in place for both education and enforcement. In 1992 the federal Office of Government Ethics published its "Standards of Ethical Conduct for Employees of the Executive Branch" and in 1993 began annual mandatory ethics training for employees of all departments of the Executive Branch. Since 1990 at least 15 states have passed major ethics legislation. In recent years, Chicago, New York City, and Los Angeles have adopted comprehensive ethics laws (by the City Council, by the approval of a new charter, and by a ballot proposal respectively). All three cities now have active Ethics or Conflict of Interest Boards and full-time staff.

Efforts to clarify standards of government ethics appear to be based largely on one fundamental principle of public service: government decision-making should put the public good above private interests. The details regarding financial disclosure, avoidance of possible conflicts of interest, restrictions on certain future employment, and limits on campaign contributions are various efforts to protect this commitment to promote the public good over private interests.

While more and more attention has been focused on ethical principles and standards for those in government service, very little has been done in a systematic way to clarify and articulate standards of ethics for those who seek to influence government officials and election outcomes. There have been legal restrictions placed on the acceptance of campaign contributions and on the acceptance of gifts from lobbyists, it is true, but as an outgrowth of government ethics, not as an outgrowth of lobbying or citizenship ethics.

The chapter on "Business in the Political Process" in *Business, Government, and Society* (Steiner and Steiner, 1994) closes with a hypothetical case regarding a U.S. Senate campaign and the offer of a large oil company to run, on their own, $350,000 worth of media ads for one of the candidates (a legal practice). As the case is written, the primary ethical issue is the one faced by the *candidate* (whether to accept massive support from a particular company). Students are not led to ask whether the *company* should refrain from such an undertaking. One discussion question does ask whether such independent expenditures by corporate PACs should be curbed, but asking the question whether such actions should be curbed defines the issue as one facing legislators and the public, not as an issue facing the company or the PAC. The case study recognizes that political candidates might, for ethical reasons, choose to refuse campaign assistance that is legal. It does not seem to recognize as clearly that businesses might, for ethical reasons, choose to forgo political activity that is legal and designed to further their goals.

As the above case suggests, many people recognize that conscientious politicians need to wrestle with how to prevent themselves from being unduly influenced by private interests (their own private interests or someone else's private interests). As a society, we are able to identify many of the ethical issues regarding good government and can articulate what is at stake. There seems to be no similar facility in recognizing and raising the ethical issues faced by conscientious managers regarding their firm's Political Action Committee or lobbying activities.

In *The Lobbyists*, Jeffrey Birnbaum, a veteran *Wall Street Journal* reporter, has provided an inside look at how corporate lobbyists operate in Washington. The book is an opportunity and an invitation to reflect upon the ethics of corporate lobbying.

The Story of Modern Day Corporate Lobbyists

During the 101st Congress (1989-1990), Birnbaum observed nine powerful lobbyists, nine men who allowed themselves to be followed for all or part of the two years as they went about their work of trying to influence Congress. The book was originally published in 1992. The 1993 version is only slightly updated and revised.

Birnbaum describes his book as telling "the story of the modern-day corporate lobbyist." (p.4) It is an intriguing story. Individual personalities and specific episodes are described in some detail, and these little stories, taken together, tell the big story. The details need not engage us here; the big story can be briefly summarized.

CITIZENSHIP AND DEMOCRACY: A REVIEW ARTICLE 255

Sometimes the public's concern about undue influence is expressed as a fear that powerful corporations and their lobbyists "buy" votes in Congress through their campaign contributions and through the "wining and dining" of legislators. The reality, as described in *The Lobbyists*, is more subtle.

Birnbaum compares the lobbyists' trade with the board game "Go:" the object is to surround the opponent completely and to cut off any avenue of escape. "Blocking the decision-maker at every turn is the object of any successful lobbying campaign. Equally important is not to allow the decision-maker to know that he or she is being entrapped." (p. 4) Lobbying is powerful, but it is also discreet.

Lobbyists are successful in affecting the political process because they are successful in becoming an important part of the process. They provide lawmakers with information that lawmakers cannot get easily otherwise; lobbyists contribute and raise money that legislators need for re-election; they assist staff in drafting or revising legislation; they accompany lawmakers at many social and speaking events; they become friends with legislators. "The fact that lobbyists are everywhere, all the time, has led official Washington to become increasingly sympathetic to the corporate cause." (p. 4) Some lawmakers are, in effect, largely shut off from other perspectives.

Lobbyists sometimes become an important part of a legislator's lifestyle. From hunting weekends to business investments to campaign fund-raising to shaping legislation, many legislators and corporate lobbyists spend time together around common interests. The fact that many lobbyists were formerly employed in the federal government also contributes to the close relationships that have developed between lawmakers and corporate lobbyists.

The focus in *The Lobbyists* is on the actual ways in which corporate lobbyists do their work. Because of that, it is easy to get focused on the methods used to influence legislation. It is important to remember, though, that lobbyists are not setting their own agenda; they are employed by corporations and trade associations to work for particular business interests. As Wayne Thevenot, one of the lobbyists featured by Birnbaum, said about a disagreement between two business groups about proposed legislation: "I don't have a dog in that fight, and don't have a position. I will have a position as soon as I have a dog." (p. 32) Discussing socially responsible lobbying with an exclusive focus on hired lobbyists is like discussing socially responsible advertising with an exclusive focus on advertising agencies. A good starting point for thinking about lobbying ethics may be reflection on the appropriate role and goals of corporations in their political activity.

Ethics and Corporate Political Activity

Political activity by business is often discussed in terms of the "right" to be involved politically. "Business has a legitimate right to participate in a political process, just as consumers, labor unions, environmentalists, and others do." (Frederick, Post, and Davis, 1992) The implication is that business should be involved in political activity precisely because there are others who are active and who are expressing other points of view.

Defenders of corporate Political Action Committees sometimes make reference to James Madison's comments on special interests in *The Federalist Papers*:

> American democracy depends on active and diversified participation by special interests. As long as many interest groups are active in the system, they will check one another and in that way, one or a few select groups cannot dominate the system. (Quoted in Ford, 1994)

One can agree that democracy thrives when different points of view are being publicly advocated and yet not conclude that the system of lobbying and campaign financing that has evolved contributes to a healthy democracy. A question that may need much more attention is the question of what sorts of interests a business should pursue and promote through its political activity.

Mark Sagoff often makes a distinction that may be relevant here. He points out that our role as consumers is not the same as our role as citizens. In acting as consumers, we seek to acquire what we want for ourselves; each follows his or her own conception of the good life. In acting as citizens, on the other hand, we work with others to promote the good society. (Sagoff, 1986) In the terms used in discussions of public service ethics, to act as a consumer is to seek one's private interests; to act as a citizen is to seek the public good. To act conscientiously as a citizen is to be willing to subordinate private interests to the public good.

Seeking one's private interest is appropriate at times, but always or frequently acting as a consumer when one should be acting as a citizen is a threat to the well being of the whole community. Shaping public policy is one of those activities more appropriately understood as citizen activity than as consumer activity. As was pointed out above, we recognize this clearly in government ethics, where public service responsibilities are largely defined as putting the public good above private interests. When individuals and organizations seek to shape public policy, they should, it would seem, hold themselves to the same standard of putting the public good above private interests. When a business makes the decision to try to shape public policy through lobbying, it becomes involved in activity where, it could be argued, decision-making should be directed by the public-good-over-private-interests understanding of responsibility. While business decisions are generally made in the pursuit of private interests, lobbying and other political activity should, perhaps, be understood as a different type of activity, an activity to be governed by different goals and standards.

Birnbaum reports that Robert Malott, the CEO of FMC Corporation, quoted the comment of Reginald Jones, former CEO of General Electric, to explain why he was in Washington on a lobbying trip: "I can do more for General Electric by spending time in Washington and assisting in the development of responsible tax policy than I can by staying home and pricing refrigerators." (p. 197) The question that needs to be examined more deeply is whether one should be pursuing the same goals in lobbying as in managing the daily business of the company. Is the public good being served by lobbying undertaken as an extension of normal business activity?

Responsibility for Good Government

Businesses are involved in the political process because the decisions made in the political arena have significant consequences for business enterprises and for the economy. Unless businesses express their interests clearly and forcefully, it is argued, public policy that affects business may be too much influenced by other groups, such as labor unions, consumer groups, and environmentalists.

This interest-group model of democracy provides us with the image of a legislator surrounded by special interest groups, each of which is trying to persuade him or her that their concerns need to be addressed. The legislator is expected to listen to these various groups, but to rise above all the special interests and to act, almost heroically, for the public good.

Good government does require that public servants put the public good above private interests, but the burden should not be placed all on the government official. Government ethics rules can be very helpful in reminding public servants of the need to protect against undue influence on the part of those promoting private interests, but it seems unrealistic to expect that public officials will (be able to) act for the public good when they are surrounded by groups and individuals seeking private interests.

If organizations and individuals reduce citizenship activity to the pursuit of private interests, all the ethics rules in the world are not likely to produce good government. In a real sense, politicians in a democratic society mirror that society. If the interest groups that lobby the government are simply pursuing their private interests, the best that can be expected of government officials is that they be independent in judging what interest to endorse. The independent endorsement of one private interest over another is not, however, to be equated with working for the public good. As was noted above, the responsibility of public servants is to work for the public good, not private interests, *whether those private interests are their own or someone else's.*

Democracy and Unequal Power

Even those who raise no question about the corporate pursuit of private interests in lobbying may recognize that democracy and the good of society are threatened when some interests groups have much more influence than others. As William Frederick and his co-authors put it:

> The principal danger arising from corporate political activity is that corporations may wield too much power. If that power were to " tip the scales" unfairly in favor of business and against the many pluralistic interests in society, both business and society would be losers. (Frederick, Post, and Davis, 1992)

Birnbaum's story strongly suggests that corporate lobbyists *do* have undue influence in promoting the interests of their clients. As was noted earlier,
they dominate the attention of legislators by their constant presence. In
addition, one of the major avenues to access is to make campaign contributions; many of the details in Birnbaum's story relate to campaign fund
raising. The connection between contributions and influence is clear.

> Few lobbyists entered the fray in Washington without first making sure they
> had a ready hoard of dollars to spread around. PAC and personal political
> contributions were expected of anyone who wanted to get his point across.
> Though money rarely bought votes outright, it did buy the lobbyist the chance
> to make his views known, a chance not everyone had. Access to the powers
> that be was rationed, and the size of one's political pocketbook was important
> to making the cut. (p. 161)

In the discussion of the danger of corporations wielding too much power,
Frederick and colleagues conclude that a "careful use of business influence
is therefore an ideal goal to be worked for...." (Frederick, Post, and Davis,
1992) In the corporate lobbying efforts chronicled in *The Lobbyists*, there is
little indication of a goal to avoid undue influence. Indeed, if it is appropriate to consider interest-group democracy as a contest among groups representing different private interests, then there is no reason to do anything
other than to seek to "win."

In order to limit lobbying to a "careful use" of influence, it would seem
that a corporation (or any other organization) must acknowledge that there
is a public good that they are responsible for promoting, a public good that
is not equated with their private interests and that, at least at times, super-
sedes their private interests. Understanding lobbying as an extension of the
business pursuit of private interests inspires no reason to limit one's influence. Understanding lobbying as a citizenship responsibility to work for the
good of the larger community might, on the other hand, be more compatible
with voluntary restraints on the use of influence and power.

Not Martyrdom, But a Vision

Birnbaum describes the persistent pursuit of campaign money as bothersome even to many lobbyists. They, too, are caught up in a system they think
they cannot control. Campaign fund-raising functions are an important
opportunity to be seen and to make an impression and lobbyists think,
therefore, that they have no real choice. As Wayne Thevenot said about the
possibility of passing up a fund-raising reception:

> It's a hell of a risk to take. And we're part of the process. I don't write the
> campaign-financing rules. But it's the system, and I'm not going to play the
> martyr and try to change it singlehandedly. I'm just going to play it until they
> change it. (p. 169)

Some who read *The Lobbyists* may conclude that what is described is
simply the way the system works; one might as well learn to play success-

CITIZENSHIP AND DEMOCRACY: A REVIEW ARTICLE 259

fully in this arena until the rules change. Others may react differently: the system as it is presently working is not acceptable; it benefits the powerful and the wealthy at the expense of others.

Those of us who think that *The Lobbyists*, along with other such accounts of the influence of powerful interests in Washington, makes a compelling case for change are not necessarily asking individuals or corporations to be martyrs. What is needed, though, may be a new vision, an understanding that things could be different. Addressing the ethics of corporate lobbying is not just thinking about how to maintain some personal integrity in a potentially corrupting system. It is also thinking about how corporations should, ideally, understand their proper role in the political process. Until the vision changes, the rules of the game are not likely to change.

Bibliography

Ford Motor Company. "PAC News: A Newsletter for All Ford U.S. Salaried Employees." March, 1994.

Frederick, William C., Post, James E. and Davis, Keith. *Business and Society: Corporate Strategy, Public Policy, Ethics*. Seventh Edition. New York: McGraw Hill, 1992.

Sagoff, Mark. "At the Shrine of Our Lady of Fatima, or Why Political Questions Are Not All Economic." In VanDeVeer, Donald and Pierce, Christine (eds.). *People, Penguins, and Plastic Trees: Issues in Environmental Ethics*. Belmont, CA: Wadsworth Publishing Company, 1986.

Steiner, George A. and Steiner, John F. *Business, Government, and Society: A Managerial Perspective*. Seventh Edition. New York: McGraw Hill, 1994.

[39]

A Framework for the Ethical Analysis of Corporate Political Activity

WILLIAM D. OBERMAN

T o read a newspaper today is to reinforce a general sense that more than one of society's major institutions has lost its moral compass. At the heart of many of the ongoing scandals and disputes is the apparent corruption that exists at the nexus of the relationship between business and government. There is a feeling that politicians and policy can be bought, that the public can be manipulated or distracted, that the sometimes quite naked pursuit of self-interest drives government, and that the money and power of corporations overwhelm those who would challenge their dominance. The notion of representative government, the policy outputs of which reflect the interests of a diverse plurality of groups, appears a cruel illusion.

Of course, this feeling is not new. The power and privilege of business, especially of big business, has long been viewed by many as a threat to democracy. The reconciliation of the concentration of wealth and resources in business organizations with democratic political ideals and theory has always been problematic. This led Charles Lindblom, for example, to conclude his well-known work, *Politics and Markets*, with the statement that "The large private corporation fits oddly into democratic theory and vision. Indeed, it does not fit."[1] The enormous resources of the large corporation, combined with its unique power to threaten disinvestment, were

William D. Oberman is an assistant professor of business administration at Pennsylvania State University, Mont Alto Campus.

seen by Lindblom as placing it in such a dominant position relative to other political actors that it became the "major specific institutional barrier to fuller democracy."[2] Other significant commentators have identified business's power to control the policy agenda or the public consciousness as the major threats to democracy.[3] The theme of big business as a threat to democracy continues to be echoed and amplified.

Regardless of the extent to which claims of business domination of government policy can be proven true, it is clear that the resources necessary for influencing government policy are not evenly distributed across all existing or potential interest groups. Businesses and business groups are often in privileged positions relative to opposing interests. It is also clear that businesses will and must remain permanent players in the political system. Businesses have constitutional guarantees of freedom of speech and petition. They have direct fiduciary duties to protect and advance the interests of their stockholders (and, possibly, other economically dependent stakeholders) when these interests can be affected by government action or inaction. At a more abstract level, it can be argued that they have a duty to represent the functional requirements of economic productivity in the process of creating balanced public policy.

Given that groups representing business interests will remain active players in the political system, what can be done to mediate the real and perceived risk of business domination? Many of the critics of business would claim that radical change is necessary. Even if this change were desirable, practically speaking, it is not going to happen. The Revolution is nowhere in sight. Adjustments to the legally enforced rules of the game, such as campaign finance reform, are narrow in scope and limited by the First Amendment, as well as by the motivated and creative legions of political operatives searching for loopholes and workarounds.

A partial answer may look to internal reform of the participants themselves. To do this we must begin thinking about a framework for ethical behavior in an imperfect and competitive political system. Such a framework would be based on the recognition that an ideal form of democracy is not a current option and that politics is a competitive enterprise. It is not expected that standards emerging from such a framework would reform the system, but at least they would provide a practical starting point for considering the ethics of corporate political involvement.

In this paper, we offer a preliminary version of a framework that identifies moral and ethical questions associated with business political involvement in an imperfect democracy. Incorporating recent work on corporate political activity and strategy, along with elements of traditional ethical analysis, this framework will structure questions rather than provide answers. The objective is to identify the questions that must be asked of corporate political action if we are to maintain a functioning representative democracy. We begin with a brief look at corporate political activity as it has been conceptualized in the academic management literature.

CORPORATE POLITICAL ACTIVITY

The subject of corporate political activity (CPA) has received considerable attention from business scholars in recent years. In an extensive review of the CPA literature, Getz[4] identified no fewer than nine streams of theorizing—drawn from the disciplines of political science, economics/political economy, and organization science—that have informed this research. Our present objective is not to engage in another general review, but rather to point out a few significant organizing trends and concepts.

The first is the movement toward developing a theory of political strategy that can be integrated with general business or corporate strategy. Beginning with the work of Miles and Cameron,[5] scholarly research on corporate political strategy accelerated throughout the late 1980s and '90s. Yoffie, Wood, Keim and Baysinger, and Mahon laid the foundations,[6] together with important volumes edited by Marcus, Kaufman, and Beam and by Mitnick.[7] Representative articles published in high-quality journals include the following: Baron, stressing that strategy formulation must consider both market and nonmarket (especially governmental) components of a firm's environment; Schuler and Rehbein, examining the organizational characteristics that affect the willingness and ability of a firm to engage in political action; Mahon and McGowan, analogizing to Porter's five-force model of business, treating issues as products and political influence as currency; Hillman and Hitt, developing a decision-tree model of how firms formulate political strategy; and Schaffer and Hillman, considering the effects of diversification on political strategies.[8]

Two interesting theoretical perspectives include agency theory[9] and the resource-based theory of the firm.[10] From the agency point of view, the goal of CPA is to convert public officials into "agents" of the firm who will serve the firm's interests in formulating and implementing public policy. Firms use political activity to create and control these agents. The agency approach in this context was pioneered by Mitnick and has been developed by Keim and Baysinger, as well as Getz.[11] Mahon extended the idea, describing indirect, "manufactured agents."[12] Manufactured agents could be public interest groups, indirectly or secretly funded by the corporation, who ideally believe that they are representing the public interest but in so doing are additionally representing the interests of their corporate "manufacturer."

The resource-based theory of the firm attributes long-term performance to possession of valuable, rare, inimitable, and non-substitutable resources.[13] In the past decade it has emerged as an important paradigm in strategic management thought. Oberman[14] has sought an integration of market strategy and political strategy by introducing the concept of "institutional resources" to recognize some strategically important resources that belong to society—such as governmental institutions, officials (as above), policies, belief systems—and can be "borrowed" and exploited by individual companies in the pursuit of competitive advantage.

A characteristic of the CPA research described earlier is that little attention is paid to the wider implications of rolling together market and political strategy. In economic theory, market behavior is regulated by market competition; in pluralist political thought[15] political behavior is regulated by competing coalitions of interest groups. In practice, competition is an imperfect guarantor of the public interest in both realms. Given that the rules of the games for both areas are written in the political realm, we should be less sanguine about celebrating combined corporate and political strategy.

In reviewing the body of CPA research, Shaffer[16] noted that the emerging, organization-focused, managerial perspective on business-government relations differs from the traditional approach in this neglect of societal concerns. Traditionally, the subject has been analyzed from perspectives based in political science, sociology, and economics. The overriding concern has been with the impact of business-government relations on society and on representative democracy. Although critiques of the political involvement of business obviously still abound, they are generally not to be found in the CPA literature. The objective of recent CPA research has been to describe and conceptualize business political activity as a strategic response to the environment, not to question or seek to limit that response. It would seem that this research stream has reached a sufficient level of maturity that normative considerations can be entered into the mix.

We can draw upon this literature itself to structure a framework to introduce normative considerations. Shaffer and Hillman describe the ability of firms to influence public policy as their political capital. This capital is said to depend on two sets of factors: (1) reputation and social legitimacy, and (2) investment in the capability to implement effective political strategies by developing access to decision makers, knowledge, and expertise. Similarly, Mahon and McGowan tied legitimacy and access to political influence. These ideas were joined together by Oberman[17] in a process model of political resource development (Figure 1).

FIGURE 1   Process Model of Political Resource Development

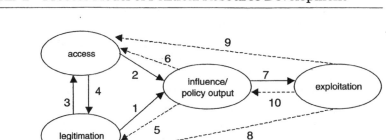

Legitimation strategies
Path 1. "right makes might"
Path 3-2. "right gains entrée"

Access strategies
Path 2. "ear of the king"
Path 4-1. "right by association"

Control and feedback strategies
Path 5-1. "control of public consciousness" or "might makes right"
Path 6-2. "control of public agenda" or "might shuts out dissent"

(Source: Oberman, 2002)

The numbered paths in the model represent possible political strategies, but of importance here are the components: access, "legitimation" (the process of seeking legitimacy), influence, and exploitation. Access to governmental decision makers can derive from, among other things, hiring the right political consultants or lobbyists, political action committee (PAC) contributions, the constituency-based interests of decision makers, or elite social connections. The long-term development of access-related political resources is termed the "relational" approach to political strategy by Hillman and Hitt, the building of "relationships across issues and over time so that when public policy issues arise that affect their operations, the contacts and resources needed to influence this policy are already in place."[18]

Legitimation involves bringing the position of the company into alignment with a view of the public interest held by at least some influential segment of society. This can be done by aligning the company's mission, goals, and any sociopolitical claims it might make with such a view. Alternatively, a firm might seek to align public *perceptions* of its sociopolitical claims with such a view, or even to change the public perception of what is legitimately in the public interest.

As depicted in Figure 1, access and legitimacy have an interactive relationship and each can reinforce or undercut the other. Together they determine a company's (or other political actor's) ability to influence public policy. Feedback from influence can also positively or negatively affect access, and legitimation as success is compounded or abused. Exploitation refers to the actual use of political influence to build competitive advantage and profitability. This too, can feed back to access, legitimation, and/or influence.

The four components of this model represent different areas in which normative questions should be introduced into the developing theory of corporate political activity and strategy. Following a discussion of the normative standards to be employed, we present a framework for ethical political competition that combines the normative questions with these components.

NORMATIVE STANDARDS

As noted in the introduction, political competition and democracy are imperfect. If we apply an absolute standard of representative fairness, we would be hard-pressed to approve of any competition among actors with unequal resource endowments. Because we must live with the current system, we should find ways to improve the functioning of democracy within it. We must look for the best standard of representative democracy we can reasonably hope for in an unfair and imperfect world. This standard may exist in the notion of "political contestability."

Political contestability—In an analysis of Edwin Epstein's seminal work on corporate political activity, Mitnick[19] recalled the metaphor of "elephants among chickens" (which Epstein had borrowed from Andrew Hacker) to capture the advantaged position of large corporate interests relative to others in the political process. The problem is how to maintain a reasonably level playing field on which both elephants and chickens can compete. In this analysis, Mitnick introduced the concept of "political contestability" as an analog to market contestability in the economics literature.[20] A contestable political system may not mirror classic democracy, but would "still permit a contest for influence and control."[21] The "test of democracy" is "not if its rules seem fair, but that its system is contestable."[22] Reasoning from a Rawlsian "veil of ignorance," Mitnick delineated the requirements of a contestable political system as respecting the popular will (i.e., being representational), possessing a neutral bias, and incorporating shared democratic values. In terms of process, such a system would allow mobilization of support for various positions; permit broad access; incorporate due process, openness, and timely consideration of issues; provide for the possibility of change; and be widely viewed as legitimate.

Although Mitnick sees contestability as a property of the structure of a political system, the concept can serve as a basis for laying out a framework of rules for ethical corporate political involvement. Under these rules, the prime standard for judging the ethics of a given action would be its effect on system contestability. This line of reasoning is somewhat related to Freeman and Gilbert's[23] development of the idea of the "implicit morality of the marketplace" (IMM). Freeman and Gilbert defined IMM as "the set of imperatives that any market actor must obey to ensure the operation of free enterprise and, accordingly, the attainment of Pareto optimality,"[24] and used it to turn the basic theoretical assumptions of perfect competition into obligations for economic actors. (Of course, they found that

corporate strategy violated IMM, as well as common morality.)
Political contestability and its analog, economic contestability,
are less stringent standards than perfect democracy or perfect
competition. The conversion of contestability from a set of systemic
assumptions to a foundation for behavioral obligations would not
require near the unrealistic degree of self-denial of IMM. IMM was
proposed as method of critiquing economics-based approaches to
corporate strategy, not as a serious set of guidelines for behavior.
The political contestability–based framework to be presented later
is meant to be a workable structure for questioning and guiding
political behavior.

The ethics of contestability—How can the assumptions of contestability be converted into a set of ethical obligations for corporate
political actors? A logical place to begin is with the three commonly
identified approaches to ethics in Western thought: consequentialist
(teleological), nonconsequentialist (deontological, including Kantian
and rights-based), and justice-oriented. These are well known and
employed in standard business ethics texts and models and were
combined by Cavanaugh, Moberg, and Velasquez [25] in a well-known
ethical decision-making framework. They also align well with the
ends and process requirements of contestable systems delineated
by Mitnick. It is proposed here that political activity be evaluated in
light of these three approaches, with the limiting standard being
maintenance of contestability. Advantaged actors in the system are
held to be under an obligation to pay attention to the effects of their
actions on contestability and to refrain from those actions that may
damage it. The "meta-ethic" here is the preservation of a contestable
system of democratic representation. It should be noted before
we proceed that our primary concern here is not with obviously
unethical instances of outright graft and bribery, but with the typical
functioning of corporate political activity.

A FRAMEWORK FOR ETHICAL POLITICAL ACTION

Figure 2 presents a framework for evaluating the ethics of political
action in a contestable, if imperfect, democracy. It is built around
the four components of the process model for political resource
development and the three traditional approaches to ethics. To

---

FIGURE 2 Framework for Evaluating the Ethics of a Political Action

---

	Consequences for representation in a contestable system (maintenance of effective and efficient representation)	**Rights and duties in a contestable system** (maintenance of shared democratic values)	**Justice in a contestable system** (maintenance of system legitimacy and possibility of change)
Access	Does action reduce representation in political decision-making process below level of contestability?	Does action attempt to deny right of participation to others?	Does action contribute to perennial exclusion of some groups from political decision-making process?
Legitimation	Does action reduce rationality of political decision-making process below level of contestability?	Does action attempt to deceive and manipulate public?	Does action contribute to perennial exclusion of some groups/ positions from opportunity for legitimization?
Influence/ Exploitation	Does action tend to increase entry barriers to other participants reducing level of contestability?	Does action ignore rights of public and other interests?	Does action contribute to perennially unfair distribution of benefits and burdens of policy?

simplify things slightly, we have combined the exploitation of influence with influence itself, leaving us with a three-by-three matrix. Action taken or contemplated in each phase of the process of political resource development must be evaluated according to the three criteria before it can be judged to be ethical. Consequentialist analysis is concerned with the direct effects of the action on the quality and degree of representation in the system. (It is assumed here that a functioning, representative democracy will serve utilitarian ends.) The rights analysis concentrates on adherence to fundamental democratic values that undergird the system and are necessary to its proper functioning. Political rights are seen as among the most fundamental of these values. Justice-oriented analysis looks at longer-term patterns and whether they effectively disenfranchise and disadvantage segments of the population.

Access—Access to politicians and other government officials can be developed, among other ways, through PAC contributions, the employment of professional lobbyists, or the exploitation of elite social ties. The resources available for gaining this access are unequally distributed, but the key question is how much inequality creates an unacceptable tilt in the playing field. When should business investment in the access-building, relational political strategies described by Hillman and Hitt be considered unethical?

A political action aimed at gaining access to a governmental decision maker can, in an absolute and a relative sense, diminish another group's representation and participation. This situation is of concern under all three ethical approaches. Access available to other groups must be sufficient to provide them with effective representation. The rights of even small minorities must be respected. No group may be constantly shut out, and conversely, no group can always dominate. If a corporate political action serves to diminish other groups' access to government, it is ethically suspect.

The focus of a consequentialist analysis of corporate political action seeking access would be on the maintenance of sufficient representation to preserve system contestability and produce a sound, balanced public policy. Although it may not be necessary or possible for all groups to have equal access, it is necessary in the interest of both good decision making and maintaining contestability that all viable points of view are heard and all significant interests represented. This can be seen primarily as an efficiency/effectiveness concern.

From a theoretical perspective, the rights of representation and participation for all go beyond the concern for creating efficient and effective public policy. However, in practice, access is a limited resource that will be rationed in some way. The question is whether the rationing is such that it violates the rights of holders of a particular interest. When a political action on the part of a business is *intended* to deny access to others, it can be considered plainly unethical. When denial of access is not the intent but nonetheless the outcome, the action is still morally suspect. Careful consideration must be given to attempts to build relational capital with decision makers when that capital can function as an "entry barrier" to others seeking to form similar relations with public officials. Particular consideration must be given when the same groups seem to be repeatedly denied access.

When political rights are denied to an individual or group, not only is there direct injury to that person or group, but also there is the potential for the broader erosion of the shared democratic values that allow a representative form of government to function. Society's various interests may agree on little else, but they must agree on the rules and rights inherent in the democratic contest or there can be no such contest. The real or perceived denial of equal opportunities for participation of some interests can destroy confidence in the system. Many will view the system itself, not just one particular outcome, as unjust. The sense of legitimacy will be lost; some may no longer even attempt to gain access and may not feel morally bound by governmental laws and policies. Over time, threats to contestability will only be compounded.

In order to meet the test of ethical acceptability, no political action aimed at gaining access to governmental decision makers may reduce representation beneath the level necessary to produce efficient and effective policy, seek to deny any group representation or participation on an issue, or contribute to the perennial exclusion of any group from participating in the political system.

Legitimation—Businesses (and other interests) generally seek legitimacy within the political system by attempting to bring public perceptions of themselves and/or their issue positions into alignment with important social values. Associated efforts may be made to delegitimize opponents and/or their issues by making them seem out of alignment with important social values or not "mainstream." This process involves communicating with (or through) the public rather than directly with government decision makers. Students of public policy have long understood that this communication tends to be based on emotion rather than logic. Endeavors are made to associate the group or its issue position with positive, emotionally powerful symbols and link opponents and their positions to negative symbols.[26] Manipulating the public understanding or definition of an issue so as to cue the proper emotions and influence the public's perception of the issue's significance and level of technicality can increase public support of a position, decrease support for an opponent's position, or put an issue on or off the public agenda.[27]

Political communication often takes the form of political or advocacy advertising. Kaid has cataloged a number of "major ethical concerns" about political advertising, including the cost of communications, the focus on emotion rather than logic, the oversimplification of arguments, the failure to disclose sources of information, the ambiguity of messages, the use of "technological tricks," and the frequently negative tone.[28] Each of these concerns can diminish the ability of citizens to make rational decisions about public policy issues and/or discourage participation.

A good illustration of the level of political discourse is the 1993–1994 debate surrounding the Clinton health-care plan. A study of the role of the media in this debate sponsored by the Robert Wood Johnson Foundation[29] found that the combined $50 million spent on advertising by both sides was primarily aimed at creating anxiety and fear. The ads were negative and did not address the substantive arguments of opponents, and more than a quarter of print ads and half of broadcast ads were judged by the researchers to be unfair, misleading, or false.[30]

Certainly, the process of seeking legitimacy in the public forum is an ethical minefield. From a consequentialist standpoint, if one side has the financial resources to define the issue and the terms of the debate, there may be no effective debate. If opponents do not have an opportunity to make their case, there can be no contest. Even if adequate resources exist on both sides of issues to allow debate, if debate is at the level of symbolic posturing and informed by half-truths, how truly can it serve the public interest? Efforts to manipulate public opinion based on half-truths and deceptions treat citizens as means rather than ends, to put it in Kantian terms, and constitutes an obvious violation of basic rights. Such efforts also violate the shared democratic value of a belief in an informed citizenry capable of self-government. In a system in which only the richly endowed can engage in political communication, some groups may never have the ability to legitimize themselves or their positions.

Yet, things are not cut and dried. As in the health-care debate, there are often two or more sides to issues employing the same emotion-based strategy. If one side, in the name of ethics, refrained from this behavior, would it reduce contestability and be antidemocratic in itself? Some may argue that emotion is as valid a criterion for decision making as logic, especially when the emotional appeal cuts to core values. A negative ad in and of itself is not necessarily bad, if it contains valuable information. And, the conventional wisdom among political scientists actually discounts the effects of political advertising, holding that it merely serves to reinforce existing beliefs—studies have shown electoral outcomes are far more attributable to such variables as the state of the economy than to campaign activities.[31]

The ideal means of seeking legitimacy is presentation to the public, in an open forum, of an honest, informative analysis of the implications of the various public policy options associated with an issue, allowing those who disagree the freedom and opportunity to respond. This is the ideal; the question is how far from that ideal can powerful interest groups stray and not undermine the contestability of the system? When choosing corporate political communications strategies, this must be the foremost ethical consideration.

In order to meet the test of ethical acceptability, no political action aimed at gaining legitimacy may seek to reduce the capacity of the system for making a rational public policy decision on the issue, deceptively manipulate public opinion on the issue, or contribute to the perennial exclusion of any group.

Influence—When is it acceptable for a private interest to make public officials into its "agents" as described by Mitnick, Keim and Baysinger, and Getz? Two criteria would have to be met to make this acceptable: (1) the private interest and the public interest would have to coincide to such an extent that the agent/public official serves both with the same action, and (2) the agent/public official intends his or her action to be in the public interest. This would be an easier judgment if the public interest was clearly understood—actions that diverged would obviously be wrong. However, the public interest is usually not clearly understood. Is there a single communal public interest? Is the public interest an aggregate of diverse group interests? Is the public interest defined by the winner of the last political contest?[32] In a legal, if not an absolute, sense, the latter is generally answered in the affirmative in representative, legitimate, democratic systems. The political contest registers the will of the people.

If the public interest is defined by the winner of the last political contest, whatever public officials do, assuming it is in line with governmental policy and does not emanate from personal whim or corrupt influence, would by definition be done in the public interest. In other words, if you win the contest for access and legitimacy, you define the public interest. At the most general level, for example, if liberals are in power, dealing with environmental concerns may be defined as more in the public interest than economic productivity; if conservatives are in, economic concerns make take precedence. In a representative democracy, accepted by its citizens as legitimate, the losing side may not agree with the definition but will be prepared to acquiesce (or at least obey the law) until the next vote.

Thus, the public interest and the question of the moral acceptability of public officials as private agents cannot be separated from contestability. If the system is biased and not contestable, no definition of the public interest that emerges from it can be accepted at face value. Such a system is likely to produce policies that not only favor the dominant group at the expense of the rest of society but, given the interrelationship of influence, access, and legitimacy, further entrench the dominant group in its position of power. Many will lose faith in the capacity of the system to register their interests and may cease to feel a duty to accept government policy. While the dominant group more deeply entrenches itself within the system, the system itself is discredited. Taken to the extreme, this represents a serious threat to democratic government.

To meet the test of ethical acceptability, political influence may not be used to restructure the rules of system or general political practice to decrease participation, to violate shared democratic values or the basic rights of other groups, or to support an unfair distribution of benefits and burdens.

DISCUSSION

In this paper, we have offered a framework for structuring ethical questions about corporate political involvement. Although the three main ethical traditions in Western thought were drawn upon, the limiting standard was the maintenance of political contestability. It was recognized that political resources are distributed unequally but that representative democracy can still function if the system remains contestable. Fundamentally, the standard of contestability maintenance is a guide to how much inequality can be tolerated before contestability is lost.

Unfortunately, the framework presented here can only draw attention to the ethical questions involved in business involvement in politics in representative democracy—it cannot provide definitive guidelines. Those who formulate corporate political strategy and direct corporate political action will have to address these questions or risk forever diminishing representative democracy. Clearly, the voice of business must be heard in public policy debates, but it cannot drown out the voices of other interests.

The mechanisms through which a delicate balance of representation without domination can be achieved are not entirely obvious. Perhaps they already exist and concerns about business dominance of the political process have been greatly exaggerated. After all, business interests are divided on many, if not most, issues, diluting the threat of domination.[33] What is obvious, however, is that the appearance of dominance can be almost as damaging to representative democracy as the substance of dominance. Both undercut contestability by shrinking participation and calling democratic values into question. It may be naive to suggest that the efforts of individual business leaders to employ an ethical framework (such as that provided in this paper) when approaching government can improve the functioning of democracy. However, this is essentially the same situation faced in all areas of business ethics and, for that matter, in ethical behavior in general. Resisting the temptation to rationalize actions taken in one's self-interest as being for the greater good, being willing to live within a certain core value system, and respecting the rights of others even if one does not respect their beliefs or behaviors are necessary constraints for maintaining a civil society. Maintaining a functioning representative democracy requires the same.

NOTES

1. C. E. Lindblom, *Politics and Markets* (New York: Basic Books, 1977), 356.

2. Ibid.; for a more recent discussion from the same perspective, see N. J. Mitchell, *The Conspicuous Corporation: Business, Public Policy, and Representative Democracy* (Ann Arbor: University of Michigan Press, 1997).

3. P. Bachrach and M. Baratz, "Two Faces of Power," *American Political Science Review* 57 (1962), 947–52; S. Lukes, *Power: A Radical View* (London: Macmillan, 1974).

4. K. A. Getz, "Research in Corporate Political Action: Integration and Assessment," *Business & Society* 36 (1997), 32–72.

5. R. H. Miles and K. S. Cameron, *Coffin Nails and Corporate Strategies* (Englewood Cliffs, NJ: Prentice Hall, 1982).

6. D. Yoffie, "Corporate Strategy for Political Action," in *Business Strategy and Public Policy*, ed. A. E. Marcus, A. E. Kaufman, and D. R. Beam (New York: Quorum, 1987); D. J. Wood, *Strategic Uses of Public Policy: Business and Government in the Progressive Era* (Marshfield, MA: Pitman, 1986); G. D. Keim and B. D. Baysinger, "The Efficacy of Business Political Activity: Competitive Consideration in Principal-Agent Context," *Journal of Management* 14 (1988), 163–80; J. F. Mahon, "Corporate Political Strategy," *Business in the Contemporary World* 2 (1989), 50–62.

7. A. E. Marcus, A. E. Kaufman, and D. R. Beam, *Business Strategy and Public Policy* (New York: Quorum, 1987); B. M. Mitnick, *Corporate Political Agency: The Construction of Competition in Public Affairs* (Newbury Park, CA: Sage, 1993).

8. D. P. Baron, "Integrated Strategy: Market and Non-market Components," *California Management Review* 37 (1995), 47–65; D. A. Schuler and K. Rehbein, "The Filtering Role of the Firm in Corporate Political Involvement," *Business & Society* 36 (1997), 116–39; J. F. Mahon and R. A. McGowan, "Modeling Industry Political Dynamics," *Business & Society* 37 (1998), 390–413; A. J. Hillman and M. A. Hitt, "Corporate Political Strategy Formulation: A Model of Approach, Participation, and Strategy Decisions," *Academy of Management Journal* 24 (1999), 825–42; B. A. Shaffer and A. J. Hillman, "The Development of Business-Government Strategies by Diversified Firms," *Strategic Management Journal*, 21 (2000), 175–90.

9. For a review relevant to organization theory see K. M. Eisenhart, "Agency Theory: An Assessment and Review," *Academy of Management Review* 14 (1989), 57–74.

10. B. Wernerfelt, "A Resource-Based View of the Firm," *Strategic Management Journal*, 5 (1984), 171–80; J. B. Barney, "Firm Resources and Sustained Competitive Advantage," *Journal of Management* 17 (1991), 99–120.

11. B. M. Mitnick, "Political Contestability," in *Corporate Political Agency: The Construction of Competition in Public Affairs*, ed. B. M. Mitnick (Newbury Park, CA: Sage, 1993); ———, *The Theory of Agency: The Concept of Fiduciary Rationality and Some Consequences* (unpublished PhD diss.,

University of Pennsylvania, 1974); Keim and Baysinger, "The Efficacy of Business Political Activity: Competitive Consideration in Principal-Agent Context"; K. A. Getz, "Corporate Political Tactics in a Principal-Agent Context: An Investigation into Ozone Protection Policy," in *Research in Corporate Social Performance and Policy, 14*, ed. J. E. Post (Greenwich, CT: JAI, 1993).

12.   J. F. Mahon, "Shaping Issues, Manufacturing Agents: Corporate Political Sculpting," in *Corporate Political Agency: The Construction of Competition in Public Affairs*, ed. B. M. Mitnick (Newbury Park, CA: Sage, 1993).

13.   Barney, "Firm Resources and Sustained Competitive Advantage."

14.   W. D. Oberman, "Strategy and Tactic Choice in an Institutional Resource Context," in *Corporate Political Agency: The Construction of Competition in Public Affairs*, ed. B. M. Mitnick (Newbury Park, CA: Sage, 1993); ———, "Corporate Political Strategy and the Resource-Based View of the Firm: A Consideration of the Dynamics of Political Resource Development," (presented at the International Association for Business & Society Conference, Victoria, BC, 2002).

15.   For example, D. Truman, *The Governmental Process* (New York: Knopf, 1951).

16.   B. A. Shaffer, "Firm Level Responses to Government Regulation: Theoretical and Research Approaches," *Journal of Management* 21 (1995), 495–514.

17.   Oberman, "Corporate Political Strategy and the Resource-Based View of the Firm."

18.   Hillman and Hitt, "Corporate Political Strategy Formulation," 828.

19.   E. M. Epstein, *The Corporation in American Politics* (Englewood Cliffs, NJ: Prentice Hall, 1969). B. M. Mitnick, "Chasing Elephants Among Chickens on a Tilted Field: Pluralism and Political Contestability in the Work of Edwin Epstein," in *Research in corporate social performance and policy, 12*, ed. J. E. Post (Greenwich, CT: JAI, 1991); ———, "Political Contestability."

20.   For example, W. J. Baumol, J. C. Panzar, R. D. Willig, and others, *Contestable Markets and the Theory of Industry Structure* (New York: Harcourt Brace Jovanovich, 1982).

21.   Mitnick, "Political Contestability," 22.

22.   Ibid., 21.

23.   R. E. Freeman and D. R. Gilbert, *Corporate Strategy and the Search for Ethics* (Englewood Cliffs, NJ: Prentice Hall, 1988); C. McMahon, "Morality and the Invisible Hand," *Philosophy and Public Affairs* 10 (1981), 247–72.

24.   Freeman and Gilbert, *Corporate Strategy and the Search for Ethics*, 113.

25. G. F. Cavanaugh, Moberg D. J., and M. Velasquez, 1981, "The Ethics of Organization Politics," *Academy of Management Review* 6 (1981), 363–64.

26. M. Edelman, *The Symbolic Uses of Politics* (Urbana: University of Illinois Press, 1964); C. D. Elder and R. W. Cobb, *The Political Use of Symbols* (New York: Longman, 1983).

27. E. E. Shattschneider, *The Semi-Sovereign People* (New York: Holt, 1960); R. W. Cobb and C. D. Elder, *Participation in American Politics: The Dynamics of Agenda Building* (Baltimore, MD: Johns Hopkins University Press, 1972).

28. L. L. Kaid, "Ethical Dimensions of Political Advertising," in *Ethical Dimensions of Political Communication*, ed. R. E. Denton Jr. (New York: Praeger, 1991).

29. K. H. Jamieson and J. N. Cappella, *Media in the Middle: Fairness and Accuracy in the 1994 Health Care Reform Debate* (Philadelphia: Annenberg Public Policy Center, University of Pennsylvania, n.d.).

30. Interestingly, it was also found that most of this advertising was not national in scope, but concentrated on the Washington, DC, and New York areas, presumably aimed at politicians and members of the national news media. This would have the dual purpose of creating a strong impression on decision makers and opinion leaders, while employing the national media to repeat the messages across the country free of charge as they reported the campaign on the evening news.

31. For a discussion and an opposing point of view, see S. Iyengar and A. F. Simon, "New Perspectives and Evidence on Political Communication and Campaign Effects," *Annual Review of Psychology*, 51 (2000), 149–69.

32. For a review and typology of the many conceptions of the public interest, see B. M. Mitnick, *The Political Economy of Regulation: Creating, Designing and Removing Regulatory Forms* (New York: Columbia University Press, 1980).

33. D. Vogel, *Fluctuating Fortunes: The Political Power of Business in America* (New York: Basic Books, 1989).

Part XI
Corruption (Corruption and Strategy)

[40]

CORRUPTION AND CHANGE: THE IMPACT OF FOREIGN DIRECT INVESTMENT

CHRISTOPHER J. ROBERTSON* and ANDREW WATSON
College of Business Administration, Northeastern University, Boston, Massachusetts, U.S.A.

This study examines influences on the level of corruption in countries from a strategic perspective. Corruption is one of the country-level influences on market entry, investment, and other decisions fundamental to strategic management at the international level. The study examines the impact on corruption of change in levels of foreign direct investment (FDI). It uses the Corruption Perceptions Index (CPI) scores computed by Transparency International for 1999 and 2000. Results indicate that the more rapid the rate of change in FDI, the higher the level of corruption. Higher levels of perceived corruption are associated with each of two dimensions of national culture: uncertainty avoidance and masculinity. Research and managerial implications are also discussed. Copyright © 2004 John Wiley & Sons, Ltd.

INTRODUCTION

"Corruption levels are perceived to be as high as ever in both the developed and developing worlds"

Chairman Peter Eigen of Transparency International, Paris, June 27, 2001

Fundamental to international strategy are decisions involving selection of countries in which to do business, and the extent of investment in each country. One of the factors influencing the foreign direct investment (FDI) decision is the level of corruption in the host country (Mauro, 1995; Wei, 2000). Indeed, in some regions of the world engaging in corruption is essentially unavoidable (Getz and Volkema, 2001). Patterns of corruption have triggered recent public scandals in countries such as France, Indonesia, and Argentina. The United

States is not untainted by private payments for corporate gain, as evidenced by many recent examples of political contributions to gain favorable rulings by government agencies and bribes to secure construction projects. These questionable practices affect investment patterns at the firm level, and hence, in aggregate, at the country level. Thus they are of relevance to firms, governments, and scholars of international strategy (Cassel, 2001; Hosmer, 1994, 2000).

Fittingly, international studies of corruption have burgeoned in recent years (e.g., Husted, 1999; Volkema and Chang, 1998). This new wave of empirical research has finally begun to supplement the more developed conceptual and model development arm of cross-cultural corruption research (Davis, Johnson, and Ohlmer, 1998; Robertson and Fadil, 1999; Wines and Napier, 1992). The German anti-corruption group Transparency International has contributed greatly to empirical corruption research, particularly by publishing the Corruption Perceptions Index (CPI) on an annual basis since 1995. The strategic nature of foreign market

Key words: corruption; change; foreign direct investment
*Correspondence to: Christopher J. Robertson, College of Business Administration, Northeastern University, 313 Hayden Hall, Boston, MA 02115, U.S.A. E-mail: c.robertson@neu.edu

analysis and FDI decisions, and the sheer weight that corruption patterns have on these decisions, reinforces the relevance of corruption research to strategic management.

Two developed streams, and one burgeoning stream, are apparent in the literature that seeks to explain between-country differences in corruption. One of these streams provides an account of corruption in terms of economics (e.g., Shleifer and Vishny, 1993; Wei, 2000). The second stream provides an account of corruption in terms of national culture (e.g., Wines and Napier, 1992). These two streams have recently started to mingle (e.g., Getz and Volkema, 2001; Husted, 1999), thus producing a third, integrative, stream. We regard this third stream as particularly relevant to strategic decision making, since it simultaneously considers 'hard' (economic) and 'soft' (cultural) variables.

The current study is a contribution to this integrative third stream of research. It is distinctive within the stream in that it focuses on change, with a keen eye on the impact of changes in FDI on shifting corruption patterns. This research line differentiates itself from extant research in two ways. First, it is dynamic, in that it focuses on change in, rather than level of, FDI. Second, while building on research that examines the impact of corruption on FDI, and acknowledging this impact, the current study examines the link from a different perspective: it identifies the impact of change in FDI on corruption. This multidimensional focus on change, FDI, and corruption is clearly exploratory in nature. Thus, the overall objective of this paper is to determine if the speed of FDI inflows and outflows influences corruption patterns. A secondary objective is to examine the influence on corruption of those dimensions of national culture most relevant to change.

INFLUENCES ON CORRUPTION PATTERNS

A broad range of definitions of corruption has been proposed by both scholars and practitioners. For our purposes we employ the definition developed by Getz and Volkema (2001: 9): 'the abuse of public roles and resources for private benefit or the misuse of office for nonofficial ends.' The most common forms of corruption in international business that affect strategic maneuvering are bribery, extortion, and embezzlement. In the context of this paper we refer to corruption in the general sense, as a comprehensive term for the myriad forms of corrupt activities that occur on a global scale. Moreover, it should be noted that we are measuring *perceived corruption* using the Transparency International data (We describe this and other measures in the Methods section).

Many scholars of corruption have elected to examine this phenomenon from an economic perspective (i.e., Brunetti, 1995; Mauro, 1995; Nye, 1979; Shleifer and Vishny, 1993; Rose-Ackerman, 1999). Mauro (1995), for example, found that corruption has a negative effect on investment, thus resulting in less economic growth. Goudie and Stasavage (1997) concluded that corruption is, in part, a result of the level of efficiency in a country. Corruption has also been found to have a positive impact on economic growth and development (Nye, 1979). The economists have developed two fundamental arguments against bribery and corruption. First, corruption has a *disincentive* effect on investment, since it increases the risk and uncertainty faced by potential investors (Getz and Volkema, 2001), as well as adding bribes and other dubious expenses to the costs of doing business.

Second, corruption has *distortionary* effects (Goudie and Stasavage, 1997). In particular, monies paid for bribery are inefficiently allocated resources. Shleifer and Vishny argue that corruption is 'much more distortionary and costly than its sister activity, taxation' (Shleifer and Vishny, 1993: 599). Corruption, unlike taxation, must usually be kept secret, and there is a cost to this secrecy that has no counterpart in the realm of taxation. This highlights the managerial relevance of corruption in a country; in assessing the cost of doing business in a particular country, firms and their managers should consider the level of corruption even more carefully than the level of taxation.

Corruption has also been studied from a cultural perspective. While numerous researchers have developed conceptual models and propositions that support culture's influence on corruption and ethics (i.e., Vitell, Nwachukwu, and Barnes, 1993; Wines and Napier, 1992) few empirical studies of this relationship have been performed. Robertson *et al.* (2002), in a study of managers from Chile, the United States, Australia, and Ecuador, concluded that culture does indeed influence the variation in ethical judgments across borders. Ralston *et al.* (1993) found that Hong Kong and U.S. managers shared few cultural similarities in their perceptions of ethical behavior. Conversely, Abratt, Nel. and Higgs (1992) examined the ethical beliefs of managers from South Africa and Australia and determined that culture had no impact on ethical beliefs. Other studies have been conducted, but there appears to be no consistency in methodology, sample selection, or level of analysis.

While the economic and cultural aspects of culture are further along in the literature, few researchers have attempted to blend these two areas into a more comprehensive analysis. Two recent studies have mixed the economic and the cultural. Husted (1999) examined the impact of income per capita and culture on corruption and he found that a significant inverse relationship exists between income per capita and perceptions of corruption. A number of relationships between culture and corruption were also identified. Getz and Volkema (2001) developed and tested a model that included culture, economic factors, and corruption. They concluded that economic adversity was positively related to corruption and that culture played a moderating role.

The concept of change has been essentially overlooked in economic, cultural, and mixed studies of corruption. And while corruption is generally assumed to be a predictor of investment flows, few scholars have challenged the direction of this relationship. In this article, we link corruption to change. Change, although rarely studied by corruption researchers, resonates with numerous cross-cultural issues and has been recently examined in light of such themes as championing strategies, trade missions, and economic development (Ralston *et al.*, 1997; Shane and Venkataraman, 1996; Shane, 1995; Wilkinson and Brouthers, 2000). Changes in country-level wealth can be attributed to increases and/or decreases in foreign direct investment. Indeed, additional factors also affect this relationship between income and investment. Variables such as the abundance of natural resources (oil in Venezuela), the level of innovation (the hi-tech sector of Bangalore in India), governmental philosophy on trade (the level and scope of trade barriers), and the cultural tendencies (such as nationalism, language abilities, education, and cultural distance) as well as other factors influence investment decisions and patterns (Getz and Volkema, 2001; Guillon, 2000; Husted, 1999; Puffer and McCarthy, 1995). Based on numerous economic, historical, and geopolitical factors,

nations experience varying degrees of FDI annually (Kogut and Singh, 1988).

While the impact of FDI on corruption patterns is essentially unknown, an analysis of data and global trade patterns reveals that a relationship is quite plausible. For example, due to its glasnost policy in the late 1980s Russia experienced a major jolt in FDI immediately after the fall of Communism and the break-up of the Soviet Union in 1991. Since the Soviet Union's collapse corruption in Russia has been rampant (Puffer and McCarthy, 1995). Other former Communist nations, such as Estonia, the Czech Republic, and Poland, which experienced a more gradual, incremental flow of FDI, have consistently maintained a much lower degree of corruption.[1] It appears that the speed and magnitude of foreign investment could very well play a role in country-level corruption patterns.

While Husted (1999) concluded that industrialization makes a difference, FDI was not included in his analysis. We go a step further in our assertion that the *speed* of industrialization makes a difference. Earlier studies have recognized that speed makes a difference in phenomena such as the adoption of unfamiliar values or technologies (Ralston *et al.*, 1997; Shane, 1995). When a country is inundated with a disproportionate level of FDI in a short period of time, a jolt to the moral framework is more likely because of the sheer multitude of trade values that are involved.

The theory of *moral intensity* has a strong footing on each side of the economic and cultural debate about corruption. This theory also addresses the notion of timing and change. The basic premise of moral intensity is its focus on the moral issue, rather than the moral agent or the organizational context (Jones, 1991). According to Jones (1991) moral intensity consists of six components: the magnitude of the consequences, social consensus, probability of effect, temporal immediacy, proximity, and concentration of effect. Three of these subparts are conceptually linked to our theoretical position in this study. The first is social consensus, which is defined as the degree of social agreement that a proposed act is evil or good (Jones, 1991). The second is temporal immediacy, or the length of time between the present and the onset of

---

[1] The 1999 and 2000 CPI rankings for these nations are as follows: 1999, Estonia 27th, Czech Republic 39th. Poland 44th, Russia 82nd; 2000, Estonia 27th, Czech Republic 42nd, Poland 43rd, Russia 82nd.

388   *C. J. Robertson and A. Watson*

consequences of the moral act in question (Jones, 1991). The third is proximity, which is the feeling of nearness (social, cultural, psychological, or physical) that the moral agent has for victims of the immoral act in question (Jones, 1991). Cultural and economic perceptions of different issues are likely to vary depending on the varying weight of each of the moral intensity components.

HYPOTHESES

The first relationship that we seek to examine is that a large increase in FDI flowing into a country will result in a higher level of corruption. An increase in FDI by definition represents a larger amount of foreign money flowing into the country, and hence an expansion of the opportunities for bribery (Smarzynska and Wei, 2000). Take the example of Ecuador, a nation that adopted the U.S. dollar as its currency in 2000 and has experienced a resurgence of economic growth and an influx of FDI. Ecuador's economy grew by 5.4 percent in 2001 yet *corruption* went up; Ecuador's 2001 corruption 'clean' score dropped by 13 percent, and the country fell from 74th to 79th in the overall rankings (www.transparency.org). Spikes in FDI may indeed create more opportunities for corruption in the short run. Further, FDI is likely to represent an eagerness on the part of foreign firms to take an opportunity presented by the target country. This eagerness may tempt host country nationals to resort to corruption as a means of sharing in the opportunities for profit presented by their own country.

In order to move from prediction to hypothesis, it is necessary to be more specific about the nature of the relationship between change in FDI and perceived corruption. Based on this relationship we present three hypotheses (Hypotheses 1a, 1b, and 1c), similar in that each is consistent with the prediction, but different in the shape of the line linking the two variables. Each arc has been plotted on a graph (Figure 1) ranging from hypothetical points negative 10 to positive 10, with a midpoint of zero. Therefore, Figure 1 illustrates the three hypotheses and the corresponding lines, which we refer to as: (a) linear; (b) V-shaped; and (c) U-shaped.

The first of these relationships is the simplest translation of the above rationale into a hypothesis. According to Jones (1991) and his notion

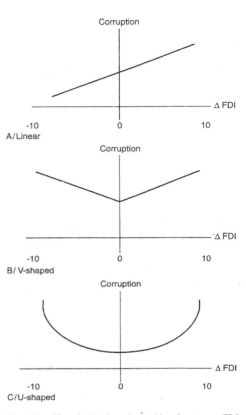

Figure 1. Hypothesized relationship between FDI change and corruption

of temporal immediacy, people tend to discount the impact of events that occur in the future. The consequences of occurrences, such as rapid changes in FDI, that are closer to the present tend to carry more moral weight (Jones, 1991). Thus, this hypothesis is consistent with literature that supports a linear link between corruption and antecedents such as economic adversity (Getz and Volkema, 2001), and income per capita (Husted, 1999). Therefore:

Hypothesis 1a: The more rapid the rate of change in FDI into a country, the higher the perceived level of corruption.

The next plausible relationship between FDI change and corruption is V-shaped. The shape of the corresponding graph is similar to that of the linear relationship for increases in FDI, but different for decreases. This prediction incorporates the absolute value of the FDI rate of change, thus capturing both inflows and outflows of FDI. Thus, not only do increases in FDI lead to higher corruption but decreases in FDI do as well. In theory, a rapid withdrawal or drop-off in FDI creates a situation in which resources become scarce. Fewer contacts and joint venture partners are now available and the competition for foreign monies creates an environment in which corruption may flourish. Clearly the current crisis in Argentina is an example of what happens when foreign investors pull out. The collapse of the Argentine economy in late 2001, combined with a 5-year recession and political turmoil, has led to a rapid decrease in FDI levels and a jolt in corruption (Moore, 2002). Further, as income per capita drops, due to less wealth created by foreign investors, corruption goes up (Husted, 1999). Based on this rationale:

Hypothesis 1b: The more rapid the increase or decrease in FDI into a country, the higher the perceived level of corruption.

The third possible form of the relationship resembles the second, in that there is a point of inflection in the line. However, this third line is smoother than the second (see Figure 1, and compare b and c). Moreover, it illustrates that the effect of change in FDI on corruption is more than linear, in that it shows particularly strong effects on corruption when the change in FDI is large. This is consistent with the above discussion of abrupt 'jolts' as having a marked effect on corruption. Therefore:

Hypothesis 1c: The perceived level of corruption increases with the square of change in FDI into a country.

We now turn from our economic antecedent to our cultural antecedents of corruption. The moral intensity components, social consensus and proximity support the notion that culture plays a role in ethical behavior (Jones, 1991). With our focus on change we consider the dimensions of culture most relevant to change: uncertainty avoidance and masculinity (Hofstede, 1997). Moreover, the speed with which the FDI occurs serves as a catalyst to this relationship between corruption

and uncertainty. This relationship between uncertainty avoidance and corruption has been examined and tested—but prior tests have not controlled for change in FDI. Getz and Volkema (2001) supported the hypothesis that higher uncertainty avoidance leads to higher corruption. For example, Husted, (1999: 345) views corruption as 'a mechanism to reduce uncertainty,' and his results appear to validate this assertion. He does, however, acknowledge that prior research (Cohen, Pant, and Sharp, 1996) suggests that the relationship between uncertainty avoidance and corruption may work in the opposite direction. There are therefore grounds for concern about the robustness of the link between uncertainty avoidance and corruption. Of particular relevance here is that this has yet to be explored in the presence of the additional variable of rate of change in FDI. The next of our hypotheses is a prediction that the link will be robust.

Hypothesis 2: The higher the level of uncertainty avoidance in a country, the higher the perceived level of corruption.

A positive relationship between masculinity and corruption has also been established (Getz and Volkema, 2001; Husted, 1999). The idea here is that the masculine values of assertiveness, aggressiveness, and materialism tend to associate with a higher degree of corruption than do feminine values, which tend to be more social (Hofstede, 1997). While Hofstede's primary level of analysis is the cultural level, his work does relate to the wealth of studies that have focused on how men and women differ (Gilligan, 1982). Of course, a masculine culture can indeed include women, and a feminine culture men, yet it is the masculine trait of materialism that is the primary driver of the link to corruption. Greed and lust for the accumulation of individual wealth are traditional pillars of corruption (Husted, 1999). Hence, in masculine cultures, actions tend to be biased toward acquisition, even when the actions involve corruption. Again, the hypothesis states a test of the robustness of the link between culture and corruption when change in FDI is present in the model:

Hypothesis 3: The higher the level of masculinity in a country, the higher the perceived level of corruption.

METHODOLOGY

Measures

The data set for the study was procured from Transparency International, World Bank, and other published, archival sources (see full listing in Table 1). Our examination of the link between FDI and corruption differs from that of prior researchers in that corruption is our dependent variable, rather than our predictor variable. We

measured corruption using the Corruption Perceptions Index (CPI) scores computed by Transparency International. In the interest of robustness we took measures for 2 years: 1999 and 2000.

Transparency International computes the CPI annually as a composite of a number of independent surveys (see Table 2 for a list; also Transparency International publishes an online comprehensive background paper on the CPI methodology each year. The paper can be found at www.transparency.org). These surveys differ

Table 1.   Data sources

Data	Source
CPI	Transparency International, www.transparency.de
BPI	Transparency International, www.transparency.de
GNP total	World Bank, www.worldbank.org (1998, 1999)
GNP per capita	World Bank, www.worldbank.org (1998, 1999)
Hofstede's scores	Geert Hofstede. *Cultures and Organizations: Software of the Mind*, 1991
FDI	World Bank, www.worldbank.org (1998, 1999)
Government consumption as a % of GDP	*International Financial Statistics Yearbook* (1998, 1999)
Total consumption as a % of GDP	*International Financial Statistics Yearbook* (1998, 1999)

Table 2.   Transparency international sources for 2000 CPI

Source	Year(s)	Coverage	Respondents
Political and Economic Risk Consultancy (PERC)	1998	12 Asian countries	Expatriate executives
PERC	1999	12 Asian countries	
PERC	2000	14 countries	
Institute for Management Development (IMD)	1998	46 countries	Executives in domestic and foreign firms
IMD	1999	47 countries	
IMD	2000	47 countries	
Economist Intelligence Unit (EIU)	2000	115 countries	Experts: EIU staff
International Crime Victim Survey (ICVS)	1999/2000	11 countries	General public
World Bank	1999	20 transition economies	Senior executives
Freedom House	1998	28 transition economies	Experts: FH staff and academics
World Economic Forum (WEF)	1998	53 countries	Business leaders; domestic and international firms
WEF	1999	59 countries	
WEF	2000	59 countries	
WEF (Africa competitiveness report)	1998	20 African countries	
WEF	2000	26 African countries	
Political Risk Services (PRS)	2000	140 countries	Experts: PRS staff

Note 1: The sources used differ from year to year. Hence the CPI allows cross-sectional comparisons, but not longitudinal comparisons.
Note 2: The table is based on the Appendix to Lambsdorff (2000).

with respect to respondents and items used, but are strongly correlated (Lambsdorff, 2000). Target questions typically include questions that range from the frequency of corruption in various contexts (such as obtaining permits, avoiding taxes) to the common occurrence of bribery to politicians, senior civil servants, and judges. Moreover, all of these sources employ a degree of corruption measure which adds consistency and reliability to the final compiled scores (Lambsdorff, 2000). In most cases, the sample designs are restricted to business practitioners who are local residents.

The CPI score for 1999 includes 99 countries and 80 for 2000. We used Husted's (1999) transformation of the CPI in order to make values of this corruption variable more intuitive: we inverted the 0 to 10 scale by subtracting each country's score from 10, thus making a 10 the most corrupt country and a 0 the least corrupt. The CPI has been a focal variable in a number of recent international studies of corruption and its validity appears to be strong (i.e., Getz and Volkema, 2001; Heidenheimer, 1996; Husted, 1999; Volkema and Chang, 1998).

The independent variables for the study fall into two categories: change in FDI variables and cultural variables. We computed three FDI change variables, one for each of the hypothesized relationships (i.e., linear, V-shaped, and U-shaped). The first, linear change in FDI, was computed by taking the raw changes from one year to the next. For example, FDI into Argentina changed from U.S. $6.670 billion in 1998 to $23.929 billion in 1999, and so for Argentina, *FDI linear change* took the value 2.59 [(23.929 -6.670)/6.670]. This variable therefore captures our construct of developmental speed, with the opportunities for corruption that it presents, that has been employed in Hypothesis 1a. The *FDI V-shaped change* variable was created by taking the absolute value of *FDI linear change*, thus capturing both the positive and negative flow of FDI. The *FDI U-shaped change* was created by squaring the *FDI linear change* variable. The FDI figures, for 1998 and for 1999, were obtained from the World Bank statistical unit (www.worldbank.org).

Due to the varying speed in which FDI, and its accompanying influences, assimilates into a society we intentionally calibrated a 1- and 2-year lag-time between the independent and dependent

variables. Thus we collected 1998 data for all control variables, with the exception of Hofstede's earlier measures, which are assumed to be constant. We then collected FDI figures for 1998 and 1999, and CPI scores for 1999 and 2000. This enabled us to determine if timing is also an issue in our hypotheses.

The two cultural predictor variables, Masculinity and Uncertainty Avoidance, were based on Hofstede's (1997) cultural dimension scores from an earlier multinational study of cultural values. Although Hofstede's measures have been criticized as being less useful over time (Sivakumar and Nakata, 2001), recent studies (e.g., Brouthers and Brouthers, 2001; Chandy and Williams, 1994; Shane, 1995) have upheld the theoretical and empirical value of his constructs and measures.

Additional control variables consisted of Gross National Product, GNP per capita, Government Consumption as a percentage of GNP, FDI as a percentage of GNP, and Hofstede's variable power distance.[2] We selected these particular control variables, since they are both consistent with prior macro-level studies of FDI and Corruption, and also make theoretical sense in our regression model (Guillon, 2000; Husted, 1999; Wilkinson and Brouthers, 2000). We lagged the control variables in the same way as the predictor variables; hence we used 1998 data.

RESULTS

The means, standard deviations, and correlations are presented in Table 3. The mean GNP per capita was U.S. $7914, which compares to U.S. $5770 by Getz and Volkema (2001) and U.S. $12,828 by Husted (1999). Although the correlations between corruption and GNP per capita, and corruption and power distance, indicate a potential for multicollinearity, our use of the robust method of OLS hierarchical regression to test the hypotheses generally prevents any undue influences (Husted, 1999). Nevertheless, we followed up with diagnostic statistical collinearity tests that measure Variance Inflation Factor (VIF), which is provided

---

[2] We initially included individualism in our analysis but, since it was insignificant in our initial model, and in order to be consistent with Husted (1999), we decided not to include this variable in our final model. The variance explained by individualism was not significant and there was no material effect on the significance of our results.

392   *C. J. Robertson and A. Watson*

Table 3.   Descriptive statistics and correlations

Variable	Mean	S.D.	1	2	3	4	5	6	7	8	9	10
1. Corruption	5.39	2.35	1.00									
2. GNP per capita	7914	10844	−0.85***	1.00								
3. GNP	75.4	919.7	−0.25**	−0.40***	1.00							
4. Consumption	0.16	5.39	−0.42***	−0.32**	−0.03	1.00						
5. Power distance	56.35	22.07	0.71***	0.60***	0.16	0.66***	1.00					
6. Masculinity	48.58	19.00	0.22	0.02	−0.31*	0.24	−0.09	1.00				
7. Uncertainty	66.69	25.00	0.43**	0.30*	0.04	0.13	−0.22	0.01	1.00			
8. Linear FDI Δ	0.18	1.04	−0.04	−0.19	−0.20*	0.20	0.11	−0.10	0.13	1.00		
9. V-shaped FDI Δ	0.61	0.85	−0.03	0.07	0.12	−0.20	0.07	0.08	−0.02	0.85***	1.00	
10. U-shaped FDI Δ	1.09	4.80	−0.10	−0.01	0.05	−0.26*	0.12	0.02	−0.08	0.81***	0.90***	1.00

Note 1: Two-tailed tests; Ns ranged from 43 to 102; * $p < 0.05$; ** $p < 0.01$; *** $p < 0.001$.
Note 2: Scores are based on 1998 figures except Corruption; CPI, 1999; CPI 2000.
Note 3: GNP per capita in thousands; GNP in billions; Government size equals total government consumption as a % of GDP.

Table 4.   Results of hierarchical regression analysis for CPI 1999

	Model 1	Model 2	Model 3	Model 4
Control variables				
GNP per capita	−0.73***	−0.72***	−0.71***	−0.71***
GNP	0.05	0.03	0.03	0.04
Consumption	−0.12	−0.05	−0.06	−0.05
Power distance	0.11	0.15	0.12	0.13
FDI per capita	−0.09	0.01	−0.03	−0.02
Predictor variables				
Masculinity		0.24**	0.20*	0.25**
Uncertainty		0.17**	0.16*	0.17*
Linear change in FDI		0.17**		
V-shaped change in FDI			0.14*	
U- shaped change in FDI				0.15*
Model R^2	0.81	0.86	0.85	0.85
ΔR^2		0.05*	0.04*	0.04*
F	23.99***	23.31***	21.89***	21.93***

Note: One-tailed tests for the significance of t; all Beta coefficients are standardized.

by the SPSS software. The results of these tests revealed that our VIFs ranged from 1.09 to 1.96 (and all tolerance levels above 0.51). According to Fox (1991), a VIF of above 4.0, or a tolerance level below 0.25, may indicate the potential for multicollinearity; thus the concern in our models appears minimal.

In Tables 4 and 5 the results from our hierarchical regression analyses are presented. An independent model was run for each dependent variable (CPI 1999 and CPI 2000) and each model consisted of four stages where control variables were entered in stage 1 and predictor variables in stages 2, 3, and 4. The results indicate support for Hypotheses 1a, 1b, and 1c, for both the 1999 and 2000 models. Thus it appears that changes in foreign direct investment lead to higher perceived

levels of corruption in a country. Further, our results indicate that the linear, V-shaped, and U-shaped relationships are all plausible. For the 1999 Corruption Perceptions Index the overall models were significant (F ranges from 21.89 to 23.31; $p < 0.001$) and the *FDI linear change* variable was significant at the 0.01 level ($\beta = 0.17$). *FDI V-shaped change* ($\beta = 0.14$, $p < 0.05$) and *FDI U-shaped change* ($\beta = 0.15$, $p < 0.05$) were also significant. This pattern held for the 2000 CPI model as well (F ranges from 19.98 to 20.35; $p < 0.001$) with significant parameter estimates for all three FDI predictor hypotheses. Moreover, the R^2 (1999 = 0.85; 2000 = 0.86) and ΔR^2 for both models was strong and significant.

Hypothesis 2 posited that higher levels of uncertainty avoidance are related to higher perceived

Table 5. Results of hierarchical regression analysis for CPI 2000

	Model 1	Model 2	Model 3	Model 4
Control variables				
GNP per capita	−0.69***	−0.65***	−0.64***	−0.63***
GNP	0.02	0.03	0.01	0.01
Consumption	−0.08	−0.03	−0.04	−0.02
Power distance	0.16	0.22	0.21*	0.21
FDI per capita	−0.12	−0.06	−0.08	−0.07
Predictor variables				
Masculinity		0.22*	0.21*	0.22*
Uncertainty		0.14*	0.14*	0.15*
Linear change in FDI		0.16*		
V-shaped change in FDI			0.14*	
U-shaped change in FDI				0.15*
Model R^2	0.82	0.86	0.86	0.86
ΔR^2		0.04*	0.04*	0.04*
F	22.49***	20.35***	19.98***	20.07***

Note: One-tailed tests for the significance of t; all β coefficients are standardized.

levels of corruption. The results from Tables 4 and 5 also support this hypothesis. The uncertainty variable was significant in both models (1999 $\beta = 0.17$, $p < 0.01$; 2000 $\beta = 0.14$, $p < 0.05$) which is indicative of a strong relationship between this cultural dimension and corruption perceptions, even when change in FDI is controlled for.

As predicted in Hypothesis 3, a positive significant relationship was identified between masculinity and CPI (1999 $\beta = 0.24$, $p < 0.01$; $\beta = 0.22$, $p < 0.05$) which suggests that nations that embrace masculine values, such as materialism and assertiveness, tend to have a higher degree of perceived corruption.

One additional relationship identified by the models is noteworthy. The link between GNP per capita and CPI was highly significant in both models (1999 $\beta = -0.72$, $p < 0.001$; 2000 $\beta = -0.65$, $p < 0.001$) which is consistent with prior research (Getz and Volkema, 2001; Husted, 1999). This finding emphasizes the strength of this relationship despite the inclusion of additional control and predictor variables.

DISCUSSION

The purpose of this study was to incorporate the concepts of change and foreign direct investment into the cross-cultural corruption research stream. In particular, we posited that the rate of change of FDI would influence national perceived levels of corruption. The empirical support for Hypotheses 1a, 1b, and 1c lends credence to our claim and this finding may be an intriguing crossroads for future corruption and international strategy research. One road for future research may lead to further investigation of the relationship between FDI and corruption; for example, does this relationship differ between geographic regions? Another road may lead to further investigation of the relationship between change, culture, and corruption. For example, if two diverse cultures, such as Vietnam and Bolivia, both experience a rapid influx of FDI will corruption patterns be similar or different? And why? Future research can help to better pinpoint which arc, from Figure 1, best describes the nature of this relationship for a given region.

Prior work in this domain has assumed that FDI flows are affected by the level of corruption. While we agree that this direction exists, the possibility of a bidirectional relationship, with FDI flows affecting corruption, has been essentially overlooked. The idea of cultural convergence, where developing nations are becoming more westernized as a result of foreign MNC influence, also supports this claim. Certainly some MNCs are taking a few questionable practices with them into the developing world. We have also added to other related research domains. In the Foreign Direct Investment literature, for example, the concept of cultural distance has had three primary thrusts: to explain the target investment location, to predict the most favorable entry mode, and to account for success

(Shenkar, 2001). Our validation of the robustness of the relationship between uncertainty avoidance, a subconstruct of cultural distance, and corruption adds to this stream by extending the set of viable dependent variables. This contribution is important to managers faced with various target FDI destinations, each with a varying degree of cultural distance and corruption.

A number of implications for practitioners are plausible based on our findings. The OECD's recent approval of an antibribery pact by 32 nations speaks to the importance of corruption in the international community (Husted, 1999). As developed industrialized nations continue to try and level the bribery and corruption playing fields developing countries will be forced to respond, otherwise FDI opportunities may be squandered. Indeed, an understanding of how FDI and uncertainty relate to corruption can aid policy developers in both governmental and private enterprise settings. For example, if a manager at a multinational firm that is considering a potential market is aware that market has a pattern of high corruption followed by a massive influx of FDI, certain procedures and protocols for dealing with local contacts may need to be adjusted depending on the current economic situation.

Our study has additional implications for managers. They may, for example, elect to rethink the validity of their corporate codes of ethics in countries that have experienced a massive influx of FDI or are in dire economic straits. They may also hesitate to jump on an FDI bandwagon, such as the one that hurtled into Russia in the 1990s. Eagerness to get in on the action, and fear of being left out while their counterparts in other firms are seizing what appears to be a golden opportunity, are understandable. But this eagerness should be tempered with awareness that the large increase in FDI may change the target country in ways that make it more difficult for MNCs to conduct business there. In particular, it may tempt host country nationals into behaviors that are perceived as corrupt by firms and their managers. Nevertheless, the impact of cataclysmic events, such as the largest bankruptcy filing in U.S. history as a result of Worldcom's financial cover-up, on global ethical standards cannot be underestimated. Indeed, the nations which are typically senders of FDI, rather than receivers, possess many moral responsibilities as well.

As with any study, a few limitations are worth mentioning at this point. Similar to earlier studies (Getz and Volkema, 2001) we employed the CPI as our proxy for corruption. Although this construct is based on numerous submeasures it captures only perceptions of corruption. Thus, actual behavior and activity are overlooked. Indeed, examining actual behavior, through national crime statistics for example, also presents problems due to strong national variations in legal code enforcement and conviction. Interestingly, Singapore's very high per capita conviction rate of bribery is misleading when compared to lower rates in developing countries in Africa and Latin America (Lambsdorff, 2000). The use of residents and nonresidents in the CPI composite score may also create some level of response bias. The use of Hofstede's (1997) dimensions has also been criticized, yet remains a strong proxy for culture in international business research (Brouthers and Brouthers, 2001). Also, a large percentage of the nations in our sample period experienced increases in FDI during the period and clearly the timing of any macro-level study is reflected in the findings.

Future research opportunities in this area are plentiful. Husted (1999) conceded that his study took a static approach to corruption and failed to examine the impact of changes in economic development or culture on changes in the level of corruption. While we have addressed the dynamic part of changes in economic development in the current study, we have also retained a static measure of culture. Future researchers may elect to incorporate, simultaneously, changes in economic development, culture, and corruption. The possibility of corruption leading to changes in various cultural variables is also a worthy area of future research, yet will have to wait until a more current, reliable, measure of culture emerges.

Analysis of the country of origin of the FDI is also a priority for future research. Here again, Transparency International does a service to the research community and to other communities by collecting data and making them available. The Bribe-Payers Index (BPI) is the supply-side counterpart to the demand-side measure we use in the current research (i.e., the CPI). Further, the destination (business sector, and public vs. private) of investment within the receiving country origin of the FDI, the particular mode of entry, and the local/foreign ownership ratio may all play an influential role in the speed and scope of changes in perceptions of corruption. In sum, any attempt to reconcile actual and perceived corruption in the international context will likely be well received by scholars and practitioners alike.

ACKNOWLEDGEMENTS

The authors are grateful to Elena Dionysiou, Marcelo Perez-Verzini, and Marie Sibaud for research assistance.

REFERENCES

Abratt R, Nel D, Higgs N. 1992. An examination of the ethical beliefs of managers using selected scenarios in a cross-cultural environment. *Journal of Business Ethics* 11: 29–35.

Brouthers K, Brouthers LE. 2001. Explaining the national cultural distance paradox. *Journal of International Business Studies* 32(1): 177–189.

Brunetti A. 1995. Political variables in cross-country growth analysis. Working paper, Harvard University, Cambridge, MA.

Cassel D. 2001. Human rights and business responsibilities in the global marketplace. *Business Ethics Quarterly* 11(2): 261–274.

Chandy P, Williams T. 1994. The impact of journals and authors on international business research. *Journal of International Business Studies* 25(4): 715–728.

Cohen JR, Pant LW, Sharp DJ. 1996. A methodological note on cross-cultural accounting ethics research. *International Journal of Accounting* 31(1): 55–66.

Davis M, Johnson N, Ohlmer D. 1998. Issue-contingent effects on ethical decision-making: a cross-cultural comparison. *Journal of Business Ethics* 17: 373–389.

Fox J. 1991. *Regression Diagnostics*. Sage: Newbury Park, CA.

Getz KA, Volkema RJ. 2001. Culture, perceived corruption, and economics. *Business & Society* 40(1): 7–30.

Gilligan C. 1982. *In a Different Voice: Psychological Theory and Women's Development*. Cambridge, MA: Harvard University Press.

Goudie A, Stasavage D. 1997. Corruption: The Issues. Working paper, Organization for Economic Cooperation and Development: Paris.

Guillon M. 2000. Business groups in emerging economies: a resource-based view. *Academy of Management Journal* 43(3): 362–380.

Heidenheimer A. 1996. The topography of corruption: explorations in a comparative perspective. *International Social Science Journal* 158(3): 337–347.

Hofstede G. 1997. *Cultures and Organizations: Software of the Mind*. McGraw-Hill: New York.

Hosmer L. 1994. Strategic planning as if ethics mattered. *Strategic Management Journal*, Summer Special Issue 15: 17–34.

Hosmer L. 2000. It's time for empirical research in business ethics. *Business Ethics Quarterly* 10(1): 233–242.

Husted B. 1999. Wealth, culture, and corruption. *Journal of International Business Studies* 30(2): 339–360.

International Financial Statistics Yearbook. 1998. International Monetary Fund: Washington, DC.

International Financial Statistics Yearbook. 1999. International Monetary Fund: Washington, DC.

Jones TM. 1991. Ethical decision making by individuals in organizations: an issue-contingent model. *Academy of Management Review* 16(2): 366–395.

Kogut B, Singh H. 1988. The effect of national culture on choice of entry mode. *Journal of International Business Studies* 19(3): 411–432.

Lambsdorff J. 2000. Background paper to the 2000 Corruption Perceptions Index. *Transparency International* September 2000.www.transparency.org.

Mauro P. 1995. Corruption and growth. *Quarterly Journal of Economics* 110(3): 681–712.

Moore L. 2002. Argentine victims of crime fight back. *The Boston Globe* May 19: A4–A5.

Nye JS. 1979. Corruption and political development: a cost–benefit analysis. In *Bureaucratic Corruption in Sub-Saharan Africa: Causes, Consequences, and Controls*, Ekpo M (ed). University Press of America: Washington, DC; 57–79.

Puffer S, McCarthy D. 1995. Finding the common ground in Russian and American business ethics. *California Management Review* 37(2): 29–46.

Ralston DA, Gustafson DJ, Cheung FM, Terpstra RH. 1993. Differences in managerial values: a study of U.S., Hong Kong and PRC managers. *Journal of International Business Studies* 24(2): 249–276.

Ralston DA, Holt DH, Terpstra RH, Kai-Cheng Y. 1997. The impact of national culture and economic ideology on managerial work values: a study of the United States, Russia, Japan, and China. *Journal of International Business Studies* 28(1): 177–207.

Robertson C, Crittenden W, Brady M, Hoffman J. 2002. Situational ethics across borders: a multicultural examination. *Journal of Business Ethics* 38(4): 327–338.

Robertson C, Fadil P. 1999. Ethical decision making in multinational organizations: a culture-based model. *Journal of Business Ethics* 19(4): 385–392.

Rose-Ackerman S. 1999. *Corruption and Government*. Cambridge University Press: Cambridge, U.K.

Shane S. 1995. Uncertainty avoidance and the preference for innovation championing roles. *Journal of International Business Studies* 26(1): 47–68.

Shane S, Venkataraman S. 1996. Renegade and rational championing strategies. *Organization Studies* 17: 751–771.

Shenkar O. 2001. Cultural distance revisited: towards a more rigorous conceptualization and measurement of cultural differences. *Journal of International Business Studies* 32(3): 529–535.

Shleifer A, Vishny R. 1993. Corruption. *Quarterly Journal of Economics* 108(3): 599–618.

Sivakumar K, Nakata C. 2001. The stampede toward Hofstede's framework: avoiding the sample design pit in cross-cultural research. *Journal of International Business Studies* **32**(3): 555–574.

Smarzynska B, Wei S. 2000. Corruption and composition of foreign direct investment: firm-level evidence. National Bureau of Economic Research: Washington, DC.

Transparency International. www.transparency.org [15 January 2002].

Vitell S, Nwachukwu S, Barnes J. 1993. The effects of culture on ethical decision-making: an application of Hofstede's typology. *Journal of Business Ethics* **12**: 753–760.

Volkema R, Chang S. 1998. Negotiating in Latin America: what we know (or think we know) and what we would like to know. *Latin American Business Review* **1**(2): 3–25.

Wei S-J. 2000. How taxing is corruption on international investors? *Review of Economics and Statistics* **82**: 1–11.

Wilkinson T, Brouthers LE. 2000. Trade shows, trade missions and state governments: increasing FDI and high-tech exports. *Journal of International Business Studies* **31**(4): 725–734.

Wines W, Napier N. 1992. Toward an understanding of cross-cultural ethics: a tentative model. *Journal of Business Ethics* **11**: 831–841.

World Bank. www.worldbank.org [15 January 2002].

[41]

INCREASING FIRM VALUE THROUGH DETECTION AND PREVENTION OF WHITE-COLLAR CRIME

KAREN SCHNATTERLY*
Carlson School of Management, University of Minnesota, Minneapolis, Minnesota,

White-collar crime can cost a company from 1 percent to 6 percent of annual sales, yet little is known about the organizational conditions that can reduce this cost. Previous governance research has examined the link between block holders, boards of directors, or CEO compensation and fraud. In this study, these traditional measures of governance are found to have little impact. Instead, operational governance, including clarity of policies and procedures, formal cross-company communication, and performance-based pay for the board and for more employees, significantly reduces the likelihood of a crime commission. Copyright © 2003 John Wiley & Sons, Ltd.

INTRODUCTION

The economic impact of fraud is immense. Estimates of the cost of white-collar crime to companies in the United States range from $200 billion (Touby, 1994) to $600 billion per year (Association of Certified Fraud Examiners (ACFE), 2002). This is massively greater than street crime losses of $3–4 billion (Baucus and Baucus, 1997) and total economic loss to victims of personal and property crimes of $15.6 billion (Bureau of Justice Statistics, 1999). Fraud can significantly impact the financial performance of a firm as it can cost a typical company between 1 percent and 6 percent of annual sales (Hogsett and Radig, 1994; Touby, 1994; ACFE, 2002). White-collar crime alone causes 30 percent of new business failures (Agro, 1978), without regard to the quality of the firms' strategy or assets.

Fraud has brought down many apparently well-performing firms. Enron, Sunbeam, Cendant, and Waste Management are some of the most recent and spectacular examples. Even before Enron's collapse, the U.S. Securities and Exchange Commission was investigating more companies than ever for possible accounting fraud (Roland, 2001). The ability to prevent fraud, or value loss through fraud, has become a potential source of competitive advantage and improved financial performance for firms in today's economy.

This paper investigates whether firms' governance systems influence the probability of white-collar crime. Governance systems comprise not only the board of directors and the CEO, but also operational systems within the firm through which management can influence the firm. Components of these systems have been examined with respect to their role in strategy process[1]

Key words: fraud; crime; governance; internal control
*Correspondence to: Karen Schnatterly, Carlson School of Management, University of Minnesota, 321 19th Avenue South, Minneapolis, MN 55455, U.S.A.

[1] Process has to do with 'how' a firm gains a competitive position (Schendel, 1992), and relates to an understanding of both how to develop these processes to 'develop good strategy, and then go on to develop those processes necessary to use the strategy to operate the firm' (Schendel, 1992: 3).

588   *K. Schnatterly*

(Marginson, 2002), but not with regard to their impact on crime.

The investigation includes what might constitute failure of governance as well as providing some direction as to what might constitute more effective governance. Understanding or identifying the variation in governance systems between firms with crime and those without it provides insight toward the reduction of white-collar crime in all companies.

The governance differences between firms with crime and those without it is investigated using a sample of 114 firms, composed of matched pairs of firms, half with announced white-collar crimes and half without from 1988 to 1998. The key findings are that a firm's clarity of policies and procedures, formal communication, and contingent pay for employees are associated with less white-collar crime. Additionally, audit committees, contingent pay for board members, and codes of conduct are also associated with fewer crimes. No other board- or CEO-level variables, such as CEO compensation or percentage of outsiders on the board, have any impact on crime. This paper contributes to the literature on fraud research and to our understanding of the process of reducing fraud in organizations.

THEORY AND HYPOTHESES

Previous governance research has not addressed crime extensively, and the few studies that have generally focused on board-level variables rather than the organizational conditions that encourage or prevent crime. The researchers who have studied different operational governance mechanisms have generally done so one at a time. This study integrates the research of board-level variables with the multiple streams included in operational governance research to develop a set of mechanisms that may impact the occurrence of white-collar crime.

Previous governance research is largely derived from agency theory and has focused primarily on the structure of ownership (Abrahamson and Park, 1994), the board of directors (Abrahamson and Park, 1994; Beasley, 1996; Kassinis and Vafeas, 2002), or CEO compensation (Boyd, 1994). This research found that governance structure could influence white-collar crime. For example, Alexander and Cohen (1999), studying 78 public firms

with crimes committed during 1984–90, find that crime occurs less frequently among firms in which management (officers and directors) has a larger ownership stake. They conclude that penalizing shareholders through both corporate fines and the negative stock price reaction on announcement deters crime, and corporate crime tends not to benefit shareholders *ex ante*.

The focus of this previous research is critical, since boards of directors are the 'apex of the decision control systems of organizations' (Fama and Jensen, 1983: 311). However, there are other theory-inspired mechanisms beyond the board, the CEO, and the structure of ownership to monitor and control management. Fama and Jensen (1983: 310) argue that mutual monitoring systems and decision hierarchies supported by 'organizational rules of the game, for example, accounting and budgeting systems' are critical for efficient decision control and monitoring of management. There has been much less work in the area of 'organizational rules' or operational governance and, as a result, there is a need to link previous governance research with that of the organizational rules of the game.

This study examines what might constitute operational governance and how it might impact the occurrence of white-collar crime in a firm.

Operational governance

Fama and Jensen (1983) mention mutual monitoring, accounting, and budgeting systems as critical for ensuring that management's decisions are made with the interests of the shareholder in mind. Jensen and Meckling (1976: 308) include 'budget restrictions, compensation policies, operating rules, etc.' as important in monitoring management. These systems represent agency theory's ideas of the organizational rules of the game. This is related to the research on internal control. Internal control helps assure effectiveness and efficiency of operations, reliability of financial information, and compliance with applicable laws and regulations (Kinney, 2000).

These 'organizational rules of the game' have also been researched under the term 'management control.' Management control is the broad term that is related to the budgeting, planning, and accounting systems in a firm. Management control gives managers 'an explicit tool for strategy implementation' (Daft and Macintosh, 1984: 63) and 'involves target-setting, activity-monitoring, and deficiency-correcting activities' (Daft and Mac-intosh, 1984: 63). Management control can also be considered 'the process by which managers influence other members of the organization to implement the organization's strategies' (Anthony 1988: 10).

The quality or success of the management or internal control can affect the possibility of employee misconduct in a firm. For example, Leatherwood and Spector (1991) find that enforcements reduced employee misconduct. They find that inducements play a role as well, and that both enforcements and inducements have independent (not interactive) effects on reducing the likelihood of employee misconduct.[2] Russell (1995) argues that widespread corporate fraud often requires a failure in internal control or operational governance systems. Some of the characteristics of a company at high risk for fraud are: weak, loose, or no enforced internal controls; poor financial and operational planning; poor company loyalty, low morale and work motivation; unusual turnover; or rapid company expansion.

This research demonstrates that operational governance mechanisms influence crime commission.

As these mechanisms reduce crime, they have the ability to improve firm performance, as do the high-level mechanisms. The next section discusses these mechanisms individually and explores their ability to impact crime commission. Figure 1 illustrates this relationship.

Operational governance mechanisms

Many employees have the opportunity to commit white-collar crimes. In fact, several studies have shown that 30 percent of employees plan to steal, 30 percent may give in to temptation occasionally, and only 40 percent would resist this temptation[3] (Hogsett and Radig, 1994). While management may not be able to affect the 30 percent who plan to steal, they can affect the 30 percent who may occasionally give in to temptation by understanding the role of operational governance.

An accounting system comprises 'the methods by which financial data about a firm or its activity are collected, processed, stored and/or distributed' (Bruns, 1968: 470). The activities of collecting and processing are potential sources of error. Indeed, 'errors and inaccuracy in the process of measuring, counting and reporting are inevitable' (Bruns, 1968: 472). Better systems can reduce the degree of error. Better systems can also lead to less opportunity for funds or inventory to be redirected

---

[2] Their definitions are: enforcements (monitoring, auditing, etc. to detect, and penalties, suspension, or prosecution to deter) and inducements (contingent compensation, options, profit sharing, used mostly to align interests of agent with principal).

[3] Bologna (1980) found 20 percent to be honest, 20 percent to be dishonest, and 60 percent to be as honest as the situation allows.

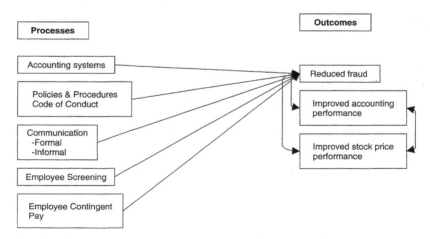

Figure 1.   Operational governance mechanisms, fraud reduction and firm performance

for personal use. An accounting system that is designed only to provide reasonable assurance that errors and inaccuracies are few can be seen as a weak system when compared to a system that frequently faces self-examination, modification, extensive employee training, and a sense of organizational responsibility for better reporting.

Firms have in place many policies to reduce or discourage fraud, beyond the accounting system. Ineffective written policies can contribute to the incidence of white-collar crime (Turner and Stephenson, 1993; Russell, 1995; Hooks *et al.*, 1994). Bell *et al.* (1998) find that where management frequently overrides controls and does not segregate duties, audit differences classified as fraud are more prevalent. Indeed, 'lax management attitudes, particularly toward internal controls, have frequently been linked to fraud and its detection'(Holmes *et al.*, 2002: 85).

A company that has clear divisions of responsibility, has communications geared toward company-wide understanding of policies and procedures, has a required management program that reinforces the importance of key policies, procedures and systems, and has a company-wide program designed to identify, analyze, and address basic problems in the workplace can be said to have clearer policies and procedures than a firm that pays less attention to ongoing education and training in what constitutes the corporate policies and procedures.

Thus, two foundational components of an operational governance system are the accounting system and the policies and procedures within the firm (Fellner and Mitchell, 1995). Thus:

Hypothesis 1: The stronger a firm's accounting system, the less likely it is to have white-collar crime.

Hypothesis 2: The clearer a firm's policies and procedures, the less likely it is to have white-collar crime.

A code of conduct is a policy or procedure that is specifically targeted to reduce unethical behavior. As such, it deserves special attention. Lack of a code of conduct can contribute to white-collar crime (Turner and Stephenson, 1993). In addition, clear expectations of behavior, company loyalty, and management integrity may strongly influence the incidence of white-collar crime (Mitchell *et al.*,

1996; Russell, 1995; Hooks *et al.*, 1994). The existence of a code of conduct can help with the explicit nature of the expectation of behavior (Turner and Stephenson, 1993). Clear expectations reduce uncertainty about choices of actions. Employees, in many cases, desire more detail as to what is acceptable within a firm (Weeks and Nantel, 1992; Pascale, 1985).

Previous research has found that just having a code of ethics may not necessarily reduce commission of a crime. Instead, a code needs to be comprehensive. The more specific it is, the more likely it is to reduce illegal behavior. Mitchell *et al.* (1996) found that the mere presence of a code of conduct has no impact. In a study of 63 organizations, Key, Messina, and Turpen (1998–99) find that executives at firms with known or suspected occurrences of fraud identified poor internal controls and weak ethics policies as the two primary contributors. When the ethics code is specific and consistently enforced, it reduces the opportunity for commission of a fraud and makes it difficult for employees to rationalize prohibited behavior. Fifty-three percent of the 1000 members of the Institute of Management Accountants' cost management group believe that a strong, comprehensive ethics policy reduces the overall cost of internal control (*Journal of Accountancy*, Anonymous, 1994). Such a policy would include a clearly articulated code, management training in following the code supplemented by an annual review, and communication of the code to all employees. Thus the following hypothesis that the quality of the code of conduct can impact crime commission:

Hypothesis 3: The stronger and more comprehensive a firm's code of conduct, the less likely it is to have white-collar crime.

Organizational communication is a 'system binder' that facilitates internal control and stability (Almaney, 1974). Communication is also 'integral to each phase of the accounting cycle and to the overall understanding of the operational processes of the organization' (Fellner and Mitchell, 1995: 80). Fraud involves concealment and communication fosters openness (Hooks *et al.*, 1994). More organization-wide communication, and greater intensity of communication, can reduce occurrences of fraud. For example, upward communication, such as face-to-face meetings or letters with management feedback, can preempt some problems or alert management early to their presence (Ettore, 1995).

Communication not only flows up or down, but laterally and diagonally as well (Sonnenberg, 1991). Lateral relations facilitate interunit communications. Lateral relations are not communication events *per se*; rather, they provide an opportunity for communication to exist. Without these opportunities, communication would be much more difficult. Lateral relations consist of joint work in teams, task forces and meetings (Ghoshal, Korine, and Szulanski, 1994; Hoskisson, Hill, and Kim, 1993). Job rotation and management development programs can also facilitate lateral relations. These procedures are also a powerful tool for organizational socialization (Gupta and Govindarajan, 1991; Martinez and Jarillo, 1989). Communication can occur on a formal basis, with the intention to communicate about certain topics. These are often occasions arranged by the organization, for example a training event involving geographically dispersed employees, a job rotation program, or several employees whose job it is to compare divisions and transfer methods and practices throughout the organization. Communication can also be informal or ad hoc, outside of the company's express purpose. Such informal communication can occur at the training event mentioned above, during a break, for example. Such communication can also occur at any team meeting. It is hypothesized that both forms of communication can have an impact on crime:

Hypothesis 4: The more formal communication opportunities a firm has, the less likely it is to have crime.

Hypothesis 5: The more a firm provides opportunity for informal communication, the less likely is it to have crime.

White-collar crime reduction should begin with the careful screening of potential employees, which may identify some of the potentially problem individuals (Stavros, 1998; Martin, 1998; Turner and Stephenson, 1993; Gardner, 1998). A potential employee's former employment, educational record, financial situation, and criminal record can all be checked. Such an exercise can reveal 'red flags' (Stavros, 1998). The care that companies take during the hiring process can vary: '... many employers base their hiring decision on their "gut

feeling" about a person. More often than not, that instinctive response is accurate ... but not always' (Stavros, 1998: 31). Careful employee screening can reject employees who have higher than normal proclivities to illegal behavior. Thus:

Hypothesis 6: The more attention the firm pays to employee screening, the less likely it is to have crime.

An employee at any level may pursue opportunistic behavior at the expense of the organization. Direct supervision cannot monitor all employee behavior. Instead, peer (or mutual) monitoring may partially substitute. Mutual monitoring can be encouraged through gainsharing programs, and supported through certain organizational characteristics. For example, reward systems can be structured so that the acts of individuals in the group threaten all group members (Trevino and Victor, 1992). Mutual monitoring supported by a mutual reward system tends to be associated with lower labor costs, high productivity, good product quality (Schuster, 1984), and improved employee attitudes (Hatcher, Ross, and Collins, 1989). 'Employees are more likely to steal if they feel a company was unfair to its employees' especially if they feel personally mistreated (Buss, 1993: 37). When an employee stock ownership system has meaningful equity, information, and influence, it produces psychological ownership, which leads to a bonding or integration of the employee–owner with the organization (Pierce, Rubenfeld, and Morgan, 1991). Thus:

Hypothesis 7: As a greater percentage of the employees in the firm are rewarded for firm performance, the less likely the firm is to have white-collar crime.

METHODOLOGY

Sample creation

In this study, the firms that have committed white-collar crime were identified through a Lexis-Nexis search of *The Wall Street Journal* from January 1, 1988 to December 31, 1998.[4] Articles were

---

[4] The crime-related search terms were obtained from a listing of the types of white collar crimes in *Fraud: Bringing Light*

eliminated that (1) did not discuss economic crime within the firm; (2) dealt with an economic crime either committed outside the United States or committed by a foreign firm within the United States; or (3) discussed economic crime in private firms. This elimination left 204 articles containing an announcement of a white-collar crime. Firms in the defense, financial services, power (energy), or healthcare (related to Medicare fraud) industries were also eliminated. These industries have extensive regulation and so occupy an environment where what might be a 'gray' crime in another industry is 'black' in the industries mentioned, or where it is difficult to separate an intentional fraudulent act that can be prosecuted in a civil or criminal court from an unintentional error or another form of violation. For example, a data entry error may lead to a Medicare fraud charge without any fraudulent intention. The energy firms are often charged with environmental crimes. While these may be genuine crimes, often it is difficult to separate the environmental violation from the civil or criminal violation. There were 161 occurrences remaining in the sample following this filter.

The firms named in these announcements were then checked for data availability. The U.S. Securities and Exchange Commission (SEC) requires public firms to publish annual reports, 10Ks and proxy statements. These were gathered for the firms for which these documents existed. The SEC data were gathered for the year prior to the announcement of the crime. This was to ensure that the firm governance conditions were those that coexisted with the crime. If a company committed a separate crime twice in the time window, they and their match were entered twice, once for each year. The final sample represents 77 occurrences of crimes representing 57 firms. Eight firms had two crimes in the time window included in this study—two had three crimes, one had four crimes, and one had six. Table 1 illustrates the filtering process.

Matched-pair design is an acceptable method when studying why otherwise similar subjects have

Table 1.   Generation of the crime-firm sample

Filter	Number remaining
First search	Tens of thousands of articles
Economic crime, in U.S., by U.S. firm, public company	204 announcements of separate crimes
Not defense or healthcare or financial services or power industry	161 announcements of separate crimes
Data availability and reasonable match	77 announcements of separate crimes, 57 firms

different outcomes.[5] In this case, one member of a pair had a crime announcement, and one member did not. Characteristics used to match firms included primary industry, asset size, and similar numbers of industries (4-digit SIC codes) outside of the primary industry. These characteristics were recorded for the 'crime firms' in the year prior to the announcement of the crime. In order to find the best matches, I first generated a complete list of the firms in the primary 4-digit SIC code in that same year. Then I identified all firms in that 4-digit SIC code that were half as large to twice as large in asset size as the crime firm. This list of firms was compared with the descriptions of the businesses either in Hoover's corporate descriptions or in the beginning of the 10K for each firm. The firm with the closest description in terms of primary industry and other industries if the firm was somewhat diversified was selected. This second step in matching was necessary as SIC codes are often not very informative and sometimes only distantly related to the primary business of the firm. In some cases, when a firm's business description did not match its SIC code, it was rematched in the SIC code that was a better description of its business. For example, Cendant (which was CUC at the time

---

to the Dark Side of Business by Albrecht, Wernz, and Williams (1995). The list of terms generated from this book's comprehensive description is as follows: fraud, kiting (false checks—a form of embezzlement), skimming (a form of embezzlement), lapping (a form of embezzlement), bilking, embezzling, larceny, theft, kickbacks, overbilling, swindling, price fixing, bid rigging, racketeering, defraud, fraudulent.

[5] Matched-pair design is most common in epidemiology, where the focus is more on what might be associated with contracting a particular disease. In these cases, individuals are matched on age, gender, socioeconomic status, ethnicity, etc. In this case, 'crime' is the disease, and firm characteristics substitute for individual characteristics. Matched-pair design also has implications for the methodology employed, which will be discussed later. A discussion of the methods can be found in Holford (2002). Previous studies incorporating a matched-pair design include McConaughy *et al.* (1998), who paired founding family controlled vs. low managerial ownership firms, and matched on sales and industry, and Teece (1981), who paired on low vs. high performance and matched on product lines and sales.

the crime was committed) is classified in SIC code 4724 (travel agencies), and its match is Damark. Damark is classified in SIC code 5961 (catalog and mail order houses). Below are excerpts from their 10Ks:

> CUC International Inc. (the 'Company') is a membership-based consumer services company, providing consumers with access to a variety of services. These memberships include such components as shopping, travel, auto, dining, home improvement, lifestyle, vacation exchange, credit card and checking account enhancement packages, financial products and discount programs. (CUC, 1995, 10K, p. 3)

> Damark's products and services are offered through mail order catalogs and a variety of membership clubs which provide members discounts on travel, hospitality, entertainment and merchandise purchased through its catalogs. (Damark, 1995, 10K, pp. 2–3)

Some of the matches are for firms that are some distance apart in asset size. However, the scopes of diversification of the firms are similar, they are in identical businesses, and there was no closer match. Size was also controlled for in the empirical tests.

Measurement of variables

Most of the variables used in this study are combinations of numbers readily found in the firm's annual reports, proxy statements or 10Ks. For example, the percentage ownership of the CEO or the number of meetings of the board of directors is easily found and are unambiguous numbers. The other variables are much more difficult to generate.

A modified form of content analysis is used for the operational governance variables in order to find references to particular characteristics of the firm, and then code those references on a scale of 1 to 7, based on details about those characteristics. This procedure analyzed the context of the words, not the number of times certain words appeared or their position in a sentence as in traditional content analysis.

Content analysis has been previously used in organizational research. Traditionally, it involves identifying constructs of interest, determining what terms are included in that construct, then counting the occurrence of those terms in sample documents that are interpreted as indicating the degree of the presence of the original constructs (see Popping, 2000, for an historical review of the evolution of content analysis). Most organizational research that has used content analysis has primarily used annual reports and a dictionary to search for terms in the annual reports. The number of occurrences of the terms was then quantitatively analyzed (Arndt and Bigelow, 2000; Bowman, 1984; Abrahamson and Park, 1994).

For this study, content analysis software was used to retrieve each mention of a firm's accounting system. Then, based on the context of the terms, or the description of the variable in question, I scored the strength of that variable on a 1 to 7 scale. I term this method 'content-context analysis.' Table 2 shows the variables for each theoretical grouping and the outline of the measures used for the content-context analysis variables.

Specifically, for each company and year (crime as well as noncrime firms), electronic versions of the SEC documents were imported into a qualitative data analysis software package called NUD*IST.[6] Using NUD*IST, nodes, or files, were created for each variable, and a scoring dictionary was developed to use for the search terms. A text search function was created to find the words in the dictionary in all the documents and to retrieve the line that the word appeared in, as well as 10 lines on either side for the context. The retrieved text was saved at the node (or in the file) belonging to that variable. For example, in searching for references to a firm's accounting system, I searched for references to accounting or internal controls. Any reference that was not relevant was deleted. For example, in searching for policies and procedures, one of the search terms is 'document'. In downloading the electronic documents from the Securities and Exchange Commission, each electronic document includes the term 'document' in the header as well as the 'document date,' reflecting the date the document was completed. Neither of these references have anything to do with that particular firm's policies or procedures. This process can be repeated without creating inconsistencies.

The retrieved text was reviewed and any noninformative text was deleted. Any reference that would belong elsewhere was also deleted. For example, there would often be references

---

[6] QSR NUD*IST (1997) from Qualitative Solutions and Research Pty Ltd.

594   *K. Schnatterly*

Table 2.   Summary of operating governance variables and measures

Theoretical grouping	Variable	Measure
Organizational rules	Accounting system	Scale 1–7; higher numbers represent more communication throughout the company as to maintaining the integrity of the accounting system, as well as periodic reviews and changes
	Policies and procedures	Scale 1–7; higher numbers represent more communication of policies throughout the organization, training, clear responsibility, formalization.
Communication	Liaison roles (formal communication)	Scale 1–7; higher numbers represent greater company-wide interaction among employees
	Teams (informal communication)	Scale 1–7; higher numbers represent greater use of teams, and more cross-functional or cross-geographic use
Code of conduct	Code of conduct	Scale 1–7; higher numbers represent more specific codes, with greater company-wide education and management responsibility
Employee screening	Employee screening	Scale 1–7; higher numbers represent more background checking for qualifications, better interviewing and recruiting
Incentive alignment	Contingent pay for employees	Scale 1–7; higher numbers represent more contingent pay available to more employees

to policies and procedures near accounting references. Policies and procedures is a separate variable, and the references were filed there instead. For each company there are several paragraphs on the accounting system that were generated by search words.

These paragraphs were read and assigned a value from 1 (meaning weak, few controls or cross-checks, selecting which principles to use, little top management attention beyond formal signing off) to 7 (strong, controls that are reviewed and changed, top management attention and interest). The company name or its crime status was not known during the coding process. This method is similar to the case survey method employed in Larsson and Finkelstein (1999). In that study, they developed a 5-point scale to convert qualitative data into quantitative data.

Each company ended up with the highest score they obtained from any one document. In other words, if a company was being scored for their accounting system, and if they received a 4 on the proxy statement, there was no information in the annual report, and a 5 in the 10K, this company would be awarded a 5. The numbers were not averaged or totaled for several reasons. First, there is a significant amount of repetition between 10Ks and annual reports. Generating a total or an average would not have reflected this repetition. For example, a firm could receive a 5 based on information in the annual report, and a

5 based on an identical paragraph in the 10K. If this was summed, the firm would receive a 10 (assuming no information in the proxy statement), but the 10 would reflect identical information, not additional, new information above a 5 category. Second, each document, in general, has a different focus. The annual report's focus is to shareholders and anyone interested in the company, the 10K to regulators and analysts, and the proxy statement to voting shareholders (some individuals, mostly institutions). As a result, averaging would take away some of the information contained in the scores. For example, a firm receiving a 3 for Code of Conduct from the annual report, and a 0 elsewhere, would end up with a 1 overall. Third, the amount of repetition (as mentioned in point one) vs. the amount of unique information per documents (point two) varies significantly over the measures. As a result, in order to not over-reward repetition, and yet maintain some variance between levels of variables, I chose to use only the highest number from each firm.

The specific operational governance variables are directly related to the hypotheses. They include information on the accounting system, on the written policies, procedures, job descriptions, whether or not there are liaison roles or permanent or temporary teams, and the extent of integration within the firm (Martinez and Jarillo, 1989; Hoskisson *et al.*, 1993; Gupta and Govindarajan, 1991). Appendix 1 shows the search terms for each content-context variable as well as text excerpts that reflect the range of each variable. Appendix 2 contains the scoring system for each content-context variable.

In order to assure quality in my coding scheme, a second rater coded a random subsample of the data set. For a random subset of approximately 20 percent, I generated 16 random numbers between 1 and 77 to identify 16 random crime firms and their matches for a total of 32 firms (20.8% of the entire sample; 10–15% has been considered sufficient (Fan and Chen, 2000)). I then retrieved the text from the original searches for these firms across all the content-context variables: accounting system, policies and procedures, code of conduct, formal communication, informal communication, employee screening, employee contingent compensation, and audit committee strength. I trained a second coder on the process and scoring sheet. The coder was not informed as to which firms were crime firms and which were not. We adopted a consensus approach for variables where the two coders disagreed. This method follows Larsson and Finkelstein (1999). The consensus approach allowed us to reexamine the scales and our own reasoning. The coding scales were critical to ultimate resolution of disputes. Percent agreement ranged from 84.38 percent to 100 percent, where 65 percent is considered a benchmark (Larsson and Finkelstein, 1999: 21), with kappas of 0.81 to 1.00, where greater than 0.60 is considered substantial agreement (Stata 7.0 Reference Manual H-P, 2001: 150). See Table 3 for the information by variable.

Controls

The variables used to control for traditional governance mechanisms include blockholders (Coffey and Fryxell, 1991), CEO duality (Boyd, 1995; Finkelstein and D'Aveni, 1994), the proportion of board insiders vs. outsiders (Hermalin and Weisbach, 1991), audit committees (McMullen, 1996; McMullen and Raghunandan, 1996), board compensation (Hermalin and Weisbach, 1991), director and CEO stock ownership (Alexander and Cohen, 1999), and CEO compensation (Boyd, 1994; Jensen and Murphy, 1990).

These variables are not only important to control for because of their extensive use in previous governance research, but also because they should impact white-collar crime commission. For example, an independent board is more likely to be better at monitoring and reducing financial statement fraud (Beasley, 1996) because more outside directors may be more likely to prevent management from making self-serving decisions (Fama, 1980). Beasley (1996) finds that firms that have not committed financial statement fraud have boards with more outside members than firms that have committed fraud. As outside directors' ownership in the firm increases, outside member tenure on the board increases and number of outside directorships in other firms decreases, the likelihood of financial statement fraud decreases. Additionally, Abrahamson and Park (1994) find that the presence of outside directors, large institutional shareholders (institutions that own 5% or more), and accountants (as seen in the presence of qualified audits) limits concealment of negative organizational outcomes, whereas small institutional owners (owning less than 5%) and outside-director-shareholders promote it.

The audit committee of a board has responsibility for interacting with the internal and external auditors and for assuring the quality of the financial reporting. McMullen (1996) finds that firms with earnings restatements, shareholder litigation,

Table 3. Interrater reliability measures

Variable	Agreement	Expected agreement	Kappa	S.E.	Z	Prob > Z
Accounting System	84.38%	15.82%	0.8144	0.0745	10.93	0.000
Policies and procedures	93.75%	19.34%	0.9225	0.0845	10.92	0.000
Code of conduct	96.88%	51.27%	0.9359	0.1015	9.22	0.000
Formal communication	96.88%	62.30%	0.9171	0.1109	8.27	0.000
Informal communication	90.63%	28.03%	0.8697	0.0984	8.84	0.000
Employee screening	100.00%	54.69%	1.0000	0.1203	8.31	0.000
Employee contingent pay	93.75%	27.54%	0.9137	0.0962	9.49	0.000
Audit committee	75.00%	19.04%	0.6912	0.0838	8.25	0.000
All variables together	91.41%	22.16%	0.8896	0.0297	29.91	0.000

SEC enforcement actions, illegal acts, or auditor turnover were less likely to have an audit committee than firms without these problems. DeFond and Jiambalvo (1991) find companies without audit committees were more likely to overstate earnings. Both of these studies imply that audit committees signal the likelihood for better financial reporting and fewer financial reporting problems.

CEOs can also be chair of the board. These are both powerful roles. If the roles of CEO and chair are separate, there may be more objective assessment of the performance of the CEO (Boyd, 1994). Vigilant boards may tend to favor separation of these roles because it reduces the possibility of entrenchment by the CEO. Entrenched CEOs may have so much power that they can use the firm to further their own interests, rather than the shareholders', and can hamper the board's independence and ability to monitor (Beatty and Zajac, 1994). This constraint reduces the possibility that

the board can execute its governance role (Rechner and Dalton, 1991; Mizruchi, 1983).

Zajac and Westphal (1994) find that firms treat incentive alignment and monitoring as substitutes for each other, although Tosi, Katz, and Gomez-Mejia (1997) find that incentive alignment is a more powerful mechanism than monitoring for ensuring that agents act in the interests of owners. This alignment of agents' and principals' interests can be achieved through contingent compensation contracts (Jensen and Murphy, 1990). Table 4 summarizes these variables and their measures.

Other controls included are for firm size and past performance. Firm size may be an important predictor of illegal activity (Baucus and Near, 1991; Daboub *et al.*, 1995). Larger firms are more likely to be investigated and not necessarily more likely to commit crimes. Also, larger firms can more easily absorb penalties for illegal acts and

Table 4.   Summary of control variables and measures

Theoretical grouping	Variable	Measure
Structure of ownership	Largest owner	The largest 5%+ shareholder alone
	CEO stock ownership	Measured as the percentage of shares of the firm held by the CEO
	Stock held by the board	Measured as the percentage of stock held by the directors and officers of the company
Structure of the board of directors	Board insiders	Measured as the number of insiders divided by the total number of board members
	Board compensation	Measured as the yearly pay received by board members, assuming the member attended all regular meetings and was not on a committee
	Board compensation type	Scale 1–7, flat annual fee to highly contingent
	Number of meetings	The number of regular and special meetings in the past year of the board of directors
Audit committee	Number of meetings of the audit committee	The number of meetings in the past year of the audit committee
	Outsiders on the audit committee	The number of outsiders on the audit committee divided by the total number of audit committee members
	Strength of audit committee	Scale 1–7; higher numbers represent more independent committees, with more responsibility and authority
CEO	Number of roles	1 = CEO, 2 = CEO + Chair, 3 = CEO + Chair + President
	CEO flat compensation	Measured as the natural log of the CEO's salary and bonus
	CEO flat vs. contingent compensation	Measured as the salary, bonus, and other annual compensation divided by the dollar value of any options, stock or other long-term incentive pay
Other	Firm size	Number of employees
	Past performance	Past 3 years ROA Past 3 years change in market value

the stigma of illegal acts than can smaller firms (Hill *et al.*, 1992).

Poor performance may increase the possibility of a crime. If crime improves the short-run performance of the employee's division or organization and poor performance in the short run increases the employees' probability of job loss, then the incentive to commit a crime is increased (Alexander and Cohen, 1996). The crime may be either to improve the perception of the division's performance or to appropriate assets for personal use prior to job loss. These variables are also in Table 4.

Estimation method

The first test is a binary logit model with crime as the dependent variable. In this case, crime = 0 in the cases of the firms without announced crime, and crime = 1 if there is any crime. As this is a matched-pair design, I employed a form of logit that allows for a stratified sample (data coming from two nonindependent groups). Additionally, to explore the idea that firms with more crime have weaker governance systems, the second test is an ordered logit model with the number of crimes committed as the dependent variable (0 to 6).[7] An ordered logit model allows multinomial dependent variables and is recommended when the dependent variables have some kind of natural ordering, in this case fewer crimes to more crimes.[8] The ordered logit model was also structured to allow for a stratified sample (data coming from two nonindependent groups).

One reason for the importance of the ordered logit model is that, throughout the sampling and testing, there has been an implicit assumption that firms that have not had an announcement of a crime have not had a crime. This is an unproven assumption. Accordingly, the ordered logit model will provide some idea of the progressive differences between firms with crime = 0, crime = 1, up to crime = 6. If there are progressive weakening governance systems, then the sampling technique, while not perfect, will be supported.

---

[7] I also ran models allowing crimes to be 0–2+ (or 0 crimes, 1 crime, 2 or more crimes) and 0–3+, as there are only two firms that had four or more announcements, and four that had three or more.

[8] Stata 7 reference manuals, Reference H-P, p. 451.

EMPIRICAL RESULTS

Descriptive statistics

For the control and governance variables, there is wide variation in many of the variables, indicating very different structures of firms. Table 5 shows the descriptive statistics. For example, the percentage of the firm held by the largest owner ranges from less than 5 percent of the firm to 90 percent, with the average at 13 percent. Similarly, the percentage of insiders on the board ranges from 7 percent to 100 percent, with the average at 33 percent. Some firms' boards met only once during the year, while others met 17 times, with the average at 7.5 meetings per year, with most boards meeting seven or eight times. In the area of CEO compensation, some CEOs receive no contingent compensation; some other CEOs receive 37.8 times their flat salary in contingent compensation (options, restricted stock). The average for all the firms in the sample is that CEOs receive 4.3 times their flat salary in contingent compensation. CEOs own 6 percent of the firm, on average, and boards own 12 percent, on average. These numbers range from essentially 0 percent to 90 percent and 95 percent, respectively.

Audit committees for the firms in the sample are mostly comprised of outsiders, but there are some audit committees with only insiders. Audit committees met three times a year, on average, with some committees meeting nine times, and others not at all.

With regard to the operational governance variables that were generated through the content analysis and range from 0 or 1 to 7, accounting systems, policies and procedures, and employee contingent pay average around 3.5 or 4, with standard deviations of 1.2 to 2. Formal communication, informal communication, code of conduct, and employee screening variables averaged 1.6 to 2.5, with standard deviations of 1.1 to 1.8.

Correlations

Table 6 shows the correlations. All the correlations discussed below are significant at the 0.05 level or greater. The crime variables are significantly correlated with a number of interesting governance and control variables. For example, of the control variables, more insiders on the board, CEO, block and board ownership are positively correlated with crime occurrence. Board compensation

Table 5.   Descriptive statistics

Variable	Obs.	Mean	S.D.	Min.	Max.
1. Crime	154	0.50	0.50	0	1
2. # of Crimes	154	0.95	1.41	0	6
3. Accounting System	154	4.10	2.04	0	7
4. Policies & Procedures	154	3.53	1.75	0	7
5. Code of Conduct	154	2.40	1.76	1	7
6. Formal Communication	154	1.95	1.60	1	7
7. Informal Communication	154	2.47	1.67	1	7
8. Employee Screening	154	1.61	1.16	1	7
9. Employee Contingent Pay	154	3.40	1.15	0	6
10. % Largest Owner	154	0.13	0.15	0	0.9
11. % Owned by CEO	154	0.06	0.14	0	0.9
12. % Owned by the Board	154	0.12	0.18	0	0.95
13. % Insiders	154	0.33	0.16	0.07	1
14. Ln(Board Salary)	154	10.62	1.32	0	13.59
15. Board Salary Type	154	4.07	1.49	0	7
16. # Meetings of the Board	154	7.47	2.78	1	17
17. # Meetings Audit Committee	154	2.95	1.45	0	9
18. % Outsiders on Audit Committee	154	0.90	0.20	0	1
19. Audit Committee Strength	154	4.39	1.38	0	7
20. # Roles CEO	154	2.30	0.57	1	3
21. Ln(CEO Flat Pay)	154	13.75	1.41	0	15.99
22. CEO Contingent/Flat	154	4.31	6.41	0	37.82
23. Size (Employees)	132	79.21	112.60	0	520
24. ROA Past 3 years	132	0.06	0.06	−0.16	0.22
25. Change in Market Value Past 3 years	132	1.60	4.91	−0.74	44.88

measured as both level of pay and as extent of stock- and option-based pay and audit committee strength are negatively correlated with the crime variables. These variables are not correlated with the number of crimes committed. Only the number of meetings of the board, the number of roles of the CEO, and the CEO's flat compensation are positively correlated with the number of crimes committed. Size is positively correlated with the number of crimes, but not the initial occurrence, and past performance measured as ROA is negatively correlated with the number of crimes, but not the initial occurrence. Past performance measured as the change in market value of the firm is not correlated with either of the crime variables.

The accounting system, policies and procedures, formal and informal communication, code of conduct, and contingent pay for employees are all negatively correlated with the occurrence of a crime. Policies and procedures, formal and informal communication are also negatively correlated with the number of crimes committed.

From the correlations, it appears that certain governance components 'go together,' and that they may be able to impact crime occurrence. It can be seen from the descriptive statistics that there are wide distributions of these variables, so that crime and noncrime companies look very different, and that these differences appear to be related to occurrences of crime.

Operational governance hypothesis testing

Logistic regressions

Table 7 shows the results of the logistic regressions on crime and number of crimes, clustering the pairs of firms together by announcement. Table 7 also shows logistic regressions when the number of crimes runs from 0 to 3+ and 0 to 2+. In other words, when the categories are 'no crime,' 'one crime,' 'two crimes' and 'three or more crimes,' or 'none,' 'one' and 'two or more crimes.' This preserves our ability to see if firms with multiple crimes are different, while increasing the representation in each of the 'more crimes' categories. For example, there is only one firm that committed six crimes, so the logistic regression on number of crimes only has one company in level 'six.'

Table 8 shows the results of the regressions clustering by firms. In other words, the firm that

Table 6. Correlations

Variable	1	2	3	4	5	6	7	8	9	10	11	12
1. Crime	1											
2. # of Crimes	0.6809**	1										
3. Accounting System	-0.2811**	0.0495	1									
4. Policies & Procedures	-0.5499**	-0.3877**	0.4670**	1								
5. Code of Conduct	-0.2075**	0.0127	0.6572**	0.4643**	1							
6. Formal Communication	-0.4154**	-0.2973**	0.0838	0.4503**	0.0702	1						
7. Informal Communication	-0.4254**	-0.3359**	0.1237	0.4982**	0.2173**	0.5452**	1					
8. Employee Screening	-0.1352	-0.1235	0.1586*	0.2255**	0.0198	0.1347	0.0489	1				
9. Employee Contingent Pay	-0.3296**	-0.0494	0.3427**	0.2764**	0.3049**	0.0721	0.2685**	0.1092	1			
10. % Largest Owner	0.1770*	0.0511	-0.1878*	-0.0923	-0.1655*	-0.0936	-0.0915	0.0348	0.0208	1		
11. % Owned by CEO	0.2099**	-0.0400	-0.3476**	-0.2001*	-0.2452**	-0.1216	-0.1340	-0.0015	-0.0911	0.5406**	1	
12. % Owned by the Board	0.2046*	-0.0522	-0.2763**	-0.1388	-0.2630**	-0.1051	-0.1067	0.0198	-0.0191	0.7809**	0.7460**	1
13. % Insiders	0.1613*	-0.0599	-0.2574**	-0.1555	-0.2424**	-0.1279	-0.0495	-0.0826	-0.0475	0.2638**	0.2699**	0.4061**
14. Ln(Board Salary)	-0.1739*	-0.0386	0.1679*	0.2059*	0.1303	0.0170	0.1571	0.0334	0.2411**	-0.1932*	-0.3590*	-0.2749**
15. Board Salary Type	-0.3286**	-0.0578	0.2993**	0.3238**	0.3264**	0.0868	0.2654**	-0.0483	0.2783**	-0.1972*	-0.3477**	-0.4136**
16. # Meetings of the Board	0.0843	0.1942*	0.1596*	-0.0594	0.2058*	-0.1237	-0.1057	-0.1360	-0.0512	-0.3386**	-0.2552**	-0.3568**
17. # Meetings Audit Committee	-0.0180	0.1081	0.2125*	0.0032	0.1626*	-0.0605	0.0374	0.0074	0.0245	-0.0894	-0.1791*	-0.1293
18. % Outsiders on Audit Committee	-0.1178	-0.0751	0.2344**	0.1075	0.2065*	0.0117	0.0520	0.1084	0.2092**	-0.1230	-0.1452	-0.1964*
19. Audit Committee Strength	-0.3203**	-0.0816	0.5093**	0.4772**	0.4028**	0.3371**	0.3413**	0.1037	0.2509**	-0.2469**	-0.2685**	-0.3424**
20. # Roles CEO	0.0455	0.1629*	-0.0882	-0.0683	-0.1331	0.0598	0.0013	0.2260**	-0.0151	-0.0358	0.0598	-0.1059
21. Ln(CEO Flat Pay)	0.0821	0.1857*	0.1846*	0.0485	0.1792*	0.0575	0.1383	0.0250	0.0534	-0.1247	-0.2246**	-0.1928*
22. CEO Contingent/Flat	-0.0035	0.0203	0.2630**	0.1021	0.2186**	-0.0876	0.0604	-0.0453	0.0010	-0.1918*	-0.2126**	-0.2088**
23. Size (Employees)	0.1260	0.4714**	0.3730**	0.1357	0.5029**	0.0427	0.0153	-0.1981*	0.2483**	-0.0532	-0.2360*	-0.1915*
24. ROA Past 3 Years	-0.1352	-0.2262**	0.0518	0.0726	0.0684	-0.0058	0.1033	0.0758	0.1290	-0.0821	0.0393	0.0655
25. Change in Market Value Past 3 Years	0.0793	-0.0083	-0.2072*	-0.1465	-0.1129	-0.1179	-0.0650	0.1811*	-0.0421	0.1107	-0.0236	0.0899

$* p < 0.05; ** p < 0.01.$

Table 6. (*Continued*)

Variable	13	14	15	16	17	18	19	20	21	22	23	24	25
1. Crime													
2. # of Crimes													
3. Accounting System													
4. Policies & Procedures													
5. Code of Conduct													
6. Formal Communication													
7. Informal Communication													
8. Employee Screening													
9. Employee Contingent Pay													
10. % Largest Owner													
11. % Owned by CEO													
12. % Owned by the Board													
13. % Insiders	1												
14. Lnt(Board Salary)	−0.1462	1											
15. Board Salary Type	−0.4238**	0.5185**	1										
16. # Meetings of the Board	−0.2985**	0.1320	0.1278	1									
17. # Meetings Audit Committee	−0.1407	0.1011	0.0474	0.3946**	1								
18. % Outsiders on Audit Committee	−0.3941**	0.2395**	0.3393**	0.1828*	0.1596*	1							
19. Audit Committee Strength	−0.3212**	0.1941*	0.4823**	0.1188	0.0985	0.2883**	1						
20. # Roles CEO	−0.2768**	−0.0415	0.0208	0.0389	0.0820	0.0596	0.0254	1					
21. Lnt(CEO Flat Pay)	−0.1806*	0.1184	0.1909*	0.0649	0.1263	0.1341	0.2100**	−0.0823	1				
22. CEO Contingent/Flat	−0.2026*	0.2091**	0.2529**	0.1737*	0.0855	0.0517	0.1855*	0.0508	0.1644**	1			
23. Size (Employees)	−0.2062*	−0.0416	0.2002*	0.2919**	0.1494	0.1812*	0.2390**	−0.0392	0.1769*	0.1849*	1		
24. ROA Past 3 Years	0.1974*	−0.0317	−0.1542	−0.0882	0.0683	−0.0217	−0.0654	−0.0361	−0.0668	0.0515	−0.0821	1	
25. Change in Market Value Past 3 Years	0.1092	0.0374	−0.0815	−0.1868*	−0.0896	0.0474	−0.0719	0.1530	−0.0287	−0.1054	−0.1305	−0.1175	1

* $p < 0.05$; ** $p < 0.01$.

Table 7. Logistic regressions on crime independent variables, clustering by announcement

Variables	Crime Model 1	Crime Model 2	# of crimes Model 1	# of crimes Model 2	Crimes 0–3+ Model 1	Crimes 0–3+ Model 2	Crimes 0–2+ Model 1	Crimes 0–2+ Model 2
Controls								
% largest owner	3.76	4.95	4.21	6.49	3.85	5.95	2.75	4.02
	(2.50)	(5.32)	(2.47)	(3.98)	(2.24)	(3.68)	(2.04)	(3.33)
CEO Triality	0.54	1.11	0.57	0.50	0.39	0.31	0.39	0.67
	(0.45)	(0.72)	(0.42)	(0.44)	(0.41)	(0.43)	(0.40)	(0.46)
% Insiders	1.75	1.02	1.16	−0.67	1.24	−0.37	1.56	−0.21
	(2.03)	(2.70)	(1.43)	(1.54)	(1.39)	(1.46)	(1.51)	(1.61)
Board Salary Type	−0.48*	−0.55	−0.37*	−0.60*	−0.40*	−0.69*	−0.41*	−0.66*
	(0.21)	(0.28)	(0.18)	(0.28)	(0.18)	(0.28)	(0.19)	(0.28)
Ln(Board Salary)	−0.01	0.24	−0.06	0.20	−0.07	0.21	−0.11	0.22
	(0.31)	(0.37)	(0.23)	(0.32)	(0.22)	(0.30)	(0.24)	(0.30)
# Meetings of the Board	0.29*	0.18	0.20	0.15	0.20	0.15	0.30	0.22
	(0.13)	(0.13)	(0.13)	(0.11)	(0.12)	(0.11)	(0.15)	(0.13)
CEO Contingent/Flat Pay	0.02	−0.02	0.01	−0.02	0.02	−0.02	0.03	−0.01
	(0.04)	(0.07)	(0.04)	(0.04)	(0.04)	(0.04)	(0.04)	(0.06)
Ln(CEO Flat Pay)	0.71*	1.03	0.79*	0.81	0.78*	0.76	0.63*	0.56
	(0.30)	(0.79)	(0.32)	(0.46)	(0.31)	(0.43)	(0.29)	(0.41)
% owned by CEO	3.21	−4.66	0.48	−1.96	0.33	−2.10	0.67	−3.93
	(3.72)	(6.26)	(1.74)	(1.90)	(1.79)	(2.01)	(2.13)	(2.44)
% Owned by the Board	0.53	5.15	−2.12	−4.59	−2.08	−4.62	−0.19	−0.75
	(2.40)	(5.43)	(2.33)	(4.19)	(2.19)	(3.98)	(2.16)	(3.88)
% Outsiders on Audit Committee	0.29	−2.18	−1.06	−4.72**	−1.54	−5.45**	−1.01	−4.54**
	(1.45)	(1.91)	(1.06)	(1.34)	(1.12)	(1.44)	(1.13)	(1.47)
# Meetings Audit Committee	−0.23	−0.41	−0.16	−0.71*	−0.15	−0.62*	−0.23	−0.61*
	(0.20)	(0.30)	(0.16)	(0.30)	(0.16)	(0.28)	(0.19)	(0.26)
Audit Committee Strength	−0.49*	0.49	−0.44*	0.63*	−0.46**	0.57	−0.51*	0.55
	(0.23)	(0.38)	(0.18)	(0.31)	(0.18)	(0.29)	(0.22)	(0.31)
Size (Employees)	0.00*	0.01*	0.01**	0.02**	0.01**	0.02**	0.01**	0.03**
	(0.00)	(0.01)	(0.00)	(0.00)	(0.00)	(0.00)	(0.00)	(0.01)
ROA Past 3 Years	−7.17	−5.35	−7.71**	−5.33	−7.26**	−4.39	−6.01*	−2.99
	(4.56)	(4.22)	(3.00)	(4.47)	(2.92)	(4.19)	(3.04)	(3.71)
Change in Market Value Past 3 Years	0.03	−0.09	0.01	−0.07*	0.02	−0.06	0.04	−0.05
	(0.04)	(0.06)	(0.03)	(0.04)	(0.03)	(0.03)	(0.03)	(0.04)
Governance variables								
Accounting System		−0.19		0.20		0.18		0.10
		(0.18)		(0.17)		(0.16)		(0.14)
Policies & Procedures		−0.74*		−0.82**		−0.73**		−0.67**
		(0.37)		(0.23)		(0.21)		(0.24)
Code of Conduct		−0.37		−0.92**		−0.90**		−0.85*
		(0.44)		(0.36)		(0.36)		(0.38)
Formal Communication		−1.07		−1.33**		−1.33**		−1.35**
		(0.61)		(0.39)		(0.39)		(0.41)
Informal Communication		−0.09		−0.41		−0.40*		−0.39*
		(0.25)		(0.21)		(0.20)		(0.18)
Employee Screening		0.19		0.75**		0.70**		0.60**
		(0.32)		(0.24)		(0.21)		(0.23)
Employee Contingent Pay		−0.85**		−0.48		−0.58*		−0.71**
		(0.30)		(0.25)		(0.25)		(0.27)
Pseudo R^2	0.29	0.61	0.18	0.46	0.19	0.48	0.24	0.54
Chi square	41.68**	112.8**	46.49**	132.8**	43.84**	107.33**	45.1**	65.32**

The entries in the table are coefficients, with standard errors in parentheses. *$p < 0.05$; **$p < 0.01$

602   *K. Schnatterly*

Table 8.   Logistic regressions on crime-independent variables, clustering by company

Variables	Crime Model 1	Crime Model 2	# of crimes Model 1	# of crimes Model 2	Crimes 0–3+ Model 1	Crimes 0–3+ Model 2	Crimes 0–2+ Model 1	Crimes 0–2+ Model 2
Controls								
% largest owner	3.76	4.95	4.21	6.49	3.85	5.95	2.75	4.02
	(2.66)	(5.38)	(2.75)	(3.97)	(2.46)	(3.68)	(2.15)	(3.29)
CEO Triality	0.54	1.11	0.57	0.50	0.39	0.31	0.38	0.67
	(0.53)	(0.73)	(0.58)	(0.55)	(0.58)	(0.53)	(0.51)	(0.51)
% Insiders	1.75	1.02	1.16	−0.67	1.24	−0.37	1.56	−0.21
	(2.16)	(2.76)	(1.47)	(1.62)	(1.45)	(1.52)	(1.59)	(1.64)
Board Salary Type	−0.48	−0.55	−0.37	−0.60*	−0.40	−0.69*	−0.41	−0.66*
	(0.26)	(0.29)	(0.27)	(0.30)	(0.29)	(0.31)	(0.27)	(0.29)
Ln(Board Salary)	−0.01	0.24	−0.06	0.20	−0.07	0.21	−0.11	0.22
	(0.33)	(0.38)	(0.28)	(0.34)	(0.26)	(0.31)	(0.27)	(0.31)
# Meetings of the Board	0.29*	0.18	0.19	0.15	0.20	0.15	0.30	0.22
	(0.14)	(0.13)	(0.14)	(0.12)	(0.14)	(0.12)	(0.16)	(0.14)
CEO Contingent/Flat Pay	0.02	−0.02	0.01	−0.02	0.02	−0.02	0.03	−0.01
	(0.04)	(0.07)	(0.04)	(0.04)	(0.03)	(0.04)	(0.04)	(0.06)
Ln(CEO Flat Pay)	0.71*	1.03	0.79*	0.81	0.78*	0.76	0.63	0.56
	(0.34)	(0.80)	(0.35)	(0.60)	(0.34)	(0.57)	(0.34)	(0.46)
% owned by CEO	3.21	−4.66	0.48	−1.96	0.33	−2.10	−0.67	−3.93
	(3.93)	(6.36)	(1.85)	(1.97)	(1.90)	(2.10)	(2.29)	(2.44)
% Owned by the Board	0.53	5.15	−2.12	−4.59	−2.08	−4.62	−0.19	−0.75
	(2.59)	(5.47)	(2.70)	(4.29)	(2.56)	(4.08)	(2.50)	(3.86)
% Outsiders on Audit Committee	0.29	−2.18	−1.06	−4.72**	−1.54	−5.45**	−1.01	−4.54**
	(1.77)	(1.92)	(1.39)	(1.31)	(1.56)	(1.42)	(1.45)	(1.37)
# Meetings Audit Committee	−0.23	−0.41	−0.16	−0.71*	−0.15	−0.62	−0.23	−0.61*
	(0.20)	(0.30)	(0.18)	(0.34)	(0.18)	(0.32)	(0.20)	(0.28)
Audit Committee Strength	−0.49	0.49	−0.44	0.63	−0.46	0.57	−0.51	0.55
	(0.28)	(0.38)	(0.24)	(0.32)	(0.24)	(0.31)	(0.28)	(0.32)
Size (Employees)	0.00	0.01*	0.01*	0.02**	0.01	0.02**	0.01*	0.03**
	(0.00)	(0.01)	(0.00)	(0.00)	(0.00)	(0.00)	(0.00)	(0.01)
ROA Past 3 Years	−7.17	−5.35	−7.71*	−5.33	−7.26*	−4.39	−6.01	−2.99
	(4.80)	(4.32)	(3.50)	(4.78)	(3.29)	(4.43)	(3.27)	(3.81)
Change in Market Value Past 3 Years	0.03	−0.09	0.01	−0.07	0.02	−0.06	0.04	−0.05
	(0.04)	(0.06)	(0.03)	(0.04)	(0.03)	(0.04)	(0.03)	(0.04)
Governance variables								
Accounting System		−0.19		0.20		0.18		0.10
		(0.19)		(0.18)		(0.17)		(0.15)
Policies & Procedures		−0.74*		−0.82**		−0.73**		−0.67**
		(0.37)		(0.24)		(0.22)		(0.24)
Code of Conduct		−0.37		−0.92*		−0.90*		−0.85*
		(0.43)		(0.36)		(0.36)		(0.38)
Formal Communication		−1.07		−1.33**		−1.33**		−1.35**
		(0.62)		(0.40)		(0.41)		(0.43)
Informal Communication		−0.09		−0.41		−0.40*		−0.39*
		(0.26)		(0.21)		(0.20)		(0.19)
Employee Screening		0.19		0.75**		0.70**		0.60*
		(0.33)		(0.26)		(0.23)		(0.25)
Employee Contingent Pay		−0.85**		−0.48		−0.58*		−0.71*
		(0.32)		(0.29)		(0.29)		(0.30)
Pseudo R^2	0.29	0.61	0.18	0.46	0.19	0.48	0.24	0.54
Chi square	35.17**	109.64**	35.73**	157.14**	34.99**	113.06**	34.94**	66.37**

The entries in the table are coefficients, with standard errors in parentheses. *$p < 0.05$; **$p < 0.01$

had six announcements is in the sample six times, as is its match. In Table 8, the clustering method accounts for the nonindependence across the pairs as well as within the pairs of these observations.

I run two models for each dependent variable to capture the difference between traditional governance variables and operational governance variables. Model 1 for each of the models consists of the control variables, while Model 2 adds in the operational governance variables.

The data do not support Hypothesis 1, that the strength of the accounting system reduces the incidence of crime, in either the binary or ordinal estimation. In contrast, there is strong support for Hypothesis 2—that clear policies and procedures reduce the likelihood of crime. Hypothesis 3, that a stronger and more complex code of conduct reduces the likelihood of crime, is partially supported. It is not significant in the binary regression, but it is negative and significant in the ordinal models. Formal communication, Hypothesis 4, is also partially supported. As is the case with the code of conduct, formal communication is not significant in the binary model, but is in the ordinal models. Informal communication, Hypothesis 5, is weakly supported, as there is no support in the binary model or the full number of crimes models, but informal communication is negative and significant in the two reduced number of crimes models. Employee screening actually appears to increase the likelihood of crime in the ordinal models, the opposite of Hypothesis 6, and receives no support in the binary model. Employee contingent pay appears to reduce the occurrence of a crime, but not the number of crimes in the full crime model. However, employee contingent pay is negative and significant in both reduced number of crimes models, somewhat supporting Hypothesis 7.

With regard to the control variables, block ownership, the number of roles of the CEO, the percentage of insiders on the board, the level of pay of the board, the amount of contingent pay the CEO receives (options, restricted stock), CEO or board ownership levels have no impact on the likelihood of crime, in any of the binary or ordinal models, in either the control or the full versions of the models, and regardless of method or grouping the data.

The number of meetings of the board is only significant in the binary crime model, and only when run with the other controls, and becomes insignificant in the full model, as well as in all forms of the ordinal regressions. The level of the CEO's flat pay is positive and significant in the control versions of the models only, with the exception of the ordinal control regression in Table 8 on crime scaled as 0–2+. When the operational governance variables are added, this result disappears.

The percent of outsiders on the audit committee and number of meetings of the audit committee have similar results. Neither is significant in any version of the binary regression. Both become negative and significant in the ordinal models, but only in the full versions of the models, not the control versions of the models. The exception is in the regression on crime as a range of 0–3+ in Table 8, where the number of meetings of the audit committee becomes insignificant. A greater percentage of outsiders on the audit committee and more meetings of this committee do not appear to impact the likelihood of a first crime; rather they may help prevent subsequent crimes. Audit committee strength is significant only in Table 7, and only for the control versions of the models, not for any of the full versions of the models.

Board salary type (a higher number means more contingent components) is negative and significant in all ordinal models in Table 7, as well as the binary control model. It is negative and significant in the full versions of the ordinal models in Table 8, but not the control versions of the models or either of the binary models. The more the board is paid through contingent methods, the less likely there is to be crime.

Size is positive and significant in all models in Table 7, and most of the models in Table 8. The change in market value over the past 3 years is negative and significant only in the full version of the ordinal model on number of crimes. Performance measured as ROA over the past 3 years is negative and significant in all the ordinal models in Table 7, but only in the control versions of the models, not the full models. It is only negative and significant in two of the three ordinal models in Table 8, again in the control versions of these models, not the full versions.

Marginal effects

In order to assess the relative impact of these variables on the occurrence of crime, I generated the marginal effect of each variable in the control version of the model and then the full model on the binary crime variable. Table 9 shows these results.

604   K. Schnatterly

Table 9.   Marginal effects of independent variables on crime as a binary dependent variable

Variable	Model 1: Control model	A move from the mean to:	Changes the pr(crime) by y%	Model 2: Full model	A move from the mean to:	Changes the pr(crime) by y%	Variable means
% Largest Owner	0.94	0.23	0.09	1.21	0.23	0.12	0.13
# Roles CEO	0.13	1	−0.17	0.27	1	−0.35	2.3
% Insiders	0.44	0.43	0.04	0.25	0.43	0.03	0.33
Board Salary Type	−0.12	5	−0.11	−0.13	5	−0.12	4.07
Ln(Board Salary)	−0.03	11.62	0.98	0.06	11.62	1.06	10.62
Dollar Translations of Logs		111,302			111,302		40,946
# Meetings of the Board	0.07	9	0.11	0.04	9	0.06	7.47
CEO Contingent/Flat	0.01	5	0.01	−0.01	5	−0.001	4.31
Ln(CEO Flat Pay)	0.18	14.75	1.20	0.25	14.75	1.28	13.75
Dollar Translations of Logs		2,545,913			2,545,913		936,589
% Owned by CEO	0.8	0.16	0.08	−1.14	0.16	−0.11	0.06
% Owned by the Board	0.13	0.22	0.013	1.26	0.22	0.126	0.12
% Outsiders on Audit Committee	0.07	0.8	−0.007	−0.53	0.8	0.05	0.90
# meetings Audit Committee	−0.06	4	−0.06	−0.1	4	−0.11	2.95
Audit Committee Strength	−0.12	6	−0.19	0.12	6	0.19	4.36
Size (Employees)	0.00	0.00	0.00	0.00	0.00	0.00	79.21
ROA past 3 years	−1.79	0.16	−0.18	−1.31	0.16	−0.131	0.06
Change in Market Value Past 3 Years	0.01	2.6	0.01	−0.02	2.6	−0.02	1.60
Accounting System				−0.05	5	−0.05	4.14
Policies & Procedures				−0.18	5	−0.26	3.52
Code of Conduct				−0.10	4	−0.16	2.38
Formal Communication				−0.26	3	−0.27	1.95
Informal Communication				−0.02	4	−0.03	2.51
Employee Screening				0.05	3	0.07	1.61
Employee Contingent Pay				−0.21	5	−0.34	3.39

*Model coefficients reflect a % change in the Pr(crime) for a 1-unit change in the independent variable away from its mean. Subsequent columns translate that into units and percentages.

Marginal effects can be interpreted as the change in the probability of crime for each unit change in the independent variables. These effects were computed based on the independent variable's mean value. In the control version of the model, increasing the share ownership of the largest owner, insider representation on the board, board salary level, number of meetings of the board, CEO compensation, both level and contingent components, CEO and board ownership increase the probability of crime. Decreasing the number of roles of the CEO, paying the board more with contingent pay, increasing outsider representation on the audit committee, the number of meetings of the audit committee and the audit committee strength decrease the probability of crime. Higher historical ROAs decrease the probability of crime while greater positive historical changes in market value increase the probability of crime.

In the full version of the model, many of the results are similar, or show magnitude but not direction changes. Direction changes are seen in the level of CEO compensation, CEO share ownership and historical market value variables from positive to negative. Outsider representation on the audit committee and audit committee strength also change sign from negative to positive.

For the operational governance variables, the percentage changes in crime based on a move from the variable mean to the next significant level up were calculated, as these are scale variables and noninteger numbers have no meaning. An increase in all of these except employee screening reduces the probability of crime.

DISCUSSION

Previous organizational research has not addressed crime extensively, and the few studies that have done so have generally focused on board-level variables rather than the organizational conditions that encourage or prevent crime. The researchers who have studied different operational governance mechanisms have generally done so one at a time. This study integrated this previous research of board-level variables with the multiple streams included in operational governance research to develop a set of mechanisms that have the possibility to impact occurrence of crimes in companies.

In this study, operational governance mechanisms appear to dominate more traditional governance mechanisms in the prevention of white-collar crime. Clarity of policies and procedures was persistent in its significance, while formal communication, the code of conduct, and employee contingent pay were significant in most models.

Clarity of policies and procedures may be significant because the clearer it is to employees what their job actually is, and what to refer to others, the less likely they are to cut corners. By moving from a mean of 3.53 to 5 on policies and procedures, a firm can reduce the probability of white-collar crime by 26 percent. By finding the interpretation of these numbers in Appendix 2, it can be seen that this means that moving from a discussion

of systems (variable = 3), or clear policies in one division (variable = 4) to communicating policies throughout the firm and an emphasis on training accordingly (variable = 5) will reduce the probability of crime by 26 percent.

Similarly, moving from a score of 2 to a score of 3 in formal communication represents moving from large group activities rarely done in the same location to having smaller groups who meet by necessity somewhat often. This shift can reduce the probability of crime by 27 percent. This may be significant because the more individuals in the company know about what others are doing, the less likely they are to commit a crime.

Stronger and more comprehensive codes of conduct may reduce numbers of crimes, or the possibility of a second crime occurring, by making clear what constitutes appropriate behavior. By moving from a 2.4 to a 4 on code of conduct moves the probability of crime down 16 percent. This means moving from a focus on compliance in the code to an acceptance of corporate social responsibility and citizenship and clarity that top management know the code of conduct.

Finally, as more employees receive performance-based rewards for their effort, the less likely they are to commit a crime. Essentially, by making performance bonuses or profit sharing available to all employees reduces the probability of crime by 34 percent. This could indicate less inclination on the part of the employee to 'steal from themselves' by reducing the profit of a division through crime. It could also indicate a greater likelihood of a colleague to report a fellow employee for a crime. Finally, it could also indicate a greater sense of 'ownership' on the part of the employee, and could create a feeling of being appreciated, thus reducing the likelihood of crime.

The employee contingent pay variable is focused on 'all employees,' not the CEO or top management team alone. This finding does not support more options compensation for top management teams, as can be seen in the lack of significance of the variable that captures the impact of options paid to the CEO. Indeed, the marginal effect of increasing options for the CEO increases the probability of crime in the control model, and has a trivial negative marginal effect in the full model.

Employee screening is positive and significant in the ordinal models. This may indicate that as the emphasis on 'hiring the best talent' increases, competition among individuals, new hires as well as old ones, may increase. As this happens, the tendency to cut corners may increase, especially after one crime has been committed. It may be that this variable measures the competitive nature of the firm's culture and not the attention paid to hiring qualified, honest individuals. The marginal effect of this variable is positive and reflects that when a firm moves from care in hiring financial and audit staff to a focus on recruiting depth, the probability of crime increases 7 percent.

The accounting system's marginal effect is such that moving from implementation of new control procedures based on recommendations to a more proactive system that does systematic review and modification will reduce the probability of crime by 5 percent.

Of the control variables, a number of these change signs or significance levels when run as just controls compared to the full models. For example, board salary type is negative and significant across the ordinal full models in Table 8, but not the control versions of those models or either binary model. This indicates that the more the board is paid in stock and options, the less likely the firm is to have multiple crimes. If the board does not own a significant percentage of the firm, then contingent compensation aligns the board members' incentives with the goals of the firm. This finding cannot be interpreted as the more the board gets paid, the more seriously they take their job, as the level of board salary is not significant. This is the strongest result involving the control variables. The marginal effect of board salary type is that as soon as the board is paid in options, the probability of crime is reduced 12 percent.

The magnitude of the CEO's salary is only positive and significant in the control versions of the models, and not in the full versions. This is cautionary in that if laws were changed based on current assumptions about CEO compensation, they would be misdirected. Similarly, the number of meetings of the board is positive and significant only in the control versions of the binary models.

While none of the ownership variables are significant in the logit models, there are some interesting marginal effects results. More ownership by the largest owner increases the probability of crime. For example, a move from the largest owner owning 13 percent to owning 23 percent increases the probability of crime by 12 percent. More ownership by the CEO (from 6% to 16%) decreases the probability of crime by 11 percent, while a similar increase in board ownership increases the probability of crime 13 percent.

As the CEO sheds roles, or serves only as CEO, and not as CEO and chair of the board, the probability of crime declines by 35 percent. This clearly supports the previous research that finds that too much power in the CEO's hands leads to less objective assessment and greater entrenchment (Boyd, 1994; Beatty and Zajac, 1994).

Audit committee strength is negative and significant in the control versions of the models in Table 7, but insignificant in the full versions of the models, as well as insignificant in all versions in Table 8. However, a greater percentage of outsiders on the audit committee and more audit committee meetings appear to reduce the likelihood of multiple crimes. This might be because a corporate reaction to a first crime is to focus on the audit committee. These results are interesting when taken in tandem with the finding on audit committee strength. This collection of variables seems to indicate that if an audit committee is mostly outsiders and meets frequently, then a charter or 'job description' is excessive. Interestingly, the marginal effect of audit committee strength in the full model is that a move from a 4 to a 5 increases the probability of crime by 19 percent. Decreasing outsider representation (from 90% to 80%) increases crime 5 percent and moving from 3 to 4 audit committee meetings reduces crime by 11 percent. This is an important finding especially if investors look to audit committees to monitor the financial integrity of the firm. This result indicates that some of the policy-making is misplaced, especially that which deals with committee charters.[9]

Past performance is only significant in the control model on number of crimes. This significance goes away in the full model. The change in market value is only negative and significant in the full model on the number of crimes in Table 7. Economic conditions of the firm do not appear to encourage or discourage crime. This may be because there are either pressures at extremes of performance, both good and bad, or that there are pressures all the time to commit crime. Because the sample is matched firms, and prior performance does not have an impact, there is something about

---

[9] The New York Stock Exchange adopted changes in listing standards for NYSE-listed firms, including a policy requiring key committee charters. August 16, 2002, www.nyse.com.

the firm itself, not its environment that creates the increased probability of a crime to be committed. The discussion about whether poor performance drives crime or good performance drives crime is secondary to the necessary discussion about what exactly is it internal to the firm that drives crime.

There are two key sets of findings. First, the findings show that there are mechanisms that managers can use to reduce the possibility of white-collar crime occurrence. Clear policies and procedures and designated liaison roles along with a strong, comprehensive code of conduct and more contingent pay for more employees are associated with fewer occurrences of crime. Contingent pay for board members is also associated with a reduction in the number of crime occurrences.

Second, given the differences in results between control and full models, traditional governance researchers should be careful about the use of their variables. Pseudo R^2s increased significantly between the control and full models. While the number of meetings of the board and the level of the CEO's salary are the only variables that are significant in both control versions of the models and not in either of the full versions, the fact that they do become insignificant indicates an omitted variable bias. It seems clear that governance research must reach down inside the firm to be able to speak to fraud reduction.

Limitations

One limitation of this study is that the sample is dependent on having a crime allegation be announced. Most corporations prefer to hide crimes. Many more crimes are committed but not announced than announced. The most serious implication for this is the question: Are the non-crime firms really crime-free? For example, has one firm announced a crime because it has a better detection system, and so more crimes are likely to be discovered in that firm, but that firm does not have more crimes *per se* than its matched firm, which has a poorer detection system, and so may have *more* crimes. This issue is less powerful as long as the relationship is that firms with more crimes, and more serious crimes, are the 'crime firms,' and the 'noncrime firms' have fewer, or less serious crimes. This is addressed in part through the use of the ordered logit model. As discussed, the results indicate firms with more crimes have less clear policies and procedures, weaker formal

communication, and less employee contingent pay than firms with fewer crimes. This result is consistent with the results of the binary logit model.

A second limitation is a result of the limitations of content analysis. If a firm did not mention anything with respect to the variables being measured in the annual report, 10K or proxy statement, the company was not credited with that activity. For example, a firm could have a code of conduct, but if it did not mention it in the SEC documents, it was scored as not having one. While this overlooked some firms' activities, it can also be said that if they do not choose to mention it in these documents, the firms do not think it is all that important. These are required documents, so every public firm produces them. As a result, there is no availability bias. As long as what the company reports or describes in these documents is consistent with the activities of the firm, then the results will hold.

A limitation, not with the study, but with the interpretation of some of the marginal effects numbers, is that the scoring system for the content-context numbers is not linear. In other words, while '3' means more than '2' and '4' means more than '3', the difference from 2 to 3 in activities in the firm may be different from the distance from 3 to 4. The strongest statement the marginal effects provides is a relative magnitude difference in the impact on reduction of crime in the firm. Start with the activities that have the highest marginal effects.

CONCLUSION

This paper contributes to both the corporate crime literature and the strategy literature. It also contributes to practice in that this study generates a set of operational governance components that have the potential to reduce crime and its associated costs to the firm.

The contributions to the strategy literature include definitional and measurement contributions. I created a broader and deeper definition of operational governance that incorporates previous research in the traditional governance area. The resulting mechanisms are measurable, so future research can include precise descriptions of governance mechanisms that will enable deeper understanding through comparisons and large sample studies.

The findings that some of the operational governance mechanisms are more powerful in explaining crime than traditional governance mechanisms is also a contribution, and has a role in the debate over reforms to the current system. If outsider ('independent') board members, for example, have no impact on crime, then placing the responsibility for past or future crimes in their hands is not appropriate and will not have the intended effect.

In the arena of managerial practice, an ability to reduce the damaging impact of a crime is significant. If a firm reduces internal frauds only a little, losing 3 percent of sales vs. 6 percent (the average estimate: Hogsett and Radig, 1994; Touby, 1994; ACFE, 2002) this represents a significant increase in profit margin. Employing the operational mechanisms discovered in the study to reduce crime can have a significant impact on firm performance.

This study can also guide investors who are concerned about the quality of the firm in which they are investing. An assessment across the key variables can give an indication of the likelihood of that firm to be prone to crime.

ACKNOWLEDGEMENTS

The author thanks Norm Bowie, Phil Bromiley, Robert Doljanac, Scott Johnson, Gautam Kaul, C. K. Prahalad, J. Myles Shaver, Jim Walsh, and Mary Zellmer-Bruhn for comments and suggestions. She also thanks participants in a colloquium at the University of Minnesota for their comments.

REFERENCES

Abrahamson E, Park C. 1994. Concealment of negative organizational outcomes: an agency theory perspective. *Academy of Management Journal* **37**(5): 1302–1334.

Agro D. 1978. White collar crime: we cannot afford it! *Government Accountants Journal* **28**(Spring): 53–57.

Albrecht WS, Wernz GW, Williams T. 1995. *Fraud: Bringing Light to the Dark Side of Business*. Irwin: New York.

Alexander C, Cohen MA. 1996. New evidence of the origins of corporate crime. *Managerial and Decision Economics* **17**(4): 421–435.

Alexander C, Cohen MA. 1999. Why do corporations become criminals? Ownership, hidden actions and crime as an agency cost. *Journal of Corporate Finance* **5**(1): 1–34.

Almaney A. 1974. Communication and the systems theory of organization. *Journal of Business Communication* **12**(1): 35–43.

Anonymous. 1994. Ethics policies help reduce internal control costs. *Journal of Accountancy* **177**(4): 14.

Anthony RN. 1988. *The Management Control Function*. Harvard Business School Press: Boston, MA.

Arndt M, Bigelow B. 2000. Presenting structural innovation in an institutional environment: hospitals' use of impression management. *Administrative Science Quarterly* **45**: 494–522.

Association of Certified Fraud Examiners. 2002. Fraud statistics web page. http://www.cfenet.com/media/statistics.asp [24 June 2002].

Baucus MS, Baucus DA. 1997. Paying the piper: an empirical examination of longer-term financial consequences of illegal corporate behavior. *Academy of Management Journal* **40**(1): 129–151.

Baucus MS, Near JP. 1991. Can illegal corporate behavior be predicted? An event history analysis. *Academy of Management Journal* **34**(1): 9–36.

Beasley MS. 1996. An empirical analysis of the relation between the board of director composition and financial statement fraud. *Accounting Review* **71**(4): 443–465.

Beatty RP, Zajac EJ. 1994. Managerial incentives, monitoring and risk bearing: a study of executive compensation, ownership and board structure in initial public offerings. *Administrative Science Quarterly* **39**: 313–335.

Bell TB, Knechel WR, Payne JL, Willingham JJ. 1998. An empirical investigation between the computerization of accounting systems and the incidence and size of audit differences. *Auditing: A Journal of Practice and Theory* **17**(1): 13–38.

Bologna J. 1980. Motivated climate prevents white collar crime. *Journal of Systems Management* **31**(10): 36–39.

Bowman EH. 1984. Content analysis of annual reports for corporate strategy and risk. *Interfaces*. **14**(1): 61–71.

Boyd BK. 1994. Board control and CEO compensation. *Strategic Management Journal* **15**(5): 335–344.

Boyd BK. 1995. CEO duality and firm performance: a contingency model. *Strategic Management Journal* **16**(4): 301–312.

Bruns WJ Jr. 1968. Accounting information and decision-making: some behavioral hypotheses. *Accounting Review* **43**(3): 469–480.

Bureau of Justice Statistics website. 1999. National Crime Victimization Survey. http://www.ojp.usdoj.gov/bjs/abstract/cvusst.htm [24 June 2002].

Buss D. 1993. Ways to curtail employee theft. *Nation's Business* **81**(4): 36–37.

Coffey BS, Fryxell GE. 1991. Institutional ownership and dimensions of corporate social performance: an empirical examination. *Journal of Business Ethics* **10**(6): 437–444.

Daboub AJ, Rasheed AMA, Priem RL, Gray DA. 1995. Top management team characteristics and corporate illegal activity. *Academy of Management Review* **20**(1): 138–170.

Daft RL, Macintosh NB. 1984. The nature and use of formal control systems for management control and strategy implementation. *Journal of Management* **10**(1): 43–66.

DeFond ML, Jiambalvo J. 1991. Incidence and circumstance of accounting errors. *Accounting Review* **66**(3): 643–745.

Ettore B. 1995. An ounce of prevention. *Management Review* **84**(4): 6.

Fama EF. 1980. Agency theory and the theory of the firm. *Journal of Political Economy* **88**(2): 288–307.

Fama EF, Jensen MC. 1983. Separation of ownership and control. *Journal of Law and Economics* **26**(2): 301–326.

Fan X, Chen M. 2000. Published studies of interrater reliability often overestimate reliability: computing the correct coefficient. *Educational and Psychological Measurement* **60**(4): 532–542.

Fellner BS, Mitchell LL. 1995. Communication: an essential element in internal control. *Healthcare Financial Management* **49**(9): 80–82.

Finkelstein S, D'Aveni RA. 1994. CEO duality as a double edged sword: how boards of directors balance entrenchment avoidance and unity of command. *Academy of Management Journal* **37**(5): 1079–1108.

Gardner R. 1998. How well do you really know whom you hire? *CPS Journal* **68**(3): 62–64.

Ghoshal S, Korine H, Szulanski G. 1994. Interunit communication in multinational corporations. *Management Science* **40**(1): 96–110.

Gupta AK, Govindarajan V. 1991. Knowledge flows and the structure of control within multinational corporations. *Academy of Management Review* **16**(4): 768–792.

Hatcher L, Ross TL, Collins D. 1989. Prosocial behavior, job complexity, and suggestion contribution under gainsharing plans. *Journal of Applied Behavioral Science* **25**(3): 231–249.

Hermalin B, Weisbach MS. 1991. The effects of board composition and direct incentives on performance. *Financial Management* **20**(4): 101–112.

Hill CWL, Kelley P, Agle BR, Hitt MA, Hoskisson RE. 1992. An empirical examination of the causes of corporate wrongdoing in the United States. *Human Relations* **45**(10): 1055–1076.

Hogsett RM, Radig WJ. 1994. Employee crime: the cost and some control measures. *Review of Business* **16**(2): 9–14.

Holford T. 2002. *Multivariate Methods in Epidemiology*. Oxford University Press: New York.

Holmes SA, Langford M, Welch OJ, Welch ST. 2002. Associations between internal controls and organizational citizenship behavior. *Journal of Managerial Issues* **14**(1): 85–99.

Hooks KL, Kaplan SE, Schultz JJ, Ponemon LA. 1994. Enhancing communication to assist in fraud prevention and detection. *Auditing: A Journal of Practice and Theory* **13**(2): 86–130.

Hoskisson RE, Hill CWL, Kim H. 1993. The multidivisional structure: organizational fossil or source of value. *Journal of Management* **19**: 269–298.

Jensen MC, Meckling WH. 1976. Theory of the firm: managerial behavior, agency costs and ownership structure. *Journal of Financial Economics* **3**: 305–360.

Jensen MC, Murphy KJ. 1990. Performance pay and top-management incentives. *Journal of Political Economy* **98**(2): 225–264.

Kassinis G, Vafeas N. 2002. Corporate boards and outside stakeholders as determinants of environmental litigation. *Strategic Management Journal* **23**(5): 399–415.

Key S, Messina F, Turpen R. 1998–99. Keeping employees honest. *Ivey Business Quarterly* **63**(2): 68–71.

Kinney WR Jr. 2000. Research opportunities in internal control quality and quality assurance. *Auditing* **19**: 83–90.

Larsson R, Finkelstein S. 1999. Integrating strategic, organizational and human resource perspectives on mergers and acquisitions: a case survey of synergy realization. *Organization Science* **10**(1): 1–27.

Leatherwood ML, Spector LC. 1991. Enforcements, inducements, expected utility and employee misconduct. *Journal of Management* **17**(3): 553–569.

Marginson DE. 2002. Management control systems and their effects on strategy formulation at middle-management levels: evidence from a UK organization. *Strategic Management Journal* **23**(12): 1019–1031.

Martin J. 1998. An HR guide to white collar crime. *HR Focus* **75**(9): 1–3.

Martinez JI, Jarillo JC. 1989. The evolution of research on coordination mechanisms in multinational corporations. *Journal of International Business Studies* **20**(3): 489–514.

McConaughy DL, Walker MC, Henderson GV Jr, Mishra CS. 1998. Founding family controlled firms: efficiency and value. *Review of Financial Economics* **7**(1): 1–19.

McMullen DA. 1996. Audit committee performance: an investigation of the consequences associated with audit committees. *Auditing: A Journal of Practice and Theory* **15**(1): 87–103.

McMullen DA, Raghunandan K. 1996. Enhancing audit committee effectiveness. *Journal of Accountancy* **182**(2): 79–81.

Mitchell TR, Daniels D, Hopper H, George-Falvy J, Ferris GR. 1996. Perceived correlates of illegal behavior in organizations. *Journal of Business Ethics* **15**(4): 439–455.

Mizruchi MS. 1983. Who controls whom? An examination of the relation between management and boards of directors in large American corporations. *Academy of Management Review* **8**(3): 426–436.

New York Stock Exchange. 2002. www.nyse.com [16 August 2002].

Pascale R. 1985. The paradox of 'corporate culture': reconciling ourselves to socialization. *California Management Review* **27**(2): 26–42.

Pierce JL, Rubenfeld SA, Morgan S. 1991. Employee ownership: a conceptual model of process and effects. *Academy of Management Review* **16**(1): 121–144.

Popping R. 2000. *Computer-Assisted Text Analysis*. Sage: Thousand Oaks, CA.

Rechner PL, Dalton DR. 1991. CEO duality and organizational performance. *Strategic Management Journal* **12**(2): 155–160.

610 *K. Schnatterly*

Roland N. 2001. SEC examining 40 large firms for accounting fraud. *Los Angeles Times* 7 July.

Russell RC. 1995. Understanding fraud and embezzlement. *Ohio CPA Journal* **54**(1): 37–39.

Schendel D. 1992. Introduction to the Summer 1992 Special Issue on 'Strategy process research'. *Strategic Management Journal*, Summer Special Issue **13**: 1–4.

Schuster M. 1984. Cooperation and change in union settings: problems and opportunities. *Human Resource Management* **23**(2): 145–161.

Sonnenberg FK. 1991. Internal communication: turning talk into action. *Journal of Business Strategy* **12**(6): 52–55.

Stata Reference Manual. 2001. Release 7. Stata Press: College Station, TX.

Stavros JA. 1998. The forgotten factors in preventing employee fraud: employee screening. *Pennsylvania CPA Journal* **69**(1): 30–33.

Teece DJ. 1981. Internal organization and economic performance: an empirical analysis of the profitability of principal firms. *Journal of Industrial Economics* **30**(2): 173–199.

Tosi HL, Katz JP, Gomez-Mejia LR. 1997. Disaggregating the agency contract: the effects of monitoring, incentive alignment, and term in office on agent decision-making. *Academy of Management Journal* **40**(3): 584–602.

Touby L. 1994. In the company of thieves. *Journal of Business Strategy* **15**(3): 24–35.

Trevino LK, Victor B. 1992. Peer reporting of unethical behavior: a social context perspective. *Academy of Management Journal* **35**(1): 38–64.

Turner DL, Stephenson RG. 1993. The lure of white-collar crime. *Security Management* **37**(2): 57–58.

Weeks WA, Nantel J. 1992. Corporate codes of ethics and sales force behavior: a case study. *Journal of Business Ethics* **11**(10): 753–761.

Zajac EJ, Westphal JD. 1994. The costs and benefits of managerial incentives and monitoring in large U.S. corporations: when is more not better? *Strategic Management Journal*, Winter Special Issue **15**: 121–142.

APPENDIX 1: TEXT SEARCH TERMS AND TEXT EXCERPTS OR EXAMPLES

Variable	Text Search Terms	Excerpts
Accounting System	Accounting, Internal	From companies that only print their auditor's statement to companies that say 'To assure that financial information is reliable and assets are safeguarded, management maintains an effective system of internal controls and procedures, important elements of which include: careful selection, training, and development of operating and financial managers; an organization that provides appropriate division of responsibility; and communications aimed at assuring that Company policies and procedures are understood throughout the organization. In establishing internal controls, management weighs the costs of such systems against the benefits it believes such systems will provide. A staff of internal auditors regularly monitors the adequacy and application of internal controls on a worldwide basis. To insure that personnel continue to understand the system of internal controls and procedures and policies concerning good and prudent business practices, the Company periodically conducts the management's Stewardship Program for key management and financial personnel. This program reinforces the importance and understanding of internal controls by reviewing key corporate policies, procedures, and systems.'
Policies and Procedures	Policy, Policies, Duty, Duties, Manual, Training, Process	From no discussion or mention to companies that discuss organizational responsibilities, formalized procedures, ongoing training, job descriptions, periodic self-analysis to keep policies updated.
Liaison Roles (formal communication)	Meeting, Conference, Retreat, Contact, Feedback, Rotation, Interaction	From no discussion or mention to 'Last year we made progress in implementing a new worldwide employee training strategy. This revitalization of employee training and development is a major investment in our employees to help them achieve their full potential. As an example, we have established an education and conference center in New Brunswick that will provide training for our people from all parts of the world.' 'She rotates international general managers meetings quarterly among countries. To maintain close contact as the company grows, (her) Open Door policy provides a forum for all members of the worldwide sales and marketing organization to make suggestions, comments or complaints directly to her.' 'The Thursday morning meeting is a multi-disciplinary effort to track the progress of all new products under development. Keeping open lines of communication among disciplines has accelerated the product development process-an industry-leading average of 18 months from inception to market. For nearly ten years, (he) has also held a daily meeting for key members of his staff-a brief encapsulation of what has happened in the operations area over the past 24 hours.'
Teams (informal communication)	Team	From no discussion or mention to 'No football team, no baseball team, no political party or fraternity or church group, no hockey team or choir or orchestra could have a team that displays the excellence and camaraderie that our ... (company does).' 'Whether the task is performing a ... procedure or running a corporation, it is teamwork that gets the job done.'

(*continued overleaf*)

Variable	Text Search Terms	Excerpts
		'A 14-year veteran of (the company, he) knows something of both teamwork and the bottom line. His far-reaching umbrella covers all of finance and accounting, as well as management information systems, legal affairs and administration. It is the job of his people to create legal and financial harmony in a company that does business in 50 states and nearly 60 countries. And they are true disciples of the team approach. In the operations realm, for example, they work closely with engineers to develop standard costs, assist in efficient inventory management and collaborate with members of quality control so that every finished product can be traced back to the smallest component part.'
Code of Conduct	Conduct, Behavior, Integrity, Responsibility, Principles, Credo	From no discussion or mention to 'We believe that it is essential for the company to conduct its business affairs in accordance with the highest ethical standards, as set forth in the (company's) Business Conduct Guidelines. In addition, the Audit Committee reviews the Company's adherence to its Business Conduct Guidelines in compliance with federal procurement laws and regulations.' 'As we conduct ourselves in the pursuit of our existing businesses and in the growth of our businesses in an ethical and moral way, we must also fulfill our commitments to our government, to our society and to ourselves as individuals. In one sense, ethics involves the point of view that suggests we live in a glass bowl, and we should feel comfortable with any actions we take, if they were shared publicly. Further, we will conduct our affairs within the law. Should there be evidence of possible malfeasance on the part of any officer or member of management, each person must feel the responsibility to communicate that to the appropriate party. This is a commitment that each of us must undertake and not feel that it is a high-risk communication, but that it is expected and, indeed, an obligation.'
Employee Screening	Employee Screening, Applicant Testing, Hiring, Select, Recruit	From no discussion or mention to 'But our strategy for managing and sustaining that growth has remained constant: we select and hire people with a record of exceptional achievement in school and business, then give them respect and the freedom to pursue their own high standards of excellence.' 'Our recruiting, training and development, and performance appraisal processes received continued emphasis during the year. The depth of our management team benefits the company and we maintain our commitment to having the best talent in (our industry).' 'Having the best talent in (our industry) is our most important priority. All of our human resource activities—recruiting, compensation, training, performance appraisal, development—support that commitment. New in 1991 is a significantly enhanced executive development and training program responsive to the needs of our "top schools/best in class" college recruits.'
Contingent Pay for Employees	ESOP, Employee Stock Bonus, Profit Sharing, Retention, Promotion, Discount, Incentive	From no discussion or mention to performance-based bonuses, options or stock (beyond an ESOP) to all employees.

Variable	Text Search Terms	Excerpts
Audit Committee	Audit Committee	From no mention of an Audit Committee, or just the mention of its existence to 'The Audit Committee of the Board of Directors is composed solely of directors who are not officers or employees of the Company. The Audit Committee's responsibilities include recommending to the Board for stockholder approval the independent auditors for the annual audit of the Company's consolidated financial statements. The Committee also reviews the audit plans, scope, fees, and audit results of the auditors; reports on the adequacy of internal accounting controls; non-audit services and related fees; the company's ethics program; status of significant legal matters; the scope of the internal auditors' plans and budget and results of their audits; and the effectiveness of the Company's program for correcting audit findings. Company personnel, including internal auditors, meet periodically with the Audit Committee to discuss auditing and financial reporting matters.' 'The duties of the Audit Committee are (a) to recommend to the Board of Directors a firm of independent accountants to perform the examination of the annual financial statements of the Company; (b) to review with the independent accountants and with the Controller the proposed scope of the annual audit, past audit experience, the Company's internal audit program, recently completed internal audits and other matters bearing upon the scope of the audit; (c) to review with the independent accountants and with the Controller significant matters revealed in the course of the audit of the annual financial statements of the Company; (d) to review on an annual basis whether the Company's Statement of Business Conduct and Corporate Policies relating thereto has been communicated by the Company to all key employees of the Company and its subsidiaries throughout the world with a direction that all such key employees certify that they have read, understand and are not aware of any violation of the Statement of Business Conduct; (e) to review with the Controller any suggestions and recommendations of the independent accountants concerning the internal control standards and accounting procedures of the Company; (f) to meet on a regular basis with a representative or representatives of the Internal Audit Department of the Company and to review the Internal Audit Department's Reports of Operations; and (g) to report its activities and action to the Board at least once each fiscal year.'

APPENDIX 2: DICTIONARY AND SCORING SHEET

Accounting system

1 Reasonable assurance
2 Costs vs. benefits
3 Internal auditor evaluates and reports on adequacy and effectiveness, emerging accounting issues
4 New control procedures implemented, based on recommendations
5 Systematic review and modification
6 Communication throughout company, selection, training, development of qualified personnel
7 6+ more procedures, including organizational responsibility

Policies and procedures

1 Only basic
2 Training of sales people
3 Discussion of systems or examination of process (not necessarily around a profitability issue, e.g., efficiency)

4 Evidence of comprehensive, understood procedures in one division, or manager training, or quality assurance
5 Policies communicated throughout company, selection, training
6 Well-defined organizational responsibility and communication, qualified people
7 Clear organizational responsibility, formalized procedures, training to update

Code of conduct

1 None, no mention
2 Compliance
3 Social responsibility, corporate citizenship mention
4 Top management know it
5 Annual review re: code, communication to all key employees, to read, understand, and certify no violations
6 Top management training
7 Company-wide training and understanding

Formal communication

1 No mention
2 Large group, remote locations
3 Sales groups, or smaller, with limited responsibility
4 Mid level, limited cross-company
5 Cross-company cooperation and interaction
6 Managers with open doors and rotating meetings, or rotating managers
7 Training employees from all over the world in one place

Informal communication

1 No mention
2 Mention, but large, generic team, or only TMT
3 Mention of use of small teams
4 Cross-functional teams, product development, small teams
5 Team structure, products with management, strategy focus
6 Limited teams, careful selection, full participation, training
7 Teams rotate across function or geography, cross-functional management teams

Employee screening

1 No mention
2 Of financial and audit staff
3 Recruiting depth
4 Emphasis on checking qualifications
5 Training staff to interview
6 Recruiting process important, emphasized
7 6+ emphasize best talent

Employee contingent compensation

1 Employee savings plan/basic retirement plan
2 Options to key employees or 401K and post-retirement benefits to all
3 Options to key employees and 401K and post-retirement benefits to all
4 Promotion from within
5 Bonus or profit sharing available to many
6 Bonus or profit sharing available to all
7 Options or stock available to all

Board salary type

1 Flat
2 Flat + committee
3 + attendance/meeting
4 + retirement package
5 + options
6 + (stock or charity death benefits)
7 + stock and charity death benefits

Audit committee strength

1 No mention
2 Select auditors
3 + generic review, scope, plans, adequacy
4 + meet without management
5 Results discussed, overall quality financial reporting
6 Actions required, reviews, changes, other matters
7 Related to Business Conduct Code/ethics program, suggestions, recommendations
8 Reviews legal matters, company's program for correcting audit findings, etc.

Part XII
Poverty (the Effects of Business on Poverty)

[42]

*Improving the lives of the billions of people at the bottom
of the economic pyramid is a noble endeavor.
It can also be a lucrative one.*

Serving the World's Poor,
Profitably

by C.K. Prahalad and Allen Hammond

CONSIDER THIS BLEAK VISION of the world 15 years from now: The global economy recovers from its current stagnation but growth remains anemic. Deflation continues to threaten, the gap between rich and poor keeps widening, and incidents of economic chaos, governmental collapse, and civil war plague developing regions. Terrorism remains a constant threat, diverting significant public and private resources to security concerns. Opposition to the global market system intensifies. Multinational companies find it difficult to expand, and many become risk averse, slowing investment and pulling back from emerging markets.

Now consider this much brighter scenario: Driven by private investment and widespread entrepreneurial activity, the economies of developing regions grow vigorously, creating jobs and wealth and bringing hundreds of millions of new consumers into the global marketplace every year. China, India, Brazil, and, gradually, South Africa become new engines of global economic growth, promoting prosperity around the world. The resulting decrease in poverty produces a range of social benefits, helping to stabilize many developing regions and reduce civil and cross-border conflicts. The threat of terrorism and war recedes. Multinational companies expand rapidly in an era of intense innovation and competition.

Both of these scenarios are possible. Which one comes to pass will be determined primarily by one factor: the willingness of big, multinational companies to enter and invest in the world's poorest markets. By stimulating commerce and development at the bottom of the economic pyramid, MNCs could radically improve the lives of billions of people and help bring into being a more stable, less dangerous world. Achieving this goal does not require multinationals to spearhead global social development initiatives for charitable purposes. They need only act in their own self-interest, for there are enormous business benefits to be gained by entering developing markets. In fact, many innovative companies – entrepreneurial outfits and large, established enterprises alike – are already serving the world's poor in ways that generate strong revenues, lead to greater operating efficiencies, and uncover new sources of innovation. For these companies – and those that follow their lead – building businesses aimed at the bottom of the pyramid promises to provide important competitive advantages as the twenty-first century unfolds.

Big companies are not going to solve the economic ills of developing countries by themselves, of course. It will also

take targeted financial aid from the developed world and improvements in the governance of the developing nations themselves. But it's clear to us that prosperity can come to the poorest regions only through the direct and sustained involvement of multinational companies. And it's equally clear that the multinationals can enhance their own prosperity in the process.

Untapped Potential

Everyone knows that the world's poor are distressingly plentiful. Fully 65% of the world's population earns less than $2,000 each per year – that's 4 billion people. But despite the vastness of this market, it remains largely untapped by multinational companies. The reluctance to invest is easy to understand. Companies assume that people with such low incomes have little to spend on goods and services and that what they do spend goes to basic needs like food and shelter. They also assume that various barriers to commerce – corruption, illiteracy, inadequate infrastructure, currency fluctuations, bureaucratic red tape – make it impossible to do business profitably in these regions.

But such assumptions reflect a narrow and largely outdated view of the developing world. The fact is, many multinationals already successfully do business in developing countries (although most currently focus on selling to the small upper-middle-class segments of these markets), and their experience shows that the barriers to commerce – although real – are much lower than is typically thought. Moreover, several positive trends in developing countries – from political reform, to a growing openness to investment, to the development of low-cost wireless communication networks – are reducing the barriers further while also providing businesses with greater access to even the poorest city slums and rural areas. Indeed, once the misperceptions are wiped away, the enormous economic potential that lies at the bottom of the pyramid becomes clear.

Take the assumption that the poor have no money. It sounds obvious on the surface, but it's wrong. While individual incomes may be low, the aggregate buying power of poor communities is actually quite large. The average per capita income of villagers in rural Bangladesh, for instance, is less than $200 per year, but as a group they are avid consumers of telecommunications services. Grameen Telecom's village phones, which are owned by a single entrepreneur but used by the entire community, generate an average revenue of roughly $90 a month – and as much as $1,000 a month in some large villages.

Customers of these village phones, who pay cash for each use, spend an average of 7% of their income on phone services–a far higher percentage than consumers in traditional markets do.

It's also incorrect to assume that the poor are too concerned with fulfilling their basic needs to "waste" money on nonessential goods. In fact, the poor often do buy "luxury" items. In the Mumbai shantytown of Dharavi, for example, 85% of households own a television set, 75% own a pressure cooker and a mixer, 56% own a gas stove, and 21% have telephones. That's because buying a house in Mumbai, for most people at the bottom of the pyramid, is not a realistic option. Neither is getting access to running water. They accept that reality, and rather than saving for a rainy day, they spend their income on things they can get now that improve the quality of their lives.

Another big misperception about developing markets is that the goods sold there are incredibly cheap and, hence, there's no room for a new competitor to come in and turn a profit. In reality, consumers at the bottom of the pyramid pay much higher prices for most things than middle-class consumers do, which means that there's a real opportunity for companies, particularly big corporations with economies of scale and efficient supply chains, to capture market share by offering higher quality goods at lower prices while maintaining attractive margins. In fact, throughout the developing world, urban slum dwellers pay, for instance, between four and 100 times as much for drinking water as middle- and upper-class families. Food also costs 20% to 30% more in the poorest communities since there is no access to bulk discount stores. On the service side of the economy, local moneylenders charge interest of 10% to 15% *per day*, with annual rates running as high as 2,000%. Even the lucky small-scale entrepreneurs who

get loans from nonprofit microfinance institutions pay between 40% and 70% interest per year–rates that are illegal in most developed countries. (For a closer look at how the prices of goods compare in rich and poor areas, see the exhibit "The High-Cost Economy of the Poor.")

It can also be surprisingly cheap to market and deliver products and services to the world's poor. That's because many of them live in cities that are densely populated today and will be

> Markets at the bottom of the economic pyramid are fundamentally new sources of growth for multinationals. And because these markets are in the earliest stages, growth can be extremely rapid.

even more so in the years to come. Figures from the UN and the World Resources Institute indicate that by 2015, in Africa, 225 cities will each have populations of more than 1 million; in Latin America, another 225; and in Asia, 903. The population of at least 27 cities will reach or exceed 8 million. Collectively, the 1,300 largest cities will account for some 1.5 billion to 2 billion people, roughly half of whom will be bottom-of-the-pyramid (BOP) consumers now served primarily by informal economies. Companies that operate in these areas will have access to millions of potential new customers, who together have billions of dollars to spend. The poor in Rio de Janeiro, for instance, have a total purchasing power of $1.2 billion ($600 per person). Shantytowns in Johannesburg or Mumbai are no different.

The slums of these cities already have distinct ecosystems, with retail shops,

small businesses, schools, clinics, and moneylenders. Although there are few reliable estimates of the value of commercial transactions in slums, business activity appears to be thriving. Dharavi–covering an area of just 435 acres– boasts scores of businesses ranging from leather, textiles, plastic recycling, and surgical sutures to gold jewelry, illicit liquor, detergents, and groceries. The scale of the businesses varies from one-person operations to bigger, well-recognized producers of brand-name products. Dharavi generates an estimated $450 million in manufacturing revenues, or about $1 million per acre of land. Established shantytowns in São Paulo, Rio, and Mexico City are equally productive. The seeds of a vibrant commercial sector have been sown.

While the rural poor are naturally harder to reach than the urban poor, they also represent a large untapped opportunity for companies. Indeed, 60% of India's GDP is generated in rural areas. The critical barrier to doing business in rural regions is distribution access, not a lack of buying power. But new information technology and communications infrastructures – especially wireless–promise to become an inexpensive way to establish marketing and distribution channels in these communities.

Conventional wisdom says that people in BOP markets cannot use such advanced technologies, but that's just another misconception. Poor rural women in Bangladesh have had no difficulty using GSM cell phones, despite never before using phones of any type. In Kenya, teenagers from slums are being successfully trained as Web page designers. Poor farmers in El Salvador use telecenters to negotiate the sale of their crops over the Internet. And women in Indian coastal villages have in less than a week learned to use PCs to interpret real-time satellite images showing concentrations of schools of fish in the Arabian Sea so they can direct their husbands to the best fishing areas. Clearly, poor communities are ready to adopt new technologies that improve their economic opportunities or their quality of life. The lesson for multinationals:

C.K. Prahalad is the Harvey C. Fruehauf Professor of Business Administration at the University of Michigan Business School in Ann Arbor and the chairman of Praja, a software company in San Diego. Allen Hammond is the CIO, senior scientist, and director of the Digital Dividend project at the World Resources Institute in Washington, DC.

Don't hesitate to deploy advanced technologies at the bottom of the pyramid while, or even before, deploying them in advanced countries.

A final misperception concerns the highly charged issue of exploitation of the poor by MNCs. The informal economies that now serve poor communities are full of inefficiencies and exploitive intermediaries. So if a microfinance institution charges 50% annual interest when the alternative is either 1,000% interest or no loan at all, is that exploiting or helping the poor? If a large financial company such as Citigroup were to use its scale to offer microloans at 20%, is that exploiting or helping the poor? The issue is not just cost but also quality–quality in the range and fairness of financial services, quality of food, quality of water. We argue that when MNCs provide basic goods and services that reduce costs to the poor and help improve their standard of living–while generating an acceptable return on investment–the results benefit everyone.

The Business Case

The business opportunities at the bottom of the pyramid have not gone unnoticed. Over the last five years, we have seen nongovernmental organizations (NGOs), entrepreneurial start-ups, and a handful of forward-thinking multinationals conduct vigorous commercial experiments in poor communities. Their experience is a proof of concept: Businesses can gain three important advantages by serving the poor–a new source of revenue growth, greater efficiency, and access to innovation. Let's look at examples of each.

Top-Line Growth. Growth is an important challenge for every company, but today it is especially critical for very large companies, many of which appear to have nearly saturated their existing markets. That's why BOP markets represent such an opportunity for MNCs: They are fundamentally new sources of growth. And because these markets are in the earliest stages of economic development, growth can be extremely rapid.

Latent demand for low-priced, high-quality goods is enormous. Consider

the reaction when Hindustan Lever, the Indian subsidiary of Unilever, recently introduced what was for it a new product category–candy–aimed at the bottom of the pyramid. A high-quality confection made with real sugar and fruit, the candy sells for only about a penny a serving. At such a price, it may seem like a marginal business opportunity, but in just six months it became the fastest-growing category in the company's portfolio. Not only is it profitable, but the company estimates it has the potential to generate revenues of $200 million

per year in India and comparable markets in five years. Hindustan Lever has had similar successes in India with low-priced detergent and iodized salt. Beyond generating new sales, the company is establishing its business and its brand in a vast new market.

There is equally strong demand for affordable services. TARAhaat, a start-up focused on rural India, has introduced a range of computer-enabled education services ranging from basic IT training

to English proficiency to vocational skills. The products are expected to be the largest single revenue generator for the company and its franchisees over the next several years.[1] Credit and financial services are also in high demand among the poor. Citibank's ATM-based banking experiment in India, called Suvidha, for instance, which requires a minimum deposit of just $25, enlisted 150,000 customers in one year in the city of Bangalore alone.

Small-business services are also popular in BOP markets. Centers run in

Uganda by the Women's Information Resource Electronic Service (WIRES) provide female entrepreneurs with information on markets and prices, as well as credit and trade support services, packaged in simple, ready-to-use formats in local languages. The centers are planning to offer other small-business services such as printing, faxing, and copying, along with access to accounting, spreadsheet, and other software. In Bolivia, a start-up has partnered with

---

The World Pyramid

Most companies target consumers at the upper tiers of the economic pyramid, completely overlooking the business potential at its base. But though they may each be earning the equivalent of less than $2,000 a year, the people at the bottom of the pyramid make up a colossal market–4 billion strong–the vast majority of the world's population.

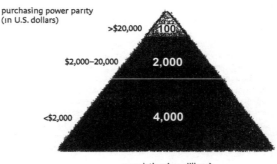

purchasing power parity (in U.S. dollars)

>$20,000   **100**

$2,000–20,000   **2,000**

<$2,000   **4,000**

population (in millions)

---

the Bolivian Association of Ecological Producers Organizations to offer business information and communications services to more than 25,000 small producers of ecoagricultural products.

It's true that some services simply cannot be offered at a low-enough cost to be profitable, at least not with traditional technologies or business models. Most mobile telecommunications providers, for example, cannot yet profitably operate their networks at affordable prices in the developing world. One answer is to find alternative technology. A microfinance organization in Bolivia named PRODEM, for example, uses multilingual smart-card ATMs to substantially reduce its marginal cost per customer. Smart cards store a customer's personal details, account numbers, transaction records, and a fingerprint, allowing cash dispensers to operate without permanent network connections – which is key in remote areas. What's more, the machines offer voice commands in Spanish and several local dialects and are equipped with touch screens so that PRODEM's customer base can be extended to illiterate and semiliterate people.

Another answer is to aggregate demand, making the community–not the individual–the network customer. Gyandoot, a start-up in the Dhar district of central India, where 60% of the population falls below the poverty level, illustrates the benefits of a shared access model. The company has a network of 39 Internet-enabled kiosks that provide local entrepreneurs with Internet and telecommunications access, as well as with governmental, educational, and other services. Each kiosk serves 25 to 30 surrounding villages; the entire network reaches more than 600 villages and over half a million people.

Networks like these can be useful channels for marketing and distributing many kinds of low-cost products and services. Aptech's Computer Education division, for example, has built its own network of 1,000 learning centers in India to market and distribute Vidya, a computer-training course specially designed for BOP consumers and available

in seven Indian languages. Pioneer Hi-Bred, a DuPont company, uses Internet kiosks in Latin America to deliver agricultural information and to interact with customers. Farmers can report different crop diseases or weather conditions, receive advice over the wire, and order seeds, fertilizers, and pesticides. This network strategy increases both sales and customer loyalty.

Reduced Costs. No less important than top-line growth are cost-saving opportunities. Outsourcing operations to low-cost labor markets has, of course, long been a popular way to contain costs, and it has led to the increasing prominence of China in manufacturing and India in software. Now, thanks to the rapid expansion of high-speed digital networks, companies are realizing even greater savings by locating such labor-intensive service functions as call centers, marketing services, and back-office transaction processing in developing areas. For example, the nearly 20 companies that use OrphanIT.com's affiliate-marketing services, provided via its telecenters in India and the Philippines, pay one-tenth the going rate

for similar services in the United States or Australia. Venture capitalist Vinod Khosla describes the remote-services opportunity this way: "I suspect that by 2010, we will be talking about [remote services] as the fastest-growing part of the world economy, with many trillions of dollars of new markets created." Besides keeping costs down, outsourcing jobs to BOP markets can enhance growth, since job creation ultimately increases local consumers' purchasing power.

But tapping into cheap labor pools is not the only way MNCs can enhance their efficiency by operating in developing regions. The competitive necessity of maintaining a low cost structure in these areas can push companies to discover creative ways to configure their products, finances, and supply chains to enhance productivity. And these discoveries can often be incorporated back into their existing operations in developed markets.

For instance, companies targeting the BOP market are finding that the shared access model, which disaggregates access from ownership, not only widens their

The High-Cost Economy of the Poor

When we compare the costs of essentials in Dharavi, a shantytown of more than 1 million people in the heart of Mumbai, India, with those of Warden Road, an upper-class community in a nice Mumbai suburb, a disturbing picture emerges. Clearly, costs could be dramatically reduced if the poor could benefit from the scope, scale, and supply-chain efficiencies of large enterprises, as their middle-class counterparts do. This pattern is common around the world, even in developed countries. For instance, a similar, if less exaggerated, disparity exists between the inner-city poor and the suburban rich in the United States.

Cost	Dharavi	Warden Road	Poverty premium
credit (annual interest)	600%–1,000%	12%–18%	53X
municipal-grade water (per cubic meter)	$1.12	$0.03	37X
phone call (per minute)	$0.04–$0.05	$0.025	1.8X
diarrhea medication	$20	$2	10X
rice (per kilogram)	$0.28	$0.24	1.2X

customer base but increases asset productivity as well. Poor people, rather than buying their own computers, Internet connections, cell phones, refrigerators, and even cars, can use such equipment on a pay-per-use basis. Typically, the providers of such services get considerably more revenue per dollar of investment in the underlying assets. One shared Internet line, for example, can serve as many as 50 people, generating more revenue per day than if it were dedicated to a single customer at a flat fee. Shared access creates the opportunity to gain far greater returns from all sorts of infrastructure investments.

In terms of finances, to operate successfully in BOP markets, managers must also rethink their business metrics – specifically, the traditional focus on high gross margins. In developing markets, the profit margin on individual units will always be low. What really counts is capital efficiency – getting the highest possible returns on capital employed (ROCE). Hindustan Lever, for instance, operates a $2.6 billion business portfolio with zero working capital. The key is constant efforts to reduce capital investments by extensively outsourcing manufacturing, streamlining supply chains, actively managing receivables, and paying close attention to distributors' performance. Very low capital needs, focused distribution and technology investments, and very large volumes at low margins lead to very high ROCE businesses, creating great economic value for shareholders. It's a model that can be equally attractive in developed and developing markets.

Streamlining supply chains often involves replacing assets with information. Consider, for example, the experience of ITC, one of India's largest companies. Its agribusiness division has deployed a total of 970 kiosks serving 600,000 farmers who supply it with soy, coffee, shrimp, and wheat from 5,000 villages spread across India. This kiosk program, called e-Choupal, helps increase the farmers' productivity by disseminating the latest information on weather and best practices in farming, and by supporting other services like soil and water testing, thus facilitating the supply of quality inputs to both the farmers and ITC. The kiosks also serve as an e-procurement system, helping farmers earn higher prices by minimizing transaction costs involved in marketing farm produce. The head of ITC's agribusiness reports that the company's procurement costs have fallen since e-Choupal was implemented. And that's despite paying higher prices to its farmers: The program has enabled the company to eliminate multiple transportation, bagging, and handling steps – from farm to local market, from market to broker, from broker to processor – that did not add value in the chain.

Innovation. BOP markets are hotbeds of commercial and technological experimentation. The Swedish wireless company Ericsson, for instance, has developed a small cellular telephone system, called a MiniGSM, that local operators in BOP markets can use to offer cell phone service to a small area at a radically lower cost than conventional equipment entails. Packaged for easy shipment and deployment, it provides stand-alone or networked voice and data communications for up to 5,000 users within a 35-kilometer radius. Capital costs to the operator can be as low as $4 per user, assuming a shared-use model with individual phones operated by local entrepreneurs. The MIT Media Lab, in collaboration with the Indian government, is developing low-cost devices that allow people to use voice commands to communicate – without keyboards – with various Internet sites in multiple languages. These new access devices promise to be far less complex than traditional computers but would perform many of the same basic functions.[2]

As we have seen, connectivity is a big issue for BOP consumers. Companies that can find ways to dramatically lower connection costs, therefore, will have a very strong market position. And that is exactly what the Indian company n-Logue is trying to do. It connects hundreds of franchised village kiosks containing both a computer and a phone with centralized nodes that are, in turn, connected to the national phone network and the Internet. Each node, also a franchise, can serve between 30,000 and 50,000 customers, providing phone, e-mail, Internet services, and relevant local information at affordable prices to villagers in rural India. Capital costs for the n-Logue system are now about $400 per wireless "line" and are projected to decline to $100 – at least ten times lower than conventional telecom costs. On a per-customer basis, the cost may amount to as little as $1.[3] This appears to be a powerful model for ending rural isolation and linking untapped rural markets to the global economy.

New wireless technologies are likely to spur further business model innovations and lower costs even more. Ultrawideband, for example, is currently licensed in the United States only for limited, very low-power applications, in part because it spreads a signal across already-crowded portions of the broadcast spectrum. In many developing countries, however, the spectrum is less congested. In fact, the U.S.-based Dandin Group is already building an ultrawideband communications system for the Kingdom of Tonga, whose population of about 100,000 is spread over dozens of islands, making it a test bed for a next-generation technology that could transform the economics of Internet access.

E-commerce systems that run over the phone or the Internet are enormously important in BOP markets because they eliminate the need for layers of intermediaries. Consider how the U.S. start-up Voxiva has changed the way information is shared and business is transacted in Peru. The company partners with Telefónica, the dominant local carrier, to offer automated business applications over the phone. The inexpensive services include voice mail, data entry, and order placement; customers can check account balances, monitor delivery status, and access prerecorded information directories. According to the Boston Consulting Group, the Peruvian

Ministry of Health uses Voxiva to disseminate information, take pharmaceutical orders, and link health care workers spread across 6,000 offices and clinics. Microfinance institutions use Voxiva to process loan applications and communicate with borrowers. Voxiva offers Web-based services, too, but far more of its potential customers in Latin America have access to a phone.

E-commerce companies are not the only ones turning the limitations of BOP markets to strategic advantage. A lack of dependable electric power stimulated the UK-based start-up Freeplay Group to introduce hand-cranked radios in South Africa that subsequently became popular with hikers in the United States. Similar breakthroughs are being pioneered in the use of solar-powered devices such as battery chargers and water pumps. In China, where pesticide costs have often limited the use of modern agricultural techniques, there are now 13,000 small farmers – more than in the rest of the world combined – growing cotton that has been genetically engineered to be pest resistant.

Strategies for Serving BOP Markets

Certainly, succeeding in BOP markets requires multinationals to think creatively. The biggest change, though, has to come in the attitudes and practices of executives. Unless CEOs and other business leaders confront their own preconceptions, companies are unlikely to master the challenges of BOP markets. The traditional workforce is so rigidly conditioned to operate in higher-margin markets that, without formal training, it is unlikely to see the vast potential of the BOP market. The most pressing need, then, is education. Perhaps MNCs should create the equivalent of the Peace Corps: Having young managers spend a couple of formative years in BOP markets would open their eyes to

the promise and the realities of doing business there.

To date, few multinationals have developed a cadre of people who are comfortable with these markets. Hindustan Lever is one of the exceptions. The company expects executive recruits to spend at least eight weeks in the villages of India to get a gut-level experience of Indian BOP markets. The new executives must become involved in some community project – building a road, cleaning up a water catchment area, teaching in a school, improving a health clinic. The goal is to engage with the local population. To buttress this effort, Hindustan Lever is initiating a massive program for managers at all levels – from the CEO down – to reconnect with their poorest customers. They'll talk with the poor in both rural and urban areas, visit the shops these customers frequent, and ask them about their experience with the company's products and those of its competitors.

In addition to expanding managers' understanding of BOP markets, companies will need to make structural changes. To capitalize on the innovation potential of these markets, for example, they might set up R&D units in developing countries that are specifically focused on local opportunities. When Hewlett-Packard launched its e-Inclusion division, which concentrates on rural markets, it established a branch of its famed HP Labs in India charged with developing products and services explicitly for this market. Hindustan Lever maintains a significant R&D effort in India, as well.

Companies might also create venture groups and internal investment funds aimed at seeding entrepreneurial efforts in BOP markets. Such investments reap direct benefits in terms of business experience and market development. They can also play an indirect but vital role in growing the overall BOP market in sectors that will ultimately benefit the multinational. At least one major U.S. corporation is planning to launch such a fund, and the G8's Digital Opportunity Task Force is proposing a similar one focused on digital ventures.

MNCs should also consider creating a business development task force aimed at these markets. Assembling a diverse group of people from across the corporation and empowering it to function as a skunk works team that ignores conventional dogma will likely lead to

should look beyond businesses to NGOs and community groups. They are key sources of knowledge about customers' behavior, and they often experiment the most with new services and new delivery models. In fact, of the social enterprises experimenting with creative uses

> To operate successfully in developing markets, managers
> must rethink their business metrics – specifically,
> the traditional focus on high gross margins.

greater innovation. Companies that have tried this approach have been surprised by the amount of interest such a task force generates. Many employees want to work on projects that have the potential to make a real difference in improving the lives of the poor. When Hewlett-Packard announced its e-Inclusion division, for example, it was overwhelmed by far more volunteers than it could accommodate.

Making internal changes is important, but so is reaching out to external partners. Joining with businesses that are already established in these markets can be an effective entry strategy, since these companies will naturally understand the market dynamics better. In addition to limiting the risks for each player, partnerships also maximize the existing infrastructure – both physical and social. MNCs seeking partners

of digital technology that the Digital Dividend Project Clearinghouse tracked, nearly 80% are NGOs. In Namibia, for instance, an organization called School-Net is providing low-cost, alternative technology solutions – such as solar power and wireless approaches – to schools and community-based groups throughout the country. SchoolNet is currently linking as many as 35 new schools every month.

Entrepreneurs also will be critical partners. According to an analysis by McKinsey & Company, the rapid growth of cable TV in India – there are 50 million connections a decade after introduction – is largely due to small entrepreneurs. These individuals have been building the last mile of the network, typically by putting a satellite dish on their own houses and laying cable to connect their neighbors. A note of caution,

Sharing Intelligence

What creative new approaches to serving the bottom-of-the-pyramid markets have digital technologies made possible? Which sectors or countries show the most economic activity or the fastest growth? What new business models show promise? What kinds of partnerships – for funding, distribution, public relations – have been most successful?

The Digital Dividend Project Clearinghouse (digitaldividend.org) helps answer those types of questions. The Web site tracks the activities of organizations that use digital tools to provide connectivity and deliver services to underserved populations in developing countries. Currently, it contains information on 700 active projects around the world. Maintained under the auspices of the nonprofit World Resources Institute, the site lets participants in different projects share experiences and swap knowledge with one another. Moreover, the site provides data for trend analyses and other specialized studies that facilitate market analyses, local partnerships, and rapid, low-cost learning.

however. Entrepreneurs in BOP markets lack access to the advice, technical help, seed funding, and business support services available in the industrial world. So MNCs may need to take on mentoring roles or partner with local business development organizations that can help entrepreneurs create investment and partnering opportunities.

It's worth noting that, contrary to popular opinion, women play a significant role in the economic development of these regions. MNCs, therefore, should pay particular attention to women entrepreneurs. Women are also likely to play the most critical role in product acceptance not only because of their childcare and household management activities but also because of the social capital that they have built up in their communities. Listening to and educating such customers is essential for success.

Regardless of the opportunities, many companies will consider the bottom of the pyramid to be too risky. We've shown how partnerships can limit risk; another option is to enter into consortia. Imagine sharing the costs of building a rural network with the communications company that would operate it, a consumer goods company seeking channels to expand its sales, and a bank that is financing the construction and wants to make loans to and collect deposits from rural customers.

Investing where powerful synergies exist will also mitigate risk. The Global Digital Opportunity Initiative, a partnership of the Markle Foundation and the UN Development Programme, will help a small number of countries implement a strategy to harness the power of information and communications technologies to increase development. The countries will be chosen in part based on their interest and their willingness to make supportive regulatory and market reforms. To concentrate resources and create reinforcing effects, the initiative will encourage international aid agencies and global companies to assist with implementation.

All of the strategies we've outlined here will be of little use, however, unless the external barriers we've touched on—poor infrastructure, inadequate connectivity, corrupt intermediaries, and the like – are removed. Here's where technology holds the most promise. Information and communications technologies can grant access to otherwise isolated communities, provide marketing and distribution channels, bypass intermediaries, drive down transaction costs, and help aggregate demand and

buying power. Smart cards and other emerging technologies are inexpensive ways to give poor customers a secure identity, a transaction or credit history, and even a virtual address – prerequisites for interacting with the formal economy. That's why high-tech companies aren't the only ones that should be interested in closing the global digital divide; encouraging the spread of low-cost digital networks at the bottom of the pyramid is a priority for virtually all companies that want to enter and engage with these markets. Improved connectivity is an important catalyst for more effective markets, which are critical to boosting income levels and accelerating economic growth.

Moreover, global companies stand to gain from the effects of network expansion in these markets. According to Metcalfe's Law, the usefulness of a network equals the square of the number of users. By the same logic, the value and vigor of the economic activity that will be generated when hundreds of thousands of previously isolated rural communities can buy and sell from one another and from urban markets will increase dramatically – to the benefit of all participants.

HARVARD BUSINESS REVIEW

• • •

Since BOP markets require significant rethinking of managerial practices, it is legitimate for managers to ask: Is it worth the effort?

We think the answer is yes. For one thing, big corporations should solve big problems – and what is a more pressing concern than alleviating the poverty that 4 billion people are currently mired in? It is hard to argue that the wealth of technology and talent within leading multinationals is better allocated to producing incremental variations of existing products than to addressing the real needs – and real opportunities – at the bottom of the pyramid. Moreover, through competition, multinationals are likely to bring to BOP markets a level of accountability for performance and resources that neither international development agencies nor national governments have demonstrated during the last 50 years. Participation by MNCs could set a new standard, as well as a new market-driven paradigm, for addressing poverty.

But ethical concerns aside, we've shown that the potential for expanding the bottom of the market is just too great to ignore. Big companies need to focus on big market opportunities if they want to generate real growth. It is simply good business strategy to be involved in large, untapped markets that offer new customers, cost-saving opportunities, and access to radical innovation. The business opportunities at the bottom of the pyramid are real, and they are open to any MNC willing to engage and learn.

1. Andrew Lawlor, Caitlin Peterson, and Vivek Sandell, "Catalyzing Rural Development: TARA-haat.com" (World Resources Institute, July 2001).

2. Michael Best and Colin M. Maclay, "Community Internet Access in Rural Areas: Solving the Economic Sustainability Puzzle," *The Global Information Technology Report 2001–2002: Readiness for the Networked World*, ed., Geoffrey Kirkman (Oxford University Press, 2002), available on-line at http://www.cid.harvard.edu/cr/gitrr_030202.html.

3. Joy Howard, Erik Simanis, and Charis Simms, "Sustainable Deployment for Rural Connectivity: The n-Logue Model" (World Resources Institute, July 2001).

[43]

POVERTY AND THE POLITICS OF CAPITALISM

R. Edward Freeman

1 Here's a way to think about poverty.[1] People who live in poverty do so because they have few opportunities to pull themselves up by their bootstraps. In fact the gap between rich and poor has increased in recent times due to the more wholesale adoption of capitalist practices around the world. The institutions of business and government conspire to give the poor a Hobson's choice of minimal wage McJobs or unemployment. Neglect of both urban ghettoes and the rural poor has been systematic, if not conscious. The very idea of capitalism reinforces the notion that some are meant to be poor and some are meant to be rich. Such a system must be overridden at times by government to help the poor cope with their lot. The only solution is a massive redistribution of income and a system of capitalism that is severely restrained. All of this is at best highly unlikely. Even if there were such a redistribution policy we could not count on *government* to execute it fairly.

2. Here's another way to think about poverty. Terrible as it is, those in poverty have a way out: the market system. If they are willing to work hard, albeit sometimes for low wages, and be imaginative, they can use the wonderful power of capitalism to capitalize on the fruits of their labor. So many are in poverty largely because of *government*. Governments constrain the efficient allocation of goods and services provided by capitalism, by artificially creating prices for labor and goods such as agricultural products, that hurts the poor. There are not as many jobs as there should be, and prices of key commodities such as food are too high. Government has hurt the poor even more by creating a safety net on which they have come to rely. The "welfare culture" prevents the poor from bootstrapping their way out of poverty to the middle class. The only solution is to get government out of the picture and to let markets work.

3. Neither of these scenarios, which represent the current discourse about poverty, government and capitalism, is very interesting. They rest on shopworn, useless metaphors about business and government, and they obviously stereotype those who live in poverty. Yet the discourse is louder today than in recent times, and the volume is related to the severity of the problem: the problem that we have an outmoded story about ourselves, one that we desperately need to drop.

4. The old worn-out story goes like this. Business is fundamentally about economics and competition. Think of business as a battlefield on which the lonely corporate warriors keep a constant vigilance against the onslaught of competition. Recently, this battlefield has moved beyond geopolitical borders and is global in nature. War is hell and so is business. The drive to compete must be strong if one is to enjoy the sweet nectar of corporate success. If everyone acts in their own self-interest solely, then a better world will be created as if by magic (or an invisible

hand). Being selfish is a virtue in business, and looking out for one's own interest is mandatory. In short, business is populated by a bunch of greedy little bastards out to do each other in before it is done to them. Call this story "Cowboy Capitalism".

5. That the story of Cowboy Capitalism is a living presence in our culture in undeniable. Daily we are treated to claims of companies and governments working on being more competitive. The academic literature of business schools is replete with war-like language and imagery. Under the current doublespeak of reengineering and restructuring, companies are laying off thousands of once loyal employees so that they can "compete in the new global arena".

6. That the story of Cowboy Capitalism is indeed shopworn is more controversial. Those on the left certainly see it as shopworn because they presume capitalism to be immoral from the start. For those on the right it is subtler. On the one hand they want business to be a celebration of the human spirit, but on the other they want to escape the moral consequences of business. The language of capitalism doesn't clearly admit to moral discourse, and this makes capitalism as bothersome to the right who want to presume it to be right as it is to the left who want to presume it to be wrong.[2]

7. In *Race Matters* Cornell West has suggested that the dichotomy of left and right is bankrupt when it is applied to the intersections of the problems of racism and poverty.[3] Liberals assume that the causes are structural in nature and that the solution is better structures, while conservatives assume that the problem is internal to the character of poor people with the only hope to be better people. While West believes that we certainly need better structures and that we need more people to bootstrap their way out of poverty, he identifies a different alternative for our discourse. Because he sees poverty and hopelessness as intimately connected he calls for a politics of conversion within a prophetic framework to restore hope and to offer the possibility of creating some meaningful future. A politics of conversion offers hope that people can struggle together to find meaning, and a prophetic framework builds in moral assessment from the beginning. Now West is proposing such a framework as necessary to address the African American experience in the United States, but I want to suggest that it has a broader application. (I want to do this without minimizing the differences between the problems of racism and poverty, and certainly without suggesting that the African American experience is solely or even essentially defined by poverty.) It is ironic that West sees no role for capitalism in this prophetic framework, for I want to suggest that if we can retell the story of capitalism in a particular way we can see how the prophetic framework can gain even more power and applicability.

8. Imagine a world in which workers routinely vote on big decisions that a company faces, such as where to locate a factory. In this world employees set their own salaries, have no time clocks or expense reports, and there is little hierarchy. Factories in this world contain employees and independent entrepreneurs (some of whom used to be employees) all working beside each other. Indeed, the CEO of the business simply does not know how many people work there and is unsympathetic

POVERTY AND THE POLITICS OF CAPITALISM 33

to those who want to know. Routinely the borderlines between company and customer, company and supplier, even company and competitor are crossed. Imagine that when the workers go on strike (there are still unions in this world) they use the company cafeteria to plan strategy. The company does not cut off their benefits during the strike, which is over rather quickly. Welcome to SEMCO, a Brazilian firm that has carved a successful business by applying the principles of democracy, profit sharing, and information openness.[4]

9. Imagine a world in which workers do all of the hiring and firing of employees. Workers constantly meet in teams to set production schedules, plan new business opportunities, and do quality control. If consumers have a problem, workers responsible for the problem personally contact the consumer. Workers share in the profits in this world, and they have salaries tied to their own improving skills and knowledge. Workers go to classes to learn about topics from budgeting to international economics. There aren't any supervisors in this world. The workers do it themselves. There are a few "coaches" who see their job as helping the workers. Welcome to Johnsonville Sausage, a Wisconsin firm that has applied many of the same principles as SEMCO.

10. Imagine a world where there are no layoffs. In this world there is a corporate university at which people are required to spend at least 2-3 weeks per year. If someone's skills become obsolete they are simply offered retraining. This large corporation regularly reinvents itself every few years. Its quality of products is among the highest in the world, and it is known for its attention to quality. Such an emphasis started after some lone soul stood up at a large meeting and was extremely critical of the corporation and its products. Rather than being executed, this manager became a hero. Welcome to Motorola, a global leader in cellular telephones and other high tech businesses.

11. What these examples have in common is that they point the way to a new story about capitalism. The new story goes like this. Corporations are places where stakeholders pursue their joint interests. Stakeholders are simply groups like suppliers, customers, employees, financiers, and communities. The interests of these groups are joint. One thrives when all thrive, and when the interests of one group are systematically discounted over time, all suffer. In a relatively free political system, these discounted groups seek political remedies to the discounting of their interests. Such remedies are often ineffective and expensive to all. Corporations are governed by their stakeholders, and while there may be many different governance schemes, depending partially on circumstances, each scheme must pay attention to the interests of each party and to their joint concerns. Directors of corporations have a duty of care to stakeholders, and managers are the agents of multiple principals. Call this story, "Stakeholder Capitalism" or "Managing for Stakeholders".

12. There is a lot more to be said about this story.[5] Suffice it here to say that Stakeholder Capitalism envisions a world where business and ethics are inextricably intertwined, where values and virtues are a part of corporate life, and where

hopelessness and despair are replaced by a solidarity that comes from the joint achievement of shared aims. Stakeholder Capitalism seeks to transform the old story of "anything goes" capitalism into a prophetic framework.

13. While some may suggest that Stakeholder Capitalism is hopeless idealism, I want to insist that such a viewpoint is mired in the old story about business. For every story of corporate greed that reaffirms the old story, we are increasingly finding people enacting the new one: Entrepreneurs, executives and employees who have stopped listening to the whispers in their ear that business and social life are separate.[6] If you have doubts read about the Social Venture Network, Businesses for Social Responsibility, the GEMI Initiative, the Business Enterprise Trust, and countless others.

14. Some will say that there is no new story, that the companies like the Body Shop and Ben and Jerry's are just using ethics as a marketing tool, that all of this is just "wink, wink, nudge, nudge, I say, I say" in the spoofing tradition of Monty Python. Rake in the profits and laugh all the way to the bank. But, business is not hagiography. This is not a contest between saints and sinners, no matter what journalists say. The new story is about possibility; it is about attempting to redescribe our institutions and ourselves so that we can live better. Such redescriptions cannot "escape" the past or be outside of space and time and culture. The fact that the Body Shop may sometimes go too far in the interests of financiers does not negate the fact that all Body Shop employees are required and paid to do community service. It says only that we are trying to enact this new story in a far from perfect world with far from perfect creatures: human beings.

15. Some will say that Stakeholder Capitalism can never be realized under the current law of the land. And, surely this is right in those cases where the law prevents directors and managers from acting in stakeholder interests. Surely the law needs to be changed. But, if we look hard enough we will find companies managing for stakeholders in spite of the law-not as acts of civil disobedience, but because the old story enacted in law is irrelevant.

16. The new story of Stakeholder Capitalism is less about law and economic theory, and more about what we need to expect from the institution of business. If we come to expect that companies raise the level of the least well off, or that they act out of respect for the earth, or that they manage the web of relationships in which they are enmeshed, then we are most of the way towards realizing the new story. Both the law and theory will follow shortly. If the only possibility is to expect Cowboy Capitalism, then we had better get used to the rather tiresome laments of the left, and the grating rasp of the right, locked in a conversation that goes nowhere.

17. The problematic of poverty is complex. But, we cannot make progress with a political philosophy that either ignores the real institution of business, or makes 19th Century assumptions about it, or more cruelly still, simply accepts the oppressive story that has been told as the one that is necessarily so. Such a new political philosophy must take Johnsonville Sausage, Motorola, Merck and others into account, not as exceptional acts of altruism, but as part of the everyday mosaic of business, as pointing us to what it is possible for humans to accomplish.

POVERTY AND THE POLITICS OF CAPITALISM   35

Endnotes

[1] The style is shamelessly borrowed from Richard Rorty's essay "Philosophy as a Kind of Writing," in *Consequences of Pragmatism* (Minneapolis, MN: University of Minnesota Press, 1982).

[2] I have tried to give a more careful analysis of this phenomenon of the role of ethics in capitalism in "The Politics of Stakeholder Theory: Some Future Directions," *Business Ethics Quarterly*, Volume 4 Number 4, pp. 409-421.

[3] Cornell West, *Race Matters* (Boston, MA: Beacon Press, 1993).

[4] For more information on SEMCO see Ricardo Semler, "Managing Without Managers," *Harvard Business Review*, Volume 89, Number 5, 1989, pp. 76-84; and, Ricardo Semler, "Why My Former Employees Still Work for Me," *Harvard Business Review*, Volume 94, Number 1, 1994, pp. 61-72. For a version of these principles as applied in the United States see "Jack Stack (A) and (B)" a case study published by the Business Enterprise Trust, available from Harvard Business School.

[5] I have tried to work out pieces of this new story in a number of places. See R. Edward Freeman and Daniel R. Gilbert, Jr., *Corporate Strategy and the Search for Ethics* (Prentice Hall, 1988); Freeman and Jeanne Liedtka, "Stakeholder Capitalism and the Value Chain," *European Management Journal*, (1997), Vol 15, No. 3, 286-296; Freeman, "The Politics of Stakeholder Theory," *Business Ethics Quarterly*, (1996) Vol. 4 No. 4; and Freeman, "Understanding Stakeholder Capitalism," *Financial Times*, July 26, 1996.

[6] I have tried to understand some of the complexities here in an essay, "The Business Sucks Story," *The Darden School Working Papers*, University of Virginia, Charlottesville, VA.

[44]

Stalking the Poverty Consumer:
A Retrospective Examination
of Modern Ethical Dilemmas

Ronald Paul Hill

ABSTRACT. This research takes a retrospective look at modern consumption opportunities of the U.S. poor from both sides of the marketing exchange relationship. The paper opens with a critical assessment of the consumer-behavior literature and its primary focus on middle-class Americans. The next section profiles the impoverished and their purchasing habits and closes with a summary of how both have changed over the last forty years. Then a theoretical account is presented using consumer literature from the same timeframe. The paper ends with a discussion of common business practices and moral dilemmas that have continued over these decades, along with an ethical paradigm involving distributive justice to guide future management tactics.

Introduction

The middle-class image of American consumers projected through the various advertising media disguises the fact that millions of poor people in the United States must also enter the marketplace and purchase goods and services. (Sturdivant, 1969, p. 3)

Several generations of U.S. researchers have investigated the topic of consumption during the previous forty years. From the sociology of consuming to psychological perspectives of consumer decision making, a vast body of literature has

Ronald Paul Hill is the (Rev.) John B. Delaunay, C.S.C. Professor of Social Responsibility, Dr. Robert B. Pamplin, Jr. School of Business Administration, The University of Portland. His research focuses on a variety of poverty subpopulations and their strategies for coping with consumer restriction in their daily lives. A summary of his research is contained in Surviving in a Material World: The Lived Experience of People in Poverty, *University of Notre Dame Press.*

developed that helps business organizations, nonprofits, government agencies, and consumer advocates understand why people buy (Holbrook, 1995). Topics of inquiry have included processing of information contained in commercial promotions, decision making in the face of a number of distinct alternatives/choices, utilization of goods and services once they are acquired, and dispossession of what remains after a product's useful life has been extinguished (*Journal of Consumer Research*).

While this viewpoint may aptly depict consumption for middle-class consumers, it fails when applied to people at the bottom of the socioeconomic scale (Hill, 2001a). Instead of abundance and too much, their consumer world is defined by restriction and too little (Alwitt and Donley, 1997). Such communities are beset with high levels of unemployment, decaying infrastructure, and a lack of affordable goods and services, which exacerbate major social ills such as drug abuse, crime, and homelessness (see Porter, 1995). The resulting restrictions in product availability and income sources lead to an imbalance in exchange that favors business over poor consumers (Alwitt, 1995).

The purpose of the paper is to take a retrospective look at modern consumption by impoverished U.S. citizens from both sides of the exchange relationship. The next section describes who are poor consumers, their purchasing habits, and how both have changed over the last forty years. Then a theoretical account of how impoverished consumers behave is presented using literature from the same timeframe. Next the paper discusses common practices and moral dilemmas of businesses that have served this population over these decades, and it closes with an ethical paradigm involving distributive justice to guide business tactics.

The poverty consumer

Who they are

During the 1960s, a group of business researchers examined the characteristics and purchasing habits of poverty consumers. For example, Holloway and Cardozo (1969) used 1960 Census data to provide an in-depth look at the 36 million impoverished people in the U.S. at the start of President Johnson's War on Poverty. While there were more poor whites than non-whites (78% versus 22%), people of color were over represented among the impoverished (10% of the total/22% of the poor). Most of the poor were urban dwellers (54%), but the incidence of rural poverty was higher (28% of the total/46% of the poor). Additionally, people over 65 were more likely to be poor (14% of the total/34% of the poor), along with those who lived in female-headed households (10% of the total/25% of the poor). According to the authors, a surprisingly large number were employed (49%), earning less than a living wage.

Other studies conducted during the same period investigated various categories of spending by impoverished consumers compared with the nonpoor. Richards (1966) notes that basic necessities such as food, shelter, and medical care required a larger share of the poor's expenditures, while clothing and transportation took a smaller share. However, Andreasen (1975) reveals that the same-era impoverished consumer allocated approximately an equivalent percentage for discretionary items such as recreation and tobacco. The combination of high relative levels of spending on necessities without compensating savings on less essential purchases meant the poor "must dissave . . . withdraw savings, sell assets, or undertake debt obligations" (p. 34).

A review of the data contained in the Survey of Consumer Expenditures, 1960 (*Bureau of Labor Statistics Report No. 238-12*) reveals a few discrepancies (see Table I). For example, food did require a decreasing percentage of expenditures as annual income rose; however, housing took a significant upturn in the highest income bracket and medical care leveled off at incomes above $6000. Additionally, tobacco took a slight downturn as a percentage of money spent as annual income increases, while leisure activities grew slightly as a percentage of expenditures across income categories. Nonetheless, the prognosis that the poor must dissave in order to survive is clear given that the ratio of income after taxes to expenditures is less that 1 for the

TABLE I
Average annual expenditures in selected product categories for 1960

Item	Income ranges					
	Under $2000	$2000–$2999	$3000–$5999	$6000–$9999	$10000–$14999	$15000–and over
% of families	7.1	9.3	39.5	33.6	8.1	2.4
After tax income	$1425	$2521	$4597	$7594	$11716	$21933
Average expenses	$1878	$2809	$4608	$6852	$9704	$14661
Income/expenses	0.76	0.90	1.00	1.11	1.21	1.50
Food/expenses	0.32	0.30	0.27	0.26	0.24	0.21
Housing/expenses	0.32	0.31	0.29	0.28	0.27	0.30
Medical/expenses	0.10	0.08	0.07	0.06	0.06	0.06
Tobacco/expenses	0.03	0.02	0.02	0.02	0.01	0.01
Leisure/expenses	0.02	0.03	0.04	0.04	0.05	0.05

Source: Survey of Consumer Expenditures, 1960.

two income categories below $3000, representing 16.4% of all families.

A resurgence of scholarly interest in poverty occurred in the 1990s, resulting from the economic instability of the late 1980s and the welfare reform movement spawned by the Republicans' "Contract with America" (Andreasen, 1993; Hill and Macan, 1996). In these accounts, 35 million Americans were classified as poor, including 35% of female-headed households and 20% of all children (Shea, 1995). Twelve million Americans were described as the hyper-poor, surviving on less than half the poverty-level income (Hill and Stephens, 1997). Approximately 4.9 million of these people were children.

As America enters the 21st century, the U.S. Census Bureau (2000) reports that the latest expansion has improved these numbers significantly. Nonetheless, poverty remains a vexing social problem – 32.3 million people are officially poor, representing approximately 12% of the total population. Almost 17% of children and 10% of the elderly are impoverished. Minority groups and people of color suffer the most, with just less than 25% of Hispanics and Blacks living below the poverty line. Female-headed households are still more likely to be impoverished than their dual-parent counterparts (28% and 5% respectively), even though an increasing number

of the poor (74%) are employed. Despite other improvements, the hyper-poor as a percentage of the total population remains unchanged, with the absolute number rising to about 13 million.

Recent accounts of spending and spending priorities among the poor are quite similar to the reports from the 1960s and 1970s. For instance, low-income consumers spend less in absolute dollars than their more affluent counterparts in all categories of consumption, but they spend a higher percentage of their income on necessities (Mergenhagen, 1996). This is particularly true for housing, food, and medical care (Alwitt and Donley, 1996). As a result, many among the poor face chronic cash deficits, especially those living on the social welfare system (see Edin, 1993 for more details). The U.S. Census Bureau (2000) found that the average income deficit among the poor is $6687 annually.

Data from the Consumer Expenditure Survey 1998 reveal some significant differences between this scholarship and current consumption reality (see Table II). While money spent on housing, food, and health care as a percentage of total expenditures tends to decrease across income categories, there is a data "bubble" showing a temporary rise at the lower end of the scale in all cases. This increase may be due to differences within categories of the number of retirees, college students, self-employed adults, and

TABLE II

Average annual expenditures in selected product categories for 1998

Item	Income ranges								
	Under $5000	$5000–$9999	$10000–$14999	$15000–$19999	$20000–$29999	$30000–$39999	$40000–$49999	$50000–$69999	$70000–over
% of families	0.05	0.10	0.11	0.09	0.14	0.12	0.09	0.14	0.16
After tax income	$1738	$7636	$12155	$16951	$23596	$32393	$40890	$53802	$97419
Average expenses	$17502	$14838	$19958	$22810	$27941	$33616	$39934	$49376	$73786
Income/expenses	0.10	0.52	0.61	0.74	0.85	0.96	1.02	1.09	1.32
Food/expenses	0.17	0.18	0.15	0.15	0.15	0.15	0.14	0.13	0.12
Housing/expenses	0.35	0.39	0.37	0.35	0.33	0.32	0.30	0.29	0.30
Medical/expenses	0.049	0.079	0.083	0.094	0.066	0.055	0.052	0.044	0.039
Tobacco/expenses	0.013	0.014	0.012	0.011	0.010	0.010	0.008	0.007	0.004
Leisure/expenses	0.052	0.038	0.045	0.039	0.043	0.043	0.049	0.053	0.054

Source: Consumer Expenditures Survey, 1998.

families with small children, all of whom consume and report income differently (Mergenhagen, 1996). Similar breaks from a straight-line increase or decrease occur for the discretionary product categories of leisure activities and tobacco. More importantly, however, the ratio of after tax income to expenditures is much less than 1 for several categories (60% of the population), and they fail to reach equivalence until income rises to $40 000 or more. Cannibalizing savings breaches this income shortfall, as well as borrowing from relatives and friends, illegal and unreported work activities, and loans based on equity in homes, automobiles, and other limited assets.

In summary, a comparison across the previous four decades confirms that the total number and percentage of Americans who are poor decreased over time, with particularly good news for the elderly. Unfortunately, the plight of female-headed families remains troublesome, contributing to high levels of poverty among children and minority groups. Additionally, while the percentage of income dedicated to food has decreased, the relative cost of healthcare is a mixed bag and housing has increased. As a result, the income to expenses ratios for several lower socioeconomic groups in the U.S. have worsened over time, suggesting that the poor must dissave at an increasing rate despite working more. With the gap in disposable income between the highest and lowest quintile of the population at a seventy-five year high, some scholars predict that this situation will not change significantly in the near future (Hill and Stephens, 1997).

How they behave

The behavior of impoverished consumers surfaced as an important topic for business scholars following the publication of *The Poor Pay More* by David Capolvitz (1963). In this volume, the author explored the plight of the urban poor as consumers of major durable products purchased on credit. Impoverished consumers are portrayed as willing victims whose limited education and intellectual skills make them vulnerable to area merchants' easy credit terms that

mask high interest rates. Caplovitz was surprised to find that the poor preferred new versus used and more expensive versus more economical furniture and appliances better suited to their financial situation. Such preferences led him to conclude that impoverished consumers practice "compensatory consumption" as a way to make up for their inability to advance their social status by different means.

Other scholars viewed this situation differently. For example, Irelan and Besner (1966) believe that the poor value the same material possessions and share the same goals for material accumulation as the remainder of society. As a result, they are not so much compensating as seeking a share of societal wealth. Thus, the primary distinction between poor and nonpoor consumers is not their values and goals but their ability to actualize them.

This difference in impoverished consumers' ability is a direct outcome of their relative poverty. As Holloway and Cardozo (1969, p. 5) note, "the poor, then, employed or jobless, lack adequate income which makes it difficult or impossible to provide themselves with proper housing, education, medical services, and other necessities of life." Negative emotional consequences of their deprivation include a sense of powerlessness to affect their future consumer lives, alienation from the primary consumer culture, and apathy in the face of exploitation (Irelan and Besner, 1966; Sturdivant, 1969). The resulting fatalism is particularly damaging to one's self-esteem in a society that measures individual success through the display of material goods (Andreasen, 1975).

These positions notwithstanding, poverty consumers' strategies for coping with their circumstances suggest a surprising resourcefulness. While authors such as Caplovitz (1963) see an inherent irrationality in the purchasing habits of impoverished consumers, Richards (1966) concedes that these behaviors may have an underlying logic when viewed in the context of their communities' marketing systems. In fact, Holloway and Cardozo (1969, p. 55) go so far as to state that the poor "have developed shopping strategies to obtain the best assortment of products they can within budgets limited in size and flexibility." Additionally, Andreasen (1975, p. 40) believes that even excessive debt obligations by the poor are "a result of careful calculations of the consequences of their actions" that seek to maximize material abundance.

Current research attempts to summarize and expand these findings through additional study of the poor. Based on an investigation of the consumer lives of welfare mothers, Hill and Stephens (1997) present a three–dimensional model of impoverished consumer behavior (see Figure 1). This model recognizes the unique characteristics of the marketing system in poverty communities, the negative emotional consequences for poor consumers, and subsequent coping strategies. Implicit in this perspective is the belief that the impoverished improve their quality of life through a wide range of emotional and behavioral approaches. Thus, rather than passively accepting their circumstances as a "fruitless struggle" (Sturdivant, 1969, p. 20), the poor actively attempt to exert some control within their consumer world.

Lee et al. (1999) advance this paradigm through their research involving the rural poor. In their study of health care delivery in Appalachia, the authors find that the impoverished have resource strengths (e.g., social capital or community) as well as resource deficits (e.g., economic and cultural capital) that play different roles in exchange relationships with providers. Public policy makers interested in improving the consumer lives of the poor are urged to pass legislation that is resource sensitive, recognizing the inherent benefit of building on strengths instead of compensating for weaknesses.

Using a decade of ethnographic research on the material lives of the poor, Hill (2001b) developed a consumer cycle of poverty with five stages that is consistent with the consumer resource concept. Helplessly falling into greater poverty reveals that the poor experience the descent into abject impoverishment as beyond their control. Hitting bottom with no place left to bounce shows that the poor recognize when they reach the lowest point in their material lives, leaving them unable to meet their consumer needs as well as assuming a deviant label. Finding the resolve to fight a deviant label demonstrates that the poor eventually shun their negative classifications (e.g., welfare mother) and seek to restore their sense of self through empowering attitudes and behaviors. Community support to the rescue displays the critical role played by local communities in marshaling the resources necessary to improve the quality of life of the poor. Finally, tenuous present/uncertain future suggests that, even with the full power of an impoverished community's resources supporting them, the opportunity for the poor to sustain themselves materially in the long run remains in question.

In summary, early scholarship suggests that the poor make irrational purchase decisions in an attempt to compensate for their lack of adequate resources and consumption opportunities. However, the preponderance of research over the past forty years disputes this perspective. Instead of compensating, impoverished consumers share the same material goals as their more affluent counterparts and are seeking their share of societal wealth. While a cross-section of these investigations reveal the negative emotions

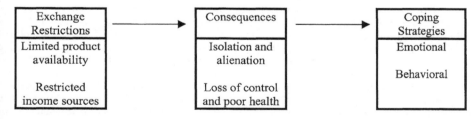

Exchange Restrictions	Consequences	Coping Strategies
Limited product availability	Isolation and alienation	Emotional
Restricted income sources	Loss of control and poor health	Behavioral

Source: Hill and Stephens, 1997, p. 37

Figure 1. A three-dimensional model of impoverished consumer behavior.

experienced by the poor, these studies also demonstrate a surprising resourcefulness in their attempt to gain control over their consumer lives. Of course, their ability to advance or maintain their standard of living remains in doubt, and the most recent research presents a cycle of consumer poverty that shows the material circumstances of the poor may vary significantly over time.

The poverty marketplace

Early research findings

Most early investigations of the marketing system within impoverished communities concentrated attention on marketers' inability to serve adequately the needs of the poor. Such neighborhoods were described as lacking the income base necessary to attract a variety of retailers, resulting in fewer competitors, higher prices, lower quality, and a smaller assortment of goods and services (Andreasen, 1975). As James Baldwin aptly notes "Anyone who has ever struggled with poverty knows how extremely expensive it is to be poor" (Sturdivant, 1969, p. 1).

Some of these accounts suggest that marketplace deficiencies were the fault of the impoverished, whose chronic cash shortages made them poor economic risks (Holloway and Cardozo, 1969). As a consequence, marketers who served poor communities charged a premium, resulting in lower value (quality/price ratio) for impoverished consumers than available in more affluent neighborhoods. Additionally, their relative poverty increased the need for credit in an environment where legitimate lenders rarely existed, causing the poor to borrow from "sources of outrageous consumer exploitation" (Andreasen, 1975, p. 36).

Once again, the work of Caplovitz (1963) provides a telling example. In the poverty communities where his research took place, he encountered an adaptation of the traditional credit system that was tailored to the needs of the poor. Through this system, an abundance of expensive products could be obtained on easy credit terms. Thus, poor consumers who lacked access to televisions, record players, appliances,

and furniture were able to acquire them for a small down payment and low weekly fees.

This availability notwithstanding, Caplovitz also discovered that merchants disguised the high interest rates inherent in these transactions in order to circumvent state laws. For example, a typical consumer was rarely provided with an installment contract and, instead, was given only a card containing the weekly payment. Consequently, poor consumers had no way of distinguishing between the cost of the product and the cost of credit within these transactions. However, even if consumers were able to determine that they were being taken advantage of, their only choice was "doing without or relying on credit and therefore paying more" (1963, p. 98).

Caplovitz concluded that the poverty marketplace is "a deviant one, in which unethical and illegal practices abound. Nevertheless, it can persist because it fulfills social functions that are presently not fulfilled by more legitimate institutions" (1963, p. 180). Under these circumstances, exploitation of the poor is an inevitable consequence of living in a restricted consumer world (see Andreasen, 1975). Even consumer education efforts designed to show the impoverished this inequity would have little impact since no legitimate alternative to exploitation exists.

Current research findings

In the 1990s, renewed interest in poverty by consumer researchers revived scholarship involving the imbalance in exchange relationships that favors the position of marketers over that of consumers (Alwitt and Donley, 1996). For example, scholars at the Haas School of Business, University of California at Berkeley found that prices for an assortment of items typically purchased by consumers was 41% higher in a poor neighborhood than the lowest available prices in a more affluent community (Bell and Burlin, 1993). Residents of the poor neighborhood complained that the quality and variety of this bundle were inferior and that prices were increased at various times during the month to correspond with the delivery of food stamps and social security and welfare checks.

Andreasen (1993) suggested that these inequities are the result of several limitations, including mobility and transportation barriers to shopping outside of impoverished neighborhoods, and a lack of access to banking services, especially credit and checking accounts, by the poor. Rhoda Karpatkin (1999), former President of Consumers Union, also recognized the impact of these marketplace restrictions, emphasizing their influence on the rise of subprime lending within poverty communities. Described as "fringe banking" in the July 1998 issue of *Consumer Reports*, such loans account for a growing percentage of equity loans generally, but most especially among the poor.

These loans are predominantly of three types. The first is subprime mortgage loans where high-interest loans are approved as a function of homeowners' equity rather than their ability to make regular payments. These payments are often well above homeowners' available disposable income, making eventual foreclosure highly likely. The second is car-title lending or car-title pawn, a practice that requires car owners to turn over title to their vehicles in exchange for cash. Debtors maintain usage as long as timely payments are made; however, interest rates as high as 25% per month have resulted in repossession from many poor consumers. Finally, the third involves the rent-to-own (RTO) industry, a marketplace of three million consumers who spend $3 billion annually at 7,500 stores nationally. Similar to the merchants studied by Caplovitz, RTO retailers make a wide variety of products available to poor consumers at many times the manufacturers' suggested prices and at undisclosed interest rates.

Research by Hill et al. (1998) on the RTO marketplace examined why poor consumers were willing to subject themselves to the form of price discrimination inherent in these transactions. In order to establish an understanding of the rationale for purchase by poor consumers, the three named defendants in the Wisconsin RTO usury case of *Burney et al. v. Thorn Americas Inc. et al.* were interviewed. The interviewer's guide for this study was developed from these data,

with additional help from several professionals who were familiar with the RTO industry. Subsequently additional data were gathered from forty RTO consumers living in the same poverty communities as the defendants.

One clear point of consensus among interviewees was that a primary consideration in their selection of RTO retailers is the easy credit arrangements that enable them to acquire products they otherwise could not obtain. Another aspect of this accessibility is the speed of the transaction. According to interviewees, a RTO customer can stop by anytime, see something he or she needs or wants, and have it delivered that afternoon. Contrary to the arguments of the industry, interviewees stated that terminability, or the ability to return merchandise after making one or more payments, was not important to their decision to shop at RTO outlets.

Most believed that termination goes against their original intention of eventual ownership when entering their RTO contracts, and that it would just make it necessary to acquire the same products elsewhere or go without. Another common reason for not terminating is that consumers believed that they had invested too much money toward ownership to stop making payments. They felt that ending such contractual relationships with RTO outlets would be like throwing money away.

These data reveal that poor consumers' entry into exchange relationships with RTO retailers was based on access to merchandise they ultimately hoped to own, to the exclusion of their ability to terminate RTO contracts. Additionally, a perceived lack of alternative sources of supply (e.g., discount retailers) suggests that their willingness to pay the higher prices charged by RTO retailers was not a function of consumer ignorance but of serious marketplace restrictions (i.e., a lack of credit and mobility barriers).

In summary, early and current research findings show an imbalance in the marketing exchange relationship that favors businesses over poor consumers. As a result, impoverished neighborhoods contain marketplaces with fewer competitors, higher prices, expensive and deceptive credit arrangements, lower quality, and smaller assortments than their complement in more affluent communities. Some early scholars suggest that fault lies with impoverished consumers themselves, who traditionally lack the resources necessary to entice retailers and represent poor credit risks. Others across the era believe marketplace imbalance results in some predatory business tactics designed to take advantage of the restrictions faced by the poor. Regardless, the consumption choices for the impoverished are simple – either accept this shoddy arrangement or forgo need satisfaction.

An ethical paradigm for serving impoverished consumers

Rawlsian theory and distributive justice

According to Rawls (1971), a theory of distributive justice should provide a set of standards that can evaluate the distribution system within a society (also see Freeman, 1999). The premise behind such a system is that a satisfactory existence for any person is dependent upon the cooperation of all members of society. Thus, the division of material abundance should be acceptable to everyone, regardless of social position. No one should feel that "they or any of the others are taken advantage of, or forced to give in to claims which they do not regard as legitimate" (Rawls, 1993/1958, p. 17).

Rawls refers to his representation of distributive justice as "Justice as Fairness" (Rawls, 1971, 1993). Its guiding principles are derived from the original position, a situation in which people are unaware of their relative status among peers. In such an environment, individuals who select principles of justice

> are free, equal, rational, knowledgeable about human nature and society, concerned about promoting their own well being, mutually disinterested, and ignorant of their own identity and place in society (Nathanson, 1998, p. 84).

An outcome of the original position is that no one has a relative advantage in the establishment of principles of justice. Since everyone lacks knowledge of their true position, they are unable

to develop principles that favor their particular circumstances. Rawls (1993/1958) views these restrictions as consistent with a situation in which an enemy has the ability to assign one's place in society. Therefore, an individual would ensure that conditions are reasonable even in the worst possible circumstances.

This position results in principles of justice that delineate the ethical distribution of the primary goods of society (Zajac, 1995). In his early work, Rawls (1993/1958, p. 6) presented two fundamental principles: "first, each person . . . has an equal right to the most extensive liberty compatible with a like liberty for all; and second, inequalities are arbitrary unless it is reasonable to expect that they will work out for everyone's advantage." While subtle in its tone, the second principle is a direct attack on the ethical paradigm of utilitarianism, which allows greater advantages for one group in society to outweigh disadvantages for another group (Ball, 1986). Under the veil of ignorance, no one is aware of his or her relative status in society and, therefore, no one is willing to accept the downside risk of absolute poverty.

Over many years, Rawls revised his theory to respond to a variety of criticisms (see Daniels, 1989), but the first principle continues to advocate for basic rights and responsibilities while the second concentrates on social and material inequalities (Rawls, 1993). The latter became known as the difference principle and "holds that social and economic inequities, for example, inequities of wealth and authority, are just only if they result in compensating benefits for everyone, and in particular the least advantaged members of society" (Rawls, 1971, pp. 14–15). Also referred to as the maximin criterion, this principle suggests that distributive justice exists only if inequities maximize the situation of the least advantaged segment, described "solely in terms of relative income . . . with no reference to social position" (p. 98). Thus, those who are better off socially and economically must help others compensate for inequities, especially undeserved inequalities such as childhood poverty.

Lessons for business practice

The literature review of the previous forty years suggests a lack of distributive justice from a Rawlsian perspective. Impoverished consumers are aware of and face severe restrictions in their local marketplaces, including higher prices, poor credit terms, lower quality goods, and smaller assortments than available in more affluent communities. These inequities reduce their ability to actualize important consumption needs relative to wealthier consumers, demonstrating that the poor experience few compensating benefits from the material advance of the well to do.

Both the early work of Caplovitz (1963) and the more recent RTO investigation by Hill et al. (1998) demonstrate that unscrupulous individuals and organizations take advantage of impoverished consumers by operating outside the legitimate and ethical market system. However, Karpatkin (1999, p. 119) shows that in recent years such business practices are no longer limited to "fly-by-night desperados. The companies that engage in predatory lending are now close to or part of mainstream corporate America." For instance, she accused a subsidiary of Ford Motor Company of high-interest asset-based lending, along with Union Planters Corporation, one of the largest banks in America. Additionally, she revealed that Associates First Capital Corporation, recently charged by the Federal Trade Commission with violating lending laws, has institutional investors that include American Express Financial Corp., JP Morgan & Co., Banc One Corp., and Dreyfus Equitable Cos. This case has yet to be settled in U.S. District Court.

Alwitt and Donley (1996) suggest three mechanisms to improve the balance in marketplace exchanges that advance Rawlsian distributive justice: increases in what poor consumers have to exchange, decreases in the exchange power of marketers, and adjustments by marketers of the product mix offered to the impoverished. While some progress has been made in the exchange power of poor consumers (e.g., growth in the minimum wage), poverty levels among female-headed households, people of color, and the hyper-poor remain high. Additionally, legislative solutions that reduce the relative power of

business over the poor have proved difficult to enact and enforce (see Hill et al., 1998 for an example). As a result, improving the quality and quantity of goods and services that businesses bring to exchange relationships with impoverished consumers may be the best possible solution. This resource-sensitive approach would improve social capital and community by making a wider variety of products available within poor neighborhoods at affordable prices.

While this perspective is consistent with Rawlsian justice and may seem ethically responsible, does it also represent sound corporate policy? Consider the case of Dollar General, a discount retail chain. Dollar General provides an assortment of groceries and general merchandise at more than 4000 stores located in smaller communities at prices that are 20% to 40% below retailers such as Wal-Mart and Kmart (Barron, 1999; Howell, 1999). Their mission is "A Better Life for Everyone," and it is actualized through an explicit attempt to identify with and satisfy the needs of low-income consumers. As a result, 46% of their customers have gross incomes below $20 000 a year, and the typical customer is a mother in a family of three who spends less than $10 per shopping trip (Howell, 1999).

Their altruism and social consciousness notwithstanding, Dollar General management has discovered that this strategy is in the best interest of their stockholders as well. Earnings improved 26% to $182 million in 1998 on sales that increased 23% to $3.2 billion (Barron, 1999). Additionally, Dollar General's 5.7% net profit margin is significantly ahead of Wal-Mart's net profit margin of 3.2%. With this success, Dollar General continues to expand profitably, adding 500 new stores a year in smaller towns and communities where impoverished consumers have fewer marketplace options.

Concluding comments

Forty years of scholarship involving impoverished consumers in the U.S. reveals a legacy of broken material dreams among the poor that results in a lower standard of living and a reduced quality of life. While poverty may be the most important causal factor for this deleterious situation, business practices that take advantage of the ensuing marketplace imbalance is an unethical response. Distributive justice demands that businesses search for ways to improve the plight of the impoverished by increasing their accessibility to products at reasonable prices within their communities. The experiences of discount retail chains such as Dollar General provide an appropriate role model of corporate as well as moral success.

Acknowledgements

The author would like to thank the Editor and anonymous reviewers for their suggestions and support, and Dr. Pamplin for his financial generosity.

References

Alwitt, L. F.: 1995, 'Marketing and the Poor', *American Behavioral Scientist* **38**(4), 564–577.

Alwitt, L. F. and T. D. Donley: 1996, *The Low Income Consumer: Adjusting the Balance of Exchange* (Sage, Thousand Oaks, CA).

Alwitt, L. F. and T. D. Donley: 1997, 'Retail Stores in Poor Urban Neighborhoods', *Journal of Consumer Affairs* **31**(1), 139–164.

Andreasen, A. R.: 1975, *The Disadvantaged Consumer* (The Free Press, New York).

Andreasen, A. R.: 1993, 'Revisiting the Disadvantaged: Old Lessons and New Problems', *Journal of Public Policy & Marketing* **12**(2), 270–275.

Ball, S. W.: 1986, 'Economic Equality: Rawls Versus Utilitarianism', *Economics and Philosophy* **2** (October), 225–244.

Barron, K.: 1999, 'Wal-Mart's Ankle Biters', *Forbes* (October 18), 86–92.

Bell, J. and B. M. Burlin: 1993, 'In Urban Areas: Many of the Poor Still Pay More for Food', *Journal of Public Policy & Marketing* **12**(2), 260–270.

Caplovitz, D.: 1963, *The Poor Pay More* (The Free Press, New York).

Daniels, N.: 1989, *Critical Studies on Rawls' "A Theory of Justice"* (Stanford University Press, Stanford).

Edin, K.: 1993, *There's a Lot of Month Left at the End of the Money: How Welfare Recipients Make Ends Meet in Chicago* (Garland Publishing, New York).

Freeman, S.: 1999, *Collected Papers: John Rawls* (Harvard University Press, Cambridge).

Hill, R. P.: 2001a, 'Surviving in a Material World: Evidence from Ethnographic Consumer Research on People in Poverty', *Journal of Contemporary Ethnography* **30**(4), 364–391.

Hill, R. P.: 2001b, *Surviving in a Material World: The Lived Experience of People in Poverty* (University of Notre Dame Press, South Bend, IN).

Hill, R. P. and B. Adrangi: 1999, 'Global Poverty and the United Nations', *Journal of Public Policy & Marketing* **18**(2), 135–146.

Hill, R. P. and S. Macan: 1996, 'Consumer Survival on Welfare with an Emphasis on Medicaid and the Food Stamp Program', *Journal of Public Policy & Marketing* **15**(1), 118–127.

Hill, R. P., D. L. Ramp and L. Silver: 1998, 'The Rent-to-Own Industry and Pricing Disclosure Tactics', *Journal of Public Policy & Marketing* **17**(1), 3–10.

Hill, R. P. and D. L. Stephens: 1997, 'Impoverished Consumers and Consumer Behavior: The Case of AFDC Mothers', *Journal of Macromarketing* **17**(2), 32–48.

Holbrook, M. B.: 1995, *Consumer Research: Introspective Essays on the Study of Consumption* (Sage, Thousand Oaks, CA).

Holloway, R. J. and R. N. Cardozo: 1969, *Consumer Problems and Marketing Patterns in Low-income Neighborhoods: An Exploratory Study* (Graduate School of Business Administration, Minneapolis).

Howell, D.: 1999, 'Dollar General Eyes Growth', *Discount Store News* (June 21), 3, 53.

Irelan, L. M. and A. Besner: 1966, 'Low Income Outlook on Life', in L. M. Irelan (ed.), *Low Income Lifestyles* (U.S. Department of Health, Education, and Welfare, DC), pp. 1–8.

Karpatkin, R. H.: 1999, 'Toward a Fair and Just Marketplace for All Consumers: The Responsibilities of Marketing Professionals', *Journal of Public Policy & Marketing* **18**(1), 118–122.

Lee, R. G., J. L. Ozanne and R. P. Hill: 1999, 'Improving Service Encounters Through Resource Sensitivity: The Case of Health Care Delivery in an Appalachian Community', *Journal of Public Policy & Marketing* **18**(2), 230–248.

Mergenhagen, P.: 1996, 'What Can Minimum Wage Buy?', *American Demographics* (January), 32–36.

Nathanson, S.: 1998, *Economic Justice* (Prentice-Hall, Upper Saddle River, NJ).

Porter, M. E.: 1995, 'The Competitive Advantage of the Inner City', *Harvard Business Review* **73** (May–June), 55–71.

Rawls, J.: 1971, *A Theory of Justice* (Belknap Press, Cambridge).

Rawls, J.: 1993/1958, 'Justice as Fairness', in C. K. Rowley (ed.), *Social Choice Theory Volume III: Social Justice and Classical Liberal Goals* (Edward Elgar Publishing, Brookfield, VT), pp. 3–33; *Philosophical Review* **67**, 164–194.

Rawls, J.: 1993, *Political Liberalism* (Columbia University Press, New York).

Richards, L.: 1966, 'Consumer Practices of the Poor', in L. M. Irelan (ed.), *Low Income Lifestyles* (U.S. Department of Health, Education, and Welfare, DC), pp. 69–83.

Shea, M.: 1995, *Dynamics of Economic Well-being: Poverty, 1990 to 1992* (U.S. Department of Commerce, DC).

Sturdivant, F. D.: 1969, *The Ghetto Marketplace* (The Free Press, New York).

U.S. Census Bureau: 2000, *Poverty in the United States* (U.S. Department of Commerce, DC).

Zajac, E. E.: 1995, *Political Economy of Fairness* (MIT Press, Cambridge).

13247 Sandalwood Court,
Lake Oswego,
OR 97035-6766,
U.S.A.
E-mail: hill@up.edu

Part XIII
Knowledge (Intellectual Property and Knowledge Strategy)

[45]

A Pluralistic Account
of Intellectual Property

D. B. Resnik

ABSTRACT. This essay reviews six different approaches to intellectual property. It and argues that none of these accounts provide an adequate justification of intellectual property laws and policies because (1) there are many different types of intellectual property, and (2) a variety of incommensurable values play a role in the justification of intellectual property. The best approach to intellectual property is to assess and balance competing moral values in light of the particular facts and circumstances.

KEY WORDS: Hegel, intellectual property, justice, Locke, pluralism, privacy, utilitarianism

1. Introduction

There have been numerous disputes about the interpretation, scope, and justification of intellectual property (IP) ever since its emergence as an important aspect of the political economy more than two centuries ago. In the last two decades, controversies have arisen regarding the patenting of animals, plants, DNA, computer chips, and computer software; copyright protection for websites, computer screen displays, digitally recorded music, and computer databases; trademark infringement for Internet domain names, the ownership of traditional knowledge, and the application of international IP treaties to drugs that are used to treat HIV and other

David B. Resnik, JD, PhD, is a Professor of Medical Humanities at the Brody School of Medicine at East Carolina University and the Director of New Programs at The Bioethics Center of University Health Systems of East Carolina. He is the author of four books and more than 80 articles on the philosophy of science and medicine, bioethics, and research ethics.

infectious diseases that affect developing countries.[1] Although these disputes raise a variety of legal, moral, economic, and political issues, most of them also touch on the most fundamental issue in IP law and policy: how should society balance public vs. private control of information?[2]

To discuss intellectual property issues, it is important to have a framework for thinking about the justification of IP laws and policies. This essay will review several different approaches to IP and argue that no single approach can provide an adequate account of IP. The essay will argue that a pluralistic approach provides the best account of IP, because (1) there are many different types of IP; and (2) there are a variety of incommensurable moral values that have a bearing on the IP regime, such as autonomy, privacy, utility, and justice. The best way to resolve disputes about IP laws and policies is to assess and balance these competing values in light of the particular facts and circumstances.

This essay will develop its thesis as follows. Section 2 will give an overview of IP and discuss the different types of IP. Section 3 will explore six different approaches to IP and discuss their shortcomings. Section 4 will defend a pluralistic approach to IP and respond to some potential objections.

2. What is intellectual property?

Property is simply a collection of legal rights to control some thing (Honore, 1977; Dreyfuss, 1989).[3] The legal system defines the types of objects that may be treated as property as well as the scope of rights with respect to those objects. For example, a homeowner has legal rights to possess, use, modify, destroy, transfer, sell, or rent the house. Various laws and regulations may prohibit the homeowner from painting his house purple, operating a business from his home, or keeping a horse in his backyard.

Since properties are collections of legal rights, the property regime is a social institution that serves particular purposes in society (Feinman, 2000).[4] We tend to think of objects, such as, land, as the properties, but these objects only have their status as property in relation to people in society. If no people were around, land would not be someone's property; it would just be *the land*.[5] We mark borders and create deeds to represent the social and legal status of a person's rights and duties with respect to the land. Thus, the concept of property is a three-place relationship between an object, an individual (i.e. a person, group of people, or corporation), and society.

Property rights protect a variety of individual interests, ranging from the interest in secure housing (i.e. home ownership) to the interest in animal companionship (i.e. pet ownership). Perhaps the most significant interests that property rights protect are economic ones: without property rights, individuals cannot participate in a market economy. Thus, properties can be bought, sold, rented, or leased for a price (or market value). Commodities are objects that societies treats as alienable, i.e. their control can be transferred from person to person; commensurable, i.e. they can be compared to other commodities via a common metric; and fungible, they can be replaced by something else of the same type without a loss of value (Black's Law Dictionary, 1999). Some objects that have a market value are can be regarded as incomplete commodities, i.e. they are either not alienable, or not commensurable, or not fungible (Radin, 1996). For example, a rare painting has a market value even though it is not fungible. Human labor has a market value even though it is not alienable.

Societies have developed and changed property laws in order to protect and promote individual interests under changing technological, social, and economic conditions. In Medieval Europe, feudalism was the dominant political economy,

and the land was the most important type of object that people would possess, use, rent, buy, or sell. Property laws recognized and protected economic interests in land and defined rights with respect to real property. During the Renaissance, the feudal system broke down and created a class of merchants who were able to trade their goods and services on the market. To protect economic interests in harvested crops, livestock, and other goods and services, laws were developed to recognize moveable property (May, 1998). During the scientific and industrial revolutions, the political economy came to depend more on the application of information and ideas, and the legal system gave more extensive recognition to IP. England passed its first patent statute in 1623 and its first copyright statute in 1710. The U.S. adopted its first copyright and patent statutes in 1790 (Miller and Davis, 2000; Foster and Shook, 1993).

To see why societies found it necessary to develop IP laws, consider property rights with respect to a book. In a world without copyright laws, if an author produces a book manuscript, he can only own the actual pages of the manuscript and has no property rights to the text itself. When the author sells his book manuscript to the publisher, he has transferred all of his rights to the publisher with respect to the book. Likewise, if the publisher sells a copy of the book, he has transferred all of his rights to the buyer. Similar problems would arise for inventions in a world without patent laws and trademarks in a world without trademark laws. It would seem that people have important interests worth protecting that extend beyond their interests in tangible things; they also have interests in intangible things, such as the ideas written on paper or the information embodied in inventions. In order to recognize these interests in ideas and information, it became necessary to create a new category of property, intellectual property.[5]

Intellectual properties, unlike tangible properties, require special legal protection because they are non-exclusive: two people can possess and use the same item of intellectual property without preventing each other from possessing or using it (Hettinger, 1989). For example, two people can both use and possess the

same computer program, poem, manufacturing
method, or the same song at the same time.
IP laws allow people to gain exclusive control
over objects that are non-exclusive (May, 1998).
The reason why intellectual properties are non-
exclusive is that information and ideas have no
particular location in time and space: they are
abstract objects.[6] Although some writers, such
as Barlow (1994), believe that it is impossible to
protect IP in the information age, due to its ease
of transmission, businesses and governments have
developed many technological and legal methods
for protecting IP, such as access restrictions,
encryption, water-marking, licensing agreements,
and infringement lawsuits (NAS, 2000).

The most common legally recognized forms
of IP are copyrights, patents, trademarks, and
trade secrets (Miller and Davis, 2000; Foster and
Shook, 1993). Many different countries have
enacted laws and signed international treaties that
define these rights and their scope. All of these
laws distinguish between privately owned information and information that is in the public
domain. Copyrights give authors of original
works the right to exclude others from copying
those works without the author's permission;
patents give inventors the right to exclude others
from making, using, or commercializing their
inventions without the inventor's permission;
trademarks give the trademark holder the right
to exclude others from using a symbol that he
uses to distinguish his business or its products;
and trade secrecy laws allow businesses to
protect confidential business information (Paine,
1991).

There are other types of IP in addition to
these four traditional categories. Confidential,
personal information, such as medical records or
psychiatric records, financial data, credit reports,
or purchasing data also can be regarded as IP.
Companies are now using information technology to acquire private information about individuals in order to enhance their advertising and
marketing. Someone who discloses or acquires
private information about a person without that
person's consent violates that person's interests
in controlling that information. One might argue
that a useful way of protecting privacy interests
is to treat private information as IP (Samuelson,

2000). Treating confidential information as IP
gives individuals the right to bargain with others
over access to their private information. If private
information is treated as IP, then individuals can
also enforce their privacy rights by suing viola-
tors for property-related torts, such as theft,
trespass and conversion.

Finally, intellectual credit might also be
regarded as a form of IP. For example, plagiarism
can be viewed as a form of theft because the
plagiarizer uses someone else's words or ideas
without giving that person proper citation or
attribution (LaFollette, 1992). Although plagiarism may involve a violation of copyright laws,
it may not. For example, someone who plagia-
rized all the ideas from a book without actually
copying the book would be guilty of plagiarism
even though they had not violated copyrights.
Thus, rules that prohibit plagiarism could also be
viewed as IP laws.

In the last two decades, the boundaries
between the different forms of intellectual
property have started to break down as a result
of advances in technology (NAS, 2000). For
instance, copyright laws evolved as a means of
protecting printed matter, while patent laws
evolved as a way of protecting practical inventions. Computer programs might be treated as
copyrightable, patentable, both, or neither. One
might argue that programs are copyrightable
because they are original works that are fixed on
tangible media, such as magnetic disks. On the
other hand, since programs are useful inventions,
one might argue that they should be patentable.
Computers have also blurred the lines between
copyright law and privacy law, since many people
store private information on computers or use
the Internet to communicate private information. Some have argued that the traditional
boundaries between different types of intellectual
property are not based on any fundamental metaphysical distinctions and reflect only pragmatic
concerns (Drahos, 1996).

Regardless of whether society treats a type of
information as falling within the domain of copyright, patent, trademark, trade secrecy, privacy,
or plagiarism laws, society must still come to
terms with a fundamental question common to
all intellectual property rules: what is the optimal

balance of public vs. private control of information? All intellectual property laws allow for the private ownership of some information while relegating a great deal of information to the public domain. For example, a patent gives the inventor a monopoly on his invention, but the monopoly is limited by the patent period (usually 20 years). When the patent expires, the invention enters the public domain. Copyright laws include a "fair use" exemption that allows for some unauthorized copying: information that is "fair use" is in the public domain. Both patent laws and copyright laws prohibit private control of some types of information. For instance, one cannot patent a basic idea or a law of nature, and one cannot copyright an idea or a fact. Even privacy laws define a realm of information about a person that is publicly known or available, and therefore, not private.

3. Accounts of intellectual property

The two most influential approaches to justifying and interpreting IP laws during the last 200 years of jurisprudence have been libertarianism and utilitarianism (Miller and Davis, 2000). This essay will examine these theories before considering other approaches.

3.1. *The libertarian approach*

The 17th century British philosopher John Locke developed a libertarian approach to property, which has been expanded by modern libertarians, such as Nozick (1974). According to Locke (1980), all people have natural rights to life, liberty, and property, and the sole reason for the existence of government is to protect these rights. Legal rights, under the Lockean approach, are based moral rights. The only justifiable legal restrictions on individual rights are those that are required to prevent individuals from violating each other's natural rights. Restrictions on rights are not justified as a means of promoting social goals, such as utility or a just distribution of resources (Nozick, 1974). Property rights are some of the most important natural rights pro-

tected by the state. People have property rights with respect to their own bodies and the products of the labor. People can acquire new property through social transactions, such as bartering, buying, selling, or giving, or through the process of original acquisition. Original acquisition occurs when a person adds his or her labor to something found in nature. Locke conceived of a world in which there is common property (or nature) given to all people. People are justified in claiming ownership of the products of their labor because they have mixed their labor with those products, they have removed them from nature, and they have added value to them. Property rights therefore protect individual interests relating to the investment of labor. According to Locke (1980),

> Whatsoever then he removes out of the state that nature hath provided, and left it in, he hath mixed his labor with, and joined it to something that is his own, and thereby makes it his property (p. 19).

Locke's labor-mixing theory fits many but not all types of intellectual property (Kuflick, 1989, Dreyfuss, 1989). It makes the most sense when applied to original works and inventions where people have invested time and effort in their products, such as books, paintings, airplanes, and new drugs. It also would seem to apply, to a lesser extent, to other business activities that involve the investment of labor, such as trademarks and trade secrets.

However, the labor-mixing theory has some shortcomings that make it an inadequate approach to IP. There are numerous examples where the degree of IP protection that people should receive does not correspond to the amount of labor they have invested in a particular intellectual property. First, consider two authors: author A works for four year researching and writing a book on the history of aviation, and Author B works for 4 weeks writing a Romance novel. Author A has invested 50 times more labor in his work than Author B, but we would still say that they both should have the same amount of IP protection. Copyrights protect authorship: if you are the author of an original work, then you get full protection. It makes no legal or practical sense to expand or restrict the scope of copyrights based on the amount of labor invested.

Second, consider two would-be inventors: inventor A and inventor B are both working for seven years to develop a new water desalination process. Inventor A develops the process and submits it to the patent office before Inventor B. According to patent law, Inventor A would receive the patent, not Inventor B. Patents are awarded for novelty, not labor (Miller and Davis, 2000). To satisfy the novelty requirement, the patent applicant must show that his invention has not been previously disclosed, invented, used, or otherwise reduced to practice. It is possible that an inventor might labor for years developing an invention that has already been patented or disclosed in the prior art. If the patent office finds that this prior disclosure has occurred, then it will deny the applicant the patent, irrespective of the quality or quantity of the labor he has invested. Although this rule does not conform to libertarian approach, it can be justified on utilitarian grounds because it rewards inventors for creating things that society does not already have and it encourages inventors to make a careful review of the prior art before submitting an application (Miller and Davis 2000).

Third, consider personal privacy. An individual might invest virtually no labor in some private information, but we would still protect this information. For example, a person usually does not invest any of his own labor in acquiring a genetic disease or obtaining a social security number. Both of these types of information come into existence before birth or shortly thereafter, yet we should regard them both as private information as well as intellectual property.

Another problem with the labor mixing theory is that it does not offer useful guidance for allocating intellectual credit. Many original works, such as movie scripts, computer programs, and scientific papers have dozens of authors. One might argue that it would not be fair to use labor investment as a basis for assigning intellectual credit for projects with many laborers, since intellectual credit should also depend on the significance of one's contribution (Shamoo and Resnik, 2002). For example, suppose that a senior investigator spends 50 hours designing an experiment, preparing a grant proposal, and writing up the results. Suppose that three students and three technicians each invest 200 hours carrying out the experiments. The senior investigator would have contributed only 4% of the labor to the project, but one might still argue that he would deserve to be the first author on the paper, since his contribution was more important than the other contributions.

3.2. The utilitarian approach

Utilitarianism is by far the most influential approach to IP because it plays a major role in most legal decisions concerning IP. Indeed, a utilitarian argument for patents and copyrights appears in Article 1, Section 8, Clause 8 of the US Constitution (1787):

> Congress shall have the power. . . . To promote the progress of science and the useful arts, by securing for limited times to authors and inventors the exclusive rights to their respective discoveries.

In the last two centuries, courts have interpreted this passage rather broadly to include a wide variety of original works and inventions, ranging from machines and chemical processes to photographs and databases. Judges and legislators have also taken a utilitarian approach to trademark and trade secrecy laws (Dreyfuss, 1989).

Judges and legal scholars have not probed the philosophical foundations of the utilitarian approach to IP in great depth, although some philosophers, such as Hettinger (1989) and Kuflik (1989), have written about this approach to IP. To understand the utilitarian approach, it will be useful to give a brief explication of the views of the 19th century English philosopher and economist John Stuart Mill, the most influential utilitarian thinker. According to Mill, all morals are founded on utility or "the greatest happiness principle," i.e. that "actions are right in proportion as they tend to promote happiness; wrong as they tend to produce the reverse of happiness" (Mill, 1979, p. 7). Although Mill defined "utility" in terms of happiness, other utilitarians have equated "utility" with the "satisfaction of preferences" or other values (Scheffler, 1988).

Mill was also a staunch defender of human freedom, and he argued that rules that protect individual rights can be justified on the grounds that they promote the overall social good (Mill, 1956, 1979). According to Mill:

> Justice is a name for certain classes of moral rules which concern the essentials of human well-being more nearly, and are therefore of more absolute obligation, than any other rules for the guidance of life. . . . The moral rules which forbid mankind to hurt one another (in which case we must never forget to include a wrongful interference with each other's freedom) are more vital to human well-being than any maxims (Mill, 1979, p. 58).

According to Mill, there are two types of moral rules, rules of expediency (or prudence) and rules of justice.[7] Although both types of rules can be justified on the basis of their role in promoting social utility, rules of justice are more absolute than mere rules of expediency because they protect individual liberties and interests. Since people have interests in property, rules of justice should protect those interests. Mill also observes that injustice occurs when a person is deprived of his "personal liberty, his property, or any other thing which belongs to him by law" (Mill, 1979, p. 42), and that injustice also consists in "taking or withholding from any person that to which he has a moral right" (Mill, 1979, p. 43). Thus, even though Mill was a utilitarian, he believed that justice requires the protection of property.

From a utilitarian perspective, IP rights can be justified insofar as they promote the greatest balance of good/bad consequences for society (Kuflik, 1989; Svatos, 1996). These rights maximize social utility by providing authors and inventors (and entrepreneurs and investors) with incentives and rewards, which encourage the development of science, technology, industry and the arts. This essay will not engage in a debate about the definition of "utility;" it will assume that the development of science, technology, industry, and the arts will promote utility, however that term is defined.

Utilitarian arguments depend heavily on empirical premises relating to the connection between means and ends. If an argument for adopting rule X is that it is likely to produce outcome Y, then one needs evidence that demonstrates a causal or statistical relationship between X and Y. One of the standard criticisms of the utilitarian view of morality is that one often cannot make reliable predictions about the consequences of actions or policies (Scheffler, 1988). Many utilitarians reply to these critiques by drawing on evidence from economics, psychology, and social sciences to buttress their arguments for specific policies. Although the utilitarian justification for IP is now the dominant paradigm for evaluating laws and policies, many critics have challenged its empirical assumptions. For the utilitarian argument to succeed, one must be able to show that the good consequences of granting people exclusive control over information outweigh the bad consequences (Hettinger, 1989). Economists and social scientists have studied patents and copyrights to determine whether these legal protections have positive effects on science, industry, and the economy. Many different studies document that IP promote scientific discovery, technological innovation, and economic development.[8]

Even though there is good evidence for the utility of IP in general, it still might be the case that in particular circumstances some types of IP protection produce more harm than good. For example, under U.S. patent law, a company may decide to develop and patent an invention in order to keep it off the market. The U.S. does not require inventors to make, use, or commercialize their inventions or license others to do so; it does not have a compulsory licensing law (Miller and Davis, 2000). Under U.S. law it is also possible to patent an invention that has only harmful uses. The U.S. does not have a law that allows its patent agency to deny patent applications that are against the public morality.

The utilitarian view therefore requires policy analysts, legislators, government agencies, and the courts to continually examine the benefits and harms of various types of IP and make adjustments in the law in order to maximize social utility (Hettinger, 1989). Furthermore, technological advances often have a profound impact on the utility of the intellectual property regime, and laws or polices may need to be changed in order to deal with these developments. For example, advances in computing and information technology have required policy analysts, political leaders, and the courts to re-examine IP rights as they apply to computer programs, electronic databases, web pages, and email (NAS, 2000).

Since utilitarianism relies so heavily on empirical evidence, one might argue that theory cannot serve as firm foundation for IP due to its epistemological uncertainties. How can society adopt rules that maximize utility if it cannot predict the consequences of adherence to these rules? It is worth noting that Mill anticipated these epistemological problems with utilitarianism:

> Again, defenders of utility often find themselves called upon to reply to such an objection as this – that there is not time, previous to action, for calculating and weighing the effects of any line of conduct . . . that mankind have still much to learn as to the effects of actions on the general happiness, I admit and rather earnestly maintain. The corollaries from the principle of utility, like the precepts of every practical art, admit of indefinite improvement, and, in a progressive state of the human mind, their improvement is perpetually going on (Mill, 1979, pp. 23–24).

Here Mill gives the standard reply to epistemological difficulties with utilitarianism: we can and should gather more evidence to reduce uncertainty and improve our understanding of the connection between means and ends.

However, the utilitarian account of IP suffers problems that are more fundamental than these epistemological difficulties. One standard objection to utilitarianism is that it does not provide an adequate account of individual rights or distributive justice (Rawls, 1971). Sophisticated utilitarians try to answer these objections by arguing that a well-designed system of moral rules will protect individual rights and will take into account fairness in the realm of distributive justice (Scheffler, 1988). This essay will consider questions of justice later. For now, it will be instructive to see how utilitarians have difficulty providing an account of individual IP rights.

For example, consider the right to claim authorship of an original work, such as a book.

Under U.S. copyright law, if you transfer your copyrights to a publisher, you still have the right to be listed or cited as the author of the book. By acquiring copyrights to the book, the publisher does not acquire the right to list someone else as the author of the book (Miller and Davis, 2000). Your rights to intellectual credit are not alienated by this transaction. Most people would agree that this is a morally justified law; there are good moral reasons why authors should still retain the right to claim authorship (Weckert, 1997).

How would a utilitarian approach this issue? To justify this policy, a utilitarian would have to argue that this rule maximizes utility. The utilitarian might argue that the rule gives authors the guarantee that they will still receive intellectual credit for their works, even when they have transferred their financial rights to another party. While it is possible to fashion some type of utilitarian justification for this policy, it is not at all clear that this argument is sound, since we lack evidence that this policy is likely to promote utility. Indeed, utilitarian arguments may support the opposite conclusion, i.e. that utility is best served by allowing those who purchase copyrights from authors to negotiate for rights to intellectual credit. Thus, if we believe that there are good moral reasons for allowing authors to retain their rights to claim intellectual credit for their works when they transfer copyrights, then the best rationale for our support of this policy probably appeals to non-utilitarian considerations.

One final problem with the utilitarian approach is that it does not provide a convincing account of trade secrets and private, personal information (Paine, 1991). Although trade secrets have solid legal protection, they may, in fact, produce more harm than good, depending on the circumstances. A utilitarian would hold that secrets should be disclosed when disclosure promotes utility, but one might argue that companies and individuals have a right to not disclose their secrets even when disclosure would be socially beneficial. For example, suppose a company has developed a new type of engine that is burns 50% less gasoline existing internal combustion engines. Although society would benefit from having access to this engine, the company decides to not patent or develop the engine but to keep its trade secret in order to continue selling its current line of automobiles. Or consider a patient who has a very rare blood type and could help many people if he donated blood. The patient does not want to donate blood and wants to keep his blood type a secret in order to avoid guilt or harassment. If we accept the premise that individuals and companies have a right to protect their secrets even when society would benefit from disclosure, then we may find it difficult to account for this intuition if we also accept the utilitarian approach to IP. According to Paine, "respect for voluntary disclosure decisions and respect for confidential relationships" provide the best account of trade secrecy laws (Paine, 1991, p. 257).

3.3. *Hegel's self-expression theory*

Several political philosophers and legal theorists, such as Radin (1993), Waldron (1988), and Rawls (2001) have drawn inspiration from the 19th century German philosopher Friedrich Hegel's ideas about freedom, self-expression, and property. According to Hegel, property provides a canvas for the development, expression, and realization of one's self. A person must define him or her self in relation to the physical and social world, which is a world that is separate from the self (Avineri, 1972; Rawls, 2000). A person can define his or her self by manipulating and controlling objects in this separate world. In order to ensure that people can have control over objects, society should recognize property rights:

> A person must translate his freedom into an external sphere in order to exist as Idea. . . . The rationale of property is to be found not in the satisfaction of needs but in the supersession (sic) of the pure subjectivity of personality. In his property a person exists for the first time as reason. Even if my freedom is here realized first of all in an external thing, and so falsely realized, nevertheless abstract personality in its immediacy can have no other embodiment save one characterized by immediacy (Hegel, 1976, pp. 41–42).

Since human freedom requires that a person be able to express him or her self in the world and develop a life plan, property rights can be justified on the grounds that they are a necessary means of realizing human freedom (Waldron, 1988; Rawls, 2000). A person exercises his or her freedom (or autonomy) by controlling physical objects as well as information. Denying a person control over property is one way of restricting that person's autonomy (Dworkin, 1988).

Hegal's theory develops an important insight about property: we need property to express ourselves in the world. The self-expression theory fits examples where the property in question reflects a person's unique knowledge, creativity, insight, skill, or genius. If the person has poured him or her "self" into the object, then the object should be his or her property. Some examples of these highly personal creations include poems, diaries, paintings, songs, sculptures, as well as gardens, houses, rooms, and musical instruments.

On the other hand, Hegel's theory also has several shortcomings. The expression of one's self is a relevant moral consideration, but it is not the sole reason for granting property rights with respect to that object. To defend this point, let's begin with a definition of "self-expression" as "the expression of one's unique knowledge, experience, or talents in an object." For example, a poem may express a person's unique experiences; a pottery bowl may express a person's unique talents, etc. Thus, self-expression implies a degree of creativity, but it does not require genius. Different activities therefore have different degrees of self-expressiveness, ranging from highly expressive activities, such as, writing poetry, to less expressive activities, such as, working on an assembly line. Although there is some general sense in which we express ourselves in everything we do, we need some way of distinguishing between activities that are highly self-expressive and those that are not, otherwise the Hegelian theory would imply the absurd conclusion that we can assert property rights over almost anything, including the air we breath.

The self-expression theory, like the labor-mixing theory, makes the most sense in cases where there is a single person connected to the property. But this theory is unable to provide us with a satisfactory account of collaborative efforts. As noted earlier, many intellectual products result from the efforts of many different people. Consider the Beatles' song "Hey Jude," for example. Is that song the expression of John Lennon, Paul McCartney, Ringo Starr, George Harrison, or Brian Martin (the producer)? Or consider the sequencing of the human genome. Who is uniquely connected to that enormous research project?

A second problem with the self-expression theory is that many properties, including intellectual properties, are produced through automation. Many modern factories are entirely automated, with machines replacing people. Automation is also common in biochemistry, molecular biology, electrical engineering, and software design. Automated DNA sequencing devices have played a key role in sequencing the mouse, human, yeast, and other genomes. The computer industry has developed machines that can design software as well as computer chips. There is also computer-generated music, art, animation, and so on. Although automation does not entirely remove human expression from the production of information, it waters down the unique contributions of individual human beings and undermines the argument that any particular product is a reflection of a person's special knowledge, experience, or talents.

Third, our current IP laws often do not reflect the self-expression theory. It is possible to obtain a copyright or a patent despite minimal self-expression. For example, if you randomly take a series of photographs of a building by just pointing my camera at the building and clicking, you will have copyrights over those photos because you will be the original author of those photos, even though none of those photos may reflect your unique ideas, talents, or experiences. In copyright law, originality is important but personal expression is not. Although some creativity is required, it is possible to obtain a copyright with only a modicum of creativity (Miller and Davis, 2000). While the condition of novelty found in patent law sounds like it has something to do with self-expressiveness, an invention can satisfy this condition without exhibiting a great deal of self-expressiveness.

Some patented inventions are based on the routine application of methods used in bio-chemistry and molecular biology. For example, one can patent a chemical, such as a DNA sequence, by using routine laboratory procedures to create an isolated and purified form of the chemical. Our current IP laws indicate a concern for utility or liberty, rather than self-expression.

3.4. *The privacy approach*

According to the privacy approach, some types of IP can be justified because they promote personal or corporate privacy (Samuelson, 2000; Paine, 1991). Trade secrecy laws allow businesses to protect economically valuable, confidential business information, if the business makes an effort to protect the secret (Foster and Shook, 1993). An employee who illegally divulges a trade secret can face criminal prosecution for violation of trade secrecy laws or civil litigation for breach of contract. Inventors are also allowed to use trade secrecy to protect their inventions prior to submitting a patent application. One advantage of trade secrecy is that there are no statutory limitations on the secrecy period: you can keep information a secret as long as you are successful in preventing it from entering the public domain (Foster and Shook, 1993). On the other hand, trade secrecy laws do not prohibit competitors from using legitimate means, such as independent research or reverse engineering, to discover trade secrets.

As noted earlier, one might also argue that confidential personal information, such as medical records, can also be regarded as a type of IP. Indeed, pharmaceutical companies are often interested in gleaning information from medical records for the purposes of conducting research or developing marketing techniques (Orentlicher, 1997). Someone who discloses medical information without consent may violate the person's privacy rights as well as his property rights. The same point would also apply to invasions of the person, such as using their name, signature, or face without permission. Someone who uses a person's face to advertise a product without his permission not only violates privacy rights, he also violates property rights (Gold, 1996).

One potential objection to the privacy theory is that we do not need to view private information as intellectual property, since this information already has adequate protection under existing trade secrecy and privacy laws (Samuelson, 2000).[9] However, one might argue that private information shares some common characteristics with other forms of IP, because it is naturally non-exclusive and it often has commercial value. In order to ensure that people can have exclusive rights to possess and control private information, the government should grant property rights in private information.

A second objection to the privacy theory is that it does not apply to trade secrets, since people, not corporations, have privacy rights. Corporations are not moral agents and, therefore, should have no moral rights. On the other hand, a strong case can be made that corporations should have moral rights even though they are not conscious beings. Corporations have legal and moral duties relating to their relationships with employees, investors, consumers, and society at large. Since corporations have moral and legal duties, they should also be accorded moral rights. Since a corporation is a legal entity but not a conscious person, it may have less than the full scope of rights granted to a person. At the very minimum, a corporation must have some rights to conduct business and take actions to protect its financial interests. Trade secrecy rights would seem to fall within the scope of corporate rights (Hamilton, 2000).

A third objection to this theory is that this is not really an independent theory of IP, since privacy can be justified by appealing to other important values, such as freedom, social utility, and so on. For instance, one might argue that all privacy rights are grounded in the right to autonomy or the right not to be harmed. To test this conjecture, imagine a situation in which we would say that privacy rights have been violated even though autonomy has not been violated and the person has not been harmed. Consider a mentally retarded patient with no family or friends. Since he is unable to express any opinions or desires about the disposition of his medical records, sharing his medical records without his consent does not violate his autonomy. Let's also assume that sharing his records will also not harm him in any way, since he has adequate medical insurance, will not suffer additional stigma, etc. Nevertheless, one might argue that sharing his medical records with people who do not need to see those records to treat his condition violates his privacy, even though this sharing of information does not violate his autonomy or even cause him any direct harm.

Thus, one can make a good case that some IP is justified on the grounds that it protects privacy. However, while this justification offers us some important insights about IP, it has only limited applications because many of the objects that we regard as IP are not private. Trademarks, for example, are often highly public displays seen by millions of people. Someone who uses McDonald's trademarked arches in their own business is clearly not violating the privacy of this business. We protect trademarks in order to enable businesses to distinguish their products and services, which promotes economic efficiency and development (Miller and Davis, 2000). Many copyrighted works, such as famous songs or books, are also highly public.

3.5. *Egalitarian approaches*

The last approach this essay will consider attempt to deal concerns about IP's effects on distributive justice. Wreen (1998) expresses this concern:

> Even if the argument from social utility is correct in saying that patents do make for appreciable social utility, such utility is not enough to show that patents are justifiable. There are considerations of equity having to do with intranational (sic) competition that have to be taken into account and there are considerations of equity – and utility – having to do with international competition that also have to be taken into account (Wreen, 1998, pp. 444–445).

Wreen is concerned about how IP may contribute to socioeconomic disparities within a particular nation and among different nations.

He argues that a theory of IP should address important concerns about the distribution of the benefits of IP.

Most of the scholarly and jurisprudential discussions of IP focus on the tension between individual rights and the public good and do not deal explicitly with questions of justice. On the other hand, many of the current controversies of IP, such the debate about affordable medications in the developing world and the high cost of prescription drugs in the developed world, raise questions concerning distributive justice (Resnik, 2001c; Brody, 1996). Thus, it is worth considering a theory of IP that attempts to deal with questions of distributive justice.

One approach that deals explicitly with these sorts of issues is the Marxist perspective on IP. This essay has not raised the question of whether property in general (or intellectual property in particular) is morally justified. It has assumed that property is necessary in order to protect individual interests in a market economy. However, Marxists object to both capitalism and private property rights. According to the Marxist view, there should not be any tangible or intangible private property. Marxists regard private property as immoral for at least two reasons. First, private property alienates workers from their labor and therefore allows the bourgeoisie to exploit the proletariat. Second, since private property enables capitalists to accumulate wealth, it leads to inequitable distributions of social goods: the rich getter richer but the poor remain poor. In an ideal Marxist state, labor is not exploited, personal property does not exist, and social goods are distributed on the basis of need. All property belongs to the state, not to individuals (Marx, 1974, 1996; Marx and Engels, 1998).

Marxism represents a polar extreme on the problem of balancing public vs. private control of property. For Marxists, the scale is tilted completely toward public control; there is no private control. Very few IP scholars, IP attorneys, or judges adopt a Marxist approach to IP. Martin (1995) is an exception. He argues that IP rights lead to social injustices, such as exploitation of poor countries and poor people. The world would be much better off, according to Martin, if there were no IP.

Responding to Marxist critiques of private property is beyond the scope of this essay. However, Marxists raise an important problem for all approaches to IP: how can IP laws and policies promote a just distribution of benefits and burdens in society? The late John Rawls (1971, 1993, 2001) defends an approach to property that attempts to address problems of distributive justice in society. Although Rawls did not write about intellectual property, it is worth considering how his views would apply to IP. Since his view is quite complex, this essay will present an abbreviated version of his approach to property.

Rawls' theory develops a conception of justice that applies to the basic structure of society, which includes the family, the legal system, the government, property, and other social institutions (Rawls, 1971, 2001). A just society, according to Rawls, is a well-ordered, fair system of social cooperation and reciprocity, over time, given the fact of reasonable pluralism. "Reasonable pluralism" means that members of society do not all accept a single comprehensive moral, religious, or philosophical doctrine (Rawls, 2001). Rawls attempts to develop a conception of justice that can be supported by a "reasonable overlapping consensus" among different members of society (Rawls, 1993, p. 15).

To identify and justify the principles that constitute this conception of justice, Rawls uses an argument strategy known as the Original Position (OP) (Rawls, 1971, pp. 118–126). In the OP, hypothetical contractors are assembled to develop principles that will shape the basic structure of society. Rawls places the contractors behind a Veil of Ignorance to ensure that their judgments will be fair and impartial: they do not know who they are or will be in that society when the veil is lifted (Rawls, 1971, pp. 136–142). According to Rawls, the parties in the OP would adopt two principles:

> Each person will have the same indefeasible claim to a fully adequate scheme of equal basic liberties, which scheme is compatible with the same scheme of liberties for all (Rawls, 2001, p. 42). . . . Social and economic inequalities are to satisfy two basic conditions: first, they are to be attached to offices

and positions open to all under conditions of fair equality of opportunity; and second, they are to be to the greatest benefit to the least-advantaged members of society (the difference principle) (Rawls, 2001, pp. 42–43).

Rawls also argues that the first principle takes precedence over the second, and the first part of the second principle takes precedence over the second part. Thus, although Rawls allows for some social and economic inequalities in societies, these are not permitted if they interfere with the scheme of basic liberties or undermine fair equality of opportunity (Rawls, 1971, p. 43).

The right to property is one of the basic liberties incorporated in the first principle. Rawls defends what he calls a narrow rather than a wide conception of property; a libertarian would defend a wide conception of property (Rawls, 1971, pp. 270–274). Rawls recognizes that a right to property can be justified because it gives a person a sense of independence and self-respect, but he also holds that this right can be limited when it is not necessary perform this function (Rawls, 2001, p. 114). Thus, Rawls would support social policies that limit property rights, provided that these policies do not undermine a person's independence and self-respect. Various limitations on IP rights, such as the "fair use" exemption in copyright law, and the 20-year patent term, would be consistent with Rawls' approach to justice.

Rawls could also develop an argument that many types of IP are justified because they benefit the least advantaged members of society in the long run. Patents and copyrights stimulate the development of new technologies and creative works, which eventually benefit the least advantaged members of society. Although it seems unfair that only rich people can afford new inventions when they are first developed, these inventions soon become affordable as a result of expiring patents, increasing competition, and improvements in manufacturing. For example, electronic calculators have dropped in price from a few hundred dollars each in 1970 to a few dollars each (or less) in 2003.

The chief advantage of the Rawlsian approach to IP is that it provides a framework for responding to concerns about social justice related to the IP regime. Another advantage of the approach is that it attempts to come to terms with the problem of pluralism: he recognizes that different people in society have different moral, religious, and philosophical beliefs and he attempts to develop a political conception of justice that would be acceptable to people with diverse values. A third advantage of Rawls' approach to IP is that his principles of justice attempt to forge a compromise between several influential theories that address property rights, including libertarianism, utilitarianism, and egalitarianism.[10] The main weakness of Rawls' theory is that it represents a compromise position that may satisfy none of the different conflicting approaches to IP. Libertarians may object that Rawls does not given enough weight to property rights, utilitarians can argue that Rawls does not pay enough attention to the importance of maximizing utility, and egalitarians may complain that Rawls does not go far enough in ensuring socioeconomic equality. It is impossible to please everyone all of the time.

4. A pluralistic approach

This essay has reviewed six different approaches to IP and has argued that none of them provide an adequate account of IP. Each approach emphasizes a different value or goal that is served by the IP regime. These values include: autonomy (or freedom), privacy, utility, and justice. Each approach has its strengths and weaknesses. For example, the libertarian approach is strong on autonomy but weak on justice and utility. The utilitarian approach is strong on utility but weak on autonomy and justice. The privacy approach is strong on privacy but weak on justice and utility. Therefore, there are reasons to consider an alternative approach to IP.

One argument for the pluralistic approach is that the other approaches provide an inadequate account of IP. In addition to this negative reason, there are two positive reasons for preferring the pluralistic approach to the six alternatives. The first reason is that IP is highly diverse. IP is highly diverse because there are many different ways of controlling and taking an interest in information. As noted in Section 2, IP includes copyrights, patents, trade secrets, private information, and intellectual credit. Although most commentators focus on how IP protects economic interests, IP also protects interests in authorship and intellectual credit, freedom, and privacy. The second reason for preferring a pluralistic approach is that modern democratic societies are pluralistic (Rawls, 1993, 2001). People come from different ethnic and cultural backgrounds and have different moral, philosophical, and religious beliefs. Given this high degree of diversity, we should not expect that a "one size fits all approach" would provide an adequate account of intellectual property (or any other type of property, for that matter).

If there are good reasons for considering a pluralistic approach, we need to understand how a pluralistic approach would resolve IP disputes. The first step is to define "pluralism." Pluralism, for the purposes of this essay, is the view that people disagree about basic moral values and that these values are incommensurable, i.e. they cannot be compared or through a common metric or currency (Gutmann and Thompson, 1996). These basic values include some of those already discussed in this essay, such as autonomy, privacy, utility, and justice. A pluralist holds that it is impossible to calculate how much autonomy is worth in terms of utility or vice versa. There is no algorithm for assigning weights to these different values for the purposes of making trade-offs when they conflict.

A pluralistic approach holds that disputes about IP result from conflicts among basic values. IP disputes cannot be resolved by appealing to any single value. To resolve IP disputes, one must weigh and balance the different values that are at stake in the situation and determine which one should have priority. Another way of making this same point is that these basic values imply *prima facie* moral obligations. Moral agents should honor their *prima facie* obligations unless they have competing *prima facie* obligations. When *prima facie* obligations conflict, moral agents must make a fair and impartial choice that takes into consideration their competing obligations in light of the facts and circumstances that create the

dilemma (Ross, 1930; Beauchamp and Childress, 2001).

Since the pluralistic approach does not endorse a scheme for ranking values or obligations, the priority assigned to any particular value may vary from one situation to another. For example, utility should have the highest priority in disputes about patents, since the legal and social function of the patent system is to promote the progress of science and the useful arts. Other considerations, such as privacy or autonomy, should have a lower priority in patent disputes. On the other hand, utility should have a much lower priority in disputes about privacy, since privacy laws have been designed to protect individual interests, not to promote utility. Justice should have a high priority in resolving disputes about the allocation of intellectual credit, since authors and inventors want to be treated fairly, i.e. to receive credit where credit it due. However, justice could play less of a role in trademark disputes, since the purpose of trademarks is to promote commerce and industry.

For an example of how to apply the pluralistic approach to a particular case, consider access to affordable medications in the developing world (Resnik, 2001c). Most of the 25 million people in sub-Saharan Africa who have HIV cannot afford any of the patented prescriptions drugs used to treat their condition and do not have access to these medications. In order to deal with this public health problem, many developing nations have considered using the compulsory licensing provisions in the Trade Related aspects of Intellectual Properties (TRIPS) agreement to allow generic drug companies to manufacture these medications without obtaining a license from the patent holders, which would greatly reduce the cost of these drugs. TRIPS is an international IP treaty, sponsored by the World Trade Organization, that sets minimum standards for patent and copyright protection and provides a mechanism for resolving IP disputes. TRIPS includes a provision that allows signatory countries to override patent rights (through compulsory licensing) in order to address national emergencies. Developing countries have argued that they should be able to use the national emergency exception in TRIPS in order to deal with the HIV pandemic. Pharmaceutical companies in developing nations have opposed indiscriminate use of this exception on the grounds that this could undermine IP protection for patented drugs.

A pluralistic approach to this problem would proceed as follows. First, one should identify the important values at stake in this issue. On first glance, it would appear that this issue raises questions about justice (i.e. access to medications), autonomy (i.e. the right to control intellectual property), and utility (i.e. the best consequences for society, technology, and industry). Patent laws currently establish a good balance between autonomy and utility by placing a 20-year limit on the term of patent and limiting the scope of patents. One might argue that there needs to be an emergency exception to the patent regime in order to deal with extremely burdensome short-term inequities, such as poor access to vital medications. Thus, justice requires that national patents laws and international treaties include an exception to deal with national emergencies. However, utility places some strict limits on this exception because a very broad exception could lead to abuses that would undermine patent protection and decrease incentives for investment in research and development. Thus, the pluralistic approach would address this difficult and complex issue through a careful balancing of three values – utility, autonomy, and justice – in light of the facts and circumstances of the case.

Before concluding, this essay will consider two objections to the pluralistic approach.

First objection: pluralism is inconsistent because it gives priority to different values in different circumstances. To achieve consistency, an account of IP should provide a ranking of values. Pluralism does not do this. Hence, it is inconsistent.

Reply: Even though pluralism gives priority to different values in different circumstances, it is consistent because it provides a principled reason for shifting the priority of values. Consistency in moral reasoning requires that similar cases should be treated similarly and that different cases should be treated differently (Beauchamp and Childress, 2001). If two cases

are factually different, then one can justify a different ranking of values based on this difference.

Objection: Pluralism is not a very useful guide to jurisprudence or policy formation. Judges, policy-makers, legislators, and voters need a simpler approach with a clear decision-procedure. For example, utilitarianism is a very practical theory because it provides a simple framework for weighing benefits and risks. Pluralism introduces too many values and considerations into IP law and policy and makes the analysis unnecessarily complicated.

Reply: Pluralism is a more complex than some approaches, but it is still practical. Moreover, the approach is politically realistic. Debates about social policy are seldom framed in simple terms, such as costs vs. benefits. More often than not, judges, policy-makers, legislators, and voters must wrestle competing basic values. Balancing competing values is not as simple as assessing benefits and risks, but it is a realistic and practical approach.

5. Conclusion

This paper has examined and critiqued six different accounts of IP and argued for a pluralistic approach. According to pluralism, a variety of fundamental moral values, such as utility, autonomy, privacy, and justice, play a role in justifying IP laws and policies. To settle IP disputes, one must weigh and consider these different values in the light of the particular facts and circumstances. The paper has also discussed two reasons why pluralism provides the best account of intellectual property. First, intellectual property is highly diverse; and, second, people accept different moral, philosophical, and religious beliefs. Since we live in a pluralistic society in which many different people want to control information for many different reasons, a pluralistic approach to IP is politically and technologically realistic and morally sound.

Acknowledgment

The author would like to thank John Davis and anonymous reviewers for useful comments.

Notes

[1] Intellectual property laws pre-date the industrial era. See Miller and Davis (2000), Drahos (1996). For more on some of these disputes, see Drahos (1996), Resnik (2001a, b, c), National Science Foundation (2000), Shiva (1996), Andrews and Nelkin (2001), Radin (1996).

[2] The question of balancing public v. private control is not unique to intellectual property law or property law, for the matter.

[3] Although I am careful to distinguish between the "objects of property rights" and "property rights," common usage conflates these two distinct ideas. I will sometimes follow the common way of talking about property in this essay, despite the fact that I think that it is important to distinguish between these two ideas.

[4] I am adopting a position known as legal positivism: legal rights and obligations exist within a particular political system and are defined by codes, statutes, judicial rulings, and actions within that system. A legal system need not conform to an independent moral code or "natural law" in order to be considered a legal system (Hart, 1961). I will not consider the question of whether there are natural, moral rights. See Glendon (1991).

[5] I am assuming some form of metaphysical realism as well: there is a world of physical objects that exists independently of human beings. By "property" I do not mean "property" in the ontological sense of these term, e.g. properties such as solidity, density, color, shape, etc.

[6] The legal term "intangible" is similar to the philosophical term "abstract." An intangible property is a property that lacks a physical or corporeal existence, such as stock options or mechanical designs (*Black's Law Dictionary*, 1999). In philosophy, an abstract object is an object that does not have physical properties, such as a number or geometric figure. However, although all intangible properties are abstract objects, not all abstract objects are intangible properties: the number 4 is an abstract object but no one can claim ownership of that number.

[7] Moral theorists distinguish between act-utilitarianism and rule-utilitarianism (Scheffler, 1988). Act-utilitarians hold that we should perform the action that is likely to produce the greatest overall utility, while rule-utilitarians hold that we should act according to a rule (or system of rules) that is likely to produce the greatest overall utility. On my reading of Mill, he is a rule-utilitarian: Mill is defending a system of moral rules on the basis of their connection to the principle of utility.

[8] For more information on the social, economic, scientific, and technical impacts of IP, see May (1998), Svatos (1996), Merges (1996), Pejovich (1996), Dreyfuss (1989), Nelkin (1985).

[9] The legal right to privacy provides a basis for the right to refuse medical care, the right to an abortion, and other choices involving personal liberties. In some ways this legal right is a bit of misnomer because it encompasses a wide variety of rights to be left alone. For further discussion, see Gross (1993).

[10] Although Rawls regards his own theory as a form of egalitarianism, it is a watered down version of egalitarianism, since it allows for socioeconomic differences between people. Marxism offers a robust egalitarianism, since it holds that there should be no socioeconomic differences among people.

References

Andrews, L. and D. Nelkin: 2001, *Body Bazaar* (Crown Publishers, New York).

Avineri, S.: 1972, *Hegel's Theory of the Modern State* (Cambridge University Press, Cambridge).

Barlow, J.: 1994, 'The Economy of Ideas: A Framework for Rethinking Patents and Copyrights in the Digital Age', *Wired Magazine* 2(3), 1–5. Available at: www.wired.com/wired/archive/2.03/economy.ideas.html.

Beauchamp, T. and J. Childress: 2001, *Principles of Biomedical Ethics*, 5th ed (Oxford University Press, New York).

Black's Law Dictionary, 7th ed.: 1999 (West Publishing, St. Paul, MN).

Brody, B.: 1996, 'Public Goods and Fair Prices: Balancing Technological Innovation and Social Well Being', *Hastings Center Report* 26(2), 5–11.

Drahos, P.: 1996, *A Philosophy of Intellectual Property* (Aldershot, Dartmouth, NH).

Dreyfuss, R.: 1989, 'General Overview of the Intellectual Property System', in V. Weil and J. Snapper (eds.), *Owning Scientific and Technical Information* (Rutgers University Press, New Brunswick, NJ), pp. 17–40.

Dworkin, G.: 1988, *The Theory and Practice of Autonomy* (Cambridge University Press, Cambridge).

Feinman, J.: 2000, *Law 101* (Oxford University Press, New York).

Foster, F. and R. Shook: 1993, *Patents, Copyrights, and Trademarks*, 2nd ed. (John Wiley and Sons, New York).

Glendon, M.: 1991, *Rights Talk* (The Free Press, New York).

Gold, R.: 1996, *Body Parts: Property Rights and the Ownership of Human Biological Materials* (Georgetown University Press, Washington, DC).

Gross, H.: 1993, 'Privacy and Autonomy', in P. Smith (ed.), *The Nature and Process of Law* (Oxford University Press, New York), pp. 708–714.

Gutmann, A. and D. Thompson: 1996, *Democracy and Disagreement* (Harvard University Press, Cambridge, MA).

Hamilton, R.: 2000, *The Law of Corporations* (West Publishing, St. Paul, MN).

Hart, H.: 1961, *The Concept of Law* (Clarendon Press, Oxford).

Hegel, F.: 1976 [1821], *The Philosophy of the Right*, Knox, T. (trans.) (Oxford University Press, Oxford).

Hettinger, E.: 1989, 'Justifying Intellectual Property', *Philosophy and Public Affairs* **18**, 31–52.

Honore, A.: 1977, 'Ownership', in P. Smith (ed.), *The Nature and Process of Law* (Oxford University Press, New York), pp. 370–375.

Kuflik, A.: 1989, 'Moral Foundations of Intellectual Property Rights', in V. Weil and J. Snapper (eds.), *Owning Scientific and Technical Information* (Rutgers University Press, New Brunswick, NJ), pp. 29–39.

LaFollette, M.: 1992, *Stealing into Print* (University of California Press, Berkeley, CA).

Locke, J.: 1980 [1764], *Second Treatise of Government* (Hackett, Indianapolis).

Martin, B.: 1995, 'Against Intellectual Property', *Philosophy and Social Action* **21**(3), 7–22.

Marx, K.: 1974 [1844], *Economic and Philosophic Manuscripts* (Progress Publishers, New York).

Marx, K.: 1996 [1867], *Das Kapital* (Regnery Publishing, New York).

Marx, K. and F. Engels: 1998 [1848], *The Communist Manifesto* (Signet Books, New York).

May, C.: 1998, Thinking, Buying, Selling: Intellectual Property Rights in Political Economy', *New Political Economy* **3**(1), 59–78.

Merges, R.: 1996, 'Property Rights Theory and the Commons: the Case of Scientific Research', *Social Philosophy and Policy* **13**, 145–167.

Mill, J.: 1956 [1859] *On Liberty* (Liberal Arts Press, New York).

Mill, J.: 1979 [1861] *Utilitarianism* (Hackett, Indianapolis).

Miller, A. and M. Davis: 2000, *Intellectual Property: Patents, Trademarks, and Copyright* (West Publishing, St. Paul, MN).

National Academy of Sciences (NAS): 2000, *The Digital Dilemma* (National Academy Press, Washington, DC).

Nelkin, D.: 1985, *Science as Intellectual Property* (MacMillan, New York).

Nozick, R.: 1974, *Anarchy, State, and Utopia* (Basic Books, New York).

Orentlicher, D.: 1997, 'Genetic Privacy in the Patient-Physician Relationship', in M. Rothstein (ed.), *Genetic Secrets* (Yale University Press, New Haven, CT), pp. 77–92.

Paine, L.: 1991, 'Trade Secrets and the Justification of Intellectual Property', *Philosophy and Public Affairs* **20**, 247–263.

Pejovich, S.: 1996, 'Property Rights and Technological Innovation', *Social Philosophy and Policy* **13**, 168–180.

Radin, M.: 1993, *Reinterpreting Property* (University of Chicago Press, Chicago).

Radin, M.: 1996, *Contested Commodities* (Harvard University Press, Cambridge, MA).

Rawls, J.: 1971, *A Theory of Justice* (Harvard University Press, Cambridge, MA).

Rawls, J.: 1993, *Political Liberalism* (Columbia University Press, New York).

Rawls, J.: 2001, *Justice as Fairness: A Restatement* (Harvard University Press, Cambridge, MA).

Rawls, J.: 2000, *Lectures on the History of Moral Philosophy* (Harvard University Press, Cambridge, MA).

Resnik, D.: 2001a, 'DNA Patents and Scientific Discovery and Innovation: Assessing Benefits and Risks', *Science and Engineering Ethics* **7**(1), 29–62.

Resnik, D.: 2001b, 'DNA Patents and Human Dignity', *The Journal of Law, Medicine, and Ethics* **29**(2), 152–165.

Resnik, D.: 2001c, 'Developing Drugs for the Developing World: an Economic, Legal, Moral, and Political Dilemma', *Developing World Bioethics* **1**(1), 11–32.

Ross, W.: 1930, *The Right and the Good* (Clarendon Press, Oxford).

Samuelson, P.: 2000. 'Privacy as Intellectual Property?', *Stanford Law Review* **52**, 1125–1172.

Scheffler, S.: 1988, *Consequentialism and its Critics* (Oxford University Press, New York).

Shiva, V.: 1996, *Biopiracy: The Plunder of Nature and Knowledge* (South End Press, Boston, MA).

Svatos, M.: 1996, 'Biotechnology and the Utilitarian Argument for Patents', *Social Philosophy and Policy* **13**, 113–144.

US Constitution: 1787, Article 1, Section 8, Clause 8.

Waldron, J.: 1988, *The Right to Private Property* (Clarendon Press, Oxford).

Wreen, M.: 1998, 'Patents', in Chadwick, R. (ed.), *Encyclopedia of Applied Ethics*, Vol. 3 (Academic Press, New York), pp. 435–447.

East Carolina University,
Brody School of Medicine,
2s-17 Brody Medical Sciences G Building,
NC 27858-4354 Grenville, U.S.A.
E-mail: resnikD@mail.ecu.edu

[46]

Dissolving the digital dilemma: meta-theory and intellectual property

Alan E. Singer [a] and Jerry Calton [b]

[a] *Department of Management University of Canterbury Christchurch, New Zealand*
Tel.: +64 3 3667001; Fax: +64 3 3642020;
E-mail: aes@mang.canterbury.ac.nz
[b] *University of Hawaii, Hilo, Hawaii, USA*
Fax: +1 808 974 7685;
E-mail: jcalton@pahuleka.uhh.hawaii.edu

The contemporary worldwide dissensus and dilemma concerning the nature and enforcement of intellectual property rights, can be informed by metatheory. Policy in this area can be depicted as a resultant of narrowly-defined interests of stakeholder groups. It can also be described in terms of rational deliberations, that span scenarios and strategies, as well as the spectrum of social science theories and metatheories. The case for weaker IPR policy regimes then becomes quite compelling. Such regimes institutionalise relatively tight limitations on the scope, duration and applicability of patents and copyrights. They can be understood and justified in terms of cautious policy-level interventions in an ecology of knowledge. They are also oriented towards human development and higher ideals. More generally, such contributions from metatheory to public policy and business strategy have been rather sparsely documented, yet they are very timely.

Alan E. Singer is an associate professor at the Department of Management, University of Canterbury. He has degrees in Mathematics (Queens College, Oxford) Psychology (Birkbeck College, London), a Doctorate in Management (Canterbury) and a Diploma in Education (Oxford). He worked in the UK private sector (from 1975) before taking up a lectureship in New Zealand, in 1982. He has over 100 publications, including articles in Strategic Management Journal, Human Systems Management, Journal of Business Ethics, OMEGA, Psychology & Marketing, Decision Sciences, Accountancy, etc., with the book 'Strategy as Rationality' (Avebury Series in Philosophy. 1996). He is co-editor (with Professor Werhane) of 'Business Ethics in Theory and Practice' (Kluwer, 1999) and is on the editorial boards of HSM, Journal of Business Ethics, and the forthcoming Journal of Internationalisation. He teaches strategic management and business ethics, separately and concurrently.

Jerry M. Calton, Ph.D., is an associate professor of management at the University of Hawaii-Hilo. He is the Immediate Past President of the International Association for Business & Society (IABS). His research and publications are concerned with stakeholder theory. dialogic learning, reflective management practices, and ethical norm-generating processes associated with building and maintaining trust in knowledge creation and collaborative problem-solving activities.

1. Introduction

Napster, Versity and *Amazon* are but a few of the dot-com names currently associated with the dissensus surrounding intellectual property rights (IPR). Amidst claims of unfairness, made by some of the world's richest individuals and most powerful lobby groups, many other scientists, and policy advisors have used words like absurd, ludicrous, or crazy, when describing some of the more questionable effects and side-effects of current IPR regimes. It is quite apparent, to say the least, that new conceptual frameworks and philosophical understandings are needed to guide policy and provide direction, in this area. The present paper attempts to fulfill that need.

In the following section, IPR policy is described and depicted as a resultant of narrowly construed interests of various stakeholder groups. Policy formation is then re-described (Section 3) in terms of rational deliberations and discussions. These span applied considerations, such as scenarios, generic strategies and business models (Sections 4 and 5), as well as deeper theoretical and meta-theoretical frameworks (Sections 6 and 7). It turns out that the latter can quite richly inform IP policy (Section 8), first by recasting the problem in terms of an ecology of knowledge, then prescribing cautious intervention in that ecology, in ways that uphold human ideals and developmental goals.

2. Stakeholder analysis

For several years, particularly in Europe and USA there has been a great deal of well-financed political lobbying activity, directed at the strengthening and coordinating (or 'harmonising') IPR regimes. Specifically, powerful stakeholder groups have lobbied for stronger and more universal copyright and patent laws, with the necessary enforcement mechanisms. These 'groups' include professional legal associations, accountancy institutes, media and related industry associations (Fig. 1), as well as security and defense-related industries and organisations.

Numerous arguments and reasons for strengthening IPR regimes have been deployed (e.g. [45], *et seq*), in a protracted campaign to justify stronger regimes and to persuade the key players. Some of these arguments are briefly set out below. Then, in similar spirit to the recently published National Research Council (US) report (which appeared after this paper was first drafted), several counter-arguments are set out. When these are placed in the context of an exposure of the strategic interests (and hence also the likely biases) of the various stakeholder groups, the result is a much more critical account of strong regimes.

2.1. Legal groups

The legal profession can be depicted as a major stakeholder in strong regimes (Fig. 1). To the extent that it is viewed as a self-sustaining and self-interested entity (rather than public-interest-oriented) the language of business strategy can be invoked. Legal groups can be described as attempting to shape the fu-

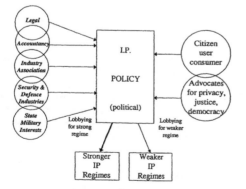

Fig. 1. Stakeholders in IP regimes.

ture of cyberspace, so that it becomes a future competitive space. Strong regimes are advocated, since these can be expected to create a vast potential 'space' for litigation. A great many business and social activities, indeed all forms of communication in cyberspace potentially lie within the ambit of 'strong' IPR laws.

As with other grand strategies, the strategic 'shaping' of cyberspace can be achieved, in part, by promulgating an ideology. In this case it is an ideology of capitalism, that retains, as far as possible, the traditional spectrum of property rights, including IPR (e.g., [15,24]. Accordingly, in policy forums, stronger IPR regimes have been justified with reference to the need for capital accumulation and financial returns from investment-intensive products (e.g., high first-copy-cost programs). Reference has also been made to the benefits that users (misleadingly called consumers), allegedly derive from these products.

These 'ideological' arguments can be countered, in quite standard ways that refer to market imperfections or inefficiencies. These include externalities and public goods, but extend to the entire economics-ethics nexus involving justice, social relations, alienation and development (e.g., [30,31]). Counterarguments of this more general type have only rarely been voiced in policy forums on IPR. They are briefly elaborated in Section 6 (below).

2.2. Accountancy institutes

The accountancy profession, also viewed as a self sustaining entity, is in a rather similar strategic position. Their 'future competitive space' is for valuation activity, rather than litigation. In the last 20 years or so, a gap has opened up between business asset valuations based upon historic costs (or realisable-values) and the much higher total market capitalisation. For example, in the U.S., in the year 2000, the book value of tangible assets (for non-financial corporations) was 31% of market capitalisation, compared with 83% in 1978 (Blair and Kochan, 2000, pp. 1–2.) The greater the information intensity, or level of embedded knowledge within a business entity, the greater the gap. The existing gap, or space, has already been filled by a variety of market offerings, as accounting firms have produced differentiated and highly priced methodologies for valuing business intangibles.

The self-serving dimensions of this strategy become quite apparent, when one considers the feasible alternative accounting practices, that might serve the broader public interest more directly. For example, financial reporting can still be based upon historic costs, whilst intangibles such as leadership, knowledge, capacity to innovate, and other competencies (the so-called intellectual and structural capital of a business) can be described, in plain natural language. This might be perfectly adequate for public reporting and strategic analysis. Furthermore, if this were normal practice, capital markets might arrive at fundamental valuations of knowledge-based entities that incorporate a more detached (and hence less biased) view of the macro-environment. Most significantly, in the present context, this 'view' would incorporate a range of possible futures for IPR regimes, including those likely to best serve the public interest. In practice, this level of detachment and objectivity in business valuation is rare.[1]

2.3. Producers and distributors

Industries such as music, software, broadcasting and pharmaceuticals have lobbied for stronger IPR regimes. In addition to the arguments deployed by the various professional groups (e.g., concerning investment-intensity, product quality, etc.) they have also expressed some specific managerial and operational concerns. These include the effect of (currently illegal) replications on product-management and relationship-marketing, as well as dilution of trademark (discussed subsequently, in Section 4).

The former 'concerns' arguably reflect an element of gamesmanship. Faults in replicated software packages, sometimes purchased at less than 1% of the full retail price, are vastly more likely to be attributed to the 'pi-

---

[1] The very idea of 'objectivity' is especially problematic here. A view from the left sees that the promulgation of IC language, with the measurement of IC, is a blatant attempt to capture all human knowledge production practices in economic terms; to dollarise human thinking, so to speak. As such it is subject to the standard critique that the mere act of 'dollarising' reduces value (e.g., the value of sex is the price of a prostitute, etc.). Furthermore, expressive (identity-related) dimensions are lost, when knowledge production is captured. Indeed, ultimately, humans might have to pay to think. A starkly contrasting view from the right (Rutledge 1997; cited by O'Connor 2000, p. 370) sees that 'IC is a potential Trojan horse for those who want stakeholders, not stockholders to control our companies; and social agendas, not performance to drive business decisions'. With this very different perspective, companies must resist measurement and reporting of human capital to the extent that they are reluctant to be accountable for goals relating to employees and other stakeholders. Meanwhile, canny consultants who themselves profit from selling IC methodology (as indicated in the text) can deploy either one of the above arguments to counter the other, as necessary for their own purposes! This is but one example, with typical consequences, of the contemporary climate of 'dissensus' discussed further in Section 7.

rate' provider, than to the original producer. With regard to the management and marketing practices, producers and distributors are ignoring the potential benefits to themselves and others from weaker IPR regimes. For example, if producers forced themselves to accept weak IPR regimes, they would have to become more innovative, at the level of their management practices and marketing strategies (Section 3). This in turn might serve their longer term and broader interests quite well. Accordingly, producers of digital works face a problem of rational self control, or weakness of will, as in the classical story of Ulysses who deliberately bound himself to the mast of his ship, to avoid temptation.

2.4. Military and security interests

Military and security related organisations also have a stake in IPR policy. Innovation, particularly in the area of information technology, increases a state's military power, especially its intelligence capability. Accordingly, military forces of nation states have an interest in policies that maximise the rate of technological innovation. This 'interest' does not, by itself, indicate any particular direction of lobbying, with respect to strong *versus* weak IPR regimes. This is because the effect of regime strength on rate of innovation *per se* remains ambiguous. The open source software movement and the public science genome projects, to mention just two examples, indicate how weak regimes might also be conducive to high quality innovation.

However, military and security related industries have a more specific interest, in particular types of innovation: those that can be directly applied to activities such as command and control, security and surveillance. Strong IPR regimes serve these interests, because they can be expected to increase the market demand for exactly these types of technological innovation, in order that compliance with the IPR laws be monitored and controlled. At the same time there is some degree of public support, in many democracies, for activities such as censoring dangerous web-sites, or surveillance of high-crime areas, etc. Yet it is far from clear, to say the least, that an emphasis of technological advance in these areas broadly serve the public interest, on balance. For example, such innovations and practices are not necessarily conducive to increasing the quality of life, nor to eliminating the causes of crime, nor even to overall economic development, to the extent that individual freedoms might be at stake (e.g., [31]).

2.5. *The public interest*

To date, commercial and security interests have dominated the IPR policy making process (Fig. 1). There has been an inevitable downplaying of public-interests issues such as civil liberties and personal freedoms. Furthermore, traditional arguments supporting copyright and involving the public interest, such as ensuring 'the variety and dissemination' of literary and artistic works (books), are no longer deployed by any of the above stakeholder groups, since they have simply lost force in the context of contemporary technologies, such as the internet. At the same time, the news media, who are themselves producer-stakeholders, have tended to ignore the entire story of the 'digital dilemma', or else they have simply broadcast industry adverts that support strong regimes. As a result, the issue has not been presented to the public as being particularly contentious. It has been framed as an esoteric field of commercial law and as such it has never been prominent in any public election campaign.

This situation might change. At the grassroots level, so to speak, some not-for profit/public-interest groups have recently proclaimed a mission to make the voice (or interests) of users and citizens heard, on this matter. Meanwhile, popular movies such as *Enemy of the State* might have also raised awareness of some related public policy issues. At the level of policy experts, an article in *Harvard Business Review* [42] called for a new system of IPR, a few years ago. More recently, the report of the U.S. National Research Council [25] stated that 'the average citizen. . . will surely be incredulous as lawyers descend with cease and desist orders as they learn to program', (thereby infringing software patents).

More generally, there are signs of a worldwide public re-awakening to the potential dangers of totalitarian corporatism (e.g., [15,23]), that might accompany the growth of the global knowledge economy. Within developing nations in particular, advocates for development and distributive justice (e.g., [29]) have been increasingly willing to express concerns about the exploitation that is possible under strong IPR regimes, not to mention more general concerns about distributive justice in the global context.

3. **Rational deliberations**

The various arguments deployed by stakeholder groups, together with the counter-arguments, can be

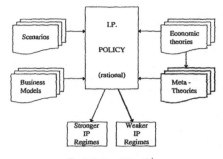

Fig. 2. Rational IP policy.

expanded with reference to possible business practices, such as scenario building and design of new business models, as well as available social science theories and metatheories (Fig 2). These are set out in the following sections.

In contrast to the political process depicted in Fig. 1, this extended rational or deliberative process (Fig. 2) appears to support the case for weaker IPR regimes, particularly with respect to the copyrighting and patenting of digital sequences. For example, various scenarios (Section 4) indicate the basic feasibility and common sense aspects of weak regimes, in which these rights are restricted. The 'business models' (Section 5) then represent various ways in which business can capture revenue and appropriate profit, in the presence of competition, but in the absence of copyright and patent protection. The limitations of traditional economic and legal arguments for having strong IPR regimes (e.g., incentives for innovation, capital formation, quality works etc.) are then briefly set out in Section 7, followed by the distinctive contributions from metatheory. The latter enable us to recast the digital dilemma in terms of an ecology of knowledge, in which cautious regulatory intervention shaped around human ideals can be of universal benefit. Several specific policy recommendations then follow.

4. **Scenarios**

The design or re-design of IPR regimes requires creative thinking and the generation of new feasible (but not necessarily optimal) alternatives. Scenarios and heuristics are often used for this purpose. One simple set of scenarios can be constructed by envisioning possible worlds, in which co-produced *rival* and *non-rival* goods are variously priced to users at (a) zero,

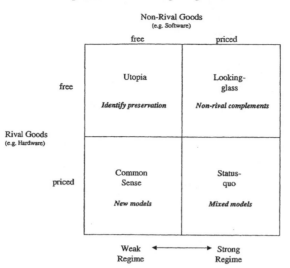

Fig. 3. Non-rival goods, prices and strategies.

or (b) greater than zero (Fig. 3). Rival goods, such as hardware and in -person services, are like a cake, that must be divided up. Non-rival goods like software, are such that their use by one entity does not necessarily have to deprive another. For both types of good, however, their availability (i.e., the total size and quality of the 'cake') can depend on the way that it is in fact divided up and used. The four resulting scenarios are described below, where they are referred to as: (i) *status quo*, (ii) looking glass, (iii) common sense, and (iv) *utopia*. Each scenario corresponds with some distinctive business strategies, or business-models.

4.1. Status-quo

Current IPR regimes motivate a varied mixture of business strategies. For example, a small business that co-produces or co-transforms a non-rival good (co-transformer seems a more accurate description), such as digital music, or a software program, might adopt a promotional strategy that focuses on geographic segments, within strong-IPR jurisdictions. A business with particularly high first-copy costs (movies, high end software) might pursue a hyper-competitive strategy, or other 'new' strategies (Section 5) that capture revenue without any IPR protection, whilst simultaneously lobbying through industry associations for the expansion (globalisation, harmonisation, etc.) of stronger regimes.

4.2. Common sense

Here, rival goods (e.g., hardware) are priced, so they can be efficiently allocated, subject to standard limitations; but non-rival goods (e.g., a digital download) are free. This is essentially the world according to *Napster*. It is 'common sense', only insofar as an average three-year-old child can quickly grasp the 'no-deprivation' aspect (of the replication of non-rival goods). By this age, the concept of object-permanence is quite well understood, with the social benefits of sharing, soon following on. This scenario is incomplete, as it leaves open the question of incentives for innovation, or arrangements for production. For example, within this scenario, an entity that 'produces' a digital sequence might use the new business models (Section 5) or design even newer ones, in order to capture revenues and appropriate profit. Alternatively, some not-for-profit arrangements might apply at the systemic level (as in the production and distribution of this article).

4.3. Looking-glass

In this scenario, the role of money and prices seemingly oppose 'common sense'. Hardware is given away free, with profits flowing from the software. This is in line with a prediction, reportedly made over 20 years ago, by a spokesperson at the Apple Computer company. The prediction has not quite become a reality, but it remains intriguingly feasible, especially if stronger regimes do develop. Rival goods (hardware) become so cheap, due to economies of scale and scope in physical production and distribution, that it becomes worthwhile to create an installed base that is free to the user. Again, profits are appropriated from the non-rival (digital) complements. High-tech hardware (and even rival services) becomes, in effect, part of a public good infrastructure. This strategy of rival/non-rival reversal can work within weak regimes, by using the 'new models'; but it is risky, because the time based advantage is seriously eroded by reverse engineering of the installed base. It is therefore quite dependent upon strong regimes.

4.4. Utopia

In Utopia, all goods are free. Robots tirelessly produce and distribute every conceivable market offering, satisfying human material and informational needs and desires. Radically different institutional structures and productive relationships can then develop. In particular, traditional priorities for exchange give way to concerns about identity and self-expression, as well as 'in person' social relations. Accordingly, those IP rights that specifically serve to uphold identity, reputation and integrity, take on a renewed priority. These rights are the moral rights of authorship, with protection against the dilution of identity-related symbols (that we currently think of as 'trade' marks) as well as protection against the disruption of social communications.

Taken together, the four scenarios serve to challenge and disrupt the historically determined and mainstream attitudes, mental models, frames and discourses, within which IPR policy has been crafted. This frame-breaking, in turn, is a necessary first step towards establishing a subsequent contribution from meta-theory. The 'disruption' also highlights the dynamic qualities of the entire system. Already the balance between the objectives of capital accumulation (needed for investment-intensive works) and the provision of public goods has manifestly shifted; but these scenarios suggest that it is likely to continue to do so. The dynamic nature of technological innovation demands an equally 'dynamic' response by IPR legislators and by businesses. The next section indicates how the latter might be achieved, in practice.

5. Business models

The 'common sense' and 'utopian' scenarios envision weak IPR regimes, but they are made quite feasible by the existence of various methods for capturing revenue from co-produced digital sequences, that depend on market forces and new technologies, rather than IPR regulations. In Table 1 these 'methods' (models, strategies, etc.) are listed, together with some examples. The particular principles of revenue-capture and profit-appropriation, with the limitations of each method, are also briefly mentioned. For example, the excludability strategy, which involves encryption, works for an interval of time before countermeasures become available (if sought); but it reduces share of mind. Extreme customisation reduces the demand for any re-distribution; but the strategy itself is easily copied. A business-to-business sale or license can result in a situation where the user (business entity) has an incentive not to re-distribute, etc.

The methods or models based upon *rival-complements* are potentially the most significant. Here, revenues are captured from rival (material, service) goods, that complement the co-produced DS. Such strategies might become very common, in future. Given some anticipatory planning, co-producers of (non-rival) digital sequences can still appropriate profits (as distinct from super-profits in global winner-take-all markets), despite the inevitable widespread replication and re-distribution. This is because the original producer of a digital work often retains at least two competitive advantages: (i) a unique early-mover advantage, and (ii) a distinctive competence in the shape of a more thorough understanding of the digital product and how it might be used and complemented. The latter 'understanding', is but one form of interaction between embedded and explicit knowledge. Such interactions are likely to form a fundamental (but abstract) building block for the industrial structures of the future (e.g., [28]).

Rival-complement strategies are essential to the 'common sense' and 'utopia' scenarios, but they also have wider implications concerning the feasibility of a new and more advanced form of knowledge-capitalism: one that is upheld by weak IPR regimes. In this form, efficient markets for rival goods (material, personal service, public-event, etc.) exist at a super-structure level, where money and price is used to mediate exchanges (i.e., of rival goods); but co-production of non-rival goods takes place within an ecology of knowledge that subsumes a vast pool of readily accessible and free digital patterns (including programs and algorithms) as well as human minds.

Table 1
Business models in weak regimes

Strategy or 'model'	Example	Captures revenue by	Limitation on revenue stream
1. Excludability	Encryption.	Interval of time before counter-measures devised.	Retards shadow diffusion and share of mind. Consumer resistance.
2. Exclusivity	Position as a status good.	Remove incentives to re-distribute.	Rarely feasible.
3. Mass/extreme customisation	Personalised newspaper, 'Collection of music tracks'.	Reduces demand for re-distribution.	Strategy is easily copied.
4. Niche in industrial markets	Audio (encoder sold to radio station).	B2B sale (or license), broadcaster increases advertising revenues.	Listeners can re-package, remove adverts, etc.
5. In-formation	CAD-CAM program for automated factory.	B2B sale or license.	Can be replicated for collaborating businesses, or sites.
6. Target inelastic segment segment	Sell high-end software to businesses that want immediacy, quality and service.	Value-added in the segment.	Short time window.
7. Low price/mass market	Cheap CDs	Easier to buy than to copy. Low margin/high volume.	Competition, 'normal' profits from commodity.
8. Hyper-competitive, disruption and cannibalisation	Free version, sell upgrade(s)	Combination of other methods (e.g., immediacy).	Combination of other limits, but these are side-stepped.
9. Rival-complements	----------------------	------ *See Text* ----------------------	

5.1. Innovation

Fortunately, there are several variants of the rival-complement business model. To generate these (and perhaps discover new ones) heuristic devices can be used, to stimulate creativity. For example, in the matrix depicted in Fig. 4, each type of market offering (i.e., digital download, material good, service, or social/public event, etc.) is paired off with each type of complement, under various possible pricing strategies. The exercise of filling in the cells of the matrix (here left to the reader) then generates new combinations of strategy-attributes.

The 'business model generator' is a morphological analysis tool, of the type more commonly used to identify novel combinations of product attributes (e.g., size, colour, etc.). This heuristic fosters innovative thinking, at the abstract level of business methods, as distinct from the level of the market offering itself. Weak regimes increase the incentives for this type of innovation. Looking further ahead, as technology inevitably progresses towards the production of powerful virtual-reality systems, the distinction between behaviour of producer and behaviour of product, as well as the dis-

tinction between the various categories of product in the matrix, will become increasingly blurred. This, in turn, will necessitate continual renewal and innovation at the level of business practices and regulatory policies.

6. Knowledge economics

In various policy forums, stakeholders in strong regimes have deployed standard economic arguments, that advance their interests. These refer to (i) innovation, (ii) corporate profitability and capital accumulation, as well as (iii) aggregate-level benefits or 'welfare' outcomes, associated with efficient markets. It is then claimed, with the support of selected theory (e.g., [41]), that strong regimes can contribute positively to all of these measures.

With regard to innovation, the claimed effect can be challenged, in several ways. As already mentioned, weak IP regimes are also likely to stimulate innovation, with respect to new business models and methods. Secondly, there has been abundant innovation by public-interest oriented entities, such as the networked open-source software movement and the human genome project. This success, in turn, might be explained with reference to the diversity of motives and contexts that foster human creativity and productivity (e.g., [20]). Finally, in strong regimes, the patenting of software processes, can unfortunately retard innovation [25], by providing a (crazy) disincentive to producers to stay fully appraised of *all* the latest industrial patents (to ensure that they do not *knowingly* violate patents, as they develop software.)

With regard to capital formation and aggregate welfare, systematic counter-arguments are readily available from standard critiques of neoclassical economic models (e.g., [30]). In addition, alternative models and theories of how markets for information-intensive goods can operate also support the case for weak regimes (e.g., [2,9,18,21] to mention a few). The critiques and models refer to factors such as (a) the effects of externalities, particularly positive network externalities created by the connectivity premium (e.g., the more copies of a program, the more useful each one becomes) and the sociality premium (e.g., people like to discuss the product); (b) the widespread use of strategies whose purpose is to create and then exploit market imperfections; (c) monopolistic tendencies, with the associated distributive justice concerns (e.g., [6,11]). These are acute, given the increasing-returns, winner-take-most phenomena, that are quite common for information-intensive products in global markets.

Finally, there is a general need for regulations that prevent tragedies-of-the-commons and that can ensure the production of public goods. Here, it is obvious that strong regimes can be expensive to administer, hence arguably reducing the availability of other public goods (i.e., they are socially inefficient), whilst to the extent that information-dispersion is constrained in any way (e.g., [11]), or that access to existing knowledge is limited, the overall rate of production of new knowledge can be retarded.

Theories and models of information economics, which formalise some of these concerns, have only rarely been invoked in the context of policy forums and political lobbying (e.g., [10]). When they have been discussed (e.g., [25]), the result has been nothing more than an appeal for empirical data, to indicate how to best manage the various tradeoffs that are expressed in those models. For example, it might be possible to quantify the lost contribution from unauthorised replications and compare this with the contribution gained indirectly from the resulting increased share of mind, in various markets. Similarly, the costs and benefits of maintaining additional trade secrets (including the loss of employee freedom, etc.), might be estimated and compared with cost of IPR litigation.

However, this research approach, aimed at informing policy, itself confronts several rather fundamen-

Priced After

	Digital Download	Physical/Material	Service by Person	Social/Public Event
Free First — Digital Download	e.g. Share-wave	?		
Physical/Material	?	?		
Service by Person				
Social/Public Event				

Free After

Priced First	Digital Download	Physical Material
Service by Person	Digital Download	Physical Material
Social/Public Event — Digital Download	?	?
Physical Material	?	

Fig. 4. A business model generator.

tal limitations. First there is a standard critique of all such cost-benefit analysis approaches (e.g., [22]). Next, there is an inevitable or a *priori bias* in the behaviour of the researcher, as discussed in the following section. Finally, policies that attempt to strike a balance between various sets of costs and benefits also have to take into account the dynamic and chaotic patterns of change in the system.

Knowledge economics, with knowledge based strategy (e.g., Von Krogh Roos and Slocum, 1994 [43]; Nonaka and Takeuchi, 1995 [26]; Grant, 1997 [8]) is more directly concerned with the transformation of information into explicit and tacit forms of knowledge, for the purpose of creating (economic) value. The question can then be asked (e.g., Calton, 1999 [42]) as to who *owns* this is process and its outputs, with the resulting return from investment in various forms of capital? Strong IPR regimes seek to preserve proprietary knowledge as something owned exclusively by shareholders. As such they tend to weaken the motivation and trust of employees who directly engage in, or who have become, the knowledge creation process. Accordingly, a broadened notion of ownership, reflected in practices such as employee stock options, might increase the economic value of the firm, as well as the rate of innovation.

To summarise the overall contribution from Economics, it now appears that those who attempt to measure and model the effects of alternative IPR policies, for the purpose of informing policy-makers, are not only standing on a shaky and contested platform, they are also aiming at rather elusive and erratically-moving targets. A possible way of managing these higher level (meta-theoretic) constraints is set out below.

7. Meta-theories

Metatheories can now richly inform IP policy and business practices. These include (i) the metatheory of representative practices [1] (ii) various synergy-oriented frameworks (e.g., [34,35]), and (iii) ecological/recursive thinking [3]. These are briefly outlined below, with policy implications outlined in subsequent sections.

7.1. Representative practices

This metatheory sets out a way of classifying research programs within social science academic disciplines, particularly sociology. The same framework can now also be applied, pragmatically, to any type of knowledge creation process, or research approach, including those falling within the ambit of current IP law. This metatheory describes and depicts all types of knowledge as claims made by social communities, rather than explicit patterns or digital sequences. For example, the situation depicted in Fig. 1 (above) can be re-described as a process involving knowledge claims, made by the various stakeholder communities, that refer to the possible effects of stronger IPR regimes.

The classification scheme (Fig. 5) involves two dimensions: 'consensus-dissensus' and 'local-elite'. The 'consensus' pole locates all knowledge production practices that advance a dominant discourse. For example, the adaptation of traditional IP laws, with reference to neo-classical economic concepts and legal precedent, belongs here. The 'dissensus' pole, in contrast, locates knowledge production practices that are oriented towards disruption, or replacement of a domi-

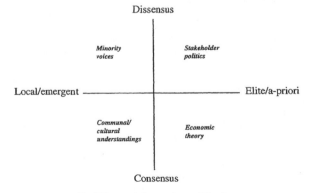

Fig. 5. Representative practices and IP policy.

nant discourse. Here we might find newspaper articles that mockingly report some of the more comical aspects of strong IPR enforcement (such as prosecuting suppliers of plastic lemons, or cakes decorated with cartoon characters, etc.), or web chatrooms on the subject of *copyleft* and open source, or business practices that deliberately disrupt markets, not to mention academic critical management theories.

The 'elite/*a-priori*' pole locates claims that rest upon privileged insights. Closed door meetings, where managerialist and legal language is readily deployed, belong here. The resultant claims, or outcomes of such meetings, are not only biased, but the 'bias' is a priori; it is built in before the discussions even begin. Finally, the 'local/emergent' pole locates forms of knowledge that have arisen entirely within an identifiable community. Traditional 'tribal' knowledge about medicinal qualities of local fauna (cf. [29]), localised constellations of property rights that incorporate duties of care, such as those conferred on canoe 'owners', by Yurok Indians (cf. [24]), as well as distinctive cultural schemata such as the Chinese understanding of ideas being 'in the air' (quoted in [25], p. 57), all belong near this pole of the metatheory.

The two axes of the system (Fig. 5) create a conceptual space in which to locate four distinctive research approaches, or knowledge production practices. These are the normative (e.g., economic theory), the critical (e.g., critical management theory), the dialogic (e.g., minority and radical voices) and the interpretive (i.e., communal understanding). The overall contribution of the metatheory to IP policy is then similar to its earlier contribution to Sociology. First, it *draws attention* to the various types of knowledge, making it quite apparent that there are indeed many alternatives to the dominant discourse. Put differently, it symbolises and hence advances an epistemological pluralism. Secondly, it places the four poles (and the four quadrants) on an *apparently equal* footing. Minority voices, local knowledge and distinctive community-wide understandings do not have to be excluded or discarded, as the products of some less developed minds or cultures. Indeed, in designing policy, it might be rather unwise to do so. Given the rather explicit limitations of the dominant theoretical discourse, as well as the manifest exclusivity of the mainstream stakeholder discussions and forums, the alternative 'claims' and 'forms of knowledge' are now seen to be an important component of any comprehensive rational policy deliberations; all the more so if the policy is intended to foster economic, social and human development, in a global setting (cf. [31]).

7.2. Synergy-orientation

Synergy orientation refers to a generic pattern observable within various streams of theory and research in the social and managerial sciences (e.g., [34,35]). A single concept, such as utility maximisation (or economic capital formation, or shareholder-value, etc.) is challenged by an alternative account that involves multiplicity, such as plural rationality (or the multi-capital framework, or the stakeholder model, etc). Next, the relationships, or meta-relations, between the singular and plural approaches become the focus of yet further theory development. Typically, at this stage, trade-offs are specified. Finally, new approaches to theory and practice are outlined (Table 2), involving some type of synthesis, or synergy. Of the various 'synergy-oriented' frameworks, the multi-capital framework, plural-rationality and stakeholder learning dialogues are particularly relevant to IP policy, as briefly indicated below.

The stakeholder claim that strong regimes encourage economic capital formation, can be challenged by an alternative account of the effects of IP regimes on social, human and ecological forms of capital. Social capital refers to communities, trust, and identity (e.g., [47]); human capital is the knowledge and capabilities embedded within individuals and collectivities; ecological capital refers to the 'nature-produced inputs' to all types of productive processes. The dominant discourse has implicitly assumed that the goal of IP policy is to increase the level of economic capital (although exactly how to do that remains contested), but it also assumes that the levels of the other forms of capital will increase as partial consequence, or later. Furthermore, this subsequent increase will at least compensate for any temporary reduction in their levels, caused by the limitations mentioned in the previous section (e.g., externalities, increased litigation, etc.). A synergy oriented approach seeks ways of adding simultaneously to *all* the forms of capital, in mutually reinforcing ways. According to the multi-capital framework, IP policy should be designed to foster this 'orientation'.[2]

---

[2]The synergy oriented approach to strategy formulation is consistent with the 'triple bottom line' for measuring corporate financial, social and ecological performance. This methodology, which might also be regarded by some as a 'Trojan Horse' has been developed by social-choice mutual funds, such as Trillium Asset Management (formerly Franklin Research and Development; see www.frdc.com) so that socially aware and active investors can monitor and reward companies that pursue a broader or more synergistic approach.

A similar prescription for IP policy also flows from the general theory of rationality. A rational-utility-maximising entity engages in the 'limited' and 'constrained' behaviours described earlier (Section 6). A hyper-rational entity (in the sociological sense of the term), in contrast, is one that continually designs new patterns and structures that enable a synthesis of the distinctive forms of rationality (e.g., [38]). Accordingly, such an entity attempts to designs ways of generating income (utility), whilst also maintaining identity (expressive rationality), promoting distributive justice (deliberative rationality) and improving social relations (sociality). According to the plural-rationality framework, IP policy should be designed with a view to fostering and encouraging this type of strategic behavior.

The generic pattern is once again evident, within a general theory of optimality and optimisation (e.g., [46]). There are many distinctive forms of optimality, each of which can be associated with particular strategic behaviours [37]. For example, an economically optimal strategy, such as the strategies of the stakeholder groups described earlier (e.g., creating future markets, promulgating ideology, etc.) can be distinguished from a systemic ethical strategy that aims to directly increase the level of co-production of (classical) human-goods, such as health, friendship, justice and wealth, etc. An optimally-designed IP policy would therefore

foster attempts at synthesis of these two types of strategy.

There are also quite a few qualitative accounts of synergy-oriented behaviour, such as *moral imagination* (e.g., [44]) and *stakeholder learning dialogues* (e.g., [7,16,19]). The latter describes how the position of a single stakeholder group can lead onto a discussion involving multiple stakeholders, exactly as in Fig. 1. Here, political interests prevail. Such discussions are often settled by premature closure (such as the pushing through of strong IPR laws), leaving some stakeholders muted and perhaps resentful. An alternative account recasts this 'discussion' as an interaction of disembodied propositions, Here stakeholders are replaced by their respective points of view, so that power-relations are (seen to be) held in abeyance. Thus far, this is very similar to the Habermasian ideal speech situation. However, according to Issacs' contemporary account, the next step is towards a *generative* discourse, or a 'learning dialogue'. At this level, dialogic engagement between people operating from different mindsets moves on to the creation and design of new solutions and new understandings. Furthermore, the participants in such a 'generative' discourse experience a subjective sense of flow, commonly associated with the highest levels of human performance.

The primary contribution of the various synergy-oriented metatheories to IP policy lies in the renewed emphasis that all of them place on *continually design-*

Table 2

Synergy orientation and intellectual property

Synergy-oriented framework	Components or elements	Synergy or Synthesis	Implication for IP policy. Regimes should ...
Multi capital framework	Economic	Designed	... foster accumulation of all the
	Human	Synergies	forms of capital
	Social		
	Ecological		
Plural-rationality	Utility – max	hyper-	... foster utility, identity, social
	Expressive	rationality	relations and distributive justice
	Reflective		
	Deliberative		
	Sociality		
Multiple optimality	Maximisation,	Economic,	... foster profit and human
	Economic optimal	optimum	goods
	Strategy, Human		
	goods, systemic-		
	ethical, Optimum		
Others	Moral imagination,	Creative thinking and	... avoid closure continual re-
	Stakeholder – synthesis	generative discourse	design
	Stakeholder – learning dialogue		

ing policies that foster the 'synergies', or overcome the tradeoffs, mentioned earlier. This is a rather similar message to that conveyed by Paul Hawken in the books *Ecology of Commerce* [16] and *Natural Capitalism* [17], but these referred to the production of rival (material) goods, with the associated problem of environmental externalities.

8. Recursivity

It is perhaps no coincidence that in telling the story of generative discourses, Isaacs [19] invoked several metaphors of ecology. For it has become increasingly apparent that theories, metatheories, meta (meta-(theories)) and so on, are themselves unfolding at ever higher levels of generality, mutual support and integration. For example, the synergy-oriented frameworks are not only similar to each other (despite quite different lineage), they can also be placed relative to each other. For example, economic capital and utility-maximisation correspond with 'economic theory' in the representative practices framework. In addition, the metatheories can be directly deployed in practice, as aids to creative design, or for stimulating moral imagination and generative discourse. Thus, recursivity (self-reference) has now become quite apparent in almost all research approaches aimed at understand human social and economic systems.

This is significant for policy makers. As information technology continues to advance, political interventions in systems of production, exchange and transformation will increasingly have to confront the many kinds of paradox that are associated with recursivity, reflexivity and self-reference. This has already happened, as the distinction between digital products and digital processes that produce those 'products' (variously copyrightable and patentable under strong regimes), has already become highly problematic, in law, not to mention in strategy. It is inevitable that the more fundamental and traditional economic distinction between a product and a productive-entity (e.g., a firm), will gradually disappear, as firms become deconstructed, so to speak (e.g., [12]). As abstract patterns co-produce other patterns, with the occasional intervention of human minds, they generate a partly-abstract ecology that grows ever more complex. In contrasts, strong IPR regimes have been shaped with the physical economy and economic forms of rationality in mind (i.e., preference relations amongst rival objects of choice), coupled to tradition public policy concerns

(such as quality and dissemination of works). It is not surprising that attempts to enforce these regimes often invite incredulity and mockery, whilst their more extreme manifestations are being described, publicly, as absurd and ludicrous.

8.1. Ecology

The metaphor or theme of an ecology is also detectable within the above metatheories. For example, in the multi-capital framework, the concepts of ecological and economic production are synthesised by a process that involves the exercise of 'moral imagination' and design. Also, the 'human capital' component incorporates individual and collective minds, that can be seen, or see themselves, as part of an ecology that encompasses mind and nature (e.g., [3,4]). Finally, the stakeholder learning dialogue is described [19] as a process from which new meanings *unfold*, like a tree unfolds from a seed, or indeed, like a computer image (of a tree) that unfolds from a mathematical 'seed', used in fractal image de-compression techniques.

Accordingly, the broader theme of 'ecology' is emerging almost everywhere, as an aid to practical sense making in the new world of business and public policy. Ecological thinking and discourse looks set to become the next grand narrative, or meta-(meta-(theory)). The term is already quite used widely in business practice, where phrases like 'product and service ecology' have quickly gained share of mind, amongst educated consultants; but it might also now be poised to displace (and inform) economic theories, so that it comes to dominate. This might provide yet further guidance to political and judicial elites, as they periodically re-design IPR regimes. If this happens, recursivity will, in effect, have replaced utility, as the new foundation, or 'seed' from which enlightened policy interventions and productive practices eventually unfold. Gregory Bateson would surely not be at all alone in approving the corresponding ideological transitions and theoretical adaptations.

9. Policies

An IP regime that intervenes in an ecology of knowledge can be likened to a deliberate intervention in a natural ecology, by a region's gardeners, farmers, breeders and bio-engineers. These entities breed crops, in-form products, design AIDS drug cocktails, produce and distribute GM rice, etc. Such activities can, in turn, be conceptualised in at least two distinctive ways:

(i) as an *intrinsic* part of an ecology: that is, the practices are part of a grand ecological system that subsumes human minds and nature;

(ii) as *transcending* ecologies and operating from a vantage point of dominion over nature, in ways that are distinctively human, moral, or spiritual.

With the latter interpretation, issues such as justice, freedom and truth telling (i.e., the concerns of citizens) become distinctive policy goals, representing the viewpoint that humans are indeed above the beasts, in some respects. This, in turn, carries some specific implications for IPR policies, as follows.

9.1. Justice and freedom

Strong IPR regimes tend to shift power from citizens to corporations, from labor to capital (e.g., when a company claims copyright over a creation of an employee, cf. [6]) and from poor to rich (e.g., LDC's *versus* Hollywood). It is not surprising that governments of some LDC's worry about being marginalised, or excluded from the so called 'new economy'. Strong regimes also tend to increase the motivation and the capabilities of all states and corporation to monitor the private behaviour of citizens, creating the spectra of corporate totalitarianism. To the extent that individual freedom is a constitutive part of development (e.g., [31]) strong regimes are profoundly limiting. In contrast, weaker regimes (e.g., short duration copyrights, limited patents, selected jurisdictions, etc.) are more likely to contribute to a more just and democratic political climate, without necessarily retarding development and efficiency.

9.2. Moral rights

Weak regimes can uphold the moral rights of identification of authors and the collective or corporate producers of digital works. If an entity simply replicates a digital work it ought not to pose as, nor claim to be, the original producer. Original producers should be identified and cited as necessary (as for example in this article). The essence of these 'moral rights' is not utility maximisation; rather it is the upholding of the identities of human individuals and groups (i.e., expressive rationality). In a world in which boundaries are continually shifting, enforcement of moral rights is highly likely to gain popular acceptance and respect, in contrast to the contempt and frustration frequently displayed towards aspects of strong regimes. Put differently, weak IPR regimes would also be democratic regimes.

9.3. Education

Programs of copyright education (or *mis*-education) have been proposed, in order to persuade citizens to comply with strong IP regimes. This can be seen as a rather blatant attempt to impose an 'elite consensus' (Section 7), that is not only highly ideological, but also manifestly opposes 'common sense' (Section 2). Not many people were amused by recent TV images of clowns dressed up in animal costumes, stomping heavily on perfectly good 'pirated' music CDs, in a city square. Such attempts at persuasion or indoctrination of young people are rather unlikely to succeed, since most children already know that (i) copying someone else's work and then changing the name of the author is wrong; but that (ii) replicating a work with the author's name still on it, say, in a school newsletter, is a good and moral thing to do. It obviously honours and dignifies the author, without causing deprivation. On the other hand, some children might be pleased indeed by the idea that teaching some mathematical algorithms, or programming techniques, might be illegal under strong regimes, as it might violate some patented digital process.

9.4. Truth-telling

Strong IP regimes tend to strengthen the position of large media corporations (hence the lobbying, depicted in Fig. 1). Such entities can offer *edu-tainment* (and perhaps some form of interactive job training and assessment), but they can also offer subtle ideological propaganda, misleading statements and re-written histories. To the extent that weaker regimes make it easier to disrupt the winner-take-most market structures in the broadcasting industry, the risks posed by combining excessive market power and political power are reduced. To the extent that governments seek to uphold truth, in its varied forms, but in the public interest, a network of publicly funded, public-interest oriented entities might serve as an accreditation agency. Such an entity might assess and critique the information, by invoking alternative frames and mental models, upholding minority points of view, or by appealing to other scientific, evidential and pragmatic criteria.

10. Conclusion

Current political interventions in the ecology of knowledge appear to be the resultants of lobbying activities, motivated by quite narrow self interest and justified in myopic and rather ideological ways. A more enlightened self interest, coupled to human concerns for justice, freedom and development, provides rational justification for weaker IPR regimes. In the short term, there is indeed an opportunity for profit-seeking businesses to be players in a tragedy of the electronic commons, or to 'ride the crazy horse until it drops', as one manager recently put it. In the longer term, it might be possible to co-produce a vast and accessible knowledge ecology, cultivated with humanity and ethics in mind. A more traditional economy of rival goods can continue to exist, as a superstructure. The present state of affairs, which has been variously described as crazy, absurd, ludicrous and incredulous, might turn out to be nothing more than a brief but remarkable historical aberration; like the alchemists, or the Spanish Inquisition. But there is certainly no guarantee. As a first step, visionary business leaders can quickly invoke the new business models. At the same time, concerned citizens can voice support for weaker regimes, whilst enlightened legislators can design and re-design cautious interventions, as prescribed and justified the metatheories outlined in this paper.

References

[1] M. Alvesson and S. Deetz, Critical theory and postmodern approaches to organisational studies, in: *Handbook of Organisational Studies*, 1998, pp. 191–217.

[2] W.B. Arthur, Increasing returns and the new world of business, *Harvard Business Review*, July-Aug., 1996, 100–109.

[3] G. Bateson, *Steps to an Ecology of Mind*, Chandler, NY, 1972.

[4] G. Bateson, *Mind and Nature: A Necessary Unity*, Wildwood, London, 1979.

[5] M.M. Blair and T.A. Kochan, eds., *The New Relationship: Human Capital and the American Corporation*, Brookings Institution Press, Washington, DC.

[6] J.M. Calton, Who owns the knowledge creation processes of learning organisations? A pragmatic ethical exploration, Paper presented at *IABS*, Paris, 1999.

[7] J.M. Calton and S. Payne, Making time for talk: stakeholder learning dialogues, Paper presented at the *Academy of Management* meeting, Toronto, 2000.

[8] R. A. D'Aveni with R. Gunther R., *Hypercompetition: Managing the Dynamics of Strategic Maneuvering*, Free Press, New York, 1994.

[9] A.V. Deardorff, Welfare effects of global patent protection, *Economica* 59 (1992), 35–51.

[10] G. Dempsey, Revisiting intellectual property policy: information economics for the information age, *Prometheus* 17(1) (1999), 33–40.

[11] T. Donaldson, Staking and ethical claim to intellectual property, Paper presented at *IABS*, Paris, 1999.

[12] P. Evans and T.S. Wurster, Strategy and the new economics of information, *Harvard Business Review*, Sept.-Oct., 1997.

[13] K.E. Goodpaster, Business ethics and stakeholder analysis, *Business Ethics Quarterly* 1 (1991), 1.

[14] R.M. Grant, The knowledge based view of the firm: implications for management practice, *Long Range Planning* (June) (1997), 451.

[15] C. Handy, The citizen corporation, *Harvard Business Review*, Sept.-Oct., 1997, 26–28.

[16] P. Hawken, *The Ecology of Commerce*, Wisenfield & Nicolson, London, 1993.

[17] P. Hawken, *Natural Capitalism*, Wisenfield & Nicolson, London, 1999.

[18] E. Helpman, Innovation, imitation and intellectual property rights, *Econometrica* 61(6) (1993), 1247–1280.

[19] W. Isaacs, *Dialogue and the Art of Thinking Together: A Pioneering Approach to Communicating in Business and in Life*, Currency, NY, 1999.

[20] J. Kao, *Jamming: the Art and Discipline of Business Creativity*, Harper Collins, 1996.

[21] K. Kelly, *New Rules for the New Economy*, Fourth Estate, London, 1999.

[22] S. Kelman, Cost-benefit analysis: an ethical critique, *Regulation*, Jan.-Feb., 1981, 74–82.

[23] C.B. Macpherson, *The Rise and Fall of Economic Justice*, OUP, Oxford, 1985.

[24] S.R. Munzer, *A Theory of Property*, Cambridge studies in philosophy and law, CUP, Cambridge, 1990.

[25] National Research Council (2000). *The Digital Dilemma: Intellectual Property in the Information Age*, Committee on Intellectual Property Rights and the Emerging Information Infrastructure, (US) National Academy Press, Washington, 2000.

[26] I. Nonaka and H. Takeuchi, *The Knowledge Creating Company: how Japanese Companies Create the Dynamics of Innovation*, OUP: New York, 1995.

[27] M.A. O'Connor, Comment on Bassi *et al.* In: M.M. Blair and T.A. Kochan, eds., *The New relationship: Human Capital and the American Corporation*, Brookings Institution Press, Washington DC, 2000.

[28] J.L. Sampler, Redefining industry structure for the information age, *Strategic Management Journal* 19 (1998), 343–355.

[29] V. Shiva and R. Holla-Bhar, Piracy by patent: the case of the Neem tree, in: *The Case Against the Global Economy*, J. Mander and E. Goldsmith, eds, Sierra Club Books, 1996, pp. 146–159.

[30] A. Sen, *On Ethics and Economics*, Blackwell, Oxford, 1987.

[31] A. Sen, *Development as Freedom*, OUP, Oxford, 1999.

[32] A.E. Singer, J. Calton and M.S. Singer, Profit without copyright, *Small Business Economics* (Special issue on internationalisation of enterprise), 2000.

[33] A.E. Singer, Metamodelling, in: *Encyclopedia of Life Support Systems*, M Zeleny, ed., UNESCO, Paris, 2001.

[34] A.E. Singer, Synergy orientation and intellectual property, in: *On the Threshold of the Millenium*, S.M. Natale, A.F. Libertella and G. Hayward, eds, University Press of America, Lanham & Oxford, 1999, pp. 67–79.

[35] A.E. Singer, Synergy-orientation and the third way, in: *Business Ethics: Contributions from Asia and New Zealand*, P. Werhane and A. Singer, eds, Kluwer Academic, Dordrecht, 1999.

[36] A.E. Singer, Education without tradeoffs, in: *Business Education: A Value-Laden Process*, S.M. Natale and G. Hayward, eds, University Press of America, Lanham & Oxford, 1997, pp. 67–79.

[37] A.E. Singer, Optimality and strategy, *International Journal of Operations and Quantitative Management* **2**(2) (1996), 111–126.

[38] A.E. Singer, Competitiveness as hyper-strategy, *Human Systems Management* **1** (1995), 163–178.

[39] A.E. Singer, Strategy as moral philosophy, *Strategic Management Journal* **15** (1994), 191–213.

[40] R. Tarnas, *The Passion of the Western Mind: Understanding the Ideas that Have Shaped our Worldview*, Ballantine Books, NY, 1996.

[41] D.J. Teece, Capturing value from knowledge assets: the new economy, markets for know-how and intangible assets, *California Management Review* **40**(3) (1998), 55–79.

[42] L.C. Thurow, Needed: a new system of intellectual property rights, *Harvard Business Review* (Sept.–Oct.) (1997), 95–103.

[43] G. Von Krogh, J. Roos and K. Slocum, An essay on corporate epistemology, *Strategic Management Journal*, Special Issue **15** (1994), 53–71.

[44] P.H. Werhane, *Moral Imagination and Management Decision Making*, Oxford University Press, NY, 1999.

[45] WIPO, *Worldwide Symposium on the Impact of Digital Technology on Copyright and Neighbouring Rights*, Harvard University, 1993 (*et seq*).

[46] M. Zeleny, Rethinking optimality: eight concepts, *Human Systems Management* **15** (1996), 1–4.

[47] M. Zeleny, Human and social capital: pre-requisites for a sustained prosperity, *Human Systems Management* **14** (1995), 279–282.

[47]

INTELLECTUAL PROPERTY RIGHTS, MORAL IMAGINATION, AND ACCESS TO LIFE-ENHANCING DRUGS

Patricia H. Werhane and Michael Gorman

Abstract: Although the idea of intellectual property (IP) rights—proprietary rights to what one invents, writes, paints, composes or creates—is firmly embedded in Western thinking, these rights are now being challenged across the globe in a number of areas. This paper will focus on one of these challenges: government-sanctioned copying of patented drugs without permission or license of the patent owner in the name of national security, in health emergencies, or life-threatening epidemics. After discussing standard rights-based and utilitarian arguments defending intellectual property we will present another model. IP is almost always a result of a long history of scientific or technological development and numbers of networks of creativity, not the act of a single person or a group of people at one moment in time. Thus thinking about and evaluating IP requires thinking about IP as shared rights. A network approach to IP challenges a traditional model of IP. It follows that the owner of those rights has some obligations to share that information or its outcomes. If that conclusion is applied to the distribution of antiretroviral drugs, what pharmaceutical companies are ethically required to do to increase access to these medicines in the developing world will have to be reanalyzed from a more systemic perspective.

Introduction

Although the idea of intellectual property (IP) rights—proprietary rights to what one invents, writes, paints, composes or creates—is firmly embedded in Western thinking, these rights are now being challenged across the globe in a number of areas.[1] These challenges include:

- Widespread copying of music and other works of art without permission
- "Knock-off" copies of designer products
- Counterfeit versions of well-known drugs and other products
- The copying of products by reverse engineering
- Challenges to gene patenting and genetic engineering
- Conflicting ownership claims to products developed from tacit knowledge of indigenous populations

- Government-sanctioned copying of patented drugs without permission or license of the patent owner in the name of national security, in health emergencies, or in life-threatening epidemics.

This paper will focus on the last challenge. It will weigh two seemingly opposing values: the value of intellectual property protection and the value of increasing access to antiretroviral drugs for HIV/AIDS to indigent infected patients. It will examine three different models of intellectual property rights. Part I will discuss two models of intellectual property rights apparently embraced by the pharmaceutical industry, the first grounded in traditional Western defenses of property rights and the second appealing to well-defended utilitarian justifications. In part II we shall present another way to think about intellectual property that both challenges and preserves this Western tradition. We shall then apply our arguments to the issue at hand: the protection of intellectual property rights garnered by new drug development in light of pandemics such as HIV/AIDS. How does one fund new drug development if patents are threatened and at the same time take on corporate responsibilities to provide access to HIV drugs in less developed countries?

Part I: The "Traditional Intellectual Property Rights" Mental Model

Enlightenment Age thinkers, including Locke, Hume, Smith, and Jefferson, recognized property rights among other fundamental rights of human beings. With the advent of the industrial revolution and the expansion of technology it became apparent that ideas as well as material property needed to be protected (Resnik 2003). Jefferson, in particular, defended patent protection because it encourages invention and creativity by protecting ownership of new ideas, and allows the inventor or creator to reap benefits from that idea, just as the farmer benefits from good agricultural practices on her land (Jefferson 1813). Unlike the farmer, the inventor should be encouraged to make public her or his innovation while protecting the right to copy or reproduce the invention. Jefferson defended intellectual property protection on two rather different grounds. The first, from the rights perspective of Locke (Locke 1764), held that inventors have rights to what they create. If a person or company creates a patentable (i.e., new, useable and not obvious) process or product, because of the creativity and work involved, the person or organization has rights to that process or product, just as she has right to land she has bought and developed. The second defense was on more utilitarian grounds that without protection of intellectual property, inventers will be less likely to be creative since they would not be able to reap honor or other benefits from their inventions. Jefferson contended that these should be time-limited protections so that others could eventually use those inventions to develop other things. (Jefferson 1813).

Thus there evolved a set of patent and copyright laws that "protect some (or most) products of the human mind *for varying periods of time*, against use by others of those products in various ways" (Vaver 2000: 621, our italics). Many nations, including the United States, have developed complex trademark, copyright, and patent laws to protect intellectual property. Genetically engineered products, designs, trade secrets,

INTELLECTUAL PROPERTY RIGHTS AND ACCESS TO DRUGS 597

plant breeder rights, databases, and a variety of other forms of intellectual property are also protected by various laws, as least in most Western developed countries (Vaver 2000: 622).[2]

Despite the legal treatment of intellectual property (IP) rights as time-limited protected claims in most Western countries, these rights are sometimes assumed to be perfect rights, a view that violation or destruction of copyrights, trademarks, or patents are always wrong without exception. Ayn Rand argues for one version of this view:

> Patents and copyrights are the legal implementation of the base of all property rights: man's right to the product of his mind. . . . [P]atents are the heart and core of property rights, and once they are destroyed, the destruction of all other rights will follow automatically, as a brief postscript. (Rand 1966: 125, 128)

Rand contends that IP rights are the most basic rights; without them all other rights are threatened. If this is true, then intellectual property rights might even preempt other important rights, say, to life and liberty. Thus, Rand's defense of the critical nature of IP rights as the basis of the protection of other rights would seem to argue against any action that would dilute intellectual property rights, even, for example, to save the lives of people afflicted with HIV/AIDS.

Utilitarian Arguments for Intellectual Property Rights

There are a number of strong arguments for the protection of intellectual property from a utilitarian point of view. It is commonly argued that protection of intellectual property is critical for the continued discovery, creation and development of new ideas. Few people will write new material, create new art, or invent new products without such protections, because there would be little in the way of honor, recognition, or profit in such activities (Jefferson 1813). Many inventers and companies argue that they have rights to patent protection to control access to that process and product because without such protections there will be few incentives for new product or idea development (Clemente 2001; Hughes, Moore, and Snyder 2002).

There are other facets of a utilitarian defense of intellectual property. Patent protection, for example, is contended to be particularly important to pharmaceutical companies, whose survival and creativity depends on large amounts of money for research and development. Patent protection allows companies to develop ideas, to profit from that development, and thus to gain funds for further research and development. Without this protection, pharmaceutical companies argue, there would be less incentive to take risk and fewer breakthrough drugs in the future. Patients and consumers would be the ultimate losers, companies contend.

In a paper titled "'Napsterizing' Pharmaceuticals," Hughes, Moore, and Snyder consider the view that, in the short term, consumers would be much better off if we eliminated present patents on drugs, thereby increasing competition with generic products. Costs of all drugs would be lower. However, as they demonstrate, in the long run we would all be worse off. This is because with lower revenues, pharmaceutical companies could not put as much money into the research and development that is critical for the development of new products. So gradually the development of new drugs would decline, and fewer new life-saving and life-enhancing treatments would be available to future generations (Hughes, Moore, and Snyder, 2002).

There is a fourth set of utilitarian arguments defending IP protections. C. L. Clemente, a senior vice president at Pfizer Corporation, contends that without intellectual property protection, companies such as Pfizer, which depend on patent protection for profits and product development, will not go into countries such as India because, through reverse engineering, Indian companies could copy their products (Clemente 2001). Indeed, according to Clemente, one early 1990s World Bank survey of international executives shows that tax rates and intellectual property protection were the main factors in determining global corporate investment decisions (World Bank 1999). Thus, lack of intellectual property protection, by discouraging investment and development, will widen the gap between the developed and developing countries. As Dr. Harvey Bale of the International Federation of Pharmaceutical Manufacturers Associations (IFPMA) put it:

> [w]ithout strong and effective global intellectual property rules, the gap between developed and developing countries will only grow in the future. (Bale 2002)

This is also the argument of the World Intellectual Property Organization (WIPO). In a new book sponsored by the WIPO, Director General Kamil Idris argues that the transformation of natural resources and products produced by indigenous populations into intellectual property and the protection of those ideas and others with a rule of law can contribute substantially to the wealth of any nation (Idris 2003; World Intellectual Property Organization 2003).

Part II: A "Network of Intellectual Property Relationships" Mental Model

Before continuing our discussion, let us step back and outline a set of assumptions from which our analysis derives. As we have argued at length elsewhere, all our experiences are socially constructed through a series of mental models or mind sets that frame our experiences. We do not simply take in experiences as if our minds were receptacles or "blank tablets." Rather, we focus, organize, select, and censor even our simplest perceptions so that all our experiences are framed by complex socially learned mindsets or cognitive schema. Mental models take the form of schema that frame the experience through which individuals process information, conduct experiments, and formulate theories. This conclusion is based on a commonly (although not universally) held assumption that human beings deal with the world through mindsets or mental models. Although the term is not always clearly defined, "mental model" encompasses the notion that human beings have mental representations, or cognitive frames, that structure the stimuli or data with which they interact, and these frameworks set up parameters though which experience, or a certain set of experiences, is organized or filtered (Senge 1990: chap. 10; Gentner and Whitley 1997: 210–11; Gorman 1992; Werhane 1999).

The "traditional intellectual property rights" model is one way to frame our thinking, a mindset or mental model, a social construction of experiences that predominates in developed countries. But it is only one worldview, and it raises at least three sets of problems. While protection of IP is important because of the proprietary rights to what one discovers or creates, to argue that intellectual property rights are inviolable or should not be destroyed is less plausible, *particularly* from a human rights perspective. If the most basic rights are those of life, liberty, and/or the right not to be harmed (or, as Henry Shue has argued, these rights are to survival, security and liberty [Shue 1996]) these most basic rights override property rights, or should do so, such as during crises such as the threat of death by HIV/Aids (Tuck 1979; Thurow 1997). Even in the United States, where patent laws grant "exclusive" rights, health and security concerns have "trumped" intellectual property rights on occasion. For example, after the anthrax scares in 2001 and 2002, the allegedly inviolable nature of IP rights was brought into question by the U. S. government. The antidote for anthrax is a highly powerful antibiotic called Cipro, patented and manufactured exclusively by Bayer. During the anthrax scare, on the grounds of a national emergency, the U. S. government threatened to override Bayer's patent of Cipro and license its manufacture elsewhere. Thus, even in a country that espouses the traditional-rights model of IP protection, patents can be overridden in cases of national emergencies or life-threatening events. Accordingly, from a traditional rights perspective, IP is a prima facie time-limited right that can and should be overridden particularly when rights to life or liberty are at stake.

In addition, there are two other interrelated problems with a traditional view of IP. First, when do individual and by extension, corporate intellectual property rights interfere with innovation? That is, when is an inventor prohibited from using the ideas of others to develop his own? Second, how do we acknowledge and give credit for the myriad of scientific developments and discoveries that precede and influence the development of a particular idea? Most new ideas do not drop out of the sky; they are the result of years, perhaps centuries of investigations that lead to the latest invention. So how do we account for these connections? These questions are not merely of intellectual importance; how one deals with them affects our conclusions concerning aid to indigent and dying HIV patients. In the next paragraphs we shall elaborate on each of these issues. Then we shall present an alternative to what we have called the traditional view of intellectual property. Note, however, that we are addressing our concerns to intellectual property. Our arguments may or may not apply similarly or equally to other property rights, but that is a consideration for another study.

Addressing the first issue, in a recent publication the pharmaceutical company Pfizer links its intellectual property rights (its ownership of patents) to control of the *processes* that produce these products as well as to any products produced from those processes (Clemente 2001). But in another article, recalling Garrett Hardin's earlier worries about the tragedy of the commons,[3] Michael A. Heller and Rebecca S. Eisenberg argue that some intellectual property protections, in particular, patent protections of biomedical and software innovations, have created what they call the "tragedy of the anticommons" (Heller and Eisenberg 1998).

Patent laws protect ownership and control while making the patent itself public knowledge. It is the *control* of the use of knowledge that Heller and Eisenberg challenge. Heller and Eisenberg argue that in some cases (although not in every case) overprotection of IP rights creates a "resource . . . prone to underuse . . . a 'tragedy of the anticommons'—when multiple owners each have a right to exclude others from a critical resource [or essential element of a process or technology] and no one has an effective privilege of use" (Heller and Eisenberg 1998: 698). Focusing on biomedical research, Heller and Eisenberg contend that privatization and patenting of IP in biomedicine can create fragmented overlapping patents for discoveries and restricted access to these fragments, access that is necessary for and linked to, other research. For example, patent protection of DNA sequences and gene fragments can block their use in other applications or research, except via expensive licensing agreements or through bundling multiple patents and licenses. The lack of immediate availability of such research and/or the expenses of licensing agreements can produce barriers that often discourage research development.

It is usually argued that patent protection protects company discoveries out of which commercial products can be developed, thus funding the research and development. We contended that that was a viable utilitarian defense of IP in the last section. However, extending such ownership rights in the form of patenting, depending on the phenomenon in question, can have the opposite effect as well, according to Heller and Eisenberg. By prohibiting others from using that idea to develop or create new products, in some cases at least, commercialization of new and needed drugs could thus be blocked. Although the judgment as to when overprotection of rights occurs is on a case-by-case basis, in the case of antiretroviral drugs for HIV, the creation of simpler drug therapies (e.g., 1–3 pills per day) from the usual "cocktail" of three different drugs taken several times a day, was slow in developing because of the patent protections surrounding each separate drug. Heller and Eisenberg have no solution for this problem except to suggest that public policy should "seek to ensure coherent boundaries of upstream patents and to minimize restrictive licensing practices that interfere with downstream product development." (Heller and Eisenberg 1998: 701). This is a vague solution, at best, and the issue of the anticommons is better addressed through rethinking the question of ownership rights, without which control is not possible, the second problem to which we alluded above.

Control (or not) of what one has patented is clearly linked to ownership, and exclusive control of what one has discovered or created depends on exclusive ownership rights. But that may be an issue. IP protection is allegedly granted to the source of the innovative idea. But what is that source? Is it the person who created or discovered the idea? The innovator of an idea or the person or company who developed it? Some companies, universities, and other institutions, through employee agreements, receive patents for product and processes their researchers develop on the grounds that they funded the project and will market it.

But ownership of IP as depicted as "mine" or as the sole proprietorship of a company presents an overly simplistic picture. The development of IP—a so-called new idea or creation— is a result of a network of interrelationships, discoveries, research and development, and exchanges of ideas, some passed down over time. IP phenomena are not single or even corporate creations; they are results of a buildup of research and exchange of ideas. Centuries of research made the discovery of DNA

INTELLECTUAL PROPERTY RIGHTS AND ACCESS TO DRUGS 601

possible; the idea did not merely come from the minds of Watson and Crick. Out of the discovery of DNA came years of research and networking relationships underlying the human genome projects. This is the case of every "new" scientific discovery or technological innovation. IP claims, at least in science, are derived from series of other intellectual property developments and a complex chain of human creativity. Even if only two people discovered DNA (and that in itself is a questionable conclusion), the discovery could not have been possible without the contributions of thousands of researchers, foundations, dollars, and companies, and a long history of overlapping and interrelated research.

While credit for the final "aha" might be given to the person or group of persons who brought the idea to fruition, simple patent protection may not be the proper vehicle for protecting this discovery or creation, since the property in question has many ancestral "owners." IP is a result of numbers of inputs, not all of which can ever be acknowledged or traced. AZT, for example, was first synthesized in 1964 by Dr. Jerome Horwitz at the Detroit Institute of Cancer Research as a cancer drug. Since it was ineffective for cancer, the compound was shelved and never patented by Dr. Horwitz. Later, Drs. Samuel Broder and Hiroaki Mitsuya at the National Institutes of Health tested the efficacy of the product on humans after it was rediscovered at Burroughs Wellcome (now GlaxoSmithKline). Other contributors include Dr. Janet Rideout, who isolated the compound, and Dr. Martha St. Clair, who tested the drug in mice. These women were helped by Phillip Furman and Sandra Lehrman at Burroughs Wellcome. Then Burroughs Wellcome patented AZT as a marketable HIV drug (Felsenthal 1993: 1).

Recognizing how IP develops from a complex web of interrelationships tracks its causal origins. At the same time the nature of these relationships might help us in recrafting our normative views about that kind of property. Part of this recrafting is parsing out the distinction between ownership, control, and sharing that is different from the traditional IP rights view. This parsing out, in turn, requires that we challenge the traditional IP model, and such challenges require a great deal of moral imagination.

What do we mean by moral imagination? Elsewhere, Werhane has defined moral imagination as

> the ability in particular circumstances to discover and evaluate possibilities not merely determined by that circumstance, or limited by its operative mental models, or merely framed by a set of rules or rule-governed concerns. (Werhane 1999: 93)

Moral imagination is by and large a facilitating reasoning process that helps us out of a particular framing box, leading us to refocus our attention, to criticize, revise, and reconstruct other operative mental models, and to develop more creative normative perspectives. Moral imagination requires the ability to disengage—to step back from a particular situation and take on another perspective, or at least, to begin a critical evaluation of the situation and its operative mind sets. Thus part of being morally imaginative is to perceive the ethical dimensions of a managerial or corporate situation. Of course, no one and no company can ever disengage completely. Our revisions, critiques, and evaluations are still context-driven by historical circumstances, culture, surrounding political and social pressures, and values perspectives.

Moral imagination, however, is not merely "second guessing." It also should entail developing fresh solutions based on revised or even different mind sets. To be morally imaginative involves evaluating these new possibilities or solutions from a normative perspective, judging not only the possibilities but also the way in which they are framed and the kinds of outcomes they are likely to produce (Werhane 1999).

Moral imagination, then, entails a three–stage process. Moral imagination is initiated from a particular experience, situation, or dilemma. For the events we focus on in this paper, moral imagination is triggered by the HIV/AIDS crisis, and the difficulties attending the manufacture and distribution of, and remuneration for, antiretroviral drugs, particularly for indigent patients in less developed countries. During this initial process, one becomes aware of the character, context, situation, or event at hand. One also becomes cognizant that something is amiss or one faces questions that do not suggest easy answers, as we outlined above. Then, if imagination is functioning, one becomes aware of the mental models or mind sets in which the situation is imbedded and the possible moral conflicts that may arise in this context—in this case the conflicts between a traditional mind set that values IP protection and an altruistic mind set of the community that imagines the pandemic can be solved by merely giving drugs away. These conflicts are coupled with various "blame" mindsets that attribute the pandemic to questionable sexual behavior, poor government oversight and the absence of a rule of law, and/or negligence by those who produce HIV/AIDS drugs.

In the next stage of moral imagination one begins to critically discuss the situation, its dominant mental models and the alternatives that present themselves, e.g., the either-or choices that seem to stop further dialogue. In this stage one has to rethink IP as developing from a series of networking processes. These processes not only account for the causal conditions under which the idea is discovered; they also challenge claims to exclusive ownership of the idea by the final discoverer. If IP develops out of knowledge relationships, broadly conceived (including scientific knowledge sharing), then one's ownership claims to the final "aha" are not absolute and carry responsibilities to communities out of which the idea was developed. This is because the new knowledge—the invention or discovery—is not an isolated idea but rather the idea overlaps and shares content with its predecessors.

The third set of processes involving stepping out of this situation and its scripts, moving beyond the either-or impasses and working toward a solution that was not evident when the processes began, often a solution that involves another mental model or worldview heretofore only latently available in the situation and context (Werhane 1999: chap. 5). For example, Kenneth Goodman challenges the idea that patents and copyrights are necessary as incentives for creativity. He contends that the conclusion that patenting creates incentives for inventors, researchers, and companies should be subjected to reexamination. According to Goodman "the history of research shows that [at least] university research for centuries yielded major results without the incentive of patents and still does" (Goodman 1993: 588). Moreover, he suggests, the sharing of information may yield more ideas than its control. Notice that it is

INTELLECTUAL PROPERTY RIGHTS AND ACCESS TO DRUGS 603

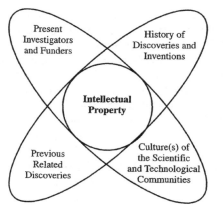

Figure 1

the restrictions on sharing, not patenting per se, that is at issue. In scientific circles worldwide there is a tradition of sharing new information, new discoveries, and new inventions. This sharing of knowledge ordinarily has one proviso: recognition for the final "aha," is given proper credit. For example, Einstein is always credited with the first formulation of the theory of relativity and his famous equation, $e=mc^2$, but neither is protected from sharing so that advances in the theory have been flourishing ever since his early publications.

What we propose is the following: The approach to IP as an individual or corporate proprietary right leads to oversimplified thinking. IP is almost always a result of a long history of scientific or technological development and numbers of networks of creativity, not the act of a single person or a group of people at one moment in time. Moreover, the resulting IP, its content, shares characteristics with its predecessors. It is not a unique idea. Thus thinking about and evaluating IP requires not merely recognizing that IP rights are prima facie rights, but also that it may be necessary to think about IP as shared rights. While credit can be given to the final discoverer or discoverers as just that—the final discoverer in a chain of inventions and ideas—exclusive control of processes and products is at issue. A network approach to IP challenges a traditional model of IP. This approach is crucial in thinking about IP, both in its development and in multicultural settings, because of the network of interlocking relationships out of which ideas develop and because the resulting IP consists of a collection of previous ideas, now repackaged. This idea of IP as a networked phenomenon is not a new proposal; it has been suggested in the law and economics literature for some time (e.g., Merges and Nelson 1990; Merges 1998; and Ordover 1991), but it has not been carefully incorporated into the mind sets of individuals and companies when they defend their IP rights.

There are many good reasons for protecting intellectual property. But we need to disengage ourselves from mind sets that contend that property rights of any form "trump" other basic rights, as we argued in part I. Now we are arguing further that discovery and creativity are results of multiple sets of events, networking, interactions, and other discoveries. That historical and networking trail needs to be acknowledged even while giving credit to Watson and Crick for discovering the double-helix structure of DNA, for instance. Watson and Crick's "discovery" was a reformulated or reworking of a collection of related previous discoveries, all of which were necessary for that discovery. Indeed, some have argued that there is a collection of people who should have shared the Nobel Prize for that discovery. AZT is even a clearer example. Burroughs Wellcome developed it for commercial use, but was not responsible for its original formulation. Because of that interdependence of ideas and their incestuous similarities, patent and copyright laws should themselves not be so restrictive as to create a tragedy of the anticommons.

Part III: IP Rights, Corporate Responsibilities, and Access to HIV Drugs in Less-Developed Countries

The Dilemmas

By law, IP rights are time-limited conventions. If IP rights are not the most basic rights that can "trump" others, they can be overridden in life-threatening emergencies or worldwide epidemics, and indeed we have seen examples of that. IP develops out of, and is dependent upon networks of relationships rather than being a result of a one-time discovery. It would appear, then, that we should arrive at the following conclusions. In times of life-threatening epidemics such as the worldwide HIV epidemic IP rights can be overridden with justification. Moreover, since IP develops from a network of interlocking relationships and shares critical characteristics with other IP, rights to IP are, in some sense, shared rights. It follows that the owner of those rights has some obligations to share that information or its outcomes since the owner's discovery came out of a network of shared ideas *and* shares overlapping content. If that conclusion is applied to thinking about the distribution of antiretroviral drugs, what are pharmaceutical companies ethically required to do to increase access to these medicines in the developing world?

Patents are not protected in at least two-thirds of those less-developed countries with high HIV infections (Attaran and Gillespie-White 2001). These countries, then, *could*, in theory, make generic versions of antiretroviral drugs without violating their own laws. So either the IP issue is a "red herring" in this debate, or the problem is much more complex.

The reality is that most countries with high rates of HIV/AIDS have no money to buy medicines. In most sub-Saharan African countries with HIV infections, countries that account for two-thirds of world-wide infections, the question of whether or not they have laws protecting intellectual property is irrelevant. There is little in the way of financial resources, except in South Africa, to underwrite the manufacture of drugs, even generic drugs. There is also no money to finance the purchase of HIV drugs. Worse, in most of these countries, with the possible exceptions of Botswana and South Africa, there is little in the way of medical infrastructure in place to distribute and monitor the use of these drugs. Ideally, one's government should be the first resort for such protections. But in most sub-Saharan countries there is little in the way of funding for health care and almost no enforcement of a rule of law. So the responsibilities of

INTELLECTUAL PROPERTY RIGHTS AND ACCESS TO DRUGS 605

less developed country governments to their citizens have to be reconceived for each country involved in this crisis, and the responsibility for addressing the pandemic becomes expanded beyond borders.

Even if pharmaceutical companies sacrifice some revenues and stop worrying about patent infringement, companies dealing in the developing world cannot simply give away HIV drugs: There is no place to send the medicines, no central authority, no distribution channels, and no competent health care professionals to administer and monitor drug use, nor are adequate delivery and follow-up systems in place in most of these countries. Even if the drugs reached the ill, without medical assistance, the medicines might be misused. Giving away the drugs even in countries with a semblance of a medical system is dangerous because often these drugs get into the black market. They are then diluted and/or sold back to developed countries at discount prices. For instance, according to one report, as much as two-thirds of the AZT now virtually given away in many African countries by GlaxoSmithKline, finds its way back to Europe through black markets (Friedman, den Besten, and Attaran 2003: 241). This reduces revenues for pharmaceutical companies in major markets, and reduces funds available for R&D on new treatments.

Another complication arises out of the mission of pharmaceutical companies. These companies are in the business of reducing pain and/or curing disease. This is what they do, and if they do it well, focusing on customers as their primary stakeholders, they are ordinarily profitable. These companies are always faced with a series of dilemmas. Which research should they fund? Which diseases should they concentrate on? And if they have a drug or set of drugs that are effective, how do they serve infected communities that have no money to pay for these drugs? The dilemma is acute in the case of HIV. Although HIV/AIDS is fatal, we have effective life prolonging and life-enhancing drugs to address this disease. Isn't the responsibility of companies that have these drugs to give them away to their indigent patients? Isn't that part of their mission?

There are other alternatives. Countries could be encouraged to focus on prevention: the use of condoms and/or abstinence. This sort of program has been somewhat successful in Uganda in reducing infection rates, but men in most of these areas of the world are loath to use condoms. The growing use of female condoms in many countries has helped stem the spread of HIV but this, too, is a small step. Companies could focus on drugs for pregnant women and newborns, a project that GlaxoSmithKline and other companies have done. However, even if those drugs get to infected mothers (and not to the black markets) and newborns were not infected, without continued antiretroviral treatment an infected mother's life span is short, and thousands of children are orphaned every year. Companies could license the production of their products or develop joint ventures, but again, to and with whom? Companies could develop a vaccine, and there are a number of such initiatives in process. However, an effective vaccine is probably ten years away. In the meantime, under the present circumstances, if nothing is done by 2020, it is projected that approximately 100 million people will have died of HIV/AIDS (Dugger 2003).

So, what should companies with antiretroviral drugs do? These companies did not start or perpetuate the HIV epidemic, and surely the countries in which this disease flourishes have responsibilities to their citizens to address this problem. Faced with what appear to be overwhelming challenges, this appears to be an "either/or" dilemma. Either these companies could follow the easy path of doing nothing, or, given the mission of pharmaceutical companies, the overwhelming extent of this pandemic, the pressure of their researchers and public opinion to address the HIV epidemic, the hopelessly poor countries in which the epidemic is prevalent, and the efficacy of HIV drugs, they could simply give the drugs away.

Networks, Moral Imagination, and an Alliance Model

The previous discussion of issues surrounding the HIV pandemic in sub-Saharan Africa, like the initial analysis of IP, was too simplistic. We have presented the pandemic as either-or dilemmas, but the issues are much more interrelated and intractable. This pandemic presents unique challenges. It presents challenges to pharmaceutical companies, not to their expertise or to the quality of their products, but to their way of thinking through IP and its implication for these ethical issues. The pandemic presents similar challenges to those governments, donor organizations, and NGOs that deal with these issues on a daily basis and to other individuals, governments, and international organizations that at least pay lip service to the problem.

To wrestle with this issue requires that companies, governments, donor organizations, and NGOs re-think their traditional approaches to problems in less developed countries and revise their standard operating procedures or traditional mind sets that have worked well in other situations. What is needed is a networked approach to thinking about intellectual property and IP protection and new thinking about drug distribution and disease control, along with a great deal of moral imagination. Such an approach could create a template for future corporate, government and donor activities for this pandemic.

Dealing in a creative way with the HIV/AIDS pandemic, like our analysis of IP, involves appealing to the third stage of moral imagination. This pandemic is embedded in a complex network of relationships themselves embedded in a complex set of systems and subsystems, including the diverse cultures and practices of indigenous people in every infected country; distribution issues; financing and funding challenges; pressures from shareholders, the media, and NGOs, and the ever present worry about protection of patents. For pharmaceutical companies with antiretroviral drugs, to protect their patents and address this crisis requires more of companies than we ordinarily expect. It requires developing and implementing a truly systemic approach to IP and to the HIV pandemic that gives good moral reasons for addressing this issue and then engages companies, donor organizations, NGOs, local villages, and countries. Such a multiple perspectives systems approach should include the following:

1. There are a number of good moral reasons why pharmaceutical companies with antiretroviral drugs have responsibilities to impoverished communities with widespread infection rates of HIV/AIDS. First, and most obviously, from the point of view of rights and justice, responding to the needs of infected and impoverished communities is the right thing to do. Unless one

INTELLECTUAL PROPERTY RIGHTS AND ACCESS TO DRUGS 607

imagines that IP rights override the right to life, it is difficult to justify ignoring this pandemic. The Good Samaritan argument, while not applicable to every situation, suggests that if we see someone in need and we are capable of helping, we have obligations to do so. This is because we all live in an interdependent global community [no longer separate communities, if they ever were] where interactive involvement is necessary for survival, preventing the spread of disease, and well-being. Analogously, no new drug could have ever been developed without these social interactions; thus obligations also arise because of the intellectual debts we have to each other. This does not imply, however, that companies should give away their HIV/AIDS drugs until they go bankrupt. Their responsibilities to employees, paying customers, shareholders and future generations who will benefit from new drug development, must be weighed as well. But to do nothing is unacceptable, and today almost every pharmaceutical company with antiretroviral drug protocols is engaged in some philanthropic project in Africa

2. If, as we suggested in part II, drug development like all IP, is a result of an interactive networking set of processes and overlapping ideas, then obligations, at least imperfect obligations, exist to continue that sharing activity since a company's ownership of an idea is in fact a shared dependency on predecessor discoveries. There is no practical means to recognize all or even very many of the ancestors of any idea. Yet one has intellectual debts that can be translated into a forward-projecting set of obligations to other scientists and to communities in which drug development is encouraged, permitted, and needed. In an interdependent global community these obligations become more widespread.

3. In dealing with the pandemic 'on the ground,' a multi-perspective analysis, spelling out the networks of relationships and viewing them from the perspective of each kind of relationship is critical (Mitroff and Linstone 1993). This would include an attempt to understand these issues from the point of view of pharmaceutical companies with antiretroviral drugs, from country and cultural perspectives, from the perspectives of traditions, funding agencies, NGOs and delivery mechanisms, and from the global perspective of the pandemic.

Consider, for example, the alliance model developed by Mary Ann Leeper, COO of the Female Health Company, a for-profit company that distributes female condoms to protect women against HIV infection in over 100 less-developed countries (Yemen and Powell 2003). The model was developed in response to a huge demand by women first in Zimbabwe and now in many other countries for protection against infection in cultures where men are adverse to condom use. The dilemma for this small company was obvious. The company had a fine product, a large customer demand for the female condom, and adequate supplies. But, the customer base was extremely poor, and as we have mentioned, governments in countries with high infection rates, at least in Africa, have little or no funds for this or any other product. So Dr. Leeper began finding donor organizations to support supplying this product. She solicited monies from UNAID, USAID, DFID, social marketing organizations that deeply discount products such as condoms, and other international organizations. But even with funding for the product, the company was faced with a second challenge: getting governments in these countries to support or at least not oppose the distribution of the product. And there was a third challenge: training villagers and local health personnel on how to use the product and how to instruct others. By working with NGOs, the Female Health Company is gradually overcoming this problem through training and education, village by village in the 100 countries where it distributes it product (Yemen and Powell 2003). Figure 2 represents this alliance model graphically.

The Female Health Company's Alliance Model

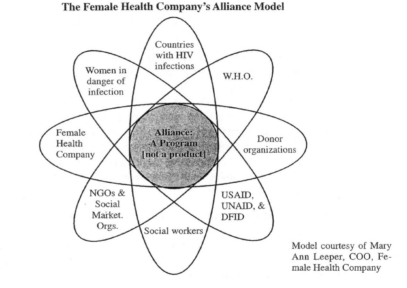

Model courtesy of Mary Ann Leeper, COO, Female Health Company

Figure 2

4.   An evaluative perspective, prioritizing the value priorities of each stakeholder and of the pandemic.

This evaluative approach has been adapted by Merck and the Gates Foundation. Merck has partnered with the Botswana government and Gates Foundation in its HIV project in Botswana. It could not merely give its HIV drug, Crixivan, away, even if it were willing to do so. Although Botswana has better medical facilities and a more stable government than most of the rest of sub-Saharan Africa, its complex culture is such that education, medical infrastructures, and monitoring are not adequate, nor are tribal traditions aligned with modern medical treatment (Weber, Austin, and Barrett 2001).

INTELLECTUAL PROPERTY RIGHTS AND ACCESS TO DRUGS 609

5. A multi-stakeholder model for structural change that will attack and work
    to alleviate the pandemic by distributing [but not avoiding] the risks and
    responsibilities.

In Tanzania, Abbott Laboratories Fund has partnered with the Tanzanian government
and the Axios Foundation (a U.S. NGO) in a multi-year multi-million dollar project to
upgrade and improve the medical care infrastructure, train health care professionals,
and to expand access to treatment for HIV infected citizens (Abbott 2003).

An alliance model entails thinking of IP as a shared right and the enterprise of
distribution as a program, not merely as delivering a product. Employing this model
requires proactive corporate initiatives, because these initiatives have not been forthcoming by those countries with widespread epidemics. One has to find international
donor organizations for funding, elicit government cooperation in the countries most
afflicted with HIV, and work with NGOs to set up delivery, medical, and monitoring
systems. The model requires developing alliances with local and state governments,
NGOs, and donor organizations, and it requires hands-on interaction in the infected
communities. It requires training local villagers to deliver and monitor drug intake.
This is currently being done in Haiti where hundreds of local people are being trained
in the rudiments of drug delivery and sent out to villages daily to deliver and monitor
drug use by the HIV infected (Dugger 2003: 1). This model is also being tried by
the World Health Organization in a number of other countries (Altman 2003: A6).
And of course, companies have to provide the drugs and monitor the process of delivery and use themselves. Otherwise the drugs will go onto the black market or into
the hands of unscrupulous people. Without a systems approach the Female Health
Company, Merck, Abbott, and even the Gates Foundation will fail, whether or not
IP is preserved. And such an approach requires a great deal of moral imagination to
think "out of the box" so to speak, that one's consumers are not paying customers,
that product distribution requires more than merely marketing or sales, and that even
charity—giving products away—is not always a good solution.

A hands-on alliance approach to drug distribution in LDCs protects company
patents and insures that products are to be used properly and by those for whom the
program is aimed, because companies are in control of distribution and use. At the same
time it acknowledges limits to IP rights by sharing its products (and in some cases, as
in Brazil, its processes). But is it unfair to those of us who pay full price for drugs or
who pay for this giveaway through buying other expensive drugs? We would argue
that it would be unfair if we lived in a global egalitarian society where everything is
distributed equally and if we adapted that model as the fairest for distributive justice.
But we neither live nor will live in such a society, nor, as Ronald Dworkin argued some
years ago, is equal distribution always the fairest method. Dworkin argues, in brief,
that the fairest means of societal distribution is not based merely on equality but rather
on the principle of treating every individual as an equal. So for example, if I have a
small supply of medicine and three children, I give the medicine to the sickest. This
is because that sick child is disadvantaged and needs to be brought up to the healthy
status of the others (Dworkin 1977: 273). Similarly providing transportation to people

who otherwise cannot get to the voting booths is not unfair to those who can for the same reasons. So those indigent people dying of HIV/AIDS are owed more than the rest of us just to bring them up to the same level, that is, the level of the living. This would be unfair only if they could provide for themselves; but they cannot.

Despite good moral reasons for engaging in such programs, we might ask the more practical question of "why do this?" Pharmaceutical companies are not responsible for the HIV/AIDS pandemic. Nor are their corporate charters located in any of the most infected countries. How can we hold companies responsible for something they did not do in out-of-the-way places where they have no customer base? From a practical point of view, these programs take a great deal of time, effort, and ingenuity, and positive outcomes are slow to be realized. In Botswana, for example, so far, Merck and the Gates Foundation are providing treatment for only about 40,000 HIV-infected persons (Goering 2005). In Tanzania, Abbott has only begun to make a difference for the two million HIV-infected persons in that country (Abbott 2004). Other companies who are engaging in these processes are also finding that this enterprise is enormously difficult.

HIV/AIDS is a worldwide pandemic that endangers all of us. It is an infectious disease, with ever-evolving new biological forms. So even from a self-interested perspective, companies and countries that can participate in this process should do so if only for their own long-term interests. We are all threatened by this disease. HIV/AIDS is destroying the young middle-class population in sub-Saharan Africa. This is a tragic loss to these economies, a loss to companies marketing to these people, and a long-term loss to global economic development, so important for free enterprise.

From the point of view of the importance of IP, pharmaceutical companies depend on the creativity of others as data from which new drugs are developed. While they need to recoup their expenses and profit from drug development, they have obligations as a result of the interdependence of ideas. And by protecting rather than sharing, they may create an anticommons for the development of a new drug. So the fact of IP creates obligations to others and to oneself. Finally, pharmaceutical companies and their sisters in biotech define themselves as being in the business of *health care*. To have developed a drug that actually prolongs lives of very sick people and then to disregard the needs of indigent ill patients belies the very mission, the heart, of these companies. Thus, those with viable drug treatments cannot ignore this need.

Conclusion

Jefferson's goal in setting up the U.S. patent system was to provide limited protection for the innovator in exchange for publication of the idea, in a form where others could improve on it. Following his lead, we conclude that intellectual property is a form of community-developed property with naming opportunities and limited rights for the final discoverer/creator, but not absolute rights to further development and use. Exclusive proprietary control of knowledge ignores the distinctive features of intellectual property as forms of innovation with many historical, social, and cultural ancestors and thousands of parents, cousins, sisters, brothers, and aunts. Moreover,

INTELLECTUAL PROPERTY RIGHTS AND ACCESS TO DRUGS 611

from a rights perspective, when millions of lives are at stake, not to share benefits is morally unthinkable.

Such a conclusion assumes that intellectual property protection is a prima facie right that is important, but not inviolable. It is advisable for societies to grant certain IP rights in order to stimulate creativity, but these societies have the obligations to acknowledge the interdependence of IP and to create barriers to anticommons that either prevent the development of new ideas or preclude drug distribution to needy ill communities.

HIV/AIDS is not simply a problem for countries with high infection rates. It is a disease that is spreading worldwide. It is a global issue that requires a global systems approach. Drug distribution is not merely the responsibility of companies who have these drugs; yet because HIV is controllable with drugs, it is a responsibility they cannot avoid. The HIV/AIDS pandemic represents an international emergency analogous to, but much larger than, the anthrax scare, where individual rights may have to be overruled—but where it is reasonable for the individual firm to expect to be involved in a partnership and to formulate some protection for its patents. Networked thinking about IP and a systems alliance model can achieve these ends. The challenge today is to operationalize these alliances globally before the projections of 100 million HIV deaths becomes a reality.

Notes

1.   Some of this thinking was stimulated by Bryan Maxwell from his unpublished thesis at the University of Virginia: "Access to Life: The Conflict between Public Health and Intellectual Property Protections on HIV/AIDS Drugs in Developing Countries," 2002. We also want to thank the editors of *Business Ethics Quarterly*, and, in particular, George Brenkert, for extensive editorial suggestions for this paper, as well as Michael Ryan, who is editing this special issue. A different version of the paper will be published in *Ethics and the Pharmaceutical Industry*, ed. Michael Santoro. Cambridge: Cambridge University Press, 2006.

2.   Copyright laws protect the ownership name, but give the right to copy, with the proper citation. But patent laws are different, since with a patent one controls the right to share or copy the information! Similarly, registered trademarks protect the trademark for owner use only.

3.   Hardin argued that we ordinarily overuse unowned, public, or shared resources since they are "free" to each of us and thus no one has incentives to conserve (Hardin 1968).

References

Abbott Laboratories. 2003. "Tanzania Care." www.tanzaniacare.org.
———. 2004. *Touching Lives: 2003 Global Citizenship Report*.
Altman, Lawrence K. 2003. "W.H.O. Aims to Treat 3 Million for AIDS." *New York Times* (December 1), A6.
Attaran, Amir, and Lee Gillespie-White. 2001. "Do Patents for Antiretroviral Drugs Constrain Access to Treatment in Africa?" *Journal of the American Medical Association* 286: 1886–92.

Bale, Harvey E., Jr. 2002. "Patents and Public Health: A Good or Bad Mix?" *Pfizer Forum*, www.pfizerforum.com.

Bollier, David, Stephanie Weiss, and Kirk Hanson. 1991. "Merck &. Co, Inc.," Harvard Business School Case 9-991-021.

Clemente, C. L. 2001. "Intellectual Property: The Patent on Prosperity." *Pfizer Forum*, www.pfizerforum.com/english/clemente/shtml.

Curti, Andrea M. 2001. "The WTO Dispute Settlement Understanding: An Unlikely Weapon in the Fight Against HIV." *American Journal of Law and Medicine* (December 22): 469–80.

Dugger, Celia W. 2003. "Rural Haitians Are Vanguard in Battle." *New York Times* (November 30), A1.

Dworkin, Ronald. 1977. *Taking Rights Seriously.* Cambridge, Mass.: Harvard University Press.

Felsenthal, Edward. 1993. "Patent Quagmire: Who Invented AZT? Big Bucks Are Riding On What Sleuths Find." *Wall Street Journal* (October 21), 1.

Friedman, Michael A., Henk den Besten, and Amir Attaran. 2003. "Out-Licensing: A Practical Approach for Improvement of Access to Medicines in Poor Countries." *The Lancet* 361: 341–44.

Gentner, Dedre, and Eric W. Whitley. 1997. "Mental Models of Population Growth," in *Environment, Ethics, and Behavior*, ed. Max Bazerman, David Messick, Ann Tenbrunsel, and Kimberley A. Wade-Benzoni. San Francisco: New Lexington Press.

Goering, Laurie. 2005. "Botswana'a Blanket HIV Care Can't Cover All Fears," *Chicago Tribune* (March 6), 1.

Goodman, Kenneth, 1993. "Intellectual Property and Control.": *Academic Medicine* 68(9): 588–92.

Gorman, Michael. 1992. *Simulating Science.* Bloomington: Indiana University Press.

Hardin, Garrett. 1968. "The Tragedy of the Commons." *Science* 162: 1243–45.

Heller, Michael A., and Rebecca S. Eisenberg. 1998. "Can Patents Deter Innovation? The Anticommons in Biomedical Research." *Science* 280: 698–701.

Hughes, James. W., Michael J. Moore, and Edward A. Snyder. 2002. "'Napsterizing' Pharmaceuticals Access, Innovation, and Consumer Welfare." National Bureau of Economic Research Working Paper 9229.

Idris, Kamil. 2003. *Intellectual Property: A Tool for Economic Growth.* Geneva: World Intellectual Property Organization.

Jefferson, Thomas. 1813. "Letter to Isaac McPherson," reprinted in *The Life and Selected Writings of Thomas Jefferson*, ed. A. Kock and W. Peden. New York: Modern Library, 1972.

Locke, John. 1764, 1983. *The Second Treatise of Government*, ed. Peter Laslett. Cambridge: Cambridge University Press.

Maxwell, Bryan. 2002. "Access to Life: The Conflict Between Public Health and Intellectual Property Protections on HIV/AIDS Drugs in Developing Countries." Unpublished thesis, University of Virginia.

Merges, Robert. 1998. "The Control of Strategic Alliances: An Empirical Analysis of Biotechnology Collaborations," *Journal of Industrial Economics* 46: 125–56.

Merges, Robert P., and Richard Nelson. 1990. "On the Complex Economics of Patent Scope." *Columbia Law Review* 90: 832–50.

INTELLECTUAL PROPERTY RIGHTS AND ACCESS TO DRUGS 613

Mitroff, Ian, and Harold Linstone. 1993. *The Unbounded Mind*. New York: Oxford University Press.

Ordover, Janusz A. 1991. "A Patent System for both Diffusion and Exclusion." *Journal of Economics Perspectives* 5: 43–60.

O'Reilly, Kevin. 2003. World Health Organization (WHO) UNAID data. http://www.who/.

Rand, Ayn. 1966. *Capitalism: The Unknown Ideal*. New York: New American Library.

Resnik, D. B. 2003. "A Pluralistic Account of Intellectual Property." *Journal of Business Ethics* 46: 319–35.

Senge, Peter. 1990. *The Fifth Discipline*. New York: Doubleday.

Shue, Henry. 1996. *Basic Rights*, second edition. Princeton, N.J.: Princeton University Press.

Thurow, Lester C. 1997. "Needed: A New System of Intellectual Property Rights." *Harvard Business Review* 75 (September–October): 95–103.

Tuck, Richard. 1979. *Natural Rights Theories*. Cambridge: Cambridge University Press.

Vaver, David. 2000. "Intellectual Property: State of the Art." *Law Quarterly Review* 116: 621–37.

Weber, James, James Austin, and Diana Barrett. 2001. "Merck Global Health Initiatives (B): Botswana." Harvard Business School Case 9-301-089.

Werhane, Patricia H. 1999. *Moral Imagination and Management Decision-Making*. New York: Oxford University Press.

World Bank. 1999. www.worldbank.org.

World Intellectual Property Organization. 2003. "Intellectual Property: A Lever for Economic Growth," *WIPO Magazine* (September/October): 2–8.

Yemen, Gerry, and Elizabeth Powell. 2003. "The Female Health Company (A) and (B)." Charlottesville: University of Virginia, Darden Business Publishing, UVA-BC-0146-7.

Part XIV
Systems (Systemic and Holistic Approaches)

[48]

MANAGERIAL MORAL STRATEGIES—IN SEARCH OF A FEW GOOD PRINCIPLES

EDWARD SOULE
Georgetown University

The goal of this article is to help managers, students, and scholars contend with moral business problems by urging efforts to develop an adequate "managerial moral strategy." Integrative social contract theory (ISCT) is arguably the most promising candidate available, but a critical analysis reveals a shortcoming: it lacks sufficient moral content. Alleviating this weakness requires the formulation of the moral principles applicable to management. Doing so will elevate the usefulness and the influence of ISCT and the business ethics enterprise generally.

BUSINESS ETHICS AND MANAGEMENT PRACTICE

The business ethics enterprise has achieved stunning successes, including a burgeoning body of literature and a place in business school curricula. These accomplishments have come in a relatively short time period, which Bowie (2001: 20) estimates to be no more than twenty-five years. But these academic achievements have not translated into similar successes in terms of influence on management practice—at least the influence is less pronounced than in some kindred fields of practical or applied philosophy (e.g., biomedical ethics). This disappointment has more explanations than it does solutions, and this brief discussion is not, in and of itself, a remedy. Rather, it contributes to a solution by highlighting a weakness in the business ethics literature and by urging and detailing a new emphasis for future research. To date, the business ethics literature is of two varieties: some authors focus on isolated commercial practices, whereas others take aim at the entire range of commercial and managerial practices. Of interest here is the latter variety because, if successful, these comprehensive moral frameworks hold the promise of enhancing the useful-

ness and thereby increasing the influence of business ethics on the practice of management.

These comprehensive moral frameworks, which I refer to here as *managerial moral strategies* (or, simply, *moral strategies*), provide systematic *analysis, criticism,* and *guidance* relative to business decisions. Among other things, analysis involves identifying the morally salient factors of a given case. Criticism and guidance require an argument about what morality demands in the precise context of an individual case. Several scholars have advanced competing projects that differ in terms of their moral justification or the basis upon which they claim moral authority and command obedience.[1] Some, referred to as *monastic moral strategies,* appeal to the authority of one (but only one) of the major moral theorists of philosophy: Aristotle, in the case of Solomon (1992, 1999), and Kant, in the case of Bowie (1999). Others appeal to a philosophical school of thought: social contract theory, in the case of Donaldson and Dunfee

I thank Tom Beauchamp, George Brenkert, Larry May, Dennis Quinn, and Cathy Tinsley, for reviewing different versions of this paper, and associate editor Arthur Brief, for his patient guidance. This paper has also benefited from the thoughtful criticism of three anonymous *AMR* reviewers.

[1] I ignore the most primitive such strategies found in introductory business ethics textbooks. Derived from the "traditional" moral theories of philosophy, these strategies are hobbled by their abstract complexity and lack of coherence. In a survey of this literature, Derry and Green (1989) note nine different approaches to overcome these flaws. Since that survey several creative efforts have been advanced (Beauchamp & Bowie, 1993: 43; Boatright, 1993: 25; Dienhart, 2000: 126) that are appropriate for the constraints of an introductory textbook. But the moral strategies discussed here, free of these constraints, hold more promise for practical application.

(1994, 1995, 1999), and American pragmatism, in the case of Buchholz and Rosenthal (1998) and Rosenthal and Buchholz (2000). All of these projects are important contributions, and none deserves idle criticism. However, for the sake of the business ethics enterprise, it is desirable that at least one of them satisfy the pedagogical and practical requirements that business students and managers could reasonably expect of them. Yet, there are reasons to doubt whether any do. In the interest of space, I contend only with Donaldson and Dunfee's integrative social contract theory (ISCT), arguably the most prominent and promising of the group.[2]

I begin by proposing and defending criteria for an adequate moral strategy. I then subject ISCT to these criteria and explain why it fails to satisfy them. The failure is one of normative content—the moral standards, principles, or values the theory advances. I argue that the normative content of ISCT is too vague to serve the needs of students and practitioners. However, vagueness can be cured, and I argue that doing so will require formulating moral principles—not as one among several possible remedies but as perhaps the only conceivable way to simultaneously respect the commitments of ISCT but also to realize its significant promise. It is beyond the scope of this paper to develop those principles. Hopefully, by identifying this problem and by pinpointing the nature of the solution, future researchers will formulate the moral principles applicable to management.

To differentiate this investigation from the hoary debate regarding corporate social responsibility, I offer one brief point of clarification. In one of the more subtle treatments of this debate, Hasnas (1998) claims that there are three normative theories in the business ethics literature: stockholder, stakeholder, and social contract. Albeit popular in the literature, there are two reasons for ignoring this taxonomy in the context of this investigation. First, Hasnas is interested in a narrow issue: whether business has any "social responsibility," meaning "ethical obligations . . . to expend business resources in ways that do not promote the specific purposes

for which the business is organized" (1998: 21). Although this is an important and interesting question, it does not exhaust the universe of moral business problems. Moral strategies (like ISCT) address this broader range of problems—from workplace diversity to bribery.

But, second, as Hasnas aptly explains these theories, it is apparent that two of them—stockholder and stakeholder—are not moral theories in and of themselves. Rather, they are morally agnostic management strategies. Asserting that either of them has moral standing—that managers are morally obliged to follow one or the other—requires an argument based on a moral and not a strategic reason. For example, this is what Evan and Freeman (1995) do when they appeal to (Kant's) respect for persons as a reason why stakeholder theory is morally required. That such an appeal is necessary is evidence that stakeholder theory provides no moral significance independent of Kant's or someone else's ethics. Managerial moral strategies are self-contained projects; they provide users with the resources to evaluate the morality of managerial models like stockholder or stakeholder theory. But the two should not be confused.

CRITERIA FOR ADEQUACY

I begin by asking "What is the purpose of a moral strategy and why bother to develop one in the first place?" Warnock (1971) claims that moral theorizing is worth the effort if it promises to relieve what he calls the "human predicament." Relative to the commercial world, this predicament can be derived from two observations. First, business involves a competitive struggle for scarce resources (be they material possessions, positions, status, power, and so forth), and, as is the case with most human struggles, opportunities abound for harmful wrongdoing and injustice. Second, some of the rewards of commercial competition are so crucial to living a good life that most people are obliged to engage in the struggle. In a similar vein, Frankena argues that promoting "some kind of cooperation or social activity between human beings" is the proper end of morality (1970: 158). Based on these and other such results-based views, moral strategies would be worth the effort if, at a minimum, they could

---

[2] As evidence for this claim, a special issue of *Business & Society Review* was devoted to ISCT, and a special edition of *Business Ethics Quarterly* was devoted to social contract theory, in which ISCT received special attention. I thank an anonymous *AMR* reviewer for reminding me of this.

contribute to relieving the pernicious aspects of commercial life (e.g., harm and injustice).

So what must a moral strategy be and how must it function in order to minimize the ill effects of commercial behavior? As a tool for analysis and criticism, it should illuminate, clarify, and thereby direct attention to the moral stakes in business decisions. But also, as a useful guide, it should have something to say about what morality demands in particular circumstances. Yet, as DeGeorge (1999: 20) emphasizes, such guidance is only possible if decision makers are confronted with legitimate and compelling moral reasons for behaving one way versus another. Accordingly, as explained below in greater detail, these four criteria (there may be others) are, in order, comprehension, comprehensiveness, specificity, and contextual relevance. Without satisfying these criteria it is unlikely that a moral strategy will provide a basis for satisfactory analysis, criticism, and guidance. In one way or another, the authors of moral strategies endorse some or all of these criteria and advance them as reasons why their project is superior to the others. Accordingly, they are not intended to be contentious or to somehow unfairly "stack the deck."

Comprehension

Students and managers must be able to understand a moral strategy if they are to use it to analyze, criticize, or guide business decisions. For this reason, Solomon (1999) urges a moral strategy based on virtue ethics because it is cast in the language of inspiration and excellence—familiar concepts to people in business. Likewise, Donaldson and Dunfee (1999: viii) cite management familiarity with the language of social contract theory—obligation and responsibility—as a virtue of ISCT. Alternatively, Solomon derides a strategy based on Kantian ethics as inaccessible and impractical insofar as "we [ordinary people] don't actually do ethics that way" (1992: 83). If those intended to use a moral strategy cannot understand what it means, much less what is expected of them, its intended purpose is illusive at best.

Comprehensiveness

Beauchamp and Childress (1994: 30) explain that solving moral problems involves identify-

ing a specific norm that commands one's obedience in the special context of a particular case. And, as Donaldson and Dunfee observe, "Managers are situated in a web of (sometimes) conflicting loyalties and duties—some legal (contractual and otherwise) and others personal (e.g., friendships, familial obligations, and so forth)" (1995: 87). Consequently, it is imperative that any systematic approach to solving moral business problems provide a sufficiently broad range of normative content to contend with this complexity; it cannot be simplistic or one dimensional. Business cases often involve several morally salient factors, and adequacy demands that a moral strategy be comprehensive in terms of the norms that it brings to bear on concrete cases. Simplistic exhortations about not lying and cheating are grossly inadequate. But so are any other approaches that fail to incorporate the full range of moral language and justifiable moral intuitions and norms that business actors legitimately employ.

Specificity

But, by the same token, a moral strategy should be specific in terms of what counts as a morally salient factor in a case—what it is that should be identified and picked out of the myriad facts and circumstances of a business event. If a moral strategy is to explain and contribute to the solution of moral problems, it must engage clearly explicated norms. But such content cannot be unlimited. Judgments regarding rules, practices, policies, punishments, rewards, and so forth are the everyday fare of business. To the extent that they are moral judgments, the people making them cannot be expected to consider an overly burdensome number of alternatives. Thus, beyond clarity, people need a limited number of moral considerations. A criterion of specificity or definiteness does not imply simplistic or trite rules, and it does not imply that being specific by limiting the universe of applicable norms will automatically resolve every difficult moral problem. Some of them defy resolution by any means. The claim is a more humble one that an adequate moral strategy needs some limit in terms of the extent of relevant moral content.

The preceding criterion of comprehensiveness ensures that specificity will not degenerate into oversimplification. These two criteria—compre-

2002 *Soule* 117

hensiveness and specificity—combine to require sufficient depth of moral content with limits based on the realities of practical application.

Contextual Relevance

Finally, an adequate moral strategy needs to be relevant to the context of commercial life. Marcus Singer (1961) argues that circumstances (in part) dictate moral obligations, and the more special the circumstances, the more specific the resulting moral duties are. The importance of context is reflected in Solomon's view that a moral strategy should take into account the "ground-level, role-specific aspects of one's position in the company and, at the same time, one's place in the overall community" (1992: 163). Of course, this means that a moral strategy must address the complicated loyalties and obligations of some business roles. But it also means that the relationship between business, society writ large, and the law must be considered. Some ethical issues are confronted by business people as individuals. Others are confronted by society and are occasionally resolved by law—commercial regulation in particular. Adequacy demands that a strategy be relevant to the entire context in which a business operates.

ISCT

As the name implies, ISCT derives its moral authority from contracts or consensual agreements among free parties. But its authors acknowledge that some voluntarily agreed upon practices are immoral. To guard against such morally rogue agreements, ISCT's authors develop a higher-order normative authority—hypernorms—as the ultimate arbiter of moral legitimacy. So, consensual agreements among business people (microsocial contracts) enjoy only prima facie (or tentative) moral standing. They can be overridden by hypernorms (macrosocial contracts) or the "norms by which all others are to be judged" (Donaldson & Dunfee, 1999: 44).

This is a good strategy insofar as it situates ISCT between two combatants in an internecine philosophical battle. On one side are philosophical liberals with strong attachments to the individual—his or her freedom and rights. On the other side are communitarians who criticize liberals for (supposedly) failing to appreciate the crucial role that communities play in constituting the individual and the legitimate commitments that individuals have to them.

By granting moral legitimacy to locally emergent norms but subjecting those norms to the higher-order test of hypernorms, ISCT carefully maneuvers its way across this philosophical minefield. Moreover, this strategy puts ISCT beyond harm's way of some potentially fatal criticism of moral relativism, the theory that ethical questions should be understood only in the context of particular communities and not universally. Hypernorms answer that criticism, and for these and other reasons, ISCT holds significant promise.

However, this strategy also makes ISCT less of a social contract theory than most other projects in that tradition of political philosophy. Hypernorms do the moral "heavy lifting" within ISCT by providing the foundational justification for why ISCT should command obedience. Traditionally, social contract theorists have assigned this role to something else: human nature, for Hobbes (1946), and human rationality, for Rawls (1971). Consequently, hypernorms deserve special attention. Although there are three different types of hypernorms—procedural, structural, and substantive—the focus here is on the substantive ones that "specify fundamental conceptions of the right and the good" (Donaldson & Dunfee, 1999: 52). They are defined as

> a thin universal morality, principles so fundamental that, by definition, they serve to evaluate lower-order norms. Defined in this way and reaching to the root of what is ethical for humanity, precepts we choose to call "hypernorms" should be discernible in a convergence of religious, political, and philosophical thought, or at least it is a reasonable hope that we should discern such a convergence (Donaldson & Dunfee, 1999: 43).

Later, the definition is modified slightly to provide that "the convergence of religious, cultural, and philosophical beliefs around certain core principles [is] an important *clue* to the identification of hypernorms" (Donaldson & Dunfee, 1999: 59; emphasis added).

Some have found fault with ISCT on the (supposed) basis that hypernorms amount to mere convention (Mayer, 1994; Mayer & Cava, 1995; Rynning, 1996). In light of the imperial role hypernorms play within ISCT, this criticism strikes

118   *Academy of Management Review*   January

at the moral justification for the entire strategy. The authors of ISCT respond that

> whatever the final answer to the question of whether hypernorms have sources in nature as immutable verities, or instead reflect the common humanity of global citizens as similar solutions are found to shared problems across the world, that answer is not critical to their value within ISCT. Instead, their existence is specified and recognized within the macrosocial contract, enabling decision makers to engage in a search for relevant hypernorms within given contexts. The importance of the concept and its role within ISCT is sufficient to allow for some ambiguity in their specification and identification (Donaldson & Dunfee, 1999: 52).

This debate over the moral justification of hypernorms will not be settled here. I rehearse it as a way to uncover a more profound problem: although the authors of ISCT argue at length about why hypernorms should command moral authority, and notwithstanding the ample criteria, sources (philosophic and otherwise), and methodology for identifying them, they do not specify them. One "structural" hypernorm (necessary social efficiency) is thoroughly explicated, and several procedural hypernorms (e.g., rights of voice and exit) are spelled out. But the all-important "substantive" hypernorms—those conceiving the right and the good that stand in judgment of all other norms (including the structural and procedural hypernorms)—are only abstractly described or tentatively suggested (e.g., respecting human dignity).

The final sentence in the foregoing quote admits to some "ambiguity" in the "specification and identification" of hypernorms, but this is a serious understatement. In fact, ISCT only describes hypernorms and provides a methodology for locating them. Until these hypernorms are identified and explicated, ISCT will be a very thorough, enlightening, and important exercise in moral justification, but it will fail to satisfy criteria of specificity and comprehension applicable to an adequate moral strategy. Consequently, it is questionable whether the theory can meet the practical needs of users trying to make morally problematic decisions.

To illustrate this flaw, consider the example (Donaldson & Dunfee, 1999: 61) of the Saudi practice of excluding women from certain occupations. In defending the possibility of locating a relevant hypernorm, the authors of ISCT make reference to the "standards of the United Na-

tions, the International Labor Organization, the laws of many countries, major philosophies, and religions" (Donaldson & Dunfee, 1999: 61–62). Based on the presumptive moral authority of these sources and their "convergence" on a standard of economic opportunity, Donaldson and Dunfee conclude that "the hypernorm [of holding the Saudi practice morally illegitimate] is established" (1999: 61–62). Some (Husted, 1996; Mayer & Cava, 1995; Shaw, 2000) have argued that identifying hypernorms is not nearly so straightforward, but the authors of ISCT have responded that it can be as long as the issue is clearly specified (as is, say, the denial of economic opportunity) and if one is willing to perform rigorous empirical investigation of the relevant sources (Donaldson & Dunfee, 1999: 63–68).

This dispute is telling. If informed scholars have difficulty and disagreements over the identification of hypernorms, it may be unrealistic to expect managers or students to root them out successfully. One need not object to the fundamental assertion of ISCT—that hypernorms are "out there" if we just look for them—to find this portion of the project troubling. The task of identifying hypernorms is not a simple one, and for the following three reasons it is inadvisable to consign their search to ISCT users, whether they be scholars, students, or managers.

First, the sources suggested for finding hypernorms (Donaldson & Dunfee, 1999: 69–73) are neither readily accessible nor easily understood. In the case of employment discrimination, neither United Nations (UN) standards nor pronouncements of the International Labor Organization (ILO) are obvious to everyone. And particularly in the case of UN documents, burdened with florid and cryptic bureaucratic language as they are, discerning normative guidance is not always easy. Moreover, as related by some (Bell, 1996; Iyer, 1999; Moody, 1996; Perry, 1997), there are reasons to question the international consensus claimed in some UN pronouncements.

Second, in ISCT it is assumed that nongovernmental organizations (NGOs) are at least a tentative source of hypernorms (provided they converge on other widely embraced norms). But considering the nature of NGOs and their incessant proliferation, there are reasons to doubt their moral authority and to dash any hopes for consensus. For almost every NGO, including the ILO, there is an ideologically opposite NGO—for every "Greenpeace" there is a "Chlorine Chemistry Council." Yet users of ISCT are asked to view these organizations as sources of normative guidance when their pronouncements converge. To the extent that this is a rarity for most commercial disputes, NGOs seem to invite as much confusion as they do resolution of complex moral problems.

Third, ISCT contains an important empirical element: observing various sources of normative guidance (philosophical guidance, religious guidance, NGO pronouncements, and so forth) in order to find convergence around a single norm. If one can demonstrate that a norm is widely held and endorsed from several different sources, then one can at least tentatively qualify it as a substantive hypernorm. This is the feature of ISCT that has been criticized as dangerously close to treating morality as convention. But from a practical standpoint, empirical investigations of this sort raise concerns that are perhaps more worrisome than are accusations of conventionalism. The chances for carelessly or opportunistically locating wrong, rogue, or conveniently self-serving hypernorms are significant. At a minimum, these three reasons suggest that identifying hypernorms could be much more complicated and fraught with the risk of error and manipulation than the authors of ISCT suggest.

Specificity and comprehension demand that an adequate moral strategy provide the operative norms—not only a methodology for developing and justifying them or an abstract description. For the unconvinced, consider what is perhaps the hallmark of twentieth-century political philosophy, *A Theory of Justice* (Rawls, 1971). This work can be understood as performing two interrelated and fully dependent tasks: it carefully justifies (morally) what justice consists of, *and* it specifies the principles of political justice. Moral justification occupies most of the book, as Rawls develops theoretical claims, models, devices, and procedures (i.e., the original position, the veil of ignorance, and a formalized account of human reason) for testing claims about justice. Now, imagine that Rawls had provided this elaborate justification of political justice but left it to his readers to discern the operative principles. That is, suppose that his readers had to determine which principles of justice the free and rational deliberators behind the veil of ignorance would choose.

Had Rawls done this, his book would remain a potent framework as to how one morally justi-

fies political justice. But readers of *A Theory of Justice* would not necessarily arrive at the same principles of justice as Rawls (e.g., equality of basic rights and the difference principle). And readers would not necessarily conclude that justice demands the same basic political institutions that follow from Rawls' principles of justice. In short, without cogently specifying the principles, *A Theory of Justice* would not be ambiguous so much as it would be a partial account of political justice.

The specific normative content—principles of justice—cannot be derived in any straightforward manner from the framework Rawls constructs to morally justify them. Moral justification is important because it gives moral authority to the content—in this case, the principles of justice. Likewise, ISCT mounts a rigorous justification for why hypernorms should command obedience and why microsocial contracts should be subservient to them. But it does not specify them. Consequently, the debate over whether hypernorms are morally justified or not is a distraction from the more fundamental problem that ISCT lacks normative content where it needs it most—at the commanding height of substantive hypernorms.

Notwithstanding the tone of this discussion, my criticism does not suggest a fatal flaw in ISCT but, rather, a missing piece. Its authors set out to *describe* and *justify* ISCT (Donaldson & Dunfee, 1999: 74), a daunting and humbling endeavor as philosophical projects go, and their accomplishment is beyond admirable. But description and justification are different from and cannot be substituted for normative content if a moral strategy is to serve as a guide. Simply put, users have to do things in deriving moral content that are inherently prone to error, selfish opportunism, and so forth. In the case of managers, ISCT requires that they do things that they have not been trained, nor are inclined, to do. Having said all of this, I also believe that the authors' thoughtful construction of ISCT and the literature that has followed in its wake provide the resources and methodology to remedy this weakness.

AN APPEAL FOR MORAL PRINCIPLES

Thus far, ISCT has been characterized as a framework or a methodology for morally justifying the normative elements of a moral strategy, which should prompt the question "Just exactly what would count as sufficient normative content for a moral strategy?" Answering this question requires briefly retracing the genesis of ISCT. In its nascent formulation the authors of ISCT expressed frustration with extant business ethics projects and set about remedying the situation (Donaldson & Dunfee, 1995). It is fair to assume that they rejected the possibility that *moral rules* (say, to tell the truth) could contend with the complexity and novelty of actual cases. And they explicitly rejected two of the traditional *moral theories*—one as overly general and the other for its (putatively) unrealistic cognitive demands.

Now, if moral rules are too narrow and moral theories are too general or burdensome, what remains? Between moral rules and moral theories are *moral principles*. I say (metaphorically) "between" because in one direction a moral principle serves to generate specific rules, and in the other direction it is justified by a moral theory (or by more than one of them). Incorporating moral principles into the framework of ISCT—by substituting them for hypernorms—remedies its indeterminacy in an important way. ISCT is a thoroughgoing moral justification, and justification is the hard part of developing a moral strategy. The substitution of moral principles for the conceptual apparatus of hypernorms preserves the moral foundations of ISCT but adds the clarity and specificity presently lacking in the project.

Defending this claim requires spelling out why and how moral principles would provide useful normative content to ISCT. Recall the above assertion that ISCT unrealistically and dangerously burdens its users with the chore of picking through the common morality in search of hypernorms. Consider now that this account is wrong, and instead assume that with proper training, access to the relevant literature, and the fullness of time, hypernorms *are* discoverable without risk of confusion or error. Imagine then that an expert group were to set about to locate them, not hypothetically but in response to difficult managerial problems—those outstripping their microsocial norms. Over time it is possible that they would successfully identify dozens of hypernorms before exhausting their consensus-making abilities. But dozens of hypernorms, many of which would be repetitious, might be cumbersome. So suppose that for ease of use or for pedagogical purposes, the list were

classified in some meaningful and useful way—perhaps according to essential moral cores—and culled of any duplications. Eventually, if these categories were spelled out with sufficient detail, they could be made to stand for the individual hypernorms included in them without loss of meaning. Emerging from this imaginary exercise would be a handful of principles, morally justified to the same extent that ISCT justifies the constituent hypernorms. This thought experiment is not offered as a realistic way to generate the moral principles applicable to business. Rather, it illustrates the near seamless relationship between moral principles and hypernorms, making clear how the substitution of moral principles for hypernorms leaves the vast majority of ISCT unscathed.

Creating these moral principles would appear to transform ISCT in at least three important ways. First, if the principles were clearly stated and limited in number, the project would become specific and comprehendible. Users would have substantive references for what was ultimately morally required, forbidden, or permissible. Local microsocial contracts would retain their prima facie moral standing, only now they would need to satisfy the criticism of overarching norms that were definite. Second, since the range of cases used to trigger hypernorm searches would be unlimited, it is reasonable to expect that the principles themselves would be comprehensive in nature. That is, these principles would not be constructed in the abstract but in reaction to genuine moral disputes. Finally, because the moral principles would have emerged from business cases, they would be relevant to the commercial context. In short, these moral principles would cause ISCT to satisfy the criteria for adequacy that were developed earlier.

This exercise is not a fussy concern for parsimony or ease of use. Moral principles remedy other practical limitations of hypernorms. For one, they eliminate the confusion of routine searches and the possibility of locating a rogue hypernorm. Of course, the choice of principles will raise criticism of another sort (are they the "right" ones?), but these are charges that can be defended against based on the principles themselves and how well they perform in practice. Very important, there is evidence in a kindred field of practical ethics—biomedical ethics—that debate over the "right" principles and their interpretation does not impair the effectiveness of the project itself. Such is the case in the work of Beauchamp and Childress (1994), where substantive progress in the standing and influence of this field of study was advanced by specifying and then debating the operative moral principles.

Second, moral principles offer clarity, which an abstract description of a hypernorm cannot. As an illustration, consider that hypernorms are described in one part of ISCT (Donaldson & Dunfee, 1999: 44) as having to satisfy Walzer's (1994) idea of a thin or minimal moral precept that everyone everywhere would agree to. These are explained as *negative* injunctions against killing, lying, and so forth. But then in another part of ISCT (Donaldson & Dunfee, 1999: 70), benevolence, which is hardly a negative injunction, appears as a source for generating hypernorms. Which is it? This is not a criticism of ISCT but a reflection on the difficulties of trying to describe without specifying moral content. Conflicts of this nature are inevitable at the descriptive level. Moral principles greatly reduce this conceptual confusion by making explicit the demands of morality, rather than suggesting their sources.

Third and finally, it is very difficult to move from either the definition and description or the sources and foundations of hypernorms to concrete business applications. A case in point is the hypernorm source that "[we must come to] the realization of [the importance of] benevolence" (Donaldson & Dunfee, 1999: 70). Few would challenge the moral standing of benevolence, but it is not clear what benevolence means in the context of a commercial enterprise. Ideally, the "benevolence hypernorm" needs to be contextualized to business by saying what it means in terms of management responsibility. Because hypernorms are universal constructs "reaching to the root of what is ethical for humanity," they are only a first approximation of normative content. They still require elaboration as to the context. But contextualizing a hypernorm seems tantamount to reformulating it as a moral principle.

Notwithstanding the merits of substituting moral principles for hypernorms, it is quite probable that the authors of ISCT would strenuously object to doing so. Accordingly, I now address these possible objections, beginning with the worry about narrowing morality down to simplistic theories and the expressed preference for the indeterminate and open nature of hypernorms (Donaldson & Dunfee, 1999: 12). While this fear may be legitimate with regard to traditional moral theories, it is misplaced when leveled against a group of moral principles. Articulating moral principles does not close a moral strategy to subsequent modification, and it does not limit the range of moral reasons that can be brought to bear on a problem. Although moral principles might be few in number, they could be constructed with a breadth equal to the hypernorms of ISCT.

Consider the tables of presumptive hypernorm foundations provided for users of ISCT (Donaldson & Dunfee, 1999: 70–73). A review of these sources reveals them be so repetitious that a handful of moral principles could capture the entire list. Sometimes the difference is simply a function of saying the same thing through two different disciplines. For instance, Hans Kung's theological invocation that "we share a sense of the sacredness of the individual person and his conscience" (Donaldson & Dunfee, 1999: 70) overlaps the references to Immanuel Kant's philosophical account of the same thing. A principle of *respecting the autonomy of persons*, spelled out in the context of managerial responsibility, would capture both. The Institute of Moralogy's statement that "[we must come to] the realization of [the importance of] benevolence" (Donaldson & Dunfee, 1999: 70) is captured by a principle that sets forth the meaning of *beneficence* in a commercial context. And such a principle would subsume many other references on the list. The reference to Henry Shue's enumeration of basic human needs (Donaldson & Dunfee, 1990: 73) falls under a principle of *justice* that, when made relevant to business, could capture several other of these sample hypernorm sources. The hypernorm sources provided in ISCT are quite thoughtful and extensive, and they appear to be much more open than moral principles could possibly be. But they need not be if the principles are carefully formulated.

Another reason the authors of ISCT would resist substituting moral principles for hypernorms is their view that by leaving the moral content unspecified, the theory is more open and accommodating to evolutionary changes in morality (Donaldson & Dunfee, 1999: 94). However, whether this is the case or not cannot be decided on theoretical grounds. The answer depends upon the principles themselves. If by "moral principles" an adamantine commandment of eternal duration is meant, then, of course, hypernorms would be more accommodating of a constantly emerging morality. But if, instead, the moral principles were formulated as revisable in light of ongoing evidence, deliberation, and use, then they would be equally accommodative. The notion that hypernorms are more responsive to the progression of morality than rigidly constructed moral *theories* is right. The notion that they are more responsive than moral principles depends on the characterization of the principles selected.

Alternatively, the authors of ISCT might resist moral principles for fear that those principles would impose the wrong sort of moral reasoning. They favor the process of seeking out hypernorms, because doing so "is more likely to produce results than a top-down analysis in which a simple, preexisting 'definitive' list of hypernorms is used with deductive reasoning" (Donaldson & Dunfee, 1999: 75). Now, as discussed above, there are reasons to be skeptical about whether hypernorm searches would function in this idealized fashion. But even so, it is wrong to think that ISCT avoids top-down deductive reasoning while the specification of moral principles does not. ISCT clearly avoids deductive reasoning in the *search* for hypernorms. But, then again, most any nontheological moral principle is nondeductive in that sense. For instance, the above thought experiment to derive moral principles from imaginary hypernorms was not a deductive affair. Rather, those principles emerged by considering concrete cases and then proceeding outward to the common morality. Therefore, this sense of deduction—in formulation—does not apply to moral principles any more than it does to hypernorms.

If, instead, the criticism of deductive reasoning refers to the *application* of normative guidance, it is not clear that ISCT avoids being deductive. In the case of gender discrimination, the conclusion that the Saudi practice of gender discrimination is morally illegitimate could be formulated as a deductive argument, with the hypernorm of equality of opportunity serving as the major premise. Any moral obligation that includes a moral rule, commandment, or even a hypernorm can be expressed deductively. Moral principles do not automatically impose a top-

down approach anymore than hypernorms do. In all likelihood, moral principles and hypernorms are subject to constant adjustment over time and use through a process of Rawlsian reflective equilibrium.[3] Such a process is neither top down nor bottom up; it is both.

Also, the authors of ISCT could reject moral principles on the grounds that these principles violate their communitarian attachments (Donaldson & Dunfee, 1999: 38). One goal of ISCT is to provide "moral free space" or the latitude for microsocial contracts to emerge from local cultures and practices, uninhibited by overarching principles of a fixed and determinate nature. Although the act of identifying hypernorms constrains this "space" to some degree, the authors of ISCT worry that specifying them in any thoroughgoing way is unnecessarily restrictive. But, once again, this cannot be settled ex ante. The moral principles generated in the hypothetical process described above would not diminish moral free space anymore than hypernorms would—the principles are simply another form of hypernorms. The respect for moral free space does not preclude substituting moral principles for hypernorms; it establishes *criteria* for their formulation.

There is one final reason why moral principles might be rejected as an inappropriate addition to ISCT. The ISCT authors worry that the moral conflicts in international business make it impossible to prescribe any universal constructs (Donaldson & Dunfee, 1999: 19). They describe how moral judgments in, say, Japan may need to involve consideration of factors different from those in the United States. Although it is not clear that these other factors are moral or not, this concern is not relevant to the possibility of substituting moral principles for hypernorms. Recall that hypernorms reach to the "root of what is ethical for humanity" (Donaldson & Dunfee, 1999: 44). If so, it cannot be the case that there is a hypernorm that applies to Japanese

---

[3] By "reflective equilibrium" I mean an iterative process of mutual adjustment between considered moral judgments and moral principles. As one confronts novel circumstances, he or she might consider the applicability of a moral principle, test it against his or her considered moral judgments, and make adjustments in one or the other as the case dictates. Reflective equilibrium can be thought of as a methodology for achieving a coherent belief system that squares moral beliefs with the world of experience.

humans that does not equally apply to every other human everywhere. If substantive hypernorms are a real possibility, then moral principles are equally possible. Again, international concerns are not impediments to substituting moral principles for hypernorms as much as they are considerations for formulating those principles.

In sum, there do not seem to be any good reasons for preferring the concept of a hypernorm over definitive moral principles. The challenge is in their formulation, and this is not the place for doing so. It should be apparent from this discussion, however, that the suggestive description of hypernorms and all of the other intellectual resources packed into ISCT should make that task much less daunting than it would otherwise be.

CONCLUSION

As mentioned at the outset, there are several other moral strategies besides ISCT—some morally monistic and another based on pragmatism. In the interest of space, I did not consider them here, but to dispel the impression that these projects either deliver the moral content that ISCT lacks or that they would not accommodate moral principles in the same way as ISCT, I believe a brief observation is in order. These other projects share an important feature with ISCT: they are each exercises in justification or the basis upon which the morality of human behavior should be judged. Each of them prescribes a different moral foundation derived from different dimensions of morality: Kantian deontology, for Bowie (1999); Aristotelian virtue, for Solomon (1992, 1999); and pragmatism, primarily the work of John Dewey, for Buchholz and Rosenthal (1998). Accordingly, they each make the same sort of foundational arguments that are found in ISCT, instead of articulating a succinct and comprehensive set of moral principles. But each of them could. There is no inherent conflict between moral principles and any of these three moral theories. Of course, each of them might endorse different principles, in keeping with their different philosophical attachments, although this is far from automatic.

As evidence for the way moral theories easily and naturally accommodate moral principles, consider that one of these projects, Buchholz and Rosenthal's (1998), is an application of Dewey's

pragmatic moral thinking to the business world. Consider further that Dewey engaged in a similar effort in the domain of education—a major focus of his prodigious intellectual life. In a book aptly entitled *Moral Principles in Education*, he urges that "what we need in education is a genuine faith in the existence of moral principles which are capable of effective application" (1909: 57). He proceeds to carefully formulate four such principles that are justifiable in terms of his pragmatic attachments. But none of these principles are antithetical to the other two moral theories; Kantians or Aristotelians could endorse them as well. The particular philosophical basis upon which these principles are morally justified is not crucial to the success of Dewey's project. What is important in terms of practical application is the nature of the principles themselves—their careful formulation. In the case of Dewey's educational project, there is no mistaking their clarity, relevance, and any of the other criteria this investigation began with. And there is no mistaking the influence this project had on the design of schools of education and on generations of school administrators. Hopefully, this brief discussion has done justice to the state of affairs in business ethics such that future research might target a similar endpoint in the domain of business management.

REFERENCES

Beauchamp, T., & Bowie, N. (Eds.). 1993. *Ethical theory and business* (4th ed.). Englewood Cliffs, NJ: Prentice-Hall.

Beauchamp, T., & Childress, J. 1994. *Principles of biomedical ethics* (4th ed.). New York: Oxford University Press.

Bell, D. A. 1996. The East Asian challenge to human rights: Reflections on an East West dialogue. *Human Rights Quarterly*, 18: 641–667.

Boatright, J. 1993. *Ethics and the conduct of business*, Englewood Cliffs, NJ: Prentice-Hall.

Bowie, N. 1999. *Business ethics: A Kantian perspective*. Malden, MA: Blackwell.

Bowie, N. 2001. Business ethics, philosophy, and the next 25 years. *Business Ethics Quarterly*, 10: 7–20.

Buchholz, R., & Rosenthal, S. 1998. *Business ethics: The pragmatic path beyond principles to process.* Upper Saddle River, NJ: Prentice-Hall.

DeGeorge, R. 1999. *Business ethics.* Upper Saddle River, NJ: Prentice-Hall.

Derry, R., & Green, R. 1989. Ethical theory in business ethics: A critical assessment. *Journal of Business Ethics*, 8: 521–533.

Dewey, J. 1909. *Moral principles in education.* New York: Houghton Mifflin.

Dienhart, J. 2000. *Business, institutions, and ethics.* New York: Oxford University Press.

Donaldson, T., & Dunfee, T. 1994. Toward a unified conception of business ethics: Integrative social contracts theory. *Academy of Management Review,* 19: 252–284.

Donaldson, T., & Dunfee, T. 1995. Integrative social contracts theory: A communitarian conception of economic ethics. *Economics and Philosophy,* 11: 85–112.

Donaldson, T., & Dunfee, T. 1999. *Ties that bind: A social contracts approach to business ethics.* Boston: Harvard Business School Press.

Evan, W., & Freeman, E. 1995. A stakeholder theory of the modern corporation: Kantian capitalism. In W. Hoffman & R. Frederick (Eds.), *Business ethics: Readings and cases in corporate morality:* 145–154. New York: McGraw-Hill.

Frankena, W. 1970. *Ethics.* Englewood Cliffs, NJ: Prentice-Hall.

Hasnas, J. 1998. The normative theories of business ethics: A guide for the perplexed. *Business Ethics Quarterly,* 8: 19–42.

Hobbes, T. 1946. *Leviathan.* Oxford: Blackwell.

Husted, B. W. 1996. *An empirical critique of integrative social contracts theory.* Paper presented at the annual meeting of the Society for Business Ethics, Quebec City, Canada.

Iyer, G. 1999. Approaches to ethics in international business education. In I. Gopalkrishnan (Ed.), *Teaching international business: Ethics and corporate social responsibility:* 5–20. New York: Haworth Press.

Mayer, D. 1994. Hypernorms and integrative social contracts theory. *Proceedings of the Fifth Annual Meeting of the International Association for Business and Society:* 96–100.

Mayer, D., & Cava, A. 1995. Social contract theory and gender discrimination. *Business Ethics Quarterly,* 5: 257–270.

Moody, P., Jr. 1996. Asian values. *Journal of International Affairs,* 50: 166–192.

Perry, M. 1997. Are human rights universal? The relativist challenge and related matters. *Human Rights Quarterly,* 19: 461–509.

Rawls, J. 1971. *A theory of justice.* Cambridge, MA: Harvard University Press.

Rosenthal, S., & Buchholz, R. 2000. *Rethinking business ethics.* New York: Oxford University Press.

Rynning, H. 1996. Political liberalism and integrative social contracts theory. In J. Logdson & K. Rehbein (Eds.), *Proceedings of the Seventh Annual Meeting of the International Association for Business and Society:* 113–118.

Shaw, W. 2000. Book review dialogue: Ties that bind. *American Business Law Journal,* 37: 563–585.

Singer, M. 1961. *Generalization in ethics: An essay in the logic of ethics, with the rudiments of a system of moral philosophy.* New York: Knopf.

Solomon, R. 1992. Corporate roles, personal virtues: An Aristotelian approach to business ethics. *Business Ethics Quarterly,* 2: 317–339.

Solomon, R. 1993. *Ethics and excellence: Cooperation and integrity in business.* New York: Oxford University Press.

Solomon, R. 1999. *A better way to think about business.* New York: Oxford University Press.

Walzer, M. 1994. *Thick and thin: Moral argument at home and abroad.* Notre Dame, IN: University of Notre Dame Press.

Warnock, G. J. 1971. *The object of morality.* London: Methuen.

Edward Soule is an assistant professor of management at Georgetown University. After a career as a CPA and as a senior executive in the financial services industry, he received a Ph.D. in philosophy from Washington University in St. Louis. His research focuses on normative issues in management and government policy.

[49]

MORAL IMAGINATION AND THE SEARCH FOR ETHICAL DECISION-MAKING IN MANAGEMENT

Patricia H. Werhane

1 993: GE's NBC News unit issues an on-air apology to General Motors for staging a misleading simulated crash test. NBC agrees to pay GM's estimated $1 million legal and investigation expenses.[1]

February 1994: The Justice Department brought a criminal antitrust case against General Electric, accusing it of conspiring with an arm of the South African DeBeers diamond cartel to fix prices in the $600 million world market for industrial diamonds. General Electric denied wrongdoing...[2]

April 18, 1994: Kidder, Peabody & Company ... dismissed its chief government bond trader, [Joseph Jett], during the weekend after it had uncovered fraudulent trading apparently intended to inflate the brokerage firm's profits and the trader's 1993 bonus. As a result, Kidder said $350 million in profits it recorded in the last year never existed. ....Jett, a 36-year-old managing director ... was among Kidder's most highly paid employees, earning a bonus of more that $9 million for 1993, the firm said.[3]

July 8, 1994: A study by the Project on Government Oversight, a Washington watch-dog group found that General Electric had been involved in more instances of Pentagon fraud since 1990 than any other military contractor. Although it was the fifth-largest military contractor during that period, General Electric had 16 criminal convictions and civil judgments, compared with 4 for McDonnell Douglas, the nation's largest military contractor.[4]

Even if these articles are exaggerated, incomplete, and biased against GE, and let us assume for the sake of fairness they are, these series of incidents illustrate a recalcitrant problem with which ethics and applied ethics have great difficulty. GE is a highly profitable company. It is led by Jack Welch, often cited as the best CEO in America. It has a values statement that allegedly drives company and managerial activity. Yet since the price-fixing scandals in the 1960s GE has not had an unblemished moral record. The problem is not merely a one-time weakness of will, but what I would call moral amnesia, an inability to remember past mistakes and to transfer that knowledge when fresh challenges arise.[5]

In what follows I shall argue that reasons why managers and companies do not always remember and thus learn from their mistakes are not complicated, but those reasons are crucial for moral decision-making. I shall argue that most individuals, even Joseph Jett, and most institutions such as Kidder and GE, are not without moral sensibilities or values. Rather, they sometimes have a narrow perspective of their situation and little in the way of moral imagination. They lack a sense of the variety of possibilities and moral consequences of their decisions, the ability to imagine a wide range of possible issues (e.g., that a bond trader with a rather mediocre record could achieve astonishing results), consequences, and solutions. Worse, some individuals and institutions are trapped in the framework of history, organization, culture, and tradition of which they are only at best, vaguely aware, a framework that often they allow to drive their decision-making to preclude taking into account moral concerns. It will turn out that the simple teaching and application of moral principles or rules may not alleviate this problem, since it is not always lack of logic nor ignorance of moral principles that causes moral amnesia but their specificity in application. This specificity has not so much to do with the particular situation at issue, *per se*, but rather with how the situation is perceived and framed by its protagonists.

Before making this case, I want to dispel one easy, tempting answer to the question of moral amnesia. Appealing to the moral development literature, it is tempting to imagine that Jett and perhaps even the top management at Kidder operated on the lowest level of moral development, gauging their moral judgments on the basis of self-interest and personal gain and basing their actions on whether or not they would be caught. The former Federal Reserve Chairperson, Paul Volcker argues that the common thread in these scenarios is "good, old-fashioned greed."[6] But that explanation, while probably partially true, is not altogether satisfactory, particularly since, except for Jett, the participants in these activities were hardly in need of money, and Jett specifically, stood to lose a great deal if he was caught. Jett appeared to be caught in his own self-interest, but this was primarily an interest to win and to show his past and present employers that he was good at trading. He seemed, then, to bracket moral considerations, even the question of breaking the law or being found out, except as those considerations related to the game of trading. That is, I shall contend, he lacked moral imagination.

I. Conceptual Schemes and Schema

To develop explanation of what I mean by moral imagination, I shall begin by outlining a basic but sometimes misunderstood assumption. Initiated by the thinking of Immanuel Kant, a number of philosophers have argued[7] that "our conceptual scheme mediates even our most basic perceptual experiences."[8] "Conceptual schemes ... are ways of organizing experience; they are systems of categories that give form to the data of sensation; they are points of view from which individuals, cultures, or [historical] periods survey the passing scene."[9] The idea of a conceptual scheme entails that the notion of reality as "something outside all schemes" makes no sense. To quote Hilary Putnam (and by implication Richard Rorty who quotes Putnam with approval),

... elements of what we call 'language' or 'mind' penetrate so deeply into what we call "reality" that the very project of representing ourselves as being mappers's of something 'language-dependent' is fatally compromised from the start.[10]

The pervasiveness of conceptual schemes entails "as human beings we cannot have a view of the world that does not reflect our interests and values."[11] It is the latter point upon which I wish to dwell in this paper.

These statements however, may be misleading. It is sometimes argued that conceptual schemes are incommensurable with one another so that one cannot translate from one scheme to another nor understand the concepts embedded in a scheme other than one's own.[12] If such schemes are *individually* logically distinct, then one is left with the problem of solipsism. If these schemes are institutionally, socially, culturally, or historically grounded such as to be logically incommensurable, one is faced with an issue Donald Davidson calls conceptual relativism.

The question of solipsism is an interesting one, but one I shall put aside for the sake of the arguments in this paper. Conceptual relativism is a sticker issue. Davidson describes the view as follows.

> Conceptual schemes, we are told [by conceptual relativists] are ways of organizing experience; they are systems of categories that give form to the data of sensation .... There may be no translating from one scheme to another, in which case the beliefs, desires, hopes, and bits of knowledge that characterize one person have no true counterparts for the subscriber to another scheme. Reality itself is relative to a scheme: what counts as real in one system may not in another.[13]

This type of conceptual relativist argues that certain world views or "constellation of beliefs, values, techniques, and scientific structures" are incommensurable with each other such that the views are mutually exclusive and/or conflict in such basic ways that one cannot hold two views simultaneously. More radically, one could argue that some world views would be logically incommensurable such that someone who functions in world view A could not comprehend another world view B nor communicate with those who held it.

Arguing against conceptual relativism, Davidson concludes that "[d]ifferent points of view [different conceptual schemes] make sense, but only if there is a common coordinate system on which to plot them; yet the existence of a common system belies the claim of dramatic incomparability."[14] What is meant by a "common coordinate system" would be the subject of a different paper. Wittgenstein, Rorty, and Putnam, for example, all argue, in different ways, that the common system is language.[15] What is confusing is that some philosophers do not carefully distinguish between what Davidson calls a "common coordinate system," and "different points of view," or different conceptual schemes.

This distinction, the distinction between a "common coordinate system" and "conceptual schemes," is crucial to avoid some problems arising from claims of incommensurability between conceptual schemes, and thus, to avoid some forms of relativism.[16] Wittgenstein may have had this in mind when he sometimes talks about forms of life as a language or a language game,[17] and other times as "bedrock."[18] Wittgenstein sometimes writes that forms of life are social practices, histories, or rule-following activities. Forms of life, according to this rubric, are conceptual schemes, schemes like languages that are not "private" or incomprehensible to each other. "Bedrock" (another use of the term "form of life") is the common coordinate system that we share as human beings as a condition for human activity including language, and the underlying ground for a variety of conceptual schemes.[19]

Beginning with the presupposition that "there is a common coordinate system" that is linguistic and thus not private (although different peoples have different forms of language), we can then begin to talk about conceptual schemes that are embedded in this common system. This leads to the claim that each of us perceives and experiences from a point of view, a perspective or set of perspectives, a schema or series of schemas that serve as selective organizing, filtering and focussing mechanisms. In fact, how we define the world is relative to that scheme. This is not to imply that the world does not exist apart from our constructions of it, but how we conceive the world is conceptually dependent so that whether or how it exists independent of our constructions is not answerable.[20] These various schema frame our perceptions. They focus, schematize, and guide the ways in which we recognize, react, and conceptually organize the world. Each of us has, or is capable of having a number of overlapping schemes that may function differently in different contexts. We also "color" our experiences by our emotions, interests, and focus, so that each of us has an idiosyncratic way of shaping our experiences. Nevertheless, the conceptual schemes we employ are socially learned and altered through language, religion, culture, and educational upbringing. They are shared ways of perceiving and organizing experience.

There is no one model for these schema, that is, they are not all formal concepts that structure our experience as Kant thought. Rather, these schema also take the form of images, assumptions, stories or myths, and theories.[21] For example, the art historian E. H. Gombrich demonstrates that art images influence perception and knowledge. According to Gombrich, there are a number of examples in the history of art where an artist's imaginary depiction has served as the prototype for reality. Albrecht Durer's famous woodcut of a rhinoceros showing the animal with armor served as a model for rhinoceros drawings even in natural history books for several centuries. An anonymous seventeenth century woodcut showing a whale with ears experienced a similar fate.[22]

Stories, movies, and myths shape our experiences as well. The myth that all homeless are unemployed, or alcoholics, for example, affects our perception of the homeless despite the fact that it is false. The movie *Wall Street* has altered our faith in markets, *Bonfire of the Vanities* has reshaped our perception of politicians.

According to Paul Churchland, conceptual schemes develop prototypically as well. Children learn to recognize certain prototypical kinds of social situations, and they learn to produce or avoid the behaviors Prototypically required or prohibited in each. Young children learn to recognize a distribution of scarce resources such as cookies or candies as a fair or unfair distribution. They learn to voice complaints in the latter case, and to withhold complaint in the former....[23]

Another way we deal with experience is normatively, through the concepts of what one ought to do, of what is right or wrong, good or bad, useful or destructive, etc. Moral theories, e.g., utilitarianism, deontology, etc., give us such prototypes. Moral theories are themselves conceptual schemes, systemic ways or models for thinking about normative issues, issues which themselves are schematic. So when one applies an ethical theory (or theories) to an incident such as Jett's phantom trading, one is layering another interpretation or schema on an already schematized situation. No wonder, then, that sometimes these approaches fail to trigger new thinking or decision-making by their recipients.

Our conceptual schemes function in a variety of ways. In selecting, focussing, framing, organizing, and ordering what we experience they bracket and leave out data, and emotional and motivational foci taint or color experience. These conceptual schemes are constantly under the influence of new social and cultural stimuli, hence they are subject to change. Now and again, however, our perspectives become narrow, microscopic or even fantasy driven, or a particular point of view becomes ingrained so that one begins adopt only that perspective.

This latter phenomenon is described by the former employee of Ford Motor company, Dennis Gioia, now a professor of organizational behavior. During the Pinto era Gioia was an employee at Ford in charge of recalls of defective automobiles. Gioia's job was to orchestrate their recall program, a job which included identifying problems that might require a recall and organizing the recalls themselves. Gioia had always thought of himself as an extremely moral and socially responsible person. Yet he relates how, while functioning as Recall Coordinator, he was exposed to a number of Pintos which had exploded; but Gioia failed to recommend Pinto's recall. He was convinced by his own reasoning process and by other seemingly thoughtful managers not to recall those cars because, it was argued, the evidence was not conclusive that the Pinto was defective, many subcompact autos had similar dreadful accidents, and the Pinto was a popular, best-selling auto. Gioia even drove a Pinto, and sold one to his sister. Gioia reports, "...in the context of the times my actions were *legal*; ... they were in accord with accepted professional standards and codes of conduct [at Ford]."[24]

Looking back on this scenario Gioia concludes:

My own schematized (scripted) knowledge influenced me to perceive recall issues in terms of the prevailing decision environment and to unconsciously overlook key features of the Pinto case, mainly because they did not fit an existing script. Although the outcomes of the case [Pinto] carry retrospectively obvious ethical overtones, the schemas driving my perceptions and actions precluded consideration of the issues in ethical terms because the scripts did not include ethical dimensions.[25]

In short, Gioia had learned to deal with his job-related world through a "Ford-trained" perspective. He was unable to step out of his role as Recall Coordinator and as manager at Ford to explore the ramifications of this situation. Arguably he was personally a moral person, but he did not translate common sense personal moral principles into his perception of his professional responsibilities leaving a gap between his personal morality and his performance as Recall Coordinator. This division was reinforced by the corporate culture at Ford which did not frame the issues they faced in terms that would raise questions about the viability of continuing to sell an automobile that had an obvious and dangerous defect. Worse, Gioia was not aware of the gap between his personal moral beliefs and his professional behavior, he had little realization that there was a distinctive "Ford perspective," nor did he imagine that this perspective was just that--one of a number of possible ways to deal with the Pinto.

Examining the Jett case, we see some parallels with Gioia's career at Ford. Whatever Jett's positive moral training was, it was not reinforced at Kidder. According to *Fortune*, the CEO at Kidder, Michael Carpenter, "was not licensed to manage a broker-dealer for most of the time he worked at Kidder. [Carpenter] did not take the required exams and did not register wit the SEC."[26] Nor was the head of retail sales at Kidder, Charles Sheehan licensed by the SEC. Jett's trading style, then, while not encouraged, might have been condoned. I want to suggest that Jett, (and perhaps too, Carpenter and Sheehan, and Jett's direct boss, Edward Cerullo) like Gioia, were caught up in a conceptual scheme--a scheme that placed success as the primary value. This scheme was reinforced at Kidder and GE by Jack Welch's motto "Be, #1 or #2 or get out."[27] Just as GE fails to understand why ethically questionable activities at that company persist, so, too, one begins to suspect that Jett did not take into account his own personal moral values nor the consequences of his actions when he began phantom trading at Kidder. Jett appears not to have engaged in any dialogue between his common sense moral principles and what he was doing at Kidder. As the chief bond trader Jett's perception of that scenario and his responsibilities must have been divided from his ordinary sense of what was right and wrong. There appears to have been little link between "perception of particulars [at Kidder] and a rule governed concern for general obligations."[28] Interestingly, too, Jett and his superiors at Kidder seemed to have had little sense of history. Had they simply-recalled the Salomon Brothers treasury bond scandal of 1991, they might have looked at what was happening at Kidder differently.

This leads us to a second temptation. (The first was to attribute these incidents merely to poor moral development or "good old-fashioned greed.") There is a temptation to appeal to traditional moral education, education, which if complete, would have, at the least, prevented the Kidder incident. Jett and other individuals at Kidder and its parent, General Electric, are responsible, morally responsible, for Jett's performance. They knew the risks, they pressured Jett to succeed, to be #1 or #2, without grounding that strategy in a values system. So, the story should continue, let us talk to people at Kidder and GE about professional and moral responsibility, diagnose what went wrong at Kidder, and locate the moral culprits. We will then test their stage of moral development, (e.g., are they egoists, conformists, rule followers, law-abiders, precedent setters, or philosophers) and give them a workshop in moral reasoning. We will present some ethical theories (e.g., utilitarianism, deontology, perhaps some virtue theory) with which to solve dilemmas, and illustrate problems with other cases and examples, discuss professional and institutional codes of ethics, and engage these organizations in a series of practice sessions that apply moral theories to case studies.

Therein lies the problem. GE has a values statement; it has had workshops on ethics. Yet problems persist at GE. GE's managers, it appears, have not all been uniformly motivated by the Categorical Imperative, the Principle of Utility, theories of justice, or even by a consideration of managerial virtues. This is because there is a gap between the general, (moral rules, principles, rights, and virtues), and the particular (the Kidder-Jett situation) wherein it is difficult, at best, to translate general precepts into particular applications.[29] In what follows I will argue that it is imagination, moral imagination, that bridges the gap between moral theories, moral principles, common sense morality, and practical decision-making, although the "bridge" can only be constructed from the particular. Jett lacked imagination, the moral imagination to engage in a dialogue between these two schemas of his common-sense morality and his position at Kidder, a dialogue that might have expanded his horizon of possible actions. This lack of interconnection--a form of moral amnesia--may have been endemic to the culture at GE. Perhaps the GE "script" was not rewritten after the first price-fixing scandal. Or perhaps Welch's motto, "Be Number One or Number Two..." overrode other moral considerations in Jett's mind and in the mind of others who engaged in questionable behavior at GE.

II. Moral imagination

One of the early proponents of the notion of moral imagination was Adam Smith. In the first chapter of the *Theory of Moral Sentiments* Smith argues that [h]ow selfish soever man may be supposed, there are evidently some principles in his nature, which interest him in the fortune of others...[30]
One of these "principles" is sympathy. At the same time, Smith says,

   [a]s we have no immediate experience of what other men feel, we can form
   no idea of the manner in which they are affected, but by conceiving what
   we ourselves should feel in the like situation.[31]

Sympathy, in Smith's technical use of the term, is not empathy, but rather, an agreement or understanding of sentiments.[32] When I sympathize I place myself in another's situation, not because of how that situation might affect me, but rather as if I were that person in that situation. I truly project myself into another's experience, according to Smith, in order to understand, although not experience, what another person is feeling rather than merely relate that situation to my own. Sympathy, then, is the comprehension of what another feels or might feels in a situation, but it is not an experiential or sentimental identification with that feeling.

The role of imagination is crucial for an understanding of Smith's notion of sympathy and indeed his whole moral psychology. Smith argues that each of us has an active imagination which enables us mentally to recreate feelings, passions, and the point of view of another. In this imaginative process one does not literally feel the passion of another, but one is able to "put oneself in another's shoes," so to speak, and to understand what another is experiencing from their perspective.

Imagination plays another important role. In the beginning of the *TMS* Smith sometimes talks as if sympathy is a general principle of "fellow-understanding" so that sympathy would enable me to understand the passions and interests of another even if I felt resentment or even abhorrence toward those passions or toward that person. Imagination is important in this scheme, perhaps more important than Smith admits, because it allows one to project oneself and understand what another is feeling even when one is revolted by that feeling. I might, then, understand how someone like Hanibul the Cannibal feels, although I could not approve of his feelings and passions. Smith breaks with a rationalist tradition by linking moral judgment to moral sentiment, and according to Smith, sympathy and imagination are the sources of moral judgment since one must first understand what another feels or engage in imaginative self-evaluation in order to experience a sentiment of approval or disapproval, a sentiment that is the basis for judgment.

Smith's analysis is prescient, because it forms the basis for much of the contemporary discussion of moral imagination as the ability to empathize, to understand another point of view, or be creative in ethical decision-making.[33] Smith breaks with a rationalist tradition by linking moral judgment to moral sentiment. Moreover, it is moral imagination along with sympathy that helps to discern what society ought to approve of, thus shaping moral rules out of community rather than individual values. But Smith's work is limited by his assumption that all of us deal with the world in the same way--through the conceptual scheme of a Scottish gentleman. So on that assumption one can more easily project and sympathize with another person or make self-evaluations, and actually be correct a good deal of the time. But each of us functions from a set of conceptual schemes, schemes about which most of us are only vaguely aware, and these schemes are not identical to those through which others experience. Smith's analysis introduces the notion of moral imagination, but it cannot take into account how one sympathizes with others whose view of the world is not that of a Scottish gentleman, nor can it account for how it is we can reshape our own conceptual schemes.

It is often argued that conceptual schemes provide "a cognitive framework for *understanding* information and events as well as a guide to appropriate *behavior* to deal with the situation face."[34] However, Mark Johnson in his recent book, *Moral Imagination*, while defining conceptual schemes semantically, links them to imagination. "Semantic frames ... do not simply mirror some objective reality or category. Rather, they define that reality by means of imaginative structure,"[35] according to Johnson. But why are these schema imaginative and not merely cognitive? Johnson's analysis depends on Kant's much earlier distinctions between various types of imagination. As we know, Kant is credited with the idea that all our sensations are structured through conceptual categories of the understanding, categories that originate in the mind of the perceiver but are universally the same in the minds of each of us. Kant argues that imagination is essential for organizing one's sensations into perceptions which become representations forming experience from which we derive knowledge. Kant distinguishes three kinds of imagination: reproductive imagination, productive imagination, and reflective imagination or free play. The reproductive imagination synthesizes nonrecurring sensations into representations in order to make perception and memory possible. The reproductive imagination functions somewhat like Hume's principle of association, and without reproductive imagination, according to Kant, we would merely be aware of nonrecurring sensations. The productive imagination is more active, and it has two functions. First, it structures, schematizes, and provides order to representations through the categories of the understanding so that experience is possible. Its function, then, is "to construe things sensibly present as instantiating pure concepts of the understanding."[36] It also helps to make sense out of the categories as pure categories of the understanding, so that, for example, we can think about quantity abstractly through number without having to recall the representation of sensible things.[37]

In the *Critique of Judgment* Kant expands his notion of imagination, giving it a third role, that of free reflection or free play. Kant argues that it is because we are imaginative we can freely "play" with ideas without being constricted by experience or by a particular conceptual scheme such as Kant's own categories of the understanding.[38] Hence we can "play" with different number schemes, explore the rules of multi-dimensional geometries, imagine a world without time, etc. Free reflection is the source of creativity, particularly in the realm of the aesthetic, because it is that which accounts for our mind's ability to manipulate images, experiences, and forms of the understanding.

Kant does not elaborate on an idea of *moral* imagination, indeed given the role of rationality in Kant's moral theory, this is not surprising. In fact, as Johnson reminds us, in the *Critique of Practical* Reason Kant argues that the productive imagination cannot function in moral judgment since the categorical imperative is exempt from schematization by the categories of the understanding.[39] Despite this, however, Johnson claims that moral imagination derives from Kant's notions of natural law and free reflection. Kant's use of the term "law of nature" or "universal law of nature" in the first formulation of the categorical imperative ("Act as though the maxim of your action were by your will to be a universal law of nature"),[40] Johnson argues, is the metaphorical bridge such that "universal law of nature" is the practical analog of the categorical imperative. Moral judgement, then, "involves an act of imaginative envisionment of a non-existing world (the kingdom of ends) as a means for judging a proposed maxim."[41] This metaphorical dimension or imaginative envisionment is very much like Kant's description of free reflection in the *Critique of Judgment* where the imagination makes reflective judgments about *possible* representations or concepts.[42]

Johnson defines moral imagination as "...an ability to imaginatively discern various possibilities for acting within a given situation and to envision the potential help and harm that are likely to result from a given action."[43] The term "imaginatively" refers to what Johnson in another place calls "metaphoric understanding," the "projective process in which we structure one domain by means of principles and material taken from a different kind of domain."[44] This ability, in turn, Johnson argues, depends on understanding the nature of conceptual schemes, the ability to distinguish various schema, and the capacity to envision their implications in present and new contexts.[45] From Johnson's point of view and speculating, perhaps Jett's problem was that he was so embedded in a Kidder-based managerial conceptual scheme he could not discern the scope of the "script" operating at Kidder nor its logic, nor could he envision its application in other contexts nor possible ramifications or consequences. Similarly, his superior, Edward Cerullo, was sufficiently impressed by Jett's performance that he could not imaginatively hypothesize that Jett would falsify trades, thus he missed discovering Jett's creative management of his bond trading.

Johnson is not altogether clear about the distinction between moral imagination and other forms of free reflection such as free play in aesthetics. I would argue that moral imagination, unlike free play, deals not merely with fancies but with possibilities or ideals that, if not practical, are at least in theory actualizable. Further these possibilities have a normative or imperative character, they have to do with what one *ought* to do, with right or wrong, with virtue, with positive or negative consequences, or with what common sense morality calls good or evil. This phenomenon is "imaginative" just because and only when it explores a wide range of possibilities including, most critically, new possible conceptual schemes, although it is never, of course, infallible.

The notion of free reflection or free play coupled with Kant's notion of the productive imagination are useful in thinking about another dimension of moral imagination. Moral imagination, if it is to do its work, has not merely to fantasize about fresh possibilities nor merely to think about these new possibilities from a normative perspective. The reason that Cerullo could not recognize Jett's bond trading alterations was perhaps, like Gioia at Ford, he was trapped in a schema, a perspective that affected the way in which he envisioned possibilities. From a neoKantian perspective, Cerullo's productive imagination could not abstract the kinds of schema or "concepts of the understanding" that were at work so that his free reflection could manipulate those concepts to help him get a perspective on the "script" that was in place at Kidder and in his mind. So part of the job of moral imagination, its most critical function, is to disengage us from the perspective with which we are dealing with a situation so that we will be able to consider new possibilities. I shall return to this point.

In attempting clarification on the notion of moral imagination, John Kekes, in a recent article "Moral Imagination, Freedom, and the Humanities" distinguishes four kinds of imagination: imaging, problem-solving, fantasizing, and moral imagination, "the mental exploration of what it would be like to realize particular possibilities."[46] Kekes argues that moral imagination has two aspects.

MORAL IMAGINATION AND THE SEARCH 85

> Moral imagination is, first, the threefold imaginative re-creation of possibilities [including] those that were generally available in the agents' context, those that the agents could reasonably have been expected to believe themselves to have, and those that the agents actually believed themselves to have.[47]

Moral imagination also includes a second element, the evaluation of these possibilities in terms of their moral worth, a process that is both exploratory and corrective. According to Kekes, one of the ways to develop moral imagination, that is, to expand the scope of one's beliefs and thus one's possibilities from the point of view of what a reasonable agent would do, is to engage in retrospection. This process, Kekes contends, gives one a better understanding of how one's belief structure operated, and helps on to redirect that belief structure in the future. Let us see how that might work in the case of Jett. It could be that Jett, like his predecessor in questionable bond trading, Paul Mozer at Salomon, was caught in the "game" of bond trading, and the environment at Kidder encouraged competition and success. Jett's belief structure while working at Kidder became restricted by his adopting the Kidder "script." While outsiders might argue that Jett could reasonably expected not to falsify his trading, in that situation Jett was "set up" by the situation and unable to process morally relevant information. Indeed, according to the journal, *Black Enterprise*, Jett may have been set up to be the scapegoat to distract from Kidder's year-end losses.[48]

Kekes claims that merely being aware of the fact that there as possibilities is not itself imaginative. I disagree, as evidenced in the Gioia and Jett scenarios. These cases suggest that a condition for being morally imaginative is the awareness *that* one has possibilities beyond those seemingly prescribed or proscribed by one's context or role. The importance of Gioia's retrospection was not his pathology of unrealized possibilities, but his recognition that while at Ford he was locked into a point of view that precluded being aware of new possibilities.

What, then, is moral imagination? Using Kant's distinctions as analogies, moral imagination consists of:

> (1) reproductive imagination: (a) an awareness of one's context, (b) awareness of the "script" or schema functioning in that context, and awareness of possible moral conflicts or dilemmas that might arise in that context, that is, dilemmas created at least in part by the dominating script.

The second stage of moral imagination:

> (2) productive imagination, consists in revamping one's schema to take into account new possibilities within the scope of one's situation and/or within one's role.

The third stage, the creative imagination or free reflection:

> (3) (a) the ability to envision and actualize possibilities that are not context-dependent but encouraged by or project a fresh schema, and/or (b) the ability to envision possibilities that other reasonable persons could envision. Morally imaginative free play also includes (c) evaluation: (i) envisioning how morally to justify actualizing these possibilities and/or (ii) how to evaluate both the *status* quo and these newly formulated possible outcomes.[49]

III. The Role of Narrative

A third temptation: Given this analysis, one is tempted to argue, with Johnson, that "moral understanding is fundamentally imaginative in character"[50] implying that moral imagination provides the single ground for moral decision-making and moral judgments. Johnson writes,

> Moral deliberation requires a form of reflective, creative judgment ....[51]
> The crux of this view of moral criticism as fundamentally imaginative is that moral objectivity consists, not in having an absolute "God's-eye point of view," but rather in a specific kind of reflective, exploratory, and critical process of evaluation carried out through communal discourse and practice.[52]

Johnson enriches his notion of moral imagination by arguing that the development of imagination demands the expansion of one's conceptual schemes through the use of narrative and metaphor. Appealing to narrative, in the Pinto and GE cases one sees examples of moral dilemmas embedded in the context of corporate, institutional, regulatory, legal and social relationships. To work one's way through these relationships one needs to become clear about this situation, the story it tells, and the traditions in which elements or this particular incident are embedded. In thinking about Kidder and Jett, one should think about how various elements of one's situation relate to each other, how a particular kind of business or industry such as GE is embedded in a social and regulatory tradition, the background tradition and practice of the investment banking firm and industry, United States customs, mores, common sense morality, and law, about customer expectations, and about how market conditions change that tradition and its narrative or story. In short, one should try to grasp how certain sets of activities or decisions fit within practices of GE, investment banking, our economy, world markets, and the moral, economic, and cultural fabric of our society.

Herein lies a difficulty. Without moral imagination it would appear that one cannot make the links between the practical and the theoretical. On the other hand, an overpreoccupation with moral imagination coupled with a narrative approach may succumb to the pitfall of a form of moral fantasy or a poorly conceived postmodern view of the world. According to a distorted version of postmodernism, it is not merely the case that we experience the world through a set of perspectives or conceptual schemes that "color" reality. At least sometimes we create the very world we experience, and in fact, it follows that there is no reality that we share. Rather, most of the time we create miniworlds with their own self-referential logic. Although these worlds often overlap with each other and with the worlds that others create, one is always involved in a narrative that creates "reality." Sometimes, the world one creates becomes totally reflexive such that one imagines the rules one creates do not merely apply to a particular project but are, in, fact true and refer to, and apply to what others take to be reality as well.[53] Could it have been the case that Kidder so insulated itself in its world to imagine that its traders would all "follow the rules" despite the heavily competitive atmosphere at Kidder? Did GE fail to do a self-evaluation after the price-fixing incidents and defense industry fraud cases, or did the success of Jack Welch make GE and Welch feel invincible and no longer vulnerable to public opinion and moral liability? And did Jett himself imagine trading was a game so that he was immune from legal and moral scrutiny?

Moral imagination alone, then, can create moral fantasies or justify a parochial set of values that are unable to handle a broader long-term perspective just because they are imaginative and consistent relative to a particular narrative. Narrative, while essential, does not get one out of this circle; in fact it may reinforce it. But given the role of conceptual schemes it is, at best, difficult to counteract that problem. It would appear that each of us lives merely in our own narrative, in a postmodern world wherein there are merely texts and no objective challenge of an impartial moral test.

Hence, one might ask, if it is true that all our experiences and knowledge are embedded in some conceptual scheme or another, how can one become aware of the ways in which a particular scheme functions, how one has extended a prototypical interpretation, or scripted a series of events? How can one be discriminating or imaginative except through the conceptual scheme in which one is imagining, a scheme that controls the direction of that discrimination? Nothing short of a very active "free-playing" imagination will enable one to get at a distance from one's it "script," role, or context to envision new possibilities. To be truly imaginative one must be more distanced from the situation. Yet even "at a distance" one will be within some conceptual scheme or other.

IV. Positional Objectivity

These conceptual constraints, however, are not as regressively circular as they appear. It is true that one cannot escape a point of view, a schematic way of experiencing. A true "a view from nowhere" or a genuinely opaque veil of ignorance is impossible. Such a totally a historical distanced impersonal idealized perspective would be, as Michael Sandel has suggested, no view at all.[54]

Nevertheless, if we keep in mind Davidson's distinction between the common coordinate system, conceptual schemes, or schema, the fact that we are always operating within some scheme or another does not entail a postmodern form of conceptual relativism. An appeal to what Amartya Sen calls "positional objectivity" helps to clarify this point. Sen writes,

> [w]hat we can observe depends on our position vis-a-vis the objects of observation .... Positionally dependent observations, beliefs, and actions are central to our knowledge and practical reason. The nature of objectivity in epistemology, decision theory, and ethics has to take adequate note of the parametric dependence of observation and inference on the position of the observer.[55]

Position-dependency defines the way in which the object appears "from a delineated somewhere." This "delineated somewhere," however, is positionally objective.

That is, any person in that position will make similar observations. The parameters of positionality are not merely spacial but could involve a shared schema. For example, Gioia and his cohorts at Ford all had access to the same data about the Pinto, and from their "schema" they all viewed that data similarly. Gioia's decision not to recall the Pinto could be defended as a positionally objective belief based on the ways in which managers at Ford processed information on automobile crashes. Similarly, Kidder's habits of trading, its loose enforcement of SEC licensing requirements, and what appear to be rather relaxed auditing of traders' transactions created a positionally objective schema in which Jett's trading creativity might have been perceived as "normal."

However, a positionally objective point of view could be mistaken in case it did not take into account all available information. Thus, as Sen points out and as the Jett case vividly illustrates, in most cases one need not accept a positionally objective view. Because of the variety of schema with which one can shape a position, almost any position has alternatives, almost every position has its critics. According to Sen, we often engage in "trans-positional" assessments or what Sen also calls a "constructed 'view from nowhere'." A trans-positional view from nowhere is a constructed critique of a particular conceptual scheme, and no positionally objective view is merely relative nor immune from challenge.[56] This sort of assessment involves comparing various positionally objective points of view to see if one can make coherent sense of them and develop some general theories about what is being observed. These trans-positional assessments, are *constructed* views from nowhere, because they too depend on the conceptual scheme of the assessors. From a transpositional point of view conceptual schemes themselves can be questioned on the basis of their coherence and/or their explanatory scope. Although that challenge could only be conducted from another conceptual scheme that assessment could take into account a variety of points of view. Revisions of the scheme in question might produce another conceptual scheme that more adequately or more comprehensively explained or took into account a range of phenomena or incidents.[57]

V. A Disengaged View from Somewhere

If it is not the case that each of us is always embedded in a blindly situated perspective, one needs to become imaginatively reflective without indulging in fantasy. To avoid the latter, one needs to get at a distance from a particular point of view or the point of view of one's colleagues, one's constituents, and/or the institutional or regulatory framework in which one is operating. A variety of perspectives is crucial, because unless one can disengage oneself from the context of a specific conceptual scheme, decisions are parochially imbedded such as to result in an iteration of the very kinds of decisions that invite moral failure such as at Kidder.

But how does one get at a distance from one's operative schema? This is the crux of what is interesting about moral imagination. Being imaginative allows us not merely to get a perspective on a script or mental model, it allows one to be self-reflective, to step back from one's situation and view it from another point of view. In taking such a perspective a person tries to disengage herself from the exigencies of the situation to look at the world or herself from a more dispassionate point of view or from the point of view of another dispassionate reasonable person. This is an appeal to a trans-positional view or, I would call it, a "disengaged view from somewhere." The notion of disengagement explains our ability to step aside and take another point of view, but never one that is totally without perspective or engagement. What is needed then, are challenges to one's perspective, "pushes" that jar one from one's particular point of view. Herein lies the fourth temptation--to allow an appeal to a notion of a disinterested or impartial spectator to do all the moral work. One sets up a decision model, a model for traders like Jett to follow. One begins with the situation, the existence of "creative" bond trading. One tests the risk of this alternative. Appealing to a disengaged view from somewhere one asks a number questions:

1. What would a reasonable person judge is the right thing to do in this case?
2. Could one defend this decision publicly?
3. What kind of precedent does this decision set? Would one want it
   repeated by other manufacturers, by the industry, or made into law?
4. Is this sort of trading necessary for the survival of Jett? For Kidder?
5. Is this the least worst option?

In using this sort of analysis it is clear that Jett would not pass the precedent test nor survive this process.

But there is something amiss with this analysis, devoted as I am to this approach. What is missing is the fact of Jett, his story. Here was a man in the middle of a situation where there appeared to be no way out *except* through inflating his trading profits. So unless one shakes Jett's sense of the world of trading, his Kidder-shaped biases, and his view of himself, or unless Jett does that himself, one cannot expect him to arrive at a different moral decision-making process at all.

Similarly, to argue that one needs to change the culture at Kidder, and perhaps, at GE as well, is a good argument given the series of moral mishaps at GE. And part of that change would of necessity be to put values at the core--as the driving force of decision-making at GE replacing even, Welch's motto, "Be first or second..." But to do that, to envision that, to jar the company and its divisions loose from a very old corporate culture and habits, habits that have not disappeared even after Welch's corporate reengineering of GE, would involve more than a disengaged view from somewhere.

What I am suggesting is that a less biased rational perspective, while crucial to moral imagination and moral decision-making, may not be enough, by itself, to avoid moral disasters.[58] This is neither to excuse Jett, Kidder, or GE, nor to let these individuals and institutions off the moral hook. But merely appealing to a disengaged view from somewhere alone will not to the job of corporate change.

VI. Moral Minimums

Moral imagination involves developing less partial and self-critical perspectives, and there is clearly a complex, dynamic relationship between a particular situation, one's imagination, and a "disengaged view from somewhere" since being able to be self-critical and cognizant of one's predicament and the schema operating on that predicament requires a great deal of imagination. A fruitful way to think of this approach is to imagine a dialogue between the story or narrative, say about Kidder and Jett, where questions are asked from a less engaged perspective, where older and new narratives as well as these acute questions · challenge Kidder and Jett. The idea, in brief, is to intensify the dialogue between Kidder and Jett's stories of what happened, to focus on the particular situation in the mode of disengagement, a form of imaginative analysis aimed at unearthing the schema driving the situation, without falling into fantasy or what Martha Nussbaum calls "moral obtuseness."[59]

Is this process merely constructivist? Have we returned to circularity through an appeal to mere coherence between situation, imagination, and a disengaged view from somewhere? In his well-known book *Spheres of Justice* Michael Walzer develops a pluralistic and relativistic theory of the good. Walzer argues that who we are and what we value is defined in terms of social goods. While social goods may overlap each social good has its own definition and "sphere" of application, values, and distributive criteria. Different societies or different groups within a society could have quite disparate social goods so one cannot define "basic goods," or the "human good" except contextually.

In his new book, *Thick and Thin* Walzer qualified the relativistic notion of spheres of social goods. He argues that running through the thickness of each sphere of social goods, and on a larger scale, running through each culture is a "thin theory of the good," or what Walzer also calls "moral minimums." What Walzer is arguing is that throughout history and in different cultures there is a thin thread of coherence and agreement. The agreement is less on what is *good* but rather on some at least partial universal recognition of "bads." For example, he argues, while there is wide disagreement about definitions or theories of justice, there is mutual recognition of *injustice*. While we are uncertain about the constitution of the "good life," there is widespread agreement about deficient or despicable living conditions, indecencies, violations of human rights, mistreatment, and other harms. Although Walzer was less clear about the content of these minimums, I would suggest that they are best understood as negative standards, universally agreed upon "bottom lines" beyond which it is morally questionable to act.[60]

This presents another temptation, the temptation to declare moral minimums as absolutes. But consistent with Walzer's thinking is the idea that the content of these moral minimums is subject to historical change. They are not fixed absolutes; rather they are revisable negative ideals. So a moral minimum is a candidate for a universal principle, but never elected for eternity or even for life. Moral minimums, these common "treads" of principle that reappear in different historical periods and in disparate cultures, explain how it is that we do appeal to general principles, but at the same time we appeal from a context, from a tradition or as a challenge to a tradition, and never from "nowhere." Still, the ability to step out of a situation and imagine new possibilities and the challenge of meeting moral minimums as more general standards or ideals standards preclude mere constructivist relativism or circularity.[61] Moral minimums are not merely a product of a particular tradition or a specific historical moment, and the thread of moral minimums is an appeal to standards with which to judge not merely Jett's actions and actions similar to that one, but to judge one's background tradition, common sense morality, one's alleged disengaged view from somewhere, and, even, to reflect on the minimums themselves.

VII. Moral Imagination and Reflective Equilibrium

The notion of moral imagination, the background of tradition and custom in which a situation is embedded, a disengaged view from somewhere, and a thin theory of moral minimums are all central elements of a viable moral decision-making process when that process begins with the specific and particular. It is a process not unlike what John Rawls and Norman Daniels call "wide reflective equilibrium."

The method of wide reflective equilibrium, first proposed by Rawls and later developed by Daniels, argues that moral decision-making is a process, a process that entails testing moral judgments in particular contexts against moral principles in the context of "background theories" traditions, practices, narratives, conceptual schemes and other presuppositions out of which decision-making takes place.[62] As Rawls summarizes this process,

> by going back and forth, sometimes altering the conditions of the contractual circumstances, at others withdrawing our judgments and conforming them to principle, I assume that eventually we shall find a description of the initial situation [solution or set of solutions to the decision process] that both expresses reasonable conditions and yields principles which match our considered judgments duly pruned and adjusted.[63]

According to Webster's Collegiate Dictionary "equilibrium" is "a state of balance, poise, a state of adjustment between opposing or divergent influences or elements, a state of balance between opposing forces or actions that is either static or dynamic."[64] Moral judgments are a result of a delicate balance of context, evaluation, the projection of moral minimums, and the presence or absence of imagination. The process takes into account context and tradition, a disengaged view from somewhere, and minimum moral standards is just that: a process, a dynamic process, where one challenges the presuppositions of tradition, tests one's disengaged perspective against the situation and its context, and continues to shape one's decisions and refine one's moral minimums. Such a process is seldom complete, objectivity is impossible, and infallibility of judgment is not part of the goal. Indeed, moral judgments are at best, partial solutions, solutions that serve as the starting place for new series of decisions always at risk of being challenged. The lynch-pin of this process is a highly developed moral imagination that perceives the nuances of a situation, challenges the framework or scheme in which the event is embedded, and imagines how that might be different.

Conclusion

There is more to be said about the theoretical construct of moral imagination. Instead, I shall end with a story, a true story of a small bank that succeeded in making money and making a difference, a story about the South Shore Bank of Chicago.

The South Shore Bank is located on the South Side of Chicago in an area covering a neighborhood population of about 80,000. Before the 1960s the neighborhood was made up of lower-middle class and middle class apartments and houses and one Knoblock square section of mansions. The neighborhood was primarily Jewish, and there was a tradition of staying in the neighborhood moving up to more affluent areas as one's economic status improved. In the 1960s there was a mass migration of blacks into the Northern cities and a subsequent "white flight" from certain City neighborhoods, including South Shore. By 1970 the population of South Shore was primarily black and poor and it was predicted that within 5 years the neighborhood would become one of the worst slums in Chicago. The South Shore Bank, whose deposits had been 'steadily falling to $42 million, was for sale. Because it was the last financial institution in that neighborhood regulatory statutes at that time prohibited closing or moving the bank. Now, the question, is, would you invest in such an institution? From a dispassionate perspective, from any reasonable disengaged view from somewhere, the answer is clearly no.

Despite advice to the contrary, in 1973 a group of entrepreneurs led by Ronald Grzywinski borrowed enough money to buy the institution for under $4 million. Today, still located in South Shore, this bank has assets of almost $180 million, it is profitable, although not wildly so, and its net loan losses in 1989 were the lowest for any bank of its size. Yet until recently most of its loans were to the South Shore neighborhood. (Last year it moved into a second low-income neighborhood in Chicago: the Austin neighborhood, and it has also opened a bank and a program in rural Arkansas.) How is this possible?

What the bank did was to focus its attention on housing and to loan money to people willing to rehab buildings in South Shore. It also set up a series of subsidiaries, one of which concentrates on real estate development, another on minority business enterprises, a nonprofit institution that works with state and federal programs to rehab and develop housing for low income residences, and a subsidiary that serves as a consulting firm for these other projects. It has raised money through what it calls Development Deposits, encouraging wealthy people from other neighborhoods to open accounts at South Shore. Today South Shore, still primarily black except in the mansion area which is 40/60, is a viable place to live. Drugs and gangs are virtually absent, and more than 3/4 of the residences and apartments are restored and inhabited. South Shore Bank officers do not claim to be Mother Teresas. Rather, they argue, they lent money to people and enterprises that were less risky than many Third World recipients of Big Bank loans in a neighborhood that was key to the Bank's survival.[65] Today the South Shore Bank has become a model for banking in developing neighborhoods and countries around the world.

It took imagination, moral imagination, to engage in a project that no -other Chicago bank at that time would engage in, in a neighborhood that leading sociologists had written off, and to see the low-risk element in this kind of venture, particularly when the project is neither a government project nor a charity but is a for-profit and a profitable enterprise. The Bank worked within given social conditions and banking regulations, and then reconfigured the framework of traditional "banking logic" to test the hypothesis that they could do banking under challenging circumstances and under redefined conditions. With their imaginations fully at work, they became, in Henry James words, "'finely aware and richly responsible.'"[66]

ENDNOTES

[1] Terence P. Pare, "Jack Welch's Nightmare on Wall Street," *Fortune* (September 5, 1994), p. 46.

[2] Douglas Frantz and Sylvia Nasar, "F.B.I. Inquiry on Jet Engine, New Jolt to Company Images," *New York Times* (July 8, 1994), p. Al, C3.

[3] Saul Hansell, "Kidder Reports Fraud and ousts a Top Trader," *New York Times* (April 18, 1994), p. Al.

[4] Hansel, p. Al.

[5] That this just happens in business, of course, is not true. Recently the World Medical Association elected Dr. Hans-Hoachim Sewering, an active participant in the Nazi medical profession's euthanasia activities during the Second World War, to its presidency. Jennifer Leaning, "German Doctors and Their Secrets," *New York Times* (February 6, 1993), p. 11.

[6] Quoted by Kenneth H. Bacon and Kevin G. Salwen in "Summer of Financial Scandals Raises Questions about the Ability of Regulators to Police Markets," *Wall Street Journal* (August 28, 1991), p. A10.

[7] See Patricia H. Werhane, "Introducing Morality to Thrift Decision Making," *Stanford Law and Policy Review* 2 (1990), pp. 125-131.

[8] Peter Railton, "Moral Realism," *Philosophical Review*, 95 (2), 1986, p. 172.

[9] Donald Davidson, "On the Very Idea of a Conceptual Scheme," *Proceedings of the American Philosophical Association*, 48 (1974), p. 5.

[10] Hilary Putnam, *Realism With a Human Face* (Cambridge: Harvard University Press, 1990), p. 28, requoted with affirmation by Richard Rorty, "Putnam and the Relativist Menace," *Journal of Philosophy* xc (1993), p. 443. Original text was italicized.

[11] Rorty quoting Putnam (again with approval), p. 443.

[12] See for example, Norman Jackson and Pippa Carter, "In Defence of paradigm incommensurability," *Organization Studies* 12 (1991), pp. 109-127.

[13] Davidson, p. 5.

[14] Davidson, p. 6.

[15] See Ludwig Wittgenstein, *Philosophical Investigations*, trans. G.E.M. Anscombe (New York: Macmillan and Co., 1953), Rorty, "Putnam and the Relativist Menace," pp 443-461, and Putnam, *Realism with a Human Face*.

[16] There is also some confusion in the social science literature on these distinctions. See for example, Gary Weaver and Dennis A. Gioia's paper, "Paradigms Lost: Incommensurability vs. Structurationist Inquiry," *Organization Studies*, 1994, pp. 565 - 590, which summarizes this confusion and attempts to clear it up.

[17] Wittgenstein, *Philosophical Investigations* 23, 19.

[18] *Ibid*, 217.

[19] To illustrate the question of incommensurability, let us consider a "global" conceptual scheme, for instance, a "world-view" that defines basic physical relationships such as cause and effect, or cosmic relationships between, say, the earth and the sun. As Thomas Kuhn has famously shown, a certain paradigm can function as a schema to shape one's approach to scientific data, and even to science itself, and that kind of scheme or paradigm "takes over" the way we think about nature. It would be weird to argue that the earth circled around Jupiter, for example, given what we know about the solar system and the way in which we organize that knowledge, in f act we would say that such an argument is just wrong. Another conceptual scheme that challenges those findings is, in the first instance contradictory, false, according to the structure of knowledge in that scheme, and in f act, as Copernicus learned, unaccepted by almost everyone. Copernicus' scheme e. g, that the earth rotates around the sun, brought into question the theory that the earth is the center of the universe. But it did more than that. It tried to falsify the Ptolemaic world-view by challenging its basic assumptions. As this example illustrates, one cannot hold both world-view paradigms, e.g., both the Ptolemaic and Copernican theory of the earth-sun relationship since they contradict each other. One could argue, as Kuhn does, that two "global" schemes are incommensurable with each other since they are two different ways of viewing the universe that contradict each other such that one cannot hold both theories simultaneously. Nevertheless, as we begin to accept a new scheme we understand the structure, truth claims, and status of both, and we are capable of this understanding, because of what Davidson calls a "common coordinate system." So even if it is true that one cannot hold a Copernican

and Ptolemaic view of cosmology at the same time because the two views contradict each other, they are not incommensurable in the stronger sense that one cannot comprehend both nor use the same common (linguistic) coordinate system to talk about each, although the descriptions, terminology, and meanings of terms such as "solar system" will be different in each case. This distinction between incomprehensibility and incomprehensibility is important, because if at least some conceptual schemes are incomprehensible to each other, it is at best difficult to explain how one could change one's world-view. (I am not suggesting that Kuhn thinks these global conceptual schemes are incommensurable in the strong sense, but to clarify what appear to be some misreadings of Kuhn.) See Kuhn's second edition to *The Structure of Scientific Revolutions* (Chicago: University of Chicago Press, 1970), "Postscript-1969," pp. 174-210.

[20] G.E.M. Anscombe, "The Question of Linguistic Idealism," *Essays on Wittgenstein in Honour of G. H. Von Wright*, Acta Philosophica Fennica, Vol. 28, ed. Jaakko Hintikka (Amsterdam: North Holland Publishing Co., 1976).

[21] See Peter Senge, *The Fifth Discipline* (New York: Doubleday and Company, 1990), chapter 10.

[22] E. H. Gombrich, *Art and Illusion* (Princeton: Princeton University Press, 1960), Chapter Two.

[23] See Paul Churchland, *A Neurocomputational Perspective; The Nature of the Mind and the Structure of Science* (Cambridge: MIT Press, 1989), cited in Mark Johnson, *Moral Imagination* (Chicago: University of Chicago Press, 1993), pp. 190-1.

[24] Dennis A. Gioia, "Pinto Fires and Personal Ethics: A script Analysis if Missed Opportunities," *Journal of Business Ethics* 11 (1992), p. 384.

[25] Gioia, "Pinto Fires...", p. 385.

[26] Pare, p. 42.

[27] See Noel M. Tichy and Stratford Sherman, *Control Your Destiny or Someone Else Will* (New York: HarperCollins, 1993) for various versions of this declaration.

[28] See Martha Nussbaum, "'Finely Aware and Richly Responsible': Literature and Moral Imagination," Chapter 5 of *Love-Is Knowledge* (New York: Oxford University Press, 1990), p. 157, reprinted from *Literature and the Question of Philosophy*, ed. A. Cascardi (Baltimore: The Johns Hopkins University Press, 1987), pp. 169-191.

[29] See Charles Larmore, "Moral Judgment,:" *Review of Metaphysics* 35 (1981), p. 279.

[30] Adam Smith, *The Theory of Moral Sentiments* (TMS) ed. A. L. Macfie and D. D. Raphael (Oxford: Oxford University Press, 1976), I. (I) 1. 1.

[31] *TMS* I.i.1.2.

[32] TMS I.i.1.5. See also, T. D. Campbell, *Adam Smith's Science of Morals* (London: George Allen & Unwin Ltd., 1971), Chapter 4.

[33] See, for example, Joan Callahan, "Applied Ethics," *Encyclopedia of Business Ethics* (Oxford: Basil Blackwell, 1992), and Thomas McCollough, *The Moral Imagination and the Public Life* (Chatham, NJ: Chatham House Publishers, Inc., 1991).

[34] Gioia, "Pinto Fires...," p. 385. See also, D. A. Gioia, "Symbols, Scripts, and Sensemaking: Creating Meaning in the Organization Experience," in *The Thinking Organization* ed. H. P. Sims, Jr. and D. A. Gioia (San Francisco: Jossey-Bass, 1986).

[35] Johnson, *Moral Imagination*, p. 192.

[36] Michael J. Young, "Kant's View of Imagination," *Kantstudien* 79 (1988), p. 155.

[37] See Michael Woods "Kant's Transcendental Schematism," *Dialectica* 37 (1983), pp. 201-20. Michael J. Young, "Kant's View of Imagination," *Kantstudien* 79 (1988), pp. 140-164, and Rudolph Makkreel, *Imagination and Interpretation in Kant* (Chicago: University of Chicago Press, 1990), Chapters 1-3.

[38] See Patricia H. Werhane, *Philosophical Issues in Art* (Englewood Cliffs: Prentice-Hall, Inc., 1984), pp. 192-3, Makkreel, Chapter 3, and Mark Johnson, "Imagination in Moral Judgment," *Philosophy and Phenomenological Research* xlvii (1985), pp. 265-80.

[39] See Mark Johnson, "Imagination in Moral Judgment," pp. 270-271. See also Immanuel Kant, *Critique of Practical Reason* trans. Lewis White Beck (Indianapolis: Bobbs-Merrill, 1956), p. 70.

[40] Kant,

[41] Johnson, "... Moral Judgment," p. 273.

[42] See Nathan L. Tierney, *Imagination and Ethical Ideals* (New York: SUNY Press, 1994), especially chapter 3.

[43] Johnson, *Moral Imagination*, p. 202.

[44] Johnson, "... Moral Judgment," pp. 274-5.

[45] Johnson, *Moral Imagination*, p. 198.

[46] John Kekes, "Moral Imagination, Freedom and the Humanities," *American Philosophical Quarterly* 28 (1991), p. 101.

[47] Kekes, p. 102.

[48] Gracian, Mack, "Joseph Jett Sparks Media Frenzy," *Black Enterprise*, p. 28, August 1994.

[49] See Mark Johnson, "Imagination in Moral Judgment," pp. 276-77 for a somewhat similar analysis. Johnson, however, does not use this analogy with Kant's definitions of imagination.

[50] Johnson, *Moral Imagination*, p. 217.

[51] Johnson, "Imagination and Moral Judgment," p. 277.

[52] Johnson, *Moral Imagination*, p. 217.

[53] See, for example, Thomas Vargish, "The Value of Humanities in Executive Development," *Sloan Management Review* 32 (1991), pp. 84 - 89. See also, E. Ermarth, *Sequel to History* (Princeton: Princeton University Press), 1991. *Postmodernism Philosophy and the Arts.*

[54] See Michael Sandel, *Liberalism and the Limits of Justice* (Cambridge: Cambridge University Press, 1982), especially Chapters 2 and 4.

[55] Amartya Sen, "Positional Objectivity," *Philosophy and Public Affairs* (1993), p. 126.

[56] A further buttress for this point of view is Michael Walzer's view of the self. In his recent book, *Thick and Thin*, Walzer distinguishes a "thick" and a "thin" self. If I understand Walzer's position correctly, Walzer accepts the position that all our experiences are perspectival and constructed. In addition, he argues, who we are as subjects is a late development from our socialization process. In that socialization process we develop a number interests, roles, memberships, commitments and values such that each individual is a historical and social product, a pluralistic bundle of overlapping spheres of foci, a "thick" self. In the first instance there is no self-as-such as a precritical, transcendental *cogito*, or totally ideal spectator. Self-reflection and self-criticism, what Walzer calls a "thin self," does develop, but only later out of the thick socialized self. Self-reflection arises when there are inconsistencies, disagreements or clashes between one's interests, commitments, and spheres of value, clashes that jar one into taking another point of view, a point of view that is still one's own. This "thin" self accounts for the unity and continuity of overlapping, changing "thick" selves, it is that of oneself that "perdures" though time and change. The "thin" self, then, is socially derived but not merely socially determined, a self with the ability to choose, manipulate, and even change events, and it explains our ability to get a perspective on our situation and its positive and negative features. (See Michael Walzer, *Thick and Thin* (Notre Dame: Notre Dame University Press, 1994), especially Chapter Five.)

[57] Sen, p. 130.

[58] Indeed, it is possible within a particular social/cultural/institutional context to develop a limited objectivity so that one has a closed loop of decision-making. To understand what I mean, let us look at an example. The Nestle Corporation produces some of the finest infant formula in the world. They are an international company with an excellent product, good marketing skills, and strong code of ethics. In selling infant formula world-wide Nestle was successful in a number of markets including the Far East. From a rational and impartial point of view it seemed reasonable to take the same product, same marketing skills to the Third World, in particular to Africa. Yet when they went into a new culture, East Africa, they neglected to take into account the context, a context in which most customers cannot read, clean water is an oxymoron, and medicine men are thought of as gods. So when men in white coats promoted infant formula, thousands of illiterate mothers, unable to read the directions and warnings on the label, gave up breast feeding for the powder, overdiluting it with polluted water. What appeared to be reasonable processes failed in this new context, because Nestle did not take into account traditions of African cultures nor the conceptual scheme through which an African mother projects her experiences.

[59] Nussbaum, p. 155.

[60] Walzer, *Thick and Thin*, especially Chapter One.

[61] See David Brink, *Moral Realism and the Foundations of Ethics* (Cambridge: Cambridge University Press, 1989), especially pp. 139-143 for a lengthy defense of this conclusion.

[62] See John Rawls, *A Theory of Justice* (Cambridge: Harvard University Press, 1971), especially pp. 20, 48-51; Norman Daniels, "Wide Reflective Equilibrium and Theory Acceptance in Ethics," *Journal of Philosophy* LXXVI (1979), pp. 256-281 and "On Some Methods of Ethics and Linguistics," *Philosophical Studies* 37 (1980), pp. 21-36.

[63] John Rawls, *A Theory of Justice*, p. 20.

[64] *Merriam Webster's Collegiate Dictionary* 10th Edition, p. 392.

[65] See Richard Taub, *Community Capitalism* (Boston: Harvard Business School Press, 1988) for a detailed analysis of the South Shore Bank and its development.

[66] Nussbaum, *op. cit.*, quoting from Henry James, *The Art of the Novel* (New York: Scribner, 1934), p. 62.

[50]

TOWARD THE FEMININE FIRM:
AN EXTENSION TO THOMAS WHITE

John Dobson and Judith White

Abstract: This paper concerns the influence of gender on a firm's moral and economic performance. It supports Thomas White's intimation of a male gender bias in the value system underlying extant business theory. We suggest that this gender bias may be corrected by drawing on the concept of substantive rationality inherent in virtue-ethics theory. This feminine-oriented relationship-based value system complements the essential nature of the firm as a nexus of relationships between stakeholders. Not only is this feminine firm morally desirable, but it is also economically more efficient in that trust becomes a more feasible implicit contractual enforcement mechanism. In an organizational context, therefore, from both a moral and an economic perspective, long established economic man is dominated by nascent economic woman.

The theory of the firm, as it has evolved in financial-economic theory, is premised on a single narrow concept of rationality. Within this rubric, a rational agent is simply one who pursues personal material advantage *ad infinitum*. In essence, to be rational in financial economics is to be individualistic, materialistic, and competitive. Business is a game played by individuals, as with all games the objects is to win, and winning is measured in terms solely of material wealth. Within the discipline this rationality concept is never questioned, and has indeed become the theory-of-the-firm's *sine qua non*.

Beyond the monastic cloisters of financial economics, however, it is generally recognized that there is no single "right" concept of rationality. Within the human milieu there are rationalities rather than rationality. One possible determinant of these rationality differences is gender (Gilligan, 1982). Women may tend to have a more group or "connected" concept of rationality, whereas the male rationality concept tends to be more individualistic or "separate."

The existence of these gender-driven rationality differences could clearly have implications for economic theory. In his provocative essay "Business, Ethics, and Carol Gilligan's 'Two Voices'," Thomas White (1992) addresses these and other implications. White applies Gilligan's work on gender differences in moral orientation to organizational behavior.[1] He notes that these gender differences may explain why various empirical studies find women relatively more sensitive to ethical dilemmas in business:

> On this matter it is crucial to note Kohlberg's claim that only one in four people advances to the highest stage of moral reasoning. The vast majority of men, then, probably employ 'conventional' moral thinking — an outlook that puts a premium on laws, rules, norms or conventions. The apparent ethical superiority of

> the women in the studies may suggest that ethical dilemmas in business register
> more strongly with the average possessor of an ethic or care [the connected self]
> than they do with someone at the conventional stage of an ethic of justice [the
> separated self]. (p. 57)

Thus, at the conventional levels of ethical reasoning, the connected self is
more adept at moral deliberation in business than is the separated self. But
White's observations are not limited to the moral worth of the firm. In addition,
he makes the provocative and somewhat equivocal suggestion that a feminine
moral orientation may enhance a firm's *economic* worth. He suggests that the
feminine ethic may be more attuned to the essential nature of the firm as a nexus
of relationships. A feminine firm, therefore, is both morally *and economically*
superior.

We analyze White's economic suggestion from the perspective of the theory
of the firm as developed in financial economics. In order to isolate the source
of any extant gender bias, the analysis necessarily begins with an elucidation of
the value system that underlies contemporary financial economics. This underlying value system is contained within the substantive rationality premise that
supports all financial economic theory. Consistent with White's suggestion, we
find this rationality premised on the male separated-self, as opposed to the
female connected-self. Having identified the source of the gender bias, its economic implications are evaluated to test White's intimation of the economic
superiority of the feminine firm using a reappraisal of financial contracting
equilibria in light of these two distinct moral orientations. Consistent with
White, we find the feminine firm economically more efficient that the extant
male oriented firm.

White's paper concludes by challenging future researchers to correct the gender bias underlying business theory and practice. We respond by identifying an
alternative substantive rationality premise which is logically coherent, and also
sensitive to what Gilligan identifies as the feminine ethic. It is supplied by
virtue-ethics theory. The implications of virtue-ethics theory for sculpting the
feminine firm are investigated. In essence, the economic superiority of a firm in
which agents adhere to the tenets of virtue-ethics theory stems from its ability to
sustain relationships of trust, thereby mitigating the agency costs that render
conventional financial-economic equilibria sub-optimal. The firm becomes a
nurturing community in addition to a passive contractual nexus.

The Two Voices

Carol Gilligan's (1982) *In a Different Voice* presents evidence of significant
gender differences in moral orientation. The "two voices" represent two selves.
The autonomous self separated from others in a hierarchical world is predominant among men. Ethics for this self adopts a game-like quality; the moves that
are acceptable and unacceptable are clearly defined before the game, disputes
are refereed impartially according to the abstract principle of fairness, and setting a precedent becomes worrisome.

The self that is predominant among women is the connected self, joined to
others in a web of relationships. The ethical outlook derived from this connected

self is more situational and contextual than that which a "separate" self produces. Instead of the male orientation to "rules of the game," the dynamics and expectations involved in relationships are central (White, 1992). Women tend to conceptualize moral questions as problems of care involving empathy and compassion, while men conceptualize them as problems of rights. A study conducted by Betz (1989), for example, asked a sample of men and women five questions relating to unethical behavior. The study revealed that men were more than twice as likely to be willing to engage in actions regarded as less ethical. The study also revealed that men are more likely to work long hours and break rules because men view achievement as competitive. Recent work by Ruegger et al. (1992) supports Betz's findings. They asked over one thousand business students to evaluate the ethical acceptability of each of ten different scenarios. In four of the ten responses there was no significant difference between the male and female responses. The results of the other six questions support the above findings of significant gender differences in ethical orientation. Again, the male responses tended to be rule based, viewing the problem as that of a game. The female responses were more compassion based and more contextual.

Seeing oneself from Gilligan's female perspective as "connected" means seeing oneself in relationship with others as one's primary sense of self, rather than primarily seeing oneself as separate from others and autonomous. To be connected to and in relationship with others assumes that one can know for certain one's own thoughts, feelings, and perceptions, while explicitly or tacitly acknowledging that another has his or her own similar or different thoughts, feelings, and perceptions. There is an assumption that the other may be different than oneself while simultaneously connected with oneself rather than that the other is most likely similar while separate. Another assumption is that the context of the phenomenon is essential for knowing and understanding; the context cannot be separated from the phenomenon itself. Context includes the people surrounding the situation. While a connected self assumes connection and relationship with others, there is always an awareness of the other and a relationship between two persons, requiring maintenance and sometimes repair of the relationship, however superficial or deep. The connected self may know through emotions, sense experiences, intuition, logic, authority, or some combination of these (Lewis, 1990). Logic, rationality, and impersonal objectivity may be meaningless in the presence of one's feelings, sense experiences, and, of particular importance to the present discussion, context. To a connected self, the context or environment and the person are inseparable; the person cannot exist without the context, and the context is meaningless without the person.

The separate self sees oneself as separate from others, usually in a ranked or hierarchical relationship with them. It feels the need to constantly jockey for or adjust one's position in relationship to a perception of, or an authoritative declaration of, others' positions in the hierarchy. In American culture, because there is some mobility within the hierarchy rather than positions being fixed by ranking at birth, such as caste or clan, people find that a competitive mode of interpersonal interaction is a means to maintain or elevate oneself in the ranking. Implied is an "each man for himself" ethos, supporting an individualistic culture

(Hofstede, 1981) with the accompanying tendencies for self-sufficiency, guarding against vulnerability or at least an exposure of such, caution with others, competitive, confrontational, and often combative behaviors. This mode of being in the world tends to be exclusionary rather than inclusive of others and does not lend itself towards an encompassing, compassionate, caring, considerate, and kind discourse and negotiation with others. So often it moves in the direction of a zero-sum game.

Van Nostrand (1993) characterizes the differences in the masculine and feminine forms of interpersonal behavior, further defining the separate and connected selves, respectively. The masculine form of interpersonal and group interaction takes primarily two forms, that of dominance or detachment, while the feminine forms are deference or diagnosis and detection. To use these in moral deliberations and discussions of ethical and moral dilemmas and issues in firms or organizations one can see that the results will be different, depending on the form taken, and perhaps the gender and sex of the individuals involved. Again, the particular set of circumstances in the particular situation, set within a particular environment, can affect the way of knowing, seeing, feeling, thinking, and acting, i.e., the way one "reasons" about ethical matters.

Yes, one can assume that the connected self is more trusting of others and the relationships that tie the self to others. One needs to be trusting if one sees oneself as interdependent and connected, in an inquiry and rapport-building mode rather than in a dominance, detachment, or reporting mode (Tannen, 1989, Van Nostrand, 1993). One mode is more inclusive, nurturing of relationships, leans in the direction of building community, no matter how small or large the group.

Theoretically then this can mean that once the relationships within the firm are established and means found to maintain and repair them, the costs of competition, isolation, alienation, conflict, passive-aggressive sabotage, and the enactment of counter-dependent relationships are somewhat if not entirely eliminated. In a firm where relationships are based on connected selves, cooperation, collaboration, support, nurturance, and the valuing interdependencies would seemingly decrease if not eliminate the problematic human resource costs of disciplinary actions, theft, absenteeism, poor morale and motivation.

In light of these gender differences in ethical orientation, the previous section's account of what — according to economic rationality — constitutes reasonable business behavior clearly exhibits a male gender bias. Collins et al., for example, summarize this concept of business behavior as one in which "work is a game with rules and customs geared to reward traditional *male* behavior" (1988, emphasis added). Similarly, a recent article in *Newsweek* magazine summarizes the views of various observers' that "...traditional business-school teaching methods are male-oriented" (1992, p.98). Specifically, three central attributes of the financial-economic concept of rationality favor the male orientation. First, the narrow focus on wealth maximization as the ultimate and sole end of all human endeavor. Second, the increasing use of a game-theory methodology and conceptualization to model business environments. Third, and most fundamentally, the rigid mathematical axiom approach to developing a concept of rationality reflecting a rule, rather than contextual, orientation. Thus the very foundation of business education, namely its rationality assumption, may actively deter female participation.

In the remainder of this paper, the term "feminine firm" is used to identify an organization in which the predominant moral orientation is that identified as the feminine "connected self." We do not mean to imply that the feminine firm is literally a firm owned or managed by women. It is the moral orientation of the firm, and not the actual gender of the agents therein, that is of interest here.

Isolating the Bias: Corporate Culture's Value Base

The value systems of business theory influence those of business practice. For example, Dees observes that "how concepts are introduced in an academic setting can have a significant influence on their use later on" (1992, p.38). Similarly, while commenting on the value system underlying business theory, Duska notes that "as it gets accepted as a legitimating reason for certain behavior in our form of life, it becomes subtly self-fulfilling" (1992, p.149). Bowie notes that "people change their behavior when confronted with assumptions about how other people behave" (1991, p.9).

In the current context, these assumptions about how other people behave originate in business academe. The modern business school represents the intellectual crucible of contemporary western corporate culture. It is in these institutions that the disparate and undeveloped value systems of future business leaders take shape. The behavioral models of financial economics have played an increasingly dominant role in the evolution of business education's value system (Dobson, 1991). These models can be traced to the seminal work of Coase (1937) on "The Nature of the Firm" in which the firm is depicted as a transaction-cost maximizer in a market-based system of exchange. More recently, Jensen and Meckling (1976) have succinctly defined firms as "legal fictions which serve as a nexus for a set of contracting relations among individuals" (p.310).[2] Thus, in the modern theory of the firm, the firm is no longer viewed as an atomistic unit, but rather as a complex web of explicit and implicit contracts between stakeholder groups; namely bondholders, stockholders, management, employees, customers, suppliers, and society at large.

This definition places emphasis on the agents within the firm, rather than on the firm itself. The humanizing and relationship-building implications of this shift from firm to agent have been largely ignored by financial theorists. To Merton Miller, for example, "[t]he firm...[is]...an abstract engine that 'uses money today to make money tomorrow'" (1986, p.452). The objective function of the non-human firm, namely profit or net-present-value (NPV) maximization, has simply been shifted to the human agents. Behavior is conceptualized entirely within the rubric of pecuniary value maximization and the firm is merely a tool that facilitates this pursuit. The firm is inseparable from and defined entirely within this economic rubric.

These models are built entirely on the premise that individuals' sole motivation is the accumulation of personal wealth: as Noreen observes "...the assumption

[is] that people act unreservedly in their own narrowly defined self-interest with, if necessary, guile and deceit" (1988, p.359). This rubric is defined by Bellah (1985) as "utilitarian individualism"; as an ideology it "gives legitimacy to the priority given to self over others and to the material social values of self-advancement" (Ladd, 1991, p.89). These models tend to be presented by business educators as morally or "value" neutral. But, as Bowie (1991) notes, "there is considerable confusion as to whether the profit maximization claim is a universal empirical claim, an approximate empirical claim, a heuristic assumption, or an ethical obligation" (p.14).

From his experience as a professor of business ethics, Bowie (1991) supplies anecdotal evidence that the wealth maximization assumption is construed by students as an ethical obligation. "They [business school students] believe that they will have to be unethical to keep their jobs. They believe that everyone else will put their [own] interests first" (p.9). Similarly, Marwell and Ames (1981) find that, compared to the aggregate student body, "[e]conomics graduate students are more inclined to behave in a self-interested fashion" (Bowie, 1991, p.9).

In the context of practitioners, Reich (1990) notes that "we are witnessing the creation of a purer form of capitalism, practiced globally by managers who are more distant, more economically driven — in essence more coldly rational in their decisions, having shed the old affiliations with people and place" (p.77). He goes on to conclude: "Vanishing...are the paternalistic corporate heads who used to feel a sense of responsibility for their local community. Emerging in their place is the new global manager, driven by the irrefutable logic of global capitalism to seek higher profits, enhanced market leadership, and improved stock price" (p.78). The assumptions that support this "irrefutable logic" are identified by Thaler (1992) in his recent book covering numerous *Paradoxes and Anomalies of Economic Life*:

> The same basic assumptions about behavior are used in all the firm, financial markets, or consumer choice. The two key assumptions are rationality and self-interest. People are assumed to want to get as much for themselves as possible, and are assumed to be quite clever in figuring out how best to accomplish this air. (p. 2)

In light of Gilligan's work, the gender bias inherent in this concept of *reasonable* behavior is readily apparent. Economists, particularly financial economists, have successfully promulgated the premise that their extant rationality premise defines the most *reasonable* mode of behavior within the firm. By arguing that is how people actually behave, i.e., that this is reasonable behavior, economists infer that this is how people *should* behave. Financial economics develops an implicit normative agenda. As this male oriented — separated self — rationality concept has become increasing accepted, primarily as a result of the growing size and social stature of business schools, it has evolved from a mathematically simplifying methodology to an epistemology. Collins et al., for example, summarize this epistemology as one in which "work is a game with rules and customs geared to reward traditional *male* behavior" (1988, emphasis added). Indeed, this epistemology is one based on individual adherence to strict rules of game-theoretic logic. As Rasmusen (1989) notes: "During the 1980s, game theory has become dramatically more important to mainstream economics.

Indeed, it seems to be swallowing up microeconomics..." (p.13). The game is one of individual wealth maximization, the milieu is adversarial and the firm is a passive conduit through which agents pursue their individual material ends. The firm invoked by contemporary financial-economic theory is a masculine firm.

The Cost of the Game: Evaluating the Gender Bias

Is this "masculine" firm economically optimal, or even desirable? Financial-economic theory implies that it is not. Interestingly, the inefficiencies of the "masculine firm" stem from precisely those value characteristics that identify the firm as masculine.

The contemporary theory of the firm, reflected in the financial contracting models of financial economics, engenders equilibria that are *second-best*. These equilibria are optimal (i.e., wealth maximizing) neither for the agent concerned nor for the economy in aggregate. Financial contracting models investigate the behavior of these 'male' agents within the firm. Depending upon the type of market imperfection assumed, these *rational* agents fall victim to one of two types of agency problem, adverse-selection or moral-hazard (Darrough and Stoughton, 1986).[3] The equilibria of these models thus support Bowie's intuition when he observes that "[i]t only pays to lie or cheat when you can free ride off the honesty of others.... The conscious pursuit of self-interest by all members of society has the collective result of undermining the interests of all" (1991, pp.11-12).

Note that agency costs stem from an inability on the part of agents to reliably enforce contractual agreements: even though it is self-defeating, opportunism holds sway. Indeed, any notion of a value system other than that of narrowly defined self-interest is summarily dismissed by financial economists as no more than a "'Nirvana' form of analysis" (Jensen and Meckling, 1976, p.328). This invocation of economic *man* is an invocation of Gilligan's "separated self," reflecting the archetypically male values of competition, individualism, game and rule orientation; an autonomous self separated from others in a hierarchical world (Gilligan, 1982). The idea that a different yet equally plausible type of agent — a more feminine, relationship-oriented, "connected self" type of agent — would ameliorate these agency costs is appealing. Thaler (1992) predicts such a future shift in economists' concept of rationality:

> we can start to see the development of the new, improved version of economic theory. The new theory will retain the idea that agents try to do the best they can, but these individuals will also have the human strengths of kindness and cooperation..." (p.5).

These "human strengths" have been linked explicitly to a feminine value system (Pearsall, 1986). Inadvertently, Thaler is singing the praises of economic woman over economic man.

Toward a Feminine Value Base: The Economics of Virtue

> ...[T]he presence of what are in a slightly old-fashioned terminology called virtues in fact plays a significant role in the operation of the economic system...[T]he process of exchange requires or at least is greatly facilitated by the presence of several of these virtues (not only truth, but also trust, loyalty, and justice in future dealings). (Arrow, 1975, p.15)

If the concept of rationality currently embedded in financial-economic theory were the only feasible one, then the 'separated-self' orientation would seem inevitable. In essence we would have to conclude that, in a business context at least, men are more rational than women. In *Whose Justice? Which Rationality?* MacIntyre (1988) cogently argues that there is no absolute rationality; "rationality itself, whether theoretical or practical, is a concept with a history: indeed, since there are a diversity of traditions of enquiry, with histories, there are...rationalities rather than rationality" (p.9). Although many philosophers and organizational theorists might question MacIntyre's somewhat extreme relativistic position, most would agree that the wealth maximization construct of financial economics provides too narrow a concept of substantive rationality (Simon 1965, Nesteruk 1992). Ladd (1970), for example, argues that rationality "is relative, that is, to be rational means to be efficient in pursuing a desired goal, whatever that might be" (p.497).

Once the relativistic nature of substantive rationality is accepted, the door is open to alternative value premises. One such premise is supplied by *virtue-ethics* theory. This epistemology encompasses a logically coherent and morally inclusive substantive rationality concept. Moreover, virtue ethics has been recognized as a particularly gender neutral — perhaps even feminine — philosophy (Pearsall, 1986).

Virtue-ethics theory provokes a complete reevaluation of the economic concept of substantive rationality. A recent definition of virtue is supplied by MacIntyre (1984): "A virtue is an acquired human quality the possession and exercise of which tends to enable us to achieve those goods which are internal..." (p.191). MacIntyre distinguishes between internal and external goods as follows:

> It is characteristic of what I have called external goods that when achieved they are always some individual's property or possession. Moreover characteristically they are such that the more someone has of them, they less there is for other people...External goods are therefore characteristically objects of competition in which there must be losers as well as winners. *Internal* goods are indeed the outcome of competition to excel, but it is characteristic of them that their achievement is a good for the whole community who participate in the practice. (1984, pp.190-91; emphasis added)

From a virtue-ethics perspective the moral impoverishment of economic rationality is reflected in both its failure to recognize the virtues, and in its substitution of the pursuit of external goods for the pursuit of internal goods as the agent's ultimate end. In business-ethics theory, for example, the traditional rule-based approach is increasingly being rejected in favor of the more holistic virtue-ethics approach (Bella and King 1989, Bowie 1991, Klein 1989, MacIntyre 1984, Williams and Murphy 1990). Solomon (1992), for example, argues that "[b]usiness ethicists have been looking for theory in the wrong place and, consequently, they have been finding and developing the wrong theories" (p.319).

Unlike traditional rule-based and material-acquisition-based value systems, virtue-ethics is founded in Aristotelian moral philosophy and focuses on the character and motivations of the agent, and on the agent's ability to pursue excellence through the exercise of the virtues. Klein (1989) succinctly distinguishes between these two schools by labeling them as "action-based" and "agent-based" respectively: the former tending to focus on rules-of-the-game that can be generally applied to contractual situations, whereas virtue-ethics concerns the character and motivations of the agent and recognizes the relativistic nature of rationality. Thus, with its emphasis on character, relationships, virtues, and the malleability of rules, this "agent-based" rationality rubric is much more akin to Gilligan's "connected-self" value orientation. The tie-in between virtue-ethics and feminine ethics is readily apparent (Pearsall, 1986).

In addition to arguing that virtue-ethics supplies a coherent concept of substantive rationality, MacIntyre (1988) argues that, of the various concepts of rationality, virtue ethics has proved the most robust:

> ...those who have thought their way through the topics of justice and practical rationality, from the standpoint constructed by and in the direction pointed out first by Aristotle and then by Aquinas, have every reason at least so far to hold that the rationality of their tradition has been confirmed in its encounters with other traditions...(pp.402-3)

But virtuous agents cannot operate in a vacuum, they must be *connected*. This value system assumes not only that agents believe in the existence of a *telos* in the form of quality or excellence, but also that an infrastructure exists that is structured in recognition of, and in order to attain, the *telos*; "one cannot think for oneself if one thinks entirely by oneself...it is only by participation in a rational practice-based community that one becomes rational...." (MacIntyre, 1988, p.396). Thus Aristotelian rationality is a shared rationality with a shared conception of what is ultimately desirable in all human endeavor. This shared conception must be supported by, and indeed be the *raison d'etre* of, the organizations and institutions that control and direct human activity. This infrastructure is an aspect of the *polis*: "the form of social order whose shared mode of life already expresses the collective answer or answers of its citizens to the question 'what is the best mode of life for human beings?'" (p.133). Such an infrastructure is essential for virtue-ethics:

> Aristotle is articulating at the level of theoretical enquiry a thought inherited from the poets when he argues in Book I of the *Politics* (1252b28-1253a39) that a human being separated from the *polis* is thereby deprived of some of the essential attributes of a human being...A human being stands to the *polis* as a part to its whole...For the *polis* is human community perfected and completed by achieving its *telos*. (p.96-97)

The virtue-ethics approach therefore casts business organizations in a role that is far more active and intrusive than merely a "contractual nexus" or "wealth creating machine." The firm becomes a nurturing community, a *polis* "Corporations are real communities, neither ideal nor idealized, and therefore the perfect place to start understanding the nature of the virtues" (Solomon, 1992, p.325). Solomon emphasizes the link between virtue-ethics and this expanded role of the firm as a nurturing community: "It [virtue-ethics] is an Aristotelian ethics precisely because it is membership in a community, a community with collective goals and a stated mission — to produce quality goods and/or services and to make a profit for the stockholders" (Solomon, 1992, p.321).[4] By broadening its concept of rationality to encompass behavior beyond that of narrow opportunism, business theory will be able to accommodate the notion of the firm as a *polis*.

Implicit Contracts: The Source of Feminine-Firm Superiority

The central inefficiency of the traditional invocation of the firm in financial economics is its inability to costlessly enforce implicit contracts. The ubiquity and importance of implicit contracts in financial markets is emphasized by Cornell and Shapiro (1987) who define an implicit contract as "too nebulous and state contingent to reduce to writing at reasonable cost" (1987, p.6). Examples of implicit contracts are many and varied; the most common include a producer's commitment to product quality, a stockbroker's commitment to execute a client's security transaction at the best available price, or management's commitment to act in the interests of shareholders. In addition, in recent years the international expansion of stakeholder relations has further increased the number of implicit contracts due to the difficulty of legally enforcing any type of contract transnationally. J.B. King (1988) makes this point clearly:

> As a result of our economy's increasing complexity, it is becoming more difficult and expensive to spell out and enforce mutual responsibilities through detailed contracts and administrative hierarchies...Conditions of *trust* are therefore becoming increasingly crucial to competing — and cooperating — in today's business environment. (p.480, emphasis added).

The problem inherent in implicit contracts is enforcement. The optimal strategy for either party may be to act opportunistically and renege on the contract, so both parties may have to expend significant resources on monitoring and bonding activities in an attempt to ensure compliance. In some circumstances, the costs of monitoring and bonding may be so high that contracts are not entered into unless some other enforcement mechanism can be relied upon. One alternative is the agent's desire to maintain a *reputation*. Reputation may act as an implicit contractual enforcement mechanism. For example, in the market for initial public offerings of equity (IPOs), reputable underwriters are able to sell a given issue at a higher price than their less reputable competitors (Carter and Manaster, 1990). Investors are willing to pay this higher price because the reputation of the underwriters *certifies* that the issue is of high quality. In the IPO market, reputation appears to work well as a contractual enforcement mechanism.

But reputation will not always work. If the contractual interactions are not continual, or if it is hard for one party in a contractual arrangement to verify the past actions of the other party (i.e., informational asymmetry exists), then reputation may fail as an enforcement mechanism (Rasmusen, 1989). In Diamond's (1989) model of reputation acquisition in debt markets, agents never strive to build reputations. Some merely acquire reputations for timely debt repayment through luck. Once acquired these reputations *may* be actively maintained until the endgame is reached, at which point agents revert to opportunistic behavior.

This reputation concept in financial economics assumes that agents build reputations, for trustworthiness for example, purely for economic reasons: hence the fragility of reputation-induced equilibria. But what if we move beyond financial-economic rationality and contemplate the possibility of agents building and maintaining reputations for *moral* reasons? Economic arguments have been made for the desirability of trustworthy agents (Arrow 1975, Frank 1988, Noreen 1988, and Thaler 1992). For example, Noreen recognizes the value of religion or ethical rules as contractual enforcement mechanisms. But these strictures lie beyond financial-economics' rationality concept and therefore adherence to them is hard to 'rationalize.' Thus Noreen concludes the "[b]ehavioral norms (or ethical rules) are clearly a most fragile enforcement mechanism" (p. 367): opportunistic agents have no rational *a priori* reason to abide by them.

The economic superiority of the feminine firm, therefore, derives from its broadened concept of what constitutes rational behavior, as invoked by virtue-ethics theory. To trust for trust's sake, to be virtuous for virtue's sake, now becomes entirely rational and indeed desirable for an agent pursuing moral excellence within the *polis*. Unlike the masculine firm invoked in financial-economic theory, therefore, the feminine firm will exhibit a tendency to nurture cooperation and a recognition of communal — in addition to merely individual — objectives. This tendency will dissipate the agency problems that plague financial-economics' theory of the firm. In essence, within the feminine firm, **trust** becomes a rational and feasible implicit contractual enforcement mechanism.

Given the essential nature of the firm as a nexus of communal relations, the exclusion of the feminine firm levies both a moral and an economic cost on our corporate culture. By establishing a sound logical conceptualization and justification for the feminine firm within the business disciplines, extensions of this work will help disseminate this broadened value orientation throughout business education and practice. Through its substantive rationality rubric, virtue-ethics theory provides both a conceptualization of the feminine ethic and a justification for the feminine firm.[5]

Conclusion

This paper extends the work of Thomas White on the influence of gender on firms' moral and economic performance. Specifically, we evaluate White's suggestion that a feminine value orientation may be superior, from an economic perspective, than the currently predominant masculine orientation. A necessary first step in making this evaluation is to identify the source of the gender bias, if any, within the business rubric. The source is identified as the substantive rationality assumption that underlies the theory of the firm in financial economics. This substantive rationality assumption invokes agents whose sole objective is the accumulation of personal material wealth. These agents are assumed to be opportunists, that is they pursue wealth with guile and deceit if such behavior is economically optimal.

The theory of the firm built around this assumption in financial economics views the business milieu as an individualistic competitive game. The firm is merely a passive contractual nexus that facilitates individual agents' pursuit of wealth. In light of Carol Gilligan's work on gender differences in moral orientation, this invocation of the goals and values of the individual within the firm exhibits a discernible male bias. It is more akin to Gilligan's identification of the male-oriented "separated self" than to the female-oriented "connected self." Thus the findings of this paper support White's intimation of a male gender bias in the value system underlying business theory.

We suggest this gender bias may be corrected by drawing on the concept of substantive rationality inherent in virtue-ethics theory. This theory is noted as being particularly sensitive to the female moral orientation. Virtue-ethics invokes a broader rationality construct in which individuals collectively pursue moral excellence through virtuous acts. Given virtuous agents, as opposed to opportunistic agents, the firm is cast in a role that is more active and intrusive than merely the aforementioned contractual nexus. The firm becomes an essential aspect of individuals' collective pursuit of moral excellence. This feminine-oriented relationship-based value system complements the essential nature of the firm as a nexus of relationships between stakeholders. Not only is this feminine firm morally desirable from a virtue-ethics perspective, but it is also economically more efficient in that trust becomes a more feasible implicit contractual enforcement mechanism. In an organizational context, from both a moral and an economic perspective, long established economic man is dominated by nascent economic woman.

Notes

[1] White's interpretation of Gilligan has been criticized recently by Martin and Shaw, 1993.

[2] Hu (1991) distinguishes between contractual relations (e.g., management and bondholders) and fiduciary relations (e.g., management and stockholders). He also notes, however, that the recent proliferation of new financial products has made this distinction ambiguous. Indeed, this proliferation threatens to undermine the whole concept of firms as share price maximizers: a concept that is the cornerstone of financial economics.

[3] In essence, an agency problem is a contractual impasse in which the 'principal' is unable to costlessly ensure that the 'agent' acts in the former's best interests. 'Adverse selection' concerns a situation in which informational asymmetry exists and the principal is thus unable to determine the 'type' of agent (e.g., whether the agent is inherently lazy or industrious). 'Moral hazard" concerns a simpler situation in which the principal is merely unable to control the opportunistic actions of the agent.

[4] An analogy can be drawn between the role of the *polis* in directing human endeavor, and work by North (1991), Romer (1990), and others in industrial-organization theory that highlights the importance of institutional infrastructure in guiding human activity. North notes that the entrepreneur within the firm (North uses the term "organization") is constrained and directed by the institutional infrastructure. He also notes that "[t]he subjective perceptions (mental models) of entrepreneurs determine the choices they make" (p. 5). It is the infrastructure, the *polis*, that helps sculpt these mental models: "It is the institutional framework that dictates the kind of knowledge perceived to having the maximum payoff" (p.10).

[5]Some practical techniques for altering individual firms' value-orientation are evaluated by Dobson (1992). These techniques involve essentially educating business executives as to the intrinsic value of virtuous behavior. This education takes various forms; for example, a series of workshops or the identification of 'exemplars' within the organization (i.e., individuals who, through their actions, demonstrate the virtues).

Bibliography

Allen F. and G. Faulhaber. 1989. "Signalling by Underpricing in the Initial Public Offering Market," *Journal of Financial Economics*, vol. 23, pp. 303-23.

Aristotle. *The Nicomachean Ethics*. Oxford University Press.

Arrow, Kenneth. 1975. "Gifts and Exchanges," in Phelps, E. S. (ed.), *Altruism, Morality, and Economic Theory*. New York: Russell Sage Foundation.

Barach, J. and John B. Elstrott. 1988. "The Transactional Ethic: The Ethical Foundations of Free Enterprise Reconsidered," *Journal of Business Ethics*, vol. 7, pp. 545-52.

Baumhart, Raymond C. 1961. "How Ethical are Businessmen?" *Harvard Business Review*.

Belenky, M. F., C. M. Clinchy, N. R. Goldberger, and J. M. Tarule. 1986. *Women's Ways of Knowing: The Development of Self, Voice and Mind*. New York: Basic Books.

Bella, David and Jonathan King. 1989. "Common Knowledge of the Second Kind," *Journal of Business Ethics*, vol. 8, pp. 415-30.

Bellah, Robert N., Richard Madsen, William M. Sullivan, Ann Swidler and Steven M. Tipton. 1985. *Habits of the Heart: Individualism and Commitment in American Life*. New York: Harper and Row.

Bowie, Norman E. 1991. "Challenging the Egoistic Paradigm," *Business Ethics Quarterly*, vol. 1, pp. 1-21.

Byron, W.J. 1988. "Twin Towers: A Philosophy and Theology of Business," *Journal of Business Ethics*, vol. 7, pp. 525-30.

Carter, R. and S. Manaster. 1990. "Initial Public Offerings and Underwriter Reputation," *Journal of Finance*, vol. 45, pp. 1045-1067.

Collins, N.W., Gilbert, S.K. and Nycum, S.H. 1988. *Women Leading: Making Tough Choices on the Fast Track*. New York: Stephen Greene Press/Viking.

Cornell, B. and A.C. Shapiro. 1988. "Corporate Stakeholders and Corporate Finance," *Financial Management*, Spring, pp. 5-14.

Copeland, Thomas and Fred Weston. 1988. *Financial Theory and Corporate Policy*, 3rd ed. Addison-Wesley.

Darrough Masako N., and Neal M. Stoughton. 1986. Moral Hazard and Adverse Selection: the Question of Financial Structure. *Journal of Finance*, vol. 41, pp. 501-14.

Dees, Gregory J. 1982. "Principals, Agents, and Ethics," in *Ethics and Agency Theory*, ed. Norman E. Bowie and R. Edward Freeman. New York: Oxford University Press.

DeGeorge, Richard T. 1986. *Business Ethics*, 2nd ed. New York: Macmillan.

Diamond, Douglas W. 1989. "Reputation Acquisition in Debt Markets," *Journal of Political Economy*, vol. 97, pp. 828-61.

Dobson, John. 1990. "The Role of Ethics in Global Corporate Culture," *Journal of Business Ethics*, vol. 9, pp. 481-88.

_____. 1991. "Reconciling Financial Economics and Business Ethics, " *Business and Professional Ethics Journal*, vol. 10 (Winter).

_____. 1992. "Ethics in Financial Contracting, " *Business and Professional Ethics Journal*, vol. 11, Nos. 3&4.

Duska, Ronald F. 1992. "Why Be a Loyal Agent? A Systematic Ethical Analysis," in *Ethics and Agency Theory*, ed. Norman E. Bowie and R. Edward Freeman. New York: Oxford University Press.

Eisenhardt, Kathleen M. 1989. "Agency Theory: An Assessment and Review," *Academy of Management Review*, vol. 14, pp. 57-74.

Eisler, R. 1987. *The Chalice and the Blade*. San Francisco: Harper and Row.

Etzioni, Anitai. 1988. *The Moral Dimension*. New York: The Free Press.

_____. 1991. "Reflections on Teaching Business Ethics, " *Business Ethics Quarterly*, vol. 1 (October), pp. 355-66.

Flannery, M. 1986. "Asymmetric Information and Risky Debt Maturity Choice," *Journal of Finance*, March, pp. 19-38.

Frank, Robert. 1988. *Passions Within Reason*. New York: W. W. Norton & Co.

Friedman, Milton. 1970. "The Social Responsibility of Business is to Increase its Profits," *The New York Times Magazine*, (reprinted in *Business Ethics*), by W.M. Hoffman and J. M. Moore, McGraw-Hill, 1990, pp. 153-56.

Gauthier, David. 1988. *Morals by Agreement*. Oxford: Clarenden Press.

Ghorbade, Jai. 1991. "Ethics in MBA Programs: The Rhetoric, the Reality, and a Plan of Action," *Journal of Business Ethics*, vol. 10, pp. 891-905.

Gilligan, C. 1982. *In a Different Voice*. Cambridge, MA: Harvard University Press.

Goodpaster, Kenneth E. 1991. "Business Ethics and Stakeholder Analysis," *Business Ethics Quarterly*, vol. 1, pp. 54-73.

Heckman, Peter. 1992. "Business and Games," *Journal of Business Ethics*, vol. 11, pp. 933-38.

Hoffman, Michael W. and Jennifer Mills Moore. 1990. *Business Ethics*. New York: McGraw-Hill.

Hofstede, Geert. 1991. "Motivation, Leadership, and Organization: Do American Theories Apply Abroad?", in Kolb, Rubin, and Osland, *The Organizational Behavioral Reader*. New Jersey: Prentice Hall.

Hollis, Martin and Steven Lukes. 1982. *Rationality and Relativism*. England, Oxford: Basil Blackwell.

Hunt, David E. 1987. *Beginning with Ourselves, in Practice, Theory, and Human Affairs*. Cambridge, MA: Brookline Books.

Jensen, M. C. and W. Meckling. 1976. "Theory of the Firm: Managerial Behavior, Ownership Costs and Ownership Structure," *Journal of Financial Economics*, vol. 3, pp. 305-60.

John, Kose, and D. Nachman. 1985. "Risky Debt, Investment Incentives and Reputation in a Sequential Equilibrium," *Journal of Finance*, vol. 40, pp. 863-77.

Kahneman, D., Jack L. Knetsch, and Richard H. Thaler. 1986. "Fairness and the Assumptions of Economics," *Journal of Business*, vol. 59, pp. 285-300.

Kavka, Gregory S. 1991. "Is Individual Choice Less Problematic than Collective Choice?" *Economics and Philosophy*, vol. 7, pp. 143-65.

King, J.B. 1989. "Confronting Chaos," *Journal of Business Ethics*, vol. 8, January.

Klein, Sherwin. 1989. "Platonic Virtue Theory and Business Ethics," *Business and Professional Ethics Journal*, vol. 8, no. 4.

_____. 1988. "Is a Moral Organization Possible?" *Business and Professional Ethics Journal*, vol. 7, no. 1.

Kreps, D. and R. Wilson. 1982. "Sequential Equilibria," *Econometrica*, vol. 7, pp. 863-94.

Ladd, John. 1970. "Morality and the Ideal of Rationality in Formal Organizations," *The Monist*, vol. 54, pp. 488-516.

Lasch, Christopher. 1991. *The True and Only Heaven: Progress and Its Critics*. New York: W. W. Norton.

Leland, Hayne E., and David H. Pyle. 1977. "Informational Asymmetries, Financial Structure, and Financial Intermediation," *Journal of Finance*, vol. 32, pp. 371-87.

Lewis, H. 1990. *A Question of Values*. San Francisco: Harper Collins.

Lukes, Steven. 1977. *Rationality and Relativism*. New York: Columbia University Press.

MacIntyre, Alisdair. 1966. *A Brief History of Ethics*. New York: Macmillan.

_____. 1984. *After Virtue* (2nd ed.). Notre Dame: University of Notre Dame Press.

_____. 1988. *Whose Justice? Which Rationality?* Notre Dame: University of Notre Dame Press.

Marwell, Gerald and Ruth E. Ames. 1981. "Economists Free Ride, Does Anyone Else?" *Journal of Public Economics*, vol. 15, pp. 295-310.

Milgram, S. 1974. *Obedience to Authority*. New York: Harper-Collins (quote can be found in Wolfe, Art. 1991. "Reflections on Business Ethics," *Business Ethics Quarterly*, vol. 1, No. 4 (October), pp. 409-40).

Milgrom, P. and J. Roberts. 1982. "Predation, Reputation and Entry Deterrence," *Journal of Economic Theory*, vol. 27, pp. 280-312.

Miller, Merton H. 1986. "Behavioral Rationality in Finance: The Case of Dividends," *Journal of Business*, vol. 59, pp. 451-68.

_____, and Kevin Rock. 1985. "Dividend Policy Under Asymmetric Information," *Journal of Finance*, vol. 40 (September), pp. 1031-1052.

Myers, Stewart C. 1977. "Determinants of Corporate Borrowing," *Journal of Financial Economics*, p. 5.

_____, and N. Majluff. 1984. "Corporate Financing and Investment Decisions when Firms Have Information that Investors Do not Have," *Journal of Financial Economics*, vol. 13, pp. 187-221.

Nesteruk, Jeffrey. 1992. "The Moral Status of the Corporation: Comments on an Inquiry," *Business Ethics Quarterly*, vol. 2, No. 4.

Noddings, N. 1984. *Caring, A Feminine Approach to Ethics and Moral Education*. Berkeley: University of California Press.

Noreen, Eric. 1988. "The Economics of Ethics: A New Perspective on Agency Theory," *Accounting Organizations and Society*, vol. 13, pp. 359-69.

Pearsall, Marilyn. 1986. *Women and Values: Readings in Recent Feminine Philosophy*. Belmont, CA: Wadsworth Inc.

Polanyi, Michael. 1958. *Personal Knowledge: Toward a Post-Critical Philosophy*. Chicago: University of Chicago Press.

Rasmusen, Eric. 1989. *Games and Information: An Introduction to Game Theory*. Oxford, U.K.: Basil Blackwell, Ltd.

Reich, Robert B. 1990. "Who is Us?" *Harvard Business Review*, January-February.

Roll, R. 1986. "The Hubris Hypothesis of Corporate Takeovers," *Journal of Business*, vol. 59, pp. 197-216.

Ross, S. 1977. "The Determination of Financial Structure: The Incentive Signaling Approach," *The Bell Journal of Economics*, vol. 8 (Spring), pp. 23-40.

Schwartz, Barry. 1990. "King Midas in America," in *Enhancing Business Ethics*, edited by Clarence C. Walton. New York: Plennum Press.

Simon, H. A. 1965. *Administrative Behavior*. New York: The Free Press.

Solomon, Robert C. 1992. "Corporate Roles, Personal Virtues: An Aristotelian Approach to Business Ethics," *Business Ethics Quarterly*, vol. 2, pp. 317-39.

Spence, A. 1977. "Job Market Signaling," *Quarterly Journal of Economics*, vol. 8 (Spring), pp. 23-40.

Tannen, D. 1990. *You Just Don't Understand: Men and Women in Conversation*. New York: Ballantine Books.

Thaler, Richard H. 1992. *The Winner's Curse: Paradoxes and Anomalies of Economic Life*. New York: The Free Press.

Thakor, Anjan V. 1989. "Strategic Issues in Financial Contracting: An Overview," *Financial Management*, (Summer).

Van Nostrand, C. H. 1993. *Gender-Responsible Leadership*. Newbury Park, CA: Sage Publications.

Von Neumann, J. and O. Morgenstern. 1947. *Theory of Games and Economic Behavior*, 2nd ed. Princeton, NJ: Princeton University Press.

Weizenbaum, Joseph. 1976. *Computer Power and Human Reason*. San Francisco: W. H. Freeman and Co.

White, Thomas I. 1992. "Business Ethics and Carol Gilligan's 'Two Voices.'" *Business Ethics Quarterly*, vol. 2, No. 1 (January), pp. 51-61.

Williams, Oliver E. and Patrick E. Murphy. 1990. "The Ethics of Virtue: A Moral Theory of Marketing," *Journal of Macromarketing*, (Spring), pp. 19-29.

Wolfe, Art. 1991. "Reflections on Business Ethics," *Business Ethics Quarterly*, vol. 1, No. 4 (October), pp. 409-40.

The Question of Organizational Consciousness: Can Organizations Have Values, Virtues and Visions?[1]

Peter Pruzan

ABSTRACT. It is common for organizational theorists as well as business practitioners to speak of an organization's visions, strategies, goals and responsibilities. This implies that collectivities have competencies normally attributed to individuals, i.e. to reflect, evaluate, learn and make considered choices. The article provides a series of reflections on the concept of consciousness in an organizational context. It is argued that, under certain conditions, it is both meaningful and efficacious to ascribe the competency for conscious and intentional behavior to organizations. The arguments provided are based on empirical observations, common sense and deductive reasoning.

1. Introduction

There is an apparent inconsistency in the way we tend to refer to the competencies and capacities of collectivities of purposeful individuals, what I

Peter Pruzan is Professor of Systems Science at the Department of Management, Philosophy & Politics, The Copenhagen Business School. He has been the president of a successful, innovative international business and has authored more than 100 articles and books on operations research, systems science, business ethics, value-based leadership, ethical accounting and corporate social responsibility. His professional goal is to integrate perspectives from management, philosophy and spirituality to develop operational and values-based approaches to leadership. He is active in international organizations that promote these themes and he is an advisor to corporations and governmental organizations on these matters. He is married to Kirsten, a journalist. They live north of Copenhagen and have 3 grown-up daughters.

will refer to in the sequel as *organizations*. On the one hand, within the field of management parlance, it is common to speak of an organization's visions, strategies, goals and responsibilities. These are everyday phrases employed by both organizational theorists and business practitioners. On the other hand, it is also common to attribute competencies for reflection, evaluation, learning and considered choice solely to individuals. We tend to say that these are distinguishing characteristics of human beings as opposed to other life forms. This suggests that the attributing to organizations of competencies ordinarily associated with consciousness is metaphorical rather than literal in nature.

A relevant example of this ambiguous usage of 'consciousness'[2] is to be found in the literature dealing with the field of business ethics. On the one hand, the propensity to behave in accord with one's conscience and accepted moral codes is typically attributed to individuals. On the other hand, the field of business ethics employs concepts such as organizational (shared) values, codes of ethics and corporate social responsibility.

This terminological conflict or lack of clarity is evident if we refer in particular to what may be called a prototypical American approach to the teaching and practice of business ethics. The pedagogy employed in teaching business ethics in most Anglo-Saxon business schools is designed to motivate the individual to be aware of and capable of dealing with conflicts of interest arising from the desire to promote economic efficiency while behaving in, what the *individual* experiences to be, an ethically acceptable manner. This is in contrast to a more European approach, which tends to emphasize questions of justification and *intersubjective* agreement.[3]

The individual-oriented teaching method is typically to confront the student with a series of case studies which place her/him in contexts characterized by a leader having to make choices when facing moral dilemmas (typically where economic rationality is challenged by ethical considerations). The underlying idea is, that by confronting the student with a series of virtual dilemmas, her/his ability to cope with such moral dilemmas in future "real-world" situations will be improved. The emphasis is on *decisionism* – on the evaluations and decisions made by an individual leader, even though these of course may be strongly affected by the corporate (or even national) culture.

From this perspective, it might be argued that all talk of organizational values and ethics is metaphorical (perhaps even euphemistical); although the management of an enterprise may refer to the corporation's values, virtues and visions, what they really refer to are their own emotive and evaluative bases. Using a combination of carrots and sticks, employees are cajoled and convinced that these constitute a legitimate basis for the establishment of behavioral norms. Similarly, public relations activities are designed to project to other stakeholders, including consumers, activists, regulators and the public at large, that these values, virtues and visions are indigenous to the company, that they are part of its culture.

Briefly speaking, the implicit logic, which underlies such an approach to the concept of consciousness, appears to be as follows:

1. It is individuals alone who have capabilities for reasoning, forming values and making informed decisions.
2. It is via the application of just these capabilities that members of an organization accept that its leaders have the right to define the "organization's" values, visions, etc. The argument is that although as an individual employee I have my own perceptions, evaluations, motivations, I accept that others are vested with the authority to make decisions on behalf of the organiza-

tion as a whole and that it is a condition for my relationship with the organization that I support (or at least do not act in opposition to) the "company values". This is fundamental to virtually all notions of bureaucracy, hierarchy and control.

3. Furthermore, not only do the employees accept that "our company" has an identity based on these values, but other major stakeholders may also choose to observe the company using an optic based on these values. Consumers may choose to take the values into account when making purchasing decisions, financial institutions may use these values as important criteria when making decisions as to providing lines of credit etc.

4. Therefore, it may be argued, one can speak of such concepts as corporate values, virtues and visions without this being in conflict with an underlying assumption that only individuals have consciousness. The values etc., although referred to as "corporate", are *accepted* rather than *shared*; they are labels which are communicated to employees and other stakeholders via a top-down process rather than the result of a participative process based on stakeholder dialogue.

The paper provides a series of reflections on the relevance and efficacy of an alternative perspective on terminology and reality. It will be argued that, if certain conditions are fulfilled, it is both meaningful and efficacious to ascribe the competency for conscious and intentional behavior, including formulating and expressing values and visions, to collectivities of individuals, to organizations. In addition the arguments will not only be hypothetical but also normative; it will be argued that not only *can* organizations acquire the ability for existential reflection and for self-assessment, but in addition the leaders of such collectivities *should* behave so as to promote the development of these competencies, i.e. of what we refer to as *organizational consciousness*. We note, however, that the concept of organizational consciousness to be presented has a more restricted meaning than that we often attribute to human beings. While individuals experience feelings such as pride, joy, guilt and pain in connection with their actions, we do not intend here to ascribe such emotive capabilities to organizations.

The paper is structured as follows:

A. To set the scene, I will briefly present anecdotal and logical arguments for why, in the context of enterprises in developed countries, it is important to even consider such matters at all.

B. Theoretical reasoning, backed by empirical observation, will argue that collectivities *can* and *should* develop these capabilities for existential self-reflection and considered choice.

C. Finally, information will be provided which will demonstrate the practical relevance of these thoughts to mainstream business thinking. In particular, the concept of *social and ethical accountability* will be introduced.

Before commencing, a reservation is called for. When developing the exposition, it will not be possible to avoid employing just those terms whose meaning are being investigated and defined. For example, in the case below, reference will be made to the managers' views on their enterprise's values before discussing whether it is relevant to attribute a competency for value formation to an organization.

2. Why is it important to reflect on the competencies of organizations to develop consciousness?

The following story deals with the creation of a "multinational monster". In the early 1990's I was contacted by a large, European-based multinational manufacturing company (with no activities in my own country, Denmark) and asked to develop a seminar for 49 leaders of the company from eight western countries. The CEO had heard about the research going on at the Copenhagen Business School on values-based leadership and *Ethical Accounting* in cooperation with a major Danish bank. The seminar was held at a lovely inn north of Copenhagen. It started out with lectures, which led up to a group exercise. Each of the participants was given a list

with roughly 50 "values" including such terms as success, love, honesty, trust, excitement, generosity, respect, wealth, creativity, freedom, power, professional competency, reputation, effectiveness, charity, progress, security, compassion, patience, peace, etc. I mentioned that these "values" were simply labels, words for basic cognitive-emotive categories we tend to use to justify our actions.

They were told to take a short walk by themselves in the autumn air and to reflect upon which of these – or any other values they might choose to add on – were most important for them in their daily lives together with family, friends and themselves. Then they were to discuss their views on these personal values with their colleagues. Seven groups were formed, each with seven participants. If possible, the members of each group should agree as to which are the five (anywhere from three to seven) most important values in one's personal life and write these down on flip-over paper. An hour was provided for these deliberations and discussions. Then, in a plenary session, each group was to present the personal values it had selected and to discuss their interpretation of these values, the process they went through in arriving at just these values, etc. etc.

I must admit that I was a bit nervous as to the outcome. This was the first time that I had employed such a procedure.[4] Furthermore, the company was known for its high degree of hierarchical control and its very strong short-term, shareholder orientation (at the expense of a more inclusive orientation towards broader constituencies). However, the exercise appeared to generate considerable energy and enthusiasm. It turned out that this was the first time that it was legitimate for the managers, most of whom had been recruited internally, to discuss such matters as personal values; this simply was not done and certainly not while at work!

In the afternoon, after another lecture and a "happening" by an activist group which demonstrated against the company's high levels of pollution, the exercise was repeated. The only change was that this time, instead of focusing on the individual manager's personal values, the subject was the "company's values". Not those values which were espoused in glittering brochures describing the company and its products, but those values which could be said to implicitly underlie decisions made as to such matters as hiring, evaluating and firing employees, investing in new plant and equipment, entering/leaving markets, negotiating with unions, advertising, lobbying etc. Otherwise the procedure was identical with the morning's exercise. The participants were to take a walk and reflect on the values which appeared to describe or underlie the company's actions, join their group and try and reach agreement as to the most important values which, using inductive reasoning, could be said to characterize the company's actions, write these on flip-over paper, hang the paper right next to the paper with the group's list of personal values from the morning session, and tell the other groups as to how and why those particular values were arrived at.

The result was most provocative for all present. On a large wall hung seven pairs of flip-over papers; for each of the seven groups there was one sheet of paper with the most important personal values and one sheet with the most important corporate values. It was obvious to all that there was absolutely no correspondence between these two sets of values for any of the groups. For each of the groups not only were all the words different; they simply had what one might call strongly varying "flavors". While the personal values tended to include labels such as "good health", "honesty", "love", "satisfaction/happiness", beauty and "peace of mind", the list of organizational values tended to included terms such as "success", "efficiency", "power", "competitiveness" and "productivity". This led to a series of nervous discussions. Tension was in the air. I challenged them and said that if such listings had resulted from the workers it would be quite understandable. The workers could argue that it was natural that there was a large gap between their personal values and those of the company. No one listened to them or was interested in what was important for them. But in the case on hand, the "workers" were the top management.

After an embarrassing period of silence, the CEO held a brief talk in which he announced

that he would consider resigning. He said that it dawned upon him that he was active in the construction of a monster, a corporate Frankenstein.

He did not resign! But the rest of the program was modified so as to allow discussions on such matters as: "Is it important that there is a high degree of harmony between the personal values of the employees (including the management) and the values of the organization as a whole?" "Should a company attempt to develop a code of corporate values – and if so, how – and how should it be interpreted and communicated?" "Should it be a 'top-down' expression of management's understanding of what the company should promote – or should it e.g. be based upon a dialogue process involving major stakeholders, in particular the employees – or some combination of these?"

After this experience I developed a metaphorical picture of the modern, strongly shareholder-oriented manager who, before he or she crosses the doorstep leading to the executive office, hangs his fine coat on a hanger and, unknowingly, hangs up his personal values as well. After a long day of managing, deciding, coordinating and controlling, he crosses the doorstep once again, puts on his fine coat and his personal values, and returns home to his beautiful home, his lovely family, to a fine dinner with good vintage wine, to good friends, the faithful Fido, Beethoven, enchanting love-making and beautiful nature. The picture is of a leader who unbeknownst to himself has developed a modern form of schizophrenia, where the gap between his personal values and the values he promotes in his company is so extreme that both his own health and that of the organization is threatened.

That organizational health can be threatened can be deduced from the observation that in the post-modern/information/knowledge/network society, successful enterprises will rely heavily on employees who are dedicated, creative, dynamic, independent, faithful and reliable. Considerable evidence[5] indicates that such employees seek not only traditional benefits such as good wages and opportunities for advancement, but also meaningful work in socially attractive environments in a company they can be proud of and where they feel that there exists a reasonable degree of harmony between their own values and those of the company.

That personal health can be threatened is not widely documented. However, the following story illustrates the dangers of this new type of schizophrenia. A former friend of mine was for many years the director of personnel at SAS (Scandinavian Airline Systems). Over these many years he had developed a database containing demographic statistics on the lives of a number of Scandinavian leaders in business and the public domain. One of the interesting, but highly depressing, statistics was that when a Scandinavian top manager leaves his or her job for any reason (death, sickness, gets fired, retirement etc.) the expected period of time that he/she has to live is on the order of one year! My friend lived pretty much up to his own statistics and died at the age of 63 after forced retirement at the age of 61. The hypothesis here is that business leaders find it stressing and difficult to live in a world of personal values when so much of their time and energy has been devoted to promoting values dealing with economic efficiency, growth, power, reputation, prestige. They have been used to expressing their values primarily through their work – and when that goes, their main outlet for personal identity and expression goes as well.

It is common for people to speak about wanting to have a long life characterized by a high quality of life. Such figures of speech can be extended to the corporate level. It is postulated that the leaders of most companies would want their company to be characterized by a long and good life. If this is the case, evidence exists that just as it appears to be important for individuals to pay attention to existential questions, it is also vital for companies to pay attention to corporate existential matters such as: "Who are 'we'?" "What do we stand for?" "What are our core values?" "How should we reflect upon our identity and responsibilities?" "How should we measure, evaluate and report on our identity, development and success?"

The authors of the book *Built to Last: Successful Habits of Visionary Companies*[6] researched a set of exceptional (American-based) companies that stood the test of time, the average founding date

being 1897. They studied these companies over their entire histories and compared them to a set of companies that had similar characteristics but did not attain the same stature as the truly visionary companies. They referred to the companies as visionary and exceptional rather than successful or enduring because they distinguished themselves as a very elite brand of institutions – they are characterized by being more than successful and more than enduring. According to the authors, in most cases they are known as the best in their industries and have been so for decades. Many have served as role models for the practice of management. As regards this paper, a fundamental conclusion of the study of the visionary companies was that they articulated a *core ideology*, defined by the authors as consisting of *core values* and *purposes*.

By "core values" the authors referred to "the organization's essential and enduring tenets – a small set of general guiding principles; not to be confused with specific cultural or operating practices: not to be compromised for financial gain or short term expediency." And by "purpose" they referred to "the organization's fundamental reasons for existence beyond just making money – a perpetual guiding star on the horizon: not to be confused with specific goals or business strategies."

What is important for our purposes is not which specific values and purposes characterized the individual companies, but rather the fact that the authors of this widely cited book speak so strongly of the corporate core values, which attain their importance by becoming *shared* values, and the corporate purposes. These values and purposes are described in such a way that they appear to have "objective" character. They exist, can be identified, classified etc. They are stable over long periods of time[7] and do not depend on the presence of a charismatic leader; in fact, according to the authors, many of these companies have had leaders who are far less dominating public figures than the leaders of the (good, well known, but not nearly as extraordinary) companies that the visionary companies were compared to.

What is equally important for our purposes is the fact that the companies they are compared to are characterized by the relative absence of such enduring core/shared values and purposes. It is thus implicitly argued throughout that corporations have the capability to develop competencies normally associated with consciousness – such as developing core values and purposes. And it is explicitly argued that "the visionary companies don't merely declare an ideology; they also take steps to make the ideology pervasive throughout the organization and transcend any individual leader."[8]

A tentative conclusion is that organizations appear to have the potential competency for developing qualities normally associated with consciousness such as being reflective, purposeful and values-oriented. In addition, evidence indicates that such competency and qualities can play an important role in determining organizational viability and success. Therefore, there exist good, practical reasons for seeking to establish a theoretical framework for dealing with such notions as company goals, shared values, and what a former leader (Values Coordinator) at the World Bank, Richard Barrett refers to as the "corporate soul".[9]

3. Theoretical arguments: Under what circumstances is it reasonable to ascribe to an organization the competency to develop shared values, virtues and visions – to develop corporate "consciousness"?

The presentation so far has argued that there may be good business reasons for the leaders of an organization to attempt to promote the development of sound "corporate values". The stage is now set for considering the theoretical question as to when it is meaningful to ascribe to organizations the competency and the capacity to develop qualities that we use to characterize "consciousness". Included are the ability to reflect on such existential matters as corporate identity (who are "we"?), visions (what are our fundamental reasons for existing, our ideals?) and values (what are the standards we will employ to measure, evaluate and report on how well we live up to our ideals?). In other words, we will

consider the question: Under what circumstances can a collectivity develop a self-referential capacity for integrating cognitive expressions of purpose and ideals into its vocabulary and identity?

It is unreasonable to expect that all the persons in a collectivity have the same values. Nevertheless it has become common to speak of "shared values". This terminology has intuitive appeal but is seldom made precise in the literature on organizational development and management philosophy. In a small, well-localized group, where the members know each other and have frequent contact, these are the values or standards that the group and its members agree (implicitly or explicitly) to use to evaluate whether the group's actions are acceptable. The individual members of the group – be they a local chapter of Hell's Angels or the Boy/Girl Scouts, or a gardening club, develop and employ such shared standards for behavior when functioning as a group.[10] Often these values are not only confined to the group's activities, but flow over and become more or less integrated in the members' individual identities. This is certainly the case with members of Hells Angels[11] – and is a fundamental aspiration underlying the Scout movement.

When we move from the context of a small, local group to that of a larger collectivity of individuals, what we refer to here as an "organization", shared values are the criteria and standards that the organization and its stakeholders agree to use to reflect on the organization's identity, to evaluate whether the organization's actions are acceptable and to guide its development.

That it is legitimate here to speak of shared values without referring to some aggregation of personal values has to do with the social nature and propensities of human beings. It is a common experience that when individuals, each with their own values, preferences and expectations, meet to decide on matters of importance to an organization they belong to and for which they feel a sense of responsibility, a new, implicit – and shared – value can develop amongst the participants. This shared value which emerges in the group is to serve the organization – to reinforce both its identity and the sense of responsibility they have with respect to the organization as a whole – and to arrive at decisions which are acceptable for all the participants.

There is no guarantee that this will happen. It is by no means certain that e.g. representatives from the sales and production departments of an enterprise who are meeting to coordinate plans, will be prepared to move their focus from their own department's – and their own personal – interests, and develop a more inclusive or holistic frame of reference for their decisions. A minimal condition for it to happen is the existence of a reasonable degree of mutual respect and shared perceptions and feelings as to organizational identity. These are a pre-condition for the development of a consensus-seeking dialogue where the participants are able to relate to what they jointly are willing to consider to be shared and efficacious.

3.1. On the relationship between "stakeholders" and "the organization"

Up until now the term "organization" has been used in an intuitive sense corresponding to its usage in daily language as well as in almost all literature on "organizational theory", "organizational development" and the like. In ordinary language we tend to refer to an organization as a group of people who, for any of a wide variety of reasons, choose to adhere to a set of norms, rules, goals and visions which they identify with a shared symbol, the organization's name. There are many types of organizations; companies, clubs, institutions, local governments and associations are all "organizations". It is not a pre-requisite for membership of an organization that its members know or support the organization's goals; it is not necessary that an employee of IBM work there to promote IBM's purposes and success. In fact s/he may consider her job primarily as a means of earning a livelihood or of maintaining social relationships, and may feel a very limited identity and solidarity with the organization. But at a minimum she must obey its rules and regulations if she is not to risk losing her job. And hopefully, both for her own sake and for the sake of the company, in her work and social intercourse with others at her place of work, she identifies with and supports the development and well being of IBM.

In general people do not ask the question: "what is an organization?" It is common e.g. for students at a business school as well as for their role models, successful top managers, to speak of a company's goals, visions and values without reflecting over what they really mean by "the company" and under which conditions it is meaningful to ascribe to it the capacity to develop and integrate collectively recognized cognitive qualities. It has become part of their language and culture and does not require further justification. Almost all textbooks on managerial economics implicitly equate 'the corporation's purposes, values and goals' with top management's purposes, values and goals – and implicitly or explicitly assume that a fundamental basis for these is an overall and overriding aspiration; to maximize the earnings of its owners (corporation's own nothing according to accounting theory).

However, it is argued here that if managers are to be able to preserve their personal integrity while dealing with the complexity characterizing modern technology, markets, regulations, production forms and cultures, it will be necessary for them to radically reconsider their conceptions of an organization and its competencies. For example, it is postulated that successful and viable enterprises no longer will be regarded primarily from the perspective of the owners or a small group of top managers. The shareholder orientation, which has dominated almost all literature on management, business administration, accounting and finance, is slowly but surely being supplemented by a stakeholder orientation.[12] Not because traditional economic criteria are irrelevant. But because the one-dimensional mapping of corporate effectiveness via profitability can lead to ineffectiveness seen from the perspective of its many constituencies, including the shareholders, and therefore as well from the perspective of the enterprise's long term viability, economic efficacy and "quality of life".

This is not only relevant for commercial, private enterprises, but applies as well for institutions, companies, communities and other forms of organizations within the public domain. Even though such not-for-profit organizations may lack a simple measure of economic success as is provided by the bottom line, their managers still tend to be dominated by economic rationality and steering via budgets and bureaucracies – and not by a stakeholder orientation. Without being able to reflect on and report on their success via a profit and loss statement, such organizations have an even greater need for the identity and legitimacy which can be created by a more holistic, inclusive orientation towards the many stakeholders. In other words, an organization must contribute to all its stakeholder values if its own values are to be promoted.

From a systems theoretical vantagepoint an *organization* can be considered to be a purposeful system with the following characteristics:

a) It selects the stakeholder groups it considers itself as interacting with, and

b) Its stakeholder groups chose, each based on its own shared values, to participate in an on-going existential discourse with the organization which reflects on and constitutes the organization's *identity* and its *shared values*.

In other words, an organization is here considered to be a social system with the self-referential ability to describe itself and reflect upon itself on the basis of its shared values.

An organization's values are not just an aggregation of each stakeholder group's values, even though it is a condition for organizational success that the organization's values respect and reflect its stakeholders' values. The organization's shared values are those values which emerge from the organization's on-going self-reflexive constitutive dialogue as to its identity, purpose and relationships to its stakeholders. In other words, these are not just any values, but those values which can take on a socially integrative function and can be employed to justify the establishment of organizational goals.

It would be detrimental for organizational effectiveness if its management had to refer to the values of its stakeholders whenever it had to make decisions. An organization's experience and traditions are valuable because they permit man-

agement – and the employees – to act without directly reflecting on or referring to the organization's values.[13]

Stakeholders are those parties who affect and/or are affected by an organization's behavior. They have a stake in the organization. It is common to refer for example to a company's employees, customers, owners, suppliers, competitors, local communities and financiers as major stakeholders. In most cases, these both affect and are affected by the organization. Other stakeholders might include the media, activist organizations, branch associations and the government. Typically such stakeholders affect but are relatively unaffected by the organization. In the case of a public organization such as a public hospital, the stakeholders could be the doctors, nurses, porters, administrative personnel, patients, their families, the politicians providing the funding etc.

From a systems theoretical perspective a stakeholder can be considered to be a group or subsystem which:

a) Is selected[14] by and interacts with the organization, and

b) Whose members, based on their own personal values, choose to participate in an existential discourse within the group and with the organization, which reflects on and constitutes the stakeholder group and the *stakeholder group's shared values*.

The stakeholder group's shared values are not just an aggregation of the individual members' values, even though these underlie the group's values. The group's shared values are those socially integrative values which emerge from a values-based dialogue within the stakeholder group – a reflexive discourse based on the group's mapping of itself and its environment.

For example, the employees in an organization can create a stakeholder group, the "employees" if: a) the leadership of the organization chooses to consider the "employees" as a special level of reality, it can relate to, and b) the individual workers choose to identify themselves as members of the "employees" based upon the values they share with each other and with the organization.

To avoid terminological confusion due to

using "employee" to refer to both a stakeholder group and an individual in the employment of a firm, I will now refer to the latter as a "worker", although this tends to be associated with terms like laborer.[15] An individual worker may have many values which are not "employee values". And if worker Smith leaves the firm and is replaced by worker Jones, it makes no sense to speak of a new stakeholder with a new set of values. The group is constituted based on its shared values and its self-reference. It would destroy its effectiveness, its ability to promote its shared values, if it had to appeal to all its members private values each time it had to relate to itself. And it would be destructive for its effectiveness if it had to relate to its shared values whenever it had to relate to the organization. As was the case with the organization, the stakeholder group's experience and traditions are valuable because they permit coordinated action without directly relating to its values and without formalizing the discourse.

3.2. *The role of management*

The perspective presented above on the relationship between values, stakeholders and organizations has so far avoided introducing some of the complexities which arise when considering a rather particular kind of employee, the manager or leader.

Most of the literature on a stakeholder perspective on the firm side-steps the question as to whether management should be considered to be a stakeholder in its own right, i.e. which is distinct from the stakeholder group "employees". This is a tricky question, particularly if we by "management" refer to "top management" since this group has special competencies, amongst these being the choice of which stakeholders the organization chooses to relate to!

Furthermore, since top management can act and communicate on the behalf of the organization as a whole, it is confusing to speak of management's values vis-à-vis the organization's values – and to say that management's values are at odds with the organization's values would be tantamount to criticizing it for a lack of respon-

sibility. Management has the responsibility for creating and maintaining the self-referential dialogue process which can elicit and coordinate the various stakeholder groups' values and thereby for (re)creating and coordinating the organization's shared values. In turn, via their concrete actions and their formulation of the organization's visions, strategies and goals, management affects the formation of the stakeholders' values. Finally, experience with *Ethical Accounting* indicates that managers have perceptions and values that tend to differ significantly from non-managerial employees.

For all of these reasons, it is difficult to justify categorizing (top) management as either a stakeholder in its own right or as a member of the stakeholder group "employees".

In fact, it is a challenging question whether "management" performs its functions from a platform within or outside of the organization. It can be argued that the vantagepoint of management of necessity is external to the organization; this permits it to observe and to steer the organization as a whole. And from an employee perspective, management is often less a "we" and more a "they". The power relationship between these groups is non-symmetric and can be characterized as a relationship between decision makers and decision receivers, between planners and the planned-for.

On the other hand, management's observations are observed by the employees and management can only effectively act in a close symbiosis with the employees and the organization's other stakeholders. Furthermore, managers clearly are employed by the judicial entity, the company, and are in many ways "in the same boat" as the regular employees and they live up to the common definition of a stakeholder since they "affect and/or are affected by" the organization.

Without attempting to resolve the problems associated with the special nature of management in a values-based and stakeholder perspective on the organization, I will consider one of management's major distinguishing characteristics and responsibilities as seen from such a perspective on organizational consciousness. Until now I have argued that organizations have the potential competency to develop values via an on-going, self-reflective dialogue process and that if this competency is realized, the shared values which emerge from this process can be said to be an expression of a collective consciousness. Management clearly plays a vital role in this process since it has not only the *legal* capacity to make binding decisions, but also has the potential competency to make *legitimate* decisions by acting on behalf of the organization as a whole. The question arises however as to what is required for this potential competency to be realized.

Briefly, the perspective provided here is that management has the responsibility for promoting the values of all the organization's stakeholders.[16] That is, management has a *social responsibility* that extends beyond maximizing the profits accruing to the owners. Management is no longer to be seen as being responsible only to one stakeholder, the shareholders, and it is no longer legitimate to reflect upon organizational success based on one criterion alone, profitability.

Management has in other words a responsibility for serving all the organization's stakeholders and it must relate to and promote the values of all the stakeholder groups in their interplay with the organization. This leads to a more complex – and far more realistic – perspective on management and decision making than that provided by classical economic rationality. If concepts of organizational values, visions and virtues are to be more than just metaphors, management must develop and utilize a multi-stakeholder, multi-criteria concept of the enterprise. It must reflect on, measure, evaluate and communicate corporate identity and success via the employment of an expanded repertoire of explanations. This in turn presupposes the existence of a dialogue culture, which maintains and develops the organization via a self-reflective communication process with the stakeholder groups, each with its own shared values.[17] We turn now to one such approach to developing operational tools for dealing with notions of organizational consciousness and values.

4. Operational arguments: Social and ethical accounting

The various distinctions employed so far are closely interrelated. If they are to be integrated into an organization's structure, procedures and systems, it is necessary to develop a vocabulary and tools that can support the development of the organization's self-referential capabilities. It is argued that in order to operationalize concepts of shared values, organizational consciousness and corporate responsibility, there is a need for a reappraisal of what we mean by *accountability* and *accounting*.

At present the notion of accountability is formally delineated only with respect to a corporation's legal compliance and its financial reporting to shareholders and governmental authorities – and of late to a limited degree in connection with environmental reporting. While both financial and even environmental performance are increasingly "auditable", many aspects of social impact remain uncounted, many claims regarding ethical performance remain unverified, and many aspects of a company's social and ethical performance are even unverifi*able* due to inadequate information systems.

Verifying claims as to corporate values is not simply a matter of "ethical policing". Rather, it opens up the possibility for constructive dialogue about what types of social responsibility are possible in different situations, and how they can best be achieved, evaluated and communicated. The ability to account for the social and ethical dimensions of an organization's activities may therefore be considered a pre-condition for the development of organizational consciousness and therefore of socially and ethically responsible business.

One such approach to working directly with organizational and stakeholder values is what was originally, in 1989, christened "ethical accounting".[18] Briefly stated, ethical accounting measures how well an organization lives up to its stakeholder values. But it encompasses more than just a snapshot at a particular point of time; its design, development and interpretation contribute to an on-going dialogue culture where values become vital for the organization's reproduction of its self-knowledge and identity. Compared to traditional accounting statements, ethical accounting comprises more values, addresses more stakeholders, and is developed, interpreted and employed by all the stakeholders. Therefore it is not objective. Rather, it draws a rich and informative picture of how stakeholders perceive their relationships to the organization and provides the basis for a learning process whereby values become integrated into the organization.

At present it is estimated that roughly one hundred Danish organizations more or less regularly employ ethical accounting as an important tool for contributing to organizational development and to managerial effectiveness. It is interesting to note that the majority of these users are public sector organizations: hospitals, schools, homes for the aged, local communities, city governments and the like. In fact, ethical accounting has been implemented within such rather unique areas as the care of the senile (in the municipalities of Aarhus and Copenhagen, Denmark) and in animal husbandry (in Denmark and Norway).

However, what is perhaps the most interesting development is that which is taking place internationally – with a major influence from Denmark. This development began in 1994 at a meeting of a small group of people from the U.K., Italy, the U.S. and Denmark who were enthusiastic as to the possibility of developing a common framework for various approaches to what is now called the field of social and ethical accounting, auditing and reporting (SEAAR). Unknown to the Danes who had developed ethical accounting, there already existed a recent history of attempts in other parts of the world, particularly in the U.S. and U.K., to develop metrics for measuring an organization's social performance; the approach was, and still is, referred to in most of the Anglo-Saxon world as *social auditing*. And in the mid-1990's other people were developing methodologies similar to ethical accounting and with similar motivations.[19]

However, developing such an accounting process is not without challenges. It is one thing to count and sum up financial flows, but quite another to measure the extent to which an organization promotes the values of its stakeholders. While a consensus on how to measure environmental impacts is slowly developing, views diverge on how to compute the ethical impacts of business activities.[20] This lack of accepted social and ethical accounting standards may, however, now be drawing to a close. The practices of the new generation of social and ethical accounting, auditing, and reporting that has emerged in the last five years are now converging towards a common approach that could form the foundation for global procedural standards in the future.

In recognition of this development, the Institute of Social and Ethical AccountAbility (ISEA), referred to as *AccountAbility*, was established in London in 1996. An underlying motivation was to develop a consensus on standards that can form the basis for securing a recognizable and assessable level of quality in social and ethical accounting, auditing and reporting. According to its mission statement, "AccountAbility is an international professional body committed to strengthening the social responsibility and ethical behavior of the business community and non-profit organizations. The institute will do this by promoting best practice social and ethical accounting, auditing and reporting and the development of standards and accreditation procedures for professionals in the field." The first such standards, AccountAbility 1000 (AA1000) have been available from ISEA as of November, 1999.[21] Recognition of both the growth of the field and its universality has resulted in a number of international meetings and conferences dealing with SEAAR.[22] At present, some of Europe's major corporations including Shell, British Telecom and Novo Nordisk have committed themselves to implementing SEAAR while others are in the preparatory phases.

Widespread agreement about such standards would have radical implications for corporate reporting and behavior more generally. It would bring to the "business" community (including governmental organizations, voluntary and community groups and NGO's) a new era of openness, introducing practices of transparent decision making. This would in turn reflect and reinforce the values, expectations and needs of the stakeholders and the environment with which the organizations coexist. Finally, and central to the theme of this article, it would enshrine in management and accounting practices the principle that businesses are not just judicial entities with certain fiscal responsibilities, but that they, just as individuals, have values and are socially and ethically accountable.

Notes

[1] Originally presented as an invited paper at the *World Philosophers Meet '98 – Second Parliament of Science, Religion and Philosophy*, Geneva, Switzerland, August 1998.

[2] The terms 'conscious' and 'consciousness' will be employed in the sense: "knowing what one is doing and why"; *Webster's Deluxe Unabridged Dictionary*, 2nd edition.

[3] In Europe, although many business schools emulate the American approach with its focus on the individual (potential) leader's reactions to moral dilemmas, there is a tendency to focus on a stakeholder perspective and on the processes leading to and characterizing the development of *shared* conceptions of organizational purpose, values and ethics. Regarding the situation in Denmark, see for example Pruzan, P., "Theory and Practice of Business Ethics in Denmark", in Zsolnai, L. (ed.), *The European Difference: Business Ethics within CEMS (Community of European Management Schools)*, 1998, pp. 1–15. This book presents an overview of teaching and research at a major business school in each of 8 CEMS countries.

[4] Since then the approach, in modified form, has been employed in a large number of private and public enterprises, e.g. in connection with the development of codes of shared values at the corporate, division or local level.

[5] See e.g. the report "Socialundersøgelsen 1997–98" by the Danish Association of Jurists and Economists, 1999. It is based upon interviews with several thousand Danish college students in the last year of their bachelor studies in social science fields such as economics, political science, law, sociology, business administration etc. The report shows that by far the major motivating factor as regards choice of a job is "meaningful work", number two is "the social environment" and much further down the list is "wage level" and "opportunities for leadership

responsibility". Similar results are reported on in a survey by the Fuqua School of Business at Duke University. According to this survey amongst MBA students at 10 leading American business schools, "Having a successful marriage or relationship, physical health and strong ethics are the three goals rated most highly by respondents. A successful career slots into fourth place. Making a lot of money is down in 12th position." (See the article Bradshaw, D. "Family Values Replace the Dash for Cash", *Financial Times*, 25.5.1998). Finally, reference is made to (Levering, R. and M. Moskowitz, *The 100 Best Companies to Work for in America*, Doubleday, 1993), where considerable empirical evidence is provided that companies with the best scores with respect to criteria such as job security and job possibilities, pride with respect to one's job and the company, openness and fairness, the social environment, wages and benefits were not only among the most profitable companies in America, they tended to have the lowest job turnover and the happiest employees.

[6] Collins, J. C. and J. I. Porras, *Built to Last: Successful Habits of Visionary Companies*, HarperCollins Publishers, 1994.

[7] Gioia, D., M. Schultz and K. Corley, "Organizational Identity, Image and Adaptive Instability", *Academy of Management Review* 25, 63–81, 2000 consider the relationship between stable values and corporate identity. They argue (pp. 64–65) that "the seeming durability of identity is actually contained in the stability of the *labels* used by organization members to express who or what they believe the organization to be, but that the meaning associated with these labels changes so that identity is actually mutable." Corporate identity with a sense of continuity is thus "one that shifts in its interpretation and meaning while retaining labels for 'core beliefs' and values that extend over time and context."

[8] Note that this attention to 'visionary' and 'pervasiveness' is also closely related to such less attractive concepts as 'indoctrination' and 'cult-like cultures'. The authors argue that "The visionary companies more thoroughly indoctrinate employees into a core ideology than the comparison companies, creating cultures so strong that they are almost cult-like around the ideology. The visionary companies more carefully nurture and select senior management based on fit with a core ideology than the comparison companies. The visionary companies attain more consistent alignment with a core ideology – in such aspects as goals, strategy, tactics, and organization design – than the comparison companies." (*Built to Last*, p. 71).

[9] Barrett, R., *Liberating the Corporate Soul: Work,*

Values and Leadership in the 21st Century, R. Barrett and Associates, 1998.

[10] In many groups and organizations these values are articulated in various forms such as codices. An example is the Boy Scouts' Code of Honor. Note however, that many, if not most, of the values which characterize a group can be said to be tacit values which are readily accessible and have become part of the individual member's cognitive and emotive approach to evaluating and reacting to opportunities. See Petersen, V., *Tacit Ethics – Creation and Change*, Working Paper 98-1, Department of Management and Organization, Aarhus School of Business, Aarhus, Denmark, 1998.

[11] I underscore here that the 'shared values' referred to throughout are shared within a group or organization – and are not necessarily shared by all the parties affected by them. Hells Angels and Phillip Morris (one of the 'visionary' organizations referred to in the book *Built to Last*) have developed highly effective means of legitimizing, reinforcing and supporting the operationalization of their values and purposes, even though these values and purposes are considered to be unethical by many of the parties affected by their decisions and behavior.

[12] The concept of 'stakeholder' was introduced in the management domain in the late 1970's and early 1980's (see for example Ackoff, R. L., *Creating the Corporate Future*, Wiley, 1981 and Freeman, E., *Strategic Management: A Stakeholder Approach*, Pitman, 1984). From a Danish perspective it is interesting to note that this frame of reference has been widely recognized over the last 10–15 years and serves as a fundamental concept underlying the development of *Ethical Accounting*, to be discussed shortly. For a more recent extensive analysis based on considerable first-hand experience, see (Wheeler, D. and M. Sillanpää, *The Stakeholder Corporation: A Blueprint for Maximizing Stakeholder Value*, Pitman, 1997).

[13] It must be underlined that once organizations develop a competency for conscious, intentional behavior there is no guarantee that this competency will lead to the establishment of enduring traditions that "permit management – and the employees – to act without directly reflecting on or referring to the organization's values." Much depends on e.g. whether new leaders embrace the shared values. One example is the Body Shop, which for many years has been internationally recognized for its emphasis on shared values and ethical behavior. A new leadership appears to be resulting in an erosion of the past values through their over-commoditization – and to a resultant decrease in both employee and customer faith.

Another case is from my own country, Denmark. In 2000, one of the organizations which has achieved a high degree of recognition for its work with *ethical accounting* since 1989, Sbn Bank (Spar Nord, as it is known here) experienced a major change in top management – accompanied by a major shift from corporate values as constituted and revitalized via processes of stakeholder dialogue, to values established solely by top management.

[14] The notion of 'selection' by the organization, though not consistent with many definitions of stakeholders which neglect this aspect, is vital here in this theoretical perspective on the relationships between organizations and their stakeholders. It indicates that the process of value generation, both within the stakeholder group as well as within the organization, depends on the organization's conscious choice of which groups it will deal with when reflecting on its values and identity, and which groups it will *not* deal with. The importance in a more pragmatic perspective is demonstrated in the difficulties organizations such as Nike and Monsanto faced due to their choice of whom to deal and whom not to deal with as stakeholders.

[15] This discussion indicates the difficulty arising from using a term from every-day language within a theoretical context. To avoid this problem one would have to introduce a new term, e.g. "employee group" and then speak of "employee group values". I have chosen to avoid introducing more new terms than are necessary.

[16] A business expression of this perspective can be found in the publication *Profits and Principles – does there have to be a choice?* Royal Dutch/Shell Group, 1998 and to Shell's *Statement of General Business Principles*, 1997: "Shell companies recognize five areas of responsibility: To shareholders . . . To customers . . . To employees . . . To those with whom they do business . . . To society . . . These five areas of responsibility are seen as inseparable. Therefore it is the duty of management continuously to assess the priorities and discharge its responsibilities as best it can on basis of that assessment."

[17] See e.g. Pruzan, Peter, "From Control to Values-Based Management and Accountability", *Journal of Business Ethics* 17, 1379–1394, 1998

[18] In a Danish article from 1988 my colleague, the philosopher Dr. Ole Thyssen and I proposed the development of Ethical Accounting as a means of operationalizing ethics in an organization. The article, now available in English, ("Conflict and Consensus: Ethics as a Shared Value Horizon for Strategic Planning", *Human Systems Management*, 9, 1990, pp.

135–151) was based on our work with ethics and with decision making contexts characterized by multiple stakeholders having multiple criteria for judging the performance of an enterprise. Our proposal was brought to the attention of the management of Denmark's seventh largest bank, Sbn Bank or "Spar Nord", as it is known in Denmark. The bank is a regional bank primarily serving Northern Jutland with 71 branches in 19 regional areas and with roughly 1,300 employees, 200,000 customers and 60,000 shareholders, most of whom are customers. A year earlier the bank had begun to develop its "Code of Values" based on psychological theories regarding people's basic needs. The top management was keen on developing a perspective on management and organizational development based on the values of its major stakeholders and offered us the opportunity of using the bank as a laboratory for developing ethical accounting. Under the leadership of Dr. Thorbjörn Meyer, the first ethical accounting statement was developed for the year 1989 and since then such supplements to the bank's financial statements have been developed each year. See e.g. Pruzan, P., "The Ethical Dimensions of Banking", in (Zadek, S. P. Pruzan and R. Evans, eds.), *Building Corporate AccountAbility: Emerging Practices in Social and Ethical Accounting, Auditing and Reporting*, Earthscan, London, 1997, pp. 63–84 and Pruzan, P., "The Ethical Accounting Statement" *World Business Academy Perspectives* 9, 1995, 35–46. In addition there are a large number of articles, several doctoral dissertations and three books in Danish on ethical accounting.

[19] For a historical overview as well as a presentation of the motivations and theory underlying SEAAR, reference is made to the major reference in the field: Zadek, S., P. Pruzan and R. Evans, *Building Corporate AccountAbility: Emerging Practices in Social and Ethical Accounting, Auditing and Reporting*, Earthscan, London, 1997. In addition to the historical and theoretical sections it also provides nine case studies of applications in a wide variety of organizations in the U.S., Canada, U.K., Italy, Norway and Denmark. It is primarily for people facing the practical task of handling, developing and implementing corporate social and ethical responsibility agendas although it is also targeted towards corporate stakeholders and an audience of students and researchers.

[20] This is of course not a unique challenge. The profession of judges, of doctors, and maybe at times even of financial accountants, faced equal or similar dilemmas. The best and most recent example, perhaps, is that of environmental assessors and auditors. Here was an area that until the early 1980's was primarily one of challenge and defense, the corporate body generally on the defense, with the challenges made by single-issue and community-based campaigning non-profit organisations. And yet in the space of just a few years the basis of a profession has emerged, complete with courses, accreditation procedures, standards and, increasingly, legislation.

[21] For further information on the institute and on AA1000 contact The secretariat, Institute of Social and Ethical AccountAbility, Thrale House, 44-46 Southwark Street, London SE1 1UN, England; Tel: +44 171 407 7370, Fax: +44 171 407 7388, E-mail: Secretariat@AccountAbility.org.uk, Website: http://www.AccountAbility.org.uk.

[22] A resume of the first International Conference on Social and Ethical Accountability: Balancing Performance, Ethics and Accountability, Nijenrode Castle, Holland is available in the special conference issue (nr. 5) of the quarterly journal of the Institute of Social and Ethical AccountAbility, *AccountAbility*, 5, autumn, 1997 and a series of papers presented at the conference are available in the *Journal of Business Ethics*, 17, 1998. The "1st.North American Conference on Social and Ethical Accounting, Auditing and Reporting: Standards for the New Millennium" took place in Vancouver, B.C., Canada, October 19–21, 1998. The third international conference dealing with SEAAR, "Building Stakeholder Relationships", took place November 15–16, 1999 in Copenhagen, Denmark; the foundation standard AA1000 was presented at this meeting.

Department of Management, Politics and Philosophy,
Copenhagen Business School,
Blaagaardsgade 23B,
2200 Copenhagen N,
Denmark.
E-mail: pruzan@cbs.dk

[52]

Human and Social Capital – Prerequisites for Sustained Prosperity

Milan Zeleny

Modern learning and knowledge-based corporations have realized for some time that human knowledge has become the primary form of capital in the global competitive space. Knowledge, defined as the ability to coordinate one's actions, alone and with others, effectively and purposefully, is embedded within and activated by human social and cultural institutions.

Learning to coordinate one's actions, i.e., producing, maintaining and sustaining human capital, can only take place within a requisite social infrastructure: cultural and educational institutions, family-based kinship systems and shared experiences of history, habits, values, beliefs and aspirations.

Functioning democracy is based on respect and free-market behavior is based on trust. This is why democracy and markets are to a large extent *learned behaviors*, brought forth by strong cultures and social infrastructures. Without the learned and deeply habituated respect and trust, both democracy and markets become merely gaudy and often cruel caricatures of themselves. Russia and Eastern Europe are the prime examples of today.

Only socially and culturally strong nations, rich in human capital, family values, respect and trust, can ever become prosperous – regardless of their natural, physical or financial endowments. Only the learning nations, evolving their human and social capital continually and reliably, can ever taste truly sustainable prosperity.

A wealthy nation, like a wealthy farmer, must be able to continue increasing its stock of capital. Such accumulation of the capital stock enlarges the set of alternatives and opportunities for subsequent generations, thus making current wealth sustainable.

Increased wealth also helps to generate higher income, although higher income can also be temporarily created through decreasing one's wealth and reducing the capital.

Only the poor countries, like the poor individuals, live mostly from their income while only maintaining or even dipping into their capital stock. Income based on the depletion of capital is not sustainable and should not be accepted as income [1], but only as a consumption of capital. Only the poorest of the poor consume their own substance: they eat up their own capital endowments.

It is therefore the charge and challenge of the current generations to leave the future generations with more capital per capita.

There are *at least* four basic forms of capital:

1. Man-made, produced physical assets of infrastructures, technologies, buildings and means of transportation. This is the manufactured 'hardware' of nations. This national hardware must be continually maintained, renewed and modernized to assure its continued productivity, efficiency and effectiveness.

2. Natural capital, i.e., nature-produced, renewed and reproduced 'inputs' of land, water, air, raw materials, biomass and organisms. Natural capital is subject to both renewable and non-renewable depletion, degradation, cultivation, recycling and reuse.

3. Human capital (or human resources) refers to the continued investment in people's skills, knowledge, education, health and nutrition,

abilities, motivation and effort. This is the 'software' and 'brainware' of a nation, perhaps the most important form of capital for rapidly developing nations.

4. Social capital is the enabling infrastructure of institutions, civic communities, cultural and national cohesion, collective and family values, trust, traditions, respect and the sense of belonging. This is the voluntary, spontaneous 'social order' which cannot be engineered, but its self-production (autopoiesis) can be nurtured, supported and cultivated.

All of the above capitals must be developed in balanced, harmonious ways. The last two forms are currently most significant and effective in the creation of wealth and prosperity. The vector or portfolio of capitals, its structure and profile, is more significant than its overall aggregate sum. A country that has all or most of its wealth in natural resources might become an international supplier but it will not progress itself. Although the trade-offs among the capitals are often necessary, and sometimes wise and strategically desirable, they are rarely sustainable. The optimal *capital portfolio* could be negatively affected by irreversible or too frequent tradeoffs and substitutions.

In the long run, it appears to be the social capital which provides the necessary supportive infrastructure for the human capital to manifest itself effectively. Through renewing primarily both itself and human capital, and consequently also the man-made and natural capitals, the set of opportunities is being widened for future generations.

Social capital is clearly critical [3], although one of the most neglected and ignored. This is a spontaneous social order, uncoerced and unforced civil society and culture which defines people's ability to work towards common goals and objectives in groups and organizations, form new associations and cooperative networks, dismantle and slough off the old institutions without conflict or violence. It is the *enabling environment* for human capital to become effective.

Social capital includes not only business, but also voluntary and not-for-profit associations, educational institutions, clubs, unions, media, charities and churches. A strong civic community

is characterized by a preponderance of horizontal organizations, self-reliance, self-organization and self-management, while autocratic, centralized and hierarchically vertical organizations of command are found in societies of lesser trust, low spontaneous sociability and thus lower economic performance. The State then has to compensate for the lack of reciprocity, moral obligation, duty toward community, and trust – a role for which the State is the least equipped and the least reliable institution to undertake.

Strong cultures, strong spontaneous social orders, strong levels of civic trust tend to produce higher economic performance and generate wealth, not the other way around. Strong economic performance and wealth creation are not precursors or prerequisites to strong civil societies

Nations with weak cultural and civic traditions will be generally poorer, saddled with 'strong' governments, relying crucially on their natural resources and man-made capital, neglecting the social and human spheres of existence. Wealthier and high-performing economies will be typically engendered by nations characterized by a strong, dense and horizontally structured culture of trust, cooperation and voluntary associations.

One would therefore expect the wealthiest nations to have most of their wealth embodied in social and human capital, only a lesser part in man-made or natural capital. For example, the wealthiest and the high income countries have, on average, only 16% of their total wealth in produced assets and 17% in natural capital, but some 67% in human resources.

The poorest countries are raw material exporters, having 20% of their wealth in produced assets, but 44% in natural capital and a meager 36% in human resources.

If we look at the US dollar wealth per capita and the percentages lodged in human, produced and natural capital respectively [1], we find, for example, the 'wealthy' portfolio profiles indicated in Table 1.

Japan has virtually no natural resources, yet all ten of the world's largest banks are now in Japan. The accumulated wealth is virtually all due to human and social capital investments. These can be compared with some selected 'poor' countries

Table 1
Capital portfolio profiles of 'wealthy' countries

Italy	$373,000;	82, 15, 3
Belgium	$384,000;	83, 16, 2
Netherlands	$379,000;	80, 18, 2
Japan	$565,000;	81, 18, 2
Switzerland	$647,000;	78, 19, 3
Luxembourg	$658,000;	83, 12, 4

Table 2
Capital portfolio profiles of 'poor' countries

Ethiopia	$1,400;	40, 21, 39
Sierra Leone	$2,900;	14, 18, 68
Bhutan	$6,500;	8, 7, 85
Zambia	$13,000;	9, 18, 73

Table 3
Capital portfolio profiles of some poor and developing countries

Vietnam	$2,600;	74, 15, 11
Slovakia	$33,000;	78, 17, 5
Czech Republic	$50,000;	66, 15, 19
Mexico	$74,000;	73, 11, 16
Slovenia	$111,000;	67, 16, 17

portfolios (see Table 2).

The capital portfolios in Table 2 have so little investment in human and social capital that their future prospects are quite discouraging indeed. On the other hand, there are some poor and developing countries which seem to have the right 'mix' of capitals, indicating a possible economic takeoff in the future (see Table 3).

Richer countries are generally those which invest more in their human capital, education, nutrition, health care, etc., over longer periods of time.

Some poor countries have relatively high incomes because they do not invest enough into renewing their capital portfolio, but actually consume their capital ('eat up their next-year corn-seed'). Especially the Sub-Saharan countries have recently registered very high levels of disinvestment, negative savings and capital depletion. Many countries in Eastern Europe are artificially increasing their current incomes for political reasons, but at the cost of depleting their wealth. It is quite sad to see some of these countries rapidly disinvesting in their educational, health care, nutritional and cultural endowments, nurturing corruption and the anything-goes culture, being culturally blind to

'dirty money' and myopic about their future.

This adds up to a very short-sighted and nation-damaging policy, destroying nations' social capital and wealth, virtually irreversibly.

The recent World Bank studies [1] have confirmed the leading role of human capital in economic development. With the exception of some raw material exporters, human capital exceeds both natural capital and produced assets combined: sustainable development is best achieved by investing in people. Yet, it is on less than a fifth of total wealth (man-made capital) that the bulk of current economic policies is focused.

The World Bank and other similar institutions have so far emphasized building the assorted 'Aswan dams' rather than founding technology institutes and enterprise foundations, educating people and expanding their self-reliance and self-management opportunities and abilities. That is why most of the world still remains poor after some 50 years of misplaced 'efforts'.

Many of the misguided policies are the result of naive beliefs and neo-pagan market worshipping, especially in Russia and Eastern Europe. The free-market efficiency is only one of the many by-products of preexisting moral communities.

Without such moral communities, the unfettered free market is neither conservative nor constructive but a most radically disruptive force, relentlessly dissolving the loyalty of corporations to their communities, customers to their neighborhood merchants, athletes to their teams and nations, teams to their cities, and so on. Without the culturally preformed, spontaneous social orders of trust, loyalty and reciprocity, a nation cannot achieve and maintain sustainable wealth.

America's human capital (Capital portfolio profile: $421,000; 59, 16, 25) accounts for some 60 percent – compared to only 15 percent for the produced capital – of the productive capital stock. Developing America's human capital is therefore by far the most important factor in maintaining its global competitiveness.

Lowering taxes for speculators in used cars, used goods, used stocks and used bonds cannot compare in importance with giving the tax incentives to teachers and educational institutions and thus encourage more and better people to educate nation's children. The payoffs would be incommensurable.

Buying and selling used cars is no different from buying and selling used stocks for gain: no tax incentives are needed for speculation. Also, the wave of mechanical and politically motivated deficit-cutting efforts appears to be similarly short-sighted. Cutting could turn into a useless political exercise if the creation of crucial social and human capitals is undermined and their accumulation stunted.

Contrariwise, creating a reasonable deficit by investing in the most productive, non-speculative forms of capital and assets could be a safer way towards prosperity. The United States national debt is now about 63 percent of the output, a relatively trivial phenomenon compared to Belgium's 138 percent or Italy's 122 percent (see their comparative wealth profiles above).

Politicians often argue how they, as individuals, have to balance their budget. It is typical, especially in the United States, that individuals do take out home mortgages that are *up to 300 percent* of their incomes – and these are clearly the richer, not the poorer segments of the population. The poor have only very little or no debts.

In other words, it is not how much to invest or how far to go into debt, but where and how and to what productive, non-productive or speculative purposes is the debt (and investment) applied to. This holds true for individuals, companies, economies, countries and nations.

References

[1] Serageldin, I. (1995). Sustainability and the Wealth of Nations: First Steps in an Ongoing Journey, *Third Annual World Bank Conference on Environmentally Sustainable Development*, Washington, DC, September 30.

[2] *Monitoring Environmental Progress: A Report on Work in Progress*, Environmentally Sustainable Development Series, The World Bank, September, 1995.

[3] Fukuyama, F. (1995): *Trust: The Social Virtues and the Creation of Prosperity*, Free Press, New York.

[4] Zeleny, M. (1991). Knowledge as Capital: Integrated Quality Management, *Prometheus* 9(1): 93–101.

Milan ZELENY
Graduate School of Business
Fordham University at Lincoln Center
New York, NY 10023
USA

[53]

Misery Loves
Companies: Rethinking
Social Initiatives by
Business

Joshua D. Margolis
Harvard University
James P. Walsh
University of Michigan

Companies are increasingly asked to provide innovative
solutions to deep-seated problems of human misery,
even as economic theory instructs managers to focus on
maximizing their shareholders' wealth. In this paper, we
assess how organization theory and empirical research
have thus far responded to this tension over corporate
involvement in wider social life. Organizational scholarship has typically sought to reconcile corporate social initiatives with seemingly inhospitable economic logic.
Depicting the hold that economics has had on how the
relationship between the firm and society is conceived,
we examine the consequences for organizational
research and theory by appraising both the 30-year quest
for an empirical relationship between a corporation's
social initiatives and its financial performance, as well as
the development of stakeholder theory. We propose an
alternative approach, embracing the tension between
economic and broader social objectives as a starting
point for systematic organizational inquiry. Adopting a
pragmatic stance, we introduce a series of research questions whose answers will reveal the descriptive and normative dimensions of organizational responses to
misery.●

The world cries out for repair. While some people in the
world are well off, many more live in misery. Ironically, the
magnitude of the problem defies easy recognition. With the
global population exceeding six billion people, it is difficult to
paint a vivid and compelling picture of social life. In the
extreme, Bales (1999) conservatively estimated that there are
27 million slaves in the world today, while Attaran and Sachs
(2001) reported that 35 million people are now infected with
the HIV virus, 95 percent of them living in sub-Saharan Africa.
Even more broadly, aggregate statistics both inform and
numb. Compiled from data released by the World Bank
(2002), table 1 represents the kind of snapshot that such statistics provide. It can be shocking to learn that so many people live on less than $2.00 per day, that a quarter of the chil-
dren in Bangladesh and Nigeria are at work in their nations'
labor force, or that some countries have mortality rates for
children under age five more than ten times that of the United States. Access to sanitation, let alone access to a telephone or computer, can be very limited around the world.

The picture in the United States alone is as vivid and compelling. For twenty years, Americans have lived through a
period of unparalleled prosperity. Ibbotson Associates (2000)
calculated that in real terms, a dollar invested in large company stocks in December 1925 was worth $24.79 by year-end
1979. Exactly twenty years later, that dollar was worth
$303.09. Nevertheless, the fact that the upper echelon of
society disproportionately reaped these gains is no longer
news. Even as debate persists about intercountry income
inequality (Firebaugh, 1999), Galbraith (1998), and Mishel,
Bernstein, and Schmitt (1999) provided a comprehensive picture of wealth inequality in the United States, while Conley
(1999) clearly pointed out that many black Americans have
been left out of this economic boom. Table 1 provides a comparative portrait of how the top 10 percent of the people in
each of the world's thirteen largest countries control so much

●

We thank Christine Oliver, Linda Johan-
son, our three anonymous reviewers,
Paul Adler, Howard Aldrich, Alan
Andreasen, Jim Austin, Charles Behling,
Michael Cohen, Bob Dolan, Mary Gentile,
Tom Gladwin, Morten Hansen, Stu Hart,
Nien-he Hsieh, Linda Lim, Nitin Nohria,
Lynn Paine, Gail Pesyna, Robert Phillips,
Lance Sandelands, Debora Spar, Joe
White, Richard Wolfe, and the students in
Jim Walsh's "The Corporation in Society"
Ph.D. seminar for their constructive com-
ments on earlier versions of this paper.
We also thank Marguerite Booker, John
Galvin, and Nichole Pelak for their helpful
research assistance. The Harvard Busi-
ness School, the Michigan Business
School, and the Aspen Institute's Busi-
ness and Society Program provided
invaluable support for this project.

Social Initiatives by Business

Table 1

A Snapshot of Social Life in the World's Most Populous Nations, 2000

Nation	Population in millions	% Pop. living on < $2/day	% Share of income or consumption: bottom 10% / top 10%	% Children aged 10–14 in labor force	Under-five mortality per 1000 live birth	% Rural pop. with access to improved water source	% Pop. with access to improved sanitation	Illiteracy rate among 15–24 year olds: % male/ % female	Main-line/ mobile phones per 1000 people	Personal computers per 1000 people
China	1,262.5	52.6	2.4 / 30.4	8	39	66	38	1 / 4	112 / 66	15.9
India	1,015.9	86.2	3.5 / 33.5	12	88	86	31	20 / 35	32 / 4	4.5
U.S.A.	281.6	*	1.8 / 30.5	0	9	100	100	*	700 / 398	585.2
Indonesia	210.4	55.3	4.0 / 26.7	8	51	65	66	2 / 3	31 / 17	9.9
Brazil	170.4	26.5	.7 / 48.0	14	39	54	77	9 / 6	82 / 136	44.1
Russia	145.6	25.1	1.7 / 38.7	0	19	96	*	<.5 /<.5	218 / 22	42.9
Pakistan	138.1	84.7	4.1 / 27.6	15	110	84	61	29 / 58	22 / 2	4.2
Bangladesh	131.1	77.8	3.9 / 28.6	28	83	97	53	39 / 60	4 / 1	1.5
Japan	126.9	*	4.8 / 21.7	0	5	*	*	*	586 / 526	315.2
Nigeria	126.9	90.8	1.6 / 40.8	24	153	39	63	10 / 16	4 / 0	6.6
Mexico	98.0	37.7	1.3 / 41.7	5	36	63	73	3 / 3	125 / 142	50.6
Germany	82.2	*	3.3 / 23.7	0	6	*	*	*	611 / 586	336.0
Vietnam	78.5	*	3.6 / 29.9	5	34	50	73	3 / 3	32 / 10	8.8

* Data not available.

more of each nation's wealth than those in the bottom 10 percent. Miringoff and Miringoff (1999) chronicled these same kinds of inequality data but also provided evidence that child abuse, child poverty, teenage suicide, and violent crime, as well as the number of people living without health insurance, have all increased in the United States since the 1970s. These kinds of data serve as a stimulus for outrage and reform (Korten, 1995; Greider, 1997; Wolman and Colamosca, 1997; Kapstein, 1999; Madeley, 1999).

In the face of these broad and deep problems, calls go out for companies to help. Some organizations exist solely to fight such problems. There are publicly traded companies dedicated to cleaning up waste (e.g., Waste Management, Inc.), private not-for-profit organizations dedicated to treating the sick in very difficult circumstances (e.g., Médecins Sans Frontières), and consortia of development organizations dedicated to fighting poverty, hunger, and social injustice (e.g., Oxfam International). The calls for help, however, target profit-making firms that produce goods and services—goods and services that may have little to do with ameliorating human misery. For example, all three branches of the United States government have recognized the role corporations could play in promoting social welfare. President Bush and Secretary of State Powell have asked companies to contribute to a global AIDS fund (*New York Times*, 2001), while Former President Clinton used his "bully pulpit" to urge corporations to attend to social problems (*New York Times*, 1996) and later advocated that minimum labor standards be a part of international trade agreements (*New York Times*, 1999). With the Economic Recovery Act of 1981, Congress increased (from 5 percent to 10 percent) the allowable corporate tax deduction for charitable contributions (Mills and Gardner, 1984). Even as a majority of states were adopting "other constituency statutes," statutes that allow directors to attend to factors other than shareholder wealth maximization when fulfilling their fiduciary duty (Orts, 1992), the Delaware Supreme Court endorsed this same idea in 1989 when it allowed Time Inc.'s management to reject a lucrative tender offer from Paramount Communications to pursue other non-shareholder-related interests (Johnson and Millon, 1990).

Activity beyond the halls of government that focuses on the corporation's role in society is equally intriguing. Non-governmental organizations (NGOs) have worked tirelessly in recent years to establish worldwide standards for corporate social accountability—Ranganathan (1998) listed 47 such initiatives—and investors have pressured firms to be more responsive to social problems (e.g., Carleton, Nelson, and Weisbach, 1998). Major charitable foundations and public interest groups—the Ford Foundation, the Sloan Foundation, and the Aspen Institute, to name three of the most prominent—have launched major initiatives to investigate and even encourage business investment in redressing societal ills. Public intellectuals, including leading business school academics whose prior contributions shaped the fields of corporate strategy and organizational behavior, have joined the call to encourage and guide firms in taking on a larger role in society. Porter (1995) celebrated the competitive advantage of doing business in the inner city, Kanter (1999) identified ways in which public-private partnerships advance corporate innovation, and Prahalad (Prahalad and Hammond, 2002; Prahalad and Hart, 2002) mapped the untapped economic opportunities that reside in what he called the bottom of the world's wealth pyramid.

Business leaders and firms themselves are even responding to calls for enhanced corporate social responsibility. From mavens, such as the Body Shop's Anita Roddick, to converts, such as British Petroleum's John Browne, some business leaders are preaching—and at least trying to practice—an approach to business that affirms the broad contribution that companies can make to human welfare, beyond maximizing the wealth of shareholders. On a larger scale, the United States Chamber of Commerce, representing tens of thousands of business interests worldwide, recently founded the Center for Corporate Citizenship, whose purpose is to provide an institutional mechanism to assist humanitarian and philanthropic business initiatives around the world.

The repeated calls for corporate action to ameliorate social ills reflect an underlying tension. On the one hand, misery loves companies. The sheer magnitude of problems, from malnutrition and HIV to illiteracy and homelessness, inspires a turn toward all available sources of aid, most notably corporations. Especially when those problems are juxtaposed to the wealth-creation capabilities of firms—or to the ills that firms may have helped to create—firms become an understandable target of appeals. On the other hand, a sturdy and persistent theoretical argument in economics suggests that such corporate involvement is misguided. It may be neither permissible nor prudent to devote corporate resources to redress social misery (Friedman, 1970; Easterbrook and Fischel, 1991; Sternberg, 1997). Calls for broader corporate responsibility, therefore, constitute an effort to surmount the presupposition that such corporate action is illicit. With social misery and the imperative of corporate involvement, on the one hand, and the skeptical economic rationale, on the other, attempts to mobilize corporate social initiatives reach an intense pitch. Organizational scholarship has confronted the economic argument head-on.

THE POINT OF TENSION

Appeals for corporate involvement in ameliorating malnutrition, infant mortality, illiteracy, pollution, pernicious wealth inequality, and other social ills quickly call to mind a long and contentious debate about the theory and purposes of the firm. Despite a long history of communitarian protest (Morrissey, 1989), Bradley et al.'s (1999) review of these efforts found that the neoclassical construal of the firm as a nexus of contracts has prevailed. Although organizational and legal scholars (Bratton, 1989a, 1989b; Davis and Useem, 2000; Paine, 2002) have questioned the contractarian model and sketched alternative views, they have also acknowledged the purchase this economic model of the firm has had on corporate conduct, law, and scholarship. The purpose of the firm, from a contractarian perspective, is perhaps best captured by the landmark 1919 *Dodge v. Ford* Michigan State Supreme Court decision that determined whether or not Henry Ford could withhold dividends from the Dodge brothers (and other shareholders). The court famously argued, "A business organization is organized and carried on primarily for the profit of the stockholders" (*Dodge Brothers v. Ford Motor Company,* 1919: 170 N.W. 668). The assumption that the primary, if not sole, purpose of the firm is to maximize wealth for shareholders has come to dominate the curricula of business schools and the thinking of future managers, as evidence from a recent survey of business school graduates reveals (Aspen Institute, 2002). Investigating corporate social initiatives presents a rich scholarly opportunity in part because the economic account suggests that there should be no so such initiatives to investigate in the first place.

The contractarian view of the firm or, to be more accurate, the economic version of contractarianism (cf. Keeley, 1988; Donaldson and Dunfee, 1999), challenges the legitimacy and value of corporate responses to social misery. The specific challenges come in three distinct forms: saying that firms already advance social welfare to the full extent possible, saying that the only legitimate actors to address societal problems are freely elected governments, or saying that if firms do get involved, managers must warn their constituencies so they can protect themselves from corporate misadventures. The first point of view defends the economic contractarian model by invoking the same aim that stimulates efforts to enlist companies to cure social ills. For example, Jensen (2002: 239) argued, "200 years' worth of work in economics and finance indicate that social welfare is maximized when all firms in an economy maximize total firm value." Jensen conceded that companies must attend to multiple constituencies in order to succeed but, ultimately, firms must be guided by a single objective function: wealth creation. He argued that it is logically incoherent and psychologically impossible to maximize performance along more than one dimension—calculating tradeoffs and selecting courses of action become intractable. Although any single objective could satisfy the logical and psychological requirements, Jensen concluded that long-term market value is the one objective that best advances social welfare. Those subscribing to this view believe that if shareholder wealth is maximized, social welfare is maximized as well. In the end, the challenge for firms to invest in social initiatives is no challenge at all.

Friedman's (1970) well-known criticism of corporate social responsibility embodies the second form of criticism. He construed these investments as theft and political subversion: in responding to calls for socially responsible practices, executives take money and resources that would otherwise go to owners, employees, and customers—thus imposing a tax—and dedicate those resources to objectives that the executives, under the sway of a minority of voices, have selected in a manner that is beyond the reach of accepted democratic political processes. Friedman did not deny the existence of social problems; he simply claimed that it is the state's role to address them.

The third form of the economic argument against corporate social initiatives deems them dubious but, provided they are disclosed, unobjectionable. As long as the contracting parties are clear about the firm's intentions, even if those intentions include something other than wealth creation, Easterbrook and Fischel (1991: 36) argued, "no one should be allowed to object." They went on to conclude that "one thing that cannot survive is systematic efforts to fool participants" (Easterbrook and Fischel, 1991: 37). They were wary of corporate social investments and, like Jensen, trusted property rights and the invisible hand of the market to solve most social problems. If all contracting parties know that the firm plans to make a social investment, no matter how ill conceived, however, then those parties can decide if they want to participate in the venture. The market will ultimately sort out whether it is the best use of a firm's resources.

The point of tension between a nexus of contracts approach to the firm and those who push for corporate social involvement can thus be distilled to two central concerns: misappropriation and misallocation. When companies engage in social initiatives, the first concern is that managers will misappropriate corporate resources by diverting them from their rightful claimants, whether these be the firm's owners or, sometimes, employees. Managers also misallocate resources by diverting those best used for one purpose to advance purposes for which those resources are poorly suited. From this perspective, managers' social initiatives are akin to using a dishwasher to wash clothes. While economic contractarians may be as committed to ameliorating human misery as anyone, they see no reason for a corporation to divert its resources to solve society's problems directly. Corporations can contribute best to society if they do what they do best: employ a workforce to provide goods and services to the marketplace and, in so doing, fulfill people's needs and create wealth.

Social Initiatives by Business

The challenge facing those who advocate corporate social initiatives then is to find a way to promote what they see as social justice in a world in which this shareholder wealth maximization paradigm reigns. Although a daunting task, it has attracted many management scholars over the years. Their scholarship has attempted to sort out the relationship between shareholders, with their economic interests, and society, with its interest in broader well-being and human development. The aim has largely been to demonstrate that corporate attention to human misery is perfectly consistent with maximizing wealth, that there is, in the words of United Nations' Secretary General Kofi Annan (2001), "a happy convergence between what your shareholders want and what is best for millions of people the world over."

ORGANIZATIONAL SCHOLARSHIP ON BUSINESS IN SOCIETY

Aware of human suffering and alert to the challenge from economic contractarianism, organization theorists and empirical researchers have sought to identify a role for the firm that both attends to shareholders' interest in wealth creation and looks beyond it. In this light, empirical research has largely focused on establishing a positive connection between corporate social performance (CSP) and corporate financial performance (CFP). First appearing in 1972, these studies were offered as something of an antidote to a public conversation that was quite skeptical of corporate social responsibility (Levitt, 1958; Friedman, 1970). The now 30-year search for an association between CSP and CFP reflects the enduring quest to find a persuasive business case for social initiatives, to substantiate the kind of claims that Kofi Annan (2001) recently made to U.S. corporations: "by joining the global fight against HIV/AIDS, your business will see benefits on its bottom line." A dozen years after the publication of the first CSP-CFP studies, stakeholder theory (Freeman, 1984) began to take shape as the dominant theoretical response to the economists' challenge. It aims to establish the legitimate place for parties other than shareholders whose interests and concerns can defensibly orient managers' actions. With a body of empirical work and a rival theoretical model of the firm, organization studies has tried to respond to the economists' fundamental challenge by establishing some grounds to license direct corporate involvement in ameliorating social misery. The problem is that the resulting empirical findings and theoretical propositions restrict organizational scholars' ability to develop a more expansive approach to understanding the relationship between organizations and society. We briefly appraise the 30-year CSP-CFP empirical research tradition and the standing of stakeholder theory and use this summary and critique as a springboard to develop an alternative scholarly agenda.

The Empirical CSP-CFP Literature

Between 1972 and 2002, 127 published studies empirically examined the relationship between companies' socially responsible conduct and their financial performance. Bragdon and Marlin (1972) and Moskowitz (1972) published the first studies, with 17 other studies following during the 1970s, 30 in the 1980s, and 68 in the 1990s. In the most recent 10-year period from 1993 through 2002, researchers have published 64 new studies. Notwithstanding a long empirical history, interest in this question seems to be gaining momentum.

Corporate social performance has been treated as an independent variable, predicting financial performance, in 109 of the 127 studies. In these studies, almost half of the results (54) pointed to a positive relationship between corporate social performance and financial performance. Only seven studies found a negative relationship; 28 studies reported non-significant relationships, while 20 reported a mixed set of findings. Corporate social performance has been treated as a dependent variable, predicted by financial performance, in 22 of the 127 studies. In these studies, the majority of results (16 studies) pointed to a positive relationship between corporate financial performance and social performance. Four studies investigated the relationship in both directions, which explains why there are more results than studies. Table 2

Table 2

Relationship between Corporate Social Performance and Corporate Financial Performance in 127 Studies*

Study	Measure	
	Social performance	Financial performance
Corporate social performance as independent variable		
Positive relationship		
Anderson & Frankle (1980)	Disclosure of social performance	Market
Belkaoui (1976)	Disclosure of pollution control	Market
Blacconiere & Northcut (1997)	Disclosure of and expenditures on environmental practices	Market
Blacconiere & Patten (1994)	Disclosure of and expenditures on environmental practices	Market
Bowman (1976)	Disclosure of social performance	Accounting
Bragdon & Karash (2002)	Stewardship, systems thinking, transparency, employee growth, financial strength	Market
Bragdon & Marlin (1972)	CEP evaluation	Accounting
Brown (1998)	*Fortune* reputation rating	Market
Christmann (2000)	Survey of environmental practices	Cost advantage
Clarkson (1988)	Ratings of charity, community relations, customer relations, environmental practices, human resource practices, and org. structures based on case studies	Accounting
Conine & Madden (1986)	*Fortune* reputation rating	Perception of value as long-term investment and of soundness of financial position
D'Antonio, Johnsen & Hutton (1997)	Mutual fund screens	Market
Dowell, Hart & Yeung (2000)	IRRC evaluation of environmental performance	Accounting & market
Epstein & Schnietz (2002)	Industry reputation for environment and labor abuses	Market
Freedman & Stagliano (1991)	Disclosure of EPA and OSHA costs	Market
Graves & Waddock (2000)	KLD evaluation	Accounting & market
Griffin & Mahon (1997)	*Fortune* reputation rating, KLD evaluation, charitable contributions, pollution control	Accounting
Hart & Ahuja (1996)	IRRC evaluation of environmental performance	Accounting
Heinze (1976)	NACBS ratings	Accounting
Herremans, Akathaporn & McInnes (1993)	*Fortune* reputation rating	Accounting & market
Ingram (1978)	Disclosure of social performance	Market
Jones & Murrell (2001)	*Working Mother* list of "Most Family Friendly" companies	Market
Judge & Douglas (1998)	Survey of environmental practices	Accounting & market share

Social Initiatives by Business

Table 2 *(Continued)*

Study	Measure	
	Social performance	Financial performance
Corporate social performance as independent variable		
Klassen & McLaughlin (1996)	Environmental awards and crises	Market
Klassen & Whybark (1999)	Survey of environmental practices and TRI	Manufacturing cost, quality, speed, and flexibility
Konar & Cohen (2001)	TRI and environmental lawsuits	Accounting & market
Luck & Pilotte (1993)	KLD evaluation	Market
McGuire, Sundgren & Schneeweis (1988)	*Fortune* reputation rating	Accounting & market
Moskowitz (1972)	Observations of charitable contributions, consumer protection, disclosure, equal employment opportunity, human resource practices, South Africa operations, and urban renewal	Personal assessment
Nehrt (1996)	Timing and intensity of pollution-reducing technologies	Accounting
Newgren et al. (1985)	Survey of environmental practices	Market
Parket & Eilbirt (1975)	Survey on minority hiring and training, ecology, contributions to education and art	Accounting
Porter & van der Linde (1995)	Waste prevention practices	Accounting
Posnikoff (1997)	South Africa: divestment	Market
Preston (1978)	Disclosure of social performance	Accounting
Preston & O'Bannon (1997)	*Fortune* reputation rating	Accounting
Preston & Sapienza (1990)	*Fortune* reputation rating	Market
Reimann (1975)	Survey of attitudes toward national government, suppliers, consumers, community, stockholders, creditors, and employees	Organizational competence
Russo & Fouts (1997)	FRDC ratings of environmental practices	Accounting
Shane & Spicer (1983)	CEP evaluation	Market
Sharma & Vredenburg (1998)	Survey of environmental strategy	Operational improvement
Simerly (1994)	*Fortune* reputation rating	Accounting & market
Simerly (1995)	*Fortune* reputation rating	Accounting
Spencer & Taylor (1987)	*Fortune* reputation rating	Accounting
Spicer (1978)	CEP evaluation	Accounting & market
Stevens (1984)	CEP evaluation	Market
Sturdivant & Ginter (1977)	Moskowitz ratings of social responsiveness	Accounting
Tichy, McGill & St. Clair (1997)	*Fortune* reputation rating	Accounting
Travers (1997)	Mutual fund screens	Market
Verschoor (1998)	Espoused commitment to ethics in annual report	Accounting & market
Verschoor (1999)	Explicit statement of an ethics code in annual report	Accounting & market
Waddock & Graves (1997)	KLD evaluation	Accounting
Wokutch & Spencer (1987)	*Fortune* reputation rating, charitable contributions, corporate crime	Accounting
Wright et al. (1995)	Awards from U.S. Dept. of Labor for exemplary equal employment opportunity	Market
Non-significant relationship		
Abbott & Monsen (1979)	Disclosure of social performance	Accounting
Alexander & Buchholz (1978)	Moskowitz ratings of social responsiveness	Market
Aupperle, Carroll & Hatfield (1985)	Survey of social responsibility practices and organizational structures	Accounting
Bowman (1978)	Disclosure of social performance	Accounting
Chen & Metcalf (1980)	CEP evaluation	Accounting & market
Fogler & Nutt (1975)	CEP evaluation	Market
Fombrun & Shanley (1990)	*Fortune* reputation rating	Accounting & market
Freedman & Jaggi (1982)	CEP evaluation	Accounting
Freedman & Jaggi (1986)	Disclosure of pollution	Market
Fry & Hock (1976)	Disclosure of social performance	Accounting
Greening (1995)	EIA reports on conservation practices	Accounting & market
Guerard (1997a)	KLD evaluation	Market
Hamilton, Jo & Statman (1993)	Mutual fund screens	Market
Hickman, Teets & Kohls (1999)	Mutual fund screens	Market
Hylton (1992)	Mutual fund screens	Market
Ingram & Frazier (1983)	Disclosure of environmental quality control	Accounting

Table 2 *(Continued)*

Study	Measure	
	Social performance	Financial performance
Corporate social performance as independent variable		
Kurtz & DiBartolomeo (1996)	KLD evaluation	Market
Lashgari & Gant (1989)	South Africa: adherence to Sullivan principles	Accounting
Luther & Matatko (1994)	Mutual fund screens	Market
Mahapatra (1984)	Disclosure of capital expenditures on pollution control	Market
McWilliams & Siegel (1997)	Awards from U.S. Dept. of Labor for exemplary equal employment opportunity	Market
McWilliams & Siegel (2000)	KLD evaluation	Accounting
O'Neill, Saunders & McCarthy (1989)	Survey of directors' concern for social responsibility	Accounting
Patten (1990)	South Africa: announcement of signing of Sullivan principles	Market
Reyes & Grieb (1998)	Mutual fund screens	Market
Sauer (1997)	Mutual fund screens	Market
Teoh, Welch & Wazzan (1999)	South Africa: divestment	Market
Waddock & Graves (2000)	KLD evaluation	Accounting & market
Negative relationship		
Boyle, Higgins & Rhee (1997)	Compliance with Defense Industries Initiative	Market
Kahn, Lekander & Leimkuhler (1997)	Tobacco-free	Market
Meznar, Nigh & Kwok (1994)	South Africa: withdrawal	Market
Mueller (1991)	Mutual fund screens	Market
Teper (1992)	No alcohol, tobacco, gambling, defense contracts, or operations in South Africa; adherence to broad social guidelines	Market
Vance (1975)	Moskowitz ratings of social responsiveness	Market
Wright & Ferris (1997)	South Africa: divestment	Market
Mixed relationship		
Belkaoui & Karpik (1989)	Disclosure of social performance and Moskowitz ratings of social responsiveness	Accounting & market
Berman et al. (1999)	KLD evaluation	Accounting
Blackburn, Doran & Shrader (1994)	CEP evaluation	Accounting & market
Bowman & Haire (1975)	Disclosure of social performance	Accounting
Brown (1997)	*Fortune* reputation rating	Market
Cochran & Wood (1984)	Moskowitz ratings of social responsiveness	Accounting & market
Diltz (1995)	CEP evaluation	Market
Graves & Waddock (1994)	KLD evaluation	Accounting
Gregory, Matatko & Luther (1997)	Mutual fund screens	Market
Guerard (1997b)	KLD evaluation	Market
Hillman & Keim (2001)	KLD evaluation	Market
Holman, New & Singer (1990)	Disclosure of social performance & capital expenditures on regulatory compliance	Market
Kedia & Kuntz (1981)	Interview and survey on charitable contributions, low-income housing loans, minority enterprise loans, female corporate officers, and minority employment	Accounting & market share
Luther, Matatko & Corner (1992)	Mutual fund screens	Market
Mallin, Saadouni & Briston (1995)	Mutual fund screens	Market
Marcus & Goodman (1986)	Compliance with safety regulations	Capabilities & productive efficiency
McGuire, Schneeweis & Branch (1990)	*Fortune* reputation rating	Accounting & market
Ogden & Watson (1999)	Customer service complaints	Accounting & market
Pava & Krausz (1996)	CEP evaluation	Accounting & market
Rockness, Schlachter & Rockness (1986)	EPA and U.S. House of Representatives data on hazardous waste disposal	Accounting & market

Social Initiatives by Business

Table 2 *(Continued)*

Study	Social performance	Financial performance
	Measure	
	Corporate social performance as dependent variable	
Positive relationship		
Brown & Perry (1994)	*Fortune* reputation rating	Accounting & market
Cottrill (1990)	*Fortune* reputation rating	Market share
Dooley & Lerner (1994)	TRI	Accounting
Fry, Keim & Meiners (1982)	Charitable contributions	Accounting
Galaskiewicz (1997)	Charitable contributions	Accounting
Konar & Cohen (1997)	TRI	Market
Levy & Shatto (1980)	Charitable contributions	Accounting
Maddox & Siegfried (1980)	Charitable contributions	Accounting
Marcus & Goodman (1986)	Compliance with emissions regulations	Accounting
McGuire, Sundgren & Schneeweis (1988)	*Fortune* reputation rating	Accounting & market
Mills & Gardner (1984)	Disclosure of social performance	Accounting & market
Navarro (1988)	Charitable contributions	Accounting
Preston & O'Bannon (1997)	*Fortune* reputation rating	Accounting
Riahi-Belkaoui (1991)	*Fortune* reputation rating	Accounting & market
Roberts (1992)	CEP evaluation	Accounting & market
Waddock & Graves (1997)	KLD evaluation	Accounting
Non-significant relationship		
Buehler & Shetty (1976)	Organizational programs in consumer affairs, environmental affairs, urban affairs	Accounting
Cowen, Ferreri & Parker (1987)	Disclosure of social performance	Accounting
Patten (1991)	Disclosure of social performance	Accounting
Mixed relationship		
Johnson & Greening (1999)	KLD evaluation	Accounting
Lerner & Fryxell (1988)	CEP evaluation	Accounting & market
McGuire, Schneeweis & Branch (1990)	*Fortune* reputation rating	Accounting & market

* CEP = Council on Economic Priorities; EIA = Energy Information Association; EPA = Environmental Protection Agency; FRDC = Franklin Research & Development Corporation; IRRC = Investor Responsibility Research Center; KLD = Kinder, Lydenberg, Domini multidimensional rating; NACBS = National Affiliation of Concerned Business Students; OSHA = Occupational Safety and Health Administration; and TRI = Toxics Release Inventory. Four studies investigate the relationship in both directions but are counted as only one study: McGuire, Schneeweis & Branch (1990); McGuire, Sundgren & Schneeweis (1988); Preston & O'Bannon (1997); Waddock & Graves (1997). Marcus & Goodman (1986) contains two separate studies and is therefore counted twice.

captures the basic approaches for measuring social and financial performance and reports which authors found which results, including positive, non-significant, negative, and mixed relationships.

A clear signal emerges from these 127 studies. A simple compilation of the findings suggests there is a positive association, and certainly very little evidence of a negative association, between a company's social performance and its financial performance. A recent meta-analysis of 52 CSP-CFP studies reached this same substantive conclusion (Orlitzky, Schmidt, and Rynes, 2003). Concerns about misappropriation, and perhaps even misallocation, would seem to be alleviated. If corporate social performance contributes to corporate financial performance, then a firm's resources are being used to advance the interests of shareholders, the rightful claimants in the economic contractarian model. Concerns about misallocation recede as well. If social performance is contributing to financial performance, then the firm is being used to advance the objective for which it is considered to be best suited, maximizing wealth. Although it can be argued that a company's resources might be used to produce even more wealth, were they devoted to some activity other than CSP, studies of the link between CSP and CFP reveal little evidence that CSP destroys value, injures shareholders in a significant way, or damages the wealth-creating capacity of firms. The empirical relationship between CSP and CFP would seem to be established and the underlying economic concerns about CSP alleviated. Even as research into the relationship between CSP and CFP addresses the objections posed by economic contractarianism, however, a closer look at this research suggests that it opens as many questions as it answers about the role of the firm in society.

What appears to be a definite link between CSP and CFP may turn out to be more illusory than the body of results suggests. The steady flow of research studies reflects ongoing efforts both to resolve the tension between advocates and critics of corporate social performance and to shore up the methodological and theoretical weaknesses in past studies. There have been 13 reviews of this CSP-CFP research published since 1978, nine in the past ten years alone (Aldag and Bartol, 1978; Arlow and Gannon, 1982; Cochran and Wood, 1984; Aupperle, Carroll, and Hatfield, 1985; Wokutch and McKinney, 1991; Wood and Jones, 1995; Pava and Krausz, 1996; Griffin and Mahon, 1997; Preston and O'Bannon, 1997; Richardson, Welker, and Hutchinson, 1999; Roman, Hayibor, and Agle, 1999; Margolis and Walsh, 2001; Orlitzky, Schmidt, and Rynes, 2003). The reviewers see problems of all kinds in this research. They identify sampling problems, concerns about the reliability and validity of the CSP and CFP measures, omission of controls, opportunities to test mediating mechanisms and moderating conditions, and a need for a causal theory to link CSP and CFP. The imperfect nature of these studies makes research on the link between CSP and CFP self-perpetuating: each successive study promises a definitive conclusion, while also revealing the inevitable inadequacies of empirically tackling the question. As the acceleration in the number of studies reveals, research that investigates the link between CSP and CFP shows no sign of abating.

This continuing research tradition produces an ironic and, no doubt, unintended consequence. The CSP-CFP empirical literature reinforces, rather than relieves, the tension surrounding corporate responses to social misery. By assaying the financial impact of corporate social performance, organizational research helps to confirm the economic contractarian model and accept its assumptions. Meanwhile, the work leaves unexplored questions about what it is firms are actually doing in response to social misery and what effects corporate actions have, not only on the bottom line but also on society. The parallel conceptual work in the area of stakeholder theory arrives at the same disquieting destination.

The Theoretical Stakeholder Literature

Freeman (1984) brought a formal consideration of stakeholder relations to a burgeoning field of management scholarship

Social Initiatives by Business

twenty years ago. Tracing its indirect roots back to Adam Smith's work in the eighteenth century and a 1963 internal memorandum at the Stanford Research Institute, Freeman's ideas provided a language and framework for examining how a firm relates to "any group or individual who can affect or is affected by the achievement of the organization's objective" (Freeman, 1984: 46). Looking at the business corporation through something other than the eyes of its equity holders has inspired great efforts to translate that intuitive appeal into a theory. Donaldson and Preston (1995) counted more than a dozen books and 100 articles devoted to stakeholder theory; Wolfe and Putler (2002) counted 76 articles on the stakeholder theme published in just six journals in the 1990s. The promise of stakeholder theory to offer a cogent alternative to the economic account of the firm, however, is impeded by a set of assumptions designed to accommodate economic considerations.

Taking stock of stakeholder theory, Donaldson and Preston (1995) introduced an influential taxonomy that sorts it into three types: descriptive, normative, and instrumental. Descriptive stakeholder theory focuses on whether and to what extent managers do in fact attend to various stakeholders and act in accord with their interests. Normative stakeholder theory explores whether managers ought to attend to stakeholders other than shareholders and, if so, on what grounds these various stakeholders have justifiable claims on the firm. Instrumental stakeholder theory delineates and investigates the consequences—most notably, the economic benefits—that follow from attending to a range of stakeholders. Instrumental versions of stakeholder theory can either be descriptive, positing and investigating the beneficial consequences that accrue to the firm, such as efficient contracting (Jones, 1995), or normative, justifying the claims of stakeholders on the basis of the benefits that accrue to the firm from attending to those claims (Freeman, 1999; Freeman and Phillips, 2002; Jensen, 2002).

Whereas Donaldson and Preston encouraged greater attention to normative questions about stakeholders, the scholarship devoted to stakeholder theory has focused largely on instrumental considerations. Jones and Wicks (1999) formally proposed a convergent stakeholder theory to blend instrumental considerations with the ongoing efforts to create a normative theory. Although Freeman (1999: 235) eschewed Donaldson and Preston's tripartite division of stakeholder theory as well as the subsequent integration, he also concluded that to buttress any normative injunction for managers to attend to key stakeholders, "it is hard to see how such an argument can be connected to real firms and real stakeholders without some kind of instrumental claim." Revealing the grip that instrumental reasoning has on stakeholder theory, Post, Preston, and Sachs (2002: 19) recently defined stakeholders explicitly by the contribution stakeholders make to wealth creation or destruction: "The stakeholders in a corporation are the individuals and constituencies that contribute, either voluntarily or involuntarily, to its wealth-creating capacity and activities, and are therefore its potential beneficiaries and/or risk bearers."

It is taken to be a practical necessity that stakeholder theory revolve around consequences, financial consequences substantive enough to convince managers that stakeholders are worthy of attention (Freeman, 1999; Jones and Wicks, 1999). When those beneficial consequences are not contingent on a certain standard of stakeholder treatment, or when that treatment fails to produce those consequences, however, the range of corporate conduct that is required, or even permissible, becomes much less clear. What happens when attention to stakeholder interests yields results that diverge from the wealth maximizing ambitions of its shareholders? This is precisely what may happen when attention is directed at the effects of organizations on society and whether, for example, companies should divest their investments in South Africa (Meznar, Nigh, and Kwok, 1994), diversify the demographic composition of their boards of directors (Carleton, Nelson, and Weisbach, 1998), or join the fight to combat AIDS. Paradoxically, a stakeholder theory conceived to be practical may have left managers bereft. As Gioia (1999: 231) argued, the central challenge for managers is "how to arrive at some workable balance" between instrumental and other moral criteria. Managers confront difficult dilemmas when normative and instrumental claims do not perfectly align.

There are normative reasons to respect stakeholders, independent of the ensuing financial benefits. Those reasons may be grounded, for example, in the beneficial consequences that result for specific stakeholders. Concerns about employee dignity and self-efficacy may prompt certain kinds of managerial behavior (Shklar, 1991; Hodson, 2001). Normative justification of stakeholder claims may also be grounded in principles of fairness and reciprocity (Applbaum, 1996; Phillips, 1997, 2003), fundamental rights (Donaldson and Preston, 1995), or respect for the intrinsic worth of human beings (Donaldson and Dunfee, 1999). How do these grounds for action inform our perspective on the place of the firm in society? How can their implications for action, in the face of calls for corporate responses to ameliorate social misery, be sorted out alongside the compelling instrumental purpose of the firm to enhance material welfare and maximize wealth?

A preoccupation with instrumental consequences renders a theory that accommodates economic premises yet sidesteps the underlying tensions between the social and economic imperatives that confront organizations. Such a theory risks omitting the pressing descriptive and normative questions raised by these tensions, which, when explored, might hold great promise for new theory, and even for addressing practical management challenges. How do firms navigate their way through these tensions? How ought they to do so? Organizational inquiry must go beyond efforts to reconcile corporate responses to social misery with the neoclassical model of the firm. Rather, this social and economic tension should serve as a starting point for new theory and research.

Exploring the Antinomy

Organizational scholars and managers alike find themselves in the clutches of an antinomy (Alexander, 1988; Poole and Van de Ven, 1989). That antinomy is captured in a question Merton (1976: 88) believed every executive must face:

Social Initiatives by Business

"Does the successful business try first to profit or to serve?"
From society's perspective, creating wealth and contributing
to material well-being are essential corporate goals. But
restoring and equipping human beings, as well as protecting
and repairing the natural environment, are also essential
objectives. Companies may be well designed to advance the
first set of objectives, yet they operate in a world plagued by
a host of recalcitrant problems that hamper the second set.
These vying objectives place claims on the firm that are often
difficult to rank and reconcile. Where economic contractarians see instrumental inefficiency and illicit conduct in directing corporate resources toward redressing social misery,
those who advocate broader corporate social initiatives see
instrumental efficiency and duties fulfilled.

The antinomy reveals itself more explicitly in the face of
appeals for companies to take a more active and expanded
role in society. Some line up to warn of the danger in heed-
ing these appeals, while others point to empirical findings to
relieve concern. Both avenues of intellectual response,
already reviewed in this paper, attempt to remove the antinomy in one of two classic ways (Nussbaum, 1986: 67), either
through invalidation or through reconciliation. For example,
declarations of what the role and purpose of a firm "really" is
attempt either to validate or disqualify certain activities by
suggesting that a theory of the firm renders certain functions
and practices defensible and others not (e.g., Berle, 1931;
Dodd, 1932). Theoretical and empirical attempts at synthesis,
reflecting the second avenue of response, seek to demonstrate the mutual reinforcement of colliding conceptions of
the firm (e.g., Griffin and Mahon, 1997; Jones and Wicks,
1999). Despite these differing efforts to resolve the antinomy, declarations of what a firm's purpose truly is and efforts
to demonstrate convergence among competing conceptions
do not erase the fundamental tension.

The effort to relieve the antinomy through synthesis and reconciliation has fueled organizational scholarship for many
years. By adopting the underlying assumptions of economic
contractarianism, both instrumental stakeholder theory and
the empirical research connecting CSP and CFP offer an allur-
ing way to ease the tension with economics. The problem,
as Tetlock (2000: 23) pointed out, is that no concession to
the instrumental and wealth-enhancing model of the firm will
reconcile economic contractarians to stakeholder theory:

> Disagreements rooted in values should be profoundly resistant to
> change. . . . Libertarian conservatives might oppose the (confiscato-
> ry) stakeholder model even when confronted by evidence that con-
> cessions in this direction have no adverse effects on profitability to
> shareholders. Expropriation is expropriation, no matter how pretti-
> fied. And some egalitarians might well endorse the stakeholder
> model, even if shown compelling evidence that it reduces profits.
> Academics who rely on evidence-based appeals to change minds
> when the disagreements are rooted in values may be wasting
> everyone's time.

Aside from failing to win over opponents, substantiating the
instrumental benefits of corporate social performance may
well be immaterial for another, equally salient reason. Companies already invest in social initiatives. Moreover, these com-

panies often invest for reasons that have nothing to do with instrumental consequences. Beyond the obvious point that researchers could not investigate the CSP-CFP relationship without evidence of CSP, companies' philanthropic contributions more than quadrupled, in real terms, between 1950 and 2000 (Caplow, Hicks, and Wattenberg, 2001). The cross-industry organization Business for Social Responsibility would not be able to count 1,400 members and commission a book to document the benefits that purportedly accrue from socially responsible practices (Makower, 1994) were such practices unknown. In keeping with Tetlock's (2000) insight, the reasons executives give for these social initiatives typically have more to do with an ineffable sense that this work is the right thing to do (Holmes, 1976; Galaskiewicz, 1997; Donnelly, 2001), rather than with how these investments will increase shareholder value. These corporate practices even seem to challenge the empirical claims of economic theory. Why does corporate social performance persist despite the disadvantages that economic theory suggests it imposes on firms? The existence of CSP begs empirical explanation rather than empirical justification.

Efforts to reconcile organizational research on corporate social performance with the economic model of the firm may ultimately turn out to be counterproductive. To make room for corporate responses to societal ills, organizational theorists and researchers have acceded to economic contractarianism, relinquishing their own ideas about the problems to be investigated, the variables on which to focus, and the methods to use for gaining insight (Alexander, 1988; Hirsch, Friedman, and Koza, 1990). For example, if corporate responses to social misery are evaluated only in terms of their instrumental benefits for the firm and its shareholders, we never learn about their impact on society, most notably on the intended beneficiaries of these initiatives. Nor do we investigate the conditions under which it is permissible to act on stakeholder interests that are inconsistent with shareholder interests. The corporate initiatives that were the focus of Meznar, Nigh, and Kwok's (1994) event study of firms announcing their divestment from South Africa and the event study of TIAA-CREF's board diversity initiatives (Carleton, Nelson, and Weisbach, 1998) were both met with negative market reactions. Does that mean that firms should have stayed to work with an apartheid government or that attempts to add African Americans to boards of directors should be halted? Financial performance may not be the final arbiter of questions that implicate a range of values and concerns, even when firms are the actors. Rather than theorizing away the collision of objectives and interests, organizational scholars would do well to explore it (Alexander, 1988).

By adopting economic assumptions, organization theory and research handicaps itself in yet another way. It leaves organizations that seek to respond to these calls for social involvement bereft of prescriptive guidance for how to do so. Simply knowing that the economic tide is with them does not provide managers with insight about how to respond properly and effectively. Organizations face a troublesome reality, in which specific requests to help fight AIDS, support homeless

Social Initiatives by Business

shelters, or improve local schools may or may not generate economic gains for the firm. The field of organization studies has largely been silent about how to consider and manage the tradeoffs and dilemmas that arise when companies confront dueling expectations.

A Reorienting Perspective

The grip of economic assumptions must be released in favor of an alternative premise, one that expands the focus of organizational scholarship. We suggest adopting a pragmatic stance toward questions about the firm's role in society, one articulated most clearly by William James (1975: 97): "Grant an idea or belief to be true," it [pragmatism] says, "what concrete difference will its being true make in anyone's actual life? How will the truth be realized? What experiences will be different from those that would obtain if the belief were false? What, in short, is the truth's cash-value in experiential terms?"

The first step of James's pragmatic approach is to assume that an idea is true. In this case, we need to begin with the idea that organizations can play an effective role in ameliorating social misery. From that beginning, pragmatism then instructs us to look at the consequences of acting on this belief. Do companies really make a concrete difference in curing social ills when they act as though they can do so? The lens of research shifts away from confirming the consistency between corporate actions and economic premises about the firm. Research would instead focus on unearthing the effects that corporate actions to redress social ills actually have. The pragmatic perspective poses a second question: How can the assumed truth that companies can be effective agents, not just of economic efficiency but of social repair, be realized? How can the concrete differences be achieved? This lays out a new direction for theory. What are the conditions under which, and the processes through which, the intended beneficiaries and institutions central to a healthy society indeed benefit from these corporate actions? Systematic descriptive research is just as necessary to examine the consequences of corporate actions as it is to identify their antecedents and the processes that bring them about.

Although we are proposing an alternative starting point for inquiry into the role of the firm in society, we are not making a steadfast normative claim about the appropriate role for the firm in society. The pragmatic stance does not require that other beliefs be relinquished. Those who believe that society is best served if companies focus solely on maximizing wealth can adhere to their convictions, as can those who believe that other stakeholders beyond the shareholder deserve attention, whatever the repercussions for profitability. The aim here is to test a pragmatic belief to determine if acting on the basis of that belief produces the desired consequences. How those consequences are to be weighed and pursued relative to others is a matter for normative theory. Here too, organizational scholarship must extend its efforts.

The challenge for those who study organizations is to investigate what happens when it is assumed that instrumental efficiency and human beneficence, wealth maximization and the amelioration of social misery, and shareholder rights and stakeholder rights all matter. A normative theory of the firm will acknowledge these competing conceptions and accommodate the tension. Instead of trying to assert the legitimacy of one set of claims and deny the legitimacy of the other, or to imagine that all of these competing interests can somehow be synthetically reconciled, theorists must undertake the task of working out the principles and guidelines for managing tradeoffs. A starting point for building such a theory requires a systematic descriptive inquiry into corporations' responses to calls for an expanded role. These insights can then combine inductively with a rigorous philosophical analysis to construct a normative conception of the firm and its purpose. A descriptive research agenda lays the foundation for the inductive development of a normative theory of the firm. As we investigate how corporations do or do not respond to misery, we can think about how they ought to respond to misery.

TOWARD A NORMATIVE THEORY OF THE FIRM

The antinomy poses a fundamental question for organization theorists and managers: How can business organizations respond to human misery while also sustaining their legitimacy, securing vital resources, and enhancing financial performance? This question may best be addressed through a partnership between systematic descriptive research and inductive normative theory. We need to paint a clear and comprehensive portrait of how firms navigate these competing objectives in their responses to social ills. To do this, economic assumptions about business organizations must be dislodged, though not discarded or discounted, in favor of a pragmatic assumption that permits examination, before cross-examination, of corporate responses to misery. Here we echo a recent call in psychology to investigate complex social phenomena as they occur in the real world before moving to tests of theoretical propositions (Rozin, 2001). A portrait of corporate responses to social misery then informs normative inquiry into the antinomy itself.

Rather than stating the firm's preeminent role and purpose, defending it, and deductively deriving principles of action that follow, our inductive approach begins with the complex interplay of vying objectives, duties, and concerns. Inductive normative theorizing asks the question, How might the role, purpose, and function of the firm be specified so as to acknowledge a range of inconsistent concerns and still facilitate action? While acknowledging the conflict between social misery and economic efficiency, an inductive normative theory seeks not to resolve the conflict but to clarify the competing considerations, probe what gives them weight, and explore their relationship. The goal is to craft a purpose and role for the firm that builds internal coherence among competing and incommensurable objectives, duties, and concerns (Richardson, 1997). While the aim of our descriptive agenda is to survey the state of corporate responses to social misery, and thereby ascertain how companies do indeed navigate through the antinomy, the aim of our normative agenda is to craft a framework for how companies should navigate that antinomy.

A Descriptive Research Agenda

Firms make social investments in the face of compelling economic reasoning not to do so. The discrepancy between actual practice and the theoretically espoused purpose of the firm prompts a quest for explanation. It is a classic sense-making situation. To make sense of corporate conduct, it is especially appropriate to follow Weick's (1995: 183) counsel to "talk the walk": "To 'talk the walk' is to be opportunistic in the best sense of the word. It is to search for words that make sense of current walking that is adaptive for reasons that are not yet clear." To make sense of corporate responses to misery and discern the function of those responses, we need to understand which firms respond to which social problems, with what consequences, for both the firms and society. It is best to explore this kind of broad research terrain with a map in hand (Weick, 1995: 54–55, 121). Used as a retrospective sensemaking guide, the core theories of organizational decision making and action provide a useful map for this descriptive exploration (Janis and Mann, 1977; Weick, 1979; Tushman and Romanelli, 1985; Cyert and March, 1992). Five areas of inquiry invite descriptive research: how companies extract and appraise the stimuli for action; how companies generate response options; how companies evaluate these options and select a course of action; how the selected course is implemented; and, finally, what consequences follow from corporate efforts to ameliorate social ills. We outline orienting research questions in each of these five areas.

Appraising the stimuli. Researchers first need to understand which social ills garner attention by which firms. Organizations observe feedback from their context (Cyert and March, 1992) or enact their context in such a way (Weick, 1979) that a stimulus for action is recognized and assessed (Kiesler and Sproull, 1982). What then explains which set of issues catch a firm's attention? Janis and Mann (1977) observed that these stimuli for action often come in two forms: communications and events.

Communications to act in the social domain can come both from internal agents (Andersson and Bateman, 2000; Bansal, 2003) and external agents, whether solicited (Adkins, 1999) or unsolicited (Mannheim, 2001). Chronicling who these agents are, what communication tactics they employ, and how the different agents use different communication strategies for greater and lesser effect are all ripe research questions. More must be learned, as well, about the kind of events that trigger, or fail to trigger, corporate action. Why do firms respond to some communications and events and not others? Perhaps a set of features of triggering stimuli increase the likelihood of response. Extant theory suggests that an appellant's power, legitimacy, and urgency might determine the extent to which managers attend to a claim (Mitchell, Agle, and Wood, 1997). Alternatively, problems and solutions may simply attach themselves to organizations in a nearly inexplicable fashion (Cohen, March, and Olsen, 1972; Cyert and March, 1992: 96).

Once the features of the stimulating problems and the organizations involved are better understood, we can then examine how companies appraise this information. Organizations might frame these stimuli as a cost or investment, a burden or responsibility, a threat or an opportunity (Jackson and Dutton, 1988), or some combination of these kinds of polar extremes (Gilbert, 2003), to greater or lesser effect. In the end, descriptive inquiry can unearth the criteria that qualify certain problems for action and guide managers to select, or discard, problems to address.

Generating response options. Once a problem has been identified and enacted as warranting a response, a search ensues for a solution (Cyert and March, 1992). How do companies generate response options? The classic dichotomy between behavioral processes, in which an action option is tried and either selected or discarded based on the ensuing feedback (Levitt and March, 1988; Gavetti and Levinthal, 2000), and cognitive processes, in which options are generated and weighed in advance of behavioral trial (March and Simon, 1958; Gavetti and Levinthal, 2000), provide one lens for diagnosing how companies generate responses to social ills. Whether options are tried out first behaviorally and then assessed or cognitively formulated and then assessed before they are executed, we also need greater insight into how the plausible options are generated.

Why do companies end up considering the set of options they do? At least three possible approaches can be identified. First, a firm may deliberately appraise its assets and capabilities and then generate options that tap into these resources (Dunfee and Hess, 2000). UPS, for example, drew on its logistics capabilities when it created a technical service manual for food rescue programs (www.community.ups). Second, a firm may look to potential partners in civil society and develop a relationship that might even grow over time (Sagawa and Segal, 2000). The relationship between Timberland and City Year represents how these collaborations can deepen through the years (Austin, 2000). Finally, the process may be more externally driven and nearly automatic. Companies may identify widely practiced options that adhere to standards of accepted conduct. Galaskiewicz (1991) illuminated the deliberate construction of philanthropic institutions and ideology in Minneapolis–Saint Paul. Once established, the charitable contributions flowed at the same rate each year, regardless of who was leading the firms (Galaskiewicz, 1997).

In addition to identifying the process of generating options, the content of those options begs for systematic descriptive research. Just as the problems that stimulate corporate responses to social ills can be catalogued and analyzed for patterns, so can the content of potential corporate responses. What are companies doing in response to social ills, and what is the range of activities they consider? Two fundamental questions, bearing on the definition of the phenomenon itself, arise at this point for descriptive research. For simplici-

Social Initiatives by Business

ty, we have operated with the assumption that responses to misery are appendages to companies' core productive activity and that corporate social performance consists of responses to human misery. In examining the responses companies actually consider, both of these assumptions open themselves to inquiry. First, to what extent are companies responding with for-profit initiatives, initiatives that treat social ills akin to any other set of business opportunities, discerning a market (Prahalad and Hammond, 2002) or an emergent product class (Tushman and Romanelli, 1985) to be entered or a cost to be reduced? Alternatively, to what extent, and when, do companies respond with charitable activities decoupled from their core for-profit activities, donating some sort of resource? Second, to what extent is corporate social performance truly a response to human misery? The options companies consider, and even the problems that get pressed upon them, may invoke a role that extends beyond a narrow economic function and yet does not touch upon human misery. What is the actual proximity between corporate responses classified as social performance and efforts to redress human misery?

Evaluating options. What assessment criteria are applied to corporate efforts to ameliorate social ills? In making decisions, managers tend to follow a logic of consequences, weighing costs and benefits, or a logic of appropriateness, weighing the fit of potential options with conceptions of their (and the company's) role identity and its implications for the given situation (Cyert and March, 1992; March, 1994). Research can reveal when the criteria are applied: do companies weigh and evaluate potential options in advance of acting (March and Simon, 1958), or do they make sense of their social initiatives retrospectively (Weick, 1979, 1995), assigning a meaningful (but retroactive) explanation for why the selected course was taken?

In unearthing the criteria companies use to assess responses to human misery, descriptive research can reveal how companies wrestle with the competing expectations that contested conceptions of the firm's role and purpose impose. If consequences are used to evaluate response options, the set of consequences may reflect the ways in which conflicting conceptions of the firm's role are being negotiated. For example, what sort of return is assessed when companies evaluate options by calculating a return on investment? Perhaps companies try to calculate the financial benefits to the firm, mimicking the research conducted for over 30 years, or perhaps they employ a more expansive definition of return and focus their attention on worker morale and commitment, corporate reputation in capital and product markets, or the legitimacy gained with regulatory authorities. Alternatively, companies may evaluate the benefits for society, estimating, for example, the greatest humanitarian gain per dollar spent. If so, how is the humanitarian gain assessed? Conflicting conceptions of the firm's role and purpose may also be reflected in how the appropriateness of corporate social initiatives is evaluated. In the face of the shareholder wealth maximization ideology, using criteria of appropriateness permits consistency between this ideology and corporate social initiatives.

Enlightened self-interest (Galaskiewicz, 1991) is one such criterion. It provides economic grounds on which to validate the fit of the economic identity of the firm with virtually any option selected.

Implementation. Once problems have been identified and selected, and once response options have been generated and evaluated, a response must be implemented. How then do companies play their social role? How are such contested acts managed? Cyert and March (1992: 164) argued that "most organizations most of the time exist and thrive with considerable latent conflict of goals." Quasi-resolution of conflict is made possible, in their view, through satisficing decision rules and sequential attention to goals. Corporate efforts to respond to social ills, however, are not only in conflict with other objectives, they are themselves inherently provocative, highlighting in their very purpose their inconsistency with the firm's economic objective. Therefore, these corporate efforts pose distinct management challenges. Ameliorative initiatives are simultaneously legitimacy-seeking and legitimacy-threatening acts, adhering to one set of expectations, social in nature, while violating another, economic in nature. In addition, as companies find themselves with an elaborated moral personality (Paine, 2002), corporate social initiatives are simultaneously identity-bridging and identity-begging activities: corporate efforts to redress social ills are a means of accommodating a new construal of companies as social institutions while raising fundamental questions about the firm's purpose. Corporate social initiatives are complicated even more by their mixed motives. Managers may seek to relieve normative and coercive calls for involvement; secure their companies' legitimacy, reputation, and ability to function; and actually aid society. How are corporate efforts to redress social ills managed—executed, controlled, monitored, and disciplined—amid this crossfire of competing purposes, expectations, identities, and motives? If companies approach prospective action with cognitive maps that outline the course of action and anticipated consequences (Gavetti and Levinthal, 2000), how is the plan converted into action and directed toward the desired consequences? If companies follow a process resembling experiential search (Gavetti and Levinthal, 2000), how is that search—the trial and error process—navigated through the mixture of expectations and motives, so that the firm's intended aims are met or readjusted?

If one way of navigating equivocal situations is to design equivocal (Weick, 1979: 223–224), ambivalent (Merton, 1976), or ambidextrous responses (Tushman and O'Reilly, 2002), then companies might navigate conflicting expectations and colliding perspectives on their role with an equivocal response. Creative allocation of control and resources may provide business organizations with this sort of dexterity, enabling companies to acknowledge the social ill and gain the benefits of response while sustaining flexibility and minimizing the risks of response (Weick, 1979: 223–224). Design options include make, buy, and hybrid arrangements, each of which entails different types and degrees of investment and control.

Social Initiatives by Business

Companies may create the responses themselves, the "make" option, when they have a distinctive capability that fits a specific, evident social need (Dunfee and Hess, 2000). Charitable contributions, the "buy" option, may be the selected design option either when a firm lacks any specific capability to address a social need, yet the need is pressing, or when existing institutions have excellent capabilities in the area in which the firm seeks to invest. A "hybrid" strategy, or public-private partnership, may be the option of choice when the firm has something to give and gain from others when it makes its social investments (Austin, 2000). A highly recognizable partner, such as Amnesty International, may reduce uncertainty for managers and increase the likelihood of reputational benefits for the firm. Examples of such partnerships abound (Sagawa and Segal, 2000) and seem to be increasing (Zadek, 2001: 91). Categorizing corporate responses using this scheme of make, buy, or hybrid can provide insight into the factors that shape companies' investment and control decisions surrounding responses to social ills.

Beyond their design, little is known about how companies internally control, monitor, and discipline their social initiatives. First, how much do companies choose to invest, in total and as a percentage of available investment capital, in ameliorating societal ills? Economic logic suggests a level that meets a bare minimum for deriving benefits for the firm (Friedman, 1970), whereas behavioral research suggests that standards of fairness (Kahneman, Knetsch, and Thaler, 1986), irrational by economic standards, may shape allocation decisions. Second, corporate responses to social misery have aims distinct from other corporate activities, so corporate control of these initiatives warrants scrutiny as well. Understanding the forms of control used to steer social initiatives toward their aims and exploring how those forms of control commingle with traditional forms of financial control is central to a descriptive research agenda. The calls for the Securities and Exchange Commission to regulate disclosure of philanthropic contributions (Kahn, 1997; Bagley and Page, 1999; Gillmor and Bremer, 1999) suggest that monitoring and control mechanisms are underdeveloped. With a variety of instrumental, moral, political, and institutional considerations motivating social initiatives, we need to know how corporate social initiatives are monitored and disciplined.

Consequences. Although the financial effects of corporate social performance have been extensively studied, little is known about any other consequences of corporate social initiatives. Most notably, as calls for corporate involvement increase, there is a vital need to understand how corporate efforts to redress social misery actually affect their intended beneficiaries. Again, a first step is simply to ascertain the consequences and discern salient patterns. What are the conditions under which positive consequences result for beneficiaries? As firms become involved in fixing societal problems, we also need to know what happens to public political processes. Kahn (1997: 635), for example, was concerned about "the dangers implied by the concentration of not only the factors of production, but also communal resources in the hands of corporate management." The street protests against the work of the World Trade Organization (*Economist,* 1999) and both the International Monetary Fund and the World Bank (*Economist,* 2000) suggest that members of society are asking these same kinds of questions. Some may consider Friedman's (1970) concerns alarmist, but asking companies to advance educational reform, assist with reproductive health, and fund cancer research does give firms and their executives significant influence over public policy, typically considered to be the domain of elected officials. How do these investments affect the political sphere, most notably democratic processes and accountability? Even if these investments meet their intended humanitarian goals, they might carry unintended consequences for government functioning (Reich, 1998).

Looking beyond the content of corporate programs, the processes through which corporate activities are generated, selected, and implemented may have differential effects worth uncovering. Understanding the consequences of corporate involvement—the impact on targeted problems and on the functioning of other civil and political institutions, as well as on the firm itself—lies at the heart of questions about the relationship between organizations and societies. Research into those consequences can help highlight the tradeoffs of seeking corporate involvement, inform decisions about when to involve and when to limit such corporate involvement, and guide policies for managing the consequences when companies do get involved. Examining and evaluating these consequences, however, invites another line of inquiry, normative in nature.

A Normative Research Agenda

Business organizations operate in the face of a sometimes irreducible conflict between humanitarian needs and economic objectives. As descriptive research begins to capture what companies are doing to respond, the pressing normative question is, How *should* companies respond? Merton (1976: 88) recognized the problem almost thirty years ago: "Leaders of business have only begun to wrestle with the problem of *how* to do both in appropriate scale. For they are at work in a rapidly changing moral environment which requires them to make new assessments of purpose." When contrasted with the clear normative positions evident in economic theories of the firm, and when seen in the shadow of the stark antinomy confronting organizations, organizational scholarship seems conspicuously quiet, in need of a line of systematic philosophical investigation. This integration of philosophical inquiry into organization theory is long overdue (Zald, 1996).

Normative questions prompt two different types of inquiry (Donaldson and Preston, 1995), one reflecting the common social scientific use of the term "normative," and another, its philosophical use. The social scientific use of normative refers to instrumental and hypothetical guidance, grounded in empirical findings and theories about cause-and-effect relationships. If one wishes to bring about certain outcomes, then research suggests a set of actions that increases the likelihood of those outcomes. In light of prior findings and theoretical models that assemble those findings into orderly

Social Initiatives by Business

causal associations, normative guidance prescribes advisable behavior if an actor wishes to achieve certain outcomes.

In its philosophical sense, and the way we use it here, normative refers to the underlying justification that gives moral weight (Korsgaard, 1996b): the source of value that makes certain options, decisions, and courses of action those worthy of selection. The instrumental benefit of some courses of action is one source of philosophically normative justification, but it begs the deeper question of why those outcomes themselves are to be sought. Normative inquiry of the philosophical sort investigates how we ought to act in light of why, weighing various considerations, that is the right, just, or good course of action (Scanlon, 1992).

Normative theory is directed toward actors on the cusp of taking action. It is about clarifying and constructing the reasons and grounds that ought to inform the actor's choice of action, rather than discovering the causal explanations of what will occur as a result of the action (Putnam, 1994; Korsgaard, 1996a, 1996b). It is not about advising a course of action based on what will happen to air quality, profitability, corporate reputation, or the docility of regulators if the company lowers factory emissions. Rather, it is about why, upon considering options for action and their potential outcomes, air quality and stock price are worthy of orienting action in the first place and what the actor is to do if a course of action will damage one of those objectives. Putnam (1994: 168) concisely captured the essence of this research orientation: ". . . the agent point of view, the first-person normative point of view, and the concepts indispensable to that point of view should be taken just as seriously as the concepts indispensable to the third-person descriptive point of view." The best way to meet this challenge is to build on our descriptive work and follow a philosophical path to this new theory.

The approach to normative inquiry we propose starts with a given situation and asks the question, How should I act? (Moody-Adams, 1990; Korsgaard, 1996a: 205). An inductive approach to normative theory begins with the set of considerations—objectives, duties, and concerns—that arise in trying to answer that question. From the start, an inductive approach takes seriously the conflict among those considerations (Nussbaum, 1986: 81). The aim is to clarify each of the salient objectives, duties, and concerns in light of one another, permitting further specification of each and greater understanding of the relationship among them (Richardson, 1997). Tensions are not irritants to be removed by dismissing certain considerations or justifying the preeminence of others. Instead, the inductive approach uses tensions and inconsistencies between considerations to prompt elaboration and clarification of each objective, duty, and concern. The inductive route travels from identifying a core set of considerations (Rawls, 1971; Scanlon, 1992) to juxtaposing them so as to elaborate their moral weight and refine them (Nussbaum, 1986; Richardson, 1997), especially in light of the specific situation being examined. A framework for action is then formulated by exploring how these considerations interact with features of the situation, specifying what is obligatory, permissible, and prohibited.

To take up our specific antinomy, a first step is to identify and probe the set of objectives, duties, and concerns that arise when business organizations confront the question of whether to help redress human misery. We need to identify the central considerations underlying the initial concerns and judgments provoked by the question (Rawls, 1971; Scanlon, 1992). For example, at least three economic arguments against corporate efforts need to be explored. The first represents the claims of *property* (Hsieh, 2003), claims that give rise to concerns about misappropriation. The rightful claimants to certain resources ought not to have those resources used for purposes they neither license nor receive compensation for. Second, there are concerns surrounding *efficiency* (Donaldson and Dunfee, 1999). Resources should be devoted to purposes for which they are designed and not misallocated to purposes for which they are not well suited. Third, there are concerns of *due process,* which require that even justifiable actions be taken in accord with procedures that respect rights and afford subsequent accountability.

Juxtaposed to these three concerns are three forms of the duty to aid and respond. First, there is the duty to respond that attaches to a company when it *contributes to the conditions* that necessitate a response, conditions that create some form of cost, violation, or degradation that others bear. This is the intuitively sensible but intellectually complex terrain in which causal responsibility gives rise to moral responsibility (Hart and Honoré, 1985; Schoeman, 1987). Second, there is the duty to respond to deleterious or unjust conditions from which *a company benefits,* but to which it has not contributed (Hsieh, 2003). This is an acute extension of the domain of fair play (Rawls, 1971; Applbaum, 1996; Phillips, 1997), in which the derivation of benefits (even from unwitting parties) calls for some compensatory exchange. Even when a company compensates those from whom it has derived immediate benefits, such as assembly workers in low-wage countries, further duties may exist because those benefits are made possible by the persistence of unjust conditions (Kant, 1963: 194–195; Herman, 2002). Third, there is the *duty of beneficence* (Murphy, 2000; Herman, 2002): the duty to promote the well-being of others, in particular to provide aid to prevent or relieve suffering or dire conditions (Murphy, 2000: 3; Herman, 2002). The immediate fear is that this last source of duty has no limit. Although seemingly insatiable, the duty of beneficence has been circumscribed by philosophers (Elster, 1989: 56; Murphy, 2000; Herman, 2002; Hsieh, 2003) through what one philosopher has termed "the collective principle of beneficence" (Murphy, 2000: 7): an individual need only aid others to the extent that would be required were everyone to comply with the duty to aid others.

The purpose of inductive theory is to provide neither a way to reconcile the two sets of considerations nor a method, theory, or argument that demonstrates the dominance of one set of claims over another (Nussbaum, 1986; Richardson, 1997). It is certainly possible that when cast in one another's light, juxtaposed considerations might suggest means of reconciliation or illuminate the clear priority of some considerations

Social Initiatives by Business

over others. That would be a propitious product, but not the intended purpose of inductive normative theorizing. The aim is to understand the compelling grounds that exist for taking alternative courses of action and to refine those grounds in light of one another. To illustrate, when concern with efficiency and misallocation is juxtaposed with the duty to aid, counterintuitive conclusions may emerge. It may well be true that companies are poorly suited to respond to illiteracy or contaminated water, problems to which, in addition, a company has not contributed. But it may nonetheless be that corporate efforts to ameliorate these problems are at least permissible, if not obligatory. Under a duty of beneficence (Herman, 2002) or assistance (Hsieh, 2003), firms have grounds for assisting those in need, regardless of corporate culpability for the problem. If no other institutions are positioned or equipped as well as business organizations to respond, then concerns with misallocation look quite different from the classic case in which a more efficient response is available. The converse may also be true. For example, if the release of mercury into water can be traced directly to a company, the strongest grounds for obligatory response may exist. But concerns with efficiency and proper allocation of institutional instruments might suggest that, under some conditions, companies be left as unencumbered as possible to fulfill a wealth-producing purpose. As a result, even in those instances in which companies either have a justifiable responsibility or their involvement in redressing social misery would be valuable, society should find alternative ways to fulfill the responsibility and meet the need, so as not to dilute companies' capacity to produce wealth. The duty to aid, in this case, looks quite different in the light of concerns for the efficient allocation of societal resources.

This brief example can only outline the process of inductive normative analysis, highlighting two of its features. The first is that normative inquiry of the inductive sort requires a systematic process of setting competing objectives, duties, and concerns side by side and exploring the range of conclusions that can be drawn when interaction effects are explored. The second is that this juxtaposition and analysis requires a return to the specific content of the situation that posed the question of how to act in the first place. But then how does one proceed with the motivating question, how should the firm act? One proceeds by scrutinizing the conditions under which the vying considerations have been invoked.

If articulating the central considerations that bear on a normative question is the first step of the inductive approach, and if juxtaposing those considerations in order to refine them individually and explore their relationship is the second step, then a third step consists of working out how competing considerations are to be integrated into a course of action. Integration clarifies what is to be done, formulating a framework for action by exploring how the colliding considerations interact with features of the situation. For corporate social initiatives, three sets of features will interact with normative considerations to shape the framework for action. How a company should respond will be a function, in part, of features of the problem, features of the company—in particular, the company's relationship to the problem—and features of the impact the company's response would have.

Features of the problem. Features of the specific societal ill to which a company is considering a response include its depth and breadth. The proper corporate response to a societal ill will hinge in part on the severity of the ill's effect on essential human functioning (Herman, 2002). What is considered essential to human functioning is of course subject to debate, so it is helpful to draw on the idea of human capabilities advanced by Sen (1985, 1992, 1993) and Nussbaum (1988, 2000). Based on Aristotle's conception of the virtues, economic and anthropological research on developing countries, and political philosophy, Sen and Nussbaum identified ten domains of human capability vital "to truly human functioning that can command a broad cross-cultural consensus" (Nussbaum, 2000: 74). They include such factors as bodily health (having adequate nourishment, medical care, and shelter), control over one's environment (effectively participating in the political choices that govern one's life, holding property, and access to employment), emotions (experiencing the range of emotions essential to human life), and affiliation (having meaningful personal and work relationships of mutual recognition and dignity).

Whether the vying objectives, duties, and concerns intersect to obligate, permit, or proscribe a corporate response will hinge, in part, on the magnitude, the depth and breadth, of the problem's consequences for these central human capabilities. The preliminary assessment of depth focuses on whether the problem plagues an essential human capability. Then assessments of degree must be made. The severity of the problem must be considered: does the problem entail active impairment of a capability or failure to promote, but not active impairment of, the capability? Alongside these two assessments of depth, the breadth of the problem must also be considered. How many capabilities are affected, and how many people are affected? Sizing up the problem opens many questions. For example, it can be difficult to distinguish between an impairment and absence of enhancement. Illiteracy can be seen in either light. The line between essential capabilities and less-than-essential capabilities can also be difficult to draw. Support for the arts may reasonably fall on either side of that line. Our aim here is to sketch the process of inquiry; the absence of clear answers underscores the importance of dedicated attention to these questions.

Features of the firm. The features of the firm's relationship to the problem also bear on how a company ought to respond to a societal ill. First, there is the company's contribution to the problem. Presumably, a problem created by the firm, or one to which it has contributed sizably, will impose a stronger duty to act than a problem not of the firm's making. Second, the company's potential contribution to the problem's solution must be considered. The relevance of the firm's capabilities and resources to the societal ill being considered bears on the efficiency and effectiveness of the company's response, which in turn shape the strength of an imperative to respond. Third, the response required may vary in strength with a company's proximity to, or extent of membership in, the community in which the need arises (Herman, 2002). Finally, the duty to respond may also vary with the benefits the corporation derives from the aggrieved constituency (Hsieh, 2003). Chevron Texaco may have limited firm-specific capability to provide what Nigerian communities demand of it, but the integral presence of the company in Escravos, Nigeria and the benefits the company derives from its oil extraction facilities, even if those benefits are the result of explicit legal contracts, may obligate or at least license the firm to do more to redress societal problems there (Moore, 2002). Only systematic normative analysis can work out the imperative of a response under these conditions.

Features of the impact. The anticipated impact of a corporate response will also determine the ethical standing of that response. Features of the impact include the effects a corporate response is likely to have on the problem, on the larger society, and on the firm itself. The results of our descriptive research agenda should help decipher these impacts. These likely consequences will bear on the determination of whether a firm's response is permissible, prohibited, or even obligated. Exploring how negative consequences are to be weighed against positive consequences requires a thorough normative analysis. A company that can provide a quicker solution than a government agency to a problem may also, in so doing, weaken (or retard the development of) political institutions essential to representative democracy. How are these consequences to be weighed, not only in determining whether corporate action is permitted but, if it is permitted, in shaping how a response is selected, designed, and implemented?

Boundaries. Understanding the impact that a corporate response might have is also essential for understanding where the boundaries to corporate responses are erected. Contrary to the fears of some and the hopes of others, the moral foundations for corporate responses to misery do not necessarily dictate that social objectives be given as much attention as economic objectives. Business organizations may have duties and responsibilities that reach beyond economic ones, but this does not itself imply that those duties and responsibilities require comparable attention, advancement, or resources. There are two sorts of boundaries to consider. One set protects the recipients of aid, reflecting the negative consequences that can result from efforts to provide assistance. For example, the type and delivery of aid must aim to reverse dependence rather than reinforce it (Herman, 2002; Hsieh, 2003; Rawls, 1999: 111). The second set protects the firm's capacity to perform its primary function, or functions, reflecting the potential impairment that responding to misery can entail. If a primary function of a business organization is to produce goods and services and, in so doing, generate wealth, then the firm's capacity to perform that function receives special protection. Again, contrary to the hopes of some and fears of others, this boundary is capacious. To be clear, it is the *capacity* of the firm to perform one of its central functions that cannot be sacrificed, not actual performance of the function itself. If a company reduces its profitability or productivity in order to ameliorate misery, that is more likely to lie within the permissible boundary, whereas efforts to ameliorate misery that impair the company's capacity to be profitable or productive would more likely be prohibited.

CONCLUSION

Managers face a vexing reality. They must find a way to do their work even as seemingly rival financial and societal demands intensify. To make matters worse, each demand can be justified or explained away by a particular conception of the firm. These dueling conceptions have inspired a generation of organizational scholars to posit and demonstrate the economic benefits of corporate responses to social misery. This has left a considerable gap in our descriptive and normative theories about the impact of companies on society. The scholarly agenda we envision accepts this tension as a starting point. The dispute among justifiable but competing demands reflects the reality that firms face in society today. By honoring the dispute and exploring the tension, we offer a different starting point for organization theory and research. In the end, this new scholarship can inform managers and citizens alike as we struggle to meet these daunting challenges.

The practical significance of the research agenda before us is no less weighty than its theoretical implications. Public pressure to satisfy each set of responsibilities, to shareholders and to other stakeholders, continues to mount (Useem, 1996; Paine, 2002). Accountability, however, can distort behavior as much as it can enhance it (Lerner and Tetlock, 1999). Organization theory and research may illuminate how organizations can move closer to actual fulfillment of those responsibilities, rather than offering the mere appearance of doing so (King and Lenox, 2000). What organizational scholars have to say about corporate involvement in societal affairs seems essential, for the risks of involving companies in broad societal problems may match the risks of excluding them: corporate involvement in addressing targeted problems is no guarantee of improvement, and organizations may only further insinuate themselves into all aspects of human life (Rosen, 1985; Kunda, 1992; Willmott, 1993). Corporate involvement may well make problems worse, or even create new ones, while reducing companies' effectiveness as economic instruments.

What is being asked and expected of corporations today is increasing even as the economic contractarian model of the firm itself has revealed clear practical limitations (Gordon, 2002). The free market may not produce the inexorable march toward worldwide prosperity and well-being that is so often anticipated (Stiglitz, 2002). Even as business organizations may be imperfect instruments for advancing a narrowly construed wealth-maximizing objective, ironically, they may also be the entities of last resort for achieving social objectives of all stripes. In the face of these challenges, organization theory and research can contribute to the construction, reform, and assessment of the organizations and institutions that play such an essential role in society (Stern and Barley, 1996; Perrow, 2000; Hinings and Greenwood, 2002).

Manifest human misery and undeniable corporate ingenuity should remind us that our central challenge may lie in blending the two. The many organizational scholars who have investigated the relationship between social and financial performance have been eager to develop empirically informed theory that stimulates, if not guides, practice. Paradoxically, by acknowledging the fundamental tension that exists between the roles corporations are asked to play, organizational scholars have the opportunity to inform practice—and thereby help society—where past efforts to remove the tension have fallen short. Before rushing off to find the missing link between a firm's social and financial performance, all in hopes of advancing the cause of social performance, we need to understand the conditions under which a corporation's efforts benefit society. This asks us to question corporate social performance and competing conceptions of the firm down to their very roots. Personal values and commitments will no doubt orient the theories we prefer and the research questions we ask. To honor those values and commitments, however, we must acknowledge and question them. Such appraisals ensure the quality of our research and the integrity of our commitments.

REFERENCES

Abbott, W. F., and R. J. Monsen
1979 "On the measurement of corporate social responsibility: Self-reported disclosures as a method of measuring corporate social involvement." Academy of Management Journal, 22: 501–515.

Adkins, S.
1999 Cause Related Marketing: Who Cares Wins. Oxford: Butterworth-Heinemann.

Aldag, R. J., and K. M. Bartol
1978 "Empirical studies of corporate social performance and policy: A survey of problems and results." Research in Corporate Social Performance and Policy, 1: 165–199.

Alexander, G. J., and R. A. Buchholz
1978 "Corporate social responsibility and stock market performance." Academy of Management Journal, 21: 479–486.

Alexander, J. C.
1988 "The new theoretical movement." In N. J. Smelser (ed.), Handbook of Sociology: 77–101. Newbury Park, CA: Sage.

Anderson, J. C., and A. W. Frankle
1979 "Voluntary social reporting: An iso-beta portfolio analysis." Accounting Review, 55: 467–479.

Andersson, L., and T. Bateman
2000 "Individual environmental initiative: Championing natural environmental issues in U.S. business organizations." Academy of Management Journal, 43: 548–570.

Annan, K.
2001 "Unparalleled nightmare of AIDS." Address to the United States Chamber of Commerce, Washington, DC: http: www.un.org/News/Press/ docs/2001/sgsm7827.doc. htm.

Applbaum, A. I.
1996 "Rules of the game, permissible harms, and fair play." In R. J. Zeckhauser, R. L. Keeney, and J. Sebenius (eds.), Wise Choices: 301–325. Boston: Harvard Business School Press.

Arlow, P., and M. J. Gannon
1982 "Social responsiveness, corporate structure, and economic performance." Academy of Management Review, 7: 235–241.

Aspen Institute Initiative for Social Innovation through Business
2002 Where Will They Lead? MBA Student Attitudes toward Business and Society. Aspen, CO.

Attaran, A., and J. Sachs
2001 "Defining and refining international donor support for combating the AIDS pandemic." Lancet, 357 (January 6): 57–61.

Aupperle, K. E., A. B. Carroll, and J. D. Hatfield
1985 "An empirical examination of the relationship between corporate social responsibility and profitability." Academy of Management Journal, 28: 446–463.

Austin, J. E.
2000 The Collaboration Challenge: How Nonprofits and Businesses Succeed through Strategic Alliances. San Francisco: Jossey-Bass.

Bagley, C. E., and K. Page
1999 "The devil made me do it: Replacing corporate directors' veil of secrecy with the mantle of stewardship." San Diego Law Review, 36: 897–945.

Bales, K.
1999 Disposable People: New Slavery in the Global Economy. Berkeley, CA: University of California Press.

Bansal, P.
2003 "From issues to actions: The importance of individual concerns and organizational values in responding to natural environment issues." Organization Science, 14: 510–527.

Belkaoui, A.
1976 "The impact of the disclosure of the environmental effects of organizational behavior on the market." Financial Management, 5 (4): 26–31.

Belkaoui, A., and P. G. Karpik
1989 "Determinants of the corporate decision to disclose social information." Accounting, Auditing and Accountability Journal, 2: 36–51.

Berle, A. A., Jr.
1931 "Corporate powers as powers in trust." Harvard Law Review, 44: 1049–1074.

Berman, S. L., A. C. Wicks, S. Kotha, and T. M. Jones
1999 "Does stakeholder orientation matter? The relationship between stakeholder management models and firm financial performance." Academy of Management Journal, 42: 488–506.

Blacconiere, W. G., and W. D. Northcut
1997 "Environmental information and market reactions to environmental legislation." Journal of Accounting, Auditing and Finance, 12: 149–178.

Blacconiere, W. G., and D. M. Patten
1994 "Environmental disclosures, regulatory costs, and changes in firm value." Journal of Accounting and Economics, 18: 357–377.

Blackburn, V. L., M. Doran, and C. B. Shrader
1994 "Investigating the dimensions of social responsibility and the consequences for corporate financial performance." Journal of Managerial Issues, 6: 195–212.

Bowman, E. H.
1976 "Strategy and the weather." Sloan Management Review, 17 (2): 49–62.
1978 "Strategy, annual reports, and alchemy." California Management Review, 20 (3): 64–71.

Bowman, E. H., and M. Haire
1975 "A strategic posture toward corporate social responsibility." California Management Review, 18 (2): 49–58.

Boyle, E. J., M. M. Higgins, and S. G. Rhee
1997 "Stock market reaction to ethical initiatives of defense contractors: Theory and evidence." Critical Perspectives on Accounting, 8: 541–561.

Bradley, M., C. A. Schipani, A. K. Sundaram, and J. P. Walsh
1999 "The purposes and accountability of the corporation in contemporary society: Corporate governance at a crossroads." Law and Contemporary Problems, 62 (3): 9–86.

Bragdon, J. H., Jr., and R. Karash
2002 "Living-asset stewardship: How organizational learning leads to exceptional market returns." Reflections, 4 (1): 55–65.

Bragdon, J. H., Jr., and J. A. T. Marlin
1972 "Is pollution profitable?" Risk Management, 19 (4): 9–18.

Bratton, W.
1989a "The new economic theory of the firm: Critical perspectives from history." Stanford Law Review, 41: 1471–1527.
1989b "The 'nexus of contracts' corporation: A critical appraisal." Cornell Law Review, 74: 407–465.

Brown, B.
1997 "Stock market valuation of reputation for corporate social performance." Corporate Reputation Review, 1: 76–80.
1998 "Do stock market investors reward reputation for corporate social performance?" Corporate Reputation Review, 1: 271–282.

Brown, B., and S. Perry
1994 "Removing the financial performance halo from *Fortune*'s 'most admired' companies." Academy of Management Journal, 37: 1347–1359.

Buehler, V. M., and Y. K. Shetty
1976 "Managerial response to social responsibility challenge." Academy of Management Journal, 19: 66–78.

Caplow, T., L. Hicks, and B. J. Wattenberg
2001 The First Measured Century: An Illustrated Guide to Trends in America, 1900–2000. Washington, DC: AEI Press.

Carleton, W. T., J. M. Nelson, and M. S. Weisbach
1998 "The influence of institutions on corporate governance through private negotiations: Evidence from TIAA-CREF." Journal of Finance, 53: 1335–1362.

Chen, K. H., and R. W. Metcalf
1980 "The relationship between pollution control record and financial indicators revisited." Accounting Review, 55: 168–177.

Christmann, P.
2000 "Effects of 'best practices' of environmental management on cost advantage: The role of complementary assets." Academy of Management Journal, 43: 663–680.

Clarkson, M. B. E.
1988 "Corporate social performance in Canada, 1976–86." Research in Corporate Social Performance and Policy, 10: 241–265.

Cochran, P. L., and R. A. Wood
1984 "Corporate social responsibility and financial performance." Academy of Management Journal, 27: 42–56.

Cohen, M. D., J. G. March, and J. P. Olsen
1972 "A garbage can model of organizational choice." Administrative Science Quarterly, 17: 1–25.

Conine, T. E., Jr., and G. P. Madden
1986 "Corporate social responsibility and investment value: The expectational relationship." In W. K. Guth (ed.), Handbook of Business Strategy: 1986/1987 Yearbook. Boston: Warren Gorham and Lamont.

Conley, D.
1999 Being Black, Living in the Red. Berkeley, CA: University of California Press.

Cottrill, M. T.
1990 "Corporate social responsibility and the marketplace." Journal of Business Ethics, 9: 723–729.

Cowen, S. S., L. B. Ferreri, and L. D. Parker
1987 "The impact of corporate characteristics on social responsibility disclosure: A typology and frequency-based analysis." Accounting, Organizations and Society, 12: 111–222.

Cyert, R. M., and J. G. March
1992 A Behavioral Theory of the Firm, 2d ed. Malden, MA: Blackwell.

Social Initiatives by Business

D'Antonio, L., T. Johnsen, and R. B. Hutton
1997 "Expanding socially screened portfolios: An attribution analysis of bond performance." Journal of Investing, Winter: 79–86.

Davis, G. F., and M. Useem
2000 "Top management, company directors, and corporate control." In A. Pettigrew, H. Thomas, and R. Whittington (eds.), Handbook of Strategy and Management: 232–258. Thousand Oaks, CA: Sage.

Diltz, D. J.
1995 "The private cost of socially responsible investing." Applied Financial Economics, 5: 69–77.

Dodd, E. M., Jr.
1932 "For whom are corporate managers trustees?" Harvard Law Review, 45: 1145–1163.

Donaldson, T., and T. W. Dunfee
1999 Ties That Bind: A Social Contracts Approach to Business Ethics. Boston: Harvard Business School Press.

Donaldson, T., and L. E. Preston
1995 "The stakeholder theory of the corporation: Concepts, evidence, and implications." Academy of Management Review, 20: 65–91.

Donnelly, J.
2001 "US firms urged to lead fight." Boston Globe, June 2: A10.

Dooley, R. S., and L. D. Lerner
1994 "Pollution, profits, and stakeholders: The constraining effect of economic performance on CEO concern with stakeholder expectations." Journal of Business Ethics, 13: 701–711.

Dowell, G., S. Hart, and B. Yeung
2000 "Do corporate global environmental standards create or destroy market value?" Management Science, 46: 1059–1074.

Dunfee, T. W., and D. Hess
2000 "The legitimacy of direct corporate humanitarian investment." Business Ethics Quarterly, 10: 95–109.

Easterbrook, F. H., and D. R. Fischel
1991 The Economic Structure of Corporate Law. Cambridge, MA: Harvard University Press.

Economist
1999 "The battle in Seattle." November 27: 21–23.

2000 "Anti-capitalist protests: Angry and effective." September 23: 85–87.

Elster, J.
1989 Nuts and Bolts for the Social Sciences. New York: Cambridge University Press.

Epstein, M. J., and K. E. Schnietz
2002 "Measuring the cost of environmental and labor protests to globalization: An event study of the failed 1999 Seattle WTO talks." International Trade Journal, 16: 129–160.

Firebaugh, G.
1999 "Empirics of world income inequality." American Journal of Sociology, 6: 1597–1630.

Fogler, H. R., and F. Nutt
1975 "A note on social responsibility and stock valuation." Academy of Management Journal, 18: 155–160.

Fombrun, C., and M. Shanley
1990 "What's in a name? Reputation building and corporate strategy." Academy of Management Journal, 33: 233–258.

Freedman, M., and B. Jaggi
1982 "Pollution disclosures, pollution performance and economic performance." Omega, 10: 167–176.
1986 "An analysis of the impact of corporate pollution disclosures included in annual financial statements on investors' decisions." In M. Neimark (ed.), Advances in Public Interest Accounting, 1: 193–212. London: Elsevier.

Freedman, M., and A. J. Stagliano
1991 "Differences in social-cost disclosures: A market test of investor reactions." Accounting, Auditing and Accountability Journal, 4: 68–83.

Freeman, R. E.
1984 Strategic Management: A Stakeholder Approach. Boston: Pitman/Ballinger.
1999 "Divergent stakeholder theory." Academy of Management Review, 24: 233–236.

Freeman, R. E., and R. A. Phillips
2002 "Stakeholder theory: A libertarian defense." Business Ethics Quarterly, 12: 331–349.

Friedman, M.
1970 "The social responsibility of business is to increase its profits." New York Times Magazine, September 13: 32–33, 122, 124, 126.

Fry, F. L., and R. J. Hock
1976 "Who claims corporate responsibility? The biggest and the worst." Business and Society Review, 18: 62–65.

Fry, L. W., G. D. Keim, and R. E. Meiners
1982 "Corporate contributions: Altruistic or for profit?" Academy of Management Journal, 25: 94–106.

Galaskiewicz, J.
1991 "Making corporate actors accountable: Institution-building in Minneapolis–St. Paul." In W. W. Powell and P. J. DiMaggio (eds.), The New Institutionalism in Organizational Analysis: 293–310. Chicago: University of Chicago Press.
1997 "An urban grants economy revisited: Corporate charitable contributions in the Twin Cities, 1979–81, 1987–89." Administrative Science Quarterly, 42: 445–471.

Galbraith, J. K.
1998 Created Unequal: The Crisis in American Pay. New York: Free Press.

Gavetti, G., and D. Levinthal
2000 "Looking forward and looking backward: Cognitive and experiential search." Administrative Science Quarterly, 45: 113–137.

Gilbert, C.
2003 "Can competing frames co-exist? The paradox of threatened response." Working paper, Harvard Business School.

Gillmor, P. E., and C. E. Bremer
1999 "Disclosure of corporate charitable contributions as a matter of shareholder accountability." Business Lawyer, 54: 1007–1022.

Gioia, D. A.
1999 "Practicability, paradigms, and problems in stakeholder theorizing." Academy of Management Review, 24: 228–232.

Gordon, J. N.
2002 "What Enron means for the management and control of the modern business corporation: Some initial reflections." University of Chicago Law Review, 69: 1233–1250.

Graves, S. B., and S. A. Waddock
1994 "Institutional owners and corporate social performance." Academy of Management Journal, 37: 1034–1046.

2000 "Beyond built to last . . . Stakeholder relations in 'built-to-last' companies." Business and Society Review, 105: 393–418.

Greening, D. W.
1995 "Conservation strategies, firm performance, and corporate reputation in the U.S. electric utility industry." Research in Corporate Social Performance and Policy, Supplement 1: 345–368.

Gregory, A., J. Matatko, and R. Luther
1997 "Ethical unit trust financial performance: Small company effects and fund size effects." Journal of Business Finance and Accounting, 24: 705–725.

Greider, W.
1997 One World, Ready or Not: The Manic Logic of Global Capitalism. New York: Simon & Schuster.

Griffin, J. J., and J. F. Mahon
1997 "The corporate social performance and corporate financial performance debate: Twenty-five years of incomparable research." Business and Society, 36 (1): 5–31.

Guerard, J. B., Jr.
1997a "Is there a cost to being socially responsible in investing?" Journal of Investing, Summer, 6 (2): 11–18.
1997b "Additional evidence on the cost of being socially responsible in investing." Journal of Investing, Winter, 6 (4): 31–36.

Hamilton, S., H. Jo, and M. Statman
1993 "Doing well while doing good? The investment performance of socially responsible mutual funds." Financial Analysts Journal, Nov./Dec.: 62–66.

Hart, H. L. A., and T. Honoré
1985 Causation in the Law, 2d ed. New York: Oxford University Press.

Hart, S. L., and G. Ahuja
1996 "Does it pay to be green? An empirical examination of the relationship between emission reduction and firm performance." Business Strategy and the Environment, 5: 30–37.

Heinze, D. C.
1976 "Financial correlates of a social involvement measure." Akron Business and Economic Review, 7 (1): 48–51.

Herman, B.
2002 "The scope of moral requirement." Philosophy and Public Affairs, 30: 227–256.

Herremans, I. M., P. Akathaporn, and M. McInnes
1993 "An investigation of corporate social responsibility reputation and economic performance." Accounting, Organizations and Society, 18: 587–604.

Hickman, K. A., W. R. Teets, and J. J. Kohls
1999 "Social investing and modern portfolio theory." American Business Review, 17: 72–78.

Hillman, A. J., and G. D. Keim
2001 "Shareholder value, stakeholder management, and social issues: What's the bottom line?" Strategic Management Journal, 22: 125–139.

Hinings, C. R., and R. Greenwood
2002 "Disconnects and consequences in organization theory?" Administrative Science Quarterly, 47: 411–421.

Hirsch, P. M., R. Friedman, and M. P. Koza
1990 "Collaboration or paradigm shift?: Caveat emptor and the risk of romance with economic models for strategy and policy research." Organization Science, 1: 87–97.

Hodson, R.
2001 Dignity at Work. New York: Cambridge University Press.

Holman, W. R., J. R. New, and D. Singer
1990 "The impact of corporate social responsiveness on shareholder wealth." In L. Preston (ed.), Corporation and Society Research: Studies in Theory and Measurement: 265–280. Greenwich, CT: JAI Press.

Holmes, S. L.
1976 "Executive perceptions of corporate social responsibility." Business Horizons, 19: 34–40.

Hsieh, N.
2003 "The obligations of transnational corporations: Rawlsian justice and the duty of assistance." Business Ethics Quarterly, 14 (in press).

Hylton, M. O.
1992 "'Socially responsible' investing: Doing good versus doing well in an efficient market." American University Law Review, 42: 1–52.

Ibbotson Associates
2000 Stocks Bonds Bills and Inflation: 2000 Yearbook. Chicago: Ibbotson Associates.

Ingram, R. W.
1978 "An investigation of the information content of (certain) social responsibility disclosures." Journal of Accounting Research, 16: 270–285.

Ingram, R. W., and K. B. Frazier
1983 "Narrative disclosures in annual reports." Journal of Business Research, 11: 49–60.

Jackson, S. E., and J. E. Dutton
1988 "Discerning threats and opportunities." Administrative Science Quarterly, 33: 370–387.

James, W.
1975 Pragmatism and the Meaning of Truth. (First published in 1907.) Cambridge, MA: Harvard University Press.

Janis, I. L., and L. Mann
1977 Decision Making: A Psychological Analysis of Conflict, Choice, and Commitment. New York: Free Press.

Jensen, M.
2002 "Value maximization, stakeholder theory, and the corporate objective function." Business Ethics Quarterly, 12: 235–256.

Johnson, L., and D. Millon
1990 "The case beyond Time." Business Lawyer, 45: 2105–2125.

Johnson, R. A., and D. W. Greening
1999 "The effects of corporate governance and institutional ownership types on corporate social performance." Academy of Management Journal, 42: 564–576.

Jones, R., and A. J. Murrell
2001 "Signaling positive corporate social performance." Business and Society, 40: 59–78.

Jones, T. M.
1995 "Instrumental stakeholder theory: A synthesis of ethics and economics." Academy of Management Review, 20: 404–437.

Jones, T. M., and A. C. Wicks
1999 "Convergent stakeholder theory." Academy of Management Review, 24: 206–221.

Judge, W. Q., Jr., and T. J. Douglas
1998 "Performance implications of incorporating natural environmental issues into the strategic planning process: An empirical assessment." Journal of Management Studies, 35: 241–262.

Kahn, F. S.
1997 "Pandora's box: Managerial discretion and the problem of corporate philanthropy." UCLA Law Review, 44: 579–676.

Kahn, R. N., C. Lekander, and T. Leimkuhler
1997 "Just say no? The investment implications of tobacco divestiture." Journal of Investing, Winter: 62–70.

Kahneman, D., J. L. Knetsch, and R. H. Thaler
1986 "Fairness and the assumptions of economics." Journal of Business, 59: S285–S300.

Kant, I.
1963 Lectures on Ethics. L. Infield, trans. Indianapolis, IN: Hackett Publishing.

Kanter, R. M.
1999 "From spare change to real change: The social sector as beta site for business innovation." Harvard Business Review, 77 (3): 123–132.

Kapstein, E. B.
1999 Sharing the Wealth: Workers and the World Economy. New York: W.W. Norton.

Kedia, B. L., and E. C. Kuntz
1981 "The context of social performance: An empirical study of Texas banks." Research in Corporate Social Performance and Policy, 3: 133–154.

Keeley, M. C.
1988 A Social Contract Theory of Organizations. Notre Dame, IN: Notre Dame University Press.

Kiesler, S., and L. Sproull
1982 "Managerial response to changing environments: Perspectives on problem sensing from social cognition." Administrative Science Quarterly, 27: 548–570.

King, A. A., and M. J. Lenox
2000 "Industry self-regulation without sanctions: The chemical industry's responsible care program." Academy of Management Journal, 43: 698–716.

Klassen, R. D., and C. P. McLaughlin
1996 "The impact of environmental management on firm performance." Management Science, 42: 1199–1214.

Klassen, R. D., and D. C. Whybark
1999 "The impact of environmental technologies on manufacturing performance." Academy of Management Journal, 42: 599–615.

Konar, S., and M. A. Cohen
1997 "Information as regulation: The effect of community right to know laws on toxic emissions." Journal of Environmental Economics and Management, 32: 109–124.
2001 "Does the market value environmental performance?" Review of Economics and Statistics, 83: 281–289.

Korsgaard, C. M.
1996a "Creating the kingdom of ends: Reciprocity and responsibility in personal relations." In Creating the Kingdom of Ends: 188–221. New York: Cambridge University Press.
1996b The Sources of Normativity. Cambridge: Cambridge University Press.

Korten, D. C.
1995 When Corporations Rule the World. West Hartford, CT: Kumarian Press; San Francisco: Berrett-Koehler.

Kunda, G.
1992 Engineering Culture: Culture and Commitment in a High-Tech Corporation. Philadelphia: Temple University Press.

Kurtz, L., and D. DiBartolomeo
1996 "Socially screened portfolios: An attribution analysis of relative performance." Journal of Investing, Fall: 35–41.

Lashgari, M. K., and D. R. Gant
1989 "Social investing: The Sullivan principles." Review of Social Economy, 47: 74–83.

Lerner, J. S., and P. E. Tetlock
1999 "Accounting for the effects of accountability." Psychological Bulletin, 125: 255–275.

Lerner, L. D., and G. D. Fryxell
1988 "An empirical study of the predictors of corporate social performance: A multi-dimensional analysis." Journal of Business Ethics, 7: 951–959.

Levitt, B., and J. G. March
1988 "Organizational learning." In Annual Review of Sociology, 14: 319–340. Palo Alto, CA: Annual Reviews.

Levitt, T.
1958 "The dangers of social responsibility." Harvard Business Review, 36 (5): 41–50.

Levy, F. K., and G. M. Shatto
1980 "Social responsibility in large electric utility firms: The case for philanthropy." Research in Corporate Social Performance and Policy, 2: 237–249.

Luck, C., and N. Pilotte
1993 "Domini Social Index Performance." Journal of Investing, Fall: 60–62.

Luther, R. G., and J. Matatko
1994 "The performance of ethical unit trusts: Choosing an appropriate benchmark." British Accounting Review, 26: 77–89.

Luther, R. G., J. Matatko, and D. C. Corner
1992 "The investment performance of U.K. 'ethical' unit trusts." Accounting, Auditing and Accountability Journal, 5: 57–70.

Maddox, K. E., and J. J. Siegfried
1980 "The effect of economic structure on corporate philanthropy." In J. J. Siegfried (ed.), The Economics of Firm Size, Market Structure, and Social Performance: 202–225. Washington, DC: Bureau of Economics, Federal Trade Commission.

Madeley, J.
1999 Big Business, Poor Peoples: The Impact of Transnational Corporations on the World's Poor. London: Zed Books.

Mahapatra, S.
1984 "Investor reaction to a corporate social accounting." Journal of Business Finance and Accounting, 11: 29–40.

Makower, J.
1994 Beyond the Bottom Line: Putting Social Responsibility to Work for Your Business and the World. New York: Simon & Schuster.

Mallin, C. A., B. Saadouni, and
R. J. Briston
1995 "The financial performance of
ethical investment funds."
Journal of Business Finance
and Accounting, 22: 483–496.

Mannheim, J. B.
2001 The Death of a Thousand
Cuts: Corporate Campaigns
and the Attack on the Corporation. Mahwah, NJ:
Lawrence Erlbaum.

March, J. G.
1994 A Primer on Decision Making.
New York: Free Press.

March, J. G., and H. A. Simon
1958 Organizations. New York:
Free Press.

Marcus, A. A., and R. S.
Goodman
1986 "Compliance and performance: Toward a contingency
theory." Research in Corporate Social Performance and
Policy, 8: 193–221.

Margolis, J. D., and J. P. Walsh
2001 People and Profits? The
Search for a Link between a
Company's Social and Finan-
cial Performance. Mahwah,
NJ: Lawrence Erlbaum.

McGuire, J. B., T. Schneeweis,
and B. Branch
1990 "Perceptions of firm quality:
A cause or result of firm performance." Journal of Management, 16: 167–180.

McGuire, J. B., A. Sundgren, and
T. Schneeweis
1988 "Corporate social responsibility and firm financial performance." Academy of Man-
agement Journal, 31:
854–872.

McWilliams, A., and D. Siegel
1997 "The role of money managers
in assessing corporate social
responsibility research." Journal of Investing, Winter:
98–107.
2000 "Corporate social responsibility and financial performance:
Correlation or misspecification?" Strategic Management
Journal, 21: 603–609.

Merton, R. K.
1976 "The ambivalence of organizational leaders." In Sociological Ambivalence and Other
Essays: 73–89. New York:
Free Press.

Meznar, M. B., D. Nigh, and
C. C. Y. Kwok
1994 "Effect of announcements of
withdrawal from South Africa
on stockholder wealth."
Academy of Management
Journal, 37: 1633–1648.

Mills, D. L., and M. J. Gardner
1984 "Financial profiles and the disclosure of expenditures for
socially responsible purposes." Journal of Business
Research, 12: 407–424.

Miringoff, M., and M.-L. Miringoff
1999 The Social Health of the
Nation: How America Is Really Doing. New York: Oxford
University Press.

Mishel, L., J. Bernstein, and J.
Schmitt
1999 The State of Working America: 1998–1999. Ithaca, NY:
Cornell University Press.

Mitchell, R. K., B. R. Agle, and
D. J. Wood
1997 "Toward a theory of stakeholder identification and
salience: Defining the principle of who and what really
counts." Academy of Man-
agement Review, 22:
853–886.

Moody-Adams, M. M.
1990 "On the alleged methodological infirmity of ethics." American Philosophical Quarterly,
27: 225–235.

Moore, S.
2002 "Nigeria's new challenge for
big oil." Wall Street Journal,
26 July: A8.

Morrissey, D. J.
1989 "Toward a new/old theory of
corporate social responsibility." Syracuse Law Review,
40: 1005–1039.

Moskowitz, M.
1972 "Choosing socially responsible stocks." Business and
Society Review, 1: 71–75.

Mueller, S. A.
1991 "The opportunity cost of dis-
cipleship: Ethical mutual
funds and their returns." Sociological Analysis, 52:
111–124.

Murphy, L. B.
2000 Moral Demands in Nonideal
Theory. New York: Oxford
University Press.

Navarro, P.
1988 "Why do corporations give to
charity?" Journal of Business,
61: 65–93.

Nehrt, C.
1996 "Timing and intensity effects
of environmental invest-
ments." Strategic Manage-
ment Journal, 17: 535–547.

Newgren, K. E., A. A. Rasher,
M. E. LaRoe, and M. R. Szabo
1985 "Environmental assessment
and corporate performance: A
longitudinal analysis using a
market-determined perfor-
mance measure." Research
in Corporate Social Performance and Policy, 7:
153–164.

New York Times
1996 "Clinton prods executives to
'do the right thing.'" May 17:
1, C4.
1999 "U.S. effort to add labor standards to agenda fails."
December 3: 1, A12.
2001 "U.N. chief calls on U.S. companies to donate to AIDS
fund." June 2: 3.

Nussbaum, M. C.
1986 The Fragility of Goodness:
Luck and Ethics in Greek
Tragedy and Philosophy. New
York: Cambridge University
Press.
1988 "Nature, function, and capability: Aristotle on political distribution." Oxford Studies in
Ancient Philosophy, Supplement: 145–184.
2000 Women and Human Development: The Capabilities
Approach. New York: Cam-
bridge University Press.

Ogden, S., and R. Watson
1999 "Corporate performance and
stakeholder management:
Balancing shareholder and
customer interests in the U.K.
privatized water industry."
Academy of Management
Journal, 42: 526–538.

O'Neill, H. M., C. B. Saunders,
and A. D. McCarthy
1989 "Board members, corporate
social responsiveness and
profitability: Are tradeoffs
necessary?" Journal of Business Ethics, 8: 353–357.

Orlitzky, M., F. L. Schmidt, and
S. L. Rynes
2003 "Corporate social and financial performance: A meta-
analysis." Organization Studies, 24: 403–441.

Orts, E. W.
1992 "Beyond shareholders: Interpreting corporate constituency statutes." George Washington Law Review, 14:
14–135.

Social Initiatives by Business

Paine, L. S.
2002 Value Shift. New York: McGraw-Hill.

Parket, I. R., and H. Eilbirt
1975 "Social responsibility: The underlying factors." Business Horizons, 18: 5–10.

Patten, D. M.
1990 "The market reaction to social responsibility disclosures: The case of the Sullivan principles signings." Accounting, Organizations and Society, 15: 575–587.
1991 "Exposure, legitimacy, and social disclosure." Journal of Accounting and Public Policy, 10: 297–308.

Pava, M. L., and J. Krausz
1996 "The association between corporate social-responsibility and financial performance: The paradox of social cost." Journal of Business Ethics, 15: 321–357.

Perrow, C.
2000 "An organizational analysis of organizational theory." Contemporary Sociology, 29: 469–476.

Phillips, R. A.
1997 "Stakeholder theory and a principle of fairness." Business Ethics Quarterly, 7: 51–66.
2003 Stakeholder Theory and Organizational Ethics. San Francisco: Berrett-Kohler.

Poole, M. S., and A. H. Van de Ven
1989 "Using paradox to build management and organization theories." Academy of Management Review, 14: 562–578.

Porter, M. E.
1995 "The competitive advantage of the inner city." Harvard Business Review, 73 (3): 55–72.

Porter, M. E., and C. van der Linde
1995 "Green and competitive: Ending the stalemate." Harvard Business Review, 73 (5): 120–134.

Posnikoff, J. F.
1997 "Disinvestment from South Africa: They did well by doing good." Contemporary Economic Policy, 15 (1): 76–86.

Post, J. E., L. E. Preston, and S. Sachs
2002 Redefining the Corporation: Stakeholder Management and Organizational Wealth. Stanford, CA: Stanford University Press.

Prahalad, C. K., and A. Hammond
2002 "Serving the world's poor, profitably." Harvard Business Review, 80 (9): 4–11.

Prahalad, C. K., and S. L. Hart
2002 "The fortune at the bottom of the pyramid." Strategy + Business, 26: 1–14.

Preston, L. E.
1978 "Analyzing corporate social performance: Methods and results." Journal of Contemporary Business, 7: 135–150.

Preston, L. E., and D. P. O'Bannon
1997 "The corporate social-financial performance relationship: A typology and analysis." Business and Society, 36: 419–429.

Preston, L. E., and H. J. Sapienza
1990 "Stakeholder management and corporate performance." Journal of Behavioral Economics, 19: 361–375.

Putnam, H.
1994 "Pragmatism and moral objectivity." In J. Conant (ed.), Words and Life: 151–181. Cambridge, MA: Harvard University Press.

Ranganathan, J.
1998 "Sustainability rulers: Measuring corporate environmental and social performance." World Resources Institute: http://www.wri.org/meb/sei/state.html.

Rawls, J.
1971 A Theory of Justice. Cambridge, MA: Harvard University Press.
1999 The Law of Peoples. Cambridge, MA: Harvard University Press.

Reich, R. B.
1998 "The new meaning of corporate social responsibility." California Management Review, 40 (2): 8–17.

Reimann, B. C.
1975 "Organizational effectiveness and management's public values: A canonical analysis." Academy of Management Journal, 18: 224–241.

Reyes, M. G., and T. Grieb
1998 "The external performance of socially-responsible mutual funds." American Business Review, 16: 1–7.

Riahi-Belkaoui, A.
1991 "Organizational effectiveness, social performance and economic performance." Research in Corporate Social Performance and Policy, 12: 143–153.

Richardson, A. J., M. Welker, and I. R. Hutchinson
1999 "Managing capital market reactions to corporate social responsibility." International Journal of Management Reviews, 1 (1): 17–43.

Richardson, H. S.
1997 Practical Reasoning about Final Ends. New York: Cambridge University Press.

Roberts, R. W.
1992 "Determinants of corporate social responsibility disclosure: An application of stakeholder theory." Accounting, Organizations and Society, 17: 595–612.

Rockness, J., P. Schlachter, and H. O. Rockness
1986 "Hazardous waste disposal, corporate disclosure, and financial performance in the chemical industry." Advances in Public Interest Accounting, 1: 167–191.

Roman, R. M., S. Hayibor, and B. R. Agle
1999 "The relationship between social and financial performance." Business and Society, 38: 109–125.

Rosen, M.
1985 "Breakfast at Spiros: Dramaturgy and dominance." Journal of Management, 11(2): 31–48.

Rozin, P.
2001 "Social psychology and science: Some lessons from Solomon Asch." Personality and Social Psychology Review, 5: 2–14.

Russo, M. V., and P. A. Fouts
1997 "A resource-based perspective on corporate environmental performance and profitability." Academy of Management Journal, 40: 534–559.

Sagawa, S., and E. Segal
2000 Common Interest, Common Good: Creating Value through Business and Social Sector Partnerships. Boston: Harvard Business School Press.

Sauer, D.
1997 "The impact of social-responsibility screens on investment performance: Evidence from the Domini 400 Social Index and Domini Equity Mutual Fund." Review of Financial Economics, 6: 137–149.

Scanlon, T. M.
1992 "The aims and authority of moral theory." Oxford Journal of Legal Studies, 12 (1): 1–23.

Schoeman, F.
1987 "Statistical norms and moral attributions." In F. Schoeman (ed.), Responsibility, Character, and the Emotions: 287–315. New York: Cambridge University Press.

Sen, A.
1985 "Well-being, agency, and freedom: The Dewey lectures 1984." Journal of Philosophy, 82: 169–221.
1992 "Functionings and capability." In Inequality Reexamined: 39–55. New York: Russell Sage Foundation; Cambridge, MA: Harvard University Press.
1993 "Capability and Well-Being." In M. Nussbaum and A. Sen (eds.), The Quality of Life: 30–53. Oxford: Clarendon Press.

Shane, P. B., and B. H. Spicer
1983 "Market response to environmental information produced outside the firm." Accounting Review, 58: 521–538.

Sharma, S., and H. Vredenburg
1998 "Proactive corporate environmental strategy and the development of competitively valuable organizational capabilities." Strategic Management Journal, 19: 729–753.

Shklar, J. N.
1991 American Citizenship: The Quest for Inclusion. Cambridge, MA: Harvard University Press.

Simerly, R. L.
1994 "Corporate social performance and firms' financial performance: An alternative perspective." Psychological Reports, 75: 1091–1103.

1995 "Institutional ownership, corporate social performance, and firms' financial performance." Psychological Reports, 77: 515–525.

Spencer, B. A., and G. S. Taylor
1987 "A within and between analysis of the relationship between corporate social responsibility and financial performance." Akron Business and Economic Review, 18 (3): 7–18.

Spicer, B. H.
1978 "Investors, corporate social performance and information disclosure: An empirical study." Accounting Review, 53: 94–110.

Stern, R. N., and S. R. Barley
1996 "Organizations and social systems: Organization theory's neglected mandate." Administrative Science Quarterly, 41: 146–162.

Sternberg, E.
1997 "The defects of stakeholder theory." Corporate Governance, 5 (1): 3–10.

Stevens, W. P.
1984 "Market reaction to corporate environmental performance." Advances in Accounting, 1: 41–61.

Stiglitz, J. E.
2002 Globalization and Its Discontents. New York: W.W. Norton.

Sturdivant, F. D., and J. L. Ginter
1977 "Corporate social responsiveness: Management attitudes and economic performance." California Management Review, 19 (3): 30–39.

Teoh, S. H., I. Welch, and C. P. Wazzan
1999 "The effect of socially activist investment policies on the financial markets: Evidence from the South African boycott." Journal of Business, 72: 35–89.

Teper, J. A.
1992 "Evaluating the cost of socially responsible investing." In P. D. Kinder, S. D. Lydenberg, and A. L. Domini (eds.), The Social Investment Almanac: A Comprehensive Guide to Socially Responsible Investing: 340–349. New York: Henry Holt.

Tetlock, P. E.
2000 "Cognitive biases and organizational correctives: Do both disease and cure depend on the politics of the beholder?" Administrative Science Quarterly, 45: 293–326.

Tichy, N. M., A. R. McGill, and L. St. Clair
1997 "Introduction: Corporate global citizenship—why now?" In N. M. Tichy, A. R. McGill, and L. St. Clair (eds.), Corporate Global Citizenship: Doing Business in the Public Eye: 1–22. San Francisco: New Lexington Press.

Travers, F. J.
1997 "Socially responsible investing on a global basis: Mixing money and morality outside the U.S." Journal of Investing, Winter: 50–56.

Tushman, M. L., and E. Romanelli
1985 "Organizational evolution: A metamorphosis model of convergence and reorientation." In L. L. Cummings and B. M. Staw (eds.), Research in Organizational Behavior, 7: 171–222. Greenwich, CT: JAI Press.

Tushman, M. L., and C. A. O'Reilly, III
2002 Winning through Innovation: A Practical Guide to Leading Organizational Change and Renewal. Boston: Harvard Business School Press.

Useem, M.
1996 Investor Capitalism: How Money Managers Are Changing the Face of Corporate America. New York: Basic Books.

Vance, S. C.
1975 "Are socially responsible corporations good investment risks?" Management Review, 64: 18–24.

Verschoor, C. C.
1998 "A study of the link between a corporation's financial performance and its commitment to ethics." Journal of Business Ethics, 17: 1509–1516.

Verschoor, C. C.
1999 "Corporate performance is closely linked to a strong ethical commitment." Business and Society Review, 104: 407–415.

Social Initiatives by Business

Waddock, S. A., and S. B. Graves
1997 "The corporate social performance-financial performance
link." Strategic Management
Journal, 18: 303–319.
2000 "Performance characteristics
of social and traditional
investments." Journal of
Investing, 9 (2): 27–38.

Weick, K. E.
1979 The Social Psychology of
Organizing, 2d ed. New York:
McGraw-Hill.
1995 Sensemaking in Organizations. Thousand Oaks, CA:
Sage.

Willmott, H.
1993 "Strength is ignorance; slavery is freedom: Managing culture in modern organiza-
tions." Journal of
Management Studies, 30:
515–552.

Wokutch, R. E., and E. W.
McKinney
1991 "Behavioral and perceptual
measures of corporate social
performance." In J. E. Post
(ed.), Research in Corporate
Social Performance and Policy, 12: 309–330. Greenwich,
CT: JAI Press.

Wokutch, R. E., and B. A. Spencer
1987 "Corporate saints and sinners: The effects of philanthropic and illegal activity on
organizational performance."
California Management
Review, 29 (2): 62–77.

Wolfe, R. A., and D. S. Putler
2002 "How tight are the ties that
bind stakeholder groups?"
Organization Science, 13:
64–80.

Wolman, W., and A. Colamosca
1997 The Judas Economy: The Tri-
umph of Capital and the
Betrayal of Work. Reading,
MA: Addison-Wesley.

Wood, D. J., and R. E. Jones
1995 "Stakeholder mismatching: A
theoretical problem in empirical research on corporate
social performance." International Journal of Organizational Analysis, 3: 229–267.

World Bank
2002 World Development Indicators 2002. Washington, DC:
World Bank.

Wright, P., and S. P. Ferris
1997 "Agency conflict and corporate strategy: The effect of
divestment on corporate
value." Strategic Manage-
ment Journal, 18: 77–83.

Wright, P., S. P. Ferris, J. S. Hiller,
and M. Kroll
1995 "Competitiveness through
management of diversity:
Effects on stock price valuation." Academy of Manage-
ment Journal, 38: 272–287.

Zadek, S.
2001 The Civil Corporation: The
New Economy of Corporate
Citizenship. London: Earthscan Publications.

Zald, M. N.
1996 "More fragmentation? Unfin-
ished business in linking the
social sciences and humanities." Administrative Science
Quarterly, 41: 251–261.

Part XV
Performance (Corporate Social and Financial Performance)

[54]

Corporate Social and Financial Performance: A Meta-analysis

Marc Orlitzky, Frank L. Schmidt, Sara L. Rynes

Abstract

Marc Orlitzky
UNSW and
University of
Sydney, Australia

Frank L. Schmidt
University of
Iowa, USA

Sara L. Rynes
University of
Iowa, USA

Most theorizing on the relationship between corporate social/environmental performance (CSP) and corporate financial performance (CFP) assumes that the current evidence is too fractured or too variable to draw any generalizable conclusions. With this integrative, quantitative study, we intend to show that the mainstream claim that we have little generalizable knowledge about CSP and CFP is built on shaky grounds. Providing a methodologically more rigorous review than previous efforts, we conduct a meta-analysis of 52 studies (which represent the population of prior quantitative inquiry) yielding a total sample size of 33,878 observations. The meta-analytic findings suggest that corporate virtue in the form of social responsibility and, to a lesser extent, environmental responsibility is likely to pay off, although the operationalizations of CSP and CFP also moderate the positive association. For example, CSP appears to be more highly correlated with accounting-based measures of CFP than with market-based indicators, and CSP reputation indices are more highly correlated with CFP than are other indicators of CSP. This meta-analysis establishes a greater degree of certainty with respect to the CSP–CFP relationship than is currently assumed to exist by many business scholars.

Keywords: social responsibility, business ethics, stakeholder theory, reputation, environmental management, correlation analysis

'Can business meet new social, environmental, and financial expectations and still win?' (Business Week 1999)

Introduction

The performance of business organizations is affected by their strategies and operations in market and non-market environments (Baron 2000). The increasing power of activist groups and the media in pluralist western societies can be expected to make organizations' non-market strategies even more important. One construct that might capture a major element of these non-market strategies is corporate social performance (CSP). CSP can be defined as 'a business organization's configuration of principles of social responsibility, processes of social responsiveness, and policies, programs, and observable outcomes as they relate to the firm's societal relationships' (Wood 1991a: 693).

The impression that 'in the aggregate, results are inconclusive' regarding any theoretical conclusions about the relationship between CSP and corporate financial performance (CFP) has persisted until today (Jones and Wicks 1999: 212; cf. also Donaldson 1999; McWilliams and Siegel 2001; Roman et al. 1999). Ullmann (1985) and Wood and Jones (1995) argued that during the past three decades of empirical research on this relationship, researchers have engaged in a futile search for stable causal patterns. A number of narrative reviews and theories (for example, Aupperle et al. 1985; Griffin and Mahon 1997; Husted 2000; McWilliams and Siegel 2001; Pava and Krausz 1995; Ullmann 1985; Wartick and Cochran 1985; Wood 1991a, 1991b; Wood and Jones 1995) have proposed conceptual explanations for the existence (or lack thereof) of a causal relationship between CSP and CFP, but failed to provide clear answers. Previous reviews of this area have suggested that such factors as stakeholder mismatching (Wood and Jones 1995), the general neglect of contingency factors (for example, Ullmann 1985), and measurement errors (for example, Waddock and Graves 1997) may explain inconsistent findings. Other authors, failing to see important differences between theory and operational context, are even more pessimistic and call for a moratorium of CSP–CFP research (Margolis and Walsh 2001; Rowley and Berman 2000). Before we embark on a costly search for contingencies or abandon a line of inquiry altogether, a theoretically and empirically meaningful integration of this area might be useful. In this article, we argue that this line of inquiry contains a number of theoretical conclusions that have hitherto been overlooked or ignored by many organizational scholars.

This article presents a meta-analytic review of primary quantitative studies of the CSP–CFP relationship. Meta-analysis has proven to be a useful technique in many substantive areas where multiple individual studies have yielded inconclusive or conflicting results (for example, Damanpour 1991; Datta et al. 1992; Gooding and Wagner 1985; Schwenk 1989; see also Hedges 1987; Hunt 1997; Rosenthal and DiMatteo 2001; and Schmidt 1992 for broader reviews of meta-analysis). By statistically aggregating results across individual studies and correcting for statistical artefacts such as sampling error and measurement error, psychometric meta-analysis allows for much greater precision than other forms of research reviews. Ironically, those researchers that question the meaningfulness of the CSP–CFP research stream the most (Griffin and Mahon 1997; Margolis and Walsh 2001) have integrated the empirical evidence with the so-called 'vote-counting' technique, which, for a variety of reasons, has been shown to be invalid by many statistical experts (Hedges and Olkin 1980; Hunter and Schmidt 1990; Rosenthal 1995; Schmidt 1992). When, in 'vote counting', studies are simply coded as showing significantly positive, negative, or statistically non-significant results, conclusions are likely to be false (Hedges and Olkin 1980; Hunter and Schmidt 1990). In contrast, psychometric meta-analysis quantifies the impact of theoretical and methodological deficiencies in a given line of inquiry and is, therefore, at present, the most sophisticated research-integration technique.

The specific objectives of this meta-analysis are to: (1) provide a statistical integration of the accumulated research on the relationship between CSP and

CFP; (2) assess the relative predictive validity of instrumental stakeholder theory in the context of the CSP–CFP relationship; and (3) examine several moderators, such as operationalization of CSP and CFP (that is, measurement strategies) and timing of CSP and CFP measurement. In so doing, it builds on earlier research by: (a) including market (stock) return measures in addition to accounting returns; (b) including CSP measures other than social-responsibility audits performed by Kinder, Lydenberg, Domini & Co., Inc.; (c) responding to Waddock and Graves' (1997: 315) call for research on the temporal consistency of results, independent of the time lag chosen between CSP and CFP measures; and (d) integrating empirical results across diverse study contexts and enabling us to look for theoretical moderators and statistical artefacts that might explain the highly variable results across previous studies.

Theory and Hypotheses

Overall CSP–CFP Relationship

Instrumental stakeholder theory (for example, Clarkson 1995; Cornell and Shapiro 1987; Donaldson and Preston 1995; Freeman 1984; Mitchell et al. 1997 (the classification of these studies as exemplifying 'instrumental stakeholder theory' was made *ex post*)) suggests a positive relationship between CSP and CFP. According to this theory, the satisfaction of various stakeholder groups is instrumental for organizational financial performance (Donaldson and Preston 1995; Jones 1995). Stakeholder-agency theory argues that the implicit and explicit negotiation and contracting processes entailed by reciprocal, bilateral stakeholder–management relationships serve as monitoring and enforcement mechanisms that prevent managers from diverting attention from broad organizational financial goals (Hill and Jones 1992; Jones 1995). Furthermore, by addressing and balancing the claims of multiple stakeholders (Freeman and Evan 1990), managers can increase the efficiency of their organization's adaptation to external demands.

Additionally, according to a firm-as-contract analysis (Freeman and Evan 1990), high corporate performance results not only from the separate satisfaction of bilateral relationships (Hill and Jones 1992), but also from the simultaneous coordination and prioritization of multilateral stakeholder interests. These strategic and tactical steps may be necessary to reduce the likelihood of the organization's becoming stuck in a high-density network. High network density can reduce CFP in a number of ways (Rowley 1997). For example, in a high-density network, firms may become stuck in the role of compromiser or subordinate, depending on the degree of the firm's network centrality (Rowley 1997). Either of these roles may lead to further consumption of valuable firm resources such as time, labour, and capital. Conversely, high CSP bolsters a company's competitive advantage by weighing and addressing the claims of various constituents in a fair, rational manner. This perspective, which is primarily derived from instrumental stakeholder theory (Jones 1995), has also been identified as the 'good management theory' (Waddock and Graves 1997). Therefore, we predict that:

H1: Corporate social performance and financial performance are generally positively related across a wide variety of industry and study contexts.

Temporal Sequence

Like the 'good management theory', slack resources theory also proposes a positive association between CSP and CFP. However, it proposes a different temporal ordering — namely, that prior CFP is directly associated with subsequent CSP. Prior high levels of CFP may provide the slack resources necessary to engage in corporate social responsibility and responsiveness (Ullmann 1985; Waddock and Graves 1997). Because CSP often represents an area of relatively high managerial discretion, the initiation or cancellation of voluntary social and environmental policies may, to a large extent, depend on the availability of excess funds (McGuire et al. 1988).

   To distinguish between slack resources theory and the good management theory, the meta-analytic data set will be examined for three sets of temporal associations: (a) prior CSP related to subsequent CFP; (b) prior CFP related to subsequent CSP; and (c) contemporaneous (cross-sectional) associations. If effect sizes are highly similar across all three meta-analytic subgroups, Waddock and Graves's (1997) argument about a virtuous cycle between CSP and CFP would be supported irrespective of study context, sampling error, and measurement error. Based on prior theory and empirical findings (McGuire et al. 1990; Waddock and Graves 1997), we believe that both instrumental stakeholder theory and slack resources descriptions are accurate, such that the two constructs are related to each other reciprocally.

H2: There is bidirectional causality between corporate social performance and financial performance.

Mediating Effects

CSP may be an organizational resource that provides internal or external benefits, or both. Internally, investments in CSP may help firms develop new competencies, resources, and capabilities which are manifested in a firm's culture, technology, structure, and human resources (Barney 1991; Russo and Fouts 1997; Wernerfelt 1984). Especially when CSP is pre-emptive (Hart 1995) and a firm's environment is dynamic or complex, CSP may help build managerial competencies because preventive efforts necessitate significant employee involvement, organization-wide coordination, and a forward-thinking managerial style (Shrivastava 1995). Thus, CSP can help management develop better scanning skills, processes, and information systems, which increase the organization's preparedness for external changes, turbulence, and crises (for example, Russo and Fouts 1997). These competencies, which are acquired internally through the CSP process, would then lead to more efficient utilization of resources (Majumdar and Marcus 2001). According to the 'internal resources/learning' perspective, whether CSP behaviours and outcomes are also disclosed to outside constituents is largely irrelevant to the development of internal capabilities and organizational efficiency.

In addition, however, CSP may have external effects on organizational reputation. According to the reputation perspective, an organization's communication with external parties about its level of CSP may help build a positive image with customers, investors, bankers, and suppliers (Fombrun and Shanley 1990). Firms high in CSP may use corporate social responsibility disclosures as one of the informational signals upon which stakeholders base their assessments of corporate reputation under conditions of incomplete information (Fombrun and Shanley 1990). Furthermore, firms with high CSP reputation ratings may improve relations with bankers and investors and thus facilitate their access to capital (Spicer 1978). They may also attract better employees (Greening and Turban 2000; Turban and Greening 1997) or increase current employees' goodwill, which in turn may improve financial outcomes (Davis 1973; McGuire et al. 1988; Waddock and Graves 1997). In sum, the reputation perspective postulates reputational effects as mediators of the CSP–CFP linkage, while the internal-resources perspective proposes managerial competencies and learning as the intervening generative mechanism between a positive CSP–CFP association. Therefore, we propose that:

H3: CSP is positively correlated with CFP because (a) CSP increases managerial competencies, contributes to organizational knowledge about the firm's market, social, political, technological, and other environments, and thus enhances organizational efficiency, and (b) CSP helps the firm build a positive reputation and goodwill with its external stakeholders.

Measurement Strategy: An Important Moderator Variable

Because both CSP and CFP are such broad meta-constructs, a given study's operationalization of each construct may act as an important moderator. To test this hypothesis, the entire meta-analytic set is broken down into different CFP and CSP subsets employing different measurement strategies. This breakdown can establish whether correlations between different CSP and CFP measures are similar across subgroups, or whether different operationalizations lead to systematically different effect sizes across studies. The following section gives an overview of how CFP and CSP have been measured in the past.

The three broad subdivisions of CFP consist of market-based (investor returns), accounting-based (accounting returns), and perceptual (survey) measures. First, market-based measures of CFP, such as price per share or share price appreciation, reflect the notion that shareholders are a primary stakeholder group whose satisfaction determines the company's fate (Cochran

and Wood 1984). The bidding and asking processes of stock-market participants, who rely on their perceptions of past, current, and future stock returns
and risk, determine a firm's stock price and thus market value. Alternatively,
accounting-based indicators, such as the firm's return on assets (ROA), return
on equity (ROE), or earnings per share (EPS), capture a firm's internal
efficiency in some way (Cochran and Wood 1984). Accounting returns are
subject to managers' discretionary allocations of funds to different projects
and policy choices, and thus reflect internal decision-making capabilities and
managerial performance rather than external market responses to organizational (non-market) actions. Lastly, perceptual measures of CFP ask survey
respondents to provide subjective estimates of, for instance, the firm's
'soundness of financial position', 'wise use of corporate assets', or 'financial
goal achievement relative to competitors' (Conine and Madden 1987;
Reimann 1975; Wartick 1988).

The construct of CSP is associated with the following four broad
measurement strategies: (a) CSP disclosures; (b) CSP reputation ratings; (c)
social audits, CSP processes, and observable outcomes; and (d) managerial
CSP principles and values (Post 1991). First, CSP disclosure measurement
consists of content analysis of annual reports, letters to shareholders, 10Ks,
and a number of other corporate disclosures to the public as surrogates of
CSP. Content analysis is employed to compare units of text against particular
CSP themes in order to draw inferences about the organization's underlying
social performance (Wolfe 1991).

A second approach to measuring CSP is the use of reputational indices, such
as Moskowitz's (1972, 1975) tripartite ratings ('outstanding', 'honourable
mention', and 'worst' companies; for example, Cochran and Wood 1984;
Sturdivant and Ginter 1977) or *Fortune* magazine ratings of a corporation's
'responsibility to the community and environment' (for example, Conine and
Madden 1987; Fombrun and Shanley 1990; McGuire et al. 1988). Other
researchers (Alexander and Buchholz 1978; Heinze 1976; Vance 1975) have
developed their own reputational measures by surveying business professionals
and business students. Reputation indices are based on the assumption that CSP
reputations are good reflections of underlying CSP values and behaviours.

Social audits and concrete observable CSP processes and outcomes are the
third broad measurement category of CSP. Social audits consist of a
systematic third-party effort to assess a firm's 'objective' CSP behaviours,
such as community service, environmental programmes, and corporate
philanthropy. Objective data are the foundation for so-called 'behavioural'
measures of CSP. However, behavioural measures based on social audits may
still result in a ranking, such as the measure provided by the Council on
Economic Priorities (CEP). Various studies have used the CEP social audit
rankings of companies' pollution records (for example, Bragdon and Marlin
1972; Fogler and Nutt 1975; Spicer 1978; see also the overview of studies in
Appendix A). Although this subset of studies differs from the other three
subsets, it is still very broad. Therefore, this third group will be broken down
further to examine the instrumental effectiveness of processes of social
responsiveness.

The fourth measurement category of CSP assesses the values and principles inherent in a company's culture. Aupperle (1984) developed a forced-choice survey of corporate social orientations, drawing on Carroll's (1979) corporate social responsibility construct with its four dimensions of economic, legal, ethical, and discretionary responsibilities. The last three elements comprise the construct 'concern for society'. Volume 12 of *Research in Corporate Social Performance and Policy* (Post 1991: Part III, 265–401) reviews in greater depth the history and psychometric properties of the different CSP measures briefly delineated here (Aupperle 1991; Carroll 1991; Clarkson 1991; Gephardt 1991; Wokutch and McKinney 1991; Wolfe 1991; Wolfe and Aupperle 1991).

Differences in CSP–CFP statistical associations across these four measurement subsets may result from three sources. First, there might be 'real' (substantive) cross-study variation in correlations between CSP and CFP, as predicted by Wood and Jones's (1995) mismatching thesis. Wood and Jones (1995) argued that effects would vary depending on expectations and evaluations of CSP, which differ from one stakeholder group to another. No positive correlations would be expected between measures that cannot be linked theoretically, such as CSP disclosures and accounting-based efficiency measures of CFP. For example, Wood and Jones's (1995) review suggested that the match between market measures and market-oriented stakeholders (for example, customers) would produce significant positive results, while the correlation between market measures and charitable contributions, for instance, would not.

Alternatively, differences in correlations across variable measurement subsets may simply be a function of statistical artefacts. For example, if one measurement subgroup were found to contain many studies with very small sample sizes, this subgroup would show a relatively large random sampling error. Thus, differences in *sampling error* across measurement subgroups may explain CSP/CFP correlational differences in primary studies. In addition, *measurement error* of CFP and CSP (that is, unreliability) might act as another artefactual source of cross-study variability in correlations. If, for example, CSP disclosure measures were plagued by comparatively low psychometric quality (for example, Abbott and Monsen 1979; Ingram and Frazier 1980; Wiseman 1982), observed correlations between CSP disclosures and CFP would be systematically lower than the correlations between CFP and other, more reliable measures of CSP. Therefore, this meta-analysis hierarchically breaks down the overall data set in order to compare the relative magnitudes of correlations arising from different CSP and CFP measurement subcategories, and to test for these three possible sources of cross-study variation of correlations (substantive differences, sampling error, and measurement error). We hypothesize that:

H4a: A large proportion of cross-study variance is due to statistical or methodological artefacts (sampling error and measurement error).

H4b: Consistent with stakeholder mismatching, after accounting for statistical artefacts, there will still be differences in the statistical associations between different sub-dimensions of CFP and CSP (after correct matching).

Figure 1
Hypothesized
Relationships (*H_j*)

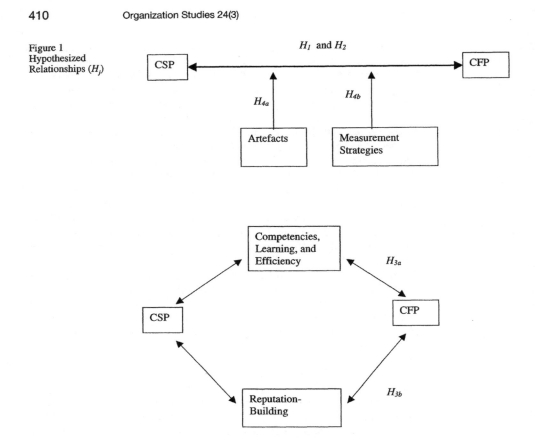

Note: CSP = corporate social performance; CFP = corporate financial performance.

Methods

Prior summaries of the CSP–CFP literature have relied mostly on narrative reviews (for example, Pava and Krausz 1995; Ullmann 1985) or the vote-counting method of aggregation (for example, Griffin and Mahon 1997; Margolis and Walsh 2001; Roman et al. 1999; Wood and Jones 1995). Narrative reviews are literature reviews that attempt to make sense of past findings verbally or conceptually. The vote-counting method refers to the cumulation of significance levels or, in the simplest case, to the tabulation of significant and non-significant findings (Hunter and Schmidt 1990; Light and Smith 1971). Both of these research integration techniques tend to draw false inferences because they do not correct for sampling and measurement error, two important study artefacts (Hedges and Olkin 1980; Hunter and Schmidt 1990). In fact, the statistical errors in the typical 'vote-counting' literature review tend to be more serious than in the average narrative review because the statistical power of the vote-counting procedure *decreases* with *increasing* number of studies reviewed (Hedges and Olkin 1980; Hunter and Schmidt 1990). Although we have known for more than 20 years that vote counting is marred by a lack of validity, the technique is still widely used today (for example, Griffin and Mahon 1997; Margolis and Walsh 2001; Roman et al. 1999; Wood and Jones 1995).

In contrast, effect-size (r) meta-analysis is a rigorous approach to external validation, which calculates population parameter estimates (ρ) by correcting for the aforementioned artefacts. The effect of sampling error is important because sample sizes that are smaller than the population cause observed sample correlation statistics r to vary randomly from the population parameter, the true-score correlation ρ. In addition, as mentioned before, measurement error (that is, unreliability) systematically attenuates observed correlations (Nunnally and Bernstein 1994).

Search for Relevant Studies

Computer searches of ABI/Inform Global and PsycINFO were conducted, using the keyword search 'organizational effectiveness and corporate social performance'. Synonyms for the former, used in separate computer searches, were 'organizational performance', 'profitability', 'economic success', and 'financial performance'. 'Corporate social performance' as a keyword search term was alternately substituted with '(corporate) social responsibility', 'corporate environmental performance', 'responsiveness', and simply 'resp?'. ABI/Inform Global gives access to the full text and images of more than 1,200 US and international business and trade journal articles (1970–current), while PsycINFO indexes abstracts of journal articles and book chapters in psychology starting in 1974. To increase the scope of our search, cross-citations from previous narrative reviews (for example, Aldag and Bartol 1978; McGuire et al. 1988: 857–860; Preston 1978a; Waddock and Mahon 1991; Wood and Jones 1995) were explored as well.

Criteria for Relevance

The studies that were deemed relevant for the meta-analysis had the following characteristics. First, the studies quantitatively examined the relationship between CSP and CFP. The reported effect size did not have to be a Pearson's product-moment correlation r, but could also be a t-test statistic or effect size d (both t and d can be transformed to r; Hunter and Schmidt 1990). Second, the studies were concerned with at least one aspect of a firm's economic performance, as circumscribed by the definition of CFP. For the purpose of this study, CFP was defined as a company's financial viability, or the extent to which a company achieves its economic goals (Price and Mueller 1986; Venkatraman and Ramanujam 1986). Third, all retrieved studies were double-checked for conformance to Wood's (1991a) definition of CSP (see Introduction above). Wood's (1991a) now classic definition is used because it is one of the most influential, helpful, parsimonious, and yet comprehensive conceptualizations of CSP. If the particular variable could not be classified as an example belonging to one of the nine subcategories of Wood's model, the study was excluded. In addition, unclear reporting of empirical results was also a reason for exclusion.

Studies of environmental management and CFP are included in the meta-analysis for several reasons. First, several studies, especially earlier ones, use environmental performance as a proxy for social responsibility. Second, stakeholder proxies, such as environmental interest groups and government agencies, may in fact give voice to, or claim a social 'stake' for, non-human nature (Starik 1995). Lastly, the business community tends to regard social responsibility as including both social and environmental performance (for example, Willums 1999). Still, the argument can be made that the literature on CSP differs from the one on corporate environmental performance in various aspects. To investigate differences between social and environmental performance, the entire set (k = number of effect sizes integrated = 388) is disaggregated into purely *social* performance measures only (that is, excluding all environmental performance measures; k = 249) and environmental measures only (k = 139).

Characteristics of Primary Studies

The most important study characteristics, such as author(s), date of study, study sample size N_i, observed r or transformed and/or partially corrected r (that is, corrected for dichotomization and unequal sample sizes in the two groups compared in a t-test), number of correlations per study, operationalization of CSP and CFP, and estimates of reliability are listed in Appendix A.

Reliability is traditionally defined as the ratio of true-score variance to observed-score variance (Traub 1994). Thus, classical measurement theory is concerned with the correspondence between observed scores and true scores. Some of the reliability coefficients used in this study are in the tradition of classical reliability theory, such as coefficient alpha. Sometimes, however, it becomes necessary to count not only variation due to item sampling, but also day-to-day variation in scores as measurement error. In classical theory, one can accomplish this task by using an alternate-forms coefficient of reliability. Generalizability theory is less restrictive in its assumptions than classical theory (Cronbach et al. 1972). The coefficient of generalizability reflects the degree to which observed scores (of CSP or CFP in this case) allow for generalization about a firm's behaviour in a defined universe of situations (Cronbach et al. 1972; Shavelson et al. 1989). Generalizability is estimated through 'alternate-forms' correlations between different CSP, and CFP, measures.

The present study estimates reliability by including coefficients of generalizability (76 percent), stability (4 percent), internal reliability (8 percent), and inter-rater reliability (12 percent). Both stability and generalizability coefficients are underestimates of reliability (Orlitzky 1998). Because of the predominance of coefficients of stability and generalizability, the meta-analysis provides conservative estimates (that is, lower-bound estimates) of the reliability of the CSP or CFP measurement instrument.

In addition to listing the reliabilities of both constructs, Appendix A shows the great variety of study contexts and operationalizations of both constructs. From the vantage point of generating cumulative knowledge, multiple operationism is an advantage because it helps determine whether a 'true' relationship exists in different industry contexts with different operationalizations of the two focal constructs (Cook and Campbell 1979; Cooper 1989; Webb et al. 1981). In past meta-analyses, integrated studies often contained broad meta-constructs as well, such as job or organizational performance, operationalized in many different ways (for example, Gooding and Wagner 1985; Ketchen et al. 1997; Roth et al. 1996; Wagner and Gooding 1987). During data collection, the inclusion criteria for relevance (see above) served as constant checks on the operationalizations' conformance to the broad conceptual definitions of CSP and CFP.

Empirically, the standard deviation of ρ serves as an indicator of cross-study heterogeneity. The percentage of cross-study variance explained by artefacts is another indicator of the degree of cross-study generalizability (Hunter and Schmidt 1990).

Statistical Conventions Used in the Meta-analysis

The meta-analysis uses Hunter and Schmidt's (1990) statistical aggregation techniques for cumulating correlations and correcting for various study artefacts in order to estimate the true score correlation (ρ) between CSP and CFP. Meta-analysis arrives at a mean true-score correlation by correcting observed correlations for sampling error (which can be written as $\sigma_e = (1 - \rho^2) / \sqrt{(N-1)}$) and for measurement error. Since sampling error varies directly with sample size, all studies are weighted by sample size N_i before correcting for the average attenuation factor (Schmidt and Hunter 1977).

Because measurement error data points are not always available for individual studies (see Appendix A), study correlations cannot be corrected individually for measurement error. Instead, correlations are meta-analysed using artefact distributions (for more details on artefact-distribution meta-analysis, see Hunter and Schmidt 1990). The moderator analyses use Hunter and Schmidt's (1990) subgrouping algorithm, as described in the Results section below.

Non-independence in any meta-analytic data set can present certain problems. Therefore, sensitivity analyses were conducted by using two other aggregation techniques. In the first sensitivity analysis, we used only one independent correlation per study, that is, composite scores. Furthermore, a second sensitivity analysis tested the stability of our transformations of effect sizes (reported t or d statistics into r).

Results

Overall CSP–CFP Relationships

As shown in the first line of Table 1, the mean observed correlation (r_{obs}) for the total set of 388 correlations and a total sample size N of 33,878

Table 1. Overall Meta-Analytic Findings (Hypothesis 1)

Relationship between…	k [a]	Total Sample Size	Sample-Size Weighted Mean Observed r (r_{obs})	Observed Variance	% Variance Explained [b]	Mean 'True-Score' r (mean ρ)	Variance of ρ [$σ^2(ρ)$]	File Drawer Analysis [c]
1. CSP and CFP (entire meta-analytic set)	388	33,878	.1836	.0646	23.89	.3648	.1896	1,037
2. CSP and CFP without CSP reputation and CFP survey measures	252	20,662	.0776	.0296	43.94	.1543	.0641	139
3.a. CSP without corporate environmental performance and CFP	249	24,055	.2301	.0638	27.04	.4671	.1891	897
3.b. Corporate environmental performance and CFP	139	9,823	.0562	.0383	40.33	.1246	.1097	17

[a] k: number of correlation coefficients meta-analysed.

[b] refers to percentage of cross-study observed variance explained by three study artefacts: sampling error, measurement error in CSP, measurement error in CFP.

[c] Hunter and Schmidt's (1990) effect size file drawer analysis: number of missing studies averaging null findings needed to bring r_{obs} down to .05.

observations is .18, with an observed variance of .06. The study artefacts of sampling and measurement error in CSP and CFP explain 24 percent of the cross-study variance of r_{obs}. After correction for sampling and measurement errors, the true score (corrected) correlation (ρ) was .36, which is twice the size of the observed correlation, with a variance (.19), which is slightly more than three times the size of the observed variance. As shown in the second line of Table 1, the relationship remains positive even after we removed studies that may be affected by response bias (survey measures of CFP) and halo (CSP reputation indices; Brown and Perry 1994); the remaining meta-analytic set showed an average observed correlation of .08 and a true-score correlation of .15. Although this true-score correlation is smaller than in the larger set including CSP reputation and CFP survey measures, it is not trivial. Thus, the meta-analytic findings support hypothesis H1.

The sensitivity analyses tend to confirm this conclusion. The first sensitivity analysis, which uses only one effect size per study (thus, $k = 52$, $N = 4924$), showed a mean observed correlation of .21 and a corrected correlation of .42. The second sensitivity analysis, on 210 product-moment correlations (k) with a total sample size of 22,218 observations (N), also showed slightly higher estimates $(r_{obs} = .20, \rho = .41)$ than the overall meta-analysis reported in Table 1. Thus, in both 'sensitivity' meta-analyses (not reported in the tables), the mean observed and corrected correlations were positive and of similar magnitude as the correlations in the entire meta-analytic set. If anything, the sensitivity analyses suggest that our meta-analytic estimates are actually conservative estimates of the relationships between CSP and CFP.

Corporate Social and Environmental Performance

Table 1 also shows analyses for two different conceptualizations of CSP. When the entire meta-analytic set was divided into two sets, that is, (a) those studies using a narrow definition of 'social' performance (thus excluding measures of environmental performance; $k = 249$, $N = 24,055$) and (b) studies of corporate environmental performance only ($k = 139$, $N = 9823$), the findings show that corporate environmental performance has a smaller relationship with CFP ($r_{obs} = .06, \rho = .12$) than do all other measures of CSP ($r_{obs} = .23, \rho = .47$), such as managerial principles and corporate reputations for minority hiring, for example. In the corporate environmental performance subset, the variances of observed and true-score correlations were also smaller than those in the 'pure' CSP subset. Furthermore, measurement error and sampling error explained more of the cross-study variance of r_{obs} in the corporate environmental performance subset than in the 'pure' CSP subset. Thus, the last two lines of Table 1 (entries 3.a and 3.b) demonstrate that the relatively lower correlation between corporate *environmental* performance and CFP is, in fact, much more consistent across industry and study contexts than the primary empirical studies would have us believe.

File Drawer Analysis

In the overall meta-analysis as in all subsequent meta-analyses, an effect size *file drawer analysis* was performed to address the possibility of availability

Table 2a. 'Good Management' Theory and Slack Resources Theory (Hypothesis 2, All measures of CSP, Incl. Environmental Performance)

Relationship between...	k [a]	Total Sample Size	Sample-Size Weighted Mean Observed r (r_{obs})	Observed Variance	% Variance Explained [b]	Mean 'True-score' r (mean ρ)	Variance of ρ [$\sigma^2(\rho)$]	File Drawer Analysis [c]
CSP and subsequent CFP	68	6,966	.1450	.0602	20.47	.2881	.1847	129
CSP and prior CFP	111	9,929	.1481	.0578	23.90	.2944	.1697	218
CSP and concurrent CFP (cross-sectional studies)	209	16,983	.2201	.0677	26.47	.4375	.1919	711

[a] k: number of correlation coefficients meta-analysed.
[b] refers to percentage of cross-study observed variance explained by three study artefacts: sampling error, measurement error in CSP, measurement error in CFP.
[c] Hunter and Schmidt's (1990) effect size file drawer analysis: number of missing studies averaging null findings needed to bring r_{obs} down to .05.

Table 2b. Hypothesis 2 'Pure' CSP Measures only

Relationship between...	k [a]	Total Sample Size	Sample-Size Weighted Mean Observed r (r_{obs})	Observed Variance	% Variance Explained [b]	Mean 'True-Score' r (mean ρ)	Variance of ρ [$\sigma^2(\rho)$]	File Drawer Analysis [c]
CSP and subsequent CFP	31	4,189	.2016	.0722	17.20	.4005	.2306	94
CSP and prior CFP	54	6,800	.2262	.0443	32.07	.4495	.1161	190
CSP and concurrent CFP (cross-sectional studies)	158	12,764	.2529	.0755	26.13	.5027	.2151	641

[a] k: number of correlation coefficients meta-analysed.
[b] refers to percentage of cross-study observed variance explained by three study artefacts: sampling error, measurement error in CSP, measurement error in CFP.
[c] Hunter and Schmidt's (1990) effect size file drawer analysis: number of missing studies averaging null findings needed to bring r_{obs} down to .05.

bias. Availability bias is one of the most common criticisms levelled against meta-analysis, in that critics of meta-analysis often suspect that published studies will report larger effect sizes than unpublished studies. File drawer analysis addresses this issue by computing the number of additional unlocated (that is, 'lost' or overlooked) studies needed to cause the correlation to decrease to a minimal critical level (r_{crit}), which is set at .05 in this study. Hunter and Schmidt (1990) present the underlying assumptions and techniques of file drawer analysis. For each correlation computed in Tables 1–4, the results of the file drawer analysis are presented in the last column. As shown in Table 1, a very large number of studies (1,037) would be needed to change the overall substantive conclusions of this meta-analysis (entry 1 in Table 1).

Temporal Sequence

Tables 2a and 2b show the results relevant to Hypothesis 2, which suggested a virtuous cycle between CSP and CFP. Consistent with that hypothesis, the primary studies supported the instrumental stakeholder and slack resources theories to about the same degree. Specifically, both the prior CFP and subsequent CFP subsets yielded observed correlations of .15, and corrected correlations of .29 (first two lines in Table 2a). Concurrent studies yielded observed and corrected correlations with CFP of .22 and .44, respectively (third line of Table 2a). Taken together, these findings suggest a virtuous cycle with quick cycle times or concurrent bidirectionality. However, the low percentages of observed cross-study variance explained by artefacts, ranging from 20 percent to 26 percent, and large true-score variances ranging from .17 to .19, indicate the presence of at least one moderator. As Table 2b shows, consistent with the overall analysis (Table 1, entries 3.a and 3.b), the results are stronger after corporate environmental measures were removed from CSP. Generally, though, the relationships reported in Table 2b confirm the conclusions of Table 2a.

Mediator Variables: Learning and Reputation

To investigate Hypothesis 3, studies were divided into two broad subsets: (a) studies that correlated both internal and external measures of CSP with only accounting CFP measures (that is, measures of *internal* resource utilization, such as ROA or ROE); and (b) studies which correlated only *externally visible* measures of CSP, such as CSP reputation or disclosures, with exclusively *external* (for example, market return or sales growth) measures of CFP. The reputational argument is further subdivided into studies correlating external indicators of CFP with: (a) reputation indices of CSP; (b) CSP disclosures in annual reports and letters to shareholders; and (c) other externally visible measures of CSP such as social audits and charitable contributions.

Based on the magnitude of the meta-analytic correlations, the meta-analysed studies support the reputation-effects viewpoint relatively more strongly than the internal viewpoint, as shown in Table 3 (compare first two

Table 3. Subset Meta-Analysis: Reputation Theory and Internal Skills Theory of CSP (Hypothesis 3)

Type of Relationship	$k^{a,d}$	Total Sample Size	Sample-Size Weighted Mean Observed r (r_{obs})	Observed Variance	% Variance Explained[b]	Mean 'True-Score' r (mean ρ)	Variance of ρ [$\sigma^2(\rho)$]	File Drawer Analysis[c]
1. Efficiency, skills, learning, and/or competency	130	12,957	.1630	.0280	49.66	.3324	.0572	294
2. Reputation theory	177	14,274	.2484	.1024	19.59	.4942	.3185	702
2.a. Reputation indexes	65	6,858	.4197	.0992	24.77	.7593	.2386	481
2.a.1. Subsequent CFP	10	1,088	.3681	.1869	15.43	.7504	.6420	64
2.a.2. Prior CFP	9	1,074	.3558	.1053	25.58	.7254	.3182	55
2.a.3. Concurrent CFP	46	4,696	.4463	.0752	51.29	.9099	.1488	365
2.b. Disclosure measures	75	4,351	.0586	.0192	93.49	.1399	.0070	13
2.c. Other	37	3,065	.1356	.0978	14.75	.2698	.3226	63

[a] k: number of correlation coefficients meta-analysed.
[b] refers to percentage of cross-study observed variance explained by three study artefacts: sampling error, measurement error in CSP, measurement error in CFP.
[c] Hunter and Schmidt's (1990) effect size file drawer analysis: number of missing studies averaging null findings needed to bring r_{obs} down to .05.
[d] Correlations in subsets 1 and 2 do not add up to 388 because assignment to type of relationship was questionable in certain cases.

lines in Table 3, that is, entry 1 with entry 2). In addition, further hierarchical breakdown of the reputation view subset indicates that CSP disclosures appear to have a low reputational impact on CFP. This statistical conclusion is generalizable across study settings because a high proportion of variance (93 percent) is explained by study artefacts (entry 2.b in Table 3). Moreover, timing of measurement (temporal sequence) is not an important moderator within the 'reputation view' argument. As was the case in the overall meta-analysis, the correlations between CSP and subsequent CFP are almost identical to the ones found between CSP and prior CFP ($\rho = .75$ and $.73$, respectively; entries 2.a.1 and 2.a.2 in Table 3). Again, the correlations are highest when CSP and CFP were measured less than a year apart ($\rho = .91$, and 51 percent of cross-study variance explained by artefacts; entry 2.a.3).

Moderator Analysis

The analyses relevant to Hypothesis 3 already alluded to an important feature of Hunter and Schmidt's (1990) meta-analytic technique; namely, detection of cross-study moderators. Because this algorithm will be used extensively in the remaining meta-analyses, a brief explanation seems in order. Hunter and Schmidt's (1990) moderator analysis consists of two distinct methods. First, the '75% rule' can be applied, stating that if 75 percent or more of the observed variance of correlations across studies is due to artefacts, then probably all of it is artefactual variance (on the grounds that the remaining 25 percent is likely due to artefacts not corrected for). Thus, in cases where 75 percent or more of the variance is explained by artefacts, including sampling error variance, moderators are unlikely to have caused a real variation in observed correlations (r_{obs}). This first method is able to detect the existence of unsuspected moderators.

The second method, which can detect discontinuous, theoretically predicted moderators, compares mean observed and true-score correlations across study domain subsets of the original entire set of studies aggregated in the meta-analysis. If in these meta-analytic subgroups, a higher percentage of variance is accounted for by study artefacts relative to the entire meta-analytic set, moderators are said to exist.

Measurement Strategy as Moderator

To examine Hypotheses 4a and 4b, the entire data set of 388 correlations was broken down hierarchically to investigate the presence of moderator effects based on the operationalizations of CSP and CFP (see Table 4a). First, CFP and CSP operationalizations were disaggregated separately. Second, the four broad CSP operationalization subsets were broken down hierarchically into the two (or three, where available) CFP measurement categories. The lowest level in Table 4a is the only one that is not confounded by lack of standardized measurement and, thus, is the most informative.

In general, Table 4a indicates that the association between CSP and CFP depends on the firm's or researcher's operational definition of each construct, or both. Accounting measures were more highly correlated with CSP than

Table 4a. Subset Meta-Analysis of Operationalization Moderator Effects (Hypothesis 4b)

Operationalization	k[a]	Total Sample Size	Sample-Size Weighted Mean Observed r (r_{obs})	Observed Variance	% Variance Explained[b]	Mean 'True-score' r (mean ρ)	Variance of ρ [$σ^2(ρ)$]	File Drawer Analysis[c]
1. CFP operationalizations	388	33,878						
1.a. Market-based	161	10,463	.0733	.0670	24.24	.1459	.1965	75
1.b. Accounting-based	205	20,984	.2070	.0478	33.87	.4215	.1282	644
1.c. Perceptual measures	22	2,431	.4471	.0727	45.64	.8885	.1525	175
2. CSP operationalizations	388	33,878						
2.a. Disclosure	97	5,360	.0438	.0189	98.47	.0871	.0011	NA
2.a.1. Market-based CFP	79	4,426	.0548	.0206	89.75	.1090	.0081	8
2.a.2. Accounting CFP	18	934	-.0085	.0077	100.00	-.0168	.0000	NA
2.b. Reputation indexes	123	12,252	.3657	.0745	34.77	.7268	.1875	777
2.b.1. Market-based CFP	45	4,291	.3593	.0965	26.64	.7141	.2730	278
2.b.2. Accounting CFP	69	6,494	.3059	.0546	39.61	.6078	.1271	353
2.b.3. Perceptual CFP	9	1,467	.6495	.0019	100.00	.9481	.0000	108
2.c. Social audits, corporation behaviours, processes, and outcomes	145	14,200	.0907	.0332	34.00	.1803	.0844	118
2.c.1. Market-based CFP	60	4,858	.0207	.0556	22.58	.0411	.1661	NA
2.c.2. Accounting CFP	82	8,652	.1312	.0188	61.79	.2607	.0277	133
2.c.3. Perceptual CFP	3	690	.0767	.0004	100.00	.1524	.0000	2
2.d. Corporation social responsibility values and attitudes	23	2,066	.1041	.0272	45.94	.2068	.0567	25
2.d.1. Market-based CFP	0	0						
2.d.2. Accounting CFP	13	1,792	.0747	.0178	44.97	.1484	.0377	6
2.d.3. Perceptual CFP	10	274	.2962	.0464	93.90	.5886	.0109	49

a k: number of correlation coefficients meta-analysed.
b refers to percentage of cross-study observed variance explained by three study artefacts: sampling error, measurement error in CSP, measurement error in CFP.
c Hunter and Schmidt's (1990) effect size file drawer analysis: number of missing studies averaging null findings needed to bring r_{obs} down to .05.

Table 4b. Further Subset Analyses of CSP in Terms of Social Audits, Corporation Behaviours, Processes, and Outcomes with CFP (Hypothesis 4b)

Type of CSP	k [a]	Total Sample Size	Sample-Size Weighted Mean Observed r (r_{obs})	Observed Variance	% Variance Explained [b]	Mean "True-Score" r (mean ρ)	Variance of ρ [$\sigma^2(\rho)$]	File Drawer Analysis [c]
Social audits	35	5,016	.1143	.0081	100.00	.2272	.0000	45
CSP behaviours:								
Philanthropic donations	17	1,283	.1463	.0642	24.60	.2907	.1867	33
Environmental assessment / forecasting	3	401	.0592	.0143	55.62	.1177	.0245	1
Issues management	3	690	.0767	.0004	100.00	.1524	.0000	2
Stakeholder management	7	513	.0717	.0105	100.00	.1425	.0000	3
Environmental management	80	6,297	.0657	.0517	25.83	.1306	.1479	25

[a] k: number of correlation coefficients meta-analysed
[b] refers to percentage of cross-study observed variance explained by three study artefacts: sampling error, measurement error in CSP, measurement error in CFP.
[c] Hunter and Schmidt's (1990) effect size file drawer analysis: number of missing studies averaging null findings needed to bring r_{obs} down to .05.

market-based measures ($\rho = .42$ as against $.15$; entries 1.b versus 1.a in Table 4a), and were particularly highly correlated with CSP reputation indices ($\rho = .61$; entry 2.b.2). In fact, overall the findings with respect to CSP operationalizations suggest that studies that used reputation indices as proxies for CSP showed the highest average correlation with CFP (ρ of .73 with a large variance of .19; entry 2.b in Table 4a). Of course, this high correlation may partially be due to halo (Brown and Perry 1994).

Furthermore, repeating the pattern of results testing reputation-theory effects (Table 3), disclosure measures appear to be only minimally related to CFP ($r_{obs} = .04$, $\rho = .09$, as shown in entry 2.a). This finding is generalizable because almost all the observed variance is explained by artefacts. Social audits, CSP processes, and outcomes are only modestly correlated with CFP ($r_{obs} = .09$, $\rho = .18$; entry 2.c). Similar mean correlations were found for the relationship between corporate social responsibility values or attitudes and CFP ($r_{obs} = .10$, $\rho = .21$; entry 2.d).

The second level in the hierarchical breakdown supports the view that differences in previous findings resulted from study artefacts, stakeholder mismatching, other theoretical mis-specifications, or lack of theory (cf. also McWilliams and Siegel 2000). As discussed above, the overall percentage of cross-study variance (in r_{obs}) explained is 24 percent. In general, this percentage tends to increase in the measurement subgroups listed in Table 4a, which suggests that studies systematically differ with respect to the distortions caused by (previously uncorrected) statistical and methodological artefacts. The fact that artefacts account for 15–100 percent of cross-study variance (the notorious 'inconsistencies' of this research stream) provides support for Hypothesis 4a.

The support for *theoretical* inconsistencies (stakeholder mismatching) becomes apparent by looking at some second-level hierarchical subgroups. First, the correlation of CSP disclosure measures with accounting CFP measures is slightly negative ($\rho = -.02$; entry 2.a.2). This small correlation supports the stakeholder mismatching thesis because there is no theoretical causal mechanism between CSP disclosures and internal (that is, accounting) CFP measures. Second, the observed and corrected correlations between (a) social audit and other observable or 'objective' (for example, dollar amount of charitable contributions) measures of CSP processes and (b) market-based measures of CFP are close to zero (Table 4a, entry 2.c.1), which again supports the stakeholder mismatching thesis. As Wood and Jones (1995: 242) argued earlier, 'There is no theory to explain why stockholders would or would not prefer a company that gives one percent of pre-tax earnings to charity, that hires and develops minority or women workers, or that ranks higher in pollution control indices.' In other words, the data suggest that capital market participants dismiss certain concrete behavioural measures of CSP (such as charitable donations), perhaps because they are perceived as direct attempts by firms to manage external impressions.

To examine the measurement moderators within subgroup 2.c even more closely, Table 4b shows results for social audits disaggregated from other CSP behaviours, which are further broken down. Two findings are noteworthy. First, social audits were consistently, but only modestly, correlated with CFP ($\rho = .23$, 100 per cent of cross-study variance explained). Second, across industry contexts, philanthropic donations were related with CFP at $\rho = .29$, which was higher than the respective correlation coefficients found for all other measures of CSP behaviours. However, the file drawer analyses (last column of Table 4b) suggest that some of the findings presented in Table 4b are not conclusive because a small number of additional studies could change our conclusions.

Discussion

Theoretical Implications

Based on this meta-analysis integrating 30 years of research, the answer to the introductory question posed by *Business Week* is affirmative. The results of this meta-analysis show that there is a positive association between CSP and CFP across industries and across study contexts. In that sense, we can confirm Frooman's (1997) conclusions, based on event studies, supporting the validity of enlightened self-interest in the social responsibility arena. The data accumulated over the past 30 years do not support the latest contingency theory in the area of corporate social responsibility (McWilliams and Siegel 2001). Like earlier research reviews, McWilliams and Siegel (2001) take inconsistent findings in primary studies at face value (that is, ignore the possible impact of sampling error and measurement error) and explain the (apparent) inconsistency with a demand/supply model of corporate social responsibility. Moreover, the temporal analysis of our meta-analysis shows that the positive association between CFP and lagged CSP (slack resources argument) does not mask a weaker negative association between CSP and lagged CFP.

Can CSP be motivated by an 'ecological selection process based on profit maximization or organizational survival' (Wholey and Brittain 1986, in Husted 2000: 33)? Husted (2000: 34) agrees with the narrative reviews in this area, stating that it is 'premature' to conclude that adaptation to market and non-market environments might force organizations to consider social issues and CSP in their day-to-day strategizing. Our meta-analysis suggests the opposite. In fact, some of our observed correlations are higher than the correlations typically found between strategy-structure fit and CFP (Amburgey and Dacin 1994; Donaldson 1987). Despite those lower correlations, the strategy-structure-performance paradigm is firmly grounded on an economic survival mechanism (across industry contexts) analogous to Hypothesis 1. On the one hand, our meta-analysis contradicts Rowley and Berman's (2000) suggestion that there cannot be a consistently positive relationship between CSP and CFP. On the other hand, in agreement with Rowley and Berman (2000), we demonstrate that the *universally positive* relationship varies (from highly positive to modestly positive) because of contingencies, such as reputation effects, market measures of CFP, or CSP disclosures.

Traditionally, researchers have worried that any positive correlations are artefactual, due to halo effects (Brown and Perry 1994, 1995; Wood 1995). However, it is important to keep in mind that the only credible halo linkage would be from CFP to CSP; that is, companies that perform better financially receive higher CSP ratings, regardless of their true underlying CSP. The meta-analytic breakdown has shown that the potential halo effect (CFP → lagged CSP correlation) does not dominate a weaker CSP → lagged CFP correlation and distort results. In fact, the two correlations are identical at two digits (.29, see Table 2a). Also, when all potentially problematic studies are removed (that is, those that measure CSP reputations only and those that measure CFP with a survey instrument), the meta-analysis still shows a non-trivial positive 'true-score' correlation of .15 (see Table 1). Furthermore, the halo argument would suggest a much higher correlation between external (market) CFP and CSP reputation than between internal (accounting) CFP and CSP reputation. In fact, however, the correlations in both subgroups were similar (entries 2.b.1 versus 2.b.2 in Table 4a).

When the CFP survey measures and CSP reputation measures are removed, the cross-study variation of r_{obs} can be shown to be increasingly a function of the artefacts of sampling and measurement error (44 percent; see entry 2 in Table 1). Thus, many of the negative findings in individual studies are artefactual, so that the generalization of a positive CSP–CFP relationship applies more broadly than previously suggested (for example, Jones and Wicks 1999; Pava and Krausz 1995; Ullmann 1985; Wood and Jones 1995). We can, therefore, state with some confidence that the association between CSP and lagged CFP is not negative. Moreover, the causation seems to be that CSP and CFP mutually affect each other through a virtuous cycle: financially successful companies spend more because they can afford it, but CSP also helps them become a bit more successful. Moreover, the file drawer analysis indicates that the present findings cannot be dismissed by availability bias.

This meta-analysis both rejects and confirms notions developed by neo-classical economists. On the one hand, it rejects the idea that CSP is necessarily inconsistent with shareholder wealth maximization (Friedman 1970; Levitt 1958). Instead, organizational effectiveness may be a broad concept encompassing both financial and social performance (Andrews 1987; Judge 1994). It is also worth noting that, according to most credible versions of stakeholder theory, shareholders are legitimate stakeholders. On the other hand, our findings also confirm the notions of libertarians such as Friedman that government regulation in the area of CSP may not be necessary. If the statistical relationship between CSP and CFP were negative, bottom-line considerations might constitute barriers to outcomes desired by the public, which in turn would make government intervention, which serves the 'public interest', a necessity. Yet, with CSP, the case for regulation and social control by governments (acting on behalf of 'society' or 'the public') is relatively weak because organizations and their shareholders tend to benefit from managers' prudent analysis, evaluation, and balancing of multiple con-stituents' preferences. Therefore, these actions are most likely adopted voluntarily, based on managers' cost-benefit analyses of a firm's investments. In contrast, 'socially responsible' command-and-control regulation may prescribe inflexible means–ends chains that are inappropriate for a particular firm's non-market and market environments (Majumdar and Marcus 2001).

Implications for Future Research

The meta-analysis helps to identify areas in which there have been relatively few studies conducted, and which warrant more research (for example, social responsibility values and market CFP; see Table 4a). Additionally, the analysis shows areas in which the unexplained variance across studies remains relatively large, so that further inquiry is needed to identify moderators (for example, CSP reputation measures and market-based CFP; see Table 4a). Moreover, Appendix A shows that the field must make a concerted effort to improve the reliability of CSP and CFP measures. In several subgroups, the percentage of variance of r_{obs} explained by measurement error (that is, low reliability) was substantial. In addition to psychometric refinements, CSP researchers must decide whether CSP 'processes' should really be regarded as a social performance measure. Including processes is equivalent to acknowledging effort. More broadly, some readers may share the authors' concern that previous studies were over-inclusive with respect to definitions of stakeholders and, thus, the CSP proxies (cf. also Roman et al. 1999). We would argue that in future studies, only social and environmental performance 'outcomes' should count as CSP and that the concept of 'stakeholder' must be more restrictive than it currently is.

Another concern that may be raised concerns the different variable CSP measures. This issue needs to be examined in future theoretical and empirical work. We believe that CSP, like CFP, is a valid theoretical construct — admittedly a meta-construct — which can be measured in a variety of ways. Like Meyer and Gupta (1994), we see the possible independence of the operationalizations as a natural outcome of differences in organizational strategies, structures, and environments. Moreover, we share the view of many meta-analysts (for example, Cooper 1989; Dalton et al. 1999; Hunter and Schmidt 1990; Smith and Glass 1977) that broad constructs can, and should, be operationalized in a number of ways. As long as researchers' choices of CSP (and CFP) measures are informed by prior judgements of their theoretical meaningfulness and subjected to peer review, then relatively low correlations across measurement categories do not present an obstacle to research integration. More important to the present case, however, is that our review of CSP generalizability coefficients shows that different CSP measures are, in fact, rather highly correlated (average $r_{xx} = .71$; Appendix A). In other words, conceptual speculations about the impossibility of meaningful integration of prior research are not supported by empirical evidence (for a detailed review of this topic, cf. Orlitzky 1998).

Overall, we reach very different conclusions than Margolis and Walsh (2001). Although we agree with some of their more definitive conclusions as to a positive CSP–CFP relationship, we also argue that our data analysis shows that interesting questions remain. The research effort does not have to be abandoned because of poor theory or poor methods in this line of inquiry. We are particularly concerned with the conclusions of Margolis and Walsh (2001) because their criticism of *other* studies is argued from the vantage point of a method (the 'vote-counting' literature review) whose lack of validity has been known for more than 20 years (Hedges and Olkin 1980; Hunter and Schmidt 1990). First, they do not take into account sampling and measurement errors. Moreover, their review relies on a binary world-view, which holds that a relationship between CSP and CFP either exists (if results are statistically positive, or negative) or does not exist (if results are mixed or statistically non-significant, which they falsely call 'zero' effects (cf. Cohen 1990, 1994)). The relationship between business and society is too important theoretically to base our conclusions on methodologically ill-advised research reviews.

Implications for Managers

Despite previous assumptions of inconclusive findings (for example, Jones and Wicks 1999; McWilliams and Siegel 2001; Roman et al. 1999; Ullmann 1985; Wood and Jones 1995), we can legitimately derive implications for corporate strategy from the meta-analysis. First and foremost, market forces generally do not penalize companies that are high in corporate social performance; thus, managers can afford to be socially responsible. If managers believe that CSP is an antecedent of CFP, they may eventually actively pursue CSP because they think the market will reward them for doing so. Top managers must learn to use CSP as a reputational lever ($\rho = .73$) and be attentive to the perceptions of third parties, regardless of whether they are market analysts, public interest groups, or the media. Whereas social audits in and of themselves are only moderately beneficial ($\rho = .23$), a company that is high in CSP may especially benefit from receiving public endorsement from federal agencies such as the Environmental Protection Agency or Occupational Safety and Health Administration. As Fombrun (1996) suggested, the key to reaping benefits from CSP is a return from reputation (cf. also Roberts and Dowling 2002).

As findings about the positive relationships between CSP and CFP become more widely known, managers may be more likely to pursue CSP as part of their strategy for attaining high CFP. These strategic management considerations would be consistent with Baron's (2000) managerial approach to the business–society interface. Baron (2000) argues that successful executives are able to integrate market strategies with non-market strategies in order to position their firm for optimal effectiveness. Baron's (2000) book offers guidelines as to how firms can strategically achieve this integration in a number of areas (such as the news media, activists, social movements, legislatures, ethics, and so on). Alternatively, social performance may increase through less deliberate decision processes, as firms emulate others that are experiencing high financial success (DiMaggio and Powell 1983). Either evolutionary process would reduce the importance of coercive control mechanisms (in the form of government regulations) for effecting public welfare and ecological sustainability. If the mental models of managers and regulators moved to this more libertarian framework, the primary role of regulations would be their signalling function with respect to prioritizing certain issues and certain constituents' claims over others.

Conclusion

Theoretically, portraying managers' choices with respect to CSP and CFP as an either/or trade-off is not justified in light of 30 years of empirical data. This meta-analysis has shown that (1) across studies, CSP is positively correlated with CFP, (2) the relationship tends to be bidirectional and simultaneous, (3) reputation appears to be an important mediator of the relationship, and (4) stakeholder mismatching, sampling error, and measurement error can explain between 15 percent and 100 percent of the cross-study variation in various subsets of CSP–CFP correlations. Corporate virtue in the form of social and, to a lesser extent, environmental responsibility is rewarding in more ways than one.

Appendix A
Overview of Studies Included in Meta-Analysis

Author(s) (year)	N_i	Observed r^b	Number of r's reported	Measure of CSP	Measure of CFP	Reliability of CSP	CFP
Abbott and Monsen (1979)	6	.60 (t)	1	Beresford's Social Involvement Disclosure scale (D)	Avg. annual % return to investors	.58	.33
Alexander and Buchholz (1978)	41, 47	−.25 to .34	4	Reputational ratings (R)	Market return on security	.66	
Anderson and Frankle (1980)	14	−.44 to .87 (t)	18	Social responsibility disclosures, dichotomized (D)	Monthly stock returns, change in EPS, change dividends/share		
Aupperle et al. (1985)	166 to 228	−.04 (t) to .13	6	Carroll's Concern for Society (CSR1)	(LT and ST) ROA (some risk-adjusted)	.86	
Belkaoui (1976)	100	−.23 to .10 (t)	24	Pollution control expenditures in ARs (SA/P/O)	Excess market return of stock		
Blackburn el al. (1994)	88	−.01 to .30	3	1989 Ratings of Council On Economic Priorities (CEP) (SA/P/O)	RAO, excess market return, EPS		
Bowman (1976)				Criterion validity of CSR1 disclosures (CSR1)		.64	
Bowman (1978)	46	.19 (t)	1	Coding of ARs for CSR1 (D)	ROSBTA	.44	
Bowman and Haire (1975)	3	.30, .35 (t)	2	CSR1 in ARs, CEP Indexes (D)	ROE		
Bragdon and Martin (1972)	12	.22 to .69	15	3 CEP Indexes (SA/P/O)	EPS growth, ROE, ROC		
Brown and Perry (1994)				KLD scores and Fortune ratings (SA/P/O, R)		.34	
Brown and Perry (1995)	119 to 232	49 to 62	10	Fortune's rating of 'responsibility to the community/environment' (R)	Composite of (1) ROA, (2) market/book value, (3) log (sales), and (4) risk		
Chen and Metcalf (1980)	18	−.04, .21	2	CEP ratings (SA/P/O)	Profitability, P/E ratio	.93	
Cochran and Wood (1984)	6	.72 to .91 (t)	9	Moskowitz reputation index (R)	OE/Assets, OE/sales, excess market valuation		.63
Conine and Madden (1987)	163	.58 to .72	9	Erdos & Morgan's Corp. Reputation Survey (R)	Perceptual/expectational survey measures		

Study	Sample size	r	k	CSR1 measure	FP measure	
Cowen et al. (1987)	10 to 15	−.25 to .18	9	Number of various CSR1 disclosures (D)	ROE	
Davidson and Worrell (1992)	51	−.09 to .24 (t)	8	Voluntary (vs. government-ordered) product recall announcements (CSP in the face of adversity) (D)	Daily security returns (mean cumulative prediction error)	
Dooley and Lerner (1994)	86	.07 to .21	4	Stakeholder orientations/emphasis (CSR1)	Firm-specific ROA/Industry's avg. ROA	
Fogler and Nutt (1975)	9	−.27 to −.02 5	3	CEP Indexes (SA/P/O)	P/E ratio	.95
Fombrun and Shanley (1990)	154	.00 to .26	9	Charitable contributions, existing separately endowed foundation (yes/no), and favourability media ratings (SA/P/O, R)	ROIC, market-to-book value ratio, yield	.88
Freedman and Jaggi (1982)	109	−.04 to .01	7	AR/10K pollution disclosure index (D)	(Cash-basis) ROA and ROE, 2 operating ratios	.15, .37
Freedman and Jaggi (1986)	56	−.15 to .32 (t)	34	Extent of CSR1 disclosure (D)	Avg. standardized market return residuals	.38
Graves and Waddock (1994)	430	.03 to .15	2	Kinder, Lydenberg, Domini (KLD) measure (SA/P/O)	ROA, ROE	
Greening (1995)	131	.01 to .22	15	4 dimensions of electric utility demand-side management (DSM) programmes, CSP reputation (SA/P/O, R)	ROA, EPS, dividend yield	.24
Griffin and Mahon (1997)	7	−.59 to .51	13	Fortune rating, KLD score, Toxics Release Inventory (TRI, reverse-coded), philanthropy (R, SA/P/O)	ROS, ROE, ROA	.35, .73 .71
Hansen and Wernerfelt (1989)	60	.60	1	Emphasis on welfare of employees and good working conditions (survey) (CSR1)	ROA — T-bill (risk-free) rate	
Heinze (1976)	28	−.34 to .51	5	National Affiliation of Concerned Business Students (NACBS) ratings of social involvement (R)	Sales growth rate, ROS, OE/sales, ROA, ROE	
Herremans et al. (1993)	38	−.13 to .48	12	Fortune 'responsibility to the community/environment' rating (R)	Abnormal market returns	.71

Appendix A *continued*
Overview of Studies Included in Meta-Analysis

Author(s) (year)	N_i	Observed r^b	Number of r's reported	Measure of CSP	Measure of CFP	Reliability of CSP	CFP
Ingram (1978)	96, 120	−.01 to .06 (t)	12	CSR1 disclosures in 5 areas (D)	Avg. monthly portfolio returns		
Ingram and Frazier (1980)	40			CSR1	Disclosures and CEP ratings (D, SA/P/0)	.15	
Jacobson (1987)	4338, 4579				ROI, stock return		.14, .23, .27, .39
Kedia and Kuntz (1981)	27, 30	−.28 to .25	5	5 measures of actual CSP outcomes (SA/P/0)	ROA	.05	
Levy and Shatto (1980)	55	.69 to .74	3	Charitable contributions to different causes (SA/P/O)	Net income		
Long and Ravenscraft (1984)					Accounting rate of return and economic rate of return		.79, .89, .89
Marcus and Goodman (1986)	22, 27	Not included b/c F-statistics unclear		Compliance with air pollution regulation	ROA, ROE		
McGuire et al. (1988)	98, 131	−.21 to .52	18	Fortune 'responsibility to community/environment' ratings (R)	Return (alpha), ROA, sales, growth, asset growth, op. income growth	.90, .47	
Newgren et al. (1985)	50	.33(t)	1	'Institutionalization' of environmental assessment (SA/P/O)	Firm P/E ratio over industry P/E ratio		
O'Neill et al. (1989)	157	−.13 to .15	4	Aupperte's Concern for Society (CSRI)	LT, ST (risk-adjusted) ROA		
Parket and Eilbirt (1975)	3	.89 to 1.00 (t)	Not included for various reasons	Response vs. Non-response to social responsibility questionnaire	Net income, ROS, ROE, EPS		
Patten (1990)	74	−.10 to .25 (t)	7	Information disclosure w.r.t. Sullivan Principles (D)	Mean abnormal (unexpected) market returns		

Study	N	r	k	CSP measure	CFP measure	
Pava and Krausz (1995)	14	-.22 to .66 (t)	7	Dichotomization based on Council on Economic Priorities rankings (SA/P/O)	Market return, P/E ratio, market-to-book value, ROA, ROE, EPS, dividend payout ratio	
Preston (1978b)	3	.50 (t)	1	Social involvement reporting (D)	Market rate of return on stock	
Reimann (1975)	19	.00 to .69	8	Osgood's semantic differential measure of public values (CSRI)	Survey goal achievement rating in comparison to other organizations	.39
Riahi-Belkaoui (1991)	139	Not included		Fortune's 'responsibility to community/environment' measure (R)	10-years' EPS growth, P/E ratio	
Roberts (1992)	130	.16, .20	2	CEP measure of social disclosure, philanthropic foundation? (Y/N) (SA/P/O)	ROA, firm growth	
Russo and Fouts (1997)	486	.13, .16	2	Franklin Research and Development corp. environmental performance ratings (SA/P/O)	ROA, firm growth	
Shane and Spicer (1983)	48	-.74 to .96 (t)	24	Dichotomized pollution-control performance index (SA/P/O)	Abnormal mean-adjusted returns	
Sharfman (1996)	varies			KLD scores, Fortune ratings, and 'social choice' mutual fund holdings (SA/P/O, R)		.33, .47
Simerly (1994)	110	.01 to .88 (t)	14	Fortune reputation scores, dichotomized (R)	EPS, share price, market value, ROE, sales/equity, ROI, sales rate	
Simerly (1995)	48	.59 (t)	1	Dichotomized Fortune survey measure (R)	ROE	
Spencer and Taylor (1987)	107, 120	-.06 to .54	20	Fortune 'responsibility to community/environment' (R)	ROA, ROS	
Spicer (1978)	18	.42, .52	2	Council on Economic Priorities report (SA/P/O)	ROE	.93
Starik (1990)	193	-.02, .14	2	7 stakeholder management strategies (survey), combined (SA/P/O)	ROI, change in revenues	.85
Sturdivant and Ginter	18, 22	.58, .72 (t)	2	Moskowitz ratings (R)	EPS growth relative to industry	

Appendix A *continued*
Overview of Studies Included in Meta-Analysis

Author(s) (year)	N_i	Observed r^b	Number of r's reported	Measure of CSP	Measure of CFP	Reliability of CSP	CFP
Turban and Greening (1997)	160	−.07 to .25	6	KLD ratings (5 dimensions), reputation (SA/P/O, R)	Profitability (ROA)	.23	.18
Vance (1975)	14, 45, 50	−.51 to −.20	3	Survey ratings, Moskowitz rankings (reverse-coded) (R)	Change in share price	.70	.66
Venkatraman and Ramanujam (1987)	86				Primary/perceptual measures of sales growth, net income growth, and ROI compared to objective secondary measures relative to industry		.36, .44, .42, .51
Waddock and Graves (1997)	469	.08 to .17	6	8 KLD dimensions (SA/P/O)	ROA, ROE, ROS		.57
Wartick (1988)	230	.05 to .10 (t)	3	Use of issues management (SA/P/O)	Survey ratings: LT investment value, soundness of financial position, and wise use of corporation assets	.75	
Wiseman (1982)	26			Social disclosures and CEP pollution audit rankings (D, SA/P/O)		.15	.37
Wokutch and Spencer (1987)	4, 8	.80 to .84 (t)	3	Philanthropy/sales and crimes: 4 cell classification (SA/P/O)	ROA, ROS	.64	
Wolfe (1991)	9 corps.			CSRI disclosures (inter-rater and test-retest rel., cnt. validity) (D)		.87, .99, .69	

[a] Classification of CSP (in parentheses): D = disclosures/content analysis; R = reputational indices; SA/P/O = social audit, process and outcome measures; CSR1 = Aupperle's and others' measures of corporate principles and values.
[b] (t): refers to transformation procedure, usually t-test statistic converted to PM r; in some cases, transformation of d to r.

Note

This article is based on Marc Orlitzky's 1998 dissertation thesis. The authors would like to thank Lex Donaldson, Steve Frenkel, Peter Hansen, David Jacobs, Barry Markovsky, Jim Price, and Jerry Rose for many helpful comments on earlier drafts.

References

References marked with an asterisk indicate studies included in the meta-analysis.

* Abbott, Walter F., and Joseph R. Monsen
1979 'On the measurement of corporate social responsibility: Self-reported disclosure as a method of measuring corporate social involvement'. *Academy of Management Journal* 22: 501–515.

Aldag, Ramon J., and Kathryn M. Bartol
1978 'Empirical studies of corporate social performance and policy: A survey of problems and results' in *Research in corporate social performance and policy*. Lee E. Preston (ed.), 1, 165–199. Greenwich, CT: JAI Press.

* Alexander, Gordon J., and Rogene A. Buchholz
1978 'Corporate social performance and stock market performance'. *Academy of Management Journal* 21: 479–486.

Amburgey, T. L., and T. Dacin
1994 'As the left foot follows the right? The dynamics of strategic and structural change'. *Academy of Management Journal* 37: 1427–1452.

* Anderson, John C., and Alan W. Frankle
1980 'Voluntary social reporting: An iso-beta portfolio analysis'. *Accounting Review* 55: 467–479.

Andrews, K. R.
1987 *The concept of corporate strategy*, 3rd edn. Homewood, IL: Irwin.

Aupperle, Kenneth E.
1984 'An empirical measure of corporate social orientation' in *Research in corporate social performance and policy*. Lee E. Preston (ed.), 6, 27–54. Greenwich, CT: JAI Press.

Aupperle, Kenneth E.
1991 'The use of forced-choice survey procedures in assessing corporate social orientation' in *Research in corporate social performance and policy*. James E. Post (ed.), 12, 269–279. Greenwich, CT: JAI Press.

* Aupperle, Kenneth E., Archie B. Carroll, and John D. Hatfield
1985 'An empirical investigation of the relationship between corporate social responsibility and profitability'. *Academy of Management Journal* 28: 446–463.

Barney, Jay
1991 'Firm resources and sustained competitive advantage'. *Journal of Management* 17: 771–792.

Baron, D. P.
2000 *Business and its environment*, 3rd edn. Upper Saddle River, NJ: Prentice Hall.

* Belkaoui, Ahmed
1976 'The impact of the disclosure of the environmental effects of organizational behavior on the market'. *Financial Management* 5: 26–31.

* Blackburn, V. L., M. Doran, and C. B. Shrader
1994 'Investigating the dimensions of social responsibility and the consequences for corporate financial performance'. *Journal of Managerial Issues* 6: 195–212.

* Bowman, Edward H.
1976 'Strategy and the weather'. *Sloan Management Review* 17: 49–58.

* Bowman, Edward H.
1978 'Strategy, annual reports, and alchemy'. *California Management Review* 20: 64–71.

* Bowman, Edward H., and Mason Haire
1975 'A strategic posture toward corporate social responsibility'. *California Management Review* 18: 49–58.

* Bragdon, Joseph H., Jr., and John A. T. Marlin
1972   'Is pollution profitable?' *Risk Management* 19: 9–18.

* Brown, Brad, and Susan Perry
1994   'Removing the financial performance halo from *Fortune*'s "Most Admired Companies"'. *Academy of Management Journal* 37: 1346–1359.

* Brown, Brad, and Susan Perry
1995   'Halo-removed residuals of *Fortune*'s "responsibility to the community and environment": A decade of data'. *Business & Society* 34: 199–215.

Business Week
1999   'The next bottom line', Asian edn, 3 May: 45–96.

Carroll, Archie B.
1979   'A three-dimensional conceptual model of corporate social performance'. *Academy of Management Review* 4: 497–506.

Carroll, Archie B.
1991   'Corporate social performance measurement: A commentary on methods for evaluating an elusive construct' in *Research in corporate social performance and policy*. James E. Post (ed.), 12, 385–401. Greenwich, CT: JAI Press.

* Chen, Kung H., and Richard W. Metcalf
1980   'The relationship between pollution control record and financial indicators revisited'. *Accounting Review* 55: 168–177.

Clarkson, Max B. E.
1991   'Defining, evaluating, and managing corporate social performance: The stakeholder management model' in *Research in corporate social performance and policy*. James E. Post (ed.), 12, 331–358. Greenwich, CT: JAI Press.

Clarkson, Max B. E.
1995   'A stakeholder framework for analyzing and evaluating corporate social performance'. *Academy of Management Review* 20: 92–117.

* Cochran, Phillip L., and Robert A. Wood
1984   'Corporate social responsibility and financial performance'. *Academy of Management Journal* 27: 42–56.

Cohen, J.
1990   'Things I have learned (so far)'. *American Psychologist* 45: 1304–1312.

Cohen, J.
1994   'The Earth is round ($p < .05$)'. *American Psychologist* 49: 997–1003.

* Conine, Thomas E., and Gerald P. Madden
1987   'Corporate social responsibility and investment value: The expectational relationship' in *Handbook of business strategy 1986/1987 yearbook*. W. D. Guth (ed.), 18–1 to 18–9. Boston, MA: Warren, Gorham, & Lamont.

Cook, Thomas D., and Donald T. Campbell
1979   *Quasi-experimentation: Design & analysis issues for field settings.* Boston, MA: Houghton Mifflin.

Cooper, Harris M.
1989   *Integrating research: A guide for literature reviews*, 2nd edn. Newbury Park, CA: Sage.

Cornell, Bradford, and Alan Shapiro
1987   'Corporate stakeholders and corporate finance'. *Financial Management* 16: 5–14.

* Cowen, Scott S., Linda B. Ferreri and Lee D. Parker
1987   'The impact of corporate characteristics on social responsibility disclosure: A typology and frequency-based analysis'. *Accounting, Organizations and Society* 12: 111–122.

Cronbach, Lee J., Goldine C. Gleser, Harinder Nanda, and Nageswari Rajaratnam
1972   *The dependability of behavioral measurements: Theory of generalizability of scores and profiles.* New York: Wiley.

Dalton, D. R., C. M. Daily, J. L. Johnson, and A. E. Ellstrand
1999   'Number of directors and financial performance: A meta-analysis'. *Academy of Management Journal* 42: 674–686.

Damanpour, Fariborz
1991   'Organizational innovation: A meta-analysis of effects of determinants and moderators'. *Academy of Management Journal* 34: 555–590.

Datta, Deepak K., George E. Pinches, and V. K. Narayanan
1992   'Factors influencing wealth creation from mergers and acquisitions: A meta-analysis'. *Strategic Management Journal* 13: 67–84.

* Davidson, Wallace N. III, and Dan L. Worrell
1992   'Research notes and communications: The effect of product recall announcements on shareholder wealth'. *Strategic Management Journal* 13: 467–473.

Davis, Keith
1973   'The case for and against business assumptions of social responsibilities'. *Academy of Management Journal* 16: 312–317.

DiMaggio, Paul J., and Walter W. Powell
1983   'The iron cage revisited: Institutional isomorphism and collective rationality in organizational fields'. *American Sociological Review* 48: 147–160.

Donaldson, Lex
1987   'Strategy and structural adjustment to regain fit and performance: In defense of contingency theory'. *Journal of Management Studies* 24: 1–24.

Donaldson, Thomas
1999   'Response: Making stakeholder theory whole'. *Academy of Management Review* 24: 237–241.

Donaldson, Thomas, and Lee E. Preston
1995   'The stakeholder theory of the corporation: Concepts, evidence, and implications'. *Academy of Management Review* 20: 65–91.

* Dooley, Robert S., and Linda D. Lerner
1994   'Pollution, profits, and stakeholders: The constraining effect of economic performance on CEO concern with stakeholder expectations'. *Journal of Business Ethics* 13: 701–711.

* Fogler, H. Russell, and Fred Nutt
1975   'A note on social responsibility and stock valuation'. *Academy of Management Journal* 18: 155–160.

Fombrun, Charles J.
1996   *Reputation: Realizing value from the corporate image.* Boston, MA: Harvard Business School Press.

* Fombrun, Charles, and Mark Shanley
1990   'What's in a name? Reputation building and corporate strategy'. *Academy of Management Journal* 33: 233–258.

* Freedman, Martin, and Bikki Jaggi
1982   'Pollution disclosures, pollution performance and economic performance'. *Omega: The International Journal of Management Science* 10: 167–176.

* Freedman, Martin, and Bikki Jaggi
1986   'An analysis of the impact of corporate pollution disclosures included in annual financial statements on investors' decisions'. *Advances in Public Interest Accounting* 1: 192–212.

Freeman, R. Edward
1984   *Strategic management: A stakeholder approach.* Marshfield, MA: Pitman.

Freeman, R. Edward, and William M. Evan
1990   'Corporate governance: A stakeholder interpretation'. *Journal of Behavioral Economics* 19/4: 337–359.

Friedman, Milton
1970   'The social responsibility of business is to increase its profits'. *New York Times Magazine,* 13 September: 33ff.

Frooman, Jeff
1997   'Socially irresponsible and illegal behavior and shareholder wealth: A meta-analysis of event studies'. *Business & Society* 36: 221–249.

Gephardt, Richard P., Jr.
1991   'Multiple methods for tracking corporate social performance: Insights from a study of major industrial accidents' in *Research in corporate social performance and policy.* James E. Post (ed.), 12, 359–383. Greenwich, CT: JAI Press.

Gooding, Richard Z., and John A. Wagner, III
1985 'A meta-analytic review of the relationship between size and performance: The productivity and efficiency of organizations and their subunits'. *Administrative Science Quarterly* 30: 462–481.

* Graves, Samuel B., and Sandra A. Waddock
1994 'Institutional owners and corporate social performance'. *Academy of Management Journal* 37: 1034–1046.

* Greening, Daniel W.
1995 'Conservation strategies, firm performance, and corporate reputation in the U.S. electric utility industry' in *Research in Corporate Social Performance and Policy, Supplement 1*, 345–368. Greenwich, CT: JAI Press.

Greening, D. W., and D. B. Turban
2000 'Corporate social performance as a competitive advantage in attracting a quality workforce'. *Business & Society* 39: 254–280.

* Griffin, Jennifer J., and John F. Mahon
1997 'The corporate social performance and corporate financial performance debate: Twenty-five years of incomparable research'. *Business & Society* 36: 5–31.

* Hansen, Gary S., and Birger Wernerfelt
1989 'Determinants of firm performance: The relative importance of economic and organizational factors'. *Strategic Management Journal* 10: 399–411.

Hart, Stuart L.
1995 'A natural resource-based view of the firm'. *Academy of Management Review* 20: 986–1014.

Hedges, Larry V.
1987 'How hard is hard science, how soft is soft science? The empirical cumulativeness of research'. *American Psychologist* 42/2: 443–455.

Hedges, Larry V., and Ingram Olkin
1980 'Vote counting methods in research synthesis'. *Psychological Bulletin* 88: 359–369.

* Heinze, David C.
1976 'Financial correlates of a social involvement measure'. *Akron Business and Economic Review* 7: 48–51.

* Herremans, Irene M., Parporn Akathaporn and Morris McInnes
1993 'An investigation of corporate social responsibility reputation and economic performance'. *Accounting, Organizations and Society* 18: 587–604.

Hill, Charles W. L., and Thomas M. Jones
1992 'Stakeholder-agency theory'. *Journal of Management Studies* 29: 131–154.

Hunt, Morton
1997 *How science takes stock: The story of meta-analysis*. New York: Russell Sage Foundation.

Hunter, John E., and Frank L. Schmidt
1990 *Methods of meta-analysis: Correcting errors and bias in research findings*. Newbury Park, CA: Sage.

Husted, Brian W.
2000 'A contingency theory of corporate social performance'. *Business & Society* 39: 24–48.

* Ingram, Robert W.
1978 'An investigation of the information content of (certain) social responsibility disclosures'. *Journal of Accounting Research* 16: 270–285.

* Ingram, Robert W., and Katherine B. Frazier
1980 'Environmental performance and corporate disclosure'. *Journal of Accounting Research* 18: 614–622.

* Jacobson, Robert
1987 'The validity of ROI as a measure of business performance'. *American Economic Review* 77: 470–478.

Jones, Thomas M.
1995 'Instrumental stakeholder theory: A synthesis of ethics and economics'. *Academy of Management Review* 20: 404–437.

Jones, Thomas M., and Andrew C. Wicks
1999 'Convergent stakeholder theory'. *Academy of Management Review* 24: 206–221.

Judge, W. Q., Jr.
1994   'Correlates of organizational
       effectiveness: A multilevel analysis
       of a multidimensional outcome'.
       Journal of Business Ethics 13: 1–10.

* Kedia, B. L., and E. C. Kuntz
1981   'The context of social performance:
       An empirical study of Texas banks'
       in *Research in corporate social
       performance and policy*. Lee E.
       Preston (ed.), 3, 133–154.
       Greenwich, CT: JAI Press.

Ketchen, David J., Jr., James G. Combs,
Craig J. Russell, Chris Shook, et al.
1997   'Organizational configurations and
       performance'. *Academy of
       Management Journal* 40: 223–240.

Levitt, T.
1958   'The dangers of social
       responsibility'. *Harvard Business
       Review*, September–October, 36:
       38–44.

* Levy, F. K., and G. M. Shatto
1980   'Social responsibility in large
       electric utility firms: The case for
       philanthropy' in *Research in
       corporate social performance and
       policy*. Lee E. Preston (ed.), 2,
       237–249. Greenwich, CT: JAI
       Press.

Light, R. J., and P. V. Smith
1971   'Accumulating evidence:
       Procedures for resolving
       contradictions among different
       research studies'. *Harvard
       Educational Review* 41: 429–471.

* Long, William F., and David J.
Ravenscraft
1984   'The misuse of accounting rates of
       return: Comment'. *American
       Economic Review* 74: 494–501.

McGuire, J. B., T. Schneeweis, and B.
Branch
1990   'Perceptions of firm quality: A
       cause or result of firm
       performance'. *Journal of
       Management* 16: 167–180.

* McGuire, J. B., Alison Sundgren, and
Thomas Schneeweis
1988   'Corporate social responsibility and
       firm financial performance'.
       Academy of Management Journal
       31: 854–872.

McWilliams, A., and D. Siegel
2000   'Corporate social responsibility and
       financial performance: Correlation
       or misspecification?' *Strategic
       Management Journal* 21: 603–609.

McWilliams, A., and D. Siegel
2001   'Corporate social responsibility: A
       theory of the firm perspective'.
       Academy of Management Review
       26: 117–127.

Majumdar, Sumit K., and Alfred A.
Marcus
2001   'Rules versus discretion: The
       productivity consequences of
       flexible regulations'. *Academy of
       Management Journal* 44: 170–179.

* Marcus, Alfred A., and Richard S.
Goodman
1986   'Compliance and performance:
       Toward a contingency theory' in
       *Research in corporate social
       performance and policy*. Lee E.
       Preston (ed.), 8, 193–221.
       Greenwich, CT: JAI Press.

Margolis, J. D., and J. P. Walsh
2001   *People and profits? The search for
       a link between a company's social
       and financial performance*.
       Mahwah, NJ: Erlbaum.

Meyer, Marshall W., and Vipin Gupta
1994   'The performance paradox'.
       *Research in Organizational
       Behavior* 16: 309–369.

Mitchell, Ronald K., Bradley R. Agle, and
Donna J. Wood
1997   'Toward a theory of stakeholder
       identification and salience: Defining
       the principle of who and what really
       counts'. *Academy of Management
       Review* 22: 853–886.

Moskowitz, Milton R.
1972   'Choosing socially responsible
       stocks'. *Business and Society
       Review* 1: 71–75.

Moskowitz, Milton R.
1975   'Profiles in corporate social
       responsibility'. *Business and
       Society Review* 13: 29–42.

* Newgren, K. E., A. A. Rasher, M. E. LaRoe, and M. R. Szabo
1985   'Environmental assessment and corporate performance: A longitudinal analysis using a market-determined performance measure' in *Research in corporate social performance and policy*. Lee E. Preston (ed.), 7, 153–164. Greenwich, CT: JAI Press.

Nunnally, Jum C., and Ira H. Bernstein
1994   *Psychometric theory*, 3rd edn. New York: McGraw-Hill.

* O'Neill, Hugh M., Charles B. Saunders, and Anne D. McCarthy
1989   'Board members, corporate social responsiveness and profitability: Are tradeoffs necessary?' *Journal of Business Ethics* 8: 353–357.

Orlitzky, Marc
1998   'A meta-analysis of the relationship between corporate social performance and firm financial performance', dissertation thesis. University of Iowa, UMI.

* Parket, I. Robert, and Henry Eilbirt
1975   'Social responsibility: The underlying factors'. *Business Horizons* 18: 5–10.

* Patten, Dennis M.
1990   'The market reaction to social responsibility disclosures: The case of the Sullivan Principles signings'. *Accounting, Organizations and Society* 15: 575–587.

* Pava, Moses L., and Joshua Krausz
1995   *Corporate responsibility and financial performance: The paradox of social cost*. Westport, CT: Quorum.

Post, James E. (ed.)
1991   *Research in corporate social performance and policy*, Vol. 12. Greenwich, CT: JAI Press.

Preston, Lee E.
1978a 'Corporate social performance and policy: A synthetic framework for research and analysis' in *Research in corporate social performance and policy*. Lee E. Preston (ed.), 1, 1–25. Greenwich, CT: JAI Press.

* Preston, Lee E.
1978b 'Analyzing corporate social performance: Methods and results'. *Journal of Contemporary Business* 7: 135–150.

Price, James L., and Charles W. Mueller
1986   *Handbook of organizational measurement*, 2nd edn. Marshfield, MA: Pitman.

* Reimann, Bernard C.
1975   'Organizational effectiveness and management's public values: A canonical analysis'. *Academy of Management Journal* 18: 224–241.

* Riahi-Belkaoui, Ahmed
1991   'Organizational effectiveness, social performance and economic performance' in *Research in corporate social performance and policy*. James E. Post (ed.), 12, 143–153. Greenwich, CT: JAI Press.

Roberts, Peter W., and Grahame R. Dowling
2002   'Corporate reputation and sustained superior financial performance'. *Strategic Management Journal* 23: 1077–1093.

* Roberts, Robin W.
1992   Determinants of corporate social responsibility disclosure: An application of stakeholder theory'. *Accounting, Organizations and Society* 17: 595–612.

Roman, R. M., S. Hayibor, and B. R. Agle
1999   'The relationship between social and financial performance: Repainting a portrait'. *Business & Society* 38: 109–125.

Rosenthal, Robert
1995   'Writing meta-analytic reviews'. *Psychological Bulletin* 118: 183–192.

Rosenthal, R., and DiMatteo, M. R.
2001   'Meta-analysis: Recent developments in quantitative methods for literature reviews'. *Annual Review of Psychology* 52: 59–82.

Roth, Philip L., Craig A. BeVier, Fred S. Switzer, III., and Jeffrey S. Schippmann
1996   'Meta-analyzing the relationship between grades and job performance'. *Journal of Applied Psychology* 81: 548–557.

Rowley, Timothy J.
1997 'Moving beyond dyadic ties: A
      network theory of stakeholder
      influences'. *Academy of
      Management Review* 22: 887–910.

Rowley, Timothy J., and Shawn Berman
2000 'A brand new brand of corporate
      social performance'. *Business &
      Society* 39: 397–418.

* Russo, Michael V., and Paul A. Fouts
1997 'A resource-based perspective on
      corporate environmental
      performance and profitability'.
      Academy of Management Journal
      40: 534–559.

Schmidt, Frank L.
1992 'What do data really mean?
      Research findings, meta-analysis,
      and cumulative knowledge in
      psychology'. *American
      Psychologist* 47: 1173–1181.

Schmidt, Frank L., and John E. Hunter
1977 'Development of a general solution
      to the problem of validity
      generalization'. *Journal of Applied
      Psychology* 62: 529–540.

Schwenk, Charles
1989 'A meta-analysis on the
      comparative effectiveness of devil's
      advocacy and dialectical inquiry'.
      Strategic Management Journal 10:
      303–306.

* Shane, Phillip B., and Barry H. Spicer
1983 'Market response to environmental
      information produced outside the
      firm'. *Accounting Review* 58:
      521–538.

* Sharfman, Mark
1996 'A concurrent validity study of the
      KLD social performance ratings
      data'. *Journal of Business Ethics*
      15: 287–296.

Shavelson, Richard J., Noreen M. Webb,
and Glenn L. Rowley
1989 'Generalizability theory'. *American
      Psychologist* 44: 922–932.

Shrivastava, Paul
1995 'Ecocentric management for a risk
      society'. *Academy of Management
      Review* 20: 118–137.

* Simerly, Roy L.
1994 'Corporate social performance and
      firms' financial performance: An
      alternative perspective'.
      Psychological Reports 75:
      1091–1103.

* Simerly, Roy L.
1995 'Institutional ownership, corporate
      social performance, and firms'
      financial performance'.
      Psychological Reports 77: 515–525.

Smith, M. L., and G. V. Glass
1977 'Meta-analysis of psychotherapy
      outcome studies'. *American
      Psychologist* 32: 752–760.

* Spencer, Barbara A., and Stephen G.
Taylor
1987 'A within and between analysis of
      the relationship between corporate
      social responsibility and financial
      performance'. *Akron Business and
      Economic Review* 18: 7–18.

* Spicer, Barry H.
1978 'Investors, corporate social
      performance and information
      disclosure: An empirical study'.
      Accounting Review 53: 94–111.

* Starik, Mark
1990 'Stakeholder management and firm
      performance: Reputation and
      financial relationships to U.S. electric
      utility consumer-related strategies',
      unpublished doctoral dissertation.
      University of Georgia, Athens.

Starik, Mark
1995 'Should trees have managerial
      standing? Toward stakeholder status
      for non-human nature'. *Journal of
      Business Ethics* 14: 207–217.

* Sturdivant, Frederick D., and James L.
Ginter
1977 'Corporate social responsiveness:
      Management attitudes and
      economic performance'. *California
      Management Review* 19: 30–39.

Traub, Ross E.
1994 *Reliability for the social sciences:
      Theory and applications*, Vol. 3.
      Thousand Oaks, CA: Sage.

* Turban, Daniel B., and Daniel W. Greening
1997 'Corporate social performance and organizational attractiveness to prospective employees'. *Academy of Management Journal* 40: 658–672.

Ullmann, Arieh
1985 'Data in search of a theory: A critical examination of the relationship among social performance, social disclosure, and economic performance'. *Academy of Management Review* 10: 540–577.

* Vance, Stanley
1975 'Are socially responsible firms good investment risks?' *Management Review* 64: 18–24.

Venkatraman, N., and Vasudevan Ramanujam
1986 'Measurement of business performance in strategy research: A comparison of approaches'. *Academy of Management Review* 11: 801–814.

* Venkatraman, N., and Vasudevan Ramanujam
1987 'Measurement of business economic performance: An examination of method convergence'. *Journal of Management* 13: 109–122.

* Waddock, Sandra A., and Samuel B. Graves
1997 'The corporate social performance–financial performance link'. *Strategic Management Journal* 18: 303–319.

Waddock, Sandra A., and John F. Mahon
1991 'Corporate social performance revisited: Dimensions of efficacy, effectiveness, and efficiency' in *Research in corporate social performance and policy*. James E. Post (ed.), 12, 231–262). Greenwich, CT: JAI Press.

Wagner, John A., II., and Richard Z. Gooding
1987 'Effects of societal trends on participation research'. *Administrative Science Quarterly* 32: 241–262.

* Wartick, Stephen L.
1988 'How issues management contributes to corporate performance'. *Business Forum* 13: 16–22.

Wartick, Stephen L., and Phillip L. Cochran
1985 'The evolution of the corporate social performance model'. *Academy of Management Review* 10: 758–769.

Webb, Eugene J., D. Campbell, R. Schwartz, L. Sechrest, and J. Grove
1981 *Nonreactive measures in the social sciences*. Boston, MA: Houghton Mifflin.

Wernerfelt, Birger
1984 'A resource-based view of the firm'. *Strategic Management Journal* 5: 171–180.

Wholey, D. R., and J. W. Brittain
1986 'Organizational ecology: Findings and implications'. *Academy of Management Review* 11: 513–533.

Willums, Jan-Olaf
1999 'Social responsibility and shareholder value'. *Business Week* (Asian Edition), 3 May: 85.

* Wiseman, Joanne
1982 'An evaluation of environmental disclosures made in corporate annual reports'. *Accounting, Organizations and Society* 7: 53–63.

Wokutch, Richard E., and E. W. McKinney
1991 'Behavioral and perceptual measures of corporate social performance' in *Research in corporate social performance and policy*. James E. Post (ed.), 12, 309–330. Greenwich, CT: JAI Press.

* Wokutch, Richard E., and Barbara A. Spencer
1987 'Corporate sinners and saints: The effects of philanthropic and illegal activity on organizational performance'. *California Management Review* 29: 62–77.

* Wolfe, Robert
1991 'The use of content analysis to assess corporate social responsibility' in *Research in corporate social performance and policy*. James E. Post (ed.), 12, 281–307. Greenwich, CT: JAI Press.

Wolfe, Robert, and Kenneth E. Aupperle
1991 'Introduction' in *Research in corporate social performance and policy*. James E. Post (ed.), 12, 265–268. Greenwich, CT: JAI Press.

Wood, Donna J.
1991a 'Corporate social performance revisited'. *Academy of Management Review* 16: 691–718.

Wood, Donna J.
1991b 'Social issues in management: Theory and research in corporate social performance'. *Journal of Management* 17: 383–406.

Wood, Donna J.
1995 'The *Fortune* database as a CSP measure'. *Business & Society* 34: 197–198.

Wood, Donna J., and Raymond E. Jones
1995 'Stakeholder mismatching: A theoretical problem in empirical research on corporate social performance'. *International Journal of Organizational Analysis* 3: 229–267.

Marc Orlitzky   Marc Orlitzky (Ph.D., University of Iowa) is Lecturer at the Australian Graduate School of Management (AGSM), which is jointly owned by the University of Sydney and the University of New South Wales. His work focuses on business ethics, human resource management, and small-group communication. Since 1997, his research has been accepted by publication outlets such as *Business & Society, Journal of Business Ethics, Research in Corporate Social Performance and Policy, Personnel Psychology, Trends in Organizational Behavior, Small Group Research, Academy of Management Review*, and *Journal of Personal & Interpersonal Loss*.
Address: AGSM, UNSW Sydney NSW 2052, Australia.
E-mail: marco@agsm.edu.au.

Frank L. Schmidt   Frank L. Schmidt (Ph.D., Purdue University) is Ralph L. Sheets Professor of Management & Organizations at the University of Iowa's Henry B. Tippie College of Business. He has authored numerous articles, book chapters, and books on meta-analysis, personnel selection, employment testing, workforce productivity, and decision theory. He is a Fellow of the American Psychological Association and a Charter Fellow of the American Psychological Society, and serves on the editorial boards of *Journal of Applied Psychology* and *Quantitative Series in the Social Sciences*.
Address: Department of Management & Organizations, W252 PBAB, University of Iowa, Iowa City, IA 52242-1000, USA.
E-mail: fschmidt@blue.weeg.uiowa.edu

Sara L. Rynes   Sara L. Rynes (Ph.D., University of Wisconsin) is John F. Murray Professor of Management & Organizations at the University of Iowa's Henry B. Tippie College of Business. She has authored more than 45 articles and book chapters on human resource strategy, recruitment and selection, careers, compensation, training, diversity, and quality management. She is a Fellow of the American Psychological Association and the Society for Industrial and Organizational Psychology, and serves on the editorial boards of *Academy of Management Journal, Journal of Applied Psychology, Personnel Psychology*, and *Frontiers in Industrial and Organizational Psychology*.
Address: Department of Management & Organizations, W252 PBAB, University of Iowa, Iowa City, IA 52242-1000, USA.
E-mail: Sara-Rynes@uiowa.edu

[55]

The Link Between Corporate Social and Financial Performance: Evidence from the Banking Industry

W. Gary Simpson
Theodor Kohers

ABSTRACT. The purpose of this investigation is to extend earlier research on the relationship between corporate social and financial performance. The unique contribution of the study is the empirical analysis of a sample of companies from the banking industry and the use of Community Reinvestment Act ratings as a social performance measure. The empirical analysis solidly supports the hypothesis that the link between social and financial performance is positive.

KEY WORDS: Community Reinvestment Act Rating, financial performance, social performance

Introduction

Attempts to scientifically examine the nature of the relationship between corporate social performance (CSP) and financial performance (FP) have established that the relationship is complex and the investigation process is theoretically and methodologically intractable (Carroll, 2000; Griffin and Mahon, 1997; Rowley and Berman, 2000). Nevertheless, a better understanding of the link between corporate social performance and financial performance (CSP-FP) would be invaluable to managers, stockholders, and, either directly or indirectly, all of the stakeholders of a corporation. Many important questions that must be answered by the stakeholders of a corporation will be affected by the nature of the CSP-FP link. For example, what resources should managers direct to socially responsible activities? How should stockholders react to resource allocations for social purposes? How can public policy best promote socially responsible

behavior? These are only a few obvious examples of the issues that are related to the CSP-FP link.

The purpose of this investigation is to extend earlier research on the relationship between corporate social and financial performance. A reasonable person might question the need for additional investigation because a rich body of evidence already exists on this topic.[1] However, previous evidence has resulted in contradictory conclusions, although a growing number of analyses indicate a positive link. Furthermore, almost all of the previous evidence was derived from samples composed of firms from multiple industries (Griffin and Mahon, 1997). Finally, various measurement issues that plague this type of research have not been resolved. This investigation is believed to make a contribution to the debate by providing empirical evidence from a single industry that has a set of unique characteristics that offer additional insights into the question and also mitigate some of the measurement problems of earlier research.

Previous empirical evidence on the CSP–FP Link

Griffin and Mahon (1997) provide a summary of the empirical evidence on the CSP-FP link that spans the twenty-five year time period 1972 until 1997. In one of the earliest papers cited by Griffin and Mahon (1997), Bragdon and Marlin (1972) asked the straightforward, but important question "Is pollution profitable?" Early empirical investigations by Vance (1975), Belkaoui

(1976), and Alexander and Bucholz (1978) tested the relationship between stock market returns and a dimension of corporate social performance. Pioneering empiricists who investigated the CSP-FP link were often interested in a single dimension of CSP, e.g. environmental pollution. Over the twenty-five year period since empirical investigation of the CSP-FP link began, many innovations in methodology were introduced. Researchers conducted cross-sectional studies over multiple industries with accounting data from large corporations as the measure of financial performance (Griffin and Mahon, 1997). The measurement of CSP moved from single dimension measures to multidimensional measures like the *Fortune* Survey of Corporate Reputation and the KLD index developed by Kinder, Lydenberg, Domini & Co., Inc. (Griffin and Mahon, 1997). Questions about the efficacy of empirical research on the CSP-FP link remain despite numerous improvements in the methodology (Griffin and Mahon, 1997; Carroll, 2000).

Griffin and Mahon (1997) summarized the findings of the numerous articles they reviewed and came to the following conclusions: (1) No definitive consensus exists on the empirical CSP-FP link, (2) While a substantial number of studies have found a negative relationship, most of these studies compared the reaction of the stock market to potential illegal activities or product problems, (3) Some studies have been inconclusive because they found both a positive and negative link in the same study, and (4) The largest number of investigations found a positive CSP-FP link. Roman et al. (1999) reviewed the work of Griffin and Mahon (1997) and concluded that the preponderance of the evidence indicated a positive relationship between CSP and FP because Griffin and Mahon (1997) included many flawed investigations that found a negative CSP-FP link.

Several empirical investigations since the review article by Griffin and Mahon (1997) have found a positive CSP-FP link. Frooman (1997) conducted a meta-analysis of 27 event studies that analyzed the relationship between stock market reaction and socially irresponsible and illegal behavior. He concluded that the market reacted negatively to firms that committed socially irre-

sponsible or illegal acts, which is evidence for a positive CSP-FP link. Waddock and Graves (1997) analyzed a total of 469 S & P 500 companies with regression analysis. A weighted composite measure of CSP similar to a KLD index was used for CSP and three accounting measures (return on equity, return on assets, and return on sales) were used for FP. Waddock and Graves (1997) included size, risk, and industry as control variables and tested various econometric specifications of the model including lagged variables. Their results supported a positive CSP-FP link. Stanwick and Stanwick (1998) conducted a regression analysis of multiple cross-sections for the years 1987–1992 with approximately 115 firms in each cross-section. They used the *Fortune* Survey of Corporate Reputation as the measure of CSP which was the dependent variable in a regression equation. The return on sales, size, and environmental performance variable based on the EPA Toxic Release Inventory Report were used as independent variables. Stanwick and Stanwick (1998) found a significant positive relationship between CSP and FP. Preston and O'Bannon (1997) compared CSP and FP for 67 large U.S. corporations over the eleven-year period 1982–1992. They used three components of the *Fortune* Survey of Corporate Reputation to represent CSP and return on assets, return on equity, and return on investment to represent FP. Preston and O'Bannon (1997) found a positive CSP-FP link.

McWilliams and Siegel (2000) tested the CSP-FP link with a regression model that used a dummy variable indicating inclusion of a firm in the Domini 400 Social Index (DSI 400) as the measure of CSP. The DSI 400 is a portfolio of socially responsible companies developed by Kinder, Lydenberg, and Domini, Inc. which developed the KLD index. McWilliams and Siegel (2000) used an average of annual values for the period 1991–1996 for 524 large U.S. corporations in a regression model that included a measure of financial performance as the dependent variable. CSP, industry, and expenditures for research and development were independent variables. The results suggest that inclusion of the research and development variable in the model causes the CSP variable to be insignificant leading McWilliams and Siegel (2000) to the conclusion that there may not be a CSP–FP link if the regression model is properly specified.

Griffin and Mahon (1997) identified several issues in the literature that they believe should be addressed in future empirical investigations. First, a large majority (78 percent) of the studies they reviewed used samples from multiple industries. The problem with this approach is that the unique characteristics of an industry make the nature of CSP unique based on different internal characteristics and external demands (Griffin and Mahon, 1997). Rowley and Berman (2000) also suggest that CSP research should be narrowly defined in operational terms to a specific industry or setting. The nature of stakeholder actions appears to be an important influence on CSP and different industries face different portfolios of stakeholders with different degrees of activity in different areas (Griffin and Mahon, 1997; Rowley and Berman, 2000). Griffin and Mahon (1997) argue that multiple industry studies confound the relationship between stakeholders and appropriate measures of CSP and FP unique to those stakeholders. The empirical investigations show that industry is an important variable in multiple industry analyses. Focusing on a single industry emphasizes internal validity rather than the external validity of multiple industry analyses. The most important contribution of the present investigation is the analysis of a large sample of firms from the same industry. While a few other studies, including Griffin and Mahon (1997), have analyzed individual industries, the samples have been small.

Another important advantage of concentrating on a single industry is that the econometric specification of the FP function can be more complete because unique characteristics of the industry can be included. Several of the econometric issues suggested by Waddock and Graves (1997) and McWilliams and Siegel (2000) are addressed in the present analysis of the banking industry.

The second issue raised by Griffin and Mahon (1997) is that multiple measures of FP should be used. Many previous investigations used only one measure of FP. They also argue that accounting measures rather than market-derived measures should be used because market measures may be picking up more than just FP. This study employs two accounting measures of FP that are recognized throughout the banking industry and are believed to accurately reflect the financial performance of banking firms.

The third issue addressed by Griffin and Mahon (1997), Carroll (2000), and many other scholars in the field, is the measurement of CSP. Griffin and Mahon (1997) and Carroll (2000) argue for multiple sources of information to produce a comprehensive metric of CSP. The CSP metric used in the present investigation of the banking industry is not represented as a complete measure of CSP but we submit that it is multidimensional and unique. The important contribution of the CSP measure is that it is a unique measurement of CSP for a specific industry that has not been used before in CSP–FP analyses.

The Community Reinvestment Act Ratings and social performance measurement

The Community Reinvestment Act of 1977 (CRA) mandated that depository institutions serve their communities (Spong, 1994). CRA was passed to insure that commercial banks meet the credit needs of the markets where they hold public charters to do business, especially the needs of low-income customers (Spong, 1994). Banks were required to provide private funding for local housing needs and economic development (Spong, 1994). The legislation is generally known as an attempt to restrict the practice of "redlining" but the act covers a broader spectrum of bank functions.

As a result of CRA, regulatory authorities are required to examine banks to develop a rating which summarizes the degree of compliance into four categories: (1) outstanding, (2) satisfactory, (3) needs to improve, and (4) substantial non-compliance (Spong, 1994). The ratings are based on twelve assessment factors: (1) Communication with members of the community to ascertain credit needs, (2) Extent of involvement by the board of directors in CRA activities, (3) Marketing efforts to make the types of credit offered known in the community, (4) The extent of loans originated in the community, (5) The extent of bank participation in government loan programs, (6) The geographic distribution of credit applications, approvals, and denials, (7) The record of branch office openings and closings and extent of service provided at the offices, (8) Practices to discourage credit applications, (9) Discriminatory or other illegal practices, (10) Participation in community development projects or programs, (11) The institution's ability to meet community credit needs, and (12) Other relevant factors which could bear upon the extent to which the institution is helping to meet the credit needs of the community (Evanoff and Segal, 1996). The CRA rating is partly based on compliance with major pieces of lending discrimination legislation such as the Fair Housing Act, Equal Credit Opportunity Act, and Home Mortgage Disclosure Act (Catalano, 1993). However, the CRA rating considers factors beyond simple compliance with the law, e.g. bank officers visiting with local customers, small businesses, community leaders, and non-profit organizations to find ways to provide needed services for the community. The board of directors is required to approve and oversee the policies designed to comply with the CRA.

Supervisory agencies have the authority to consider the level of noncompliance with the provisions of the CRA when a bank or bank holding company requests approval to acquire another institution, open or relocate an office, or create a bank holding company (Spong, 1994). Noncompliance can result in banks or bank holding companies being denied the ability to expand and merge, an important business activity in the modern banking industry (Spong, 1994). Banks are required to make their CRA ratings publicly available and keep a file which contains any public comments over the last two years (Spong, 1994). Banks with poor performance under CRA may be examined more frequently.

The core business of commercial banks is lending the deposits of customers to other customers who need loans. Meeting the credit needs of a community is central to the economic and social health of that community. The CRA rating is an indication of the social responsibility banks

exhibit in this core activity. The dimensions of social performance measured by the CRA rating are not exhaustive but do cover several of the critical facets of the external social performance of the industry.

The measurement of corporate social performance

The conceptual development of CSP has migrated from a rather narrow classical economic viewpoint articulated by Friedman (1962), among others, to a much broader view. Carroll (1979) developed one of the earlier versions of a comprehensive view of CSP. In a recent discussion of CSP, Carroll (2000) reiterated his view that CSP should be a comprehensive assessment of a firm's social performance relative to most social issues and stakeholders. The recent literature indicates that many academics support a complex, multidimensional construct (Wartrick and Cochran, 1985; Wood, 1991; Roman et al., 1999; Griffin and Mahon, 1997; Swanson, 1999; Rowley and Berman, 2000).

The problems associated with measuring a comprehensive theoretical construct of CSP are daunting. As previously mentioned, individual facets of CSP have been measured with the EPA Toxics Release Inventory, *Corporate 500 Directory of Corporate Philanthropy* data, product recalls, and illegal acts. Attempts to obtain a more comprehensive measure of CSP have relied on the *Fortune* reputation survey, the KLD index, and the Domini 400 Social Index. One problem with the more comprehensive metrics is that they do not cover enough firms to provide a large sample in one industry. The *Fortune* reputation survey is based on the opinions of senior managers that may be confounded with financial performance (Brown and Perry, 1994). The KLD index is a more comprehensive measure but is subject to questions associated with how the different components should be weighted and the fact a component can potentially be both a strength and weakness (Griffin and Mahon, 1997).

To no one's surprise, an ideal empirical measure of a comprehensive conceptual construct of CSP does not now exist. Carroll (2000) argues that unless a better empirical measure of the comprehensive construct of CSP can be developed, empirical research probably should not be done and, if done, it should not be labeled as CSP. Griffin (2000) and Rowley and Berman (2000) suggest that a universal measure may not be desirable. Griffin (2000) argues that a comprehensive measure of CSP means "that time, culture, industry, and contextual variables do not make a difference." Griffin (2000) goes on to say that a universal measure of CSP "potentially oversimplifies a complex construct". Griffin (2000) and Rowley and Berman (2000) appear to be saying that investigation of CSP in an operational setting has value.

The measure of CSP for the banking industry employed in this investigation is obviously not a universal measure. It is not a single dimension measure either. The CRA rating is a multidimensional construct distilled into a single measure that describes several aspects of social performance in a unique operational setting. The use of the CRA rating as a measure of CSP has advantages and disadvantages. We gain a fairly homogeneous set of contextual circumstances by choosing one industry e.g. limited direct pollution of the environment, a relatively homogeneous production process where product safety and employee safety are minimal concerns, similar stakeholder configurations, similar expenditures on R&D, and a constant regulatory framework.[2] The banking industry is a unique opportunity to obtain a sample with a substantial number of companies in the same industry. The methodology used to develop the social performance measure is relatively homogeneous because regulatory authorities apply a standardized procedure that assesses outcomes through on-site examinations of the organization.[3] We lose some generality as a result of holding industry constant and lose direct comparability to other research by not using a social performance measure commonly used in other research, e.g. KLD index.

Theoretical framework and hypothesis development

The link between corporate social and financial performance has been alternatively hypothesized to be positive, negative, and neutral. The ability of researchers to offer rational theoretical justification for each of the possible positions demonstrates the need for both a more unified theory and reliable empirical verification.

Waddock and Graves (1997) and Preston and O'Bannon (1997) offer a summary of previous conceptual explanations for a negative, neutral, and positive relationship between CSP and FP. A negative relationship is consistent with the neoclassical economist's argument that positive social performance causes the firm to incur costs that reduce profits and shareholder wealth (Waddock and Graves, 1997; Preston and O'Bannon, 1997). Preston and O'Bannon (1997) offer a "managerial opportunism hypothesis" as a rationale for a negative CSP-FP link. They suggest that when financial performance is strong, managers will reduce expenditures on social performance because they can increase short-term profitability and increase their personal compensation that is tied to short-term profitability. Conversely, when financial performance is poor, managers will attempt to divert attention by expenditures on conspicuous social programs.

The finding of a neutral (no) relationship is explained by the thesis that the general situation of the firm and society is so complex that a simple, direct relationship between CSP and FP does not exist (Waddock and Graves, 1997). McWilliams and Siegel (2001) argue for a neutral, or nonexistent, relationship between CSP and FP from a framework based on a supply and demand theory of the firm which assumes shareholder wealth maximization. They argue that firms produce at a profit-maximizing level, including the production of social performance. This leads each firm to supply different amounts of social performance based on the unique demand for CSP the firm experiences. In equilibrium, the amount of CSP produced by firms will be different but profitability will be maximized and equal.

Several explanations for a positive CSP-FP link exist. First, one perspective is that a tension exists between the explicit costs of the firm, e.g. interest payments to bond holders, and the implicit costs of the firm, e.g. product quality or safety costs (Waddock and Graves, 1997). Attempts by the firm to lower implicit costs by socially irresponsible actions are hypothesized to result in higher explicit costs. In a similar vein, Preston and O'Bannon (1997) describe a "social impact hypothesis" which suggests that meeting the needs of various nonowner corporate stakeholders will have a positive impact on financial performance. A second viewpoint suggests that the actual costs of CSP are minimal compared to the potential benefits to the firm (Waddock and Graves, 1997). For example, the cost of providing employee benefits may be much less than the productivity gains that result. A third argument is that good management will do most things well, including the determinants of both social and financial performance (Waddock and Graves, 1997). A fourth explanation is the financially successful firm has slack resources as a result of its superior financial performance that can be devoted to social performance (Waddock and Graves, 1997; Preston and O'Bannon, 1997). Finally, Waddock and Graves (1997) suggest that there may be a positive CFP-FP link because of a simultaneous relationship combining slack resources and good management which results in a "virtuous circle" between CSP and FP.

When no single accepted theoretical foundation with clear empirical predictions exists, hypothesis development requires some judgement. Two factors drive the hypothesis tested in this investigation. First, we find the most convincing theoretical arguments to be the slack resources hypothesis and the good management hypothesis, which predict a positive relationship. In light of these two hypotheses, the concept of a feedback process that results in a "virtuous circle" is also reasonable. Second, previous empirical evidence supports a positive link between CSP and FP. The hypothesis tested is:

H_0: The relationship between social performance and financial performance in the commercial banking industry is either zero or negative.

H_1: The relationship between social performance and financial performance in the commercial banking industry is positive.

Methodology

Sample and data

The sample was taken from all national banks examined for CRA compliance in 1993 and 1994. All banks that were assigned ratings of outstanding and needs improvement were included in the sample. Banks receiving satisfactory ratings were omitted to provide a clear separation between banks with high social performance and low social performance. No banks receiving a rating of substantial noncompliance were included because the category included a very small number of banks. The result was a total sample of 385 banks with 284 banks rated outstanding and 101 rated needs to improve. The rating and dates were taken from various news releases from the Comptroller of the Currency. The Comptroller of the Currency is a division of the U.S. Treasury that is the primary regulator of nationally chartered banks. Only national banks were used to hold the examination and regulatory process constant. The time period of 1993 and 1994 was used to hold constant the rating process as regulatory emphasis could change over time.

The CRA rating is developed for each individual commercial bank in the U.S. (Spong, 1994). Commercial banks are restricted to a limited set of activities by federal law. So, they are not involved in multiple industries, as a large conglomerate corporation will be (Spong, 1994). Individual banks may be owned by bank holding companies, which are more diversified financial service providers, but the CRA rating applies to the individual bank, not the bank holding company. The banks included in this sample are in the basic business of banking which includes accepting deposits, making loans, providing safekeeping, and making payments through checking and electronic systems. The nature of the regulatory framework, which restricts the activities of individual commercial banks, provides some assurance that the sample units are from a single industry.

The accounting data for the financial variables were taken from call reports filed with the Comptroller of the Currency. The information for the state level bank performance variables was taken from *FDIC Statistics on Banking* and the data for the local economic conditions variables were taken from *Employment and Earnings* of the Bureau of Labor Statistics, *Survey of Current Business* of the Bureau of Economic Analysis, and

Statistical Abstract of the United States. The variables used in the analysis are described in Table I.

Financial performance measures

Two measures of FP that are generally considered to capture major dimensions of financial performance in the banking industry were utilized: return on assets (ROA) and loan losses to total loans.[4] The return on assets is probably the most widely recognized measure of financial perfor-

TABLE I
Variable definitions

Variable name	Variable description
Financial performance	
Return on assets	Net operating income/Average total assets
Loan losses	Net charged-off loans/Average total assets
Social performance	
CRA rating	Dummy variable which equals 0 if CRA rating is needs improvement and 1 if the CRA rating is outstanding
Control	
Total assets	Natural logarithm of average total assets
Holding company	Dummy variable which equals 1 if the bank is an affiliate of a bank holding company and 0 if the bank is an independent bank
Assets per office	Natural logarithm of average total assets/Number of offices operated by the bank
State return on assets	Weighted-average return on assets for all banks in the state where the bank is located
State personal income	Annual percentage change in personal income for the state where the bank is located
Population	Natural Logarithm of the total population of the city where the bank is located
Cost of funds	Weighted-average rate paid on interest bearing deposits
Capital ratio	Equity capital/Average total assets
Loan ratio	Average total loans/Average total assets
Earning assets	Average interest earning assets/Average interest bearing liabilities
Overhead expenses	Total noninterest expenses/Average total assets
State bankruptcies	Annual percentage change in the number of personal and business bankruptcy petitions filed in the state where bank is located
Nonperforming assets	(Nonaccrual loans + loans 30 days or more past due + repossessed real estate)/(average total loans + repossessed real estate)
State nonperforming assets	Weighted-average ratio of (non-performing loans/Average total loans) for all banks in the state where the bank is located.

mance in the industry. Return on assets measures the ability of bank managers to acquire deposits at a reasonable cost, invest these funds in profitable loans and investments, and profitably perform the daily operations of the bank. For most banks, the largest portion of total assets is loans and the largest amount of revenues comes from interest on loans. As a result, the ability to make collectible loans directly affects net income and capital, which determine financial success. Loan losses can be a major expense for banks and the ratio of loan losses to loans is an important indicator of the success of the credit function.

Statistical procedures

The financial performance measures were calculated the calendar year preceding the calendar year in which the examination was conducted. This was done because the CRA ratings were based on the social performance of the bank in the period prior to the date of the examination. Then *t*-tests for differences in group means were calculated for the financial performance measures. The two groups were banks with an outstanding CRA rating and banks with a needs to improve rating.

Two regression equations were estimated with the financial performance measures as the dependent variable and the CRA rating as the independent variable, plus a set of control variables. The financial measures were used as dependent variables because the *a priori* profit function of a bank and the *a priori* determinants of loan losses are fairly well understood. The *a priori* determinants of the CRA rating, i.e. the measure of social performance, are not well developed. This econometric specification implies that corporate social performance, i.e. the CRA rating, causes financial performance because financial performance is the dependent variable in the equation. However, equally reasonable theoretical justification exists for the proposition that financial performance causes social performance. If the CRA rating was used as the dependent variable and financial performance as one independent variable in a regression equation, any ability to impute causation from financial performance to

social performance would be dependent on the correct specification of the other variables that determine the CRA rating. Unfortunately, these independent variables are very likely not the same as those in the profit function or loan loss function. We cannot test the proposition that financial performance causes the CRA rating by simply switching the financial performance and social performance variables in the profit function and loan loss function. Given the lack of a well developed *a priori* model of the determinants of the CRA rating, simple regression analysis cannot establish causation.[5] The regression analysis can test for the existence and direction of a relationship between FP and CSP, but not the cause of any observed relationship.

The control variables for the ROA equation were designed to hold firm size, risk, asset portfolio composition, local economic environment, holding company affiliation, level of investment in branch offices, cost of funds, and overhead expenses constant. Banks do not directly account for R&D expenditures in their financial statements but any expenditures for R&D that might exist would probably be included in overhead expenses. The control variables for the loan loss equation were included to hold constant firm size, risk of the loan portfolio, size of the loan portfolio, and economic conditions in the local loan market. Industry effects were held constant in both equations by using only firms from the same industry.

Ordinary least squares regression was used to estimate the regression parameters and standard regression diagnostics were performed to evaluate the reliability of the results (Greene, 1997).

Results

Tests for difference in group means

The results of the group means tests reported in Table II give a strong indication that the link between corporate social and financial performance is positive. The mean return on assets for the group of banks rated outstanding was 1.750 percent compared to 0.984 percent for the banks that received a needs to improve rating.

TABLE II
Tests for differences in group means

Financial performance	Social performance group	Group mean	t-value (probability)
Return on assets	Outstanding	1.750%	5.06
	Needs to improve	0.984%	(0.00)
Loan losses	Outstanding	0.478%	−3.37
	Needs to improve	0.812%	(0.00)

Note: t-values are a pooled variance estimate and probabilities are for a one-tailed test.
The sample size was 385 with 284 banks rated outstanding and 101 rated Needs to Improve.

The t-statistic for the difference in group means indicates that the probability of this difference being observed by chance was almost zero, i.e. the null hypothesis was rejected with a high level of confidence. This difference in profitability between the banks with high social performance and the banks with lower social performance is not only statistically significant but also substantial in absolute terms. The return on assets for the high CRA rated banks is almost twice the return on assets of the low CRA banks, i.e. the high social performance banks were 78 percent more profitable than low social performance banks.

The results of the group means test for loan losses also provide strong support for the hypothesis that the link between social and financial performance is positive. The mean for the loan losses variable was 0.478 percent for the banks with an outstanding CRA rating and 0.812 percent for the banks with a CRA rating of needs to improve. This indicates the high social performance banks experienced approximately one-half of the loan losses experienced by the banks with low social performance. Once again, the difference in an absolute sense is substantial. The difference in means for the two groups was significantly different from zero at the 0.001 probability level.

Regression analysis

The regression results reported in Table III support the results of the group means test. The null hypothesis of no relationship or a negative relationship between the CRA rating and return on assets was rejected at the 0.016 probability level as indicated by the positive regression coefficient for the CRA rating variable. The adjusted R-square for the regression equation was 0.227 and most of the control variables were significant at the 0.10 level which indicates the equation was reliable.

The regression equation with loan losses as the dependent variable and CRA rating as the independent variable revealed that the null hypothesis could be rejected at the 0.001 probability level. The sign of the regression coefficient for the CRA rating variable was negative which indicates better financial performance for banks with high social performance, i.e. high social performance banks had lower loan losses. The R-square of 0.198 and the fact that most of the regression coefficients in the equation were significant indicates the results of the analysis were dependable.

Implications of the results

The findings of this investigation are important because they validate a strong positive relationship between CSP and FP in a different operational setting than previously tested. These results from the banking industry corroborate the mounting body of evidence developed from large S & P 500 or Fortune 500 corporations. Much of the previous evidence for a positive relationship between CSP and FP was based on the same type of firms, i.e. large, national corporations. The fact that an analysis of a unique CSP

W. Gary Simpson and Theodor Kohers

TABLE III
Regression coefficients and statistics

Independent and control variables	Dependent variable Return on assets	Dependent variable Loan losses
CRA rating	0.354 (0.016)	−0.420 (0.001)
Total assets	0.015 (0.373)	0.109 (0.000)
Holding company	−0.251 (0.074)	
Assets per office	0.130 (0.082)	
State return on assets	1.442 (0.000)	
State personal income	−0.028 (0.251)	0.037 (0.121)
Population	0.002 (0.146)	
Cost of funds	0.116 (0.045)	
Capital ratio	−0.060 (0.001)	
Loan ratio	−0.007 (0.046)	0.008 (0.004)
Earning assets	0.017 (0.003)	
Overhead expenses	−0.008 (0.406)	
State bankruptcies		0.006 (0.479)
Nonperforming assets	−0.150 (0.000)	
State nonperforming		0.199 (0.000)
Adjusted R Square	0.227	0.198
F-Statistic	23.130	16.733
Probability	0.000	0.000

Note: The intercept term in the regression equation is not reported.
The probabilities for a one-tailed test are in parentheses.
All control variables were not used in every equation.

measure in a single industry with a sample of firms that are appreciably smaller found a positive CSP-FP link argues for the robustness of the relationship. The findings of the present analysis are also convincing because of the magnitude of the observed differences and the fact that important variables such as industry and R&D expenditures were held constant.

The results of this investigation are consistent with the theoretical constructs of corporate social performance that predict a positive CSP-FP link. Albeit, several arguments exist for a positive CSP-FP link and our evidence does not support any of these more than any other. Nevertheless, the evidence does help rule out the theoretical descriptions of the nature of corporate social performance that predict a negative and neutral CSP-FP link. This alone may facilitate the task of developing a better theoretical understanding of corporate social performance. The results of this analysis are consistent with the good management hypothesis, the slack resources hypothesis, the virtuous circle explanation, and the social impact hypothesis discussed previously. These results are also consistent with the positive cost-benefit explanation that the costs of being socially responsible are outweighed by associated improvements in productivity, or other factors, which will improve financial performance.

From the viewpoint of stockholders and managers, the results of this analysis are consistent with the view that the resources required to be socially responsible are not so high as to make the firm unprofitable. Furthermore, the possibility exists that firms may even receive a competitive advantage from social performance expenditures which create favorable stakeholder relationships (Waddock and Graves, 1997). For example, a bank could increase the probability of receiving permission from regulators to acquire another institution by investing the necessary resources in social performance to assure a good CRA rating. However, we do not prove that social performance has positive benefits for stockholders because managers may simply allocate slack resources to benefit one group of stakeholders, e.g. customers or the community, and harm stockholders by reducing the earnings available for dividends. Managers could also use slack

resources as a way to reduce conflict with various stakeholder groups to make their lives easier but reduce earnings available for the stockholders.

While negative implications for stockholders are possible when the firm has slack resources, it is equally possible that good management tends to value social performance and has the ability to create high levels of both CSP and FP. This explanation is attractive because all stakeholders benefit. Waddock and Graves (1997) argue that a positive link between CSP and FP implies that good CSP and good management are the same thing when CSP is defined in terms of the stakeholder relationships considered important to the performance of the firm and not discretionary activities, e.g. philanthropy. Recall that the activities required to receive a high Community Investment Act rating were tied to the daily activities of the firm in serving customers and the community. These activities are central to the business of banking and our evidence is consistent with the idea that good management and good CSP are the same.

Conclusion

This investigation based on data from a sample of commercial banks extends the research on corporate social performance and financial performance by providing empirical support for a positive CSP-FP link. The analysis employs a measure of social performance unique to the banking industry that has not been used in previous research. The results from the banking industry are consistent with much of the previous evidence developed from the analysis of Fortune 500 corporations. Evidence supporting a positive CSP-FP link in a unique operational setting supports the idea that a positive CSP-FP link is a universal phenomenon.

Numerous theoretical explanations have been offered to support a negative, positive, and neutral CSP-FP relationship. The implication of this research, when taken in conjunction with previous empirical evidence, is that future research efforts should concentrate on a theoretical explanation for a positive CSP-FP link. Simultaneously, empirical investigation of the

CSP–FP link in other unique operational contexts appears to be a valuable direction for future research.

One of the limitations of this analysis is that we do not test why a positive CFP–FP link may exist. The absence of an accepted theoretical construct with precise empirical predictions makes the analysis of causation difficult. Several conceptual arguments are consistent with a positive CFP–FP link but each has different implications. Empirical tests to isolate specific hypotheses that explain why a positive CSP–FP link might be observed would be a valuable direction for future research. A second and related limitation of this investigation is that we do not establish if CSP causes FP, FP causes CSP, or there is some feedback relationship. A valuable direction for future research would be the application of econometric techniques to help determine causation when a complete theory is not available, e.g. Granger-Sims Causality tests. The use of the Community Investment Act rating as a measure of CSP has some advantages, but is also a limitation because it is not a broad, comprehensive measure of CSP. We have only evaluated a few important facets of CSP. Future research to develop effective comprehensive measures of CSP would be valuable, but admittedly difficult. Another limitation is that the length of the time period covered in the study should be longer.

In spite of the limitations of this investigation and the need for additional research, the results of this analysis are encouraging because the prospect of a positive CSP–FP link means that firms can be both socially responsible and financially successful.

Notes

[1] Refer to Griffin and Mahon (1997), Roman et al. (1999), and Frooman (1997) for a summary of the previous evidence. See Griffin (2000), Rowley and Berman (2000), Swanson (1999), and Carroll (2000) for a discussion of several important issues associated with research in corporate social performance.

[2] Commercial banks do not face the same social responsibility challenges of pollution, product safety, and employee safety encountered by other firms, but they do have a social and legal responsibility because they lend to firms that pollute, produce unsafe products, etc.

[3] Griffin and Mahon (1997) argue that rating firms by independent third parties with largely objective screening criteria is an improvement over largely perceptual data, e.g. the *Fortune* survey.

[4] Return on equity (ROE) was not used because it is highly correlated with return on assets (ROA) in the banking industry. By definition ROE = ROA (Total Assets/Total Capital). The relationship between total assets and total capital is tightly regulated in the banking industry causing ROE to convey about the same information on financial performance as ROA. Almost all of the banks in the sample were smaller banks that did not have common stock traded in an active market so market returns were not used as a measure of FP.

[5] The use of econometric techniques to test for causation when *a prior* reasoning cannot provide the appropriate specification requires a procedure like the Granger-Sims causality test but this approach also has limitations (Pindyck and Rubinfeld, 1998; Greene, 1997).

References

Alexander, G. J. and R. A. Buchholz: 1978, 'Corporate Responsibility and Stock Market Performance', *Academy of Management Journal* 21, 479–486.

Belkaoui, A.: 1976, 'The Impact of the Disclosure of the Environmental Effects of Organizational Behavior on the Market', *Financial Management* 5, 26–31.

Bragdon, J. H. and J. T. Marlin: 1972, 'Is Pollution Profitable?', *Risk Management* 19, 9–18.

Brown, B. and S. Perry: 1995, 'Halo-Removed Residuals of Fortune's "Responsibility to the Community and Environment" – A Decade of Data', *Business and Society* 34, 199–215.

Carroll, A. B.: 1979, 'A Three-Dimensional Model of Corporate Social Performance', *Academy of Management Review* 4, 497–505.

Carroll, A. B.: 2000, 'A Commentary and an Overview of Key Questions on Corporate Social Performance Measurement', *Business and Society* 39, 466–478.

Catalano, J.: 1993, 'A Clearer Focus on Your CRA Examination', *ABA Bank Compliance* (Spring), 5–12.

Evanoff, D. D. and L. M. Segal: 1996, 'CRA and Fair Lending Regulations: Resulting Trends in

Mortgage Lending', *Economic Perspectives: Federal Reserve Bank of Chicago* (Nov.–Dec.), 19–43.

Friedman, M.: 1962, *Capitalism and Freedom* (University of Chicago Press, Chicago).

Frooman, J.: 1997, 'Socially Irresponsible and Illegal Behavior and Shareholder Wealth', *Business and Society* 36, 221–249.

Greene, W. H.: 1997, *Econometric Analysis* (Prentice Hall, Upper Saddle River, New Jersey).

Griffin, J. J.: 2000, 'Corporate Social Performance: Research Directions for the 21st Century', *Business and Society* 39, 479–491.

Griffin, J. J. and J. F. Mahon: 1997, 'The Corporate Social Performance and Corporate Financial Performance Debate: Twenty-Five Years of Incomparable Research', *Business and Society* 36, 5–31.

McWilliams, A. and D. Siegel: 2001, 'Corporate Social Responsibility: A Theory of the Firm Perspective', *Academy of Management Review* 26, 117–127.

McWilliams, A. and D. Siegel: 2000, 'Corporate Social Responsibility and Financial Performance: Correlation or Misspecification?', *Strategic Management Journal* 21, 603–609.

Preston, L. E. and D. P. O'Bannon: 1997, 'The Corporate Social-Financial Performance Relationship: A Typology and Analysis', *Business and Society* 36, 419–429.

Pindyck, R. S. and D. L. Rubinfeld: 1998, *Econometric Models and Economic Forecasts* (Irwin McGraw-Hill, Boston).

Roman, R. M., S. Hayibor and B. R. Agle: 1999, 'The Relationship Between Social And Financial Performance: Repainting a Portrait', *Business and Society* 38, 109–125.

Rowley, T. and S. Berman: 2000, 'A Brand New Brand of Corporate Social Performance', *Business and Society* 39, 397–418.

Spong, K.: 1994, *Banking Regulation: Its Purposes, Implementation, and Effects*, Kansas City, Federal Reserve Bank of Kansas City.

Stanwick, P. A. and S. D. Stanwick: 1998, 'The Relationship Between Corporate Social Performance and Organizational Size, Financial Performance, and Environmental Performance: An Empirical Examination', *Journal of Business Ethics* 17, 195–204.

Swanson, D. L.: 1999, 'Toward an Integrative Theory of Business and Society: A Research Strategy for Corporate Social Performance', *Academy of Management Review* 24, 506–521.

Vance, S. C.: 1975, 'Are Socially Responsible Corporations Good Investment Risks?', *Academy of Management Review* (August), 18–24.

Waddock, S. A. and S. B. Graves: 1997, 'The Corporate Social Performance-Financial Performance Link', *Strategic Management Journal* 18, 303–319.

Wartrick, S. L. and P. L. Cochran: 1985, 'The Evolution of the Corporate Social Performance Model', *Academy of Management Review* 10, 758–769.

Wood, D. J.: 1991, 'Corporate Social Performance Revisited', *Academy of Management Review* 16, 691–718.

W. Gary Simpson
Department of Finance,
College of Business Administration,
Oklahoma State University,
Stillwater, OK, 74078-0555,
U.S.A.
E-mail: simpson@okstate.edu

Theodor Kohers
Department of Finance and Economics,
College of Business and Industry,
Mississippi State University,
Mississippi State, MS,
U.S.A.
E-mail: tkohers@cobilan.msstate

[56]

Beyond Built to Last . . . Stakeholder Relations in "Built-to-Last" Companies

SAMUEL B. GRAVES AND SANDRA A. WADDOCK

In their book, *Built to Last*, Collins and Porras produced a groundbreaking study that highlighted the performance characteristics—and significant positive performance differences—between companies they termed visionary or built to last (BTL) and a control group of comparison companies.[1] Their study was based on data from the founding of each company to the early 1990s, with some companies in business for as long as 100 years. Collins and Porras compared 18 large-capitalization "visionary" companies identified in a survey of chief executives to a set of comparison companies matched to the visionary companies by industry and time of founding.

Visionary companies, according to Collins and Porras, are "built to last." They attain outstanding long-term performance through institutional mechanisms that support what the authors called "clock building" as opposed to "time telling." Shattering many myths, particularly about the goal of maximizing profits, *Built to Last* provides significant insight into what it takes to succeed over the long term. Built-to-last companies, conclude the authors, are not just organizations, they are institutions[2] in the richest sense of that word, for, as Collins and Porras put it, "they have woven themselves into the very fabric of society."[3]

Collins and Porras show that visionary companies have performed well for shareholders over long periods. The question remains, however, the extent to which these companies also attain

Samuel B. Graves and Sandra A. Waddock are professors at the Carroll School of Management, Boston College.

their extraordinary performance by working productively and positively with other primary stakeholders[4] such as customers, employees, and communities, as well as the environment.[5] Recent empirical research has suggested that there may be a positive link between the overall quality of management in a firm and its social performance, defined in terms of stakeholder relationships.[6] Called the good management hypothesis, this research suggests that the quality of management is associated with the ways companies treat certain key stakeholders on an ongoing basis. In this view, positive treatment of stakeholders is also, by extension, related to better performance outcomes, typically measured in financial terms.

In this article, we extend the work of Collins and Porras by assessing the stakeholder, as well as financial, performance of Collins and Porras' visionary and comparison companies. We explore the differences between visionary and comparison companies in their treatment of primary stakeholders. Thus, we attempted to determine whether visionary companies really did focus on "more than profits" by treating their multiple stakeholders more generously than did the comparison group

VISION, VALUES, AND SOCIAL/STAKEHOLDER PERFORMANCE

Collins and Porras define visionary companies:

> Visionary companies are premier institutions—the crown jewels—in their industries, widely admired by their peers and having a long track record of making a significant impact on the world around them. The key point is that a visionary company is an *organization*—an institution. *All* institutional leaders, no matter how charismatic or visionary, eventually die; and all visionary products and services—all 'great ideas'— eventually become obsolete. Yet visionary *companies* prosper over long periods of time, through multiple product life cycles and multiple generations of active leaders.[7]

According to Collins and Porras, the success of visionary companies results from their adherence to an immutable core ideology while stimulating progress with audacious goals that change over time. The core ideology is an established purpose and vital set of core values. In visionary companies, the core ideology remains the essence of the company's existence over time and drives operations and strategy. Visionary companies simultaneously stimulate progress and dynamic change through a mutable set of audacious goals brought alive by rich descriptions (strategies), cult-like cultures, and constant experimentation geared to meet (or create) changing needs and competitive conditions.

Core values of visionary companies encompass themes such as 3M's emphasis on innovation and integrity, Johnson and Johnson's hierarchy of responsibilities to a range of stakeholders, and Merck's emphasis on "preserving and improving human life." Collins and Porras concluded that "the critical issue is not whether a company has the 'right' core ideology or a 'likable' core ideology but rather whether it *has* a core ideology that gives guidance and inspiration to people *inside the company*."[8] Here we disagree. It appears to us that the core values on which visionary companies are based tend to be those that James MacGregor Burns, who wrote about transformational leadership,[9] would have characterized as "end values." For example, it is hard to disagree with values of integrity, service, helping humanity, meritocracy, valuing people, improving the quality of life, making contributions, and alleviating pain and disease, as end values, all associated with one or more of the visionary companies.

Still, Collins and Porras concluded from the range of values they uncovered that no specific ideological content was necessary to becoming a visionary company. Visionary companies,[10] they noted, exhibited "consistent alignment with the ideology." That is, visionary companies clearly stated what their core values were and made extensive efforts to live up to those values,[11] especially as compared to the non-built-to-last (non-BTL) companies that served as the comparison group. But no consistent set of core values was found among the BTL companies. We believe that it is not so much the content as the nature of the vision to which visionary companies adhere that makes the difference. To wit: it appears to us that the end values contained in these visions can inspire commitment to the company from a range of different stakeholders.

For example, it is clear that the values embedded in core ideology are among the set of end values that most people would find acceptable and positive, even when the company's product is repugnant. Take, for example, Philip Morris as a visionary company. One might legitimately claim that the company's participation in the tobacco industry indicates that it is pursuing the "wrong" values (harmful products). But the values expressed in its core ideology are stated not in product terms, but rather in end value terms that many individualistic Americans would likely find appealing: the right to personal freedom of choice, winning, encouraging individual initiative, opportunity to achieve based on merit, hard work, and continuous self-improvement.[12] Note that these are all positive values and that the core values of the visionary companies all tend to be expressed along similar end value lines.

Other recent thinking about strategic management has also begun to focus on the importance of a powerful (and positive) vision integrated with a strong set of core values in generating positive economic performance. For example, Hamel and Prahalad highlighted the critical role of "strategic intent" in the success of the companies that they studied.[13] More recently, Carl Anderson highlighted the importance of "values-based management" in driving organizational performance. Anderson explained the need for integrating four interdependent values-driven goals to achieve organizational success: "Over the long run, competence and learning are necessary to sustain economic performance. A strong community is fundamental to all three."[14]

Although Anderson decries the neglect of values-based management in recent management practice, others have highlighted the linkage of dominant management tools in use in recent years with underlying values that seem likely to result in better performance. For example, Jeanne Liedtka[15] has noted pointedly that many of the recent fads in management are in fact based on a common set of underlying values that influence operating practices. These approaches to organizational improvement include Senge's learning organization,[16] total quality management (which as been described as "just what the ethicist ordered"),[17] re-engineering,[18] and strategic thinking as discussed by Mintzberg.[19] As articulated by Liedtka, the values common to all these management systems include creation of a shared sense of meaning, vision and purpose, developing a systems perspective, emphasizing business processes, localizing decision making, leveraging information, focusing on personal and organizational development, and encouraging dialogue.

As Liedtka points out, the failure of so many companies in using any of these methods appears to be that, unlike Collins and Porras's visionary companies, too little has been done to assure organization-wide implementation of this common set of values-based approaches to management. Too frequently, for example, TQM, participative management techniques, reengineering, learning organizational strategies, or strategic thinking methods are tacked on to what already exists, without fundamentally changing the organization. It is possible that what the visionary companies have done is develop the organizational capability to implement and hold to their articulated vision, which incorporates both the desired picture of the future the core values support and the achievement of that vision. Working positively and productively with primary stakeholders would seem to be a core element of successfully implementing vision.

OPERATING WITH INTEGRITY: STAKEHOLDER RELATIONS

The types of visions and values embedded in the visionary companies suggest an internal consistency that sustains a company over time, through whatever strategic, competitive, or operational problems arise. Values-driven, visionary companies must also sustain positive relationships with those stakeholders who matter most to the successful realization of the vision. Operationalizing a vision may mean, for instance, ensuring high morale and productive employees, gaining the trust of customers by providing products or services that meet expectations, and working with communities so that problems are resolved mutually rather than adversarially.

Scholars have also recently noted that operating with integrity with respect to important stakeholders appears to be vital not only to successful financial performance but also to a company's broader reputation with respect to its overall quality of management.[20] Further, comprehensive reviews of the literature on the links between corporate social performance and financial performance have begun to indicate that there is potentially a positive (or at worst neutral) relationship between social performance and financial outcomes.[21] Corporate social performance (CSP) can be defined as the on-going relationships that a company has with its primary stakeholders. The definition places emphasis on day-to-day operations. That is, positive CSP means positive implementation of stakeholder relationships.

Such a definition moves understanding of CSP towards a stake-holder framing rather than a set of predominantly discretionary activities associated with philanthropy, volunteerism, or "doing good" for its own sake or, as companies like Cisco Systems have discovered, for competitive advantage.[22] Implementing daily operating practices through stakeholder relationships is likely to derive directly from the values embedded in a company's vision, that is, from what Collins and Porras termed its core ideology. Core values that are positive end values provide a sense of meaning and structure to stakeholders associated with the company. If companies are values-driven in this way, then it makes sense that BTL companies would focus on sustaining positive relationships with important stakeholders like owners, employees, customers, communities, and the environment.

One of the more interesting items of evidence adduced by Collins and Porras is the striking long-term financial performance difference between visionary (BTL) and comparison (non-BTL) companies.[23] Vision-driven BTL companies dramatically outperform the comparison group in terms of market performance, generating more than six times the comparison group and fifteen times the general market in terms of cumulative stock returns over the period of Collins and Porras' study.[24] What this means in practice is that one primary stakeholder, the owner, receives great satisfaction from visionary companies because of their long-term financial performance. Although Collins and Porras point out that many of their visionary companies, including IBM, Disney, and Motorola, have experienced hard times, the significant point is that, considered over long time periods, those companies with a "clock building" orientation will continue to outperform other companies with a "time telling" mentality.

While the BTL companies have financially outperformed the comparison group, it is important to note that the BTL group was not selected or identified on the basis of financial performance. The companies that Collins and Porras identified were to be visionary, not simply companies with superior stock performance. Collins and Porras identified the BTL group from a survey of CEOs taken in the late 1980s. In that survey, they asked the CEOs to nominate up to five "highly visionary" companies. Collins and Porras then used these nominations to compile their list by identifying the 20 most frequently mentioned companies. After eliminating companies that were founded after 1950, Collins and Porras had a final list that included 18 visionary companies. They then identified comparison companies that were founded in the same era, had similar founding products and markets, had fewer mentions in the CEO survey, and were themselves respected companies.

Most of these companies have been through peaks and valleys of performance, as noted above. Our task here, however, is to evaluate the average performance of the surviving members of these groups of visionary vs. non-visionary companies using data from a time period considerably later than that of the original selection. If positive values are actually embedded in visionary companies, then it makes sense to think that they will outperform non-visionary companies in their treatment of primary stakeholders. As noted, there is already some evidence to suggest that well-managed companies outperform less-well-managed companies in their treatment of various stakeholders.[25] Extending this logic supports our hypothesis that companies that are visionary (the BTL companies), will outperform others both financially and in the ways that they treat other primary stakeholders.

HOW WE DID THE STUDY

Data on corporate social performance (CSP) are from Kinder, Lydenberg, Domini (KLD), an independent social research firm that develops social performance ratings for interested business and investor communities. KLD's primary business is the assessment of company social performance and not investment management, although a separate investment firm does maintain a passive fund comprised of firms that have "passed" all KLD screens. To do the study we used five of KLD's stakeholder-related measures to assess primary stakeholder relationships: community relations, employee relations, treatment of the environment, product (as a surrogate for customer relations), and diversity.[26] KLD rates each of these five variables on a five-point scale from –2 to +2 and reports the data annually. Our data set covers the seven-year time period 1991–1997, the full period for which KLD had been reporting at the time of this study.

All financial performance data are from COMPUSTAT. Accounting measures of financial performance were return on equity (ROE), return on (total) assets (ROA), and return on sales (ROS). Market measures used included: 10 year *relative* total return to shareholders (a firm's 10 year total return divided by the 10 year return of its industry group), 10 year total return to shareholders, long term debt to asset ratio, and Beta (a measurement of the sensitivity of a company's stock price to the overall fluctuation in the Standard and Poor's 500 Index). The COMPUSTAT financial data are also annual, and cover the latest available eight-year time period, 1989–1996.[27]

Firms in this study are classified as either Built-To-Last (BTL) or non-Built-To-Last (non-BTL), as taken from Collins and Porras. The original Collins and Porras study included 18 BTL and 18 non-BTL firms. These were matched pairs, with the non-BTL firms serving as a control group. We have maintained that relationship in our study, but some of the 18 pairs are no longer complete. After the effects of mergers, bankruptcies, and unavailable data for one or more of our variables, we were able to retain 11 of the original 18 pairs. Companies studied are listed in Table 1, although not every one of these pairs is present in every year of the analysis. For example, the second pair, Boeing-McDonnell Douglas is lost in 1997 when the two firms merged. For any given year of the analysis, however, a minimum of eight pairs is represented.

Three types of analysis were undertaken. First, we look at the raw results in Figures 1–13, noting the immediately observable differences between visionary and non-visionary companies on both financial and stakeholder measures. Then, considering our data as a sample from a larger population, we test for statistical significance of these observed differences. Finally, we look for general trends in the companies' CSP performance over the period of the study.[28]

VISIONARY COMPANIES DO BETTER . . .

Financially

Given the long-term performance differences uncovered in the original Collins and Porras study, we expected that the BTL companies would continue to outperform the non-BTL companies financially, and we were not disappointed. As Figures 1–7 dramatically illustrate, in almost all years and on all of the measures of financial performance that we used, with the exception of beta, BTL companies outperformed the non-BTL companies. Each chart shows the average performance for the BTL group vs. the average performance for the non-BTL group. Let us explore the ways in which these two groups of companies perform with respect to the owner stakeholder.

We consider financial performance to be the fundamental way that companies "treat" their shareholders or owners. The results are striking and consistent across all measures. For example, Figure 1 shows the performance of each group for return on equity over the period 1989 to 1996. The BTL group outperforms the control

TABLE 1 Collins and Porras Visionary and Comparison Companies***

Built-to-Last Companies	Non-Built-to-Last Companies
3M	Norton
American Express	Wells Fargo
Boeing	McDonnell Douglas
Citicorp	Chase Manhattan
Ford	General Motors
General Electric	Westinghouse
Hewlett Packard	Texas Instruments
IBM	Burroughs
Johnson and Johnson	Bristol-Myers-Squibb
Marriott	Howard Johnson
Motorola	Zenith
Merck	Pfizer
Nordstrom	Melville
Philip Morris	RJR Nabisco
Procter and Gamble	Colgate
Sony	Kenwood
Wal-Mart	Ames
Walt Disney	Columbia

*As noted in the text, some of the original pairs are no longer available because of bankruptcies, acquisitions, and mergers.

** For the sake of completeness, we note the reasons why some companies are no longer in the study. The Norton Company was acquired by Saint-Gobain, a France-based world leader in the manufacture of engineered materials. Burroughs merged with Sperry in 1986 to become Unisys Corporation. Howard Johnson was acquired in 1990 by JFS, Inc., which then merged with CUC International to form Cendant Corporation. RJR Nabisco was taken private in a leveraged buyout in 1988 by KKR. Kenwood International is still operating, but is based in Tokyo and not listed in Compustat. Ames filed for bankruptcy protection in 1990, emerged in 1992, and returned to profitability in 1993. Columbia is now CBS Records Group, which was acquired by Sony and is today known as Sony Music Entertainment.

group in seven of the eight. On average, the BTL group's ROE is 9.8% higher than the comparison group. Performance differences continue when we look at return on assets (ROA), a second way of assessing shareholder treatment. As Figure 2 shows, the BTL group outperforms the control group in every year, with an average advantage of 3.55%. Similarly, the return on sales (ROS) comparison in Figure 3 shows the BTL firms outperforming non-BTL companies in each year, with an average advantage of 2.79%. Clearly, in terms of financial performance as assessed by traditional accounting-based returns, the visionary companies are treating their owners very well compared even to the excellent group of companies included in the comparison group.

Market-based measures, which emphasize explicit returns to shareholders, show similar striking results, continuing the performance pattern identified in the original study by Collins and Porras. We used ten-year relative total return to balance out both the vagaries of the market and industry performance differences. For ten-year relative total return, shown in Figure 4, the BTL group outperforms the non-BTL group in all but one year, with an average

FIGURE 1 ROE Comparison

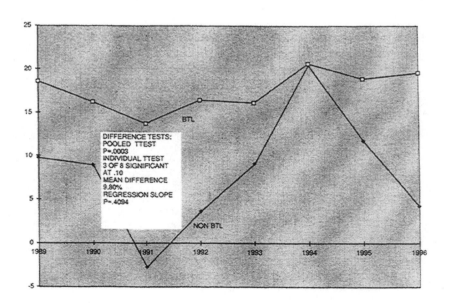

FIGURE 2 ROA Comparison

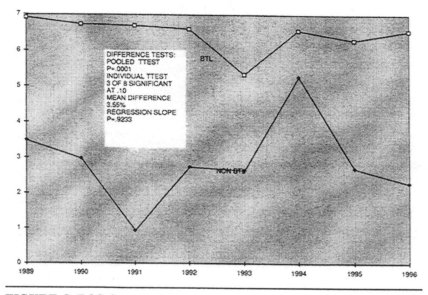

FIGURE 3 ROS Comparison

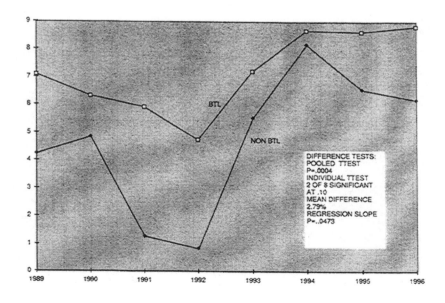

FIGURE 4 10 Year Relative Total Return Comparison

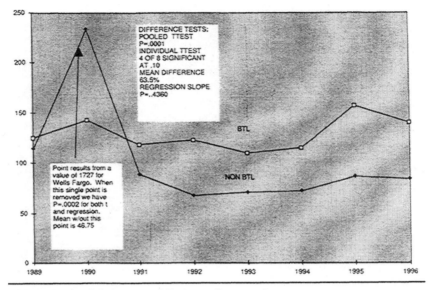

FIGURE 5 10 Year Total Return Comparison

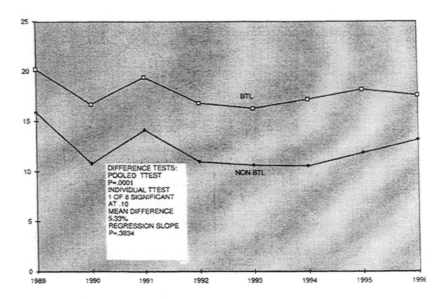

FIGURE 6 Long Term Debt Comparison

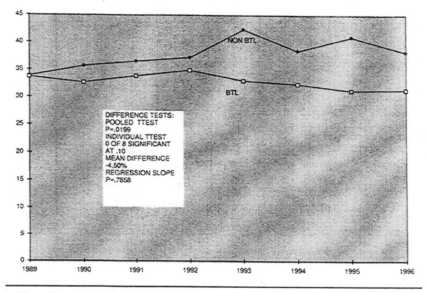

FIGURE 7 Beta Comparison

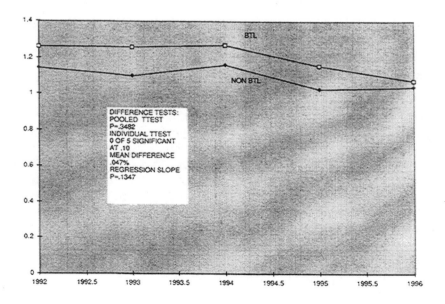

advantage of 63.5%. (Note that the very high value for the non-BTL group in 1990 results from one extremely high value for Wells Fargo for that single year. Without this point, the value would have been much lower, about 46.75%, which is consistent with the pattern evidenced in other years and would be well below the performance of the visionary company group.) Another measure of interest to shareholders is long term return, ten-year total return. Figure 5, shows that the BTL group exceeds the non-BTL group in every year on this measure as well, with an average advantage of 5.33%.

We also wanted to assess the comparative risk of visionary vs. non-visionary companies. We used long-term debt/assets and Beta, a measure of share price volatility. Here the results are conflicting. For the long term debt ratio shown in Figure 6, the difference between the two groups is small, with the non-BTL group showing a slightly higher (average difference 4.5%) debt ratio, than the BTL. Built to last companies, that is, are less risky in terms of debt load than are non-built-to-last companies, perhaps providing a sense of greater stability to shareholders. The last of the financial measures, Beta, shown in Figure 7, is the only one in which the non-BTL group shows an advantage over the BTL group. Here we see that the non-BTL group has a consistently smaller Beta (average difference 0.047), indicating a slightly lower stock market-related volatility in their share prices.

For Stakeholders

Next we turn to consideration of differences between the visionary and non-visionary companies with respect to other primary stakeholders to see whether other stakeholders also benefit more in visionary than non-visionary companies. This way of viewing CSP, as treatment of stakeholders, once again exhibits a remarkable consistency over the period of the study. In general, Figures 8 through 13 show that BTL companies do, in fact, seem to relate better to primary stakeholders than do their counterparts. This finding is particularly remarkable given the fact that all companies included in the comparison group are considered to be strong, healthy, and productive corporate citizens.

The first of the five stakeholder measures, community relations, is shown in Figure 8. Here we see that the BTL group outperforms the non-BTL group in six of seven years, with an average advantage

FIGURE 8 Community Relations Comparison

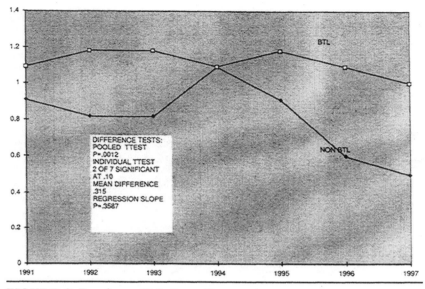

FIGURE 9 Employee Relations Comparison

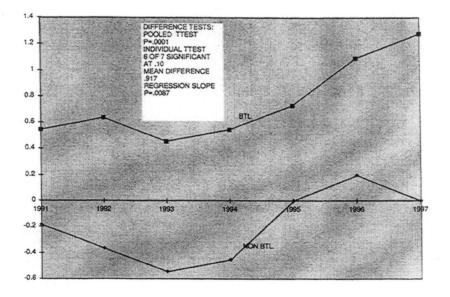

FIGURE 10 Environment Comparison

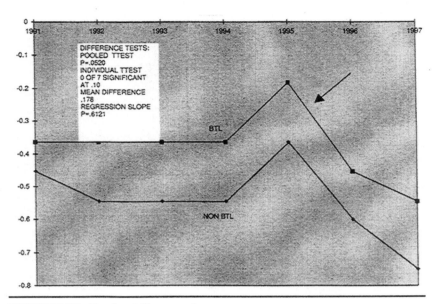

FIGURE 11 Product Comparison

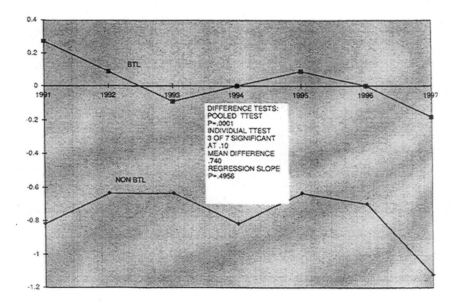

FIGURE 12 Diversity Comparison

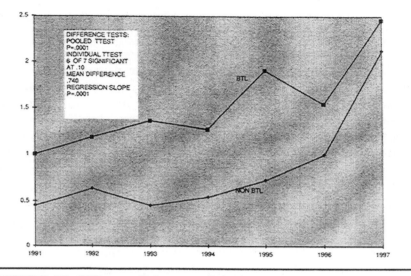

FIGURE 13 CSP-overall Average Comparison

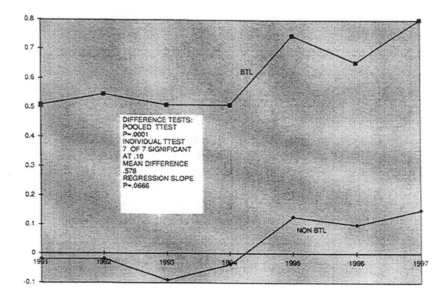

of 0.315 on the five-point CSP scale. (We note that these two curves do *not* cross over in 1994 as the eye is led to believe, but that in 1994 the groups achieved the same overall average result, then once again diverge in ensuring years.)

For employee relations the findings are even more dramatic in support of the contention that visionary companies treat primary stakeholders better than non-visionary companies do. Figure 9 shows that the BTL group outperforms non-BTL companies in each of the seven years with an average advantage of 0.917 points, a fairly dramatic difference given the scale of the measurement. Similarly, for treatment of the environment, as Figure 10 highlights, the BTL group again outperforms the non-BTL in all seven years, with an average advantage of 0.178 points, less dramatic than for the employee stakeholder but still remarkably consistent from year to year.

Since there is no direct measure for treatment of customers, we have used the product category in the KLD ratings to assess treatment of customers, in part because the measure is largely built upon product quality issues, which figure greatly in customer satisfaction. Figure 11 gives the product category for both groups, showing a large performance difference between the BTL companies and non-BTL group in each of seven years. The average advantage is 0.740 points. The last of the five CSP variables, diversity, is illustrated in Figure 12, which shows that the BTL group outperformed the non-BTL group in each of seven years, with an average advantage of 0.740 points.

Finally, we wanted to assess overall CSP so we combined all five of the stakeholder categories in an unweighted average and once again compared the performance *vis à vis* these stakeholders for visionary and non-visionary companies. The final comparison, Figure 13, shows that for this overall CSP measure, the BTL firms outperformed the non-BTL firms in each of the seven years, with an average advantage of 0.578 points.

SOME STATISTICS PROVE THE POINT . . .

We have provided mainly descriptive results based on observed financial and stakeholder scores. It is possible, however, to test for statistically significant differences between the visionary and non-visionary companies if we consider them to be samples from a larger population.[29] When we perform the *t*-tests for differences in means, we are able to provide some strong statistical evidence that the relationship we have been discussing is real, rather than random.

Results of these *t*-tests are reported in Table 2. Here again, we find strong evidence that BTL companies outperform non-BTL firms in both accounting and market-based measures, extending their long record of excellent financial performance. The pooled *t*-tests show that visionary companies outperform non-visionary companies in terms of ROE, ROA, ROS, ten-year relative total return, and ten-year total return. As might be expected from the closeness of the curves shown in Figures 6 and 7, in terms of long-term debt and Beta there are no significant differences.[30]

Among the remaining variables, we see the strongest significant difference in ROE, ROA, and 10-year relative total return. Each of these measures is strongly significant in the pooled data and visionary companies significantly outperform non-visionary companies in three or more of the eight individual years, again with the BTL companies doing better than non-BTL. Among all of the financial variables, the strongest significance is for 10-year total relative total return.

When we look at stakeholder relationships explored in this study, we see a similar pattern with respect to the statistical tests shown in Table 2. BTL companies significantly outperform non-BTL companies in most stakeholder relationships studied. BTL companies evidence significantly better scores on employee relations, community relations, product (treatment of customer), and diversity measures than do non-BTL firms. The only measure for which visionary and non-visionary companies show no difference in treatment is the environment (and that result might be considered marginally significant). Further, the year-by-year results for environment are consistent with the pooled results, with environment insignificant in all seven years. After environment, the next weakest result is for community relations. The strongest results are for employee relations, for diversity, and for overall CSP, the unweighted average of the other CSP variables.

Looking once again at the figures, we consider whether the external evaluations of stakeholder relations performed by KLD show any significant trends during the period of the study (see Table 3).

TABLE 2   T-Tests for Differences between Means

	Pooled *t*-test	Number of individual year *t*-tests with p < .10
ROE	p = .0003	3 of 8
ROA	p = .0001	3 of 8
ROS	p = .0004	2 of 8
10-year relative total return	p = .0001	4 of 8
10-year total return	p = .0001	1 of 8
Long term debt	p = .0199	0 of 8
Beta	p = .3482	0 of 5
Community relations	p = .0012	2 of 7
Employee relations	p = .0001	6 of 7
Environment	p = .0520	0 of 7
Product	p = .0001	3 of 7
Diversity	p = .0001	6 of 7
CSP average	p = .0001	7 of 7

TABLE 3   Trend Analysis: Regression Test for Slope

Variable	Sign of Slope	Significance
Community relations	NA	p = .3587
Employee relations	+	p = .0087
Environment	NA	p = .6121
Product	NA	p = .4956
Diversity	+	p = .0001
CSP Average	+	p = .0666

Here we can see that two of the individual variables, employee relations and diversity, show a significant positive trend, suggesting that *both* groups of companies have improved their relationships with these stakeholders during the period of the study. The finding on diversity, in particular, makes sense in that a great deal of attention has been devoted to diversity management programs in recent years, with numerous companies implementing programs and paying attention to the status of minority groups in both the executive ranks and on their boards. Notably, none of the stakeholder-related variables shows a statistically significantly decreasing trend over the whole period of the study.

BEYOND "BUILT TO LAST . . ."

We titled this article "Beyond Built to Last . . ." because we expected, in starting this study, that the excellent performance of visionary companies studied by Collins and Porras (1994) would spill over into stakeholder arenas. That is, the vision and values that comprise the core ideology that drives visionary companies also conceivably drive operating practices that link companies positively to their manifold stakeholders. The "beyond" implies that not only do visionary companies do well for stockholders, using traditional financial performance measures as an assessment, but that visionary companies also have better relationships with other important primary stakeholders through the operating practices that are assessed in determining corporate social performance. These positive relationships with stakeholders, and the underlying operational practices that support them, we posit, result in the overall long-term better financial performance of the company, just as Collins and Porras suggested. We will speculate below on the importance, implications, and possible meaning of these findings.

BTL companies clearly outperform non-BTL companies on all of the measures of stakeholder and financial performance. Further, despite the small sample size, most of the differences are statistically significant, though visionary companies appear to be a bit more volatile in stock performance. The impact of values-driven visionary "clockbuilding" does indeed seem to sustain itself over time as is evidenced in traditional performance measures, despite the normal bumps and hurdles of everyday competitive life. Companies, however, don't just achieve long-term financial success, as the Collins and Porras study and these findings illustrate, by focusing on financial goals alone. The stakeholder evidence is, in our opinion, most compelling.

Indeed, Collins and Porras devote an entire chapter of their book to debunking the myth that the core purpose of the corporation is to maximize shareholder—or any other form—of wealth. Highlighting the "genius of the and" rather than the "tyranny of the or," Collins and Porras emphasize that "a fundamental element of the 'ticking clock' of a visionary company is a *core ideology*—core values and sense of purpose beyond just making money—that guides and inspires people throughout the organization and remains relatively fixed for long periods of time. [Core ideology] exists paradoxically with the fact that visionary companies are also highly effective profit-making enterprises."[31] The stakeholder evidence strongly support the notion that living out values—the practices inherent in implementing strategies related to stakeholder performance—is related to the by-product of strong financial performance.

It is this commitment to a higher purpose—a set of values that allows for the building of community spirit, a sense of integrity that goes beyond mere wealth maximization, that, we believe creates the type of organization that one calls visionary. The living out of these values through stakeholder relationships that are positive simultaneously inspires commitment and performance. Thus, having a core ideology does matter, as Collins and Porras argue. But we argue that the *content* of that ideology matters as well. The visionary companies demonstrate that the chosen core ideology must be capable of bringing a range of stakeholders together for a common purpose that goes beyond the trivial or the mere material and provides a common basis for doing this work together.

In looking at the ways that visionary companies treat their primary stakeholders we believe that we have added an important new dimension to Collins and Porras' argument. Bringing a range of different important stakeholders into alignment with the vision through the adoption and implementation of progressive operating policies, which manifest the way stakeholders are treated, is a critical element, we believe, of long-term corporate success. Far from being marginal considerations, developing and maintaining good relationships with stakeholders through the positive internal and external relationship building implied by positive stakeholder relationships appears to be a key to long-term success. It appears to be the implementation of vision into daily practice that makes the sustainable difference for the visionary companies.

One conclusion that can be drawn from this study is that the BTL companies do, in fact, seem to have avoided what Collins and Porras termed the "tyranny of the or." Not only do these companies continue to perform better for shareholders in financial and market terms, but they *also* carry less debt, which can be viewed as a measure of risk, and they evidence significantly better treatment of a range of stakeholders. These data thus provide more evidence for what is termed the "good management hypothesis:" that companies that treat their stakeholders well are well-managed companies.[32] That is, we posit—and these results confirm—that there is a positive relationship between the overall quality of management of a firm and the way it treats its critical stakeholders.

Further, remember that all of the companies in this study are considered to be good, strong, and well managed companies. Collins and Porras point out that the comparison group would be like the silver and bronze medal winners in the Olympics, not just a randomly selected group of companies. With that fact in mind, the differences with respect to financial and stakeholder performance are particularly striking.

NOTES

1. See James C. Collins and Jerry I. Porras, *Built to Last: Successful Habits of Visionary Companies* (New York: HarperBusiness, 1994).

2. E.g., Philip Selznick, *Leadership in Administration: A Sociological Interpretation* (Berkeley: University of California Press, 1983).

3. Collins and Porras, 4.

4. The classic definition of stakeholders derives from R. Edward Freeman's *Strategic Management: A Stakeholder Perspective* (New York: Basic Books, 1984). See also William M. Evans, and R. Edward Freeman, "A Stakeholder Theory of the Modern Corporation: Kantian Capitalism," in T. Beauchamp and N. Bowie, eds. *Ethical Theory and Business* (Englewood Cliffs, NJ: Prentice-Hall, 1988).

5. Mark Starik has articulated a perspective incorporating environment as a primary stakeholder in "Should Trees Have Managerial Standing? Towards Stakeholder Status for Non-Human Nature," *Journal of Business Ethics* 14 (1995), 204–217. While we do not believe the environment is a stakeholder, we treat it as an important part of a company's responsibility.

6. See, for example, Sandra A. Waddock and Samuel B. Graves, "The Corporate Social Performance-Financial Performance Link," in *Strategic Management Journal* 18(4) (1997), 303–319 and "Quality of Management and Quality of Stakeholder Relations: Are They Synonymous?" in *Business and Society* 36(3) (1997), 250–279.

7. Collins and Porras, 1–2.

8.   Collins and Porras, 88.

9.   James MacGregor Burns discusses the importance of end values in what he terms transformational leaders in *Leadership* (New York: Harper Torchbooks, 1978).

10.   The terms visionary companies and "built to last" companies and their comparison counterparts are used interchangeably throughout the rest of this article.

11.   Collins and Porras, 87.

12.   Collins and Porras, 70.

13.   This research was first published by Gary Hamel and C.K. Prahalad in an article entitled "Strategic Intent" in *Harvard Business Review*, May–June (1989), 63–76 and was later summarized in the book by the same authors, *Competing for the Future* (Boston: Harvard Business School Press, 1994).

14.   See Carl Anderson, "Values-Based Management," *Academy of Management Executives* 11(4) (1997), 25–46.

15.   See Jeanne M. Liedtka, "Constructing an Ethic for Business Practice: Competing Effectively and Doing Good" in *Business and Society* 37(3) (1998), 254–280.

16.   E.g., Peter M. Senge, *The Fifth Discipline: The Art and Practice of the Learning Organization* (New York: Doubleday, 1991).

17.   See, for example, W. Edwards Deming, *Out of the Crisis* (Cambridge, MA: MIT Center for Advanced Engineering Study, 1982), and for a perspective on the ethical implications of total quality management, Cecily Raiborn and Dinah Payne's "TQM: Just What the Ethicist Ordered," *Journal of Business Ethics* 15 (1996), 963–972.

18.   The seminal work on reengineering is Michael Hammer and James Champy's 1994 book *Reengineering the Corporation* (New York: Harper Business, 1994).

19.   See Henry Mintzberg, *The Rise and Fall of Strategic Planning* (New York: Free Press, 1994).

20.   For example, see the articles by Waddock and Graves, cited above.

21.   Comprehensive reviews of the corporate social performance literature have been undertaken by Jennifer J. Griffin and John F. Mahon, "The Corporate Social Performance and Corporate Financial Performance Debate: Twenty-Five Years of Incomparable Research," *Business and Society* 36(1) (1997), 5–31; Moses L. Pava and Joshua Krausz, "The Association Between Corporate Social-Responsibility and Financial Performance: The Paradox of Social Cost," *Journal of Business Ethics* 15 (1996), 321–357; and Donna J. Wood and Raymond E. Jones, "Stakeholder Mismatching: A

Theoretical Problem in Empirical Research on Corporate Social Performance," *The International Journal of Organizational Analysis*, 3(3) (1995), 229–267.

22. Sandra Waddock and Neil Smith, "Corporate Responsibility Audits: Doing Well by Doing Good," *Sloan Management Review*, Winter 2000, 41(2), 75–83.

23. Collins and Porras, 6.

24. Collins and Porras, 5.

25. Waddock and Graves cited above.

26. See Waddock and Graves, "Quality of Management and Quality of Stakeholder Relations" article cited above.

27. The collection cycle for KLD begins on July 1st, and ends June 30th of each year. The date associated with the KLD data is the ending year. For example, 1991 KLD data were collected over the period July 1st 1990 to June 30th, 1991. The COMPUSTAT data is reported depending on the individual company's fiscal year. The reporting year for each company is the year in which a majority of the months of the company's fiscal year fall. For example, if a firm's fiscal year ends in March, the data from April 1990 to March 1991 would be reported as 1990 data. If the same firm had a fiscal year ending in July, the August 1990 to July 1991 data would be reported as 1991 data. For the companies included in this study the average firm has a fiscal year ending in month 10.1, so the data as reported should correspond fairly closely to the reporting year for most firms. When KLD and COMPUSTAT data are merged by year in this study, the correspondence should be fairly close, with the KLD data leading the COMPUSTAT data by just a few months for the average firm.

28. For the COMPUSTAT financial data the analysis covers eight years, while the KLD social performance data cover seven. Some of the analyses were performed year by year, and some were performed on the pooled data for all years. The analysis is broken into three parts. In the first part we look only at the BTL and Non-BTL companies without any attempt to make inferences beyond these observed groups. That is, we consider these groups as the entire population(s) of interest in the study. When the groups are viewed this way it is necessary only to present and observe descriptive statistics to determine whether or not differences exist between the groups. Under this interpretation, tests of significance are neither necessary nor meaningful. In the second part, we take the view that the observed firms are a sample from a larger population (the population of all visionary firms) about which we wish to make an inference. Under this interpretation, tests of significance are necessary. A technical problem arises here, however, in that the

firms studied are not a random sample from the populations, but carefully screened groups, constructed according to Collins and Porras' criteria for visionary firms. This fact introduces the potential for unknown biases in the significance tests. In the third part of the analysis, we analyze the CSP data, looking for trends, to see whether the observed groups of companies are showing any overall improvement (or degradation) in their performance on the social dimensions measured.

29.   To perform significance tests, we take the view that the observed data are samples from a larger population about which we wish to draw an inference. Consider the data for ROE, for example. If we wish to make an inference about the difference between ROE for all visionary companies vs. all other companies (BTL-type companies vs. non-BTL) we must perform a test of significance to determine whether the observed difference is statistically significant. To do this we will use t-tests (of the paired difference variety, since we have paired observations). Since these observations do not result from a random sample from the populations of interest, a bias of unknown size may be introduced into these tests. Nonetheless, for those readers who may wish to draw inferences beyond the observed companies, we provide the t-tests. The t-tests are approached in two ways, first using pooled data for all years, then performing separate t-tests for each year. When the data are pooled for all years, two assumptions are required: first, that the observations (for each measure) are randomly and independently drawn from a normal distribution; and second, that there is independence between years. When conducting the year by year t-tests, this second assumption may be dropped. The results from these t-tests are shown in Table 2. The apparent disparity between the pooled figures and the individual year-by-year figures results from the large difference in degrees of freedom. For the year by year results, with only 10 differences per year, quite a large average difference is necessary to reach a level of statistical significance. Nonetheless, one can see some consistency and draw some inferences from looking at all of the tests together.

30.   The reason that Table 2 shows that only some of the years are statistically significantly different relates as much to small sample size as to the actual differences between the groups.

31.   Collins and Porras, 48.

32.   See the two studies by Waddock and Graves, cited above, for additional empirical research behind this argument.

[57]

CORPORATE SOCIAL RESPONSIBILITY AND FINANCIAL PERFORMANCE: CORRELATION OR MISSPECIFICATION?

ABAGAIL McWILLIAMS[1]* and DONALD SIEGEL[2]
[1]School of Management, Arizona State University West, Phoenix, Arizona, U.S.A.
[2]The University of Nottingham Business School, Nottingham, U.K.

Researchers have reported a positive, negative, and neutral impact of corporate social responsibility (CSR) on financial performance. This inconsistency may be due to flawed empirical analysis. In this paper, we demonstrate a particular flaw in existing econometric studies of the relationship between social and financial performance. These studies estimate the effect of CSR by regressing firm performance on corporate social performance, and several control variables. This model is misspecified because it does not control for investment in R&D, which has been shown to be an important determinant of firm performance. This misspecification results in upwardly biased estimates of the financial impact of CSR. When the model is properly specified, we find that CSR has a neutral impact on financial performance. Copyright © 2000 John Wiley & Sons, Ltd.

In recent years, customers, employees, suppliers, community groups, governments, and some shareholders have encouraged firms to undertake additional investments in corporate social responsibility (CSR). Some firms have responded to these concerns by devoting more resources to CSR. Other companies' managers have resisted, arguing that additional investment in CSR is inconsistent with their efforts to maximize profits. The resulting controversy has induced researchers to examine the relationship between CSR and financial performance, in an effort to assess the validity of concerns regarding a tradeoff between investment in CSR and profitability.

Existing studies of the relationship between CSR and financial performance suffer from several important theoretical and empirical limitations. One major concern is that these studies sometimes use models that are misspecified in the sense that they omit variables that have been shown to be important determinants of profitability. One such variable is the intensity of R&D investment by the firm. In this paper we discuss the correlation between CSR and R&D, and how to appropriately estimate the impact of CSR on financial performance.

Key words: corporate social responsibility; firm performance; product differentiation; R&D; specification error

*Correspondence to: Abagail McWilliams, School of Management, Arizona State University West, PO Box 37100, Phoenix, AZ 85069-7100, U.S.A.

EMPIRICAL STUDIES OF CSR AND FINANCIAL PERFORMANCE

There are basically two types of empirical studies of the relationship between CSR and financial performance. One set of studies uses the event study methodology to assess the *short-run* financial impact (abnormal returns) when firms engage in socially responsible or irresponsible acts (see, for example, Clinebell and Clinebell, 1994; Hannon and Milkovich, 1996; Posnikoff, 1997; Teoh, Welch and Wazzan, 1999; Worrell, Davidson, and Sharma, 1991; Wright and Ferris, 1997). The results of these studies have been mixed. For example, Wright and Ferris found a negative relationship; Posnikoff reported a positive relationship; and Teoh et al. found no relationship between CSR and financial performance, when examining divestitures from South Africa during the Apartheid controversy (see McWilliams, Siegel and Teoh, 1999, for a discussion of these studies). Other studies are similarly inconsistent on the relationship between CSR and short run financial returns (McWilliams and Siegel, 1997, provides a theoretical and empirical critique of the use of the event study methodology for examining the impact of CSR).

A second set of studies examines the nature of the relationship between some measure of corporate social performance, CSP (a measure of CSR), and measures of *long term* firm performance, using accounting or financial measures of profitability (see, for example, Aupperle, Carroll, and Hatfield, 1985; McGuire, Sundgren and Schneeweis, 1988; and Waddock and Graves, 1997). The results from these studies have also been mixed. Aupperle et al. found no relationship between CSP and profitability, McGuire et al. found that prior performance was more closely related to CSP than was subsequent performance, and Waddock and Graves found significant positive relationships between an index of CSP and performance measures such as ROA in the following year.

The inconsistency of the results from these studies of the relationship between CSR and performance is not surprising, given the nature of the models that form the basis for the empirical estimation. For example, Waddock and Graves (1997) estimate the following econometric model:[1]

$$PERF_i = f(CSP_i, SIZE_i, RISK_i, IND_i) \quad (1)$$

where

$PERF_i$ = long-run economic or financial performance of firm i (measures of accounting profits)

CSP_i = a proxy for corporate social responsibility of firm i (based on an index of social performance)

$SIZE_i$ = a proxy for the size of firm i

$RISK_i$ = a proxy for the "risk" of firm i (debt/asset ratio)

IND_i = industry of firm i (4 digit SIC code)

The inclusion of the industry dummy (IND) is to control for some industry-level factors that have been shown to explain variation in firm performance across industries, such as economies of scale and competitive intensity.[2] We hypothesize that Equation 1 is misspecified due to omitted variables, because it does not control for a firm's rate of investment in R&D and the advertising intensity of its industry. A more appropriate specification is:

$$PERF_i = f$$

$$(CSP_i, SIZE_i, RISK_i, IND_i, RDINT_i, INDADINT_i)$$

$$(2)$$

where the additional covariates are:

$RDINT_i$ = R&D intensity of firm i (R&D expenditures/sales)

$INDADINT_i$ = advertising intensity of the industry of firm i

Excluding R&D in the econometric model is especially problematic, because there is a long standing theoretical literature linking investment in R&D to improvements in long-run economic performance (Griliches, 1979). In these models, R&D is considered to be a form of investment in "technical" capital. Investment in technical capital results in knowledge enhancement, which leads to product *and* process innovation. This innovative activity enables firms to enhance their productivity.

---

[1] Note that many studies simply examine correlation coefficients, but with causal implications.

[2] We will argue that a very specific type of industry effect—industry advertising intensity—must also be (separately) controlled for, because it is so closely associated with CSR.

Strat. Mgmt. J., **21**: 603–609 (2000)

There is strong empirical evidence to support this hypothesis, using a wide variety of measures of long-run economic performance. These results are robust to different time periods and levels of aggregation.[3] For example, using data from over 2000 firms, Lichtenberg and Siegel (1991) report a strong positive correlation between R&D investment and growth in total factor productivity. Clark and Griliches (1984) find similar results at the line-of-business level, using the PIMS database. Ben-Zion (1984), Guerard, Bean, and Andrews (1987), Guerard, Stone, and Andrews (1988), and Hall (1999) report similar positive associations between R&D, accounting profits, and long-term shareholder returns (and other proxies for long-term financial performance).[4]

If R&D has a positive impact on firm performance, then the coefficient on any variable that is strongly positively correlated with R&D will be *overestimated* when R&D is omitted from Equation 1 (Theil, 1971: 549). We hypothesize that R&D and CSP are positively correlated, since many aspects of CSR create either a product innovation, a process innovation, or both.

The link between CSR and R&D

Investment in CSR promotes product differentiation at the product and firm levels. Some firms will produce goods or services with attributes or characteristics that signal to the consumer that the company is concerned about certain social issues. Also, many companies will try to establish a socially responsible corporate image. Both of these strategies will encourage consumers to believe that, by consuming the product, they are directly or indirectly supporting a cause.

These strategies are effective with those consumers who wish to champion firms that devote resources to CSR. Consequently, many products have labels that indicate the use of certain

---

[3]See Lichtenberg and Siegel (1991) and Griliches (1998) for comprehensive reviews of existing empirical studies of the relationship between R&D and productivity growth.
[4]Evidence on the short-run impact of R&D on stock prices (event studies) is mixed. Early event studies (Chan et al., 1990, Austin, 1993) found that announcements of increases in R&D expenditures and patent awards enhance share prices. The results of recent event studies (Sundaram et al., 1996, Chung et al., 1998, and Chung and Wright, 1998) cast doubt on such broad generalizations. These authors report that the short-run stock market response to unexpected changes in R&D will depend on firm characteristics and strategic factors.

ingredients and production methods that promote CSR. For example, natural food companies place labels on their products signifying the use of organic, pesticide-free ingredients; cosmetic firms boast of animal-free testing; manufacturing companies display "made in the USA" stickers; and radio and television commercials tell us to "look for the union label." Labels that refer to CSR attributes also create new (socially responsible) product categories in the perception of consumers.

The examples above apply to process *and* product innovations, both of which are valued by some consumers. For instance, the "organic, pesticide-free" label simultaneously indicates the use of organic methods, which constitutes a *process innovation* by the *farmer*, and the creation of a new product category, or a *product innovation* by the *natural foods retailer*. If the natural foods company is vertically integrated, it engages in both CSR-related process and product innovation simultaneously. Each of these examples underscores the point that some consumers want the goods they purchase to have certain socially responsible attributes (product innovation), while some also value knowing that the goods they purchase are produced in a socially responsible manner (process innovation).

Consumer-oriented CSR may also involve intangible attributes such as a reputation for quality or reliability. The presumption is that firms that actively support CSR are more reliable and their products are of higher quality. This is especially important for food products. For example, some restaurants serve "free range" chicken and beef. "Free range" meat products are perceived to be of higher quality than conventional meat products. Presumably, this is because they have a more natural taste, due perhaps to their closer proximity to a natural state (in the sense that the animals roam more freely) or because they are not injected with hormones or antibiotics. By promoting their use of "free range" chicken and beef, restaurants signify to their patrons that they are concerned about product quality (use of the finest ingredients) and also about more humane treatment of animals.

There is strong evidence that many (but certainly not all) consumers value CSR attributes. Therefore, an increasing number of companies incorporate CSR into their marketing strategies, to exploit the appeal of CSR to key segments of the market, such as "baby-boomers" or "generation X" shoppers. We need only look at the rapid growth of such socially responsible companies as Ben & Jerry's, the Body Shop, and Health Valley to confirm the importance of CSR in marketing.

Support of CSR may also be used to create a reputation that a firm is reliable and honest, and some consumers may assume that the products of a reliable and honest firm will be of high quality. Therefore, advertising that provides information about CSR attributes may be used to create a reputation for quality or reliability or honesty—all attributes that are important, but may be difficult for consumers to determine. Such advertising makes consumers aware of product differentiation (quality) based on CSR attributes.

For example, New United Motor Manufacturing, Inc., or NUMMI, the innovative joint venture between Toyota and General Motors, was established in Fremont, California in 1984 to build small cars for both companies. The NUMMI plant implemented many of the latest Japanese "lean manufacturing" methods (process innovation), and produced the Geo Prism, the prototype for GM's new generation of small cars (product innovation). Furthermore, through its unique partnership with the United Auto Workers (UAW), NUMMI also implemented a number of progressive workplace practices, such as a strong emphasis on teamwork and employee empowerment. The bottom line is that some consumers perceived that NUMMI cars, such as the Geo Prism, were superior to traditional, American-made cars, in terms of quality and reliability. More germanely, many customers also believed that by purchasing these cars, they were demonstrating their support of progressive human resource management practices and the UAW.

The link between advertising and firm performance

The remaining independent variable in our proposed model—Equation 2- ($INDADINT_i$) is designed to serve as a proxy for the extent of product differentiation at the industry level and entry barriers that might serve to enhance firm profitability. Entry barriers are a shared asset across firms in an industry, because entry barriers are an industry level construct (McWilliams and Smart, 1993). While there is considerable debate regarding the magnitudes of industry level effects

(Powell, 1996; Rumelt, 1991; Schmalansee, 1975; Waring, 1996), the consensus is that industry factors "matter," in the sense that they explain a non-negligible percentage of the variation in profitability across firms. Thus, $INDADINT_i$ should be included in the model, along with "size" and "risk," as a control variable.

If our conjectures are true (corr (RDINT, PERF) > 0, corr (RDINT, CSP) > 0), then the consequences of omitting R&D from Equation 1 are clear. As noted in Theil (1971), if an omitted regressor, in this case RDINT, is positively correlated with both the dependent variable (PERF) and the included regressor (CSP), then the coefficient on CSP, in the misspecified Equation 1, will be overestimated.

Simply put, the positive and significant coefficient on CSP, as reported by Waddock and Graves (1997), could simply reflect the impact of R&D on firm performance. It is impossible to isolate the impact of CSP on firm performance unless the model is properly specified. A similar argument could be made for other omitted regressors, such as advertising intensity, if they are also positively correlated with CSP and firm performance.

EMPIRICAL ANALYSIS

To assess the validity of the results reported in studies that employ Equation 1 (Waddock and Graves, 1997), we estimate the model outlined in Equation 2. For this estimation, we linked Compustat data to information on corporate social performance provided to us by the firm of Kinder, Lydenberg, and Domini (KLD), which began compiling this information in May 1991. KLD provides ratings of corporate social performance, or CSP (a measure of corporate social responsibility), for portfolio managers and other institutional investors who wish to incorporate social factors into their investment decisions. Many of these social investors want to "screen" their portfolios to exclude companies that violate their social principles. In this context, CSP is defined as a (0,1) variable; a firm is either socially responsible or it is not, based on the "screen" applied. For example, an investment firm that is managing a portfolio for evangelical Christians will avoid companies in the gambling and alcohol industries.

KLD uses a combination of surveys, financial statements, articles on companies in the popular press, academic journals (especially law journals), and government reports to assess CSP along eleven dimensions: military contracting, nuclear power, gambling, tobacco, alcohol, community relations, diversity, employee relations, environment, and product quality (innovation/R&D), and non-U.S. operations (usually environment and labor relations).[5] Based on this information, the firm constructed the Domini 400 Social Index (DSI 400), the functional equivalent of the Standard and Poors 500 Index for socially responsible firms.

In order to be eligible for the DSI 400, a firm must derive less than 2% of its gross revenue from the production of military weapons, have no involvement in nuclear power, gambling, tobacco, and alcohol, and have a positive record in each of the remaining six categories. For example, a firm that implements recycling and pollution-prevention programs, provides donations to conservation organizations, and demonstrates concern for the environment in its day-to-day operations, is regarded as having a positive record along the environmental dimension. A firm that actively promotes minorities and women to top managerial positions and membership on the board of directors will receive a similar positive score along the diversity dimension. Our measure of CSP is a dummy variable, with a value of 1 if a firm is included in the DSI 400 in a given year (for having passed the "social screen"); 0 otherwise.

Our data series, created from a linkage of the KLD data and Compustat, contains 524 firms. To simplify the econometric analysis and to ensure comparability with existing studies, each of the variables in Equation 2 is computed as an average annual value for the years 1991–1996, a time period that corresponds to the overlap of the Compustat and KLD files. Table 1 presents definitions, descriptive statistics, and a correlation matrix for the three key variables: PERF, CSP, and RDINT.

Several stylized facts are evident from Table 1. The most striking results are that R&D, CSP, and financial performance all appear to be strongly positively correlated. This supports our hypothesis

that estimation of Equation 1 constitutes a specification error that may result in an overestimation of the impact of CSP on financial performance. This overestimation arises because CSP is positively correlated with R&D, which has been found to be a strong determinant of improvements in economic performance.

We argue that firm-level investment in R&D, and additional industry factors (advertising intensity as a proxy for barriers to entry) should also be included in the econometric specification. To explicitly test our hypothesis that Equation 1 is misspecified, we examine variants of Equation 2, including the rate of firm level investment in R&D and industry dummy variables (4 digit SIC) in the model (with advertising intensity included as a control variable). These findings are presented in Table 2.

The results confirm our hypothesis regarding the importance of including R&D and industry factors in a model that attempts to "explain" corporate performance. As shown in column (1), when R&D and industry factors are excluded from the model, the coefficient on CSP is positive and statistically significant. However, when R&D and industry factors are added to the model, the magnitude of the coefficient diminishes dramatically and is no longer significant. Additionally, the "fit" of the model improves, as shown by the increase in the adjusted R^2. Thus, our findings underscore the importance of using the appropriate specification when estimating the "return" on CSR investment.[6]

DISCUSSION

Over the last 3 decades, the pressure on firms to engage in corporate social responsibility (CSR) has increased. Many managers have responded to these pressures, but many have resisted. Those who resist typically have invoked the trade-off between socially responsible behavior and profitability. Management researchers have responded to this by attempting to demonstrate the effect of CSR on profitability. However, the results of

---

[5]Additional detail on the KLD file and the social "screens" is presented in Waddock and Graves (1997) and Kinder and Domini (1997).

[6]A caveat is in order. Our result of no financial impact from CSR may be a result of the lack of a good measure of CSR. We use the KLD rating system, which relies heavily on negative screens and includes philanthropic activities. A more business-oriented definition of CSR might yield a different result. We thank a reviewer for pointing this out.

608	*A. McWilliams and D. Siegel*

Table 1.	Definitions of key variables, descriptive statistics, and correlations (N = 524 firms)

Variable	Definition	Mean	Std Dev	PERF	CSP	RDINT
PERF	Financial Performance	−0.011	1.043	1.000		
CSP	Corporate Social Performance	0.619	0.345	0.356**	1.000	
RDINT	R&D to Sales Ratio	0.011	0.949	0.403**	0.449***	1.00

All variables computed as annual averages over the period 1991–1996.
*p ≤ 0.10; **p ≤ 0.05; ***p ≤ 0.01

Table 2.	Regression results from estimation of variants of Equation 2 (N = 524 firms, standard errors in parentheses)

Dependent Variable: PERF	(1)	(2)	(3)
Coefficient on CSP	0.141*** (0.052)	0.104 (0.106)	−0.062 (0.059)
Coefficient on RDINT	–	0.145*** (0.036)	0.263*** (0.050)
Industry Dummies (4 digit SIC) included	No	No	Yes
Adjusted R²	0.10	0.19	0.29

*p ≤ 0.10; **p ≤ 0.05; ***p ≤ 0.01
Note: All regressions include controls for size, risk, and advertising intensity, which are computed as annual averages over the period 1991–1996.

empirical studies of the relationship between CSR and profitability have been inconclusive, reporting positive, negative, and neutral results.

We hypothesized that this inconsistency could be due to flaws in empirical analysis. One particular flaw is econometric estimation of a misspecified model. An example of such a specification error is the equation estimated by Waddock and Graves, 1997, which is misspecified because it does not include a measure of firm-level investment in R&D. This is unfortunate, because there is a large body of empirical evidence showing that investment in R&D has a strong positive impact on profitability. We also hypothesized that R&D investment and CSR are likely to be highly correlated, because both are associated with product and process innovation. If CSR and R&D are highly correlated, an equation that includes CSP (a measure of CSR) as a determinant of firm performance, but *not* R&D will result in upwardly biased estimates of the CSP variable.

To test our hypothesis, we estimated two models. The first was the same specification as Waddock and Graves and the second was one in which we included R&D intensity. Our results confirm that CSP and R&D are highly correlated, and that, when R&D intensity is included in the equation, CSP is shown to have a neutral effect on profitability. This should not be surprising, because many firms that actively engage in CSR are also pursuing a differentiation strategy, involving complementary strategic investments in R&D. This makes it difficult to isolate the impact of CSR on performance without simultaneously controlling for R&D. Therefore, we caution readers to be wary of models that claim to "explain" firm performance, but do not include important strategic variables, such as R&D intensity.

REFERENCES

Aupperle, K., A. Carroll and J. Hatfield (1985). 'An empirical examination of the relationship between corporate social responsibility and profitability', *Academy of Management Journal*, **28**(2), pp. 446–463.

Austin, D. H. (1993). 'An event study approach to measuring innovative output: The case of biotechnology', *American Economic Review*, **83**(2), pp. 253–259.

Ben-Zion, U. (1984). 'The R&D and investment decision and its relationship to the firm's market value: Some preliminary results'. In Z. Griliches (ed.), *R&D, Patents, and Productivity*. University of Chicago Press, Chicago, IL, pp. 134–162.

Chan, S. H., J. D. Martin and J. W. Kensinger (1990). 'Corporate research and development expenditures and share value', *Journal of Financial Economics*, **26**, pp. 255–276.

Chung, K. H. and P. Wright (1998). 'Corporate policy and market value: A q-theory approach', *Review of Quantitative Finance and Accounting*, **11**, pp. 293–310.

Chung, K. H., P. Wright and C. Charoenwong (1998). 'Investment opportunities and market reaction to capital expenditure decisions', *Journal of Banking and Finance*, **22**, pp. 41–60.

Clark, K. B. and Z. Griliches (1984). 'Productivity growth and R&D at the business level: Results from the PIMS database'. In Z. Griliches (ed.), *R&D, Patents, and Productivity*. University of Chicago Press, Chicago, IL, pp. 393–416.

Clinebell, S. K. and J. M. Clinebell (1994). 'The effect of advanced notice of plant closings on firm value', *Journal of Management*, **20**, pp. 553–564.

Griliches, Z. (1979). 'Issues in assessing the contribution of R&D to productivity growth', *Bell Journal of Economics*, **10**(1), pp. 92–116.

Griliches, Z. (ed.) (1998). *R&D and Productivity: The Econometric Evidence*. National Bureau of Economic Research for the University of Chicago Press, University of Chicago Press, Chicago, IL.

Guerard, J. B., Jr., A. S. Bean and S. Andrews (1987). 'R&D management and corporate financial policy', *Management Science*, **33**, pp. 1419–1427.

Guerard, J. B., Jr., B. K. Stone and S. Andrews (1988). 'Corporate R&D expenditures, innovation, and competition in an international economy'. In R. Shrieves (ed.), *Competition in the International Economy*. Cambridge University Press, Cambridge, UK, pp. 215–250.

Hall, B. H. (1999). 'Innovation and market value', National Bureau of Economic Research Working Paper #6984.

Hannon, J. and G. Milkovich (1996). 'The effect of human resource reputation signals on share prices: An event study', *Human Resource Management*, **35**(3), pp. 405–424.

Kinder, P. and A. Domini (1997). 'Social screening: Paradigms old and new', *Journal of Investing*, **6**(4), pp. 12–19.

Kinder, P., S. Lydenberg and A. Domini (1993). *Making Money While Being Socially Responsible*. Harper Business, New York.

Lichtenberg, F. and D. Siegel (1991). 'The impact of R&D investment on productivity: New evidence using linked R&D-LRD data', *Economic Inquiry*, **29**, pp. 203–228.

McGuire, J., A. Sundgren and T. Schneeweis (1988). 'Corporate social responsibility and firm financial performance', *Academy of Management Journal*, **31**(4), pp. 854–872.

McWilliams, A. and D. Siegel (1997). 'Event studies in management research: Theoretical and empirical issues', *Academy of Management Journal*, **40**(3), pp. 626–657.

McWilliams, A., D. Siegel and S. H. Teoh (1999). 'Issues in the use of the event study methodology: A critical analysis of corporate social responsibility studies', *Organizational Research Methods*, **2**(4), pp. 350–372.

McWilliams, A. and D. Smart (1993). 'Efficiency v. structure-conduct-performance: Implications for strategy research and practice', *Journal of Management*, **19**(1), pp. 63–78.

Posnikoff, J. F. (1997). 'Disinvestment from South Africa: They did well by doing good', *Contemporary Economic Policy*, **15**(1), pp. 76–86.

Powell, T. C. (1996). 'How much does industry matter? An alternative empirical test', *Strategic Management Journal*, **17**(4), pp. 323–334.

Rumelt, R. (1991). 'How much does industry matter?', *Strategic Management Journal*, **12**(3), pp. 167–185.

Schmalansee, R. (1985). 'Do markets differ much?', *American Economic Review*, **75**, pp. 341–351.

Sundaram, A., T. John and K. John (1996). 'An empirical analysis of strategic competition and firm values: The case of R&D competition', *Journal of Financial Economics*, **40**(3), pp. 459–470.

Teoh, S. H., I. Welch and C. P. Wazzan (1999). 'The effect of socially activist investment policies on the financial markets: Evidence from the South African boycott', *Journal of Business*, **72**(1), pp. 35–89.

Theil, H. (1971). *Principles of Econometrics*. John Wiley & Sons, New York.

Waddock, S. and S. Graves (1997). 'The corporate social performance – financial performance link', *Strategic Management Journal*, **18**(4), pp. 303–319.

Waring, G. (1996). 'Industry differences in the persistence of firm-specific returns', *American Economic Review*, **86**(5), pp. 1253–1265.

Worrell, D., W. N. Davidson and V. N. Sharma (1991). 'Layoff announcements and stockholder wealth', *Academy of Management Journal*, **34**(3), pp. 662–678.

Wright, P. and S. Ferris (1997). 'Agency conflict and corporate strategy: The effect of divestment on corporate value', *Strategic Management Journal*, **18**(1), pp. 77–83.

Part XVI
Implementation (Implanting Ethical Strategy)

[58]

Modes of Managing Morality:
A Descriptive Model of
Strategies for Managing Ethics

Gedeon J. Rossouw
Leon J. van Vuuren

ABSTRACT. As an alternative to attempts to impose models of personal moral development (e.g. Kohlberg) upon organisations we propose an evolutionary model of managing ethics in organisations. The Modes of Managing Morality Model that we suggest, is based on an analysis that explains why business organisations tend to move from less complex modes of *managing ethics* to more complex modes thereof. Furthermore, it also identifies the dominant ethics management strategies that characterise each of the stages. It is done in a way that avoids claiming that the more advanced modes of managing ethics necessarily represent moral development by business organisations. Instead of claiming the organisations develop morally, we claim that organisations move through an evolutionary process of *improving their sophistication in managing ethical performance.*

KEY WORDS: business ethics, compliance, institusionalisation, integrity, management, moral development, strategy

Gedeon J. Rossouw is professor in Philosophy at RAU University in Johannesburg, South Africa. He is President of the Business Ethics Network of Africa (BEN-Africa), serves on the Executive Committee of the International Society for Business Economics and Ethics and on the Editorial Board of the Journal of Business Ethics.

Leon J. Van Vuuren is a registered industrial psychologist and associate professor in Human Resource Management at RAU University in Johannesburg, South Africa. He specialises in the institutionalisation of ethics in organisations.

Introduction

Various attempts have been made to adapt models of personal moral development – such as those developed by Piaget, Kohlberg, and Gilligan – to organisations. Logsdon and Yuthas (1997) for example developed a model of organisational moral development based on Kohlberg's six stages of moral development in which they claim that an organisation's level of moral development can by gauged by its stakeholder orientation. Petrick and Manning (1990) who also used Kohlberg's model to identify six stages of moral development in organisations have made a similar attempt. Sridhar and Camburn (1993) applied Kohlberg's model to examine if organisations can be viewed as passing through different stages of moral reasoning to explain their behaviours in the face of ethical crises. In this article we will show why these and other attempts to apply theories of personal moral development to business organisations are inappropriate.

An alternative approach to using personal cognitive moral development in describing "collective" or organisational moral development was proposed by Coleman (2000). Coleman, based his approach on insights acquired during his term as ethics officer at Texas Instruments. He identified six levels of natural ethical progress of an organisation, namely (1) commitment, (2) formulation, (3) action and feedback, (4) re-evaluation, (5) total ethical culture, and (6) total alignment and integration. He describes each level as "more ingrained, more naturally integrated, than the one before . . ." (2000, p. 1). These levels reflect an organisation's attempts to manage ethics in an increasingly concerted and sophisticated manner over time.

A similar approach is Driscoll and Hoffman's (2000) "Stages of ethical development" model. They used a pyramid diagram to reflect the causal relationship between four stages or levels of ethical development in an organisation. The stages that organisations and their people progress through, commence with *ethical awareness*, whereafter *ethical reasoning* (decision-making models and criteria) is acquired. This is followed by a confrontation between the values/behaviour gap which results in the *ethical action* stage. Finally, ethical development culminates in *ethical leadership*, which implies the cultivation of broad-based-commitment and an ethical culture.

As an alternative to attempts to impose personal moral development upon organisations we will propose an evolutionary model of managing ethics in organisations that is closer aligned to the Coleman and Driscoll and Hoffman approaches. However, the model that we propose (Modes of Managing Morality Model) goes beyond these approaches in the sense that it is based on an analysis that explains why business organisations tend to move from less complex modes of *managing ethics* to more complex modes thereof. Furthermore it also identifies the dominant ethics management strategies that characterise each of the stages. It is done in a way that avoids claiming that the more advanced modes of managing ethics necessarily represent moral development by business organisations. Instead of claiming that organisations develop morally, we will claim that organisations move through an evolutionary process of *improving their sophistication in managing ethical performance*.

1. On applying personal moral development to organisations

The empirical research done by Piaget (1948), Kohlberg (1948), Gilligan (1982) and other established that individuals typically move through a process that can be broadly described as a move from a heteronomous phase to an autonomous phase of moral decision-making. Attempts to further refine this broad description of the process of personal moral development

suggest that personal moral development starts at a pre-conventional level and then moves through a conventional level to a post-conventional level. Attempts have further been made to discern more specific stages within each of these three broad levels of moral development. The more specific these models are on the specific stages of moral development, the more controversial they tend to become.

In the above mentioned attempts to design a model of organisational moral development, either the broad phases or the more specific stages of moral development are applied and adapted to organisations. Although these adapted models all recognise the important differences between individuals and organisations, they nevertheless claim that organisations move through the same phases, levels or stages that individuals do. While the content of the phases, levels or stages are altered and renamed to reflect organisational reality, the basic structure of personal moral development still remains and is imposed upon organisations.

We believe that any attempt to impose personal moral development upon organisations is unwarranted. This is not because organisations cannot be considered moral agents. Even if one agrees with French (1979), De George (1988) and Meyers (1993) that corporations can be regarded as moral agents, that still does not imply that corporations develop morally like individuals do. That corporations decide and act collectively cannot be denied. However, corporations do not take decisions and actions in the way that individuals do. Corporate decisions and actions are the outcomes of complicated group dynamic processes in which individual members of the organisation participate. The decisions and actions therefore do not emanate from a collective personality, or a collective mind, or a collective moral state of development, but from a group dynamic process in which individuals with different personalities, minds and levels of moral development participate. The fact that certain patterns in the decisions and actions of a corporation can be discerned over time, once more does not imply that a corporation has a personality, mind, and level of moral development like individuals do. This consistency in decisions and actions only emerges because the individual members of the corporation are guided by a common set of corporate objectives and priorities.

One should thus not conclude that there is moral development in organisations simply because corporations can be regarded as moral agents in whose moral decisions and actions a certain extent of consistency can be discerned. The consistency in moral behaviour by corporations should rather be ascribed to the moral objectives and priorities that corporations collective pursue and by the strategies that they adopt in pursuing there objectives and priorities. In the remainder of this article, it will be demonstrated how specific moral objectives and priorities and the management strategies that are adopted in pursuit thereof, is a sufficient explanation for both consistency and change in moral behaviour in corporations.

In the Modes of Managing Morality Model that follows, five different modes of managing ethics are identified. The nature and distinguishing features of each mode is first described. Each mode of managing ethics, however, presents its own challenges to managing ethics. It is exactly these challenges presented by each mode that facilitate transition to the next mode of managing ethics. Although the model does not presuppose moral development within corporations, it does assume that there is an increase in the complexity of the management modes as they follow on one another. In this sense there can be distinguished between more and less advanced modes in terms of management complexity, without equating this distinction with more or less advanced stages of moral development.

The model is specifically designed to explain the changes in mode of managing ethics within medium to large business enterprises. Given the evolutionary nature of the model, the more advanced modes of managing ethics can only be expected in well-established sustainable businesses.

2. The Modes of Managing Morality model (MMM) model

A classification framework is proposed whereby an organisation can be classified as having a specific way (or *mode*) of dealing or not dealing with ethics. A mode can be described as *the predominant (preferred) strategy of an organisation to manage its ethics at a given point in time*. The preferred mode reflects the decision its leaders make to ignore ethics and to act unethically, or to actively deal with ethics in an overt manner. The mode is observable and has discernible qualitative and quantitative properties that display the organisation's strategy (conscious or not) to ignore or manage ethics. The extent to which organisations deal with ethics can obviously vary from reactive and superficial ethical window-dressing to concerted and structured efforts to institutionalise and integrate ethics. It is suggested that five relatively distinct *modes* can be discerned in describing organisations' preferred strategies for managing ethics. The model consists of the modes of (1) immorality, (2) reactivity, (3) compliance, (4) integrity and (5) total alignment. A synopsis of the modes is provided in Table I.

As is shown in Table I each mode is described in terms of (1) its nature, (2) primary purpose, (3) predominant strategy, and (4) typical challenges.

The challenges that arise within each mode provide an explanation for the change in mode of managing ethics that typically occur within organisations over time. These challenges arise when organisations sense that they may have exhausted a specific mode's potential for managing ethics. These challenges then serve as sufficiently powerful catalysts to overcome factors of inertia and provide impetus for organisations to either operate within a new and more advanced mode of ethics management, or to perhaps even revert to a previous mode. The latter may occur when the previous mode is perceived to provide a comfort zone of familiarity in dealing with (or ignoring) ethics issues. A mode may therefore produce its own self-destruction when challenges force the organisation into another mode of managing ethics.

TABLE I
The Modes of Managing Morality (MMM) model

Dimensions of comparison	Immoral mode	Reactive mode	Compliance mode	Integrity mode	Totally Aligned Organisation (TAO) Mode
Nature	Unethical conduct is good business The business of business is business, and *not* ethics	Token gesture of ethical intent is shown (a code of ethics) Unethical behaviour is ignored and remain unpunished	Commitment to manage and monitor ethics performance *Rule-based approach* to ethics Disciplining unethical behaviour	Internalisation of ethical values and standards *Value-based approach* to ethics Internal locus of (ethics) control; "Walking the ethics 'talk'"	Seamless integration of ethics in corporate purpose, strategy and operations Non-negotiable morally responsible interaction with stakeholders
Purpose	Ethics has no place in the singular pursuit of the bottom line Unethical behaviour espoused as good business	Protection against dangers of unethical behaviour Sceptics and critics are silenced (temporarily) by the existence of ethics standards	Prevention of unethical behaviour Desire to have a good ethical reputation	Raising level of corporate ethical performance Pro-active promotion of ethical behaviour Ethics of strategic importance or a competitive edge	Ethics reinforced as part of culture and purpose Ethics entrenched in discourse and decision-making
Ethics management strategy	A Macchiavellian orientation exists that denies the need to make decisions concerning ethics No concern for stakeholders No ethics management strategy or interventions	*Laissez-faire* ethics management Inability to manage ethics Corporate (ethical) values are words on paper	Transactional approach to managing ethics Code clear and comprehensive & corporate ethics management function exists Ethics management systems used Unethical behaviour punished	Transformational approach to managing ethics Stakeholder engagement Ethics "talk" prevails High-level ethics management functions and systems Managers have an ethics competence	Everyone responsible for ethics management Ethics function/office serves as "rudder" Ethical heroes celebrated, ethics stories told Elimination of discrepancies between corporate values and behaviour

TABLE I
Continued

Dimensions of comparison	Immoral mode	Reactive mode	Compliance mode	Integrity mode	Totally Aligned Organisation (TAO) Mode
Challenges	Financial consequences of immorality becomes unaffordable	Credibility problems with stakeholders	Mentality of "what is not forbidden is allowed"	Discretion granted is abused	Ethical complacency/ arrogance; moral laxness
		Susceptible to ethical scandal		Moral autonomy leads to moral dissidence	Neglect ethics induction of new employees
	Increased dissonance between personal and corporate values	Stakeholders convey frustrated expectations	Personal moral autonomy and responsibility undermined		
			Proliferation of ethical rules and guidelines	Powerful leaders undermine ethics drive	Lack of co-ordination in managing ethics
	Stakeholders experience alienation	Corporate ethical reputation below par	Employees disempowered to use ethical discretion	Lack of clear corporate identity undermines integrity mode	

2.1. *The immoral mode*

Nature. Organisations in this mode usually espouse unethical conduct as good business and ascribe to the cynical viewpoint that business ethics is an oxymoron. They embrace the popular myths (cf. Rossouw, 2002, pp. 11–21) that many corporate leaders and business ethics scholars have already dispelled during the past few decades. Examples of such myths are: "dog eats dog" (the business environment is a hostile world and you either trample on others or you yourself will be trampled on); "survival of the fittest" (the competitive nature of business means that you cannot afford to waste time on the interests of others); "nice guys come second" (a proclamation that it is impossible to be both ethical *and* successful in business); "it is not serious" (the notion that although unethical conduct is wrong, it is not really harmful to society); "when in Rome, do as the Romans do" (if it is the norm to act unethically in a certain environment, why be different?); and "all that matters is the bottom line" (the business of business is business, and *not* ethics).

Purpose. Organisations in this mode aim at maximising profit at all cost – all that matters to them is the bottom line. Such a mode dictates motives and actions beyond reasonable capitalistic greed. Where more ethically aware organisations realise that the above mentioned credos are merely myths, a central feature of immoral mode organisations is that they view some or all of these credos to epitomise good management philosophy. The myths as outlined above become implicit or even explicit credos that are viewed as part and parcel of "good business". When this happens managerial philosophies and behaviours assume unethical proportions.

Strategy to manage ethics. Immoral mode organisations are typically characterised by a Macchiavellian orientation in that management does not see the need to make decisions concerning ethics. There is therefore no commitment to deal with ethics. In such organisations there is a lack of sensitivity to ethical issues and reluctance to engage with it. Although there may be some varied dissonance about the eventual effects of unethical conduct, it is nevertheless endorsed as good business and goes unpunished.

Immoral mode organisations have little inclination to be sensitive to stakeholders' ethics expectations. Since members of immoral mode organisations generally share beliefs regarding the prevalence of myths such as those described above, the corporate culture makes little provision for an ethical way of thinking. The ethical climate is virtually non-existent in that managers and employees can be described as morally mute (Waters and Bird, 1987). "Ethics talk" is frowned upon and perceived to be wimpish behaviour that does not belong in an organisation characterised by hard-line philosophies such as a desire to be "lean and mean" and a "we take no prisoners"-orientation. Any attempts to question the ethical dimension of decisions are thwarted by peer pressure characterised by a singular focus on the bottom line.

Consequently there is an absence of a proper ethics management strategy in such organisations. No ethics management interventions exist – not even the most rudimentary ones such as a code of ethics.

Challenges. The challenges for organisations to move beyond this mode are threefold.

- The real financial consequences of immorality may become unaffordable. It may, however, also be that the perceived probable cost of immorality become an overwhelming threat in that organisations fear being found out or exposed. Change may also be triggered by scandal and the explosion of myths. In Schein's (1987, p. 289) words: "Nothing changes until the consequences of the *theory-in-use* create a public and visible scandal that cannot be hidden, avoided or denied".
- An increased dissonance between personal and corporate values may surface. Employees, for example, may develop a severe cognitive dissonance if they perceive the unethical inclination of the organisation to be contradictory to their own ethical value systems. They may then either remain in the organisation in a state of alienation and passivity, or they may move on to other companies that appear to have more sound ethics. The effects of this on the organisation's morale may be devastating.
- Other stakeholders, e.g. shareholders, customers, suppliers and the local community, may experience similar feelings of dissonance and resultant alienation – this may lead to them severing their ties with the immoral mode organisation. When this happens the organization's social network may be in danger of complete collapse.

Immoral mode organisations either continue in their ways to a point-of-no-return self-destruction, or they may be compelled by the above-mentioned challenge to rethink their preferred unethical mode and to do at least something about their ethics, albeit reactive.

2.2. *The reactive mode*

Nature. Organisations often enter a reactive mode of morality as a knee-jerk reaction to the challenges posed by the immoral mode. In order to avoid rejection such organisations make the confession to ethical business, but do not proceed beyond that (Rossouw, 1994, p. 9). The reactive mode is prompted by awareness that something needs to be done to avoid the risk and dire consequences of unethical conduct. Such organisations have a naïve belief that a show of commitment (the presence of a set of ethical values) will create a sufficient context for ethical behaviour. In the process these organisations profess to be ethical, without management compliance to its set ethical standards. This may be ascribed to an inability to manage ethics. Although reactive mode organisations make provision for ethics, unethical behaviour still prevails. A blind eye is turned towards unethical behaviour and, at best, if unethical practices are detected, they are not endorsed, but remain unpunished. Corporate ethics therefore amounts to a token gesture of ethical intent.

Purpose. Reactive mode organisations have a desire to protect themselves against the dangers of unethical behaviour in that they sense the potential risk of unethical behaviour. Of course they also fear rejection by their stakeholders. Organisations in reactive mode become sensitive to the effects unethical practices may have on their reputations. By confessing to ethical behaviour they hope to avoid threats of litigation, boycotts, strikes and shareholder alienation. The possibility of government intervention or even enforced curatorship may be another motivational force to acquire some "inoculation" against unethical behaviour. The enforcement of corporate governance standards by regulatory institutions might compel organisations into reactive morality. This mode of managing morality thus merely signifies a defensive corporate approach to business ethics. Although cognisant of the consequences of unethical behaviour, they may still condone a bending of the rules (e.g. creative accounting).

Strategy to manage ethics. Since attempts by a reactive mode organisation to manage ethics are seldom based on ethics being good business, but rather on a desire to protect against investigation and punitive action, the organisation will formulate standards that display rejection of unethical behaviour. Although value judgements exist, they lack application. There is therefore no attempt to complement formal ethical standards with compliance procedures. Nor do these organisations develop any form of corporate ethics management capacity.

Senior management of organisations in the reactive mode may obviously have a desire to mend their attitudes and ways. A result of such good intentions may be a strategic planning session that results in the generation of a number of corporate ethical values. Although these values signal a commitment to integrity, respect and organisational ethics, they do not have the impact to create an ethical context in which employees can operate. As such, they by and large remain words or statements on paper.

Ethics management interventions by reactive mode organisations are usually limited in scope and depth. Such organisations often scamper to institute some minimum measures of ethics management interventions in an effort to avoid paying a high price for immorality. This effort can at best be described as window-dressing. A feature of organisations in this mode's attempt to manage ethics is the design of a corporate code of ethics. The focus is, however, often on the final product rather than on a proper inclusive process to produce it. As such, code design is often delegated to either a single member of the organisation or to a function such as internal audit, risk management, the company secretariat or human resources. Some reactive mode organisations may engage external consultants to draft the code. It is also not uncommon for reactive mode organisations to obtain existing codes from other companies and to adapt these for their own purposes. The development of the code is an event rather than a process in the sense that it is produced in unilateral fashion without participation by relevant internal and external stakeholders. Although the code may eventually be of high quality and may have good potential for application, the code is not worth the paper it is written on insofar as application is concerned. The code is likely to remain on a shelf without assuming living document proportions. Having most probably not been involved in the code design exercise, employees are not *au fait* with the code, nor do they know how to apply its contents to the key performance areas as is expected of them vis-à-vis their job descriptions.

Ethics management in reactive organisations therefore rarely progress beyond code design interventions and can be described as *laissez-faire* ethics management, both in philosophy and in application.

Challenges. The challenges facing reactive mode organisations are the following:

- Reactive mode organisations display a gap between talking and walking ethics. This leads to a serious credibility problem with stakeholders. Both internal and external stakeholders find their expectations frustrated and have difficulty trusting an entity whose words and actions are not aligned. They are therefore likely to formally or informally convey frustrated expectations regarding the organisation's ethics.

- In the absence of the security and predictability that an ethical context can provide for employees, the organisational morale may be very fragile.
- Like organisations in the immoral mode, an organisation in reactive mode is very susceptible to scandal. Since there is a gap between espoused ethical standards and the actual behaviour of the organisation, this might easily be exploited. Dissatisfied employees may, in the absence of internal channels for dealing with ethical failures, opt for blowing the whistle on unethical practices, which in turn can trigger scandals.
- Reactive mode organisations are also likely to discover that token gestures to ethical performance does not satisfy institutional investors, consumers and talented employees. The cost associated with their lack of trust in the organisation might become a compelling factor in convincing the reactive mode organisation to revise its ethics strategy.
- Since the mere existence of a code of ethics does not guarantee ethical behaviour, nor provide the context for moral discourse, ethically aware employees might demand more pro-active engagement with ethics. They might specifically demand training in dealing with ethical dilemmas and in moral decision-making that will assist them in applying the organisation's code of ethics.

When these challenges gain sufficient momentum they have the potential of compelling the reactive mode organisation into moving beyond reactive gestures unto enforcing ethics deliberately.

2.3. *The compliance mode*

Nature. The compliance mode of managing ethics represents a substantial move away from the reactive mode. Companies in compliance mode commit themselves to monitoring and managing their ethics performance. Instead of merely having a code of ethics for the sake of pacifying stakeholders, the code becomes the standard against which the company measures its own ethical performance. Companies in this mode of managing their ethics typically express their intention to ensure that all members of the organisation abide by the ethical standards of the company. In order to ensure compliance to the code, they monitor the ethical performance of members of the organisation. When deviation from the code of ethics occurs, the company takes corrective action by disciplining or penalising the transgressors. Alternatively the company may opt for not only penalising transgression of its ethical standards, but also for rewarding those who consistently abide by its code of conduct. The compliance approach thus represents a rule-based approach to managing ethics.

Purpose. The managerial purpose of the compliance mode is to prevent unethical behaviour by the business. The driving force behind this commitment to eradicate unethical behaviour can either be found in the desire to avoid the cost and damage associated with unethical behaviour (Moon and Bonny, 2001, p. 26), or in the quest to benefit from having a good corporate ethical reputation. An example of the former is the company that insists on compliance in order to avoid costs associated with discrimination, fraud or a business scandal, while an example of the latter is the company that wishes to uses its good ethical reputation to attract investors, ethically discerning consumers or talented employees.

Management strategy. Compliance mode organisations make a conscious decision to regulate ethics and display a commitment to eradicate unethical behaviour. Given the central role of the code of ethics in the compliance mode, management first needs to ensure that the code is sufficiently clear and detailed in order to provide distinct guidance on ethics to members of the organisation. If the current code is insufficient in this regard, one can expect that it will be revised to provide clarity on ethical standards and guidelines for behaviour. Unless the code is very clear and specific, it will fail in serving as a standard for evaluating ethical performance.

The code needs to be complemented by an ethics management function that will manage and drive the process of compliance to the code. This ethics management function can be the responsibility of a dedicated corporate function created specifically for this purpose (e.g. an ethics office or compliance office) or it can be delegated to an existing management function in the company (e.g. risk management, human resource management, or internal audit). This ethics management function takes responsibility for all the processes and systems required for ensuring adherence to the code. This includes processes such as communication, training and the induction of new employees to the code. It requires that systems be designed for monitoring, appraising, and rewarding ethical performance. Also systems whereby employees can safely report unethical or morally suspicious behaviour by employees can be implemented. The management process in this mode may also include accounting, auditing and disclosure of ethics performance.

In sum, ethics management in the compliance mode may be described as a *transactional* approach – the emphasis is on rules to be complied to in exchange for withholding of punishment for non-compliance, rather than an embracing of ethical values and an entrenching of these values.

Challenges. The compliance approach may result in a number of side-effects that can potentially pose a serious challenge to the viability of this approach. These potentially harmful side-effects include the following:

- It breeds a mentality of "what is not forbidden is allowed". Given the rule-based nature of this approach, organisational members can rely merely on the existing rules for moral guidance.
- It undermines personal moral autonomy and responsibility. As the code of ethics is enforced upon the organisation, the locus of moral control resides externally in the code and in the ethics management function. The ethical values and standards

of the company are not internalised, but are imposed externally.

- Since this mode implies a comprehensive and diligent attempt to enforce ethical compliance, it may assume bureaucratic proportions over time. This can lead to a proliferation of ethical rules and guidelines for conduct. In an attempt to provide unambiguous guidance on ethical conduct, more and more directives are issued. These rules can grow so numerous that it becomes difficult to keep track of them. Should this happen, it is almost impossible to recall all the directives, and for that reason they may have very little impact on actual corporate behaviour.
- It tends to disempower employees (Sharp Paine, 2002, p. 135). A compliance approach does not rely on the moral discretion of employees, but on their almost blind adherence to the rules of conduct. This undermines their ability to cope with issues and grey areas that is not addressed in the code of ethics.

If these challenges are not adequately addressed, they can erode the viability of the compliance approach to managing ethics. If they are dealt with adequately their negative impact can be alleviated. It is, however, often exactly these challenges that facilitate the transition to the integrity mode.

2.4. The integrity mode

Nature. An integrity approach comprises a value-based approach to managing ethics. Where the compliance mode is characterised by external enforcement of ethical standards upon a business organisation, the integrity approach is marked by the internalisation of ethical values and standards. Instead of imposing ethical standards upon the organisation, it seeks to obtain the commitment of individual members of the organisation to a set of shared corporate values (Moon and Boony, 2001, p. 26). In this way the locus of control becomes internal. By ensuring that the locus of control resides within members of the organisation, less external control is required. There is thus less need for external guidance and more reliance on the discretion of individual members of the organisation to act morally responsible. This approach to managing ethics requires much more knowledge and expertise on managing ethics, since it ventures into the subtle domain of value formation and commitment. Given the delicate nature of the integrity approach to managing ethics, it is usually complemented by a limited form of a compliance approach that serves as a safety net to protect the company against gross unethical conduct.

Purpose. The purpose of the integrity approach to managing ethics is to raise the level of ethical performance of the company. Instead of merely trying to minimise incidents of unethical behaviour, it pro-actively endeavours to promote ethical behaviour. By getting organisational members to commit themselves to the corporate ethical standards and values of the company, the responsibility for ethical behaviour becomes a collective effort shared by all members of the organisation. Companies typically embark on this approach when they realise that ethical performance is of strategic importance to the company or even its competitive edge. In such cases a defensive approach that protects the company against the damage of unethical conduct is no longer deemed sufficient. To the contrary, a concerted effort in which all members of the organisation take joint responsibility for the ethics performance of the company is required.

Management strategy. The management strategy required for an integrity approach is one that facilitates the internalization of ethical standards in all members of the organisation. Such a strategy typically commences with a comprehensive and deep diagnosis of the corporate ethical culture and current state of ethical behaviour. As such a wide ranging consultative process of stakeholder engagement in which their moral expectations of the company are gauged is instituted. These expectations will be widely communicated in the company. In response to it the core ethical values of the company will be identified or be revisited. This will also be done in

a consultative and consensus-seeking manner in order to facilitate buy-in into these core values. There are two further vital components of an integrity strategy. The first is the promotion of "ethics talk". Employees need to get into the habit of discussing the ethical dimension of their work. No decision should be considered complete unless the ethical dimension thereof had been contemplated. Secondly, an integrity approach also relies heavily on the example set by the leadership of the company. If leaders are not seen to adhere to the core ethical values and standards of the company in word and deed, the integrity approach will lose credibility.

The integrity approach further requires managerial system and process support in much the same way that it is required in the compliance mode. It requires ongoing communication, training and induction of new employees. Training on moral decision-making becomes much more prominent as there is an increased reliance on the moral discretion of employees in the integrity approach. Systems for evaluating and rewarding the ethical performance of the company are also required. In an integrity approach the emphasis is on the reward of ethical behaviour, rather than on punishing unethical behaviour. It is therefore to be expected that ethical performance will be perceived as a key performance area to be included in performance management and appraisal. In addition, the aspects of ethical reporting, auditing and disclosure that were introduced in the compliance mode will remain. Once well established, the corporate ethics function may require fewer human and other resources, as there then would be a diminished need to rely on monitoring compliance to ethical guidelines.

An integrity mode of ethics management has *transformational* proportions – as such deep cultural organisational change is effected over time. Internalisation of values occurs in that employees are empowered as well as enabled to manage ethics in their own roles and jobs.

Challenges. The integrity mode also poses a number of challenges to ethics management. The most prominent being the following:

- The greater discretion granted to employees can be abused and unethical conduct can increase. Should this happen a turn towards greater compliance might occur, which in turn will erode the integrity approach. In this way the integrity approach can gradually revert to a compliance approach.
- The promotion of moral autonomy that results from an integrity approach can also lead to moral dissidence in a company. Individuals who are empowered to use their moral discretion and to act with moral courage are more likely to challenge the morality of company actions. Given the differences in personal moral values that one is likely to encounter in bigger companies, serious moral differences are more likely to emerge.
- The integrity approach relies heavily on the integrity of its leadership. If they do not set both the tone and the example, the integrity approach can easily be discredited. If the entire leadership does not endorse the core ethical values in their practical behaviour (i.e. walk the ethics talk), it can pose a serious challenge to the viability of the integrity approach. Since those leaders who undermine the integrity approach are most probably in positions of considerable power, it may be very difficult, or even impossible, to overcome the challenge that they pose.
- The integrity approach also presupposes a clear sense of corporate identity and priorities (Sharp Paine, 2002, p. 135). The individual discretion upon which the integrity approach is premised can only be properly exercised when core ethical values are aligned with corporate identity and priorities. A lack of clarity about corporate identity and priorities thus lurks as another obstacle that can jeopardize the sustainability of the integrity approach.

All these challenges can potentially be addressed within the integrity approach. Failure to do so, may result in a lapse to a compliance approach or in disillusionment with the current endeavour to manage ethics. It is however also possible that these challenges, if overcome, may give rise to a new mode of managing ethics. Since very few companies have yet ventured into this domain, one can but merely speculate about its outlines.

2.5. The Totally Aligned Organisation (TAO) mode

Nature. The TAO-mode is characterised by a seamless integration of ethics into the purpose, mission and goals of the organisation – ethics is integral to how an organisation defines itself and how things are done. Ethics is no longer viewed as just another aspect of the organisation that needs to be managed. To the contrary, it is regarded as an integral part of the company without which it would be unable to fulfil its purpose, mission and goals. This presupposes that a company in the TAO-mode will have a well-developed sense of identity and purpose premised upon non-negotiable morally responsible interaction with its internal and external stakeholders as well as its environment. Consequently ethical behaviour is regarded as strategically important and unethical behaviour is regarded as jeopardizing not only the business success of the organisation, but also as undermining its *raison de être*.

Purpose. The purpose of managing ethics in the TAO-mode is to reinforce ethics as part of the company's culture and purpose. Through ongoing conscientisation all members of the organisation are aware that ethical behaviour is not an optional extra, but is at the core of the very nature and purpose of the organisation. Ethics thus is recognised as part of business as usual and is entrenched in corporate discourse and decision-making. In this way members of the organisation become sensitive to behaviour that contradicts the ethical nature and commitment of the organisation. As they understand and are aware of the strategic importance of ethical behaviour for organisational success and sustainability, they regard unethical behaviour as high-risk behaviour and are empowered to prevent, disclose and confront such deviant behaviour.

Management strategy. The management strategy in the TAO-mode is geared towards reinforcing the essentiality of ethical behaviour for the sustained success of the organisation. It therefore becomes vitally important that all managers in the organisation play their part in reinforcing ethics as part of business as usual. All the trappings of ethics management that manifested in the integrity mode will however, still remain. The essential difference is that the managerial responsibility for ethics is no longer limited to a dedicated ethics function, but is now widely dispersed throughout the organisation and on all management levels. Ethics therefore becomes an ingrained part of line management's strategic and operational activities. Although a dedicated ethics management function and structure will most probably remain, its major responsibility will be to empower managers on all levels to integrate ethics in their repertoire of managerial skills and actions.

In the TAO-mode the congruence between the purpose, vision and ethical values of the organisation is all-important. Consequently communication gains in importance and becomes the primary managerial intervention. Through both the formal and informal communication systems of the organisation its identity and purpose and the essential role of ethics therein is continually emphasized. The vision of the company, its history as well as the stories of its former and current moral heroes are kept in circulation. Rather than focusing on either punishing unethical behaviour or rewarding ethical conduct, the focus is on celebrating organisational heroes who embody the vision, purpose and ethical commitment of the organisation.

Sustained stakeholder engagement form an integral part of managing ethics in the TAO mode. As the organisation regards morally responsible interaction with its internal and external stakeholders as part of its organisational identity, it follows that regular stakeholder engagement to determine how they are affected and how they perceive the organisation, will be a management priority. This will result in ongoing bilateral communication in which the organisation not only listens to its stakeholders' needs and expectations, but also regularly discloses its economic, social and environmental performance to stakeholders.

Part of the ethics management strategy in the TAO mode is to identify discrepancies between behaviour and organisational values. Wherever such discrepancies are detected, those responsible for the deviation of corporate norms are persuaded that their behaviour contradict and undermine the values and culture of the company. Once more this responsibility for protecting the company's ethical orientation is a widely dispersed one that is shared across all management levels of the organisation.

Challenges. The TAO-mode creates challenges of its own. Such challenges may include:

- The TAO-mode can breed a mentality of ethical complacency or even ethical arrogance. Ethical behaviour is simply accepted as the norm and therefore some may regard it as superfluous to keep on emphasising the importance thereof. This ironically can result in a situation where ethics talk start to diminish and is left to chance, rather than being monitored and managed.
- Since ethics is so well ingrained in the TAO-mode organisation it becomes almost second-nature to those members of the organisations who are steeped in its culture. They then start to assume that what is so evident to them is equally obvious to others. This may result in new entrants to the organisation not being properly inducted into the organisational culture and values. Over time this can create a subgroup in the organisation with a lesser commitment to the ethical culture of the organisation.
- The dispersion of the managerial responsibility throughout the organisation may also result in a lack of co-ordination of the ethics management effort. Because ethics management is now the responsibility of all managers, there may be no dedicated function or person to take responsibility for the ongoing co-ordination and strategic planning of corporate ethical performance. This can result in ethical discrepancies developing within the organisation. It can also undermine pro-active planning for

the sustained ethical performance of the company.

- Reliance on the capacity of organisational members to act with integrity may also result in the organisation ridding itself of rules and procedures that were originally designed to protect the company against moral failures. The absence of such rules and procedures may over time induce moral laxness that increases the risk of moral failure.

None of these challenges produced by the TAO-mode of managing ethics is insurmountable. A reluctance to address them, may however result in them becoming huge obstacles that can potentially undermine the TAO-mode of managing ethics and eventually compel management to revert to the integrity or even compliance mode.

3. Conclusion

The Modes of Managing Morality (MMM) model provides a heuristic device to assist business ethics scholars and practitioners to make sense of the differences that exist in the ways in which different organisations manage their ethics. Although it recognises that there are distinct differences between the various modes and also in the levels of managerial sophistication displayed by organisations in managing their ethics, it does not attribute these differences to variations in organisational moral development. It steers clear of the temptation to impose personal moral development models upon organisations. In this way it avoids the controversy that usually surrounds such attempts, whilst still recognising that all are not equal when it comes to sophistication in managing ethics.

For the MMM-model to become a well-entrenched interpretative and descriptive tool it needs to be subjected to empirical scrutiny. From an applied research perspective it may be particularly useful to analyse particular organisations in terms of their fit to a mode as described in the model. As such the development of quantitative and qualitative diagnostic instruments (e.g. questionnaires, focus groups, in-depth interviews,

document analysis, etc.) that can provide organisations with sufficient information to enable them to determine their current mode of managing morality, appears imminent. The results attained from such measures will also provide feedback to organisations on their current ethics performance and may facilitate further adjustments to ethics management philosophies and actions.

Further research into the dynamics that prompts organisations to proceed beyond their current mode, is also recommended. Longitudinal analyses of organisations subjected to various internal (e.g. changes in employee moral awareness) and/or external pressures (e.g. legislation) to amend their mode of managing ethics, is therefore desirable.

References

Coleman, G.: 2000, *The Six Levels of a Totally Aligned Ethics Culture*. Paper presented at the Managing Ethics in Organisations course (Centre for Business Ethics, Bentley College, Waltham, MA).

De George, R. T.: 1988, 'The Right to Work: Law and Ideology', in T. L. Beauchamp and N. E. Bowie (eds.), *Ethical Theory and Business*, 3rd ed. (Prentice-Hall, Englewood Cliffs, NJ).

Driscoll, D.-M. and W. M. Hoffman: 2000, *Ethics Matters: How to Implement Values-driven Management* (Centre for Business Ethics, Bentley College, Waltham, MA).

French, P. A.: 1979, 'The Corporation as Moral Person', *American Philosophical Quarterly* **3**, 201–215.

Gilligan, C.: 1982, *In a Different Voice: Psychological Theory and Women's Development* (Harvard University Press, Cambridge, USA).

Kohlberg, L.: 1981, *The Philosophy of Moral Development* (Harper and Row, San Francisco).

Logsdon, J. M. and K. Yuthas: 1997, 'Corporate Social Performance, Stakeholder Orientation and Organizational Moral Development', *Journal of Business Ethics* **16**, 1213–1226.

Meyers, C.: 1993, 'The Corporation, its Members, and Moral Accountability', in T. I. White (ed.), *Business Ethics: A Philosophical Reader* (Macmillan, New York).

Moon, C. and C. Bonny: 2001, *Business Ethics* (The Economist Books, London).

Petrick, J. A. and G. E. Manning: 1990, 'Developing an Ethical Climate for Excellence', *The Journal for Quality and Participation* (March), 84–90.

Piaget, J.: 1948, *The Moral Judgement of the Child* (Free Press, New York).

Rossouw, D.: 1994, *Business Ethics: A Southern African Perspective* (Southern Books, Midrand).

Rossouw, D.: 2002, *Business Ethics in Africa* (Oxford University Press, Cape Town).

Schein, E. H.: 1987, *Organisational Culture and Leadership* (Jossey-Bass, San Francisco).

Sharpe-Paine, L.: 2002, 'Venturing Beyond Compliance', in L. P. Hartman (ed.), *Perspectives in Business Ethics* (McGraw-Hill Irwin, Boston), pp. 133–137.

Sridhar, B. S. and A. Camburn: 1993, 'Stages of Moral Development in Organisations', *Journal of Business Ethics* **12**, 727–739.

Waters, J. A. and F. Bird: 1987, 'The Moral Dimension of Organizational Culture', *Journal of Business Ethics* **6**, 15–22.

Gedeon J. Rossouw
Philosophy Department,
RAU University,
P.O. Box 524,
Aucklandpark, 2006,
South Africa
E-mail: gjr@lw.rau.ac.za

Leon J. van Vuuren
Human Resource Management,
RAU University,
P.O. Box 524,
Aucklandpark, 2006,
South Africa
E-mail: ljvv@eb.rau.ac.za

[59]

Enron Ethics (Or: Culture Matters More than Codes)

Ronald R. Sims
Johannes Brinkmann

ABSTRACT. This paper describes and discusses the Enron Corporation debacle. The paper presents the business ethics background and leadership mechanisms affecting Enron's collapse and eventual bankruptcy. Through a systematic analysis of the organizational culture at Enron (following Schein's frame of reference) the paper demonstrates how the company's culture had profound effects on the ethics of its employees.

Now, when most people hear the word "Enron" they think of corruption on a colossal scale – a company where a handful of highly paid executives were able to pocket millions of dollars while carelessly eroding the life-savings of thousands of unwitting employees. Not long ago, the same company had been heralded as a paragon of corporate responsibility and ethics – successful, driven, focused, philanthropic and environmentally responsible. Enron appeared to represent the best a 21st century organization had to offer, economically *and* ethically. The questions become, how did Enron lose both its economical and ethical status? Is it because of its very size and effects? Is it the direct harm to primary and secondary stakeholders? Or, is it the worldwide media coverage that the Enron demise has drawn? These questions make the Enron case interesting to us as business ethicists.

At first sight, Enron looks like a mega-size illustration of the bad apple and/or the bad barrel disease and, hence, looks like good marketing for the business ethics business (which almost has a vested interest in such scandals and other bad examples). The problem is, however, that Enron looked like an excellent corporate citizen, with all the corporate social responsibility (CSR) and business ethics tools and status symbols in place.

Enron Ethics (an ironic expression which is used now and then, see e.g. the headings of Tracinski, 2002 or Berenbeim in *Executive action* no. 15, Feb. 2002) reads like *the* new catchword for the ultimate contradiction between words and deeds, between a deceiving glossy facade and a rotten structure behind, like a definite good-bye to naive business ethics. Enron ethics means (still ironically) that business ethics is a question of organizational "deep" culture rather than of cultural artifacts like ethics codes, ethics officers and the like. With this as a backdrop, the paper will describe and discuss how executives at Enron in practice created an organizational culture that put the bottom line ahead of ethical behavior and doing what's right. More specifically, the paper first provides a brief background on Enron and its rise and fall. Next, the paper systematically uses Schein's (1985) five primary mechanisms available to leaders to create and reinforce aspects of culture (i.e., attention focusing, reaction to crises, role modeling, rewards allocation and criteria for hiring and firing) to analyze the company's culture and leadership that contributed to it's ethical demise and filing for bankruptcy. It is our contention, that with such a point of departure one will be better prepared for a necessary discussion in our field of how to prevent an "instrumentalization" of ethics and CSR for mere facade purposes (this theme deserves and requires a paper on its own, at least).

The culture history of Enron

The Enron case is not least a good illustration of continuously updated case presentation and case discussion in the Internet age (which could deserve a paper on its own, too). Business school researchers, teachers and students alike can easily keep themselves busy for days just with sorting, structuring, checking and summarizing all the ingredients and pieces of the Enron story found on the Internet. One possible way of organizing and limiting such a task is departing from or even staying with the websites of traditional *mass media* such as CNN (see e.g. cnn.com/SPECIALS/2002/enron/), the *Wall Street Journal, Financial Times*, or of the *main stakeholders* such as the victims' enrongate.com or the remainders' enron.com. Most tempting for business ethicists is of course a closer look at the websites of the *business ethics business* (see e.g. http://www.msnbc.com/modules/enron/, businessethics.ca/enron/, caseplace.org, enronguide.com, all with lots of further links) and as the up-dated and earliest of all the academic articles and papers we can expect in the future Tonge et al., 2003; Petrick and Quinn, 2002; Cohan, 2002). In spite of (or because of) such an abundance of available information[1] we choose to tell the story once more, as a culture history in our own prose, as a background for the following illustration of how Schein's organization culture approach can lead to a better understanding of the Enron case.

Background

A company with humble beginnings, Enron began as a merger of two Houston pipeline companies in 1985. Although Enron faced a number of financially difficult years, the company managed to survive. In 1988, the deregulation of the electrical power markets took effect, and the company redefined its business from "energy delivery" to "energy broker" and Enron quickly changed from a surviving company to a thriving one. Deregulation allowed Enron to become a "matchmaker" in the power industry, bringing buyers and sellers together. Enron profited from the exchanges, generating revenue from the differences between the buying and selling prices. Deregulation allowed Enron to be creative – for the first time, a company that had been required to "operate within the lines" could innovate and

test limits. Over time, Enron's contracts became increasingly diverse and significantly more complex. As Enron's products and services evolved, so did the company's culture.

In this newly deregulated and innovative forum, Enron embraced a culture that rewarded "cleverness". Deregulation opened the industry up to experimentation and the culture at Enron was one that expected employees to explore this new playing field to the utmost. Pushing the limits was considered a survival skill.

Enron's former President and Chief Executive Officer (CEO) Jeffry Skilling actively cultivated a culture that would push limits – "Do it right, do it now and do it better" was his motto. He encouraged employees to be independent, innovative and aggressive. The Harvard Business Review Case Study: *Enron's Transformation* (Bartlett and Glinska, 2001) contains employee quotations such as ". . . you were expected to perform to a standard that was continually being raised . . .", "the only thing that mattered was adding value", or ". . . it was all about an atmosphere of deliberately breaking the rules . . ." (Bartlett and Glinska, 2001). A culture that admires innovation and unchecked ambition and publicly punishes poor performance can produce tremendous returns in the short run. However, in the long run, achieving additional value by constantly "upping the ante" becomes harder and harder. Employees are forced to stretch the rules further and further until the limits of ethical conduct are easily overlooked in the pursuit of the next big success (Josephson, 1999; cf. also similarities found in the culture at Salomon Brothers in the early 1990s, see Sims, 2000; Sims and Brinkmann, 2002).

A lot of smoke and mirrors

Enron's spectacular success, and the positive scrutiny the company was receiving from the business press and the financial analysts, only added fuel to the company's competitive culture. The business community rewarded Enron for its cleverness (and even its ethicalness) and Enron's executives felt driven by this reputation to sustain the explosive growth of the late 1990s, even when they logically knew that it was not possible. A negative earnings outlook would have been a red flag to investors, indicating Enron was not as successful as it appeared. If investors' concerns drove down the stock price due to excessive selling, credit agencies would be forced to downgrade Enron's credit rating. Trading partners would lose faith in the company, trade elsewhere, and Enron's ability to generate quality earnings and cash flows would suffer. In order to avoid such a scenario at all costs, Enron entered into a deceiving web of partnerships and employed increasingly questionable accounting methods to maintain its investment-grade status. Enron executives probably felt that they were doing the right thing for their organization.

Partnerships

Partnerships can be an easy and efficient way to raise money. However, in an effort to continue to push the value envelope Enron took partnerships to a new level by creating "special purpose vehicles" (SPVs), pseudo-partnerships that allowed the company to sell assets and "create" earnings that artificially enhanced its bottom line. Enron exaggerated earnings by recognizing gains on the sale of assets to SPVs. In some cases, the company booked revenues prior to a partnership generating significant revenues. Project Braveheart, a partnership Enron developed with Blockbuster was intended to provide movies to homes directly over phone lines. Just months after the partnership was formed, Enron recorded $110.9 million in profits prematurely, these profits were never realized as the partnership failed after only a 1,000-home pilot.

In a success culture like Enron's such behavior represented a way of least resistance. Enron employees with a self-image of being the best and the brightest and being extremely clever do not make business deals that fail. Therefore booking earnings before they are realized were rather "early" than wrong. The culture at Enron was quickly eroding the ethical boundaries of its employees.

Keeping debt off the balance sheet

The SPVs not only allowed Enron to boost earnings, but the SPV's also allowed the company to keep debt off its balance sheet. A highly leveraged balance sheet would jeopardize its credit rating as its debt-equity ratio would rise and increase its cost of capital. To avoid this, Enron parked some of its debt on the balance sheet of its SPVs and kept it hidden from analysts and investors. When the extent of its debt burden came to light, Enron's credit rating fell and lenders demanded immediate payment in the sum of hundreds of millions of dollars in debt.

This can be read as another example of ethical erosion. Enron's decision makers saw the shuffling of debt rather as a timing issue and not as an ethical one. Clever people would eventually make everything right, because the deals would all be successful in the long run. Moving debt was as easy as pre-dating a check, and would harm no one, and therefore was not an ethical issue.

Partnerships at "arm's length"

Each questionable partnership decision carried additional cleverness burdens. In order to keep information from the public, Enron had to guarantee that the Securities Exchange Commission (SEC) did not consider its partnerships as Enron subsidiaries. If the partnerships had been classified as such, in-depth disclosure and stricter accounting methods would have been required. In order to prevent potential SEC skepticism, Enron enlisted help from its outside accountants and its attorneys (Arthur Andersen, and Vinson & Elkins). The accountants and attorneys all referenced the Financial Accounting Standards Board (FASB) rule that holds that partnerships are not considered subsidiaries as long as 3% of their equity comes from outside investors and they are managed independently of their sponsors. This is commonly known as being at "arm's length". Enron crafted relationships that looked (legally) like partnerships, although they were (in practice) subsidiaries. A closer look at the partnerships would have revealed that the outside investments came from companies (like SE Thunderbird LLC) that were owned by Enron.

Conflicts of interest

Although the partnerships were classified as partnerships according to the FASB rules, Enron officials obviously had close ties with them. This raised the question about conflicts of interest. Andrew Fastow, Enron's former Chief Financial Officer (CFO), ran or was partial owner of two of the most important partnerships: LJM Cayman LP and LJM2 Co-Investment LP. Michael Kopper, a former managing director at Enron, managed a third partnership, Chewco Investments LP.

The culture of cleverness at Enron started as a pursuit of excellence that devolved into the appearance of excellence as executives worked to develop clever ways of preserving Enron's infallible facade of success. Although Enron maintained that top officials in the company reviewed the dealings with potential conflicts of interest, Enron later claimed that Fastow earned over $30 million from Enron with his companies. At some point in the bending of ethical guidelines for the good of the company, Enron's executives also began to bend the rules for personal gain. Once a culture's ethical boundaries are breached thresholds of more extreme ethical compromises become lower.

The self-reinforcing decline of Enron

In the long run, Enron's executives could not "rob Peter to pay Paul". Even if the Enron culture permitted acts of insignificant rule bending, it was the sum of incremental ethical transgressions that produced the business catastrophe. Although Enron's executives had believed that everything would work successfully in the long run, the questionable partnerships left the company extremely vulnerable when financial troubles came to light. As partnerships began to fail with increasing regularity, Enron was liable for millions of dollars it had not anticipated

losing. Promises began to come due and Enron did not have the ability to follow through on its financial obligations.[2]

The financial implosion

The partnerships that once boosted earnings and allowed Enron to prosper became the misplaced card that caused the Enron house to collapse. The stability of Enron's house of cards had been eroded by the very culture that had allowed it to be built. Enron was forced to renounce over $390 million in earnings from dealings with Chewco Investments and JEDI, another partnership. The company was also forced to restate earnings back to 1997, and the restated earnings totaled only $586 million, a mere 20% of the initially reported figures. The very results Enron had sought to prevent – falling stock prices, lack of consumer and financial market confidence – came about as a direct result of decisions that had been driven by Enron's culture.

The Enron case of ethical failure consists of more than a series of questionable business dealings. When strong company leadership would have been needed the most, Enron's leader left the company. In August of 2001, Jeffery Skilling resigned as President and CEO of Enron and sold shares of his company stock totaling $66 million dollars. Only two months later, Enron restated earnings, stock prices dropped and the company froze shares in an attempt to help stabilize the company. Enron employees, who had been encouraged to invest heavily in the company, found themselves unable to remove and salvage their investments. The company culture of individualism, innovation, and aggressive cleverness left Enron without compassionate, responsible leadership. Enron's Board of Directors was slow to step in to fill the void and individual Enron employees for the first time realized all of the ramifications of a culture with leaders that eschew the boundaries of ethical behavior.

What did the Enron executives do to mold a corporate culture that resulted in unethical behavior and the collapse of the company? The remainder of this paper drafts some answers to this question.

Leadership mechanisms and organizational culture at Enron

If corporate leaders encourage rule-breaking and foster an intimidating, aggressive environment, it is not surprising that the ethical boundaries at Enron eroded away to nothing. Schein (1985) has focused on leadership as *the* critical component of the organization's culture because leaders can create, reinforce, or change the organization's culture. This applies not the least to an organization's ethical climate (Sims, 2000; Trevino et al., 2000; Sims and Brinkmann, 2002). According to Schein (1985) there are five primary mechanisms that a leader can use to influence an organization's culture: attention, reaction to crises, role modeling, allocation of rewards, and criteria for selection and dismissal. Schein's assumption is that these five criteria reinforce and encourage behavioral and cultural norms within an organization. Our paper can be read as an illustration of Schein's assumptions. The Enron executives used the five mechanisms to reinforce a culture that was morally flexible opening the door to ethics degeneration, lying, cheating, and stealing.

Attention

The first of the mechanisms mentioned by Schein (1985) is attention. The issues that capture the attention of the leader (i.e. what is criticized, praised or asked about) will also capture the attention of the greater organization and will become the focus of the employees. If the leaders of the organization focus on the bottom line, employees believe that financial success is the leading value to consider. D. M. Wolfe, author of "Executive Integrity" even suggests that a focus on profit, "promotes an unrealistic belief that everything boils down to a monetary game" (1988). In such a context, rules or morality are merely obstacles, impediments along the way to bottom-line financial success (Sims, 2000).

One former executive of Enron has described Jeffrey Skilling as a leader driven by the almighty dollar. ". . . Skilling would say all that matters is

money. You buy loyalty with money" (Zellner, 2002). Enron executives' attention was clearly focused on profits, power, greed and influence. They wanted their employees to focus on today's bottom line. Skilling communicated his priorities to his employees overtly, both in word and deed. Consistently clear signals told employees what was important to leadership – "Profits at all costs" (Tracinski, 2002). Or with another quote from a former Enron employee: ". . . there were no rules for people, even in our personal lives. Everything was about the company and everything was supposed to be on the edge – sex, money, all of it . . ." (Broughton, 2002). In her testimony before the House Subcommittee, Sherron Watkins described Enron as a ". . . very arrogant place, with a feeling of invincibility". Still another Enron employee noted about the company's environment that ". . . it was all about creating an atmosphere of deliberately breaking the rules. For example, our official vacation policy was that you could take as much as you wanted whenever you wanted as long as you delivered your results. It drove the human resource department crazy" (Bartlett and Glinska, 2001).

Another example of today's bottom line gain mentality is Andrew Fastow's, former Enron CFO, network of questionable partnerships. These partnerships provided profit for Fastow personally, as well as for some of his more favored employees, who were aware of his actions. Fastow demanded that Enron permit him to invest in and to personally profit from the partnerships (some of his earnings were passed to associates who aided him). Such actions sent a clear message that management's attention was focused on the bottom line for the company as well as personal gain, regardless of the means to get there. When it came to Fastow's special interest dealings the Board of Directors suspended the company's Code of Ethics at least twice. This made Fastow a wealthy man at the expense of Enron (Landers, 2002).

As Stern (1992) has suggested, if the organization's leaders seem to care only about the short-term bottom line, employees quickly get the message too. How else could employees read the Enron culture than being focused on short-term when their CEO (Ken Lay) both blessed the relaxation of conflict-of-interest rules designed to protect Enron from the very self-dealings that brought the company down and participated in board meetings allowing the creation of the off-balance sheet partnerships that were part of those transactions. By late summer 2001 he was reassuring investors and employees that all was well (when he already had been informed that the company had problems with some investment vehicles that could cost it hundreds of millions of dollars, see Gruley and Smith, 2002).

Reaction to crises

The second leadership method mentioned by Schein (1985) refers to a leader's reaction to a crisis situation. Schein asserts, that a crisis tests what the leader values and brings these values to the surface. With each impending crisis, leaders have an opportunity to communicate throughout the organization what the company's values are. Enron was facing a crisis of how to sustain a phenomenal growth rate. Leaders reacted by defending a culture that valued profitability, even when it was at the expense of everything else. The off-balance sheet partnerships were tremendously risky. However, since normal growth of the stock price would have fallen short of expectations anyway, the only thing to do was to try to meet the unrealistic target profitability expectations. In such a case, an accident was waiting to happen.

Once the Enron situation came to light, the reaction from the Enron executives was telling. The executives were busy shifting the blame and pointing fingers. Jeffery Skilling even went as far as telling an incredulous Congress that despite his Harvard Business School degree and business experience he neither knew of, nor would understand the intricacies of the Enron accounting deals. (On the other hand, Skilling also was quoted on CNN saying ". . . if he knew then what he knows now – he *STILL* would not do anything differently.") Even before the issues came to light it appears that Skilling was willing to abandon the company to save his own skin as

evidenced by his mysterious resignation in August 2001 and giving only the "personal reasons" explanation for his sudden departure (and he still sold significant amounts of company stock at a premium). Both Kenneth Lay and Sherron Watkins also sold stock before prices began to dramatically plummet (Kenneth Lay claiming that he had some personal debts to pay off, Sherron Watkins referring to the September 11th terrorist attacks. Watkins also sold stock at the same time when she was making allegations of deceptive accounting practices).

Enron began systematically firing those it could lay blame on before it declared bankruptcy (Brown and Sender, 2002). A self-serving exoneration committee was employed to explain (or excuse?) the current situation (Eichenwald, 2002). After Skilling resigned from his post, Kenneth Lay returned as CEO, promising that there were no "accounting issues, trading issues, or reserve issues" at Enron (McClean, 2001). Congressional testimony, news accounts and federal investigations have told us otherwise. Throughout October 2001, Lay insisted that Enron had access to cash and that the company was "performing very well," while he failed to disclose that Enron had written down shareholders' equity by $1.2 billion, or that Moody's was considering downgrading Enron's debt ("Explaining the Enron Bankruptcy", 2002). Company insiders also referred to Loretta Lynch as "an idiot" (the Yale-educated litigator who was among the first to question Enron's practices), Bethany McLean, the *Fortune* Magazine journalist who first broke the story, was called "a looker who doesn't know anything" (Dowd, 2002).

Another crisis consists in having to admit accounting irregularities. At first, the leaders of the company tried to deny there was a problem. They next tried to cover up any evidence of a problem or any wrongdoing. They even tried to seize computers of anyone they thought was trying to expose them as well as to destroy many files thought to be guilt-inducing (Daily Press, 2002). It transitioned into a blame game as many executives tried blaming each other, saying they didn't know what was going on, or it was someone else's responsibility to know about the problems and do something about it. Both Kenneth Lay and his wife proclaimed his innocence. Lay claimed to have been unaware of the sweetheart deals, which were entirely the brainchild of Skilling and Fastow. Watkins also blamed them for the debacle, while shifting any blame from herself.

"I take the Fifth" (U.S. Congressional Hearing, 2002 – this was the response Kenneth Lay gave to the Senate Commerce Committee when asked to explain Enron's failure. Although all but one of Enron's officers (curiously Skilling) invoked the 5th Amendment right to not self-incriminate, the story has played out much like that of the Salomon Brothers and John Gutfreund fiasco in the early 1990s. Document shredding and lies, both overt and those of omission, have become the preferred strategy for Enron's management (Brown and Sender, 2002). These bold acts from Enron leadership show a poor reaction to crisis.

From anonymous whistleblowing to bankruptcy to document shredding, to suicide (Cliff Baxter) to hiding behind the 5th Amendment, the leaders at Enron have run the gamut of extremes in their reaction to the company's crisis. Willet and Always (2002) noted that "the mantra at Enron seems to be that ethical wrongdoing is to be hidden at any cost; deny, play the dupe, claim ignorance ("the ostrich instruction") lie, quit." It appears that the truth and its consequences have never been a part of the Enron culture.

Role modeling (how leaders behave)

Schein's third mechanism is the example leaders set for the acceptability of unethical behavior within an organization. Actions speak louder than words – therefore role-modeling behavior is a very powerful tool that leaders have to develop and influence corporate culture. Through role modeling, teaching, and coaching, leaders reinforce the values that support the organizational culture. Employees often emulate leaders' behavior and look to the leaders for cues to appropriate behavior. Many companies are encouraging employees to be more entrepre-

neurial – that is, to take more initiative and be more innovative in their jobs. The Scientific Foundation reports a study that showed that managers who want to change the organization's culture to a more entrepreneurial one must "walk the talk". In other words, they must demonstrate the entrepreneurial behaviors themselves (Pearce et al., 1997). This is the case with any cultural value. Employees observe the behavior of leaders to find out what is valued in the organization. Perhaps, this was the most significant shortcoming of Enron executives.

According to the values statement in Enron's Code of Ethics and its annual report, the company maintains strong commitments to communication, respect, integrity, and excellence. However, there is little evidence that supports management modeling of these values. For instance, while the first pillar of the values statement addresses an obligation to communicate, Sherron Watkins claims (quoted from the Hearing transcripts):

> I continued to ask questions and seek answers, primarily from former coworkers in the Global Finance Group or in the business units that had hedged assets with Raptor. I never heard reassuring explanations. I was not comfortable confronting either Mr. Skilling or Mr. Fastow with my concerns. To do so, I believe, would have been a job-terminating move (U.S. Congressional Hearings, 2002).

Enron's leaders' primary message about their values was sent through their own actions. They broke the law as they concentrated on financial measures and used of the creative partnerships described earlier in this paper. For example, Kenneth Lay announced to analysts on October 16, 2001 that Enron had eliminated $1.2 billion in shareholder equity by terminating a partnership created by former CFO Andrew Fastow. This arrangement allowed Enron to buy and sell assets without carrying the debt on its books, i.e. keeping Enron's credit clean and the stock price high. Such actions clearly show a self-serving attitude of Enron leadership. The executives not only condoned such unethical behavior, they initiated it and were rewarded for it. The partnerships were used to deceive investors about the enormous debt Enron was incurring. It also sent a message to employees that full and complete disclosure is not a requirement, or even recommended. If the company achieved short-term benefits by hiding information, it was acceptable.

Enron's leaders also ignored, then denied serious problems with their business transactions and were more concerned about their personal financial rewards than those of the company. For example, when the company's stock price began to drop as the problems were becoming public, the company was transitioning from one investment program to another. While the employees were unable to sell their stock, the executives were quickly selling off many of their shares. Another example is the executives' lack of integrity in communicating to the employees and investors. They maintained that the company was financially stable and that many of their emerging problems really were not too serious, even though they knew the truth and were making financial decisions to protect their personal gains.

In retrospect, the leadership of Enron almost certainly dictated the company's outcome through their own actions by providing perfect conditions for unethical behavior. Michael Josephson, President of the Josephson Institute of Ethics, aptly described these conditions as they relate to the character of leadership: "People may produce spectacular results for a while, but it is inevitable that techniques depending so heavily on fear as a motivator generate survival strategies that include cheating, distortion, and an internal competitive ethos characterized by a look-out-for-number-one attitude. . . . Just as the destiny of individuals is determined by personal character, the destiny of an organization is determined by the character of its leadership. And when individuals are derailed because of a lack of character, the organization will also be harmed" (Josephson, 1999).

Allocation of rewards

The behavior of people rewarded with pay increases or promotions signals to others what is necessary to succeed in an organization – this is what Schein calls the "allocation of rewards"-mechanism. To ensure that values are accepted, leaders should reward behavior that is consistent with the values (and actual rewards count obviously more than promised rewards, cf. Sims and Brinkmann, 2002).

The reward system created by a leader indicates what is prized and expected in the organization. This view is in line with a basic management doctrine. When an instance of ethical achievement occurs – for instance, when someone acts with integrity and honor – the organization's leaders must reward it. Such an effort sends as clear a message to the rest of the organization as when an organization rewards an employee who acts unethically (see e.g. Larimer, 1997). Enron's reward system established a "win-at-all-costs" focus. The company's leadership promoted and retained only those employees that produced consistently, with little regard to ethics. Skilling singled out one of his vice presidents, Louise Kitchen, for her results-oriented approach to Enron's online business. Kitchen had started the company's Internet-based trading business even though Skilling repeatedly turned down her requests to begin such a program. Kitchen ignored the former CEO's decision and instead used already-allocated funds to pull the new network together. Or, as a former Enron vice president who attended the meeting described it best. "The moral of this story is break the rules, you can cheat, you can lie, but as long as you make money, it's all right" (quoted after Schwartz, 2002).

The company's compensation structure contributed to an unethical work culture, too – by promoting self-interest above any other interest. As a consequence, the team approach once used by Enron associates deteriorated. Performance reviews were public events and poor performance was ridiculed (or employees were fired through a "rank and yank" process). The strongest performing units even went as far as to "ignore" company policy – granting unlimited vacation time as noted earlier as long as the work got done, ignoring Human Resources' complaints (Bartlett and Glinska, 2001).

Extremely high bonuses were doled out to executives who behaved in desirable ways, e.g. in the form of stock options) which in turn incited executives to keep the stock price up at any cost (Lardner, 2002). Annual bonuses were as high as $1 million for traders, and for executives they were even higher). Enron developed a reputation for both internal and external ruthlessness where employees attempted to crush any competition and was considered extremely aggressive for a non-investment bank (McClean et al., 2001). Additionally, the executives at Enron played favorites, inviting top performers to spend weekend vacations with the executive staff. The best workers (determined through day-to-day bottom line results) received staggering incentives and exorbitant bonuses. One example of this was Car Day. On this day, an array of lavish sports cars arrived for the most successful employees (Broughton, 2002).

Retention bonuses that were paid shortly before the company declared bankruptcy to about 500 executives ranged in value from $1,000 to $5 million (possibly as a reward for help with setting up the problematic financial partnerships that led to the company's downfall). Overall, Enron's reward system rewarded individuals who embraced Enron's aggressive, individualistic culture and were based on short-term profits and financial measures.

Criteria of selection and dismissal (how leaders hire and fire employees)

Schein's (1985) last mechanism by which a leader shapes a corporate culture, describes how a leader's decisions about whom to recruit or dismiss signals a leader's values to all of his employees. The selection of newcomers to an organization is a powerful way of how a leader reinforces culture. Leaders often unconsciously look for individuals who are similar to current organizational members in terms of values and assumptions. Some companies hire individuals on the recommendation of a current employee. This tends to perpetuate the culture because the new employees typically hold similar values. Promotion-from-within policies also serve to reinforce organizational culture.

Ken Lay placed an immediate focus on hiring the best and smartest people, those who would thrive in a competitive environment. Skilling shared Lay's philosophy. Skilling hired only Ivy-league graduates with a hunger for money that matched his. He hired people who considered themselves the best and the brightest and were out to forward their own causes. Stanford and Harvard graduates, who would have otherwise worked on Wall Street, these people were paid well to work in Texas and to build the Enron culture. Their reward for giving up the allure of Silicon Valley and Wall Street was a high salary and a large bonus opportunity.

Skilling perpetuated a focus on short-term transactional endeavors from the very beginning by hiring employees that embodied the beliefs that he was trying to instill: aggressiveness, greed, a will to win at all costs, and an appreciation for circumventing the rules. This was the same culture of greed that brought turmoil to Salomon Brothers on Wall Street in the early 1990s. Divorce rates among senior executives were sky-rocketing as well. Instant gratification, both personally and professionally, was part of the Enron culture and Skilling did everything he could to surround himself with individuals who had similar values and assumptions and fitted into the Enron culture.

The way a company fires an employee and the rationale behind the firing also communicates the culture. Some companies deal with poor performers by trying to find them a place within the organization where they can perform better and make a contribution. Other companies seem to operate under the philosophy that those who cannot perform are out quickly (Sims and Brinkmann, 2002).

Enron carried out an annual "rank and yank" policy where the bottom fifteen to twenty percent of producers were let go or fired after a formal evaluation process each year. Associates graded their peers, which caused a great amount of distrust and paranoia among employees. Enron's employee reviews added to the competition by reviewing job performance in a public forum and sending the bottom 5% to the redeployment office – dubbed the "office of shame" (Frey and Rosin, 2002). What better way to develop a distrustful work environment than to pit employees against one another and as Larry Bossidy, former CEO of Allied Signal recently noted "forced ranking promotes bad employee morale" (2002), a win-at-all costs mentality, and a willingness to cross the ethical line (Wolfe, 1988; Sims and Brinkman, 2002).

The occurrence and handling of internal whistle-blowing also tells a lot about a corporate culture. At Enron, employees who tried to blow the whistle were punished, e.g. by career setbacks and hostility (cf. e.g. not least the enrongate website). The most well-known whistle-blower, Sherron Watkins, recounted how her fears about being fired for speaking out led her to reach out to Ken Lay through anonymous warnings. She even publicly stated that Andrew Fastow tried to have her fired once he found out that she was the author of the anonymous memo to Lay (Hamburger, 2002). Watkins reported that her computer was confiscated and she was moved to another office after she submitted her letter to Kenneth Lay. Another employee, Jeff McMahon, also spoke up against the conflicts of interest seen in the off book partnerships. As a reward for his actions, he was reassigned to a new job.

On the other hand, those who closed their eyes to the wrong doings were rewarded. Or with the words of a former Enron employee: "It was very clear what the measures were and how you got promoted at Enron. That absolutely drives behavior . . . getting the deal was paramount at Enron" (Hansell, 2002). A Houston headhunter described the freedom given by Skilling when he was Enron's CEO to loyal employees metaphorically: "Once you gained Jeff's trust, the leash became really long" (Zellner, 2002).

The selection and rewards system was consistent with the culture at Enron. It promoted greed, selfishness, and jealousy within the organization. Enron's executives selected those employees who shared their aggressive, win-at-all-costs mentality. Their short-term view may have prevented them from seeing what the long-term costs of this kind of personality could be on the organization as a whole.

Final comments and suggestions for future work

The story of Enron sounds smart and stupid at the same time. Deeply defective leadership from Lay and Skilling played a significant role in creating the company's culture that led to it's undoing, and we may never know whether it was hubris, greed, psychological shock or just plain stupidity that led them to behave in the way they did (Eavis, 2001). "Consequences of unethical or illegal actions are not usually realized until much later than when the act is committed" (Sims, 2000).

Enron's house of cards collapsed as a result of interacting decision processes. The culture at Enron eroded little by little, by the trespassing of ethical boundaries, allowing more and more questionable behavior to slip through the cracks. This deterioration did not go entirely unnoticed. Individual employees at Enron, auditors at Anderson and even some analysts who watch the financial markets, noticed aspects about the Enron situation that did not seem right, long before the public became aware of Enron's transgressions. There were whistle-blowers but the Enron leaders did not listen.

What existed in Enron's culture that kept individual employees from exposing the executive wrongdoers? And what about the Enron way permitted the executives to behave the way that they did? Enron's culture is a good example of groupthink (cf. eg. Janis, 1989; Moorehead, 1986) where individuals feel extreme pressure not to express any real strong arguments against any co-workers' actions. Although very individualistic, the culture at Enron was at the same time conformist, or quoting Glenn Dickson, a former Enron Risk Manager: "The pressure was – you just didn't have a choice but to approve the deals once everybody had their heart set on that deal closing" (ABC News, 2002). Employees were loyal in an ambiguous sense of the term, i.e., they wanted to be seen as part of the star team and to partake in the benefits that that honor entailed. Some former Enron employees commented that: "loyalty required a sort of groupthink. You had to 'keep drinking the Enron Water' . . ." (Stephens and Behr, 2002). John

Alarial, a former midlevel manager at Enron noted that: "Enron's aggressive business tactics were embraced by the rank and file, . . . even if (authors addition) . . . many suspected it was a house of cards" (ABC News, 2002). Employees were focused on the bottom line and "promoted short term solutions that were immediately financially sound despite the fact that they would cause problems for the organization as a whole . . . rules of ethical conduct were merely barriers to success" (Sims, 1992).

Enron's top executives set the tone for this culture. Personal ambition and greed seemed to overshadow much of their corporate and individual lives. They strove to maximize their individual wealth by initiating and participating in scandalous behaviors. Enron's culture created an atmosphere ripe for the unethical and illegal behavior that occurred.

Two of the most important lessons to learn from the Enron culture history is that bad top management morality can be a sufficient condition for creating a self-destructive ethical climate and that a well-filled CSR and business ethics toolbox can neither stop nor compensate for such processes.[3]

Enron's new CEO, turnaround-specialist Stephen Cooper could use (or should one rather say needs to use) the same five leader' influence mechanisms (Schein, 1985) used above for a turnaround of Enron's culture and ethical climate:

Attention – Cooper needs to focus attention on improving the moral climate of the organization by looking at the long-term implications of employee's actions instead of only the most recent bottom line profits.

Reaction to Crises – Cooper should swiftly react to the crisis facing the company by complying with authorities and firing ethical wrongdoers. The company must stop the lying, covering up ethical and legal transgressions, and trying to preserve those ethical wrongdoers at any cost.

Role Modeling – Cooper must convey the image of the moral manager (Trevino et al., 2002). He must set the example of honesty and integrity for the rest of the organization.

Allocation of Rewards – Using rewards and discipline effectively may be the most powerful

way for Cooper to send signals about desirable and undesirable conduct. That means rewarding those who accomplish their goals by behaving in ways that are consistent with stated values and it must be assumed that a lack of commitment to ethical principles will ensure that employees will not be promoted.

Criteria for Selection and Dismissal – Cooper must bring employees into Enron who are committed to ethical principles and usher out all old employees connected to ethical misconduct. The company must have clear policies on the criteria for selection and dismissal that employees understand.

In other words, Enron's new CEO, Stephen Cooper, must take a proactive stance to promote an ethical climate and must be the *Chief Ethics Officer* of the organization (Trevino et al., 2000), creating a strong ethics message that gets employees' attention and influences their thoughts and behaviors. Executive commitment to ethical behavior is an important way of sustaining an ethical organizational culture (Weaver et al., 1999). Cooper must find ways to focus the organization's attention on ethics and values and to infuse the organization with principles that will guide the actions of all employees. New (and first of all credible) values could be the glue that holds things together at Enron, and these values must be communicated (by deeds) from the top of the organization. Employees must understand that any single employee who operates outside of the organizational value system can cost the organization dearly in legal fees and can have a tremendous, sometimes irreversible impact on the organization's image and culture. Employees must trust that whistleblowers will be protected, that procedures used to investigate ethical problems will be fair, and that management will take action to solve problems that are uncovered.

Our skeptical view regarding any compensatory use of the CSR and business ethics toolbox (i.e. as long as morally disputable leadership creates a bad moral climate) does not imply any radical rejection of CSR and ethics tools as such (Schein would have called such tools "secondary articulation and reinforcement mechanisms", such as "organizational systems and procedures" and "formal statements of organizational philosophy, creeds and charters", see Schein, 1985, pp. 237–242). Once tools are understood as ("secondary") catalysts for ("primary") leadership influence, it is more fruitful to ask for conditions under which ethical tools such as codes could further and reinforce a given organization's ethical climate (cf. Brinkmann and Ims, 2003, esp. table #3) and how Schein's five mechanisms could be operationalized in terms of available tools.

In our introduction we mentioned briefly Enron's image of being an excellent corporate citizen, with all the corporate social responsibility (CSR) and business ethics tools and status symbols in place. It was suggested that this was a key aspect or dimension of the Enron case, as a case of deceiving corporate citizenship and of surface or facade ethics (which also has contributed to the creation of a new word, *Enron Ethics*). As an academic field we owe the general public and the business public a thorough documentation, analysis and discussion of how Enron and other companies with a similar record and reputation could "instrumentalize" (and thus discredit) ethics and CSR for mere facade purposes.

It has also been mentioned that such a focus deserves and requires a paper on its own, at least. As an open end to this paper we should like to draft briefly a typology with moral culture types and transitions which such a paper could address, as a prolongation of the present paper and as a bridge-building towards a more self-critical business ethics business and business ethics discipline. The typology is made up of two dimensions, ethicalness of an organization culture or what has been called ethical or moral climate, and presence of business ethical tools or artifacts, such as ethics officers, codes of ethics, value state-

ments and the like. If one for practical purposes distinguishes dichotomously between low and high one ends up with a four-fold table as shown in Table I.[4]

As mentioned above, Enron looks at first sight like "type I", similar to what Kohlberg might have called moral "pre-conventionalism", like a classical business ethics case, with a typical mix of "amorality" and "immorality" (cf. for the distinction Carroll and Meeks, 1999). For headline-journalism and public opinion Enron and World.com are simply bad and rotten, one just didn't know before it was too late, and this shows once more an urgent need for more legislation and ethics. Our thesis is that Enron (and probably quite a number of other companies waiting to be discovered) is an at least as good illustration of "type II", of window-dressing ethics, with talking instead of walking, ethics as rhetoric. While "type II" looks modern or at least fashionable, "type III" looks like the old-fashioned type of moral business, from the days before the disciplines of business ethics, CSR, marketing and public relations were invented, with collective moral conscience (borrowing E. Durkheim's term) as consistent label and content, perhaps additionally communicating moral humbleness, with a touch of British understatement. The final "type IV" refers to a moral role-model business culture in the age of marketing and public relations, with walking the talk, with showing and confessing openly its collective moral conscience (call it self-reassurance, or more U.S.-style self-marketing, to put it stereotypically). In other words, a future paper should primarily deal with a documentation and criticism of "window-dressing ethics", of how to further processes towards collective moral conscience,

TABLE I
Typology of moral culture types and transitions

Presence and marketing of business ethical tools	Ethicalness of a given organization culture	
	Low	High
High	II: Window-Dressing Ethics	IV: Moral Role-Modeling
Low	I: Moral Preconventionalism (Without Disguise)	III: Collective Moral Conscience

with more or less marketing of the good examples, and of how to prevent degeneration towards "window-dressing ethics". We often wonder if we would prefer honest amorality and immorality to dishonest morality. But still, we choose to read the paper title of Tonge et al. (2003) optimistically: "The Enron story: you can fool some of the people some of the time . . .".

Notes

[1] Cf. in addition the Enron-story books for sale as of today by Amazon, see bookhttp://www.amazon.com/exec/obidos/ASIN/0471265748/millerriskadv-20/002-3887103-5927230.

[2] For example, Enron had promised CIBC World Markets the majority of the profits from Project Braveheart for ten years, or in the event of failure Enron would be obligated to repay CIBC its entire $115.2 million investment. Not only did Enron book the earnings prematurely, but it was also forced to repay CIBC its full investment.

[3] For a draft of possible "latent, negative functions" of ethical codes cf. Brinkmann and Ims, 2003, esp. table #2.

[4] Thanks to colleague Knut Ims from the Norwegian School of Business Administration for a discussion about this typology.

References

ABC News – World News Sunday: 2002, 'Profile: The Shadowy World of Enron's Corporate Culture' (January 27).

Bartlett, C. A. and M. Glinska: 2001, 'Enron's Transformation: From Gas Pipeline to New Economy Powerhouse' (Harvard Business School Press, Boston, MA).

Brinkmann, J. and K. Ims: 2003, 'Good Intentions Aside (Drafting a Functionalist Look at Codes of Ethics)', forthcoming Summer 2003 in *Business Ethics: A European Review*.

Broughton, P. D.: 2002, 'Enron Cocktail of Cash, Sex and Fast Living', *News. Telegraph.co.uk* (On-line journal) (February 13).

Brown, K. and H. Sender: 2002, Enron's Board Fires Arthur Andersen: Questions Arise About Auditor's Actions', *The Wall Street Journal* [On-line]. Available: http://wsjclassroomedition.com/tj 011802 enron.htm.

Carroll, A. B. and M. D. Meeks: 1999, 'Models of Management Morality: European Applications and Implications', *Business Ethics: A European Review* 8, 108–116.

Cohan, J. A.: 2002, 'I Didn't Know and I was Only Doing My Job. Has Corporate Governance Careened Out of Control? A Case Study of Enron's Information Myopia', *Journal of Business Ethics* 40, 275–299.

Daily Press: 2002, 'Troubles Widely Known, Exec Says' (February 15), p. A1.

Dowd, M.: 2002, 'Enron, Hollywood Version', *The Roanoke Times* (February 10), 1.

Eavis, P.: 2001, 'Enron Reaps What Its Cowboy Culture Sowed', TheStreet.com [On-line]. Available: http://www.thestreet.com/markets/detox/10004675.html.

Eichenwald, K.: 2002, 'Report Lays Out Troubles At Enron: Internal Investigation Finds Profits Overstated To Executive's Enrichment', *The New York Times* [On-line]. Available: http://www.austin360.com/aas/business/020302/3enrong.html.

'Explaining the Enron Bankruptcy': 2002, CNN.com (January 12). Available: http://www.cnn.com.html.

Frey, J. and H. Rosin: 2002, 'Enron's Green Acres', *The Washington Post* (February 25), 1.

Gruley, B. and R. Smith: 2002, 'Anatomy of a Fall: Keys to Success Left Kenneth Lay Open to Disaster', *The Wall Street Journal* (April 26), pp. A1, A5.

Hamburger, T.: 2002, 'Watkins Tells of 'Arrogant' Culture; Enron Stifled Staff Whistle-Blowing', *The Wall Street Journal* (February 15), pp. A3, C1.

Hansell, G.: 2002, 'The Fall of Enron Pressure Cooker Finally Exploded', *The Houston Chronicle* [On-line]. Available: http://www.russreyn.com/news/newsitem.asp?news=235.

Janis, I.: 1989, *Critical Decisions: Leadership in Policy Making and Crisis Management* (Free Press, New York).

Josephson, M.: 1999, 'Character: Linchpin of Leadership', *Executive Excellence* 16(8), 13–14.

Landers, J.: 2002, 'Enron Exec' Silence Is No Shock Testimony Would Have Followed Hard-hitting Report On Activities. *The Dallas Morning News* [On-line], Available: http://www.kmsb.com/business/news/506152 enron.html.

Lardner, J.: 2002, 'Why Should Anyone Believe You? What Ruined Enron Wasn't Just Accounting. It Was a Culture that Valued Appealing Lies Over Inconvenient Truths. Are You Sure Your Company

Is All That Different?' *Business 2.0* [On-line]. Available: http://www.business2.com/articles/mag/0/1640.37748.FF.html.

Larimer, L. V.: 1997, 'Reflections on Ethics and Integrity', *HRFocus* (April), 5.

Lewis, M.: 1989, *Liar's Poker* (Norton, New York).

McClean, B., J. Sung Revell and A. Helyar: 2001, 'Why Enron went Bust: Start with Arrogance. Add Greed, Deceit, and Financial Chicanery. What Do You Get? A Company that Wasn't What it was Cracked Up to Be', *Business 2.0* [On-line]. Available: http://www.business2.com/articles/mag/print/0.1643.36124.FF.html.

Moorehead, G. and J. R. Montanari: 1986. 'An Empirical Investigation of the Groupthink Phenomenon', *Human Relations* **39**, 339–410.

New York Times: 2002, 'Profits At Enron Energy Services', [On-line] (February 14). Available: http://www.nytimes.com/learning/students/pop/articles.

Pearce, J. A., II, T. R. Kramer and D. K. Robbins: 1997, 'Effects of Managers' Entrepreneurial Behavior on Subordinates', *Journal of Business Venturing* **12**, 147–160.

Petrick, J. A. and J. F. Quinn: 2002, 'Management Integrity Capacity Neglect and Enron: Stakeholder Damages and Remedies', paper presented at the 9th International Conference Promoting Business Ethics, Niagara University, Niagara Falls, NY, Oct 23–25, 2002.

Schein, E.: 1985, *Organizational Culture and Leadership* (Jossey-Bass, San Francisco, CA).

Schwartz, J.: 2002, 'Darth Vader. Machiavelli. Skilling Set Intense Pace', *The New York Times* (February 7), 1–2.

Sims, R. R.: 1992, 'The Challenge to Unethical Behavior in Organizations', *Journal of Business Ethics* **11**, 505–513.

Sims, R. R.: 2002, 'Leadership, Organizational Culture and Ethics', *Teaching Note* (Graduate School of Business, College of William and Mary, Williamsburg, VA).

Sims, R. R.: 2000, 'Changing an Organization's Culture Under New Leadership', *Journal of Business Ethics* **25**, 65–78.

Sims, R. R. and J. Brinkmann: 2002, 'Leaders as Moral Role Models: The Case of John Gutfreund at Salomon Brothers', *Journal of Business Ethics* **35**, 327–339.

Stephens, J. and P. Behr: 2002, 'Enron's Culture Fed Its Demise: Groupthink Promoted Foolhardy Risks', *Washington Post* (January 27), A01.

Stern, G.: 1992, 'Audit Report Shows How Far

Chambers Would Go For Profits', *The Wall Street Journal* (October 12), A1.

Tonge A., L. Greer and A. Lawton: 2003, 'The Enron Story: You Can Fool Some of the People Some of the Time . . .', *Business Ethics: A European Review* **12**, 4–22.

Tracinski, R.: 2002, 'Enron Ethics', *Capitalism Magazine* [On-line] (January 28). Available: http://www.capitalismagazine.com/2002/january/rwt.enron.htm.

Trevino, L. K., L. P. Hartman and M. Brown: 2000, 'Moral Person and Moral Manager: How Executives Develop a Reputation for Ethical Leadership', *California Management Review* **42**(4), 124–142.

Trevino, L. K. and K. A. Nelson: 1995, *Managing Business Ethics: Straight Talk about How to Do It Right* (John Wiley & Sons, New York).

U.S. Congressional Hearing: 2002 (February 6), Washington, DC.

Vogt, A. J.: 2002, 'Interview with Larry Bossidy: The Way It Is', *Across the Board* (May/June), 31–37.

Weaver, G. R., L. K. Trevino and P. L. Cochran: 1999, 'Corporate Ethics Programs as Control Systems: Influences of Executive Commitment and Environmental Factors', *Academy of Management Journal* **42**, 41–57.

Willet, B. and T. Always: 2002, 'For Investors, X Marks the Spot, Whether They Choose To See It Or Not', FallStreet.com [On-line]. Available: http://www.fallstreet.com/Spotlight/jan2502/htm.

Wolfe, D.: 1988, 'Is There Integrity in the Bottomline: Managing Obstacles to Executive Integrity', in S. Srivastva (ed.), *Executive Integrity: The Search for High Human Values in Organizational Life* (Jossey-Bass, San Francisco), pp. 140–171.

Zellner, W.: 2002, 'Jeff Skilling: Enron's Missing Man', *Business Week Online* (February 11).

Ronald R. Sims
Graduate School of Business,
College of William and Mary,
Williamsburg, VA 23187-8795,
U.S.A
E-mail: ronald.sims@business.wm.edu

Johannes Brinkmann
Norwegian School of Management BI,
PO Box 4676 Sofienberg,
N0506 Oslo Norway
E-mail: johannes.brinkmann@bi.no

[60]

Creating Corporate Accountability: Foundational Principles to Make Corporate Citizenship Real

Sandra Waddock

ABSTRACT. This paper explores the growing array of initiatives aimed at creating corporate accountability with the goal of attempting to uncover the foundation principles that underlie them and create a "floor" below which practices are ethically questionable. Using the Global Compact's nine principles and the work of Transparency International as guides, foundational principles seem to exist in the areas of human rights, labor standards, environment, and anti-corruption initiatives.

Introduction

Many countries, global bodies, and companies around the world are struggling with how to turn foundational principles articulated in a growing array of principles, codes of conduct, and standards from statements about what *ought* to be done in corporate practices into what *is* in the marketplace. Increasingly corporations' figurative feet are being held to the fire of social activism aimed at creating greater accountability on the part of companies for the impacts that they have, not just with respect to investors, but on others stakeholders as well. If these pressures are to effect real change, they need to be underpinned by generally agreed foundation principles that are implemented not just rhetorically in corporate codes of conduct but in day-to-day operating practice. Before that day actually comes, however, there needs to be general agreement on the fundamental principles themselves. This paper will explore some of the growing array of initiatives aimed at creating corporate accountability with the goal of attempting to uncover foundation principles that are embedded in global agreements and corporate practices.

Global brands are often targets of exposés and activist pressures (e.g., Klein, 2000; Schoenberger, ca. 2000; Schlosser, 2000) as public attention shifts from topic to topic. As early as the 1960s and 1970s environmental concerns – and the company-produced chemicals causing them – became high on the public agenda. The publication of Rachael Carson's *Silent Spring* in 1962 and the attention paid to ecological issues on Earth Day #1 in 1970 were significant events in the U.S. raising public awareness of corporate impacts on the natural environment. Other social issues came to the forefront of public opinion during this period as growth of single-issue pressure groups such as Greenpeace and Amnesty International gained momentum. Among other incidents, the consumer boycott of the Nestle Corporation for its sales of infant formula in developing nations by religious groups began in the late 1970s and culminated in Nestle's appointment of an internal infant formula audit commission. Combined with a global boycott of products from companies operating in South Africa, these and similar forms of consumer activism vividly demonstrated the usefulness of consumer movements to attempt to change corporate behavior and hold companies accountable through publicity, boycotts, and related forms of activism.

Another source of increasing pressure for corporate accountability is the social or ethical investing movement, which is now estimated by the Social Investment Forum to include some two trillion dollars in the U.S. alone. Social investing gained steady currency in the 1980s and 1990s, with socially conscious investors initially demanding that companies withdraw from South Africa. Although social investing is yet to become fully mainstream, there is sufficient investor interest with about one of every eight dollars invested in equities[1] under some form of social activism that even major investment houses like Smith Barney and large pension funds like TIAA-CREF have begun to get into the act and create social funds. In the U.S., the Dow Jones Sustainability Group Index focuses on five corporate sustainability principles: innovative technology, corporate governance, shareholder relations, industrial leadership, and social well being, with the latter category explicitly emphasizing positive corporate responsibility with respect to society. In the United Kingdom, the FTSE4Good index, launched in July 2001, focuses on three areas: environmental sustainability, positive stakeholder relationships, and upholding and supporting universal human rights. By the 1990s, corporate governance activists had also become sophisticated in their use of shareholder resolutions targeted at specific corporate practices (e.g., Rivoli, 2003; Proffit, 2000a, b; Graves et al., 2001). Shareholder activists annually submit hundreds of such resolutions, frequently aimed as negotiating tools to gain management attention even when they were withdrawn before voting.

Inside companies, outsourcing, strategic and other alliances, and just-in-time inventory management systems began to blur the boundaries between companies and their suppliers and customers during the 1980s and 1990s. Outsourcing created new global supply chains, often in developing nations, and human rights, labor, and environmental activists became concerned corporate practices in the increasingly long supply chains of consumer goods, clothing, and toy companies, among others (Rivoli, 2003). Boundaries between multinational companies and their suppliers, clear perhaps in the eyes of managers, were and are much less clear to activists wanting to create corporate accountability.

In the 1990s the rise of the Internet fueled new levels of activism and strengthened the capacity of civil society's non-governmental organizations (NGOs) to organize efforts fighting against sweatshop labor conditions, human rights abuses, child labor, anti-democratic regimes,

political infractions, and ecological damages. Anti-globalization activists continue to demonstrate these concerns when international bodies fostering free trade, like the World Bank or World Trade Organization, attempt to meet. Legal developments, consumer requirements, technological innovation, and NGO activism are increasingly geared towards sustainability guidelines and the triple-bottom line of economic, social, and ecological assessment, measurement, and reporting criteria (Elkington, 1998; European Commission, 2001), rather than traditional, more unidimensional financial reporting standards.

Finally, the work of Transparency International (TI), founded in 1995, has again and again pointed out the need to weed out corruption in government and in business, receiving global attention for its now annual country-based "corruption index" (see http://www.transparency.org/). In May 2002, TI issued the 2002 Bribe Payers Index, as a means of determining whether any progress is being made on the anti-bribery front since the ratification by many nations of the OECD's Anti-Bribery Convention two years earlier. The conclusions reached were hardly encouraging: awareness of the anti-bribery convention is generally low, while perceived bribery-paying (corruption) among companies in the 15 countries surveyed was relatively high. According to a TI spokesperson the findings "signal the rejection by multinational firms of the spirit of international anti-bribery conventions, while their actions lead to a huge misallocation of very scarce resources in developing countries."[2]

The gap between ideal and the real . . .

Demands for greater corporate transparency and accountability, as well as anti-corruption measures are fostering significant new accountability, reporting, and transparency initiatives among coalitions of business, labor, human rights, investor, and governmental bodies. Indeed, a database created by the International Labor Organization and available over the Internet lists nearly 450 websites of industry and business associations, corporate, NGO and activist groups, and consulting organizations that have developed and are promulgating a wide range of relevant policy initiatives. These initiatives include a mix of transparency and reporting initiatives, codes of conduct, principles, and fair trade agreements.[3] Responses to these demands are varied. Many companies, particularly those under NGO and social activist pressures to reform labor and human rights abuses in their supply chains, have formulated their own codes of conduct. Notable among these companies are Levi Strauss, Nike, and Reebok, all significant targets of activism.

The proliferation of standards, principles, reporting initiatives, and codes threatens confusion and continued lack of implementation unless there is a common set of principles shared among them. Below we explore whether in the emerging proliferation of initiatives, there might be a common set of foundation principles or standards that could, if actually implemented, suggest standards of management practice. The array of emerging standards suggests that there is a gap between growing public expectations from a variety of stakeholders and actual company performance else this array of initiatives would not occur. Pressures from a wide range of stakeholders appear to be pushing companies toward a common set of guidelines of what *ought* to be and away from the stark and not always pleasant realities of global competition (Frenkel, 2001; O'Rourke, 1997, 2000; Greider, 1998). But this change is happening neither quickly nor systemically as of yet, nor is it entirely clear that voluntary standards alone will satisfy corporate critics or develop what Goodpaster (2003) calls corporate conscience. As a starting point, however, one thing is clear: for standards to be effective over the long term, agreement on fundamental principles or foundational values must be found, and, as Sethi (2003) has argued, companies must be held accountable for their implementation.

The argument for foundation principles

Foundation principles, if they exist, would provide a *baseline* below which it does not make ethical sense to go. As noted, however, such principles or values make sense only if there is sufficient global agreement about the standards that they create a level playing field for companies adhering to them. For example, corporate critics ask whether a company that employed 180 forced laborers yesterday and only 160 today could really be considered to be more responsible through this reduction. Yes, there is an improvement in practice, but most people would likely agree that slavery is reprehensible under any circumstances. Fundamental or foundation principles would suggest where the "floor" but not the "ceiling" of responsible practice lies. Such baseline level behaviors, practices, and values are foundation values. *Foundation values are generally agreed standards that provide a floor of acceptable practice* going below which is ethically and managerially problematic. Donaldson and Dunfee (1999) term such general principles or values 'hypernorms' and suggest that relatively universal consensus must exist for them to exist at all. They define hypernorms to 'entail principles so fundamental to human existence that they serve as a guide in evaluating lower level moral norms' (1994, p. 265).

General agreement (by businesses) on a common set of foundational principles – a baseline or "moral minimum" (Donaldson and Dunfee, 1999) for operating practice – would be an important development in providing a level playing field for companies. Schwartz (2002), for example, argues for a set of universal moral standards, including trustworthiness, respect, responsibility, fairness, caring, and citizenship, which could underpin the development of codes and principles themselves. Agreement on foundation principles could help companies avoid the information overload and code mania that some are currently experiencing as the number and types of initiatives grow, as well as disparities between developed and developing nations (e.g., Behrman, 2001).

Donaldson and Dunfee (1999) provide a framework for core values, built upon the need

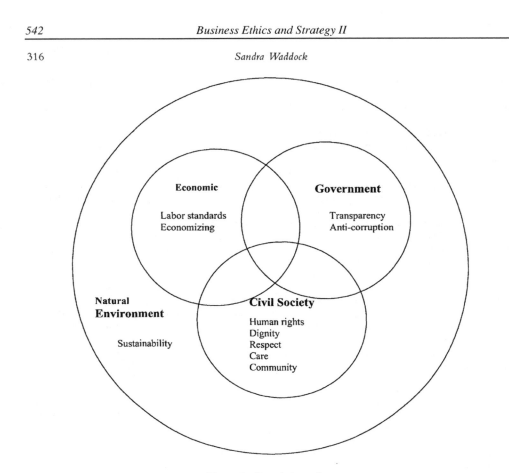

Figure 1. Foundation value.

for system integrity that builds trust and the mutual respect that emerges from Kant's categorical imperative. Donaldson (1996) argues that these basic principles of respect are useful aids for searching out commonly agreed foundation values:

- Respect for core human values, which determine the absolute moral threshold for all business activities.
- Respect for local traditions.
- Respect for the belief that context matters when deciding what is right and wrong.
  (Donaldson, 1996, p. 6).

From these guiding principles, Donaldson (see also Donaldson and Dunfee, 1999) articulates three core values derived from the work of philosophers and theologians. All involve the critical element of respect. Core or foundational principles, then need to emphasize what McGregor Burns (1978) terms end values, which ultimately, as Donaldson and Dunfee (1999) point out, respect:

- human dignity;
- basic rights; and
- good citizenship (which involves working together to support and improve the institutions on which the community depends).
  (Donaldson, 1996, pp. 7–8).

These guiding principles negotiate the tension that exists in treating people as ends, not means, and treating each individual as unique and deserving of respect and dignity, while simultaneously holding valuable the context of community or common good that makes societies work.

Spheres and related values

For purposes of discussion, let us conceive of human society as consisting of three dominant and intersecting spheres of activity: economic/business, government/political, and civil society (Waddock, 2002; Waddell and Brown, 1997; Waddell, 2000), all of which are underpinned by the natural environmental sphere from which all living beings draw life-giving resources (Waddock, 2002) (see Table I). Core purposes within each of these spheres differ, hence there are likely to be foundational values or hypernorms associated with each sphere, though these will clearly merge into other spheres as well. Businesses, operating in the economic sphere, emphasize efficiency or "economizing" (Frederick, 1995) and wealth generation. Governments, operating in the political sphere, emphasize the rule of law and establishing the "common good" through the use of coercive power through values of power aggrandizing

(Etzioni, 1961; Frederick, 1995; Waddell, 2000; Waddock, 2002). NGOs and other civil society organizations are primarily associated with relationships (generation of social capital) and community-building via "civilizing" activities (Putnam, 1993a, b; Waddock, 2002).

The long-term wellbeing of human society or civilization is necessarily and irrevocably linked to the state of the natural environment. The natural environment needs to be able to support human life if human society is to survive (though the environment will, in some form, survive in any case) (Maturana and Varela, 1998). The dominant "goal" of the environment, if the environment can be said to have a goal, is ecologizing (Frederick, 1995) since what "waste" is produced naturally is consumed as food in another part of the system. Thus, we identify three spheres of human civilization underpinned by the ecological environment or four spheres in which we need to seek foundation principles: economic, governmental, civil society, and environmental.

To the extent that foundation principles exist, chances are they exist within broad-based consensus documents, generated not from theory but from agreements by the nations of the world, such as those promulgated by the United Nations, perhaps the longest-existing multilateral global enterprise. Although a few nations may not agree with principles articulated in these

TABLE I
Sphere system goals and their implications for foundation values

Sphere	System goal	Respect for . . .	Implies . . .
Economic	Economizing	Human dignity	Respect for employees, labor standards. Respect for product/service integrity.
Government	Power aggrandizing	Basic rights	Respect for system integrity, transparency, and the rule of law.
Civil Society	Relationship	Community	Respect for local traditions, context, and basic human values.
Environment	Ecologizing	Future generations	Respect for ecological sustainability that supports human civilization.

Sources: System goals adapted from Frederick, 1995 and Waddock, 2002; core values of human dignity, basic rights, and community (good citizenship) adapted from Donaldson, 1996.

broad-based consensus documents (e.g., China on human rights), they nonetheless represent the world's best efforts to find agreed values to date. Indeed, the recent development of the UN's Global Compact, launched in 1999 by Secretary General Kofi Annan, provides significant insight into the relatively few values that may have achieved the status of global agreement that may serve as candidate for actual hypernorms. Four principles deal with labor rights and can be said to fall within the economic sphere. Two principles deal with human rights, which fall within the civil society sphere, and two are ecological principles within the environmental sphere that underpins human civilization. The "missing 10th principle" is a transparency or anti-corruption principle, which falls most dominantly within the governmental sphere, albeit its influence affects all three spheres of human civilization (Post, 2002; Vogl, personal communication). Below we will explore emerging foundation principles within each of the four spheres.

Economic sphere foundation principles

Businesses operate within the economic sphere with the dominant goal of economizing (Frederick, 1995). Since it is employees who produce the work of organizations, labor standards are certainly one important arena in which foundation principles are needed. Economizing means using resources, including human resources, in the most efficient way possible (and, in our current system at least, externalizing whatever costs can be externalized [Frederick, 2002]). In the human resource arena, economizing strategies can stand in some (at least apparent) degree of tension with respect for human dignity (Donaldson, 1996) (see Table I). Despite a growing body of evidence to the contrary (c.f., Margolis and Walsh, 2001; Wood and Jones, 1995; Pava and Krauscz, 1995; Waddock and Graves, 1997), many managers still believe that there is a trade-off between productivity and corporate responsibility. Further, in terms of management style, many managers also believe in what Pfeffer and Veiga (1999) term "failed assumptions," i.e., that treating people

with toughness and disrespect will achieve higher productivity than will treating them respectfully and well (see also Dessler, 1999).

In the economic sphere, principles derived from ILO standards and the UN Declaration on Human Rights are particularly relevant, according to Hartman et al. (2001; Hartman et al., 2003), who have extensively analyzed global documents. The International Labor Standards (ILS) of the ILO were developed with government policy in mind, targeting the development of national labor laws. Companies, of course, are subject to labor laws in countries where they have a presence, but the ILSs do not generally specifically target companies. Such standards involve the fundamental principles of respect for humans as ends, not means, and, fundamentally, for human dignity at work (e.g., Donalson and Dunfee, 1999).

The International Labor Standards cover a broad a range of areas and lack universal acceptance in their entirety; thus they lack key traits necessary to serve as a foundation for economic sphere principles. A narrower group of principles, targeted directly at companies, has more recently been articulated in the ILO's Tripartite Declaration of Principles Concerning Multinational Enterprises and Social Policy (referencing the ILO's Fundamental Principles), the OECD Guidelines for Multinational Enterprises, and the UN Secretary General's Global Compact. Each of these target a more limited number of organizational behaviors – specifically behaviors concerning issues like child and forced labor, freedom of association, and discrimination – that have been accepted as universally applicable by much of the global community.

Others have also thought about what fundamental principles might exist in each of the spheres discussed above, particularly with respect to primary stakeholders, or those stakeholders without which a business cannot exist (Clarkson, 1995; Freeman, 1984). Employees quite literally make up the business, hence deserve special consideration, particularly because employees are more directly affected by corporate operating practices than are other stakeholders. In the labor domain, some theorists suggest the need for a system of "ratcheting labor standards" (Sabel et

TABLE II
Foundation values in the spheres of human civilization and natural environment

Economic sphere	Governmental sphere	Civil society sphere	Ecological sphere
• Just and favorable working conditions, • Minimum age and working conditions for child labor, • Nondiscrimination, • Freedom from forced labor, and • Free association. *Source:* ILO Conventions, Donaldson and Dunfee, 1999; Hartman et al., 2001.	• Participation, • Decentralization, • Diversity, • Accountability, • Transparency. *Source:* Transparency International.	• Freedom of physical movement, • Ownership of property, • Freedom from torture, • Right to a fair trial, • Nondiscriminatory treatment, • Physical security, • Freedom of speech and association, • Right to at least a minimal education, • Right to political participation, • Right to subsistence. *Sources:* Donalson and Dunfee, 1999; UN Declaration on Human Rights and Environment	• Sustainability, • Precautionary (preventative) approach to environmental challenges, • Responsible and ethical management products and processes, and • Development and diffusion of environmentally sound technologies. *Sources:* Frederick, 1995; Global Compact.

al., 2000, p. 1) based on "a compact list of incontestable human rights of the workplace."

Specifically with respect to labor standards, Hartman et al. (2001) demonstrate through an analysis of existing global labor standards, that there *are* certain basic labor rights that are relatively universally acknowledged, which build on the concept of human dignity and rights identified as fundamental by Donaldson and Dunfee (1999). These minimal labor rights are derived from the UN Declaration on Human Rights, UN International Convention on Economic, Social and Cultural Rights, Caux Round Table Principles, International Labor Organization labor standards. They are operationalized by the SA 8000 labor standards, as well as being found in many corporate and business association codes of conduct. Based on Hartman et al., for labor rights, the following foundation principles may represent the minimal set of conditions and standards to which all companies' labor standards *should* (which is not to say companies always do) adhere:

• Just and favorable working conditions, including a limit to the number of hours a human should have to work each day and a healthy working environment;
• Minimum age and working conditions for child labor;
• Nondiscrimination requirements regarding the *relative* amount that a worker should be paid and the right to equal pay for equal work;
• Freedom from forced labor; and
• Free association, including the right to organize and to bargain collectively in contract negotiations

(Hartman et al., 2001).

Despite that even these minimal standards are not always achieved in practice because of economizing efforts by companies, from an economic sphere perspective, all of these foundation principles rest on the bedrock of human dignity and respect for the human capital invested by workers, treating people as ends rather than as means to an end (e.g., of profitability). The emergence of no-sweat, no child-labor, Rugmark, and related labels that signify that baseline labor standards have been met attests to a growing international consensus on such standards as the floor (moral minimum) of acceptable practices.

Governmental sphere foundation principles

Sustaining the integrity of the business and economic system demands trust in the system, particularly at the intersection between government (with its power to regulate and create the rules by which businesses operate) and business. Trust is the key to sustainable nations and a sustainable economic system. Governments have the capacity to use coercive power (power aggrandizing tendencies, Frederick, 1995) to create the system under which other types of entities exist. System integrity is fundamentally undermined by corruption and bribery, which has the tendency to make both the economic and political systems untrustworthy. Accountability in corrupt systems is nonexistent and companies that participate in corruption, which the Transparency International report cited above suggests is quite rampant, work against system integrity and the necessary foundation of trust. Transparency International (TI) and the World Bank, two global organizations working at the country level on the issue of corruption, have highlighted the need for foundational principles built on the concept of system integrity. An anti-corruption principle would thus be what Post (2002) characterized as the missing tenth principle in the Global Compact.

As stated on the TI website, there are several reasons for fostering system integrity, integrity that structures business-government relationships and ultimately fosters democracy. The reasons are:

- Humanitarian, as corruption undermines and distorts development and leads to increasing levels of human rights abuse;
- Democratic, as corruption undermines democracies and in particular the achievements of many developing countries and countries in transition;

- Ethical, as corruption undermines a society's integrity; and
- Practical, as corruption distorts the operations of markets and deprives ordinary people of the benefits which should flow from them. (Source: http://www.transparency.org/welcome.html)

Foundation principles for government (and business) as developed by TI are based on the Organization for Economic Cooperation and Development's (OECD) 1997 Convention on Combating Bribery of Foreign Officials in International Business Transactions, an internationally-agreed convention that makes bribery illegal in many nations of the world. This convention was ratified by 34 signatory countries, including the OECD countries, which account for some three-quarters of global trade by June 2001.[4] The convention makes bribery a criminal act and eliminates the deduction for bribes that was formerly allowable in some signatory nations. Using this convention as baseline guidance for ethics in practice, Transparency International fosters "integrity systems" in government, that is, a complex set of institutions, laws, and regulations aimed at fighting corruption in all of its manifestations (for more details see "The Integrity Pact" at http://www.transparency.org/activities/ip_attachm-a.html).

TI's core principles form the foundation of possible baseline principles with respect to the interactions of business and government, as well as providing some guidance for business transactions and reporting. Interestingly, TI's core principles are similar to the ethical principles of the numerous business initiatives aimed at improving management practice analyzed by Liedtka (1998), suggesting their broad applicability. TI's mission statement articulates its foundation principles as:

- Participation;
- Decentralization;
- Diversity;
- Accountability; and
- Transparency.
    (Source: http://www.transparency.org/
    activities/ip_attachm-a.html)

These principles are important because of the coercive power commanded by governments (Etzioni, 1961) to accomplish their fundamental goals of creating the rule of law to which citizens, individual and corporate, must adhere. While more authoritarian regimes might not agree with the foundational democratic values expressed by concepts of participation and decentralization, these same underlying values are, in fact, to be found in the corporate initiatives aimed at fostering effectiveness (Liedtka, 1998). Principles fostering democracy, encompass different people, nations, cultures, and personal expression. Further, many scientists recognize that biological diversity results in a healthy ecology (Maturana and Varela, 1998; Capra, 1995; Frederick, 1995). Extending this consideration to society is the basis of suggesting the value of diversity, because the diversity of local cultures differences among individuals (Donaldson and Dunfee, 1999) is also important in fostering both differentiation and integration across nations and corporations.

Civil society sphere foundation principles

Basic human rights are possible candidates for fundamental principles associated with the civil society sphere, which is the realm of "social" organizations, family, church, schools, and nongovernmental organizations. Foundation principles related to human rights are most well known from their promulgation in the UN Declaration on Human Rights, first written in 1948 and more recently updated to include basic environmental concerns as well as human rights. Based on this declaration and other sources, Donaldson and Dunfee (1999) suggest that there is significant cross cultural agreement on the following principles, all of which respect the dignity and humanity of individuals:

- The right to freedom of physical movement.
- The right to ownership of property.
- The right to freedom from torture.
- The right to a fair trial.
- The right to nondiscriminatory treatment.

- The right to physical security.
- The right to freedom of speech and association.
- The right to minimal education.
- The right to political participation.
- The right to subsistence.

(Source: Donaldson, 1989, cited in Donaldson and Dunfee, 1999, p. 68)

Some of these foundation principles are highly congruent with the labor rights identified above in the economic sphere. As with the governmental foundation principles, the foundational human rights identified by Donaldson and Dunfee (1999) also foster democratic values (i.e., the right to political participation and the freedoms of speech and association) rather than more authoritarian values. Simultaneously, these rights allow for individual, national, and cultural differences (i.e., nondiscriminatory treatment and the freedom of speech and association), in what Donaldson and Dunfee (1999) term the "moral free space" where individual differences of opinions about right and wrong exist.

It is important to note that these human rights are agreed principles about what *ought* to be and come from consensus documents from the international community. Nonetheless, these principles are not necessarily representative of the way people are *actually* treated in different parts of the world today, particularly under the pressures of global competitiveness that seek for ever-lower costs (or greater economizing efforts). Even though there is widespread agreement on these principles, as found in UN documents, there are still many countries (and companies) that are run as dictatorships, where democracy and participation are not universally valued.

Despite that participation (democracy) has been shown in multiple studies to be effective in bottom-line terms (Pfeffer and Viega, 1999), it is still not universal. Discrimination along ethnic, religious, gender, and other lines is still commonplace. Universal franchise, freedom of association, and living wage are highly contentious issues in many parts of the world. Using outdated assumptions, some managers believe that there is a trade-off between achieving some of these principles in practice and generating the most efficient operations. As a counterpoint, however, Motorola achieved considerable success with its slogan that "quality is free" (Post et al., 2002). We might as easily argue that a similar understanding could be generated about human dignity and responsible treatment of people, both at work and in civil society: "Responsibility is free." There need not necessarily be a conflict between profitable enterprise and respect for basic human values, as multiple studies on the relationship between corporate responsibility and profitability indicate (Margolis and Walsh, 2001, 2003).

More fundamentally, perhaps other values simply sometimes outweigh purely economic ones. In his important book, *Fast Food Nation*, Eric Schlosser puts the core issue starkly:

> The market is a tool, and a useful one. But the worship of this tool is a hollow faith. Far more important than any tool is what you make with it. . . . If all that mattered were the unfettered right to buy and sell, tainted food could not be kept off supermarket shelves, toxic waste could be dumped next door to elementary schools, and every American family could import an indentured servant (or two), paying them with meals instead of money. . . . The great challenge now facing countries throughout the world is how to find a proper balance between the efficiency and the amorality of the market. . . . An economic system promising freedom has too often become a means of denying, as the narrow dictates of the market gain precedence over more important democratic values. (Schlosser, 2001, pp. 260–261).

Ecological sphere foundation principles

If nature can be said to have a goal, it is likely to be what Frederick (1995) calls ecologizing. The economizing that is inherent in industrialization (Frederick, 1995) when combined with the basic ecologizing processes of nature (Frederick, 1995) points in the direction of a possible foundation value for the nature environment of:

- Sustainability or ecologizing (Frederick, 1995).

Nature, that is, wastes nothing as Frederick's (1995) extensive review of the biology literature attests. What is waste for one process becomes food for others, creating a cycle that sustains itself in creating the conditions for life on earth as we know it, or what some have called the Gaia hypothesis, the hypothesis that the earth itself is a living system (Lovelock, 2000).

The ecological or environmental sphere provides the basic elements necessary for human civilization to survive and prosper, according to biologists Maturana and Varela (1999). Though processes of industrial development sometimes disconnect us from this reality, human civilization can survive only within a narrow range of ecological conditions, though the "environment" will go on whether humans are a part of it or not. The health of the natural environment with respect to human civilization is currently threatened, largely from the impact of human beings and processes of industrialization (e.g., Diamond, 1992; Hawken, 1999; Hawken et al., 1999; Capra, 1983; Freeman et al., 2000). The need for sustainable development has never been more real (e.g., Gladwin et al., 1995; Hawken, 1999), despite the continuing emphasis in the economic system on growth, consumption, and continued use of natural resources.

The Global Compact, building on the consensus fostered through the UN's Agenda 21 and the Declaration on Human Rights and Environment, reinforces the need for sustainability by emphasizing the following core environmental principles as its foundation principles:

- Taking a precautionary (preventative) approach to environmental challenges;
- Responsible and ethical management products and processes from the point of view of health, safety and environmental aspects; and
- Development and diffusion of environmentally sound technologies.
  (Source: http://www.unglobalcompact.org/gc/ unweb.nsf/content/thenine.htm)

Although corporate and indeed human practices are currently far from sustainable (e.g., Hawken, 1999; Diamond, 1992), the growing concerns about environmental issues suggest the need for the types of foundation principles found in the Global Compact and elsewhere.

Challenge ahead: moving from principles to practice

This paper has identified a set of foundational principles for the issues of labor, human rights, system integrity, and environmental practices, based on what is contained in globally-agreed (mostly UN-based) documents. These documents by virtue of the international consensus on which they are based promulgate basic standards that arguably *ought* to be followed by the brands, retailers and their suppliers around the globe. Of course, as evidenced by a continuing stream of exposés put forward by the BBC, New York Times, *Sixty Minutes* and a host of other outlets, frequently such standards are not met. After years of hard won progress in the major industrialized countries on the range of issues covered by these foundational principles, the globalization of production and the disaggregation of supply chains appears to have brought us back full circle to some of the more egregious business practices of the past, including sweatshops, abusive working standards, and growing ecological deterioration.

Given this unsatisfactory state, it is not surprising to find a wide variety of initiatives emerging to better regulate, ensure compliance with standards, and establish some system of accountability and comparability. To avoid external regulation, many companies are engaged in voluntary initiatives to monitor their own practices through codes of conduct or by joining initiatives that attest to their adherence to foundational values. Voluntary initiatives include The Fair Labor Association (FLA), Ethical Trading Initiative, Clean Clothes Campaign, to name just a few. Some companies agree to monitor their suppliers' labor practices and submit to external verification through organizations like Social Accountability International's SA 8000 standard. Others are attempting to become more transparent through active engagement with stakeholders and living up to AccountAbility's AA 1000 series of labor/work-

place standards guidelines. Some entire industries' professional associations, including the Direct Selling Association and the Chemical Industry have started self-regulatory process, such as chemicals' Responsible Care initiative and the DSA's code of conduct to attempt to guide their members toward more responsible practices that live up to global standards and expectations.

OECD guidelines on multinationals, the Caux Roundtable's Principles, and the Global Sullivan Principles, among others, are all attempts to boost standards by promulgating global codes of conduct and what we have termed foundational principles that are widely agreed. One major initiative is the Global Reporting Initiative (GRI), which is attempting to provide reporting mechanisms for social and environmental reporting similar to those already in place for financial reporting. By 2003 about 1,000 of the estimated 70,000 transnational corporations in the world had joined this initiative. Just as new expectations and norms, standards, and regulations evolved in the U.S. and elsewhere during the early 1900s to respond to the most egregious abuses of industrialization, so today are new global mechanisms beginning to evolve that have some potential to hold companies more accountable for their practices and to meeting foundational principles.

Combined with internal responsibility management systems, these initiatives constitute the beginnings of what I have elsewhere termed a responsibility assurance system (Waddock, in press). We can see the outlines of a voluntary global system that establishes standards and enforces standards beginning to emerge, in part the result of civil society and non-governmental organization anti-corporate activism, but at this point the system is still voluntary and many critics of globalization and of the power of the modern transnational firm believe that voluntary standards will need to be complimented by mandate. For example, the Global Compact (GC), Global Reporting Initiative (GRI), SA 8000, and AA 1000 contain three core elements of responsibility assurance: standards of conduct or the foundational principles discussed above (e.g., the Global Compact), monitoring, verification, and certification processes to ensure that what companies say they are doing is what they are actually doing (e.g., AA 1000 and SA 8000), and reporting guidelines for reasonably standardized external communication of what is being done that is relatively comparable across companies and nations (e.g., GRI).

Each of the core elements of responsibility assurance addresses a different element of an important continuum that reinforces the foundational values discussed above. For example, the GC articulates nine foundation principles, as discussed above, which are supplemented by principles of respect, dignity, and care for the community as identified by Donaldson and Dunfee (1999). The GRI provides a common reporting tool that provides for comparability across companies and other institutions using it, as well as a degree of transparency not currently available. SA 8000 and AA 1000, and related International Standards Organizations (ISO) standards on environment, provide specific means for assessing company performance in the important arenas of the multiple bottom lines associated with ensuring that companies are held to higher standards than some are meeting today in the global arena. Whether these are the specific initiatives that will, in the end, create a "new business imperative" of corporate responsibility (Waddock et al., 2002) at the global level, these *types* of initiatives, along with continued activism and public pressure, are among the types that will be needed to bring about more accountable corporations that meet these basic standards of practice.

Such voluntary initiatives may never satisfy corporate critics, particularly in light of the reality that, for example, of the nearly 70,000 transnational corporations, only about 1,000 had signed the Global Compact by early 2003, and the reach of the GC hardly touches the millions of small and medium-sized enterprises in the world today. Peer pressure from companies within the same industry does have the capacity to shift corporate attention to the reporting of social and ecological as well as economic/financial performance – and what gets measured is what managers tend to pay attention to, thus, the existence and promulgation of reports does have some potential, in and of itself, to shift

attention toward foundational principles such as those discussed above. Such reports and monitoring of supply chain activities is particularly important for companies with brand reputation to protect, who have been targets of anti-corporate or anti-globalization activism, as the membership of the Fair Labor Association attests.

Further, although some companies are now voluntarily producing triple bottom line reports (Elkington, 1997) that focus on economic, social, and ecological performance, and engaging in verification of standards in their supply chain factories, some managers are questioning their usefulness – as well as whether they are even being read. New regulatory mechanisms, such as the Sarbanes-Oxley Act in the U.S., and recent legislation in France and the U.K. that mandates that pension fund managers report how they deal with ecological and social issues within their funds have far-reaching potential to shift priorities of they continue to spread to other nations, and become the norm. Although specific behaviors are not required in these European laws, the mere fact of having to report how these issues are considered draws new attention to underlying standards.

Additionally, we can make an analogy to the quality movement. Quality became a business imperative during the 1980s in part because of customer demands for better quality, in part because the Japanese had already set a high standard of quality that forced others to focus on quality, and in part because European Union companies began requiring that suppliers meet ISO quality standards (Evans and Lindsay, 1999). Perhaps it will take a similar sequence of events around corporate responsibility, underlying corporate responsibility for all companies, branded or not, to begin taking foundational principles seriously. For instance, what might be the impact of current EU companies requiring their suppliers to meet SA 8000 labor standards, to join the Global Compact and uphold the principles, reporting out using GRI standards?

Alternatively, what if several major transnational corporations that have long or extensive supply chains (e.g., Wal*Mart) or employ people on a global basis (e.g., McDonalds) determined that they – and all of *their* suppliers had to be certified as meeting foundational standards? The chain reaction of such moves would create a cascade effect, much along the lines of the quality movement, that would, in fact, make the implementation and meeting of foundational principles a way of doing business. Resultant attention from the general public, the press, and competitors could conceivably create an entirely new context in which foundational principles as related to the very stakeholders who constitute the company and without which it cannot do business are met as part of the company's basic license to operate – its fundamental social contract.

The world today is far from either voluntary or mandated assurance that foundational principles – basic human and labor rights, ecological principles, or the transparency that provides trust in the integrity of the system – are in fact being implemented. Yet, as can be seen from the sketch given above, there are forces in place that are pushing in the direction of establishing and implementing core principles to make corporate citizenship real, not just rhetoric. Only time, competitive conditions, political will, and the social movements that underlie the development of that political will, will determine whether the ultimate outcome is in the best interests of humanity – meeting the basic needs of people for respect and dignity, of human civilization for a sustainable global ecology, of democracy for systemic integrity.

Acknowledgements

I would like to acknowledge the contributions of Charles Bodwell of the International Labor Office Corporate Citizenship Programme to the original conception and ideas presented in this paper.

Notes

[1] TI Advisory Council Chairman Kamal Hossain, quoted in a TI press release, May 14, 2002, 'Russian, Chinese, Taiwanese and S. Korean companies widely seen using bribes in developing countries,' posted at:

http://www.transparency.org/pressreleases_archive/20 02/2002.05.14.bpi.en.html.
[2] See http://www.investorhome.com/sri.htm. This screen is notably broad, including shareholder resolutions, as well as direct investments in screened companies and mutual funds.
[3] See ILO's Business and Social Initiatives: http://oracle02.ilo.org:6060/vpi/VpiSearch.First?p_la ng=en.
[4] As reported at http://uspolicy.usembassy.be/ Issues/WTO/factsheet.062901.htm.

References

Behrman, J. N.: 2001 (May), 'Adequacy of International Codes of Behavior', *Journal of Business Ethics* **31**(1), 51–63.

Burns, James McGregor: 1978, *Leadership* (Harper Torchbooks, New York).

Capra, F.: 1983, *The Turning Point: Science, Society, and the Rising Culture* (Bantam Books, New York).

Capra, F.: 1995, *The Web of Life* (Anchor Doubleday, New York).

Dessler, G.: 1999 (May), 'How to Earn Your Employees' Commitment', *Academy of Management Executive* **13**(2), 58–67

Diamond, J.: 1992, *The Third Chimpanzee: The Evolution and Future of the Human Animal* (HarperPrennial, New York).

Donaldson, T.: 1996, 'Values in Tension: Ethics Away from Home', *Harvard Business Review* (September-October), Reprint # 96402, 1–12.

Donaldson, T. and T. W. Dunfee: 1994, 'Toward a Unified Conception of Social Contracts Theory', *Academy of Management Review* **19**(2), 252–284.

Donaldson, T. and T. W. Dunfee: 1999, *Ties that Bind: A Social Contracts Approach to Business Ethics* (Harvard Business School Press, Boston).

Elkington, J.: 1998, *Cannibals with Forks: The Triple Bottom Line of Sustainability* (New Society Publishers, Gabriola Island).

European Commission: 2001, *Promoting a European Framework for Corporate Social Responsibility: Green Paper* (European Communities, Luxembourg).

Evans, J. R. and W. M. Lindsay: 1999, *The Management and Control of Quality*, 4th edition (West, New York), 1999.[1] Evans & Lindsay, p. 8.

Fossum, J. A.: 1979, *Labor Relations: Development, Structure, Process* (Business Publications, Dallas).

Frederick, W. C.: 1995. *Values, Nature, and Culture in the American Corporation* (Oxford University Press, New York).

Frederick, W. C.: Forthcoming. The Evolutionary Firm and Its Moral (Dis)Contents. Business Ethics and Science, Ruffin Series No. 4, Society for Business Ethics.

Freeman, R. E.: 1984, *Strategic Management: A Stakeholder Approach* (Pitman, Boston).

Freeman, R. E., J. Pierce and R. H. Dodd: 2000, *Environmentalism and the New Logic of Business: How Firms Can be Profitable and Leave Our Children a Living Planet* (Oxford University Press, New York).

Fenkel, S. J.: 2001, 'Globalization, Athletic Footwear Commodity Chains and Employment Relations in China', *Organization Studies* 22(4), 531–562.

Friedman, T. L.: 2000, *The Lexus and the Olive Tree* (Anchor Books, New York).

Gladwell, M.: 2000, *The Tipping Point: How Little Things Can Make a Big Difference* (Little Brown & Company, Boston).

Gladwin, T. N., J. J. Kennelly and T.-S. Krause: 1995 (October), 'Shifting Paradigms for Sustainable Development: Implications for Management Theory and Research', *Academy of Management Review* 20(4), 874–907.

Goodpaster, K. E.: 2003 (March), 'Some Challenges of Social Screening', *Journal of Business Ethics* 43(3), 239–246.

Greider, W.: 1998, *One World, Ready or Not: The Manic Logic of Global Capitalism* (Touchstone Books, New York).

Graves, S.: B., K. Rehbein and S. Waddock: 2001, 'Fad and Fashion in Shareholder Activism: The Landscape of Social Policy Shareholder Resolutions, 1988–1998', *Business and Society Review* 106(4) (Winter), 293–314.

Hartman, L. P., B. Shaw and R. Stevenson: In press, 'Exploring the Ethics and Economics of Global Labor standards: A Challenge to Integrated Social Contract Theory', *Business Ethics Quarterly*.

Hartman L. P., D. G. Arnold and R. E. Wokutch: 2003, *Rising Above Sweatshops: Innovative Approaches to Global Labor Challenger* (Praeger, Westport, CT).

Hawken, P.: 1999, *Natural Capitalism: Creating the Next Industrial Revolution* (Little Brown, Boston).

Klein, N.: i 2000, *No Logo: No Space, No Choice, no Jobs, No Logo: Taking Aim at the Brand Bullies* (Picador, New York).

Kok, P., T. van der Wiele, R, McKenna and A. Brown: 2001, 'A Corporate Social Responsibility Audit within a Quality Management Framework', *Journal of Business Ethics* 31, 285–297.

Liedtka, J. L.: 1998 (September), 'Constructing an Ethic for Business Practice: Competing Effectively

and Doing Good', *Business and Society* 37(3), 254–280.

Lovelock, J.: 2000, *Gaia: A New Look at Life on Earth* (Oxford University Press, New York).

Lovins, A. B., L. H. Lovins and P. Hawken: 1999, 'A Road Map for Natural Capitalism', *Harvard Business Review* (May–June), 145–158.

Margolis, J. D. and J. P. Walsh: 2001a, *People and Profits? The Search for a Link between a Company's Social and Financial Performance* (Lawrence Erlbaum Associates, Mahwah, NJ).

Margolis, J. and J. P. Walsh: 2003, 'Misery Loves Companies: Rethinking Social Initiatives by Business', *Administrative Science Quarterly* 48, 268–305.

Maturana, H. R. and F. J. Varela: 1998, *The Tree of Knowledge: The Biological Roots of Human Understanding*, revised edition (Shambala Press, Boston).

Mills, D. Q.: 1986, *Labor Management Relations* (McGraw-Hill, New York).

Nelson, J., P. Zollinger and A. Sing: 2001, *The Power to Change: Mobilising Board Leadership to Deliver Sustainable Value to Markets and Society* (The International Business Leaders Forum and SustainAbility, Ltd., London).

O'Rourke, D.: 2000, 'Monitoring the Monitors: A Critique of PricewaterhouseCooper's Labor Monitoring', white paper, released September 28, 2000.

O'Rourke, D.: 1997. Smoke from a Hired Gun: A Critique of Nike's Labor and Environmental Auditing in Vietnam as Performed by Ernst & Young, report published by the Transnational Resource and Action Center: San Francisco, November 10th, available on the Internet at: www.corpwatch.org/trac/nike/ernst/.

Pfeffer, J. and J. F. Veiga: 1999 (May), 'Putting People First for Organizational Success', *Academy of Management Executive* 13(2), 37–48.

Post, J. E. : 2002, Comment made at the Notre Dame Conference on the UN Global Compact, April 2002.

Post, J. E., L. E. Preston and S. Sachs: 2002, *Redefining the Corporation* (Stanford University Press, Palo Alto).

Proffitt, W. T., Jr.: 2000a, Constellations Of Conflict: Investor Mobilization in The United States, 1934–1997. Northwestern University Working Paper.

Proffitt, W. T.r, Jr.: 2000b. Turning Up The Volume: Shareholder Mobilization And Field-Level Change. Presented at the Annual Meeting of the Academy of Management, Toronto, Canada.

Putnam, R. D.: 1993, 'The Prosperous Community: Social Capital and Public Life', *The American Prospect*, Spring, 13, http://epn.org/prospect/13/13putn.html.

Putnam, R. D.: 1993. *Making Democracy Work: Civic Traditions in Modern Italy* (Princeton University Press, Princeton, NJ).

Rivoli, P.: 2003 (March), 'Labor Standards in the Glboal Economy: Issues for Investors', *Journal of Business Ethics* 43(30), 223–232.

Sabel, C.s, D. O'Rourke and A. Fung: 2000. Racheting Labor Standards: Regulation for Continuous Improvement in the Global Workplace. http://web.mit.edu/dorourke/www/PDF/RLS21.pdf.

Schlosser, E.: 2001, *Fast Food Nation: The Dark Side of the All-American Meal* (Houghton Mifflin, Boston).

Schoenberger, K.: ca. 2000, *Levi's Children : Coming To Terms With Human Rights In The Global Marketplace* (Atlantic Monthly Press, New York).

Schwartz, M. S.: 2002 (November/December), 'A Code of Ethics for Corporate Codes of Ethics', *Journal of Business Ethics* 41(1/2), 27–42.

Sethi, S. P.: 2003, 'Globalization and the Good Corporation: A Need for Proactive Co-existence', *Journal of Business Ethics* 43(1/2), 21–31.

Vogl, F.: 2001. Personal communication.

Waddell, S. and L. D. Brown: 1997, Fostering Intersectoral Partnering: A Guide to Promoting Cooperation among Government, Business, and Civil Society Actors. IDR Reports, Vol. 13, No. 3.

Waddell, S.: 2000, Business-Government-Civil Society Collaborations: A Brief Review of Key Conceptual Foundations. For the Interaction Institute for Social Change, Working Paper (Cambridge, MA).

Waddock, S.: In press, 'Corporate Responsibility, Accountability, and Stakeholder Relationships: Will Voluntary Standards Be Enough', in Jonathan P. Doh and Stephen Stumpf (eds.), *Responsible Leadership and Governance in Global Business* (Edward Elgar, U.K.).

Waddock, S.: 2002, *Leading Corporate Citizens: Vision, Values, Values Added* (McGraw-Hill, New York).

Waddock, S. and C. Bodwell: 2002 (Autumn), 'From TQM to TRM: The Emerging Evolution of Total Responsibility Management (TRM) Systems', *Journal of Corporate Citizenship* 2(7), 113–126.

Waddock, S., C. Bodwell and S. B. Graves: 2002, 'Responsibility: The New Business Imperative', *Academy of Management Executive* 16(2), 132–148.

Wilber, K.: 1995, *Sex, Ecology, Spirituality: The Spirit of Evolution* (Shambala Publications, Boston).

Wilber, K.: 1996, *A Brief History of Everything* (Shambala Publications, Boston).

Willis, A.: 2003 (March), 'The Role of the Global Reporting Initiative's Sustainability Reporting Guidelines in the Social Screening of Investments', *Journal of Business Ethics* 43(3), 233–237.

Zucker, L. G.: 1986. 'Production of Trust: Institutional Sources of Economic Structure, 1840–1920', *Research in Organizational Behavior* 8, 53–111.

Boston College,
Carroll School of Management,
Chestnut Hill, MA 02467,
U.S.A.
E-mail: waddock@bc.edu

Name Index